AT THE GATE OF CHRISTENDOM

Modern life in increasingly heterogeneous societies has directed attention to patterns of cultural interactions. While scholars have often used the binary framework of persecution and tolerance to understand such interactions, this book argues that both exclusion and integration simultaneously characterized medieval non-Christian status. It compares the place of Jews, Muslims and nomad Cumans between 1000 and 1300 in Hungary, a kingdom on the frontier of Christendom.

A complex picture of non-Christian status emerges from the analysis of economic, social, legal and religious positions and roles. Existence on the frontier with the nomadic world led to the formulation of a frontier ideology, and to anxiety about Hungary's detachment from Christendom. The author uses a variety of written and material evidence, including Latin charters and laws, rabbinical responses, accounts by Muslim travellers and archaeological finds, and draws upon analogies with other areas of medieval Christendom. The study also succeeds in integrating central European history into the study of the medieval world, while challenging how the concepts of frontier societies, persecution and tolerance, ethnicity and 'the other', are currently used in medieval studies.

NORA BEREND is Assistant Lecturer in History, University of Cambridge, and Fellow of St Catharine's College.

Cambridge Studies in Medieval Life and Thought
Fourth Series

General Editor:
D. E. LUSCOMBE
Leverhulme Personal Research Professor of Medieval History, University of Sheffield

Advisory Editors:
CHRISTINE CARPENTER
Reader in Medieval English History, University of Cambridge, and Fellow of New Hall

ROSAMOND McKITTERICK
*Professor of Medieval History, University of Cambridge,
and Fellow of Newnham College*

The series Cambridge Studies in Medieval Life and Thought was inaugurated by G. G. Coulton in 1921; Professor D. E. Luscombe now acts as General Editor of the Fourth Series, with Dr Christine Carpenter and Professor Rosamond McKitterick as Advisory Editors. The series brings together outstanding work by medieval scholars over a wide range of human endeavour extending from political economy to the history of ideas.

For a list of titles in the series, see end of book.

AT THE GATE OF CHRISTENDOM

Jews, Muslims and 'Pagans' in Medieval Hungary,
c. 1000–c. 1300

NORA BEREND

CAMBRIDGE
UNIVERSITY PRESS

CAMBRIDGE UNIVERSITY PRESS
Cambridge, New York, Melbourne, Madrid, Cape Town, Singapore, São Paulo

Cambridge University Press
The Edinburgh Building, Cambridge CB2 2RU, UK

Published in the United States of America by Cambridge University Press, New York

www.cambridge.org
Information on this title: www.cambridge.org/9780521651851

© Cambridge University Press 2001

This publication is in copyright. Subject to statutory exception
and to the provisions of relevant collective licensing agreements,
no reproduction of any part may take place without
the written permission of Cambridge University Press.

First published 2001
This digitally printed first paperback version 2006

A catalogue record for this publication is available from the British Library

Library of Congress Cataloguing in Publication data
Berend, Nora.
At the Gate of Christendom: Jews, Muslims and 'Pagans' in Medieval Hungary, c. 1000–c. 1300 /
Nora Berend.
p. cm. – (Cambridge Studies in Medieval Life and Thought)
ISBN 0 521 65185 9
1. Christianity and other religions – Hungary – History. 2. Hungary – Church history.
3. Hungary – Religion. I. Title. II. Series.

BR869.54.B47 2001
305.6´09439´0902 – dc21   00–062134

ISBN-13 978-0-521-65185-1 hardback
ISBN-10 0-521-65185-9 hardback

ISBN-13 978-0-521-02720-5 paperback
ISBN-10 0-521-02720-9 paperback

TO THE MEMORY OF
ERVIN BERKOVITS
(1927–1944)

'Ut ea, que geruntur in tempore, ne cum tempore defluant et labantur, ad cautelam solent scripti patrocinio peremnari.'

(So that those things which take place in time should not flow and slip away with time, as a guarantee it is the custom to fix them forever through the protection of the written word.)

CONTENTS

List of maps	page xi
Acknowledgements	xiii
List of abbreviations	xv

	INTRODUCTION	1
1	HUNGARY: A FRONTIER SOCIETY	6
	Medievalists on the frontier	6
	Medieval Hungary	17
	Medieval Hungary on the frontier of Christendom	23
2	CHRISTIANS AND NON-CHRISTIANS	42
	Christianitas and non-Christians	42
	Jews	60
	Muslims	64
	Cumans	68
3	THE LEGAL POSITION OF HUNGARY'S NON-CHRISTIAN POPULATION	74
	The legal status of Jews	74
	The legal position of Muslims	84
	The legal status of Cumans	87
	The judicial autonomy of non-Christians	93
	The Hungarian legal system and the non-Christians	101
4	NON-CHRISTIANS IN HUNGARIAN ECONOMY AND SOCIETY	109
	Trade	110
	Financial functions and office-holding	116
	Money-lending	116

Contents

	'Public office': roles connected to the mint and treasury	120
	Non-Christian presence in agriculture	129
	Military role	140
5	CONFLICTS BETWEEN THE PAPACY AND THE KINGS	149
	'Since it is quite absurd that any who blaspheme against Christ should have power over Christians'	152
	Hungary, the Gate of Christendom: birth of a frontier ideology	163
	Political fragmentation and the Cumans	171
	Papal and royal attitudes: the role of non-Christians in Christian society	183
6	CHRISTIAN PERCEPTIONS AND ATTITUDES	190
	Christian categorization of non-Christians	190
	Christian perceptions of non-Christians	195
	Christian missionary efforts	210
7	NON-CHRISTIAN COMMUNITIES: CONTINUITY, TRANSFORMATION, CONVERSION AND ASSIMILATION	224
	The Jews	225
	The Muslims	237
	The Cumans	244
	CONCLUSION	268

Appendix 1: Hungarian kings of the house of Árpád	273
Appendix 2: Toponyms, with Latin and German equivalents	274
Appendix 3: The manuscript tradition of the Synod of Buda (1279)	275
Bibliography	277
Index	335

MAPS

| 1 | The medieval kingdom of Hungary | *page* 18 |
| 2 | Non-Christians in the kingdom of Hungary | 59 |

ACKNOWLEDGEMENTS

While writing this book, I often shared the sinking feeling of Winnie-the-Pooh climbing on to his honey-jar boat; I was not quite sure as to which of us was going to end up on the top. I thank my family, friends and colleagues who helped me to stay afloat by their advice, encouragement and support.

My affectionate thanks go to Yosef H. Yerushalmi for his support from the time I was writing my dissertation at Columbia University; and to Peter B. Golden who has generously shared his erudition, and has cheerfully encouraged me with an assortment of Turkish proverbs, Chinese wisdoms and Cuman jokes.

I am grateful to those who introduced me to fields that can be particularly bewildering for the unwary traveller: Robert Somerville to canon law, József Laszlovszky to archaeology, Lucia Travaini to numismatics. They also drew my attention to several of the works I have used. Géza Komoróczy, Peter Linehan, Zsigmond Pál Pach and the series editor Rosamond McKitterick read the entire manuscript at some stage; I am grateful for their friendship and comments, which have greatly helped me along the way. I am also indebted to those who discussed various chapters or particular problems with me: David Abulafia, János Bak, Iván Borsa, Alain Boureau, Richard Bulliet, Isabelle Cochelin, Olivia Remie Constable, David D'Avray, Tom Head, Gábor Klaniczay, László Koszta, Clare Kudera, Jacques Le Goff, Jinty Nelson, David Nirenberg, Éric Palazzo, Agostino Paravicini Bagliani, Evelyne Patlagean, Amy Remensnyder, Jean-Claude Schmitt, László Veszprémy, Patrick Zutshi. I also thank the personnel of the Hungarian National Archives and the Vatican Archives for their help in facilitating my research.

Most of the work of writing this book was carried out while I was a Research Fellow at St Catharine's College, Cambridge. I am indebted to the Fellows of the College for giving me this opportunity, and particularly to Christopher Bayly, Christopher Clark and John Thompson, its

Acknowledgements

historians, whose friendship and support far surpassed the mere dictates of collegiality.

Last, but not least, I thank Columbia University, the Memorial Foundation for Jewish Culture and St Catharine's College for their financial support.

This book is dedicated to the memory of my uncle, Ervin Berkovits, who died in a forced labour camp long before I was born. Had he lived, I hope he would have approved of this book. May it also stand in place of the tombstone he has never had.

ABBREVIATIONS

AEMAe	*Archivum Eurasiae Medii Aevi.*
AOASH	*Acta Orientalia Academiae Scientiarum Hungaricae.*
ASV	Archivio Segreto Vaticano, Vatican City.
ÁÚO	Wenzel, Gusztáv. ed. *Árpádkori új okmánytár (Codex diplomaticus Arpadianus continuatus)*. 12 vols. Pest, 1860–74.
AUSz	*Acta Universitatis Szegediensis de Attila József Nominatae.*
CD	Fejér, György. *Codex diplomaticus Hungariae ecclesiasticus ac civilis*. 11 vols. Buda, 1829–44.
CDZ	Nagy, Imre et al. eds. *Codex diplomaticus domus senioris comitum Zichy de Zich et Vásonkő*. 12 vols. Pest, 1871–1931.
Gratian	*Decretum Gratiani*, in A. Friedberg, *Corpus Iuris Canonici*, 2 vols. Leipzig: Tauchnitz, 1879–81. Reprint Graz: Akademische Druck- und Verlagsanstalt, 1959.
HO	Nagy, Imre et al. eds. *Hazai Okmánytár (Codex diplomaticus patrius)*. 8 vols. Győr and Budapest, 1865–91.
JK	Gyárfás, István. *A jász-kunok története* (The history of the As-Cumans). 4 vols. Kecskemét, Szolnok and Budapest, 1870–85. Reprint Budapest: A Jászkunságért Alapítvány, 1982.
KMTL	Kristó, Gyula. ed. *Korai Magyar Történeti Lexikon (9–14. sz.)* (Dictionary for early medieval Hungarian history: ninth–fourteenth centuries). Budapest: Akadémiai Kiadó, 1994.
MES	Knauz, Ferdinand. ed. *Monumenta Ecclesiae Strigoniensis*. 3 vols. Esztergom, 1874–1924.
MGH	*Monumenta Germaniae Historica*. Edited by Georgius Heinricus Pertz et al.
SS	*Scriptores*. 36 vols. to date. Hannover: Hahnsche Buchhandlung, 1826– .

List of abbreviations

DC	*Deutsche Chroniken*. 6 vols. Berlin: Weidmannsche Verlagsbuchhandlung, 1877–1909.
SRG	*Scriptores Rerum Germanicarum*. n.s. Cologne: Böhlau, 1922– .
Epp	*Epistolae*. 8 vols. Berlin: Weidmannsche Verlagsbuchhandlung, 1887–1937.
Leges	*Sectio IV Constitutiones et Acta Publica Imperatorum et Regum*. 11 parts. Hannover and Leipzig, 1893–1996.
MOL	Magyar Országos Levéltár (Hungarian National Archives) Budapest.
MOPH	*Monumenta Ordinis Fratrum Praedicatorum Historica*. 27 vols. to date. Edited by Benedictus Maria Reichert *et al.* Louvain, 1896– . From vol. XV, Rome: Institutum Historicum Fratrum Praedicatorum.
MZsO	Scheiber, Sándor and Ármin Friss. eds. *Magyar Zsidó Oklevéltár (Monumenta Hungariae Judaica)*. 18 vols. Budapest, 1903–80.
RA	Szentpétery, Imre and Iván Borsa. *Regesta regum stirpis Arpadianae critico-diplomatica. Az Árpád-házi királyok okleveleinek kritikai jegyzéke* (A critical register of royal charters from the House of Arpad). 3 vols. Budapest: Magyar Tudományos Akadémia, 1923–87.
Reg. Alex. IV	Bourel de la Roncière, C., J. de Loye, P. de Cenival and A. Coulon. eds. *Les Registres d'Alexandre IV*. 3 vols. Bibliothèque des Ecoles Françaises d'Athènes et de Rome. 2nd ser. Paris, 1895–1959.
Reg. Bon. VIII	Digard, G., M. Faucon, A. Thomas and R. Fawtier. eds. *Les Registres de Boniface VIII*. 4 vols. Bibliothèque des Ecoles Françaises d'Athènes et de Rome. 2nd ser. Paris, 1884–39.
Reg. Clem. IV	Jordan, E. ed. *Les Registres de Clément IV*. Bibliothèque des Ecoles Françaises d'Athènes et de Rome. 2nd ser. Paris, 1893–1945.
Reg. Greg. IX	Auvray, L. ed. *Les Registres de Grégoire IX*. 4 vols. Bibliothèque des Ecoles Françaises d'Athènes et de Rome. 2nd ser. Paris, 1890–1955.
Reg. Greg. X	Guiraud, J. and L. Cadier. eds. *Les Registres de Grégoire X et de Jean XXI*. Bibliothèque des Ecoles Françaises d'Athènes et de Rome. 2nd ser. Paris, 1892–1906.
Reg. Hon. III	Pressutti, Pietro. ed. *Regesta Honorii papae III*. 2 vols. Rome, 1888–1905.

List of abbreviations

Reg. Hon. IV	Prou, M. ed. *Les Registres d'Honorius IV*. Bibliothèque des Ecoles Françaises d'Athènes et de Rome. 2nd ser. Paris, 1886–8.
Reg. Inn. IV	Berger, E. ed. *Les Registres d'Innocent IV*. 4 vols. Bibliothèque des Ecoles Françaises d'Athènes et de Rome. 2nd ser. Paris, 1884–1921.
Reg. Ioh. XXII	Mollat, G. ed. *Jean XXII (1316–1334) Lettres communes*. 16 vols. Paris, 1904–1947.
Reg. Martin IV	Olivier-Martin, F. ed. *Les Registres de Martin IV*. Bibliothèque des Ecoles Françaises d'Athènes et de Rome. 2nd ser. Paris, 1901–35.
Reg. Nic. III	Gay, J. and S. Clémencet-Witte. eds. *Les Registres de Nicolas III*. Bibliothèque des Ecoles Françaises d'Athènes et de Rome. 2nd ser. Paris, 1898–1938.
Reg. Nic. IV	Langlois, E. ed. *Les Registres de Nicolas IV*. 2 vols. Bibliothèque des Ecoles Françaises d'Athènes et de Rome. 2nd ser. Paris. 1886–1905.
Reg. Urb. IV	Guiraud, J. ed. *Les Registres d'Urbain IV*. 4 vols. Bibliothèque des Ecoles Françaises d'Athènes et de Rome. 2nd ser. Paris, 1899–1958.
SRH	Szentpétery, Imre. ed. *Scriptores Rerum Hungaricarum*. 2 vols. Budapest: MTA, 1937–8.
TF	Györffy, György. *Az Árpád-kori Magyarország történeti földrajza* (Historical geography of Árpád-age Hungary). 4 vols. to date. Budapest: Akadémiai Kiadó, 1963–98.
VMH	Theiner, Augustinus. *Vetera Monumenta Historica Hungariam Sacram Illustrantia*. vol. 1. *1216–1352*. Rome, 1859.
VI	Liber Sextus, in A. Friedberg, *Corpus Iuris Canonici*, 2 vols. Leipzig: Tauchnitz, 1879–81. Reprint Graz: Akademische Druck- und Verlagsanstalt, 1959.
X	Liber Extra (Decretales Gregorii IX), in A. Friedberg, *Corpus Iuris Canonici*, 2 vols. Leipzig: Tauchnitz, 1879–81. Reprint Graz: Akademische Druck- und Verlagsanstalt, 1959.

INTRODUCTION

Twentieth-century events and concerns have fostered interest in the treatment of social and religious minorities in the past. As a consequence, medievalists have also set out to unravel both what was perceived or constructed as difference, and how groups regarded as different were treated. These studies have started to reveal the complexity of non-Christian positions in the Middle Ages. The analysis of the place of Jews in medieval Europe, for example, modified not only the interpretation of Jewish history, abandoning its 'lachrymose conception',[1] but also that of the dynamics of state formation and of developments within Christian theology and practice in medieval society.[2] The debate about the role and function of non-Christians in medieval Spanish history has enriched our understanding of Spanish culture.[3] There has been both an efflorescence of case-studies on local interaction between Christians and

---

[1] First challenged by Salo W. Baron, 'Ghetto and Emancipation', *Menorah Journal* 14 (1928): pp. 515–26.

[2] E.g. Salo W. Baron, ' "Plenitude of Apostolic Powers" and Medieval "Jewish Serfdom" ', in *Ancient and Medieval Jewish History* (New Brunswick: Rutgers University Press, 1972), pp. 284–307; William Chester Jordan, *The French Monarchy and the Jews: From Philip Augustus to the Last Capetians* (Philadelphia: University of Pennsylvania Press, 1989); Robert I. Moore, *The Formation of a Persecuting Society* (Oxford: Blackwell, 1987, paperback edn, 1990); Gavin I. Langmuir, *Toward a Definition of Antisemitism* (Berkeley, Los Angeles and London: University of California Press, 1990); David Nirenberg, *Communities of Violence: Persecution of Minorities in the Middle Ages* (Princeton: Princeton University Press, 1996); Robert Chazan, *Daggers of Faith: Thirteenth-Century Christian Missionizing and Jewish Response* (Berkeley and Los Angeles: University of California Press, 1989); Anna Sapir Abulafia, *Christians and Jews in Dispute: Disputational Literature and the Rise of Anti-Judaism in the West (c. 1000–1150)* (Aldershot: Ashgate–Variorum, 1998).

[3] Américo Castro, *España en su historia* (Buenos Aires: Editorial Losada, 1948; Eng. tr. *The Structure of Spanish History* (Princeton: Princeton University Press, 1954)); Claudio Sánchez-Albornoz, *El Islam de España y el Occidente*, 2nd edn (Madrid: Espasa-Calpe, 1974); Claudio Sánchez-Albornoz, *España: un enigma histórico*, 2 vols. (Buenos Aires: Editorial Sudamericana, 1956); Thomas F. Glick, *Islamic and Christian Spain in the Early Middle Ages* (Princeton: Princeton University Press, 1979); John Boswell, *The Royal Treasure: Muslim Communities under the Crown of Aragon in the Fourteenth Century* (New Haven and London: Yale University Press, 1977), pp. 402–8; David Nirenberg, 'The Current State of Mudejar Studies', *Journal of Medieval History* 24 (1998): pp. 381–89.

I

non-Christians in regions such as Spain, Sicily or Scandinavia,[4] and an increased interest in a comparative perspective: thus, comparison between the situation of Jews under Christian and under Muslim rule has yielded insight into the origins of the persecution of Jews.[5] New approaches have created new debates as well, on the nature of medieval society, on the 'other', on ethnicity.

This book compares the fate of three groups, Jews, Muslims and 'pagan' Cumans, in medieval Hungary.[6] Its aim is twofold: first, to present a case-study that contributes to our knowledge about non-Christian populations living in medieval Europe, integrating non-western European developments into analyses of the medieval world; second, to examine a variety of issues relating to the position of religious minorities in what was, as I argue in chapter 1, a frontier society. The fact that Hungary incorporated three non-Christian groups enables me to compare the treatment of the different groups by both lay and ecclesiastical authorities within one socio-economic and legal framework. Hungary is also unique in that its non-Christians settled there voluntarily. Elsewhere in this period non-Christian groups were incorporated into Christian realms as a result of conquest, as were Muslims in Reconquest Spain or 'pagans' in Livonia.[7]

Hungary, an area of Christianization only since the late tenth century, and perched – precariously, it often seemed – on the frontier between Christendom and the 'pagan' world, was characterized by a distinctive background of opportunities and tension. On the one hand, frontier existence affected the possibilities open to, and policies towards, non-Christians. On the other hand, the notion that Hungary might be detached from Christendom and integrated into the nomadic world generated apprehension about Hungarian policies towards non-Christians.

Issues raised in this book relate in part to the way in which non-Christians interacted with Christian society. What roles and what

---

[4] Such as Norman Roth, *Jews, Visigoths and Muslims in Medieval Spain: Cooperation and Conflict* (Leiden, New York and Cologne: Brill, 1994); Régis Boyer, *Le Christ des barbares: Le monde nordique (IXe–XIIIe siècle)* (Paris: Cerf, 1987); David Abulafia, 'Una comunità ebraica della Sicilia occidentale: Erice 1298–1304', in Abulafia, *Commerce and Conquest in the Mediterranean, 1100–1500* (Aldershot: Variorum, 1993), no. VIII; James M. Powell, ed., *Muslims under Latin Rule, 1100–1300* (Princeton: Princeton University Press, 1990).

[5] Mark Cohen, *Under Crescent and Cross: The Jews in the Middle Ages* (Princeton: Princeton University Press, 1994).

[6] I use 'pagan' in quotation marks as it is not an objective or coherent category; it covers a variety of experience and belief, from polytheism to shamanism, and was used by Christians and not in self-designations. Thus it reflects Christian prejudices. Cumans held animistic–shamanistic beliefs, but this was not recognized in medieval Christian texts.

[7] There were some exceptions. For example, Jews migrated from Al-Andalus to Christian Spain, but in no other Christian kingdom was the voluntary immigration of non-Christians the main form of their incorporation.

Introduction

functions did non-Christians have? Were they outcasts and outsiders? Were they marginalized or were they integral parts of society? How were they seen and defined by society around them? Analysing the history of the various non-Christian groups together, thematically, as opposed to separating the material into chapters on Jews, Muslims and 'pagans', highlights similarities and differences between the three groups and allows more general conclusions to be drawn concerning the place of non-Christians in medieval society. The chapters concentrate on economic, social, legal and religious aspects of their existence. This composite approach is a means of avoiding a mono-causal explanation of non-Christian status. It also precludes reliance on preconceived notions of what determined medieval ideas and realities concerning non-Christians. Further, these problems illuminate mechanisms within Christian society. Investigating the policies of lay and ecclesiastical powers towards non-Christians leads us to questions of economic, religious and political motivation, which cannot be encapsulated by reference to a persecuting mentality, or to tolerance.

Designating the relations between Christians and non-Christians as 'coexistence' is not an attempt to refer to some golden age of harmonious or tolerant interaction.[8] It does, however, signal that the story I tell is not simply one of persecution. As I shall show, non-Christians were not uniformly excluded 'others'. Coexistence, in its primary meaning of 'exist together (in time or place)' seems to me to describe the realities well. It subsumes both peaceful and hostile relations, until the eradication of the minorities, either by assimilation or expulsion.

A brief discussion of my choice of chronology is necessary. My starting point for the analysis of the status of non-Christians in a Christian polity is the eleventh century, when the Christian kingdom of Hungary, the framework of this study, came into being. The first two centuries, however, provide much less material than the thirteenth century. Early medieval institutions in Hungary did not produce many documents, whereas the thirteenth-century production of privileges, letters and chronicles was abundant. To cite a striking example: we possess only seven extant royal charters from the eleventh century, whereas the registers of royal charters from the thirteenth century fill almost three volumes.[9] Later centuries offer an even richer harvest of documents. Yet the problem addressed in this study – non-Christians in a Christian

---

[8] See Mark D. Meyerson, *The Muslims of Valencia in the Age of Ferdinand and Isabel: Between Coexistence and Crusade* (Berkeley and Los Angeles: University of California Press, 1991), esp. introduction and chapter I.

[9] László Fejérpataky, *A királyi kancellária az Árpádok korában* (Budapest, 1885), pp. 10–13; Imre Szentpétery and Iván Borsa, *Regesta regum stirpis Arpadianae critico-diplomatica* [*RA*], 3 vols. (Budapest: MTA, 1923–87).

society – cannot be observed so well during later centuries despite the richer general documentation. The thirteenth is the last century in which all three groups (Jews, Muslims and 'pagans') lived in medieval Hungary; it is therefore the last to be treated systematically in this study. The structure and life of non-Christian groups in Hungary were transformed in the fourteenth century, as the economic and social framework changed. Moreover, the Angevin rulers of Hungary, who came to the throne in the early fourteenth century, inaugurated policies much closer to western European models in their treatment of non-Christians. The Muslim community disappeared completely. The Cumans were integrated into local society. The Jews remained the only non-Christian group in Hungary, with changing roles. Naturally, these transformations occurred over time, and not abruptly in 1301. But as a symbolic date, 1301, the extinction of the Árpád dynasty (whose members ruled the kingdom from its beginnings), signals the end of a period. Thus only brief descriptions of the later developments are included, either to indicate how thirteenth-century trends culminated or to highlight thirteenth-century specificities.

Finally, a few words concerning the limitations imposed by the nature of the primary sources are pertinent. The main methodological problems are, on the one hand, the scarcity of documentation and, on the other, the more or less 'mute' nature of the non-Christian groups analysed in this study. The more abundant output of written sources in the thirteenth century still cannot compare with, for example, the richness of Spanish archives on Jews and Muslims. It is possible to alleviate this first problem in two ways. First, to gain additional information, it is necessary to rely not only on written sources, but also on the testimony of personal and topographical names, linguistics, iconography and archaeological finds. The latter include gravestones and coins in the case of the Jews, finds from the excavation of the one Muslim village in Hungary that has been uncovered to date, and information regarding armament, costume and religious practices that the excavation of Cuman graves has yielded. Second, the use of comparative material provides perspectives which reveal either the uniqueness of the Hungarian case, or its similarities to Christian interaction with non-Christians elsewhere. None the less, it is impossible to achieve a completely balanced analysis; for each topic there is an unequal amount of information on the three groups. Thus Jews will feature more prominently in some of the chapters, Cumans in others; the sources concerning Muslims are consistently the most fragmentary. The second problem directs the focus of this study. Many aspects of the life of medieval non-Christians, indeed their very existence in Christian countries, ultimately depended on powers external to their communities. It is

Introduction

ironic that our own knowledge of the non-Christian communities of medieval Hungary should also be so dependent on Christian sources. Although the narrative of the Latin texts is supplemented by information from the onomastic and material evidence I have described above, and occasionally by texts produced by non-Christians, the bulk of the sources reflect Christian perspectives. This work, therefore, primarily treats the ways in which non-Christians fit into an economic, legal and cultural framework created by Christians. While it can address Christian views, concepts and fears, the equivalent non-Christian experience is almost totally absent. The daily life of Hungary's non-Christian communities is irretrievably lost; apart from a few shreds of information, it is most vividly captured when assimilation had already started. The history of Christian relations with non-Christians in medieval Hungary can only be uncovered through 'the cautious inching forward by the dim light of probability and the intermittent flicker (in this remote region) of scientific method'.[10]

[10] John Fowles, *The Aristos*, rev. edn (New York: Signet Books, 1970), p. 104.

Chapter 1

HUNGARY: A FRONTIER SOCIETY

Non-Christians in medieval Hungary lived in a society that was formed by a variety of influences, many of them the result of Hungary's location on the frontier of Christendom. 'Frontier' and 'frontier society' are concepts that have become extensively used in medieval historiography and incorporate a wide variety of approaches. Conceptual clarity requires tackling the issue of definitions and interpretations in order to bring both the notion of frontier society and the place of Hungary as such a society into sharp focus.

MEDIEVALISTS ON THE FRONTIER[1]

A brief rehearsal of the history of the 'f-word'[2] is useful in disentangling the varied threads that constitute frontier studies. Paternity goes to a very unwilling figure indeed. Frederick Jackson Turner claimed that the frontier was both unique to the United States and closed forever.[3] He has precipitated an avalanche of work on frontiers in history. Yet no single aspect of the Turner thesis concerning American history has withstood critical scrutiny.[4] First the concept of the 'frontier' was transformed: instead of a

---

[1] A version of this part of the chapter was published as 'Medievalists and the Notion of the Frontier', *Medieval History Journal* 2, no. 1 (1999): pp. 55–72.
[2] Patricia N. Limerick, 'The Adventures of the Frontier in the Twentieth Century', in *The Frontier in American Culture*, ed. James R. Grossman (Berkeley, Los Angeles and London: University of California Press, 1994), pp. 67–102, see p. 72. For a discussion of frontier historiography, see also Daniel Power, 'Introduction', in *Frontiers in Question: Eurasian Borderlands 700–1700*, ed. Daniel Power and Naomi Standen (London: Macmillan, 1999).
[3] 'The Significance of the Frontier in American History' (1893) is incorporated as the opening chapter of Frederick Jackson Turner, *The Frontier in American History* (New York: Henry Holt, 1920; reprint, New York: Holt, Rinehart and Winston, 1962), pp. 1–38.
[4] Among the many books, see esp. Patricia N. Limerick, Clyde A. Milner II and Charles E. Rankin, eds., *Trails: Toward a New Western History* (Lawrence: University Press of Kansas, 1991); Patricia N. Limerick, *The Legacy of Conquest: The Unbroken Past of the American West* (New York: Norton, 1987); William Cronon, George Miles and Jay Gitlin, eds., *Under an Open Sky: Rethinking America's Western Past* (New York: Norton, 1992); Richard White, *'It's Your Misfortune and None*

wilderness to be conquered, the frontier came to be seen as a contact zone, where an interchange of cultures was constantly taking place (an approach widely used by medievalists). This has been criticized in turn; many scholars of American history now argue that only the myth of the frontier constitutes a legitimate field of study, and that the real processes should be described by other names.[5] This approach led to the introduction of the concept of the 'middle ground' instead of 'frontier', emphasizing relations and common consensus rather than two separate sides.[6]

While Americanists have been repudiating the 'frontier' as an explanatory concept, it took on a life of its own in the historiography of other periods and areas.[7] The Turner thesis and its later adaptations had perhaps more impact on historians of the Middle Ages than on anyone, apart from those working on Turner's own field, American history. This influence is ironic; Turner formulated his frontier hypothesis partly in reaction to medievalists who were arguing for a continuity of civilization between medieval and American society.[8] James W. Thompson applied the Turnerian hypothesis to medieval German history as early as 1913.[9] From Archibald Lewis's article on 'The Closing of the Mediaeval Frontier 1250–1350' (1958) to Robert Bartlett and Angus MacKay's *Medieval Frontier Societies* (1989) and beyond, many medievalists have espoused the frontier as an explanatory concept.[10] Turner and a slightly modified

---

of My Own': A History of the American West (Norman and London: University of Oklahoma Press, 1991). I thank Jill Anderson for bringing these books to my attention. On the opacity of the Turner thesis, see esp. the introduction of Limerick, *Legacy*; Patricia N. Limerick, 'The Trail to Santa Fe: The Unleashing of the Western Public Intellection', in Limerick, Milner and Rankin, eds., *Trails*, p. 63, and Gerald Thompson, 'Another Look at Frontier/Western Historiography', ibid., pp. 89–95. Comparative studies reached similar conclusions: Richard Hofstadter and Seymour Martin Lipset, eds., *Turner and the Sociology of the Frontier* (New York and London: Basic Books, 1968), esp. Lipset, 'The Turner Thesis in Comparative Perspective: An Introduction', pp. 9–14.

[5] Limerick, 'Adventures', p. 77, pointed out that by defining frontier as cultural interaction, one arrives at a general pattern of human relations, so the term has neither coherence nor utility.

[6] Richard White, *The Middle Ground: Indians, Empires, and Republics in the Great Lakes Region, 1650–1815* (Cambridge: Cambridge University Press, 1991).

[7] Walter Prescott Webb, *The Great Frontier* (Lincoln and London: University of Nebraska Press, 1986; 1st edn, 1951), has pioneered the notion that the frontier was a determining explanatory concept in the history of western civilization (for the post-1500 period). For him, the frontier (the Americas and all the territory discovered by Europeans from the late fifteenth century) was an 'area inviting entrance', providing a 'vast body of wealth without proprietors' (pp. 2, 13); it created modern culture, affecting the sciences, law, government, economics, literature, art and history.

[8] Turner's letter cited in Ray Allen Billington, *America's Frontier Heritage* (New York: Holt, Reinhart and Winston, 1966), p. 7.

[9] James Westfall Thompson, 'Profitable Fields of Investigation in Medieval History', *American Historical Review* 18 (1913): pp. 490–504.

[10] Archibald Lewis, 'The Closing of the Mediaeval Frontier 1250–1350', *Speculum* 33 (October 1958): pp. 475–83; Robert Bartlett and Angus MacKay, eds., *Medieval Frontier Societies* (Oxford: Clarendon Press, 1989), with detailed bibliography.

Turnerian approach have especially influenced historians of the Iberian peninsula, such as Charles Julian Bishko, Robert I. Burns and Angus MacKay, who have used the concept as a main interpretative tool for the development of medieval Iberian society.

The frontier has been evoked in its original Turnerian meaning of man's fight against nature with the correlated changes in the institutions and behaviour of the frontiersmen to explain agricultural expansion, monastic innovations from the fourth to the twelfth century, ranching in Extremadura, and Cistercian settlement.[11] Most medievalists add a cultural and religious dimension to the theme of fight against nature in their discussions of the 'frontier', and many focus entirely on interaction between societies. A common point of view in the latter approach is to identify militarization as the main feature of the frontier, or even of the whole society.[12] Studies on Iberian frontiers with Islam, the rise of border lords and militarization on both sides of the Arab–Byzantine frontier, or warfare in Ireland and Wales, attest to this aspect of the

---

[11] Richard E. Sullivan, 'The Medieval Monk as Frontiersman', in *The Frontier: Comparative Studies*, vol. II, ed. William W. Savage, Jr. and Stephen I. Thompson (Norman: University of Oklahoma Press, 1979), pp. 25–49, reprinted as no. VI in Sullivan, *Christian Missionary Activity in the Early Middle Ages* (Aldershot: Variorum, 1994); Charles Julian Bishko, 'The Castilian as Plainsman: The Medieval Ranching Frontier in La Mancha and Extremadura', in *The New World Looks at its History*, ed. Archibald R. Lewis and Thomas F. McGann (Austin, Tex.: University of Texas Press, 1963), pp. 47–69, reprinted as no. IV in Bishko, *Studies in Medieval Spanish Frontier History* (London: Variorum Reprints, 1980); Lawrence J. McCrank, 'The Cistercians of Poblet as Medieval Frontiersmen: An Historiographic Essay and Case Study', in *Estudios en Homenaje a don Claudio Sanchez Albornoz en sus 90 años*, ed. María de Carmen Carlé et al. (Buenos Aires: Istituto de Historia de España, 1983), vol. II: pp. 313–60. William H. TeBrake, *Medieval Frontier: Culture and Ecology in Rijnland* (College Station: Texas A. and M. University Press, 1985). Joseph L. Wieczynski, *The Russian Frontier: The Impact of Borderlands upon the Course of Early Russian History* (Charlottesville: University Press of Virginia, 1976).

[12] Elena Lourie, 'A Society Organized for War: Medieval Spain', *Past and Present* 35 (1966): pp. 54–76 prompted this approach. Although subsequent research showed that reconquest ideology did not appear in the year 711, and interaction between Christians and Muslims was more complex, considerations of the military aspects of frontiers have remained important. Eduardo Manzano Moreno, 'Christian–Muslim Frontier in Al-Andalus: Idea and Reality', in *The Arab Influence in Medieval Europe*, ed. Dionisius A. Agius and Richard Hitchcock (Reading: Ithaca Press, 1994), pp. 83–99, argued that until the early eleventh century there was no Christian–Muslim frontier in the Duero Valley; Eduardo Manzano Moreno, 'The Creation of a Medieval Frontier: Islam and Christianity in the Iberian Peninsula, Eighth to Eleventh Centuries', in *Frontiers in Question*, pp. 32–54; Peter Linehan, 'Religion, Nationalism and National Identity in Medieval Spain and Portugal', in *Religion and National Identity*, ed. Stuart Mews, Studies in Church History 18 (Oxford: Blackwell, 1982), pp. 161–99; reprinted as no. I in Linehan, *Spanish Church and Society 1150–1300* (London: Variorum Reprints, 1983); Charles Julian Bishko, 'The Spanish and Portuguese Reconquest, 1095–1492', in *A History of the Crusades*, ed. Kenneth M. Setton (Madison, Wis.: University of Wisconsin Press, 1975), vol. III: pp. 396–456, reprinted as no. III in Bishko, *Studies in Medieval Spanish*; Angus MacKay, *Spain in the Middle Ages: From Frontier to Empire 1000–1500* (London: Macmillan, 1977); Mikel de Epalza and Suzanne Guellouz, *Le Cid: Personnage historique et littéraire* (Paris: Maisonneuve et Larose, 1983), pp. 9–55; Richard A. Fletcher, *The Quest for El Cid* (London: Hutchinson, 1989).

Hungary: a frontier society

historiography.[13] The military function of frontier zones, however, does not mean either that the dynamics within the whole of society were wholly or even mostly determined by frontier warfare and preparations for it, or that warfare in itself caused the emergence of 'frontier societies'. Moreover, the idea that pre-modern frontiers were defined in military terms and that construction in border areas served military functions has come under criticism.[14] Research on the practical military value of various frontier defence systems suggests that they facilitated monitoring and control, and their function was tied to detecting the presence of, rather than stopping, the enemy. Thus deep zonal defence mechanisms existed in Spain, Rome, Byzantium and China.[15] The adoption of crusading rhetoric is also often associated with medieval military frontiers. While true for Spain (but only from the twelfth–thirteenth centuries) and the northern wars, it did not play a role in Sicily and other frontier areas.[16]

Many medievalists have emphasized that devices of arbitration, negotiation, trade and other peaceful dealings equally characterize frontier life. A variety of views exist about the nature of such frontier life, created

---

[13] E.g. Manuel González Jiménez, 'Frontier and Settlement in the Kingdom of Castile', in *Medieval Frontier Societies*, pp. 49–74; Rees Davies, 'Frontier Arrangements in Fragmented Societies: Ireland and Wales', in *ibid.*, pp. 77–100. Also see the previous note.

[14] The Great Wall of China did not keep out the barbarians; it was the manifestation of Chinese state theory: Owen Lattimore, 'Origins of the Great Wall of China: A Frontier Concept in Theory and Practice', *Geographical Review* 27, no. 4 (1937), reprinted in Lattimore, *Studies in Frontier History: Collected Papers 1928–1958* (London, New York and Toronto: Oxford University Press, 1962), pp. 97–118. The Roman policy and ideology of expansion did not admit an idea of permanent enclosures separating the empire from the rest of the world; thus there was no frontier strategy to create a defensive system of frontier lines (a '*limes*' system): C. R. Whittaker, *Frontiers of the Roman Empire: A Social and Economic Study* (Baltimore and London: Johns Hopkins University Press, 1994); Benjamin Isaac, *The Limits of Empire: The Roman Army in the East*, rev. edn (Oxford: Clarendon Press, 1992). Aline Rousselle, ed., *Frontières terrestres, frontières célestes dans l'Antiquité* (Paris: Presses Universitaires de Perpignan, 1995).

[15] Lattimore, *Studies in Frontier History*, esp. pp. 108–10, 113–16, 257; Jiménez, 'Frontier', p. 74; J. F. Haldon and H. Kennedy, 'The Arab–Byzantine Frontier in the Eighth and Ninth Centuries: Military Organisation and Society in the Borderlands', *Recueil des Travaux de l'Institut d'Etudes Byzantines* 19 (1980): pp. 79–116; Nicolas Oikonomidès, 'L'organisation de la frontière orientale de Byzance aux Xe–XIe siècles et le Taktikon de l'Escorial', in *Actes du XIVe Congrès International des Etudes Byzantines* (Bucharest: Editura Academiei Republicii Socialiste România, 1974), vol. I: pp. 285–302, see p. 300.

[16] Friedrich Lotter, 'The Crusading Idea and the Conquest of the Region East of the Elbe', in *Medieval Frontier Societies*, pp. 267–306; MacKay, *Spain*; Eric Christiansen, *The Northern Crusades: The Baltic and the Catholic Frontier 1100–1525* (London: Macmillan, 1980; 2nd edn, Harmondsworth: Penguin, 1997); David Abulafia, *A Mediterranean Emporium: The Catalan Kingdom of Majorca* (Cambridge: Cambridge University Press, 1994), chapters I and III; David Abulafia, 'The Norman Kingdom of Africa and the Norman Expeditions to Majorca and the Muslim Mediterranean', in *Anglo-Norman Studies VII: Proceedings of the Battle Conference*, ed. R. Allen Brown (Woodbridge: Boydell and Brewer, 1985), pp. 26–49, reprinted as no. XII in Abulafia, *Italy, Sicily and the Mediterranean, 1100–1400* (London: Variorum Reprints, 1987).

by the dual dynamics of war and peaceful interaction. It is often asserted that the situation was different in central areas. Sometimes 'frontier institutions' were indeed clearly distinct from those of central areas.[17] There are, however, more questionable links between other institutions and the 'frontier': not only the military orders, but also parish organization in the frontier zone, have been described as 'frontier' institutions, and McCrank even talked about a frontier religion brought to the newly Christianized lands of Catalonia.[18] Some scholars emphasize the different quality of life: a greater freedom, feelings of self-reliance, social fluidity, the fragmented nature of society and multiple loyalties in frontier zones.[19] This may be true for some areas, but in many frontier territories settlers' lives were directed by the authorities, while other frontier regions were even under condominium, that is authorities from both sides tried to extend their rule to the region.[20] The peculiar nature of frontier life has been used to explain the development of literary genres and sacred objects, and even political structures such as the Ottoman Empire.[21]

'Frontier interaction' also came to mean acculturation or religious syn-

[17] E.g. the tenth-century eastern frontier themes of Byzantium, that were smaller than central ones, had a different structure and were populated by various minority groups: Oikonomidès, 'L'organisation'. Administrative, fiscal and military frontiers of Byzantium did not overlap: Hélène Ahrweiler, 'La frontière et les frontières de Byzance en Orient', in *Actes du XIVe Congrès International des Etudes Byzantines*, vol. I: pp. 209–30, reprinted as no. III in Ahrweiler, *Byzance: les pays et les territoires* (London: Variorum Reprints, 1976). See also A. D. Lee, *Information and Frontiers: Roman Foreign Relations in Late Antiquity* (Cambridge: Cambridge University Press, 1993), on Roman frontier institutions and control.

[18] Robert I. Burns, *The Crusader Kingdom of Valencia: Reconstruction on a Thirteenth-Century Frontier* (Cambridge, Mass.: Harvard University Press, 1967); Robert I. Burns, 'The Parish as a Frontier Institution in Thirteenth-Century Valencia', *Speculum* 37 (1962): pp. 244–51, reprinted as no. VIII in Burns, *Moors and Crusaders in Mediterranean Spain* (London: Variorum Reprints, 1978); McCrank, 'Cistercians'. Peter Linehan's incisive criticism: 'Segovia: A "Frontier" Diocese in the Thirteenth Century', *English Historical Review* 96 (1981): pp. 481–508, reprinted as no. V in Linehan, *Spanish Church and Society*; Peter Linehan, 'Frontier and Frontiers in Medieval Spain', forthcoming in *The Medieval World*, ed. Peter Linehan and Janet Nelson (London: Routledge).

[19] Lourie, 'Society Organized'; Haldon and Kennedy, 'Arab–Byzantine frontier' ('self-reliance': p. 98); Lattimore, *Studies in Frontier History*; Manzano Moreno, 'Christian–Muslim Frontier', pp. 91–6; Mehmed Fuad Köprülü, *Les Origines de l'Empire Ottoman*, Etudes Orientales 3 (Paris: E. de Boccard, 1935).

[20] Thomas F. Glick, *From Muslim Fortress to Christian Castle: Social and Cultural Change in Medieval Spain* (Manchester and New York: Manchester University Press, 1995), esp. p. 166; Ahrweiler, 'La frontière', pp. 215–16.

[21] E.g. Hugh S. Graham, '"Digenis Akritas" as a Source for Frontier History', in *Actes du XIVe Congrès*, vol. II: pp. 321–9; Angus MacKay, 'Religion, Culture, and Ideology on the Late Medieval Castilian–Granadan Frontier', in *Medieval Frontier Societies*, pp. 217–43, see pp. 224–5 (ballads; with further bibliography); pp. 230–1 (objects). Köprülü, *Les Origines*; Mehmed Fuad Köprülü, *Islam in Anatolia after the Turkish Invasion (Prolegomena)* (Salt Lake City: University of Utah Press, 1993); Colin Heywood, 'The Frontier in Ottoman History: Old Ideas and New Myths', in *Frontiers in Question*, pp. 228–50.

Hungary: a frontier society

cretism.[22] Many scholars focus not merely on commerce and contacts, but on the mixing of populations from the two sides of a theoretical frontier that came to resemble each other more than their respective core societies.[23] Even ideologically hostile cultures interacted in peaceful ways that often resulted in mingling.[24]

Frontier interaction has also been understood to affect societies in their entirety. Historians of the British Isles have recourse to the term in order to discuss Anglo-Scottish and Anglo-Irish relations, and those of the crusader kingdoms in the east have debated the extent to which crusaders were affected by the customs of those they conquered. Interaction between the nomads of the steppe and their sedentary neighbours (including Rus' and Georgia) has been seen on the one hand to lead to formations of nomad states through the influence of sedentary societies, and on the other hand to force sedentary states to adapt by military or diplomatic means to the nomadic challenge on their borders.[25] Conquest and acculturation have even served as a model for analysing the development of Europe: Robert Bartlett interpreted the emergence of Europe as a consequence of the medieval extension of Christendom's frontiers. He focused on the change produced by western European expansion.[26]

'Frontier society' is an elusive concept, with many, often implicit, interpretations. For example, Fernández-Armesto defined 'frontier society' as one that is moulded and changed by new challenges and opportunities, instead of imitating and implanting an old system.[27]

---

[22] E.g. José Enrique López de Coca-Castañer, 'Institutions on the Castilian-Granadan Frontier, 1369–1482', in *Medieval Frontier Societies*, pp. 127–50; MacKay, 'Religion'; Rasa Mažeika, 'Of Cabbages and Knights: Trade and Trade Treaties with the Infidel on the Northern Frontier, 1200–1390', *Journal of Medieval History* 20 (1994): pp. 63–76; Dimitri Obolensky, 'Byzantine Frontier Zones and Cultural Exchanges', in *Actes du XIVe Congrès*, vol. II: pp. 302–13.

[23] E.g. Glick, *Islamic and Christian Spain*; Burns, *The Crusader Kingdom of Valencia*. Hugh R. Clark, 'Muslims and Hindus in the Culture and Morphology of Quanzhou from the Tenth to the Thirteenth Century', *Journal of World History* 6, no. 1 (1995): pp. 49–74.

[24] Lattimore, *Studies in Frontier History*; articles in the section 'Challenge and interaction' in Burns, *Moors and Crusaders in Mediterranean Spain*.

[25] Denis Sinor, *Inner Asia and its Contacts with Medieval Europe* (London: Variorum Reprints, 1977); Denis Sinor, ed., *The Cambridge History of Early Inner Asia* (Cambridge: Cambridge University Press, 1990); Gary Seaman and Daniel Marks, eds., *Rulers from the Steppe: State Formation on the Eurasian Periphery* (Los Angeles: University of Southern California and Ethnographics Press, 1991); Peter B. Golden, 'Nomads and their Sedentary Neighbors in Pre-Činggisid Eurasia', *Archivum Eurasiae Medii Aevi* [*AEMAe*] 7 (1987–91): pp. 41–81; Peter B. Golden, 'Cumanica I: The Qipčaqs in Georgia', *AEMAe* 4 (1984): pp. 45–87; Anatoly Khazanov, *Nomads and the Outside World* (Cambridge: Cambridge University Press, 1984; 2nd edn, Madison: University of Wisconsin Press, 1994). Criticism of Lattimore, *Studies in Frontier History*: Thomas J. Barfield, *The Perilous Frontier: Nomadic Empires and China* (Cambridge, Mass.: Blackwell, 1989).

[26] Robert Bartlett, *The Making of Europe: Conquest, Colonization and Cultural Change 950–1350* (Princeton: Princeton University Press, 1993; 2nd edn, Harmondsworth: Penguin, 1994).

[27] Felipe Fernández-Armesto, *Before Columbus: Exploration and Colonisation from the Mediterranean to the Atlantic 1229–1492* (London: Macmillan, 1987), p. 6.

Others also use the concept to characterize areas where the development of new institutions, social forms and rules takes place.[28] This Turnerian definition obscures the fact that every society relies on traditions but also changes over time. The term can equally denote societies whose peripheries (frontier zones) developed as a result of confrontation and interaction with another society, such as along the Arab–Byzantine frontier or Muslim–Christian frontier in the Iberian peninsula. 'Frontier society' is also employed in the meaning of 'conquest society', where a conquering elite rules over a subjugated native population, such as Wales.[29] Finally, 'frontier society' has been used to denote cultural interaction. Some analyses focus on the development of the frontier region alone while others focus on the transformations of an entire society.

One of the most important associations in historiography is between frontier and expansion.[30] Turner lurks behind the model of 'frontier society' that has been prevalent in Anglo-American frontier studies. This is increasingly seldom directly Turnerian,[31] but 'frontier' often conjures up images of its transformative powers and an expanding society. Thus the focus of historical analysis has often been on western European or Christian expansion and influence, conquest, and the transplantation of western customs and religion, to the detriment of analysing local development.[32] For example, Rowell has pointed out that historians have treated Lithuania as a passive partner and analysed the aims and motivations only of Christian powers.[33]

The notion of frontier regions or societies is implicitly linked to an idea that these are formed because of the existence of frontiers (in the sense of boundaries) between different states or religions. Yet the historiography of the formation of political, especially state, boundaries has often been separate from discussions of frontier regions and frontier

---

[28] McCrank, 'Cistercians', calls the whole of medieval Europe a frontier society.
[29] E.g. Davies, 'Frontier Arrangements'; Robert Bartlett, 'Colonial Aristocracies of the High Middle Ages', in *Medieval Frontier Societies*, pp. 23–47.
[30] Friedrich Ratzel, *Politische Geographie* (Munich and Leipzig: R. Oldenbourg, 1897; reprint of 3rd edn, Osnabruck: Zeller, 1974), also wrote about the expansion of frontiers.
[31] Burns's essay entitled 'The Significance of the Frontier in the Middle Ages', in *Medieval Frontier Societies*, pp. 307–30, recalls Turner's title, but argues that Turner's thesis has to be modified to be valid. The works of Ray Allen Billington especially had an important impact on the acceptance of a reformulated Turnerian approach: *Westward Expansion: A History of the American Frontier* (New York: Macmillan, 1949); *America's Frontier Heritage*; *The American Frontier Thesis: Attack and Defense* (Washington: American Historical Association, 1971), all of them reprinted many times.
[32] Christiansen, *Northern Crusades*; James A. Brundage, 'The Thirteenth-Century Livonian Crusade: Henricus de Lettis and the First Legatine Mission of Bishop William of Modena', no. XIV in *The Crusades, Holy War and Canon Law* (Aldershot: Variorum Reprints, 1991); Bartlett, *Making of Europe*.
[33] S. C. Rowell, *Lithuania Ascending: A Pagan Empire within East-Central Europe, 1295–1345* (Cambridge: Cambridge University Press, 1994).

Hungary: a frontier society

life.[34] The development of linear boundaries is generally seen as contemporary with the formation of territorial states, although its dating has been debated.[35] The development of linear frontiers is linked to the contact and confrontation of two religions and cultures in the claim that a linear boundary first developed in thirteenth-century Iberia. According to this argument, a constant contact with a different culture in densely populated areas, a material (fortified) frontier and the ideology of expanding the borders southwards, led to the emergence of the word and notion of the frontier (*frontera*) as an exact political boundary.[36] The first appearance of the word 'frontier' (as a border, but not necessarily a state boundary) has been traced to the twelfth century in Iberia, to the thirteenth century in Italy and to 1312 in France.[37] Work on the development of state boundaries in central Europe led to a detailed charting of often very mobile borders, as well as to an analysis of the diplomatic and military means by which these frontiers evolved.[38] Linear boundaries (first of smaller territorial units) developed from the twelfth century in central Europe.[39]

---

[34] Lucien Febvre, 'La Frontière: le mot et la notion', *Revue de Synthèse Historique* 45 (1928): pp. 31–44, and in Lucien Febvre, *Pour une histoire à part entière* (Paris: Ecole Pratique des Hautes Etudes, 1962), pp. 11–24; Lucien Febvre, 'Limites et frontières', *Annales ESC* 2 (1947): pp. 201–7; Bernard Guenée, 'Des limites féodales aux frontières politiques', in *Les Lieux de mémoire*, vol. II: *La Nation*, ed. Pierre Nora (Paris: Gallimard, 1986), 2: pp. 10–33; Daniel Nordman, 'Des limites d'état aux frontières nationales', in *Les Lieux de mémoire*, vol. II: 2: pp. 35–61; Daniel Nordman, *Frontières de France: de l'espace au territoire XVIe–XIXe siècles* (Paris: Gallimard, 1998); Paul Bonenfant, 'A propos des limites médiévales', in *Eventail de l'histoire vivante: hommage à Lucien Febvre* (Paris: Librairie Armand Colin, 1953), vol. II: pp. 73–9; Jean-François Lemarignier, *Recherches sur l'hommage en marche et les frontières féodales*, Travaux et mémoires de l'Université de Lille, n.s. Droit et Lettres 24 (Lille: Bibliothèque Universitaire, 1945); Pierre Toubert, 'Frontière et frontières: un objet historique', in *Castrum 4: Frontière et peuplement dans le monde méditerranéen au Moyen Age*, Actes du colloque d'Erice-Trapani, 18–25 September 1988 (Rome: Ecole Française de Rome and Madrid: Casa Velazquez, 1992), pp. 9–17; also see essays on specific frontiers in this collection.

[35] Detailed analysis of one case: Peter Sahlins, *Boundaries: The Making of France and Spain in the Pyrenees* (Berkeley, Los Angeles and Oxford: Oxford University Press, 1989).

[36] Jean Gautier Dalché, 'Islam et chrétienté en Espagne au XIIe s.: contribution à l'étude de la notion de frontière', *Hespéris* 46 (1959): pp. 183–217; André Bazzana, Pierre Guichard and Philippe Sénac, 'La frontière dans l'Espagne médiévale', in *Castrum 4*, pp. 36–59.

[37] Guenée, 'Des limites', p. 21; Michel Mollat, *Genèse médiévale de la France moderne* (Paris: Arthaud, 1977), p. 114 dates it to 1315; Max Pfister, 'Grenzbezeichnungen im Italoromanischen und Galloromanischen', in *Grenzen und Grenzregionen*, ed. Wolfgang Haubrichs and Reinhard Schneider (Saarbrücken: Saarbrücker Druckerei und Verlag, 1994), pp. 37–50.

[38] Gotthold Rhode, *Die Ostgrenze Polens: Politische Entwicklung, kulturelle Bedeutung und geistige Auswirkung*, vol. I (Cologne and Graz: Böhlau Verlag, 1955); Zdzislaw Kaczmarczyk, 'One Thousand Years of the History of the Polish Western Frontier', *Acta Poloniae Historica* 5 (1962): pp. 79–109 (for events and maps; the interpretive framework of 'German aggression' is thoroughly outdated); Paul W. Knoll, 'The Stabilization of the Polish Western Frontier under Casimir the Great 1333–1370', *The Polish Review* 12, no. 4 (1967): pp. 3–29; Hans-Jürgen Karp, *Grenzen in Ostmitteleuropa während des Mittelalters: Ein Beitrag zur Entstehungsgeschichte der Grenzlinie aus dem Grenzsaum* (Cologne and Vienna: Böhlau Verlag, 1972).

[39] Karp, *Grenzen*, pp. 113–36; 155–65.

At the Gate of Christendom

It is usually understood that in the Middle Ages frontiers were not lines but zones or regions.[40] Even Normandy, long celebrated as the first to possess a precise linear frontier, had in fact a more zonal frontier for a long time.[41] Indeed, one of the conclusions that recurs whether scholars write about the Great Wall of China, Byzantine defence systems of the seventh century, or medieval Europe, is that linear state borders were never created in practice; frontiers always remained imprecise and zonal in the pre-modern age.[42] Yet the *concept* of linear frontier existed in medieval Europe and so did frontiers delineated by border markers on the ground. It is enough to peruse charters delimiting estates in order to find detailed and very precise descriptions of the boundary line, running between such reference points as streams, clearly identified trees, road junctions, or even artificial border markers.[43] Daniel Nordman pointed out that the clearest territorial boundary lines were those that were perceived as such by contemporaries.[44] This was certainly the case for divisions between estates, as well as in defining the extent of ecclesiastical jurisdictions of dioceses. In principle the same idea could be applied to frontiers of states. From the early fourteenth century, with the development of cartography and technology, linear frontiers indeed started to develop from points fortified for defence to continuous borders, although the permanent maintenance of unchanging linear frontiers of entire states is a modern phenomenon. This is not to say that the direction of evolution was always from zonal to linear frontiers; often the two coexisted and served different ends.[45]

Since modern interest in frontiers and frontier societies has been

---

[40] Patrick Gautier Dalché, 'De la liste à la carte: limite et frontière dans la géographie et la cartographie de l'Occident médiéval', in *Castrum* 4, pp. 19–31; Bazzana *et al.*, 'La frontière', pp. 36–59; Bartlett and MacKay, eds., *Medieval Frontier Societies*.

[41] Remarks of Lemarignier to this effect: *Recherches sur l'hommage*, pp. 70–1; Daniel Power, 'What Did the Frontier of Angevin Normandy Comprise?' in *Anglo-Norman Studies* 17, ed. Christopher Harper-Bill (Woodbridge: Boydell Press, 1995), pp. 181–201.

[42] Even reflected on medieval maps: Gautier Dalché, 'De la liste', p. 21.

[43] Border markers: Bonenfant, 'A propos des limites', pp. 77–9. Linear boundaries: Reinhard Schneider, 'Lineare Grenzen – Vom Frühen bis zum Späten Mittelalter', in *Grenzen und Grenzregionen*, pp. 51–68; in France (from the twelfth c.): Guenée, 'Des limites', pp. 11–15; Central Europe: Karp, *Grenzen*, pp. 113–36; Lajos Takács, *Határjelek, határjárás a feudális kor végén Magyarországon* (Budapest: Akadémiai Kiadó, 1987). (See below for examples on medieval Hungary.)

[44] Daniel Nordman, 'Frontière, histoire et écologie', *Annales ESC* no. 1 (1988): pp. 277–83, see p. 282.

[45] Febvre, 'Frontière', p. 17, long ago criticized the idea that linear frontiers always developed from zones. Roman frontiers were imprecise and more zonal than linear, despite the presence of walls and fortifications. Yet the fact that Rome was not surrounded by a defensive frontier system was not antithetical to enclosing space, marking boundaries and having rituals connected to boundaries: these ensured that the extent of Roman rule at any given time was signalled and protected. Whittaker, *Frontiers*, esp. pp. 18–19; Isaac, *Limits of Empire*, pp. 397–8, 401, 408–18.

inspired by a variety of perceptions and ideologies, from Victorian imperialism to modern multiculturalism,[46] it is not surprising that what emerges from a survey of frontier studies is the multiplicity of implied or explicit meanings and functions of 'frontiers'. They have included interpretations focusing on expansion against nature and agricultural colonization as well as expansion against other societies, military confrontation, spheres of interaction and acculturation. The frontier can be a place, a fringe or outer boundary; a type of society or movement; and a process.[47] In fact, other words could often be substituted for 'frontier' depending on the context: conquest and colonization, land reclamation, a variety of cultural processes. It is not clear when an area ceases to be a frontier.

Therefore, when using the concept in analyses of medieval history, it is important to distinguish between its various meanings, as well as between historical construct (or interpretative tool) and medieval ideology. 'Frontiers' in the linear–zonal boundary sense delimit administrative units, whereas 'frontiers' in the sense of borderlands are places where interaction between cultures, religions or civilizations (the form of which varies) occurs. To employ the term 'frontier' in the latter meaning can be a historical construct or a reflection of medieval notions. Whether or not contemporaries conceived of territorial or ideological frontiers between various societies and religions is a question in itself. Frontier zones in this second sense often mean frontier regions of a society. Whether there was anything 'special' about these regions has to be established rather than assumed. It needs to be proved whether there was a distinct style of life characterized by militarization, violence, and norms, laws and mechanisms different from the central areas of the same society; and whether mingling between populations from the two sides of the supposed frontier progressed to the point that they resembled each other more than their respective societies. The type of interaction or the results of interaction are not predetermined in frontier situations. If we understand 'frontier' as a zone of interpenetration between two civilizations that were politically separate, it follows that the frontier disappears when a single political authority gains hegemony over the area.[48]

One should also distinguish between frontier zones (or societies with a frontier region) and societies incorporating two or more religions and cultures in one political unit. In zones of contact, where different cultures

---

[46] Lord Curzon of Kedleston, *Frontiers*, The Romanes Lecture 1907 (Oxford: Clarendon Press, 1907), compared the frontiers of the British Empire with those of the Roman Empire. On Victorian interest in Roman frontiers: Whittaker, *Frontiers*, pp. 2–4.

[47] David H. Miller and Jerome Steffens, eds., *The Frontier: Comparative Studies*, vol. I (Norman: University of Oklahoma Press, 1977); Savage and Thompson, eds., *The Frontier*, vol. II; Theodore Papadopoullos, 'The Byzantine Model in Frontier History: A Comparative Approach', in *Actes du XIVe Congrès*, vol. II: pp. 415–19. [48] Limerick, 'Adventures', p. 76.

At the Gate of Christendom

and religions interacted in hostile or peaceful ways, states often faced each other, such as Lithuania and its Christian neighbours. These, however, were separate political entities. Such interaction between two political units has to be distinguished from 'frontier society' in the sense of a zone of interaction between two or more religions or cultures within one political framework, whether or not that framework emerged as a result of conquest.

One could therefore argue against the usefulness of a 'frontier' concept that is unconnected to the formation of frontiers as political boundaries. After all, what good is a concept which was ambiguously formulated a hundred years ago and has been severely criticized ever since? As Patricia Limerick put it: 'the word "frontier" uses historians before historians can use it'.[49] Does not the term 'frontier society' conceal more than it reveals, because all societies described as 'frontier societies' are, in fact, different from each other?

Like other concepts, 'frontier' and 'frontier society' have their uses, provided they direct attention to certain questions, rather than preclude further analysis. In the case of medieval society, did the territorial concept of Christendom have an effect on notions of frontiers, and on the development of societies in the areas along the frontiers of Christendom? Theoreticians of space emphasize that each society produces its own 'space'.[50] Richard White turned Turner on his head (a move in which he was preceded by Lattimore) to argue that society created the frontier, instead of the frontier creating society.[51] There was influence in both directions; from the centre to the frontiers, and from the frontiers to the centre. In this vein, one can investigate how medieval Christendom created its own frontiers, and what types of societies emerged along these frontiers. We can distinguish three main frontiers of medieval Roman Christendom, although, naturally, there was a great variety of local difference within this broad typology. One was characterized by the contact of Christianity and Islam. The second frontier was the one with Byzantium and orthodox Christianity. Finally, towards the north and the east, Christianity encountered animistic and shamanistic populations ('pagans' from a medieval Christian point of view), some of whom were nomads. Societies emerged in these contact zones that incorporated populations of different religions and cultures: in the Mediterranean,

---

[49] *Ibid.*, p. 75.
[50] E.g. Henri Lefebvre, *La production de l'espace* (Paris: Editions Anthropos, 1974, 3rd edn, 1986); Robert David Sack, *Conceptions of Space in Social Thought: A Geographic Perspective* (London: Macmillan, 1980); Robert David Sack, *Human Territoriality: Its Theory and History* (Cambridge, London and New York: Cambridge University Press, 1986); states as *producteurs* of frontiers: Michel Foucher, *L'invention des frontières* (Paris: Fondation pour les Etudes de Défense Nationale, 1986), p. 52. [51] Lattimore, *Studies in Frontier History*, p. 490; White, *Your Misfortune*.

Hungary: a frontier society

especially in Spain, Sicily and the Holy Land during the crusades; in the Baltic lands; and in Poland and Hungary. Many modern scholars have warned us of the dangers of adopting a simplistic view (which can even be based on certain medieval sources that expound official ideologies) of Christian–Muslim or civilized–barbarian hostility. Uncovering local realities within Christendom's frontier societies is therefore important if we are to understand medieval European societies and the formation of Europe. To what extent were these societies determined by the reality of interaction (be it hostile or peaceful), and by contemporary and explicit frontier ideologies? It is important to distinguish between explicitly 'frontier' ideologies and real interaction. Medieval frontier ideologies and rhetoric themselves, as well as the realities of interaction, are important objects of analysis. Medieval Hungary developed along one of Christendom's frontiers, and in the thirteenth century produced an explicit frontier rhetoric as well. This did not entirely determine the position of non-Christians within the kingdom, but it exercised an important influence over it.

MEDIEVAL HUNGARY

Non-Christian status in Hungary would be incomprehensible without some idea of the structures and the history of the kingdom itself.[52] Two aspects of medieval Hungarian history are particularly relevant to the present study: the situation of the kingdom on the frontier of Christendom; and the character of a composite society, partly a result of this location. Thus an analysis of these characteristics of Hungarian

---

[52] Handbooks on medieval Hungary include: Gyula Pauler, *A magyar nemzet története az Árpádok korában*, 2 vols. 2nd edn (Budapest, 1899; reprint Szeged: Állami Könyvterjesztő Vállalat, 1984); Pál Engel, *Beilleszkedés Európába a kezdetektől 1440-ig* (Budapest: Háttér Lap- és Könyvkiadó, 1990); György Székely, ed., *Magyarország története*, vol. I, pts. 1 and 2: *Előzmények és magyar történet 1242-ig* (Budapest: Akadémiai Kiadó, 1984); Jenő Szűcs, *Az utolsó Árpádok* (Budapest: MTA Történettudományi Intézete, 1993); Ervin Pamlényi, ed., *A History of Hungary* (London: Collet's, 1975); Peter Sugár, ed., *A History of Hungary* (London and New York: I. B. Tauris, 1990); Gyula Kristó, *Die Arpaden-Dynastie: Die Geschichte Ungarns von 895 bis 1301* (Budapest: Corvina, 1993); Pál Engel, *The Realm of St Stephen: A History of Medieval Hungary* (London: I. B. Tauris, forthcoming). On the early history of the Magyars, see Charles R. Bowlus, *Franks, Moravians and Magyars: The Struggle for the Middle Danube, 788–907* (Philadelphia: University of Pennsylvania Press, 1995); András Róna-Tas, *Hungarians and Europe in the Early Middle Ages: An Introduction to Early Hungarian History* (Budapest: Central European University Press, 1999). Encyclopedic reference work: Gyula Kristó, ed., *Korai Magyar Történeti Lexikon (9–14. század)* (Budapest: Akadémiai Kiadó, 1994). Maps: Ferenc Glatz, ed., *Virágkor és pusztulás: A kezdetektől 1606-ig*, História Könyvtár Atlaszok Magyarország történetéhez 1 (Budapest: MTA Történettudományi Intézet, 1995). Further bibliography in my 'Hungary in the Eleventh and Twelfth Centuries', forthcoming in *The New Cambridge Medieval History*, vol. IV, pt 2, ed. David Luscombe and Jonathan Riley-Smith. C. A. Macartney, *Hungary: A Short History* (Edinburgh: Edinburgh University Press, 1962) is unreliable.

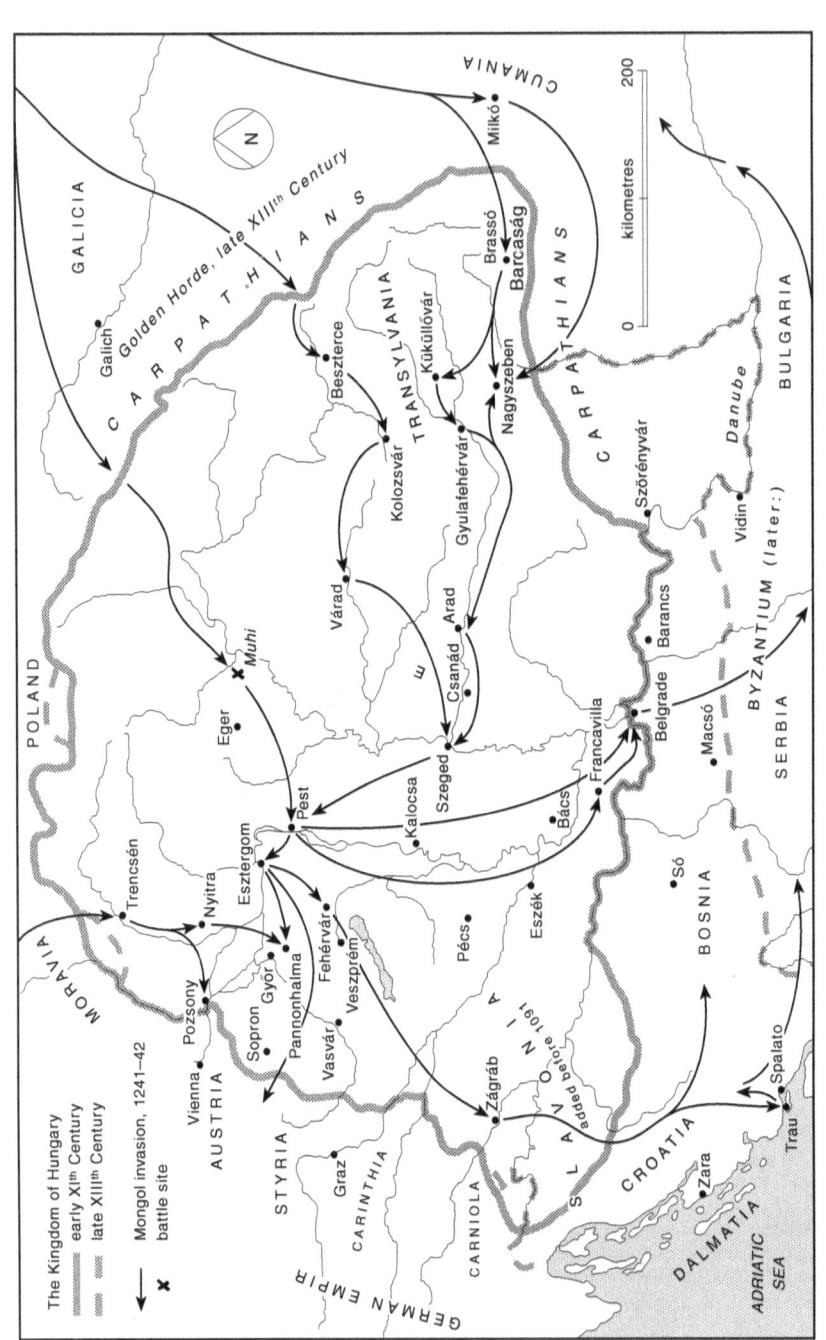

Map 1 The medieval kingdom of Hungary.

history and of the applicability of frontier theories needs to precede the examination of non-Christian presence. Hungary emerged on the frontier of Christendom. The 'Hungarians' who settled there in the late ninth century were themselves a mixture of different groups: a Finno-Ugric tribal confederation that gradually migrated from the Western Siberia–Urals region, while some tribes detached themselves and various Turkic groups progressively joined them. In the process they came into close contact with nomads and adopted steppe culture. They were also associated for a time with the Khazar Empire. Defeated by the Pechenegs, the tribal union reached the Carpathian basin in the late ninth century.

After invading the area that was to become Hungary, these tribes conducted a series of raiding expeditions well into the tenth century, reaching as far as Constantinople in the east, and the Frankish kingdoms, Iberia and Apulia in the west and south. Forced by changed economic circumstances (insufficient pasturage to support a nomad society and the impossibility of moving on) and finally by two major defeats (933 at Riade and 955 near Augsburg at the famous battle of the Lech) to settle permanently, Hungarian society underwent radical changes in the latter half of the tenth and the early eleventh centuries. The tribes were broken up, traditional leadership (chieftains and dual rulership) was eliminated and the population was subjected to a new type of monarchy. The local Slavic and other populations merged with the invaders.[53] Final settlement and Christianization went hand in hand. Byzantine as well as Roman Catholic missions, especially organized missionary work from Germany, encouraged by Prince Géza, the ruler (c. 970–97) of Hungary, resulted in the conversion of the population. Géza established close ties with the Bavarian court, inviting missionaries to his territories and marrying his son to Gisela, daughter of the Bavarian Duke Henry II, and sister of the Emperor Henry II. In the early eleventh century, Hungary emerged as a Christian kingdom, ruled by King István (Stephen, 1000/1001–38). Canonized by a local synod at the initiative of King László I in 1083, István was exalted as the founder of the kingdom and apostle of the Hungarians.

During the eleventh century Hungarian kings achieved the consolidation of the kingdom and its political–ecclesiastical independence from the Ottonian–Salian Empire. Military confrontation was complemented

---

[53] József Kovacsics, 'A történeti demográfia válaszai és nyitott kérdései az Árpád-kori népesség számára vonatkozóan', in *Magyarország történeti demográfiája I. A Honfoglalás és az Árpád-kor népessége*, ed. József Kovacsics (Budapest: Központi Statisztikai Hivatal, 1995), pp. 8–36; Loránd Benkő, 'A helynevek szerepe az Árpád-kori népességtörténeti kutatásokban', in *ibid.*, pp. 96–105; György Székely, 'A honfoglalás kori maradvány népek a Kárpát-medencében (román és német elméletek)', in *ibid.*, pp. 106–21.

by ideological formulations of sovereignty. Thus Hartvic, author of the royally commissioned *Vita* of St István in the early twelfth century, invented the legend that István received a royal crown from the pope himself, who was alerted in a vision to grant the ruler the royal insignia.[54] This buttressed the claim to Hungary's independence and equal status among the Christian kingdoms of Europe. Hartvic also incorporated a story whereby the Virgin Mary protected the kingdom, her hereditary possession, from a German attack.[55] German counter-claims included the promotion of István's Bavarian wife Gisela to the role of adviser to the king and the instrument of his conversion to Christianity.[56]

State and ecclesiastical structures that had developed in Christian kingdoms were adopted in eleventh-century Hungary, mostly according to the German model, and local institutions evolved. The main components of the new organization were two archbishoprics, dioceses, and the division of the kingdom into counties. Royal castles headed by *ispáns* (royal officials) were the centres of production and taxation, as well as of the legal and military system. In the early thirteenth century landholding patterns evolved from a mostly royal and ecclesiastical monopoly to include an ever-growing percentage of noble landholders. In the early Middle Ages the king's personal domains were more extensive than all the other lands in the country combined. Royal power rested upon the land and its inhabitants, who were in the service of the ruler. From the early thirteenth century Hungarian kings began to donate large domains to nobles as perpetual holdings. These holdings, however, were not given conditionally, so as to ensure service. As a growing portion of the lands belonged to the nobility, the kings gradually lost much of their power, together with their domains. Trade, towns and the money economy did not develop to the extent of providing sufficient income and an alternative power-base for the kings. Most towns were ecclesiastical centres (archbishoprics and bishoprics) or royal residences. They also contained communities of artisans and functioned as local markets. Some of them, however, had extensive economic roles, even including international

---

[54] 'Legenda S. Stephani regis ab Hartvico episcopo conscripta', ed. Emma Bartoniek, in *Scriptores Rerum Hungaricarum* [*SRH*], ed. Imre Szentpétery, 2 vols. (Budapest: MTA, 1937–8), vol. II: pp. 401–40, see pp. 412–14.

[55] *Ibid.*, pp. 423–4; the story is from 'Legenda Sancti Stephani Regis Maior', ed. Emma Bartoniek, in *SRH*, vol. II: pp. 377–92, see pp. 389–90. István placing Hungary under Mary's tutelage: 'Legenda Maior', p. 385 and Hartvic's 'Legenda', p. 417.

[56] 'Chronica Sigeberti Gemblacensis', ed. Ludowicus Conradus Bethmann, in *MGH SS*, vol. VI: pp. 300–74, p. 354: '1010. Gens Ungarorum hactenus idolatriae dedita, hoc tempore ad fidem Christi convertitur per Gislam sororem imperatoris, quae nupta Ungarorum regi, ad hoc sua instantia regem adduxit, ut se et totam Ungarorum gentem baptizari expeteret. Qui in baptismo Stephanus est vocatus'.

Hungary: a frontier society

trade. Urban privileges and autonomy started to develop from the status accorded to internal or foreign migrants. The *hospes* status of these (often foreign) settlers became the basis for the royal conferral of economic and legal urban rights.

Society was divided into a large number of groups with their own specific statuses, duties and privileges. There were slaves, serving-people established on the royal domains furnishing specific goods or services (*szolgálónépek*), free peasants and free men living on royal domains owing labour-service, produce and military service to the king (*várnépek*) under the higher ranking *várjobbágyok*, led by castellans (overseers, judges and military leaders in one: *várnagy*). There was a military aristocracy, which conceived of its own privileges as won by the right of conquest, claiming descent from the (often mythical) chiefs who led the tribes into the Carpathian basin in the ninth century. In fact, families, including those of German, Iberian and other immigrants, rose into the ranks of the nobility and even reached its highest rank, the barons (the distinction developed in the thirteenth century). Vassalage, with a chain of dependence, never evolved. Instead, in the latter half of the thirteenth century, it was *familiaritas* that developed in Hungary. Nobles were *familiares* of high-ranking lords; service was only rarely tied to receiving lands from the lord, the status was not hereditary and in capital crimes they came under the jurisdiction of the king.

During the thirteenth century, the social structure was becoming more unified and regulated, a process that culminated in the fourteenth century. Written charters defined the position of various groups, from peasants to nobles; a great variety of free and unfree elements began to merge into a unified serfdom; and the nobility grew more hierarchical. At the same time, the urban and monetary economy developed. Economic and social change did not occur without political upheavals. During the thirteenth century the king was confronted by the nobles, who wished to carve out more and more independence. This struggle culminated in the period of the 'kinglets' (*kiskirályok*) after the extinction of the Árpád dynasty, when a few territorial magnates, holding large parts of the country, monopolized political power before being defeated by the Angevin Charles Robert. Free men, living on royal domains prior to the early thirteenth century, were threatened by the donation of these lands to barons; they clamoured for protection. Calling themselves 'servants of the king' (*servientes regis*) they emphasized their dependence on him and thus their independence from everybody else. Only their incorporation into the nobility could safeguard their status and liberty. Their movement led to the Golden Bull of 1222, the charter of privileges that granted freedom from taxation to their domains, extensive legal privileges, restrictions on the royal donations of land and employment of 'foreigners' for the sole obligation of military service, but only in defence of the kingdom.

To argue the case for Hungary as a frontier society does not mean rehashing, in more fashionable garb, the debate concerning centre and periphery, or economic and social 'backwardness'. 'Periphery' carries connotations from its use in modern economic history and development studies: a contrast between developed, industrialized (core) countries with underdeveloped or backward regions (periphery) that supply raw materials and foodstuffs.[57] This terminology posits the interdependence of the periphery and of the core, and it is based on the analysis of the social and economic structure of the countries in question. To argue 'backwards' from modern developments is always a temptation; in this case, since Hungary did not develop a modern capitalist economy, and was industrialized late and incompletely, differences from western development in the preceding period were seen as explanations of later divergence. Moreover, political reasons often influence interpretations of the past. Thus various arguments exist about Hungary's place: that it belongs to the western world, that it has been assimilated into the east, and that it represents a unique pattern of development.

Four main trends of Hungarian historiography address the issue of Hungary's peripheral position in the Middle Ages. The first one, the so-called 'catastrophe theory', is rooted in the nationalist school of historiography.[58] This theory posits that Hungary developed parallel to western Europe, and it was because of the Ottoman conquest (1526–1686) that the country fell behind and became part of the economically and socially backward regions. The more sophisticated 'divergence theory' argues that Hungary was pushed to the periphery by the changing structure of the world economy from the late fifteenth and early sixteenth centuries. As the main trade routes shifted to the Atlantic, Hungary became integrated into the world system as a part of the agrarian periphery rather than the industrializing core.[59] The third theory recognizes late medieval changes, but stresses the existence of 'original characteristics' of Hungarian (and eastern European) feudalism from the

---

[57] These terms have been used by many authors, but became most widely known through Immanuel M. Wallerstein, *The Modern World-System: Capitalist Agriculture and the Origins of the European World-Economy in the Sixteenth Century* (New York, San Francisco and London: Academic Press, 1974).

[58] Gyula Szekfű's theory in Bálint Hóman and Gyula Szekfű, *Magyar Történet*, 5 vols., 2nd edn. (Budapest: Királyi Magyar Egyetemi Nyomda, 1935; reprint Budapest: Maecenas Könyvkiadó, 1990), vol. III: pp. 101–13, 498–9. 'the source of every later catastrophe of our history was the Turkish conquest' (p. 499).

[59] Zsigmond Pál Pach, 'The Shifting of International Trade Routes in the 15th–17th centuries', *Acta Historica Academiae Scientiarum Hungaricae* 14 (1968): pp. 287–321; Zsigmond Pál Pach, *Nyugat-európai és magyarországi agrárfejlődés a XV–XVII. században* (Budapest: Kossuth, 1963), and *Die ungarische Agrarentwicklung im 16–17. Jahrhundert, Abbiegung vom westeuropäischen Entwicklungsgang*

Hungary: a frontier society

beginning of the Middle Ages. These 'characteristics' denote developments in the Hungarian economic and social structure that were not fully fledged in comparison with western Europe.[60] The fourth theory, Jenő Szűcs's 'the three regions of Europe', distinguishes between western Europe, central Europe and eastern Europe.[61] According to Szűcs, central Europe (Bohemia, Hungary and Poland) was a region distinct from both west and east, whose social and economic structure included a mixture of elements from both, as well as local characteristics. Historical circumstances and forces drew it westwards in certain periods, eastwards at other times, but it lagged behind the west even in the most propitious periods.

These theories, whether they argue against the peripheral nature of the country in the Middle Ages, or posit it to a greater or lesser degree, all take a centre–periphery structure as their framework. This is not my aim in this book. It is necessary to distinguish between issues of 'backwardness', and questions of the kingdom's position on Christendom's frontier. The latter involves the analysis of interaction with non-Christians and of medieval views on Hungary's place in Christendom.

MEDIEVAL HUNGARY ON THE FRONTIER OF CHRISTENDOM

Hungary emerged on the Catholic–Byzantine–'pagan' frontier. After the settlement of the Hungarian tribal alliance, the country remained at the intersection of the Turkic-nomad, Byzantine and Roman Christian cultures, influenced by each, incorporating elements from each. It also became, from the beginning, a frontier society comprising a very heterogeneous population. This was a frontier existence of *la longue durée*, lasting from the tenth–eleventh centuries to the seventeenth, although the nomads to the east of Hungary disappeared and were replaced by Islam and the Ottoman Empire. How Hungarian kings coped with this frontier situation and what the consequences of living in a frontier society were for non-Christian communities constitutes the background, and some of the arguments, of this study.

A brief look at the concepts, terminology and existing structures of

---

(Budapest: Akadémiai Kiadó, 1964), claimed that the fifteenth–sixteenth c. divergence resulted in Hungary's joining eastern rather than western Europe. Péter Hanák maintained that the shifting of the trade routes pushed Hungary on to the periphery of western Europe: 'Kezdjük újra a régióvitát?' *BUKSZ* (1992, no. 4): pp. 6–10.

[60] László Makkai, 'Feudalizmus és az eredeti jellegzetességek Európában', *Történelmi Szemle* (1976, no. 1): pp. 257–77; László Makkai, 'Les caractères originaux de l'histoire économique et sociale de l'Europe orientale pendant le Moyen Age', *Acta Historica Academiae Scientiarum Hungaricae* 16 (1970): pp. 261–87.

[61] Jenő Szűcs, *Vázlat Európa három történeti régiójáról* (Budapest: Magvető Kiadó, 1983); translations: 'The Three Historical Regions of Europe: An Outline', *Acta Historica Academiae Scientiarum Hungaricae* 29 (1983): pp. 2–4, 131–84; *Les trois Europes* (Paris: Harmattan, 1985).

Hungary's borders is in order. Early medieval Hungary was surrounded by a wide area of borderlands, the *indagines regni* (vernacular *gyepű*).[62] Like European border districts since the time of the Carolingian marches, these were regions where defensive systems existed.[63] Natural and artificial obstacles hindered entry and where roads passed through the forests, stones and branches were used as barricades (*clausura, obstaculum*). In theory, entry was permitted only at gates (*porta,* vernacular *baranya* from Slavic *brana*).[64] These were described as entry and exit points.[65] Frontier guards, often from members of immigrant eastern groups, such as Pechenegs and Muslims, were settled on the *gyepű*.[66] These guards had a messenger service to send news to the king about danger on the borders.[67] The *gyepű* (*indago*) in the early medieval period often did not directly adjoin neighbouring countries but, along with the gates, was situated further towards the interior of the kingdom.[68] Beyond the *gyepű* (*ultra indagines*, vernacular *gyepűelve*), uninhabited territory stretched to the neighbouring countries. For example, Otto of Freising reported that Leopold, duke of Austria, attacked Hungary and marched as far as the obstacles protecting the country.[69]

[62] György Fejér, *Codex diplomaticus Hungariae ecclesiasticus ac civilis* [*CD*] 11 vols. (Buda, 1829–44), vol. III, pt. 2, p. 69 (*RA*, no. 420; 1225): 'compellantur ire ad incidendas indagines vulgo gepu'. Hungary's borders in the tenth and eleventh centuries: Kornél Bakay, 'Hungary in the Tenth and Eleventh Centuries', in Bakay, ed., *Sacra Corona Hungariae* (Kőszeg: Városi Múzeum, 1994), pp. 3–31, see p. 8–10. Gyula Kristó, Ferenc Makk and László Szegfű, 'Szempontok és adatok a korai magyar határvédelem kérdéséhez', *Hadtörténelmi Közlemények* n.s. 20, no. 4 (1973): pp. 639–58. 'Gyepű' in *KMTL*, with further bibliography.

[63] Julia M. H. Smith, 'Fines Imperii: The Marches', in *The New Cambridge Medieval History* vol. II, ed. Rosamond McKitterick (Cambridge: Cambridge University Press, 1995), pp. 169–89; marches elsewhere, e.g.: Lemarignier, *Recherches sur l'hommage*, p. 5; Davies, 'Frontier Arrangements', p. 80.

[64] Hansgerd Göckenjan, *Hilfsvölker und Grenzwächter im Mittelalterlichen Ungarn* (Wiesbaden: Franz Steiner Verlag, 1972), pp. 5–11; Gyula Kristó, *A vármegyék kialakulása Magyarországon* (Budapest: Magvető Kiadó, 1988), p. 112; Gyula Pauler, 'Néhány szó hadi viszonyainkról a XI–XIII. században', *Hadtörténelmi Közlemények* 1, no. 4 (1888): pp. 501–26, see p. 504.

[65] Imre Nagy et al., eds., *Hazai Okmánytár (Codex diplomaticus patrius)* [*HO*], 8 vols. (Győr and Budapest, 1865–91), vol. VIII: p. 136, no. 106 (*RA*, no. 2005; 1270): 'ultra indagines prope terminos terre nostre . . . in exitu ad Poloniam'.

[66] János M. Bak, György Bónis and James Ross Sweeney, tr. and eds., *The Laws of Hungary*, ser. I, vol. I: *The Laws of Medieval Hungary 1000–1301* (Bakersfield, Calif.: Charles Schlacks Jr, 1989), p. 15: 'custodes confiniorum, vulgo ewrii'; György Székely, 'Településtörténet és nyelvtörténet. A XII. századi magyar nyelvhatár kérdéséhez', in *Mályusz Elemér Emlékkönyv*, ed. Éva H. Balázs, Erik Fügedi and Ferenc Maksay (Budapest: Akadémiai Kiadó, 1984), pp. 311–39, see p. 315; Göckenjan, *Hilfsvölker*, pp. 12–22.

[67] Bak, *Laws*, p. 28: 'Si magna fama marchiam intraverit, comes nuntios II equis exercitualibus IIII ad regem dirigat'; Székely, 'Településtörténet', p. 313.

[68] *CD*, vol. IV, pt. 2: p. 380 (*RA*, no. 1105); vol. III, pt. 2: p. 333 (*RA*, no. 503); Gusztáv Wenzel, *Árpádkori új okmánytár* [*ÁÚO*], 12 vols. (Pest, 1860–74), vol. VIII: p. 68, no. 45 (*RA*, no. 1809). One example of *gyepű* and *gyepűelve* (with map): György Györffy, *Az Árpád-kori Magyarország történeti földrajza* [*TF*], 4 vols. to date (Budapest: Akadémiai Kiadó, 1963–), vol. II: p. 50.

[69] Otto of Freising, 'Chronicon', ed. Roger Wilmans in *MGH SS*, vol. XX: pp. 116–301, see p. 256. Székely, 'Településtörténet', p. 314.

Hungary: a frontier society

The borderlands were first organized into separate territories. Initially, there were *ispáns* ('counts') of a border county or border region.[70] As the settlement of the kingdom pushed outwards, several villages settled beyond the *gyepű* and gates; in this way 'beyond the *gyepű*' (*gyepűelve*) became a toponym in the northern and north-eastern parts of the kingdom, used for territories and estates.[71] Eventually the *gyepű* also moved outwards. Gradually these territories were incorporated into the county system, ceasing to be separate territorial organizations. In this way, the borders of the kingdom began to coincide with the borders of counties.[72] While in the west a stable frontier emerged earlier as inhabited lands on the two sides became contiguous (although border skirmishes continued),[73] wide borderlands on the eastern frontier had a prolonged existence. Almost no charters refer to the locations of the borders of the kingdom with Rus', the Cumans and the Bulgars, that is, in the north-east, east and south-east; here, the borders were fixed only at a very late stage, and the system of *gyepű*, gates, and *gyepűelve* survived much longer.[74] The frontier zone that witnessed the most constant turbulence and confrontation was not heavily settled, and therefore was the slowest to develop as a fixed border, contrary to the Iberian example. That the development pattern of borders was asynchronous is not unusual. Roman frontier strategy in the desert, where Roman police activities were essential to maintain security, differed from the one *vis-à-vis* the Persian Empire, a rival; the southern frontier of China was open and an area of expansion, while the northern frontier where the Great Wall was built was a more defensive one; the eastern frontiers of Byzantium, where two rival ideologies clashed, were more precisely defined than the western; the western border of Poland stabilized earlier than the eastern one.[75]

Terminology and imagery applied to borders within the kingdom and to the frontier of the kingdom often overlapped. Internal borders, around villages and estates, were clearly designated both on the ground and in charter descriptions, although the vocabulary for doing so varied. Village

---

[70] They were called *marchio* (adopted from charters of the German Empire) during St István's reign. By the time of King László I's so-called second law-book, this was replaced by the name *comes confinii*. Bak, *Laws*, p. 15; Kristó, *Vármegyék*, p. 61.

[71] Settlements 'extra portam existentes', 'ultra portam', 'ultra indagines': Kristó, *Vármegyék*, pp. 112–13; Kristó et al., 'Szempontok', pp. 643–4.

[72] Kristó et al., 'Szempontok', pp. 640–4. Maps and descriptions for each relevant county: TF.

[73] Fritz Posch, 'Die deutsch-ungarische Grenzentwicklung im 10. und 11. Jahrhundert auf dem Boden der heutigen Steiermark', *Südost-Forschungen* 22 (1963): pp. 126–39.

[74] Kristó, *Vármegyék*, p. 114.

[75] Foucher, *Invention*, pp. 75–6; Ahrweiler, 'Frontière', pp. 224–7; Isaac, *Limits of Empire*, pp. 19–100; Whittaker, *Frontiers*, pp. 38–59; Lattimore, *Studies in Frontier History*, pp. 85–96, 475–7; Knoll, 'Stabilization'; Rhode, *Ostgrenze Polens*.

lands were already defined by their borders in early foundation charters of ecclesiastical institutions.⁷⁶ Latin words, adopted from western usage, were current in Hungary from the eleventh century onwards: *terminus, marchia, finis, limes*. Vernacular words also appeared at that time: *megye* or *mesgye* and *határ*.⁷⁷ Borders of lands were signalled by various objects (stones, trees and so on), and were very precisely described in charters that gave detailed accounts of the perambulation (*határjárás*) that accompanied land donations or confirmations of ownership.⁷⁸ A boundary could even be drawn so that it ran through a church building.⁷⁹ The Latin word *meta* clearly indicated the assimilation of markers and borders, as it was used in both senses.⁸⁰ Border disputes occasionally led to swearing an oath about rightful ownership, which shows the aura of sacrality surrounding borders. A charter dating from 1236 tells of two people taking an oath standing on the land that was the object of litigation, with clods of earth on their heads.⁸¹ Internal boundaries, together with the notion of linear boundaries, developed elsewhere in Europe with similar precision.⁸²

---

[76] István Szabó, *A középkori magyar falu* (Budapest: Akadémiai Kiadó, 1969), p. 107: 'cum suis terminis'. On borders, ways of delimiting them and symbolic functions in a later period: Takács, *Határjelek*.

[77] *Megye*: a loan-word from a western Slavic language, probably in the tenth century; first appeared in western Hungary. Its meaning was 'border' (Latin equivalents in charters: *terminus, limitatio, margo, distinccio, meta seu signa metalia*). Prior to the first half of the thirteenth century it also took on the meaning 'border region', and 'county' (first surviving reference to *megye* as 'county': laws of King Kálmán, c. 1100): Kristó, *Vármegyék*, p. 37.

Határ, attested from 1061, meant a boundary or zone between territories, or any object or natural marker indicating this boundary. (From the verb 'press forward', *hat, hatol*: the place to which it was possible to go forwards.) *Határ* to this day means both internal borders and the frontiers of the country, as well as fields of a village; from the fifteenth century it also acquired an abstract meaning of 'final limits, bounds'. Loránd Benkő, ed., *A magyar nyelv történeti-etimológiai szótára*, 3 vols. (Budapest: Akadémiai Kiadó, 1967–76), vol. II: pp. 73–4; On the modern period: Robert J. W. Evans, 'Frontiers and National Identities in Central Europe', *International History Review* 14, no. 3 (1992): pp. 480–502.

[78] E.g. *ÁÚO*, vol. IV: pp. 307–8, no. 198. Someone buried along the border (1181): *TF*, vol. I: p. 284 (*RA*, no. 130).

[79] Imre Nagy and Gyula Tasnádi Nagy, eds., *Anjoukori Okmánytár*, 7 vols. (Budapest, 1878–1920), vol. II: pp. 491–2, no. 423 (1330).

[80] Often a ditch was made to mark a border, and by the eleventh century the vernacular Hungarian word *árok* (ditch), like *meta*, came to mean border as well: Szabó, *A magyar falu*, p. 108.

[81] Ferdinand Knauz, *Monumenta Ecclesiae Strigoniensis* [*MES*], 3 vols. (Esztergom, 1874–1924), vol. I: p. 320, no. 394; Ferdinand Knauz, *Az esztergomi főegyháznak okmánytára (Codex diplomaticus primatialis ecclesiae Strigoniensis)*, 2 vols. (Esztergom, 1863–6), vol. II: pp. 44–5, no. 59. A false oath was thought to bring swift punishment from God, a theme used by the poet János Arany, in his 'A hamis tanú' (the perjurer). A recent edn is *Arany János Balladái* (Budapest: Szépirodalmi Kiadó, 1985), pp. 93–5.

[82] E.g. Schneider, 'Lineare Grenzen'; Gautier Dalché, 'De la liste', p. 19; Christopher Wickham, 'Frontiere di vilaggio in Toscana nel XII secolo', *Castrum* 4, pp. 239–51; Sahlins, *Boundaries*, pp. 5–6; Foucher, *Invention*, p. 112 (and p. 81 for China); Lemarignier, *Recherches sur l'hommage*, p. 177; Guenée, 'Des limites', pp. 12–13. On central Europe: Evans, 'Frontiers', p. 482; Karp, *Grenzen*, pp. 113–35. Similarly for the Roman Empire: Isaac, *Limits of Empire*, p. 397.

Hungary: a frontier society

Written evidence shows a clear understanding of the existence of a frontier of the kingdom, at least among ecclesiastics and at the royal court, whence such evidence emanated. Conceptually, this frontier was both linear and zonal. Several groups of sources are significant in this respect. The frontiers of the kingdom appear in Hungarian laws, charters, chronicles and hagiography. These sources portrayed the frontier as enclosing the kingdom's territory, and separating it from neighbouring political units. For example a man of the king was sent on a diplomatic mission 'ultra terminos regni nostri', a castle was built 'in confinio regni Sclavonie', and King László IV led an army to force Cumans who left Hungary to return: 'pro reducendis Cumanis qui . . . de regno nostro aufugerant, de finibus et terminis Tartarorum . . . ultra Alpes'.[83] The main concerns associated with this frontier in the eleventh to the early twelfth centuries were the exit of inhabitants of the kingdom, and interaction with foreigners in the forms of trade and war. This notion of the frontier was linked to royal control. Those who wished to leave Hungary were to obtain a seal from the king's and *ispán*'s toll collectors who guarded the border crossings.[84] Royal permission was also necessary for trade with foreigners at the frontier.[85] This juridical and administrative aspect of frontiers, linking borders to the territorial extent of royal power, was a major factor in the development of medieval frontiers in Europe.[86] The vocabulary of entrance and exit, with a clear definition of points on the frontier but without drawing a strict linear frontier around the whole kingdom, occurred elsewhere as well.[87]

The frontier was also seen as a point of control and defence against enemies. The *gyepű* system with the border guards was to facilitate this defence. Medieval charters, chronicles and hagiography all described enemy attacks as breaching Hungary's frontiers. For example, the Czech

---

[83] *ÁÚO*, vol. IV: p. 310, no. 200 (*RA*, no. 3482). Castle: *CD*, vol. V, pt. 2: p. 125 (*RA*, no. 2426; in 1273). Cumans: *JK*, vol. II: pp. 454–5, no. 84 (*CD*, vol. V, pt. 3: p. 410; *RA*, no. 3499). Other examples: the king donates a castle built by the Czechs and occupied by the Hungarians to one of his men, 'in regni nostri confinio': *CD*, vol. VII, pt. 5: p. 590, no. CCCXCII (*RA*, no. 2565, in 1274); description 'loca ultra indagines prope terminos terre nostre existencia': *HO*, vol. VIII: p. 136, no. 106 (*RA*, no. 2005, in 1270). Another estate is 'circa confinia polonie': *Hazai Oklevéltár 1234–1536*, ed. Imre Nagy, Farkas Deák and Gyula Nagy (Budapest, 1879), p. 71, no. 61 (*RA*, no. 2523, in 1274). 'In confinio Franconie': Chronicle of the Hungarian Anonymous, in *SRH*, vol. I: p. 108.

[84] Bak, *Laws*, p. 32: 'Egressuri de Hungaria a theloneariis . . . qui exitus tenent, sigillum querant'.

[85] There was a special concern with trade in horses in the early Middle Ages. 'In confinium' and 'fines Hungarie' for borders. Laws of László I (1077–95): Bak, *Laws*, pp. 15–16; law of King Kálmán (1095–1116) in *ibid.*, pp. 28, 31–2.

[86] Guenée, 'Des limites', pp. 18–21; similar in Rome: Rousselle, ed., *Frontières*, pp. 49–50; Whittaker, *Frontiers*, esp. chapters II–III; Lee, *Information*, chapter II.

[87] S. Italy: Jean-Marie Martin, 'Les problèmes de la frontière en Italie méridionale (VIe–XIIe siècles)', in *Castrum 4*, pp. 259–76, see pp. 262–5.

King Otakar II entered the 'fines regni Hungarie' and the 'fines regni nostri' to devastate the kingdom; a man deserved a reward for his role in 'confiniorum regni nostri defensionibus'. The Hospitallers were settled 'in frontibus paganorum', 'in paganorum confiniis' to defend Hungary and spread Christianity. The *Illuminated Chronicle* described the Hungarian tribes as arriving 'in confinium regni Hungarie' at the time of the conquest of Hungary. In the thirteenth-century *Life* of St László, the Pechenegs 'confinia Ungarorum irruperunt'.[88] These examples demonstrate that there was a clear concept of the kingdom as a territorial entity, whose frontiers had to be defended, without the existence of a linear frontier all around Hungary in practice.

Finally, there are two very eloquent examples of medieval conceptualizations of a linear frontier of the kingdom of Hungary. One, a charter from 1244, describes the borders of two estates, and also mentions the frontier of the kingdom.[89] The king conferred two estates, one, 'terram in confinio Poloniae existentem'; the other 'terram in terminis Berem' (the last being a toponym). The actual delimitation of the estates is described in detail by giving the location of border markers: 'prima meta' starts at a river, the border then goes to a tree 'sub qua est meta terrea'; further on there are 'duae metae terreae', and so on. Finally the estate stretches 'ad confinia Polonorum et ibi metis terminatur'. On the other estate 'prima meta procedit in confinio Morauiae'; the charter again lists the *metae*. Thus the terminology may fluctuate slightly between different sources, but within one text there is a clear differentiation of terms for internal land borders and for the frontiers of the kingdom. The location of the border of an estate, moreover, can coincide with the border of the kingdom, showing that the notion of a linear border of Hungary existed. The other example, a passage in the *Gesta Hungarorum* of the Hungarian Anonymous (late twelfth or early thirteenth century) on *De constitutione*

---

[88] Otakar's attack: *ÁÚO*, vol. IV: p. 25, no. 9 (*RA*, no. 2364); p. 40, no. 18 (*RA*, no. 2558). Reward for defence: *HO*, vol. VIII: p. 231, no. 185 (*RA*, no. 3214). Hospitallers: *CD*, vol. III, pt. 1: p. 238 (*RA*, no. 330). *Illuminated Chronicle* (a fourteenth-century composition incorporating earlier texts): Alexander [Sándor] Domanovszky, ed., 'Chronici Hungarici compositio saeculi XIV', in *SRH*, vol. I: pp. 239–505, see p. 286. *Life* of St László: *SRH*, vol. II: p. 520. Other examples: a castle in Sopron, on the western border, 'castrum nostrum sit in confinio, et continuis vigiliis et custodiis debeat conseruari': *ÁÚO*, vol. IV: p. 254, no. 157 (*RA*, no. 3249); King András II gave land to the Teutonic Order to protect Hungary against the Cumans 'in confinio': *CD*, vol. III, pt. 1: p. 117 (*RA*, no. 275). A man participated 'in diversis expedicionibus', undertaken 'in illis partibus in defensione confini regni nostri': *HO*, vol. IV: p. 71, no. 49 (*RA*, no. 3446, in 1287). Otakar of Bohemia 'in confiniis Hungariae laceraverat': Alexander [Sándor] Domanovszky, ed., 'Simonis de Keza Gesta Hungarorum', in *SRH*, vol. I: pp. 141–94, see p. 185. The German emperor came 'ad terminos Hungarie' and encountered the 'obstacula' put up there by the Hungarians, then 'invasit fines Hungarie': 'Chronici', in *SRH*, vol. I: pp. 329, 331. In the early twelfth-century *Life* of St István by Hartvic, Germans attack 'Pannonie terminos': *SRH*, vol. II: p. 423.

[89] *CD*, vol. IV, pt. 1: pp. 345–6 (*RA*, no. 792).

Hungary: a frontier society

regni, relates a fictitious story about the ruler fixing the borders of the kingdom much like the borders of an estate.[90] The chronicler uses several different words – I would suggest, not accidentally – to convey this process. To describe how the ruler Zulta set out the borders of the kingdom of Hungary the word *meta* (which means both border-markers and borders) is used. The Anonymous depicted the drawing of borders around the 'estate' of the king – the whole kingdom – in the same way as the process of delimiting estates. To say that Zulta placed Pechenegs on these borders, the author wrote 'in confinio'. The Pechenegs were to protect the kingdom so that the Germans would not attack the borders of Hungary ('fines Hungarorum'). The chronicler used *meta* to denote a theoretical linear boundary of the kingdom, presented in the same way as the boundaries of estates that were marked by border markers; and *confinium* and *fines* to designate a frontier zone that protected the kingdom.

The terminology used for frontiers in medieval Hungary was somewhat fluid. 'In frontibus' itself, the word (*frons*) that ultimately gave us the word 'frontier', was rarely used, and when it was it conformed to usage elsewhere in Europe and meant a military front.[91] Despite partially overlapping designations, however, the frontier around the kingdom was understood conceptually as both zonal and linear. Certain terms were more associated with the frontier as a zone, such as *confinium*. Similar overlaps and differentiation occurred elsewhere in Europe; for example, Latin *fines*, French *fins* and *confins* meant a frontier zone, while the boundary line was indicated by Latin *metae*, French *bornes*, *termes*, *limites*. Spanish *frontera* meant a frontier zone, and eventually came to mean a frontier line. German *marka* was used for both linear frontier and a frontier zone, while *grenze* (from *granica* and its various forms in Slavic languages) was used for boundary line, from the original physical marker.[92]

Hungary's frontiers changed over time. As new territories were added or claimed (a claim did not always necessarily lead to real possession), the title of the Hungarian kings grew. Thus by the end of the thirteenth century, the Hungarian king was 'rex Hungarie, Dalmacie, Croacie, Rame, Seruie, Gallicie, Lodomerie, Cumanie, Bulgarie'.[93] This title does not reflect the territory effectively ruled by Hungarian kings, the extent of which changed somewhat in the eastern and southern areas. Hungarian expansion led to the attachment of Croatia in the late

---

[90] Emil Jakubovich, ed., 'Anonymi (P. Magistri) Gesta Hungarorum', in *SRH*, vol. I: pp. 33–117, see pp. 113–14: 'Dux... Zulta... fixit metas regni Hungarie ex parte Grecorum usque ad portam Wacil et usque ad terram Racy'.
[91] Febvre, 'Frontière', pp. 12–13; Guenée, 'Des limites', p. 21.
[92] Pfister, 'Grenzbezeichnungen', pp. 37–50; Karp, *Grenzen*, pp. 137–51; Febvre, 'Frontière', pp. 23–4.   [93] E.g. *ÁÚO*, vol. IV: p. 339, no. 216 (*RA*, no. 3541). Engel, *Beilleszkedés*, p. 160.

eleventh century, to that of Bosnia and territories north of Serbia gradually in the twelfth and thirteenth centuries, and to that of the area between the Danube and the Olt rivers in the early thirteenth century. Competition with Byzantium and then Venice for Dalmatian coastal cities from the twelfth century onwards was much less of a success, and attempts in Galicia and Cumania in the early thirteenth century, and in Styria in the middle of the century, failed.

Hungary was on the frontier of Christendom; its own frontiers were permeable to both hostile and peaceful interaction from east and west. Defence and military considerations were important and at times the main task of kings. However, Hungary cannot be simply defined as a militarized society, centred on war and mastering devices for arbitration and mediation.[94] Interaction both along the frontier and within the kingdom together shaped society.

Interaction with Latin Christendom, Byzantium and the nomad world influenced the formation and subsequent character of the kingdom. After the Christianization of Hungary, the links between Latin Christendom and Hungary grew ever tighter, although this did not mean the end of conflict. Attacks from the west were initiated by Salian emperors. They sent military expeditions against Hungary, often in aid of one side in civil wars (1030, 1040s), in order to extend their suzerainty to Hungary through an oath of fidelity from the king. This essentially corresponded to imperial policy towards Bohemia and Poland. Later on, the western frontier became more stable, but as the example of the Mongol invasion demonstrated, when an opportunity presented itself, this stability could be disrupted; Duke Frederick of Austria briefly annexed some of western Hungary when King Béla was defeated by the Mongols. More important than hostilities were the networks that evolved. From the beginning of the Christianization of Hungary individuals and groups arrived from all over Christendom. Missionaries from German areas (and the Byzantine Empire) went to Hungary from the tenth century onwards. Clerics and monks continued to take up residence in Hungary. Bishops and other clerics were appointed throughout the period, such as Roger who was from Italy and came to Hungary in the retinue of the papal legate Jacob in 1233, then becoming archdeacon of Várad; or Bartholomew, bishop of Pécs (1219–51) who was French.[95] Cistercians,

---

[94] Lourie, 'Society Organized'; Bartlett and MacKay, eds., *Medieval Frontier Societies*, pp. v–vi as a common characteristic of medieval frontier societies.

[95] Tibor Almási, 'Megjegyzések Rogerius magyarországi méltóságviseléséhez', *Acta Universitatis Szegediensis de Attila József Nominatae* [*AUSz*]. *Acta Historica* 86 (1988): pp. 9–14; Agostino Paravicini Bagliani, *Cardinali di curia e 'familiae' cardinalizie dal 1227 al 1254*, 2 vols. (Padua: Antenore, 1972), vol. I: pp. 126, 251–2; László Koszta, 'Un prélat français de Hongrie: Bertalan, évêque de Pécs (1219–1251)', *Cahiers d'Etudes Hongroises* 8 (1996): pp. 71–96.

Hungary: a frontier society

Premonstratensians, Franciscans and Dominicans arrived and the networks of the monastic orders brought individuals like John of Limoges to Hungary, who was abbot of the Cistercian monastery of Zirc (1208–18). Knights reached Hungary both as members of military orders and in the retinue of foreign queens; for example, in the entourage of Gertrude of Merania, first wife of András II, or Constance of Aragon, wife of King Imre. In addition, large groups of burghers and peasant settlers arrived, especially from the mid-twelfth century: Germans, Walloons, French, Italians and Flemings.[96]

Hungary was also on the frontier between Roman Catholicism and Byzantine Christianity. Byzantine influences did not cease after the conversion of the country to Roman Catholicism; they dwindled only from the thirteenth century onwards. Not only did Greek monasteries survive into the thirteenth century, but personal contacts between the royal dynasty and the court at Constantinople remained and even strengthened during the twelfth century. An outstanding example of these dynastic ties, Béla III (ruled 1172–96), was brought up in the Byzantine court. His brother, King István IV, entrusted Béla to Emperor Manuel Comnenos (1143–80), to ensure Manuel's alliance in his own fight for the Hungarian throne. Béla was engaged to Manuel's daughter, and spent his childhood as the heir apparent to the throne of Constantinople. For a few years, there was even the possibility of a united Byzantino-Hungarian empire. But Manuel finally had a son; thus Béla was given another fiancée and deprived of the right to the throne. At the time of the death of his brother, who had no children, Béla returned to be king of Hungary. The archbishop of the country refused to crown him, fearing that Greek Christianity would take the place of Catholicism in Hungary. His fears proved to be groundless: Béla, although he did keep a strong political and cultural orientation to Byzantium, established one of the most resplendent royal courts of Hungary, laying the foundations of the royal chancery and other institutions. This episode shows the importance of Byzantine influences even at the end of the twelfth century.[97]

---

[96] See chapter 3.
[97] Ferenc Makk, *The Árpáds and the Comneni: Political Relations Between Hungary and Byzantium in the 12th Century* (Budapest: Akadémiai Kiadó, 1989); Gyula Moravcsik, 'Les relations entre la Hongrie et Byzance à l'époque des Croisades', *Bibliothèque de la Revue des Etudes Hongroises* 9 (1934): pp. 1–8; Gyula Moravcsik, 'The Role of the Byzantine Church in Medieval Hungary', *American Slavic and East European Review* 6 (1947): pp. 134–51; Gyula Moravcsik, 'Hungary and Byzantium in the Middle Ages', in *The Cambridge Medieval History* (1966) vol. IV, pt. 1: pp. 566–92; Gyula Moravcsik, *Byzantium and the Magyars* (Budapest: Akadémiai Kiadó, 1970); Gyula Moravcsik, *Fontes Byzantini historiae Hungaricae aevo ducum et regum ex stirpe Árpád descendentium* (Budapest: Akadémiai Kiadó, 1984); György Székely, 'La Hongrie et Byzance aux Xe–XIIe siècles', *Acta Historica Academiae Scientiarum Hungaricae* 13 (1967): pp. 291–310; Nicolas Oikonomidès, 'A propos des relations ecclésiastiques entre Byzance et la Hongrie au XIe siècle:

As noted above, Hungary was on the eastern frontier of Christendom for *la longue durée*. The kingdom's eastern borders remained turbulent throughout the thirteenth century; processes there represented typical patterns of interaction between nomads and their sedentary neighbours. This frontier is the most significant for the present study. One of the major themes of medieval Hungarian history throughout the Middle Ages continued to be encounter with peoples – in the form of conquerors or refugees – migrating from the east. Just as the Hungarians had done, tribal alliances from the east continued to arrive at the borders of the kingdom. They were steppe nomads who were either raiding for booty, an activity that was a routine part of nomad economies, or were caught up in migrations that characterized the steppe.[98] In this way, various nomads attacked Hungary or sought entrance. The steppe background of raids and migrations has been analysed by several scholars; the elements I wish to emphasize are the mobile lifestyle of the nomads, and their capacity to forge alliances with other nomads and with sedentary states. Their mobility was based on an economy centred on livestock, 'living' on horseback, and using tents and yurts that could be moved easily. Sometimes loose formations of nomad empires arose, while other groups entered into agreements with sedentary states. In their interactions with sedentary societies, the nomads played several complementary roles. They raided for plunder, traded, entered into military alliances with their neighbours, or settled.

From the time of the establishment of the kingdom of Hungary, nomad raids swept through eastern parts of the country. For example, the *Life* of István I, the first Christian king of Hungary, recounts how István was warned by divine vision about a Pecheneg raid: 'one night suddenly awakened by some revelation, he ordered a courier to hasten . . . to Alba in Transylvania and gather all those living in the country within the fortifications of the city . . . For . . . the enemies of Christians would come upon them, that is, the Pechenegs . . . Scarcely had the messenger completed the orders of the king, when . . . the onslaught of the Pechenegs devastated everything by burning and plundering.'[99] These nomad

---

footnote 97 (*cont.*)
   le Métropolite de Turquie', in *Documents et études sur les institutions de Byzance (VIIe–XVe s.)* (London: Variorum, 1976), no. XX; Paul Stephenson, 'Manuel I Comnenus, the Hungarian Crown and the 'Feudal Subjection' of Hungary, 1162–1167', *Byzantinoslavica* 57 (1996): pp. 33–59. Relations were not always peaceful during the twelfth century; questions of territorial domination led to fights.
[98] Sinor, *Cambridge History of Early Inner Asia*; Peter B. Golden, *An Introduction to the History of the Turkic Peoples* (Wiesbaden: Otto Harrasowitz, 1992); Khazanov, *Nomads*; István Vásáry, *A régi Belső-Ázsia története* (Szeged: József Attila Tudományegyetem Magyar Őstörténeti Kutatócsoportja, 1993).
[99] 'Quadam . . . nocte repente per revelationem quandam expergefactus, veredarium quendam . . . ad Albam Transilvanam precepit festinare et omnes in rure manentes ad munitiones civitatum . . .

Hungary: a frontier society

attacks were a recurrent feature on the eastern frontier. Pechenegs, Oghuz, then Cumans, conducted plundering expeditions against Hungary; frequent entries in Hungarian chronicles testify to this: 'Three years after the coming of the Cuns, the Pechenegs . . . swam across the river Sava . . . and taking captives and plunder, carried them off to their lands.'[100] The legend of St László included a popular story about the saving of a maiden from a 'Cuman' who abducted her.[101]

The *gyepű* system could not stop large armies from attacking, but hindered small raids and served to gain time while messengers alerted the king to the danger; this was a common function of pre-modern frontier systems.[102] Chronicle accounts of the nomad raids sometimes described how the enemy broke through the *gyepű* to enter the kingdom.[103] There were various points of entry such as the pass of Borgó and Radna in Transylvania through which nomads penetrated.[104] Thirteenth-century kings adopted new methods for the protection of the eastern borders. Apart from settlements of border guards, two military orders were installed to protect especially danger-prone areas in these regions in the thirteenth century: the Teutonic Knights in 1211 to protect the Barcaság, directly adjoining Cuman lands (where eventually one of the Mongol armies entered), and the Hospitallers in 1247 to defend the eastern borders. The king, however, was not willing to cede territories for the sake of defence, and the Teutonic Order's attempts at gaining independence through direct subordination to the Apostolic See resulted in their expulsion in 1225. Despite repeated papal interventions, King András II did not permit the Knights to return. After the Mongol invasion, King Béla IV relinquished the royal monopoly on building stone castles, and nobles soon erected castles of their own. The result, however, was a significant growth of castles in the western and northern regions of Hungary, rather than the strengthening of the eastern borders.[105]

---

congregare. Predixit enim superventuros christianorum hostes, videlicet . . . Bessos. . . . Vix nuncius mandata regis complevit et ecce Bessorum . . . calamitas incendiis et rapinis cuncta devastavit'. *SRH*, vol. II: p. 423.

[100] 'Factum est . . . tertio anno post adventum Cunorum, Bisseni . . . transnataverunt flumen Zaua . . . et . . . gentem captivorum et predarum diripientes, in suam terram abduxerunt'. *SRH*, vol. I: p. 369.

[101] In *Illuminated Chronicle*, *SRH*, vol. I: pp. 368–9; Gyula László, *A Szent László-legenda középkori falképei* (Budapest: Tájak-Korok-Múzeumok Egyesület, 1993), pp. 18–20; Gábor Klaniczay and Edit Madas, 'La Hongrie', in *Hagiographies*, vol. II, ed. Guy Philippart (Turnhout: Brepols, 1996), pp. 103–60, see pp. 117–21. On pictorial representations, see chapter 6.

[102] Pauler, 'Néhány szó', p. 505; cf. above for Chinese, Iberian and other defence systems.

[103] E.g. 'pagani Cuni a superiori parte porte Meses ruptis indaginibus irruperunt in Hungariam'. *SRH*, vol. I: p. 366.   [104] Pauler, 'Néhány szó', p. 508.

[105] Erik Fügedi, *Vár és társadalom a 13–14. századi Magyarországon*, Értekezések a történeti tudományok köréből 82 (Budapest: Akadémiai Kiadó, 1977), pp. 30–1; Erik Fügedi, *Castle and Society in Medieval Hungary (1000–1437)* (Budapest: Akadémiai Kiadó, 1986), pp. 57–8; Tünde

The most important nomad incursion into Hungary was the Mongol invasion of 1241–2. It was more significant than any other medieval attack against the territory since the Hungarian conquest and remained unparalleled until the Ottoman conquest beginning in 1526. The invasion conformed to previous raids to some extent: a nomad tribal alliance broke into the kingdom, killed and pillaged, then withdrew. Yet it was not just another raid; the Hungarian term *tatárjárás* (with its connotation of directionless, protracted movement) denotes its significance. The word was not used to describe any other nomad raid; instead, the second element (*járás*) is the same that is used in the composite word that means the swarming migration of locusts (*sáskajárás*). The Mongol invasion has been likened to the forces of nature in its destructive effects both in medieval sources and modern historiography. It has long been seen as a turning point in Hungarian history. It certainly played a significant role in shaping relations to non-Christians, both by the fears it generated, and the opportunities this gave kings to manipulate these fears. It is, therefore, necessary to assess its importance, in terms of both real destruction and its impact on the medieval imagination.

The Mongols, after having overrun and pillaged or conquered the areas east of Hungary, attacked the country from several directions. The Mongol right flank, advancing through Poland, defeated the duke of Silesia's troops at Liegnitz (Legnica) and invaded Hungary from the north. The left flank entered the country through several mountain passes into Transylvania, while the main army, under the leadership of Batu, pushed through the mountain pass of Verecke (north-eastern Hungary). The Mongols advanced rapidly, destroying and plundering, through Vác to Pest, where King Béla IV was staying, trying to organize the defence of the country.[106] After some small skirmishes, the Mongol army turned back. Béla, relying on his knowledge of former patterns of invasions from the east, marched after the Mongols to chase them out of the country, probably believing that they were retreating. This retreat, however, was a part of Mongol tactics, and at the Sajó river the Hungarian army lost the battle of Muhi on 11 April 1241. The king fled to Austria and then to the Dalmatian coast. The Mongol army reached the Danube, laying siege to whatever fortified place they found in their way, killing and capturing the inhabitants of both the countryside and the cities. During the winter of 1242, they crossed the Danube, made an unsuccessful attempt to

---

footnote 105 (*cont.*)
    Wehli, 'A magyarországi művészet helyzete a tatárjárás körüli években', *Hadtörténelmi Közlemények* 104 (1991): pp. 34–44.

[106] I use the Hungarian names of cities; for Latin and German variants (when they exist), and modern names when they are different, see appendix 2.

Hungary: a frontier society

capture the king, and finally turned back and left the country as quickly as they had arrived.

The reasons and effects of the Mongol conquest are still debated today. Contemporary accounts suggest either that the Mongols wished 'to conquer the whole world' and thus Hungary was only one step on their way west, or that the Mongols intended to punish the country for having sheltered the Cumans, who were seen as disobedient servants of the Khan.[107] Scholars either took up these explanations or advanced new hypotheses: the Mongols raided Hungary as a preliminary to future conquest, or they wished to subjugate the country in order to collect taxes.[108] The reasons for the Mongols leaving the country are equally uncertain. The traditional explanation, that at the news of the Great Khan Ogodai's death Batu returned home with his troops to participate in the election of the new Great Khan, or even to be a candidate himself, has been questioned.[109] Those who argue that the invasion was a preliminary raiding

---

[107] Mongol warning to King Béla: Heinrich Dörrie, ed., *Drei Texte zur Geschichte der Ungarn und Mongolen*, Nachrichten der Akademie der Wissenschaften in Göttingen, Philosophisch-Historische Klasse 6 (Göttingen: Vandenhoeck and Ruprecht, 1956), p. 179. Eric Voegelin, 'The Mongol Orders of Submission to European Powers, 1245–1255', *Byzantion* 15 (1940–1): pp. 378–413. Matthew Paris, *Chronica Majora*, 7 vols., ed. Henry Richards Luard, Rolls Series 57 (London, 1872–84; Wiesbaden: Kraus Reprint, 1964), vol. IV: pp. 112–19, see pp. 113–14. Cf. J. J. Saunders, 'Matthew Paris and the Mongols', in *Essays in Medieval History Presented to Bertie Wilkinson*, ed. T. A. Sandquist and M. R. Powicke (Toronto: University of Toronto Press, 1969), pp. 116–32; Daniel Williams, 'Matthew Paris and the Thirteenth-Century Prospect of Asia', in *England in the Thirteenth Century*, ed. W. M. Ormrod (Stamford: Paul Watkins, 1991), pp. 51–67. Report by the Hungarian Dominican Julian that the Mongols wanted to conquer the world: Dörrie, *Drei Texte*, pp. 162–82. *The History of the World Conqueror by ʿAla-ad-Din ʿAta-Malik Juvaini*, tr. John Andrew Boyle, 2nd edn (Manchester: Manchester University Press, 1997), pp. 270–2: Batu decided to destroy the Christian kingdoms of 'Keler and Bashgird'.

[108] Examples: punitive expedition: Pauler, *Magyar*, vol. II: p. 145; Voegelin, 'Mongol Orders', p. 406; Robert E. Lerner, *The Powers of Prophecy* (Berkeley and Los Angeles: University of California Press, 1983), p. 11; Denis Sinor, 'Les relations entre les Mongols et l'Europe jusqu'à la mort d'Arghoun et de Béla IV', in Sinor, *Inner Asia*, no. X. Attempt at conquest: Ladomér Zichy, *A tatárjárás Magyarországon* (Pécs: Veszprémvármegyei Történelmi, Régészeti és Néprajzi Társulat, 1934), p. 14; Csaba Csorba: 'A tatárjárás és a kunok Magyarországi betelepedése', in *Emlékkönyv a Túrkevei Múzeum fennállásának harmincadik évfordulójára* (Túrkeve: Túrkevei Finta Múzeum, 1981), pp. 33–68, see pp. 63–4; J. J. Saunders, *The History of the Mongol Conquests* (London: Routledge and Kegan Paul, 1971), pp. 80, 84. Initial raiding expedition before conquest: Emma Lederer, 'A tatárjárás Magyarországon és nemzetközi összefüggései', *Századok* 86 (1952): pp. 327–63 (she also mentions that the Mongols wished to tax Hungary, p. 339); Ödön Schütz, 'A mongol hódítás néhány problémájához', *Századok* 93 (1959): pp. 209–32. Mihail Konsztantinovics Juraszov, 'Batu magyarországi hadjáratának jellegéről és a tatárok elvonulásának okairól', *Világtörténet*, n.s. (1989, no. 4): pp. 92–103, see pp. 98–100: the invasion started as a war of conquest, but the Mongols reduced their aims first to taxing Hungary, then to a plundering raid. See also David Morgan, *The Mongols* (Oxford: Blackwell, 1986, reprinted 1996), pp. 136–41; András Borosy, 'Történetírók a tatárjárásról', *Hadtörténelmi Közlemények* 104 (1991): pp. 3–21.

[109] E.g. Tamás Katona, ed., *A tatárjárás emlékezete*, 2nd edn (Budapest: Európa Könyvkiadó, 1987), p. 28; Hermann Kinder and Werner Hilgemann, *The Anchor Atlas of World History* (New York: Doubleday, 1974), vol. I: p. 179; J. R. S. Phillips, *The Medieval Expansion of Europe*, 2nd edn

expedition, or a purely punitive expedition, see the withdrawal of the Mongol army as a natural consequence of the character of the invasion itself.[110] Those who believe that the invasion was an attempt at conquest explain its failure by citing the unstable conditions in the hinterlands: the Rus' principalities were far from being willingly subjugated to the Mongols and thus Batu's army was constantly threatened by the upheavals at its back. An alternative or complementary explanation is that the effect of a continuous Hungarian resistance – the perseverance of some fortified castles, for example – prevented the Mongols from consolidating their power in Hungary, and finally forced them to withdraw.[111] We should not forget that the Mongols retreated of their own accord (though there continued to be periodic raids against Hungary and especially Poland) and not after a defeat.

The impact of the invasion on the country has generated intense debates. Contemporary medieval sources paint a picture of complete desolation and destruction.[112] Two schools of historiography emerged on the basis of these sources. One school accepted uncritically the image formulated by medieval authors. Thus the Mongol invasion is portrayed as a major catastrophe that left the country crippled and devastated. A calculation based on the number of abandoned villages mentioned in charters after the invasion has claimed that 50 per cent of the population died

---

footnote 109 (cont.)
(Oxford: Clarendon Press, 1998), pp. 67–8. Critics, e.g.: Csorba, 'Tatárjárás', pp. 64–5; Székely, *Magyarország története*, p. 1439; Saunders, *History of Mongol Conquests*, p. 89. See also Morgan, *Mongols*, pp. 140–1.

[110] Juraszov, 'Batu', p. 98; Lederer, 'Tatárjárás', p. 341; Schütz, 'Mongol', p. 230.

[111] Schütz, 'Mongol', p. 232; Csorba, 'Tatárjárás', p. 63; Székely, *Magyarország története*, pp. 1439–40. Szűcs, *Utolsó Árpádok*, p. 10 has suggested that the Mongols simply could not cope with western cavalry and stone fortresses. Several successful sieges attest the opposite.

[112] Ladislaus Juhász, ed., 'Rogerii Carmen Miserabile', in *SRH*, vol. II: pp. 543–88. Manuscript tradition: Tibor Almási, 'A Siralmas Ének kézirati hagyományának néhány problémája', *AUSz Acta Historica* 84 (1987): pp. 51–6. Thomas of Spalato (writes about Rogerius personally): 'Historia Salonitanorum Pontificum atque Spalatensium', ed. F. Rački, in *Monumenta Spectantia Historiam Slavorum Meridionalium*, vol. XXVI (Zagreb, 1894), pp. 132–80. Ladislaus Juhász, ed., 'Planctus Destructionis Regni Hungariae per Tartaros', in *SRH*, vol. II: pp. 589–98.

The contemporary German *Annales* from Niederaltaich claimed that Hungary was destroyed: 'A. 1241. Hoc anno regnum Ungarie, quod 350 annis duravit, a Tartarorum gente destruitur'. Philip Jaffé, ed. 'Hermanni Althanensis annales', in *MGH SS*, vol. XVII: pp. 381–407, see p. 394.

Armenian, Rus' and Mongol sources on Mongol cruelty against enemies (translations based on the original documents): Kirakos Gandzaketzi (c. 1200–71), chapters 20–6, tr. Ödön Schütz, 'Az Örmények története', in *Kelet-Kutatás. Tanulmányok az orientalisztika köréből* (Budapest: Kőrösi Csoma Társaság, 1977), pp. 255–66; Antal Hodinka, ed. and tr., *Az orosz évkönyvek magyar vonatkozásai* (Budapest: Magyar Tudományos Akadémia, 1916), pp. 410–17; Lajos Ligeti, tr., *A Mongolok Titkos Története* (Budapest: Akadémiai Kiadó, 1962), *passim* (English tr. Francis Woodman Cleaves, *The Secret History of the Mongols*, Cambridge, Mass.: Harvard University Press, 1982); According to Rashīd al-Dīn the Mongols 'seized all the territories' of Hungary: John Andrew Boyle, tr., *The Successors of Genghis Khan* (New York and London: Columbia University Press, 1971), p. 70.

Hungary: a frontier society

in the wars or starved to death in the aftermath of the invasion.[113] Those contesting this conclusion have pointed out that Hungary waged several successful wars against Austria and Bohemia soon after the invasion: such a heavy population loss would have made these victories unlikely.[114] The rapid economic development of the latter half of the thirteenth century also contradicts the image of a country in ruins and half of its population dead. Between 147 and 172 new castles were built in the years 1242–1300,[115] and twenty-two towns with full privileges were established during the thirty years following the Mongol invasion.[116] Calculated terror was part of nomad tactics in general.[117] It should not be forgotten, however, that the Mongols also stayed in the eastern half of the country for over a year; this meant that they had to provide for themselves.[118] For all these reasons, the more balanced estimate of a 15–20 per cent population loss seems more likely.[119] Some scholars have denied that the invasion left lasting effects, claiming that the chilling medieval accounts were generated not by the weight of the devastation but by the appearance of a little known and even less understood, therefore mythified, enemy.[120]

The invasion was a major turning point if we consider the deep imprint it left on the imagination of contemporaries. The Mongol invasion became year 1 of a semi-official new chronology. In numerous royal charters and other sources, events and concessions are dated in relation

---

[113] György Györffy, 'Magyarország népessége a honfoglalástól a XIV. század közepéig', in *Magyarország történeti demográfiája*, ed. József Kovacsics (Budapest: Közgazdasági és Jogi Könyvkiadó, 1963), pp. 45–62, see pp. 53–4; György Györffy, introduction in Katona, *Tatárjárás*, pp. 29–33; György Györffy, 'A honfoglalók száma és az Árpád-kor népessége', in *Magyarország történeti demográfiája I. A Honfoglalás*, pp. 37–41. Györffy draws conclusions about population loss based on mentions of 'empty villages' in charters following the Mongol invasion. Critics (see below) have pointed out methodological shortcomings: the 'empty villages' do not only reflect population loss, but also the relocation of villages, the establishment of new villages, the number of people moving into towns, etc. Moreover, not all the villages are documented.

[114] Iván Bertényi, 'Magyarország nemzetközi helyzete a tatárjárás után', in *Unger Mátyás Emlékkönyv*, ed. Péter Kovács, János Kalmár and László V. Molnár (Budapest: MTA Történettudományi Intézet, 1991), pp. 15–22; Csorba, 'Tatárjárás', pp. 64–5.

[115] Fügedi, *Vár és társadalom*, p. 25; Fügedi, *Castle*, pp. 53–4.

[116] Szűcs, *Utolsó Árpádok*, pp. 53–4. On town privileges: Erik Fügedi, 'Középkori magyar városprivilégiumok', in *Tanulmányok Budapest múltjából*, no. 14 (Budapest: Akadémiai Kiadó, 1961), pp. 17–107, esp. pp. 19–26, 56–73.

[117] Barfield, *Perilous Frontier*, p. 15; Golden, 'Cumanica I', p. 49. Bartlett describes similar practices of the Normans: *Making of Europe*, pp. 86–7.

[118] Although Spuler's assertion that the Mongols even minted money is incorrect: Bertold Spuler, *Les Mongols dans l'histoire* (Paris: Payot, 1961), p. 29; Morgan, *Mongols*, p. 139. See chapter 4 on coins.

[119] Engel, *Beilleszkedés*, p. 226; Szűcs, *Utolsó Árpádok*, pp. 5–6. Both follow István Szabó, *A falurendszer kialakulása Magyarországon (X–XV. század)* (Budapest: Akadémiai Kiadó, 1966), pp. 95, 175–9. Gyula Kristó, 'Magyarország lélekszáma az Árpád-korban', in *Magyarország történeti demográfiája I. A Honfoglalás*, pp. 42–95, see pp. 81–4: 10–15 per cent population loss.

[120] Zichy, 'Tatárjárás', pp. 5, 69–86, 109–10; Csorba, 'Tatárjárás', pp. 63–5.

At the Gate of Christendom

to the time of the invasion: 'nostrum priuilegium ante aduentum Thartarorum datum'; 'tempore Tartarorum'.[121] During the canonization process of Margit of Hungary, some witnesses gave their age by referring to the Mongol invasion, such as 'I was a child when the Tartars entered this land.'[122] The real or imaginary Tartar threat (the most common though erroneous name in medieval Europe to designate the Mongols[123]) continued to loom large throughout the thirteenth century. Even today, Hungarians say 'you aren't chased by the Tatars' when they want someone to slow down.[124]

The many aspects of the Mongol impact on Europe have been discussed extensively: from the belief that they were the people of Prester John, come to rid the world of the Muslims, to plans of alliances by rulers such as Louis IX of France; from fears for the physical safety of Christendom to an eschatological interpretation of their role, the Mongols influenced Christian perceptions and policies.[125] They also affected developments in Hungary, including relations between Christians and non-Christians. The invasion was linked to the admittance of the Cumans and to King Béla's innovation in constructing a frontier ideology (see chapter 5). There were, however, continuities as well, such as royal employment of non-Christians, before and after the invasion.

The other main form of encounter occurred when nomads settled.

---

[121] *ÁÚO*, vol. II: p. 271, no. 180 (*RA*, no. 1093); *CD*, vol. v, pt. 1: p. 161 (*RA*, no. 2120).

[122] 'Puer eram, quando Tartari intraverunt terram istam': *Monumenta Romana Episcopatus Vesprimiensis*, 4 vols., ed. Vilmos Fraknói (Budapest, 1896), vol. I: p. 347; similar: pp. 339, 344, 349, 381. György Györffy has mentioned the chronological use of the invasion in 'Budapest története az Árpád-korban', in *Budapest története*, vol. I, ed. László Gerevich (Budapest: Budapest Főváros Tanácsa, 1973), pp. 217–349, see p. 334; also Szűcs, *Utolsó Árpádok*, p. 6.

[123] The Tatar tribe was conquered by the Mongols and integrated into the tribal alliance ruled by the Mongols. The word, transformed as 'tartar', was used by most medieval authors. It was conflated with Tartaros from Greek mythology and used to prove the infernal origins of the Mongols. Denis Sinor, 'Le Mongol vu par l'Occident', in *1274: Année charnière: Mutations et continuités* (Paris: CNRS, 1977), pp. 55–72.

[124] 'nem hajt a tatár'; in Ede Margalits, *Magyar közmondások és közmondásszerű szólások*, 2nd edn (1896; reprint Budapest: Akadémiai Kiadó, 1993), p. 706.

[125] E.g. Charles F. Beckingham and Bernard Hamilton, eds., *Prester John: The Mongols and the Ten Lost Tribes* (Aldershot: Variorum, 1996); Davide Bigalli, *I Tartari e l'Apocalisse* (Florence, La Nuova Italia, 1971); C. W. Connell, 'Western Views of the Origin of the Tartars: An Example of the Influence of Myth in the Second Half of the Thirteenth Century', *Journal of Medieval and Renaissance Studies* 3 (1973): pp. 115–37; Sinor, *Inner Asia*, nos. IX, X; Jean Richard, *La papauté et les missions d'Orient au Moyen Age (XIIIe–XVe siècles)* (Rome: Ecole Française de Rome, 1977), esp. pp. 63–165; Jean Richard, 'Les causes des victoires mongoles d'après les historiens occidentaux du XIIIe siècle', in *Croisés, missionaires et voyageurs* (London: Variorum, 1983), no. XI; Lerner, *Powers of Prophecy*, chapter I; Charles Burnett and Patrick Gautier Dalché, 'Attitudes towards the Mongols in Medieval Literature: The XXII Kings of Gog and Magog from the Court of Frederick II to Jean de Mandeville', *Viator* 22 (1991): pp. 153–67; Felicitas Schmieder, *Europa und die Fremden: Die Mongolen im Urteil des Abendlandes vom 13. bis in das 15. Jahrhundert* (Sigmaringen: Thorbecke, 1994), chapters III and IV.

Hungary: a frontier society

Just as raids from the east differed from those from the west, so the settlement of nomads had special traits compared with immigration from the west. Some of the 'pagans' who periodically raided Hungary eventually settled permanently in the country. As groups were moving in search of new pastures or as a new tribal union rose to power on the steppe, some groups were forced to find new territories. Those who were pushed into or chose to go to the lands of their sedentary neighbours had to negotiate for settlement. The two major examples of this in Hungary were the arrival first of Pecheneg groups from the tenth century to the mid-twelfth century, then of the Cumans in the mid-thirteenth century. The Pechenegs arrived in several waves from the mid-tenth century, especially in the late eleventh and early twelfth centuries, after they suffered a shattering defeat by the allied Byzantine and Cuman troops.[126] The Cumans themselves were fleeing from the Mongol conquest after several heavy defeats. The choice of asking for entry into a Christian kingdom was probably motivated by previous contacts with Christian neighbours: the chieftain Kötön was the father-in-law of Prince Mstislav Mstislavich of Galicia.[127] When the dynamics of nomad migrations pushed certain groups into the territory of Hungary, they had to adapt to new circumstances. As fragments of previous tribal unions fled after massive defeats, they were not powerful enough to conquer and force entry into the kingdom. They had to reach an agreement with the ruler to settle. Motivation for the settlement of 'pagan' groups also existed on the Christian side. They ranged from ecclesiastical and royal aims of 'gaining new souls for Christendom' (an issue that will be addressed in chapters 5 and 6), to more pragmatic reasons, such as strengthening royal military power (discussed in chapters 4 and 5).

The eastern frontier was, unlike thirteenth-century frontiers with Islam in Europe, not primarily an expanding but a defensive one. At best, it extended at the eastern border of the kingdom (when raids were successfully warded off) but, at worst, it moved westwards; the mid-thirteenth-century Mongol invasion threatened to maim the country or even put an end to its existence as an independent entity. Even when the regions east of the kingdom became a part of the world of Islam, the defensive nature of the eastern frontier remained; in the sixteenth century, the Ottoman conquests pushed this frontier further west. Throughout the medieval period, the steppe overflowed into Christendom, and Hungary was at the meeting point. Immigration may

---

[126] See chapter 2.
[127] László Rásonyi, *Hidak a Dunán: A régi török népek a Dunánál* (Budapest: Magvető Kiadó, 1981), p. 120; John Fennell, *The Crisis of Medieval Russia (1200–1304)*, 5th edn (London and New York: Longman, 1993), p. 64.

At the Gate of Christendom

have been initially facilitated by geographical conditions; the Hungarian plains (Alföld) were the last extension of the steppe, allowing for a nomadic pastoral life. The fact that Hungary was on this frontier in the Middle Ages meant that new groups constantly moved into the country: people who were neither Christians nor adapted to a settled mode of life. It also meant that the main frontier experience was a defensive one, which fostered the emergence of a frontier identity from the thirteenth century that was not a triumphalist one. I shall address this issue in chapter 5; it is, however, worth noting here that to talk about Hungary as a frontier society is not entirely a modern historian's construct. However differently, the idea had already surfaced in the period under consideration.

Hungary's position at the crossroads of three civilizations also led to a mixing of peoples within the country. Raids and settlement brought a variety of groups into the kingdom from east and west. The population of the kingdom was very heterogeneous: thirteenth-century Hungary included Jews, Muslims, Cumans and other Turkic peoples, Armenians, Greek orthodox, Slavs, Italians, Walloons, French, Spaniards and different German groups. We have an eloquent, if rhetorical, statement from the early eleventh century concerning royal motivations in encouraging immigration. The *Admonitions*, attributed to St István, but written by a Venetian or Bavarian cleric at the royal court, depict an ideal Christian monarchy based on the influx of immigrants. 'As guests [meaning settlers] come from various areas and lands, so they bring with them various languages and customs, various examples and forms of armament, which adorn and glorify the royal court and discourage the pride of foreigners. For a kingdom of one language and one custom is weak and fragile. Therefore, my son, I order that you should feed them with goodwill and honour them so that they will prefer to live with you rather than inhabit any other place.'[128] The tangible benefits – loyalty, revenues and military service, in other words the preoccupation with strengthening royal power – are visible despite the lofty rhetoric. (Chapters 4 and 5 elaborate on this theme.)

Forms of interaction with other religions, cultures and peoples varied

[128] 'Sicut enim ex diversis partibus et provinciis veniunt hospites, ita diversas linguas et consuetudines, diversaque documenta et arma secum ducunt, que omnia regna [variant: regiam] ornant et magnificant aulam et perterritant exterorum arrogantiam. Nam unius lingue uniusque moris regnum inbecille et fragile est. Propterea iubeo te fili mi, ut bona voluntate illos nutrias, et honeste teneas, ut tecum libentius degant, quam alicubi habitent.' Josephus Balogh, ed., 'Libellus de institutione morum', in *SRH*, vol. II: pp. 611–27, see p. 625. Jenő Szűcs, 'Szent István Intelmei: az első magyarországi államelméleti mű', in *Szent István és kora*, ed. Ferenc Glatz and József Kardos (Budapest: MTA Történettudományi Intézet, 1988), pp. 32–53, see p. 42, emphasized political utility as István's main concern, although he interpreted the text as a reference to priests and nobles only, not to all immigrants. Hagiography also emphasized royal generosity to foreigners: e.g. *SRH*, vol. II: pp. 378–9, 387, 518 (*Lives* of Saints István and László I).

Hungary: a frontier society

between different frontier societies, and included, for example, military action, trade, scientific or artistic cooperation and intermarriage. Interaction, settlement and integration were not even uniform for the three non-Christian groups within Hungary. Various chapters take up the numerous issues connected to the place of these groups: chapter 3 addresses their legal position, chapter 4 their economic and social position, chapter 6 Christian views, and, finally, chapter 7 traces processes of assimilation and continuity.

The frontier character of Hungary sets the background for this study. The meeting of groups coming from the east (Muslims and nomads) with Jews arriving from the west took place because of Hungary's position on Christendom's frontier. The characteristics arising from this frontier situation, moreover, determined to some extent the position of these groups in the country. This book addresses questions related to the treatment of non-Christian groups in a frontier setting, but without taking as its framework the 'persecution vs. tolerance' paradigm (see chapter 2).

Hungary was not a frontier society in which rulers and ruled practised rival exclusivist religions. Although its history started with a conquest, this society was not formed by Christians conquering a population of different religious adherence. The context for Hungary's non-Christian population was thus radically different from that in most other areas along the frontiers of Christendom. They migrated into the kingdom voluntarily, rather than being incorporated through conquest, an unusual state of affairs in Europe at the time. Frontier societies have been studied to examine the interplay between the exigencies of religious exclusivism and those of reality (religious plurality).[129] Inconsistency, however, existed not just between religious ideology and reality, but within the spheres of both ideology and practical policies. The kingdom of Hungary, at the meeting point of three civilizations on the eastern frontier of Christendom, a frontier permeable to 'pagans', characterized by the dynamics of both Christian–non-Christian and sedentary–nomad interaction, and peopled by a heterogeneous society, provides a specific case-study of medieval Christian–non-Christian interaction. Yet to analyse the position of non-Christian communities in Hungary from economic, social, legal and religious perspectives brings to light the variety of Christian policies, fears and aims, both lay and ecclesiastical, whose significance extends beyond the Hungarian case to medieval Europe.

---

[129] Charles J. Halperin, 'The Ideology of Silence: Prejudice and Pragmatism on the Medieval Religious Frontier', *Comparative Studies in Society and History* 26 (1984): pp. 442–66.

Chapter 2

CHRISTIANS AND NON-CHRISTIANS

Medieval encounters with non-Christians[1] took many forms. On the frontiers of Christendom, warfare was combined with peaceful contacts and interaction; a striking example of this is the case of Frankish knights in the east, some of whom learned Arabic and adopted local customs by the second or third generation.[2] The types of contacts were also influenced by the relative position of non-Christian groups; they lived outside Christendom, they were newcomers to it as converts, or they lived within Christian Europe.[3] Hungary's non-Christians moved from within Christian Europe or from outside Christendom, and some of them became Christians. Their story can be told only in the wider context of Christian–non-Christian interaction in medieval Europe.

CHRISTIANITAS AND NON-CHRISTIANS

If we are to understand the position of medieval non-Christians, we have to take into account contemporary notions of *Christianitas*. The concept took on a variety of meanings during the Middle Ages.[4] Used to denote

---

[1] I prefer to use the value-neutral 'non-Christian' as a general grouping term, rather than 'infidel', which carries Christian prejudices.
[2] Norman Daniel, *The Arabs and Mediaeval Europe*, 2nd edn (London: Longman, 1979), pp. 202, 209.
[3] James Muldoon, *Popes, Lawyers and Infidels: The Church and the Non-Christian World 1250–1550* (Philadelphia: University of Pennsylvania Press, 1979), p. 29.
[4] Judith Herrin, *The Formation of Christendom* (Princeton: Princeton University Press, 1987); J. Rupp, *L'idée de chrétienté dans la pensée pontificale des origines à Innocent III* (Paris: Les Presses Modernes, 1939); Gerhart B. Ladner, 'The Concepts of "Ecclesia" and "Christianitas" and their Relation to the Idea of Papal "Plenitudo Potestatis" from Gregory VII to Boniface VIII', *Miscellanea Historiae Pontificiae* 18 (1954): pp. 49–77; Jan van Laarhoven, 'Christianitas et réforme grégorienne', *Studi Gregoriani* 6 (1959–60): pp. 1–98; Raoul Manselli, 'La res publica christiana e l'Islam', in *L'Occidente e l'Islam nell'Alto Medioevo*, 2 vols., Settimane di Studio del Centro Italiano di Studi sull'Alto Medioevo 12 (Spoleto, 1965), vol. I: pp. 115–47; Alberto Melloni, *Innocenzo IV: La concezione e l'esperienza della cristianità come regimen unius personae* (Genoa: Marietti, 1990); Bartlett, *Making of Europe*, pp. 250–5; Jacques Le Goff, 'Le concile et la prise de conscience de

a set of beliefs and adherence to them (that is, in opposition to Judaism), it acquired social and communal meanings, especially beginning in the ninth century. *Christianitas* was sometimes a synonym for the Church, but also, rather than referring either to the Church or to the empire, it came to mean the collectivity of the *populus Christianus* as a social and temporal, as well as spiritual unity. A geographic idea of Christendom also developed; the territorial connotations of *Christianitas* appeared in the ninth century. During the following centuries, the concept of *Christianitas* as a territory (populated by the faithful) was firmly established. This territory could be attacked, and its borders needed to be defended, which, in practice, often meant extended by conquest. The concept of a Latin Christendom under Rome emerged amidst controversies and an increasing separation between Latin and Byzantine Christianity. The notion of a territorial Latin Christendom as a cultural, social, political and religious unit under papal leadership was elaborated during and after the Investiture Conflict, and obtained its most complete form with thirteenth-century popes. A territorial Christendom, along with the enemies of this territory, became the focus of attention during the crusades. The crusades and the Spanish 'Reconquest' also established relatively long-lasting frontiers of Muslim–Christian interaction. The role of Christian kings was equated with that of defenders of Christendom. By the thirteenth century the idea of *Christianitas* was fully developed, together with its political and juridical overtones: a territorial unit to be defended and enlarged, under the leadership of the pope. Potentially, this territory could be extended to the entire world. *Christianitas* gained new importance during the thirteenth century as a universalistic political idea: the ideology of papal power. Popes Innocent III and Innocent IV played a major role in developing and enforcing this papal leadership.[5] By the end of the thirteenth century the extension (*dilatatio*) of Christendom's frontiers manifestly failed, and territorially Christendom and Europe became more or less synonymous.

As the idea of Christendom took shape, so did definitions of 'outsiders'. From a religious viewpoint – to use modern criteria – those who were professing Christians but failed to conform to Latin ecclesiastical prescriptions (that is, heretics or eastern Christians), or those who

---

l'espace de la Chrétienté', in *1274: Année charnière*, pp. 481–9; Agostino Paravicini Bagliani, *Il trono di Pietro: L'universalità del papato da Alessandro III a Bonifacio VIII* (Rome: La Nuova Italia, 1996), pp. 225–47.

[5] John A. Watt, *The Theory of Papal Monarchy in the Thirteenth Century: The Contribution of the Canonists* (New York: Fordham University Press, 1965); Colin Morris, *The Papal Monarchy: The Western Church from 1050 to 1250* (Oxford: Clarendon Press, 1989); Jane E. Sayers, *Innocent III: Leader of Europe, 1198–1216* (London: Longman, 1994).

professed a different religion from Christianity, such as Judaism or Islam, became 'outsiders'. My focus is on non-Christians in the technical sense: those professing religions other than Christianity. Without providing a detailed analysis of views about and policies towards non-Christians in medieval Europe, it is necessary to point out certain important issues and developments, especially concerning non-Christians on the frontiers of Christendom. By the eleventh century, Christian contact with non-Christians within the heartland of Christendom was limited to contact with Jews. At the frontiers of Christendom, Christians encountered other non-Christian groups as well: Muslims and 'pagans'. Moreover, Jewish–Christian relations were coloured by the special religious and theological significance of Jews to Christians. The importance of the Hebrew Bible for Christians, the dependence on Judaism as the foundation of Christianity, yet the rejection of its continued validity, and the notion that Jews served as signs and would convert at the end of time ensured that Christian attitudes to Jews would in many ways differ from those to other non-Christians.

Coexistence with Jews had a history of several centuries, and because the Christian Bible incorporated the Hebrew Bible as its 'Old Testament', a part of Jewish religious beliefs had been known to Christians. Christian ecclesiastical interest in Judaism grew in the late eleventh and twelfth centuries. Interest in Judaism as well as in Islam was restricted to a small elite in the twelfth century, mainly for purposes of biblical scholarship, scientific interest, and a type of polemic whose main aim may have been the reassurance of Christians rather than the conversion of Jews and Muslims. It led to collaborations with Jewish scholars, to works of translation of many scientific, philosophical and religious texts, and to literary dialogues between Christians and adherents of other faiths, like Abelard's *Dialogus inter Philosophum, Iudaeum et Christianum*, as well as to literary condemnations of Judaism and Islam.[6] Exegetes such

---

[6] Beryl Smalley, *The Study of the Bible in the Middle Ages*, 3rd edn (Notre Dame: University of Notre Dame Press, 1978), pp. 149–73; Gilbert Dahan, *Les intellectuels chrétiens et les juifs au moyen âge* (Paris: Cerf, 1990); Gilbert Dahan, *La polémique chrétienne contre le judaïsme au moyen âge* (Paris: Albin Michel, 1991); Anna Sapir Abulafia, *Christians and Jews in the Twelfth-Century Renaissance* (London and New York: Routledge, 1995; Abulafia, *Christians and Jews in Dispute*; Heinz Schreckenberg, *Die christlichen Adversus-Judaeos-Texte und ihr literarisches und historisches Umfeld*, 3 vols. (Frankfurt am Main: Lang, 1990–4). Charles Homer Haskins, *Studies in the History of Mediaeval Science*, 2nd edn (Cambridge, Mass.: Harvard University Press, 1927; repr. New York: Frederick Ungar, 1960); Charles Homer Haskins, 'The Translators from Greek and Arabic', in *The Renaissance of the Twelfth Century*, 6th edn (Cambridge, Mass.: Harvard University Press, 1976), pp. 278–302; Marie-Thérèse d'Alverny, 'Translations and Translators', in *Renaissance and Renewal in the Twelfth Century*, ed. Robert L. Benson and Giles Constable (Cambridge, Mass.: Harvard University Press, 1982), pp. 421–62. Abelard, *Dialogus inter Philosophum, Iudaeum et Christianum*, ed. Rudolf Thomas (Stuttgart and Bad Cannstatt: Friedrich Frommann, 1970).

Christians and non-Christians

as Andrew of St Victor consulted Jewish sages to enhance their understanding of the Bible.[7] Hostility was often inseparable from interest during these centuries: witness Peter the Venerable's vicious verbal attack on the Jews.[8] Much work has addressed the impact of the crusades on enmity towards non-Christians both in the Holy Land and within Europe.[9] Instances of understanding, cooperation (even in crime) and tolerance occasionally resulted from interaction,[10] but more often the consequence was verbal and physical violence against the tenets of other religions and their holders. During the thirteenth century, postbiblical Jewish practice and learning became a more urgent issue for ecclesiastics. Papal direction came to play an important role as well. At that time, there was a more sustained effort of enquiry into and attack of the tenets of Judaism, the Talmud (known only exceptionally by twelfth-century Christians[11]) and rabbinical literature. The organized teaching of Hebrew also began. Even before Innocent IV's vindication of papal rights to judge Jewish belief and condemn its heresies in order to ensure that Judaism did not develop beyond Old Testament tenets, the Talmud was examined for 'blasphemous' passages with the aid of Jewish converts to Christianity. Louis IX of France enthusiastically implemented papal orders concerning the investigation; in 1242 over ten thousand volumes of the Talmud were burnt in Paris (similar condemnations recurred).[12] The presence of converts eager to supply information (as early as the twelfth century) and mendicant interest in disputations led to the thorough mining of Jewish texts for more precise

---

[7] Smalley, *Study of the Bible*, pp. 149–72.

[8] Gavin I. Langmuir, 'Peter the Venerable: Defense Against Doubts', In *Toward a Definition*, pp. 197–208; Dominique Iogna-Prat, *Ordonner et exclure: Cluny et la société chrétienne face à l'hérésie, au judaïsme et à l'Islam 1000–1150* (Paris: Aubier, 1998), chapter IX.

[9] Robert Chazan, *European Jewry and the First Crusade* (Berkeley, Los Angeles and London: University of California Press, 1996; 1st edn, 1987); Jonathan Riley-Smith, 'The First Crusade and the Persecution of the Jews', *Persecution and Toleration*, pp. 51–72; Joshua Prawer, *The History of the Jews in the Latin Kingdom of Jerusalem* (Oxford: Oxford University Press, 1988, repr. Clarendon Press, 1996); Powell, ed., *Muslims under Latin Rule*; Norman Daniel, *Islam and the West: The Making of an Image*, rev. edn. (Oxford: Oneworld Publications, 1993).

[10] E.g. Jonathan Riley-Smith, ed., *The Oxford Illustrated History of the Crusades* (Oxford and New York: Oxford University Press, 1997), p. 253; Elena Lourie, 'Complicidad criminal: un aspecto insolito de convivencia Judeo-Christiana', in Lourie, *Crusade and Colonisation: Muslims, Christians, and Jews in Medieval Aragon* (Aldershot: Variorum, 1990), no. XI; Dominique de Courcelles, *La parole risquée de Raymond Lulle: entre le judaïsme, le christianisme et l'islam* (Paris: J. Vrin, 1993), pp. 58–62; Abulafia, *Christians and Jews in Dispute*.

[11] Iogna-Prat, *Ordonner et exclure*, p. 300.

[12] Dahan, *Intellectuels*, pp. 216–20 (with bibliography of previous works); Alain Boureau, 'La guerre des récits: la crémation du Talmud (1240–1242)', in *L'Evénement sans fin: récit et christianisme au Moyen Age* (Paris: Les Belles Lettres, 1993), pp. 231–51; Gilbert Dahan, ed., *Le brûlement du Talmud à Paris 1242–1244* (Paris: Cerf, 1999); Jacques Le Goff, *Saint Louis* (Paris: Gallimard, 1996), pp. 803–7; Shlomo Simonsohn, *The Apostolic See and the Jews: History* (Toronto: Pontifical Institute of Mediaeval Studies, 1991), Studies and Texts 109, pp. 300–7.

information on Judaism.[13] In the intensified effort to convert Jews, this was also put in the service of Christian missionary purposes, along with the introduction of compulsory attendance at missionary sermons. Attempts to convert did not preclude the growth of exclusionary measures. By the end of the thirteenth century expulsions had started. At the other end of the spectrum of new attitudes, Frederick II ordered an investigation to determine whether blood accusations could be true; learning about the rules of *kashrut*, he decided that they could not be.[14] Other rulers and many popes also condemned the ritual murder libel.[15]

Interaction with Muslims was more restricted both chronologically and geographically. Apart from real contacts with Muslims through a limited scientific interest, translations and the crusades, imagined characteristics played an important role in the formation of Christian views on Muslims. During the twelfth and thirteenth centuries, a variety of stereotypes was available. Views on the absurdity of the Muslim faith, on the immorality of its adherents and about Mahomet as an impostor and liar persisted throughout this period. The image of the brutal, perverse, sexually promiscuous Saracen and that of the brave and noble Muslim warrior who had a code of honour comparable to, if not better than, that of his Christian counterpart both existed, and the land of the Muslims was imagined as the resplendent East, with its rare and luxurious artefacts. At the same time, at the initiative of clerics and kings such as Peter the Venerable and Alfonso the Wise of Spain, the work of numerous translators and scholars made material on Islam available, from the Qu'ran to apocalyptic Arabic texts on the ascension of the Prophet. Moreover, contacts with Muslims changed, as they were not only military foes but came under Christian rule in Spain and the Latin east.[16]

---

[13] Dahan, *Polémique*, pp. 46–52. Robert Chazan, *Barcelona and Beyond: The Disputation of 1263 and its Aftermath* (Berkeley and Los Angeles: University of California Press, 1992); Chazan, *Daggers of Faith*. [14] Dahan, *Intellectuels*, pp. 45–6.

[15] Shlomo Simonsohn, *The Apostolic See and the Jews: Documents 492–1404* (Toronto: Pontifical Institute of Mediaeval Studies, 1988), nos. 178, 179, 181, 182, 183, 185, 188, 201, 202; Simonsohn, *Apostolic See: History*, pp. 49, 52–6.

[16] 'Ein Leben Mohammeds (Adelphus?)', in *Anecdota Novissima: Texte des vierten bis sechzehnten Jahrhunderts*, ed. Bernhard Bischoff (Stuttgart: Anton Hiersemann, 1984), pp. 106–22; Norman Daniel, *Heroes and Saracens: An Interpretation of the Chansons de Geste* (Edinburgh: Edinburgh University Press, 1989); Daniel, *Islam*; Marie-Thérèse d'Alverny, 'La connaissance de l'Islam en occident du IXe au milieu du XIIe siècle', in *L'Occidente e l'Islam nell'Alto Medioevo*, 2 vols., Settimane di Studio del Centro Italiano di Studi sull'Alto Medioevo 12 (Spoleto, 1965), vol. II: pp. 577–602; Marie-Thérèse d'Alverny, 'La connaissance de l'Islam au temps de Saint Louis', in *Septième centenaire de la mort de Saint Louis: Actes des colloques de Royaumont et de Paris* (Paris: Les Belles Lettres, 1976), pp. 235–46; Richard W. Southern, *Western Views of Islam in the Middle Ages*, 2nd edn (Cambridge, Mass.: Harvard University Press, 1978); Philippe Sénac, *L'image de l'autre: Histoire de l'occident médiéval face à l'Islam* (Paris: Flammarion, 1983); John Victor Tolan, ed., *Medieval Christian Perceptions of Islam* (New York and London: Garland, 1996).

Christians and non-Christians

These contacts fostered both a 'dream' of Muslim conversion and the growth of negative attitudes; ecclesiastical authors stated the culpability of Muslims and produced a justification for the use of violence against Muslims.[17]

Compared with the study of Islam and Judaism, the study of 'pagan' beliefs was much more complicated in this period; there were no texts to translate, and the observation of various practices did not necessarily lead to an understanding of their significance as parts of a religious system. Curious travellers and missionaries such as John of Plano Carpini and William of Rubruck, those forerunners of modern anthropologists, observed Turkic nomads and recorded their observations in colourful accounts. These contained many correct elements as well as misinterpretations, and did not lead to a comprehensive understanding of 'paganism'.[18] Different groups, with divergent beliefs and practices, were not differentiated, as the designation 'pagan' (*pagani*) itself indicates. It is not a name these people themselves would ever have used, nor does it indicate any characteristics of their beliefs. None the less, the available information on the customs and beliefs of the Baltic and Turkic 'pagans' increased, and thirteenth-century mendicants studied local languages and developed missionary methods adapted to the way of life of these populations. At the same time, the use of violence gained new adherents and justification. Taking part in northern crusades, even churchmen endorsed the use of force in baptism, when peaceful methods did not produce results.[19]

Thus by the end of the thirteenth century there was a large body of material available on both Islam and Judaism, and a growing familiarity with a 'pagan' world to the north and east of Christian countries. A more institutionalized policy of discrimination was formulated, such as

---

[17] Daniel, *Islam and the West*, pp. 134–6; Benjamin Z. Kedar, *Crusade and Mission: European Approaches toward Muslims* (Princeton: Princeton University Press, 1984); Robert I. Burns, 'Christian–Muslim Confrontation: The Thirteenth-Century Dream of Conversion', in Burns, *Muslims, Christians and Jews in the Crusader Kingdom of Valencia: Societies in Symbiosis* (Cambridge: Cambridge University Press, 1984), pp. 80–108.

[18] For example, Plano Carpini thought that the Mongol deity 'Itoga' was called 'Kam' by the Cumans: Johannes de Plano Carpini, *Ystoria Mongalorum quos nos Tartaros appellamus*, in *Sinica Franciscana*, ed. Anastasius van den Wyngaert (Quaracchi: Collegio San Bonaventura, 1929), vol. I: pp. 27–130, see p. 41; new edn: Paolo Daffinà, Claudio Leonardi, Maria Cristiana Lungarotti, Enrico Menestò, Luciano Petech, *Giovanni di Pian di Carpine: Storia dei Mongoli* (Spoleto: Centro Italiano di Studi sull'Alto Medioevo, 1989), p. 240. In fact, he equated the Mongol deity with the Cuman word for shaman: Sir Gerard Clauson, *An Etymological Dictionary of Pre-Thirteenth-Century Turkish* (Oxford: Clarendon Press, 1972), p. 625.

[19] Christiansen, *Northern Crusades*, pp. 79–88, 124; Richard A. Fletcher, *The Conversion of Europe from Paganism to Christianity 371–1386* (London: HarperCollins, 1997), esp. chapter XIV. Violence in order to convert was already used in the early Middle Ages, notably by Charlemagne against the Saxons.

measures to distinguish and separate non-Christians promulgated at the Fourth Lateran Council (1215). These were to be implemented in all of Christendom. Innocent III made crusading central to his policies, and was instrumental in restricting non-Christian influence within Europe. Restrictive policies towards non-Christians occasionally culminated in their complete exclusion. The missionary and exclusionary policies formulated under ecclesiastical and royal leadership led to, on the one hand, the choice between conversion or death in newly conquered areas like Livonia[20] and, on the other, the expulsion of Jews. These expulsions began locally from French territories for short durations. The first mass expulsion that was not reversed during the Middle Ages and affected a whole kingdom took place in England in 1290.

Innocent IV was the first pope to develop the legal basis for papal relations with non-Christians and to define their position. He insisted on their natural rights to possess and govern, while upholding the right of the pope to exercise ultimate jurisdiction over them. Innocent IV was innovative in positing that the pope was *de iure* responsible for the soul of everyone, even 'infidels', because he was the vicar of Christ to whom all belonged by right of the Creation.[21] While the trends of suppression and control characterized the whole century, at the same time there was an ever-growing desire, and corresponding effort, to send out missionaries in order to bring about the conversion of the rest of the world. Innocent IV was especially active in such missionary policy; he sent his messengers to Muslim princes and Mongol khans.[22]

On the frontiers of Christendom, interaction with non-Christians took many forms. In Spain, the 'Reconquest' produced a society with two important religious minorities, Jews and Muslims. The Norman conquest of Sicily in the late eleventh century had created a similar situation, albeit on a much smaller scale. Christian conquests in the Iberian peninsula resulted in the incorporation of an unprecedented number of Muslims into Christian Europe; for example, in Valencia Muslim households outnumbered Christian ones by about five to one.[23] Surrender charters were drawn up, giving them substantial rights.[24] Moreover, this Muslim population played a very active role; their contribution ranged from agriculture and learning to military and government affairs. Policies towards such a large number of non-Christians had to be invented. The

---

[20] Christiansen, *Northern Crusades*, for example pp. 90–1, 99.
[21] Muldoon, *Popes*, pp. 5–15, 29–48; Melloni, *Innocenzo IV*, pp. 177–87.
[22] Richard, *Papauté*, pp. 45, 69–86.
[23] Burns, *Crusader Kingdom of Valencia*, vol. II: p. 303.
[24] Robert I. Burns, 'Surrender Constitutions: The Islamic Communities of Eslida and Alfandech', in *Muslims, Christians and Jews*, pp. 54–78.

status of *mudejars* (Muslims living under Christian rule) needed to be formulated.[25] The policy of military orders to Muslims is a good example of the contradictions that characterized this phase: set up to combat Islam, the orders preferred to settle Muslim tenants on lands already acquired.[26] At the same time, the French involved in the Christian conquest of Spain represented Muslims as unambiguously evil who had to be destroyed.[27] Canon law solved this problem by assimilating subject Muslims to Jews, differentiating between those who fought against Christians and those who accepted Christian rule. Jews, mediators between two cultures and acting as councillors and officials to Christian kings, were valued and protected, although restrictive measures began to be promulgated during the thirteenth century. They held offices despite prohibitions in canon law.[28] In 1279 King Pere (Peter) even objected to Franciscans preaching in synagogues aimed at converting Jews in Valencia.[29]

At the other end of Europe, conquest linked to conversion reached the Baltic lands. This area provides an example of the discrepancy between theories of missionary activity among 'pagans' and relations to them in practice.[30] The east Baltic lands were conquered during the thirteenth century. After the defeat of the local population, missionaries were to convert those who had not been killed. Canon law would then have granted full membership in Christendom to the baptized. But the knights who carried out these conquests, even though designated agents of the propagation of the Christian faith, were not ready to give up acquiring territories and wealth in order to satisfy ecclesiastical ideals. In Livonia, for example, the Sword-Brothers killed converts and prevented others from receiving baptism in order to retain their power over newly conquered lands. They confronted the papacy over what procedures to follow. The popes wished the territory to be transformed into a state under papal power. The Sword-Brothers would have lost much of the territory and would have had to give equal rights to converts. The Teutonic Order in Prussia also spurned papal ideas and granted political freedom to a chosen few instead of to all converts. For these tribes, there-

---

[25] On the historiography: Nirenberg, 'Current state of Mudejar studies'.
[26] Leonard Patrick Harvey, *Islamic Spain 1250 to 1500* (Chicago and London: University of Chicago Press, 1990), pp. 70–1.
[27] Ron Barkaï, *Cristianos y musulmanes en la España medieval* (Madrid: Rialp, 1984), pp. 154–70; on participation: Pierre Guichard, 'Participation des Méridionaux à la Reconquista dans le royaume de Valence', in *Islam et chrétiens du Midi (XIIe–XIVe s.)*, Cahiers de Fanjeaux 18 (Toulouse: Edouard Privat, 1983), pp. 115–31.
[28] Yitzhak Baer, *A History of the Jews in Christian Spain*, 2 vols., 2nd edn (Philadelphia and Jerusalem: Jewish Publication Society, 1992), vol. I: pp. 120–9, 144–7, 325–7.
[29] Robert I. Burns, 'King Jaume's Jews: Problem and Methodology', in *Muslims, Christians and Jews*, pp. 126–41, see p. 136. [30] Christiansen, *Northern Crusades*, pp. 122–6.

fore, baptism meant subjection and not admission into Christendom as equal partners. Christian interaction with Lithuania, a politically independent 'pagan' state, was no less complex and included warfare, trade treaties and diplomatic negotiations involving the promise of conversion. Indeed, the Teutonic Knights carried on trade and negotiations with the Lithuanians while at the same time fighting against them.[31]

Hopes to reconquer the Holy Land, and then Christian successes in Iberia and in the north had provided the basis of the dual attitude towards non-Christians characteristic of the twelfth and early thirteenth centuries; namely, optimism about Christian expansion and fears of the polluting effect of contacts with non-Christians.[32] The fears resulted in attempts at separation, notably the decrees promulgated at the Fourth Lateran Council. The optimism was strikingly formulated by Peter the Venerable: 'The Christian faith . . . as truth derived from the highest truth, which is Christ . . . subjected the whole world to itself. The whole world I said, because although pagans and Saracens may exercise lordship over some parts, and although Jews lurk among Christians and pagans, nonetheless there is no part of the earth or very little . . . that is not inhabited by Christians.'[33] This optimism was perhaps at its peak in the late twelfth and early thirteenth centuries, with the belief in Prester John (or King David). The legend of the rich and powerful Far Eastern prince who would come to the aid of the crusaders was reinforced by the first news of the Mongol conquests in the late 1210s and 1220s. The Mongols were believed to be Prester John's people, having come to defeat the Muslims in the Holy Land and unite with their European brethren.[34] The final victory seemed to be tangibly near.

The second half of the same century brought a cruel awakening: Christians did not defeat the unbelievers. Instead, the latter were definitely getting the upper hand. 'Prester John' and his people turned out to be nomadic warriors who devastated and partially conquered eastern

---

[31] S. C. Rowell, 'A Pagan's Word: Lithuanian Diplomatic Procedure 1200–1385', *Journal of Medieval History* 18 (1992): pp. 145–60; S. C. Rowell, *Lithuania*, ch. III; Rasa Mažeika, 'Bargaining for Baptism: Lithuanian Negotiations for Conversion, 1250–1358', in *Varieties of Religious Conversion in the Middle Ages*, ed. James Muldoon (Gainesville: University Press of Florida, 1997), pp. 131–45; Mažeika, 'Of Cabbages and Knights'.

[32] Moore, *Formation of a Persecuting Society*, pp. 100–1. This fear of pollution continued: Nirenberg, *Communities*, chapter V and pp. 240–3.

[33] *Petri Venerabilis Adversus Judeorum Inveteratam Duritiem*, ed. Yvonne Friedman, Corpus Christianorum, Continuatio Mediaevalis, vol. LVIII (Turnhout: Brepols, 1985), p. 109; Eng. tr. Langmuir, 'Peter the Venerable', pp. 199–200. See also Iogna-Prat, *Ordonner et exclure*, esp. chapter IX.

[34] Richard, *Papauté*, pp. 66–7; Denis Sinor, 'The Mongols and Western Europe', in *Inner Asia*, no. IX, see pp. 516–18; Sinor, 'Le Mongol vu par l'Occident'; Beckingham and Hamilton, eds., *Prester John*.

Europe. Even Louis IX of France, who came close to being the embodiment of the clerical ideal of the good Christian king, failed to achieve victories in the Holy Land. Muslim success led to a crisis of Christian consciousness. The papacy increasingly came to see non-Christians as internal and external enemies of Christendom, and Jews and Muslims as a spiritual and temporal threat, undermining Christendom and plotting its destruction.[35] The Mongol attacks, the reversal of the Lithuanian conversion process with the murder of the baptized Prince Mindaugas (1263) and the 1264 Mudejar revolt in Iberia, seemed to be signals of the non-Christian threat within and without.

As the thirteenth century drew to its close, optimism about the possibility of Mongol conversion dwindled, and along with it the jubilant hope of imminent Christian triumph. Western kings and popes still focused on Christ's birthplace; success or failure in the Holy Land was fraught with symbolism. But the exploration of parts of the non-Christian world, especially the Mongol Empire, and Christian failures in the Holy Land inevitably led to the conclusion that the ultimate triumph of Christianity was not at hand. Finally, the realization had to come that the Christian world, in fact, was infinitely smaller than the non-Christian one. 'By the middle of the thirteenth century . . . it was seen that . . . there were ten, or possibly a hundred, unbelievers for every Christian. Nobody knew; and the estimate grew with each access of knowledge.'[36]

There has been reflection about the nature of medieval society that is relevant to the understanding of the position of non-Christians. Scholars have different opinions about both the degree of and reasons for medieval intolerance of 'out'-groups. Joseph Lecler has argued that the Middle Ages, as a whole, was intolerant, owing to the structure of society. He claimed that the Church, equated with Christendom, was the basis of society, within which both lay and ecclesiastical power functioned; therefore anything outside the Church was necessarily condemned, although with varying degrees of persecution.[37]

Most recent contributions concerning European views of Islam and Judaism, however, claim that medieval society was not a 'persecuting one'

---

[35] Muldoon, *Popes*, pp. 50–2.
[36] Southern, *Western Views of Islam*, p. 43. On Europe's place in the medieval world: Janet L. Abu-Lughod, *Before European Hegemony: The World System A.D. 1250–1350* (New York and Oxford: Oxford University Press, 1989). On the development of medieval cartography and knowledge of the world as mirrored in maps: Anna-Dorothee von den Brincken, *Fines Terrae: Die Enden der Erde und der vierte Kontinent auf mittelalterlichen Weltkarten* (Hannover: Hahnsche Buchhandlung, 1992).
[37] Joseph Lecler, *Histoire de la tolérance au siècle de la Réforme* (1955; repr. Paris: Albin Michel, 1994), pp. 65–124. See also Adriaan H. Bredero's views on the role of the Church and the laity in anti-Judaism: 'Anti-Jewish Sentiment in Medieval Society', in his *Christendom and Christianity in the Middle Ages: The Relations between Religion, Church, and Society*, tr. Reinder Bruinsma, 2nd edn (Grand Rapids, Mich.: William B. Eerdmans, 1987), pp. 274–318.

At the Gate of Christendom

from its beginnings. The twelfth and thirteenth centuries are usually seen as a turning point (for the worse) in relations to non-Christians. For example, Norman Daniel, focusing exclusively on matters of religion, has argued that hatred and suspicion predominated in Christian writings about Islam from the twelfth century and that even Christian toleration of subject Muslims was only intended to aid conversion.[38] Gilbert Dahan has seen both lay and ecclesiastical authorities on the offensive against Judaism and Jews in these centuries.[39] Mark Cohen has emphasized that during the thirteenth century, churchmen moved towards a policy of restriction and exclusion, while secular powers began to enforce these policies.[40] Gavin Langmuir has argued that the appearance of antisemitism in the twelfth and thirteenth centuries was due to changes in the mentality of Christians; surfacing Christian doubts rendered Jewish disbelief menacing.[41] R. I. Moore in a more general study has linked the emergence of a 'persecuting society' to eleventh- and twelfth-century social change and explained it as part of the establishment of Church and state authority. Moore has argued that as the institutional apparatus of the Catholic Church and monarchies developed in western Europe amidst rapid social and economic changes, persecution evolved as a means exercised by a central authority. Certain groups were defined as outsiders and individuals were persecuted for belonging to these groups.[42] The study of persecution continues.[43]

Several authors mention tolerance or 'toleration' of non-Christians either in the sense of allowing Jews and Muslims for some pragmatic reason to exist physically within Christendom, without converting, or in the sense of a lack of repressive measures taken against them.[44] Although several scholars have interpreted the coexistence of Christians with Muslims and Jews as indicative of the genuine tolerance of societies or rulers, the validity of this interpretation has been severely criticized for medieval Iberia and Sicily.[45] It is usually assumed, however, that the western and eastern parts of Europe developed differently in terms of the treatment of non-Christians in the Middle Ages: the former as persecut-

---

[38] Daniel, *Islam*, esp. pp. 137–45. [39] Dahan, *Intellectuels*, esp. pp. 29–41, 199–226.
[40] Cohen, *Under Crescent*, pp. 42–3. [41] Langmuir, *Toward a Definition*.
[42] Moore, *Formation of a Persecuting Society*. See also John Boswell, *Christianity, Social Tolerance, and Homosexuality: Gay People in Western Europe from the Beginning of the Christian Era to the Fourteenth Century* (Chicago: University of Chicago Press, 1980), esp. pp. 3–38, 269–95.
[43] Scott L. Waugh and Peter D. Diehl, eds., *Christendom and its Discontents: Exclusion, Persecution and Rebellion, 1000–1500* (Cambridge, Cambridge University Press, 1996); Iogna-Prat, *Ordonner et exclure*.
[44] For example Dahan, *Intellectuels*, p. 217; Daniel, *Islam*, pp. 137–9; Cohen, *Under Crescent*, p. 36.
[45] David Abulafia, *Frederick II: A Medieval Emperor* (New York and Oxford: Oxford University Press, 1992; first edn, 1988); David Abulafia, 'Monarchs and Minorities in the Christian Western Mediterranean around 1300: Lucera and its Analogues', in *Christendom and its Discontents*, pp. 234–63; Nirenberg, *Communities*, pp. 21–40.

ing societies, the latter as tolerant ones. The notion of tolerant societies has been reinforced for east-central Europe by the idea that rulers were tolerant out of economic necessity, or because of the continued nomad–pagan influences in these areas This notion is sometimes expressed in the form of a coherent argument, but often it is only an assumption that informs works more or less implicitly.[46]

Modern scholars can argue whether peaceful methods of conversion can be called 'tolerant', as opposed to the 'intolerance' of forced conversions, or whether the idea of converting non-Christians to Christianity is a sign of intolerance in itself. Most medieval Christians would have been baffled by such discussions. The missionary John of Plano Carpini's remarks show that he could conceive of religious toleration only as a ruse. In the *History of the Mongols*, a relation of his experiences, John remarked that the Mongols did not attempt to spread their religious beliefs, even though they conquered many lands. 'And since they do not follow any law in the worship of God, until now, as far as we know, they have not forced anyone to deny his faith or law . . . What they will do later we do not know; but some people think that if they will have absolute power, God forbid, then they will force everyone to bow to that idol.'[47]

Hungary, on the eastern frontier of Christendom, was one of the significant areas of interaction with non-Christians, both across the border and within the kingdom. As the following chapters demonstrate, Hungary was neither a tolerant nor a persecuting society, and the Hungarian case contributes to rethinking the complex web of factors that together determined Christian policies and attitudes to non-Christians, and the place of non-Christians in medieval Christian society.

---

[46] Sámuel Kohn, *A zsidók története Magyarországon* (Budapest, 1884), e.g. pp. 128, 138, 144; András Kubinyi, 'Nemzetiségi és vallási tolerancia a középkori Magyarországon', in *Főpapok, egyházi intézmények és vallásosság a középkori Magyarországon* (Budapest: METEM, 1999), pp. 123–38; Gyula Kristó, 'Vallási türelem az Árpád-kori Magyarországon', in *La civiltà ungherese e il cristianesimo: Atti del IV Congresso Internazionale di Studi Ungheresi Roma–Napoli 9–14 settembre 1996*, 3 vols. (Budapest and Szeged: Nemzetközi Magyar Filológiai Társaság and Scriptum, 1998), vol. II: pp. 485–96. Jerzy Wyrozumski, 'Die Frage der Toleranz im mittelalterlichen Polen', *Universitas Iagellonica Acta Scientiarum Litterarumque*, vol. MXXV Studia Germano-Polonica 1, ed. Krzysztof Baczkowski, Antoni Podraza and Winfried Schulze (Cracow: Nakl. Uniwersytetu Jagiellońskiego, 1992): pp. 7–19; Janusz Tazbir, *A State without Stakes: Polish Religious Toleration in the Sixteenth and Seventeenth Centuries* (Warsaw and New York: Kosciuszko Foundation, 1973). Germanic tolerance: Gavin Langmuir, 'From Ambrose of Milan to Emicho of Leiningen: The Transformation of Hostility Against Jews in Northern Christendom', in *Gli Ebrei nell'Alto Medioevo*, 2 vols., Settimane di Studio del Centro Italiano di Studi sull'Alto Medioevo 26 (Spoleto, 1980), vol. I: pp. 313–68, see p. 340. Poland: Léon Poliakov, *Histoire de l'antisémitisme*, 3rd edn, (Paris: Libr. Gén. Française, 1981), vol. I: pp. 388–90.

[47] 'Et quia de cultu Dei nullam legem observant, neminem adhuc quod inteleximus coegerunt suam fidem vel legem negare . . . Quid ulterius faciant ignoramus; presumitur tamen a quibusdam quod si monarchiam haberent, quod Deus avertat, facerent quod omnes isti ydolo inclinarent'. Carpini, *Ystoria*, ed. Wyngaert, p. 39; ed. Daffinà *et al.*, p. 238.

NON-CHRISTIANS IN HUNGARY

Periphery, as applied to medieval history by Jacques Le Goff,[48] acquires a geographical, cultural and religious meaning instead of denoting economic and social structures. It carries the ambivalence of liminality: it can be a place where danger lurks or, alternatively, a place of access to the divine. To be on the fringes of the medieval Christian world could entail being regarded as a barbarian; it could also be seen as a source of holiness. For example, medieval Ireland was seen as a land of barbarians, but at the same time as the site of many miraculous events.[49] For the medieval Christian, the true centre of the world was Jerusalem. From this vantage point, much of Europe was on the periphery. None the less, the frontiers of Christendom, characterized by real and imaginary encounters with non-Christians, acquired more of the ambivalent status of the 'periphery'. These were the key places for the defence and expansion of Christendom, but also those most exposed to the danger of corruption and penetration.

Hungary was both an area of recent Christianization and a meeting point of the Christian and nomad worlds, which created a unique background to the problem of non-Christians. The country was converted to Christianity in the late tenth and early eleventh centuries. As a frontier zone of medieval Christendom, Hungary – along with other frontier areas – played an important role in defence against incursions from the east (the most significant of which was the Mongol invasion of 1241–2). At the same time its eastern regions were the last extension of the steppe. Both nomadic raids and settlement were constant features of the kingdom's medieval history. In the second half of the thirteenth century both nomad conquest (the Mongol invasion and continued fear of its recurrence) and royal policies (settlement of the 'pagan' Cumans) threatened to detach Hungary from Christendom. Both Hungary's recent Christianization and its position lying astride a socio-economic and religious frontier created tension; Hungary manoeuvred between Christendom and the nomad 'pagan' world that threatened to erode Christianity.

Hungary was Christianized in the late tenth and eleventh centuries, if the criterion of 'Christianization' is the adoption of the Christian religion, customs and institutions, and not the internalization of Christian

---

[48] Lecture series at the Ecole des Hautes Etudes en Sciences Sociales, Paris, 1993–4; Jacques Le Goff, 'Centre/Périphérie', in Le Goff and Jean-Claude Schmitt, eds., *Dictionnaire raisonné de l'Occident médiéval* (Paris: Fayard, 1999), pp. 149–65. I thank Jacques Le Goff for allowing me to read the article prior to publication.

[49] Jeanne-Marie Boivin, *L'Irlande au Moyen Age. Giraud de Barri et la Topographia Hibernica (1188)* (Paris: Honoré Champion, 1993), pp. 111–45.

doctrine, elusive and controversial in itself.[50] Hungary was a latecomer to Christendom, and had first to obtain full recognition and then full status among Christian kingdoms. These developments were common to the Scandinavian and east-central European region. The battle for recognition was successful. The Hungarian ecclesiastical organization did not become dependent on the German one, unlike Bohemia and parts of Scandinavia, but formed an independent church with the archbishopric of Esztergom as its head.[51]

Internal events raised the possibility of a 'pagan' reversal as late as 1046 (the Vata revolt). At the time of Peter Damian and Odilo of Cluny, the church in Hungary was not undergoing major reform, but faced extirpation. The revolt was connected to internal strife over royal succession. Members of the dynasty who found themselves excluded from power linked their cause to an opposition to Christianity. Churches were destroyed, Christian priests were killed, and the only known theologian who worked in Hungary during that period, the Venetian-born Gerard (Gellért), was martyred by the rebels. A second, less important revolt broke out in 1061. At the beginning of the twelfth century King Kálmán (Coloman) thought it necessary to include in the prologue to his decrees a reassurance that Hungary was finally thoroughly Christianized:

the law given to our people by our holy father Stephen, that truly apostolic man, was in certain matters more harsh and in others more lenient . . . but let no one escape the rod of discipline . . . Since in the time of the said father this entire kingdom wallowed in barbaric crudity, and the rough, coerced Christian converts kicked against the admonitory prod of holy faith and answered the penitential lashes of the switch of correction with bites, it was most necessary that the coercion of holy discipline converted nominal believers to the faith while it called the already converted to account for their sins through penance. But the most Christian King [Coloman] . . . after having seen that mature faith had acquired the strength of perfect religion, wisely considered releasing the bonds of legal fetters, or rather he deemed it unseemly that the now willing soldiers of the faith, whom not even death would be able to keep from confessing the truth recently embraced, should be tormented by the fear of legal punishment.[52]

---

[50] On the debates about the concept of popular religion (partially concerned with the extent to which 'pagan' customs and beliefs were retained in Christian countries during the Middle Ages): Jean-Claude Schmitt, 'Religion populaire et culture folklorique', *Annales ESC* 31 (1976): pp. 941–53; John Van Engen, 'The Christian Middle Ages as an Historiographical Problem', *American Historical Review* 91 (June 1986): pp. 519–52.

[51] Another archbishopric, that of Kalocsa, was also established.

[52] 'a sancto patro nostro Stephano, viro quippe apostolico legem populo nostro datam in quibusdam austeriorem, in quibusdam vero tollerabiliorem . . . nec quemquam tamen absque discipline verbere dimittentem . . . Nam cum tempore predicti patris universum regnum eius barbaricis servierit incultibus, ac rudis coactusque christianos contra commoniturium sancte fidei stimulum adhuc recalcitraret, adhuc contra penitentialia ultricis virge verbera remorderet, opere pretium fuit, ut sancte discipline coactio in fidelibus quidem ad conversionem fidei, sed conversis fieret ad

Hungary became an integral part of western Christendom. Among the many examples that illustrate this are the ecclesiastical structure of dioceses, tithes paid and immunities granted to ecclesiastical institutions, papal decisions in Hungarian cases that were incorporated into canon law, and the participation of King András II in the crusade in 1217–18.[53] Yet the possibility of slipping away from Christianity remained a real or imagined danger for much of the Middle Ages. 'Pagan' influences were not eradicated by the crushing of the uprisings of 1046 and 1061. Nomads from the east continued to appear on the Hungarian scene. With Cuman settlement and the Mongol invasion, the spectre of a 'pagan' reversal still haunted the popes in the thirteenth century. From the 'Christian' perspective, Hungary was integrated into Christendom, but continued in a precarious position – which occasioned fear and manipulation.

I have chosen to compare three different non-Christian groups in Hungary, rather than writing a study of all those who did not adhere to Latin Christianity. Of the many 'pagan' groups, I selected the Cumans, because they provide the best example of the treatment and integration of 'pagans'. Over the centuries, numerous Turkic nomad groups settled in the kingdom; the most important before the Cumans were the Oghuz and the Pecheneg.[54] It seems that those who arrived in the eleventh and twelfth centuries were converted and Christianized fairly fast, but the process is not well documented. By the thirteenth century, sources no longer describe them as 'pagans', nor do papal letters complain about their behaviour, which cannot be said of the Cumans. Archaeological finds connected to Pechenegs suggest that their religious practices did not survive after the eleventh century.[55] On the other hand, Pechenegs who were priests or were engaged in activities that indicate that they were Christians were explicitly mentioned.[56] Some of the Pechenegs in

footnote 52 (cont.)
iustitiam penitentie peccati. At christianissimus rex noster [Colomanus] . . . postquam vidit adultam fidem perfecte religionis robor accepisse, legalis vinculum cathene cogitavit relaxare prudenter, utpote perpendens indignum esse, si iam spontaneum fidei militem legalis pene timor torqueret, quem nec ipsa mors ab agnite iam confessione veritatis abstrahere potuisset'. Bak, *Laws*, pp. 24–5 (Latin text and English translation).

[53] Kornél Szovák, 'Pápai-magyar kapcsolatok a 12. században', in *Magyarország és a Szentszék kapcsolatának ezer éve*, ed. István Zombori (Budapest: METEM, 1996), pp. 21–46.

[54] György Györffy, 'Besenyők és magyarok', in Györffy, *A magyarság keleti elemei* (Budapest: Gondolat, 1990), pp. 94–191; András Pálóczi Horváth, *Besenyők, kunok, jászok* (Budapest: Corvina, 1989), pp. 7–33 (Eng. tr.: *Pechenegs, Cumans, Iasians: Steppe Peoples in Medieval Hungary* (Budapest: Corvina, 1989)); Péter Havassy, ed., *Zúduló sasok: új honfoglalók – besenyők, kunok, jászok – a középkori Alföldön és Mezőföldön* (Gyula: Erkel Ferenc Múzeum, 1996).

[55] Pálóczi Horváth, *Besenyők*, pp. 32–3; András Pálóczi Horváth, 'Nomád népek a kelet-európai steppén és a középkori Magyarországon', in *Zúduló sasok*, pp. 7–36, see p. 19.

[56] E.g. Andreas Bissenus, cellarius in a monastery: *MES*, vol. I: p. 416, no. 540; Zoloch Bissenus civis Nittriensis (1265): Györffy, 'Besenyők és magyarok', p. 156; in a trial concerning the non-payment of tithes Pechenegs are mentioned together with the *Latini* (who were certainly western Christian

Hungary may have been Muslims; from the perspective of religious affiliation, therefore, their case need not be separated from that of other Muslims.[57] The existing documentation is significantly more important for the history of the Cumans than for other 'pagan' Turkic populations.

There is a long debate in Hungarian historiography concerning the As (Hungarian *jász*, also erroneously called Jazyges) who may or may not have arrived in Hungary with the Cumans.[58] The first explicit mention of As families living in Hungary, in which they are clearly designated by their own name, is in 1323, but from this description it seems that they were not newly settled in Hungary.[59] The source is a royal charter that grants special privileges to a group of As. It exempts them from the jurisdiction of a Cuman captain and raises them to the status of other As serving the king. This seems to indicate that they had lived a settled way of life there for some time. Since As were allied with the Cumans in the north Caucasian steppe, maybe they entered Hungary together with the Cumans, and were not distinguished from them for over half a century.[60] The As spoke an Iranian language clearly distinct from the Turkic Cuman.[61] Moreover, they were probably Greek Orthodox at the time of their arrival in Hungary.[62] It has been suggested that despite these

immigrants) and no accusation of 'paganism' appears (1218, 1221, 1227): *ÁÚO*, vol. I: p. 160, no. 86; Györffy, 'Besenyők és magyarok', p. 132; Theber of Keer, *probus vir* (elected judge) (1300): *CD*, vol. IX, pt. 7: p. 729, no. LXVI; the castellan Johannes Beseny of Nezda is granted permission to build a monastery in 1373: Györffy, 'Besenyők és magyarok', p. 134.

[57] 'Hysmaelitae vel Byssenii' in a text of 1196: *CD*, vol. II: p. 303 (*RA*, no. 168); Jenő Szűcs, 'Két történelmi példa az etnikai csoportok életképességéről', in *Magyarságkutatás, A Magyarságkutató Csoport Évkönyve*, ed. Csaba Gy. Kiss (Budapest: Magyarságkutató Csoport, 1987), pp. 11–27, see p. 14; Pálóczi Horváth, *Besenyők*, p. 24.

[58] Jazyg was the name of an ancient Iranian people, applied to the As during the Middle Ages. On the As in Hungary: László Szabó, *A jász etnikai csoport* (Szolnok: Szolnoki Múzeum, 1979); László Selmeczi, *A négyszállási I. számú jász temető* (Budapest: Történeti Múzeum, 1992); László Selmeczi, *Régészeti-néprajzi tanulmányok a jászokról és a kunokról*, Folklór és etnográfia 64 (Debrecen: KLTE, 1992); László Selmeczi, 'A jászok keresztény hitre térítése a XIII.–XV. században', in *Egyházak a változó világban*, ed. István Bárdos and Margit Beke (Tatabánya: Komárom-Esztergom Megye Önkormányzata és József Attila Megyei Könyvtár, 1992), pp. 159–65; Pálóczi Horváth, *Besenyők*, pp. 54–8; Havassy, *Zúduló sasok*.

[59] István Gyárfás, *A jász-kunok története* [*JK*], 4 vols. (Kecskemét, Szolnok, and Budapest, 1870–85; repr. Budapest: A Jászságért Alapítvány, 1992), vol. III: pp. 463–5. One earlier instance (1318) concerns only one individual who is a slave ('Elysabeth natione Jazonice'): György Györffy, 'Gyulafehérvár kezdetei, neve és káptalanjának registruma', *Századok*, 117 (1983): pp. 1103–34, see p. 1131, no. 22.

[60] Cuman–As alliance against the Mongols described by Ibn al-Athīr and repeated by Rašīd al-Dīn: Golden, *Introduction*, p. 288. Summary and bibliography of the view that As immigrated with Cumans: László Selmeczi, 'A jászok etnogenezise', in *Tanulmányok és közlemények*, ed. Zoltán Ujváry (Debrecen and Szolnok: Damjanich Múzeum és Kossuth Lajos Tudományegyetem Néprajzi Tanszéke, 1995), pp. 127–44.

[61] Gyula Németh, *Eine Wörterliste der Jassen, der Ungarländischen Alanen* (Berlin: Akademie Verlag, 1959); György Györffy, 'A XV. századi jász szójegyzék', in *Magyarság*, pp. 316–18.

[62] Greek names of As: Lajos Ligeti, 'A magyar nyelv török kapcsolatai és ami körülöttük van', *Magyar Nyelv* 72 (1976): pp. 11–27, see p. 24. On the conversion of As to Byzantine Christianity: Dimitri

differences they were not distinguished from the Cumans in Hungary because they were subjugated by the Cumans as a military auxiliary group, and because the Hungarians did not participate in internal Cuman affairs.[63] Another possibility is that the majority of the As lived in Moldavia and Wallachia until the end of the thirteenth century (called Alania at that time) and migrated into the kingdom later than, and separately from, the Cumans.[64] Whatever the case may be, the As were either treated together with the Cumans, and in exactly the same way as the Cumans, in thirteenth-century Hungary, or they moved into Hungary at the end of the thirteenth or the beginning of the fourteenth century, thus falling outside the scope of this study.

Heretics (in Hungary's case, Bogomils in Bosnia) are not included in this analysis either.[65] Although heretics were in some ways treated as non-Christians, two considerations led me not to incorporate them into this study. First, heretics were seen as deviant Christians, whereas Jews, Muslims and 'pagans' were judged to be – with more or less benevolence – unacquainted with or stubbornly refusing to accept Christian doctrine; in no instance were they seen as people willingly leaving the right path, as was the case with heretics. The policy towards heretics by the Central Middle Ages was to induce them to repent and return to the flock, or, failing that, to eradicate them – a policy which appears superficially similar to the one sometimes exercised towards non-Christians. Yet

footnote 62 (*cont.*)
Obolensky, *The Byzantine Commonwealth: Eastern Europe, 500–1453* (New York and Washington: Praeger, 1971), p. 178.
László Selmeczi, 'A négyszállási jász temető (előzetes közlés az 1980. évi feltárásokról)', *Communicationes Archaeologicae Hungariae* (1981): pp. 165–77, reprinted in *Régészeti-néprajzi tanulmányok*, pp. 135–64; Selmeczi, *A négyszállási I. számú* on 'Byzantine' position of the arms of skeletons, Byzantine crosses, rings and dress ornaments depicting crosses in As graves in Hungary. Non-Christian customs can also be detected in these graves, such as the remnants of fires that were lit to chase away evil spirits, and objects placed in the graves to be used in the next world ('Régészeti adatok a jászok szokásaihoz és hiedelemvilágához', in *Régészeti-néprajzi tanulmányok*, pp. 185–211 and *A négyszállási I. számú*, passim).

[63] Szabó, *Jász etnikai csoport*, pp. 26–32.
[64] Györffy, 'A Jászság betelepülése', in *Magyarság*, pp. 312–15. Lajos Ligeti, *A magyar nyelv török kapcsolatai a honfoglalás előtt és az Árpád-korban* (Budapest: Akadémiai Kiadó, 1986), pp. 417–18.
[65] Dimitri Obolensky, *The Bogomils: A Study in Balkan Neo-Manicheism* (Cambridge: Cambridge University Press, 1948); Atanasio G. Matanič, 'Correnti ereticali in Bosnia (sec. XII–XV)', in *L'Eglise et le peuple chrétien dans les pays de l'Europe du Centre-Est et du Nord, XIVe–XVe siècles*, Collection de l'Ecole Française de Rome 128 (Rome: Ecole Française de Rome and Paris: Diffusion de Boccard, 1990), pp. 267–73; James Ross Sweeney, 'Papal–Hungarian Relations during the Pontificate of Innocent III, 1198–1216', Ph.D. dissertation (Cornell University, 1971), p. 110; John V. A. Fine, Jr., *The Late Medieval Balkans. A Critical Survey from the Late Twelfth Century to the Ottoman Conquest* (Ann Arbor: University of Michigan Press, 1994), pp. 100, 131–2, 146; Zsuzsánna Kulcsár, *Eretnekmozgalmak a XI–XIV. században*, A Budapesti Egyetemi Könyvtár Kiadványai 22 (Budapest: Tankönyvkiadó, 1964). Translated sources with a historical introduction and bibliography: Janet Hamilton and Bernard Hamilton, *Christian Dualist Heresies in the Byzantine World c. 650–c. 1450* (Manchester and New York: Manchester University Press, 1998).

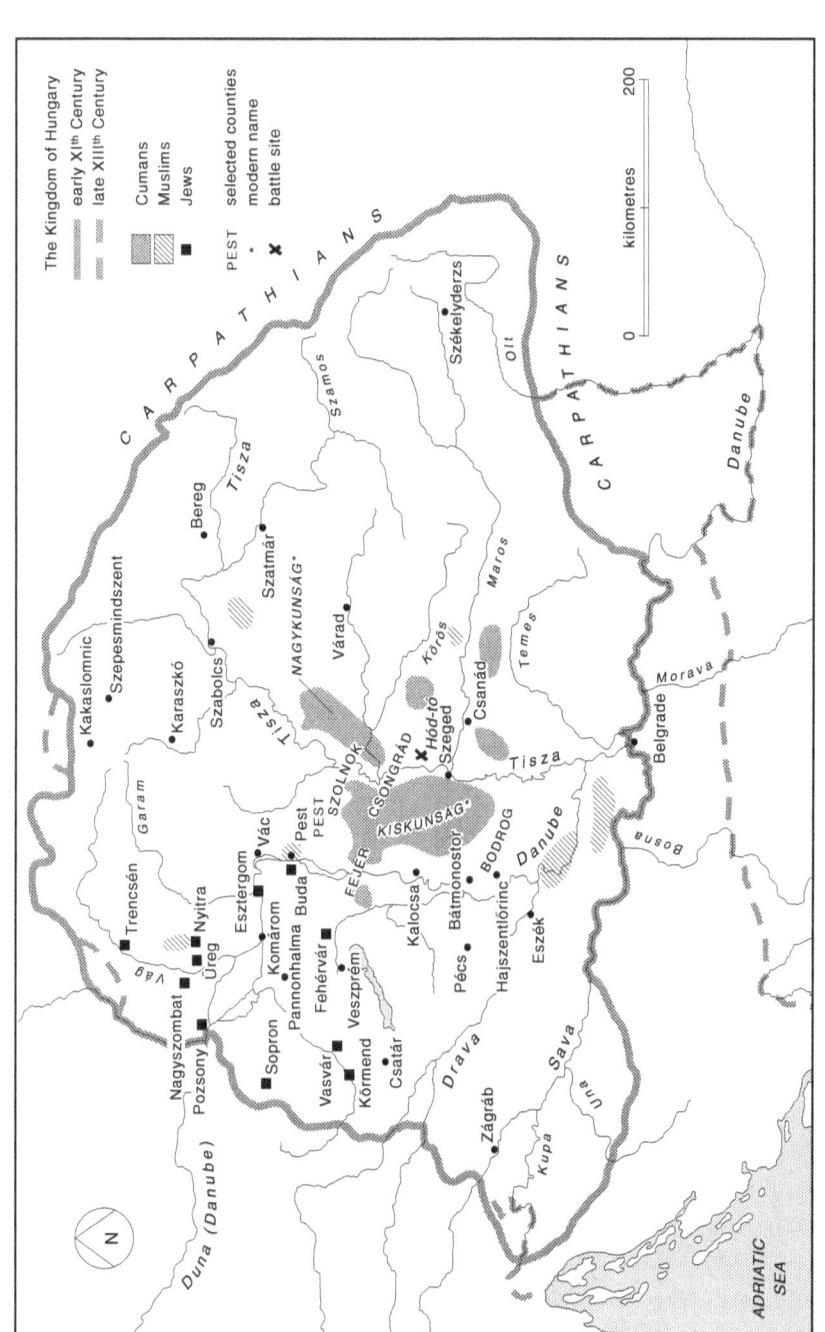

Map 2 Non-Christians in the kingdom of Hungary.

repression played a major role in the case of heretics from the moment a movement was perceived as heretical, whereas it was only one phase of Christian–non-Christian relations. Second, Hungarian policies towards Bogomils were always linked to expansion and conquest, whereas such linkage was true for only the early phase of policies towards one of the non-Christian groups, the Cumans.

Although the problems raised by the relations between Greek Christians and Latin Christendom were partially similar to those concerning non-Christians, there were significant differences as well.[66] First, their case cannot be separated from Hungarian–Byzantine political relations. Second, these groups were definitely seen as Christian by both kings and popes, even if some of their customs and rituals were called into question as erroneous.

Therefore, although sometimes comparisons could be made with other groups, I shall concentrate on those whose religion was not Christian. The non-Christians I focus on in this study arrived in Hungary in different periods and had varied backgrounds.

JEWS

Jews lived in Roman Pannonia (a territory which later became the western part of Hungary) from the third century, but continuity between them and medieval Jews cannot be proven.[67] According to one theory, the Jewish Khazars joined the Hungarian tribes and arrived in the Carpathian basin with them in the late ninth century.[68] Some groups from the Khazar Empire (called Kavars) indeed joined the Hungarians, and certain individuals professing Judaism may have merged into this tribal alliance, but the Jews of Hungary were not descendants of the Khazars. There are debates about the date of both the Khazar conversion (between 740 and 860) and the joining of the Kavars to the Hungarians (760–881); it is thus not even certain that the Kavars joined after the con-

---

[66] Gyula Moravcsik, 'Görögnyelvű monostorok Szent István korában', in *Emlékkönyv Szent István király halálának kilencszázadik évfordulóján*, 3 vols., ed. Jusztinián Serédi (Budapest: Magyar Tudományos Akadémia, 1938), vol. 1: pp. 389–422; Moravcsik, 'The Role of the Byzantine Church'; Moravcsik, 'Les relations entre la Hongrie et Byzance'; Gyula Moravcsik, 'Bizánci császárok és követeik Budán', *Századok* 95 (1961): pp. 832–45; István Pirigyi, *A magyarországi görög katolikusok története* (Budapest: Görög katolikus hittudományi főiskola, 1990), chapter VI; István Pirigyi, *A görögkatolikus magyarság története* (Budapest: IKVA, 1991), chapter I.

[67] Kohn, *Zsidók*, pp. 2–5; Sándor Büchler, *A zsidók története Budapesten a legrégibb időktől 1867-ig* (Budapest: Izraelita Magyar Irodalmi Társulat, 1901), p. 13; Alexander Scheiber, *Jewish Inscriptions in Hungary from the 3rd Century to 1686* (Budapest: Akadémiai Kiadó and Leiden: Brill, 1983), pp. 13–72.

[68] Kohn, *Zsidók*, pp. 12–24; Mátyás Gyóni, 'Kálizok, kazárok, kabarok, magyarok', *Magyar Nyelv* 34 (1938): pp. 86–92, 159–71; Raphael Patai, *The Jews of Hungary: History, Culture, Psychology* (Detroit: Wayne State University Press, 1996), p. 28.

version. How extensively Judaism was practised in Khazaria, and to what extent the converted elite followed Jewish rituals and law, is also far from certain. Moreover, whenever the conversion took place, it was the ruler who initiated it; and those who joined the Hungarian tribes were rebels against the ruler.[69] All that is certain about the origins of Jewish settlement in medieval Hungary is that by the middle of the tenth century Jews who were immigrants from German and western Slav areas lived in the country.[70]

The size of the Jewish communities of Hungary is uncertain. Estimates of the maximum number for the early sixteenth century range from 2,500 to 20,000.[71] The existing data is insufficient either definitively to support

[69] Peter B. Golden, 'Khazaria and Judaism', *AEMAe*, 3 (1983): pp. 127–56; Omeljan Pritsak, 'The Khazar Kingdom's Conversion to Judaism', *Harvard Ukrainian Studies* 2 (1978): pp. 261–81; Norman Golb and Omeljan Pritsak, *Khazarian Hebrew Documents of the Tenth Century* (Ithaca and London: Cornell University Press, 1982); D. M. Dunlop, *The History of the Jewish Khazars* (Princeton: Princeton University Press, 1954; New York: Schocken, 1967), esp. pp. 196–7; 'Kabar', in *KMTL*.

All the evidence used to support the thesis of Jewish Khazars in Hungary is questionable. Two rings with Hebrew letters were found in a Hungarian cemetery (from the second half of the eleventh c.) near villages that were probably settled by tribes from the Khazar Empire. The rings could have been imported, and the Hebrew letters are only used as an ornament, without constituting a meaningful script. Scheiber, *Jewish Inscriptions*, p. 75; Attila Kiss, '11th c. Khazar Rings from Hungary with Hebrew Letters and Signs', *Acta Archaeologica Academiae Scientiarum Hungaricae* 22 (1970): pp. 341–8. One interpretation of a runic inscription maintains that it concerns a Karaite Jew from Khazaria; there is, however, no agreement even on the language of the inscription: András Kubinyi, 'A magyarországi zsidóság története a középkorban', *Soproni Szemle* 49 (1995): pp. 2–27, see p. 2. The Byzantine Ioannes Kinnamos in his *Epitome* twice mentioned *khalisioi* in the Hungarian army: Gyula Moravcsik, *Fontes Byzantini*, pp. 202, 234. He first describes them as keeping the laws of Moses although not in a pure form, then as having the same religion as Persians. This is a reference to the *khaliz* (Muslims), not Jewish Khazars. Büchler, *Zsidók*, pp. 17–20; Béla Kossányi, 'A kalizok vallása', in *Emlékkönyv Domanovszky Sándor születése hatvanadik fordulójának ünnepére* (Budapest: Királyi Magyar Egyetemi Nyomda, 1937), pp. 355–68; Göckenjan, *Hilfsvölker*, pp. 52–6; 'kálizok', in *KMTL*.

[70] Ibrāhīm ibn Yaʿqūb (965) on Jewish merchants who travelled from Hungary to Prague: 'Relatio Ibrāhīm ībn Jaʾqūb de itinere slavico', ed. and tr. Tadeusz Kowalski, in *Monumenta Poloniae Historica*, n.s., 1 (Cracow: Polska Academia, 1946), p. 146; Chasdai ben Yitzchak ibn Shaprūt on Jews living in Hungary c. 955: Pavel Kokovcov, ed., *Yevreysko – Kazarskaya perepiska v X veke* (Leningrad, 1932), pp. 7–19, see p. 16; tr. (from Pavel Kokovcov's edition) Sámuel Kohn, *Héber kútforrások és adatok Magyarország történetéhez* (1881; repr. Budapest, Akadémiai Kiadó, 1990), pp. 10–23, see p. 19. Golb and Pritsak, *Khazarian Hebrew Documents*, p. 92.

Pauler, *Magyar nemzet*, vol. I: pp. 167, 450 (German origin). Jews from Bohemia to Hungary (1098): Cosmas, 'Chronicon Boemorum libri III usque ad annum 1125', in *Fontes Rerum Bohemicarum*, vol. II (Prague, 1874), p. 140. Also see Aleksander Gieysztor, 'The Beginnings of Jewish Settlement in the Polish Lands', in *The Jews in Poland*, ed. Chimen Abramsky et al. (Oxford: Blackwell, 1986), pp. 15–21; Jerzy Wyrozumski, 'Jews in Medieval Poland', in *The Jews in Old Poland 1000–1795*, ed. Antony Polonsky et al. (London and New York: I.B. Tauris, 1993), pp. 13–22. As I discuss in the following chapters, eleventh- to thirteenth-century sources and the synagogue of Sopron show connections to German lands.

[71] 20,000: Kohn, *Zsidók*, p. 393; 2,500–3,700: Ferenc Kováts, 'Introduction', in *Magyar Zsidó Oklevéltár (Monumenta Hungariae Judaica) [MZsO]*, ed. Ármin Friss and Sándor Scheiber, 18 vols. (Budapest, 1903–80), vol. IV: pp. XXXIII–LV, esp. p. LV; criticized as 'too high' by András

or to disprove any of these figures. No calculation has been made of the size of the eleventh- to thirteenth-century Jewish population of Hungary. By the end of the thirteenth century, Jewish communities lived in several medieval cities (Buda, Esztergom, Fehérvár, Nyitra, Pozsony, Vasvár, Körmend, Trencsén, probably Sopron and Nagyszombat) as well as in the village of Üreg (see map 2).[72] No figures exist as to the size of these communities, and the list itself may be very incomplete. Documentation on individuals and communities exists only in so far as there were legal cases recorded, privileges granted, or material remains found. Other communities may have existed without ever appearing in medieval sources. Place names referring to Jews are rare and their interpretation particularly difficult as a toponym may contain the word 'Jew' (*zsidó* in Hungarian) for several reasons. It may not be connected to Jews at all, but be a result of folk etymology: the distortion of *séd*, stream, into /z/sid, may be mistakenly seen as derived from *zsidó*.[73] Alternatively, such a toponym may indicate land that had once belonged to someone bearing the name 'Zsidó' who could be a Christian.[74] Moreover, Jewish landownership need not imply the presence of a Jewish community. Even if there was a Jewish community, it is impossible to determine the period of settlement. A name first documented in the fifteenth century, for example, may or may not point to the existence of a thirteenth-century community. Because Jews lived within existing cities and did not build their own settlements, moreover, the names of cities yield no indication of their

---

footnote 71 (*cont.*)

Kubinyi, 'A zsidóság története a középkori Magyarországon', in *Magyarországi zsinagógák*, ed. László Gerő (Budapest: Műszaki Könyvkiadó, 1989), pp. 19–27, see p. 23. Kubinyi, 'Magyarországi zsidóság', pp. 20–1.

[72] Written evidence exists except for Nagyszombat and Sopron. Tombstones were found in Nagyszombat, the earliest one surviving from 1340 (Scheiber, *Jewish Inscriptions*, pp. 137–45); therefore Jewish settlement may have existed there at least by the late thirteenth century. A synagogue was built *c.* 1300 in Sopron: Ferenc Dávid, *A soproni ó-zsinagóga* (Budapest: A Magyar Izraeliták Országos Képviselete, 1978). During the thirteenth century there are also traces of Jews living near Sopron: Miksa Pollák, *A zsidók története Sopronban a legrégebbi időktől a mai napig* (Budapest, 1896), pp. 9–11. List of thirty-six towns with Jewish inhabitants (until 1526): Kubinyi, 'Magyarországi zsidóság', pp. 18–20. Possible alternative identifications of Üreg: Gyula Wellesz, 'Izsák b. Mózes Or Zarua és az üreghi zsidók', *Magyar Zsidó Szemle* 21 (1904): pp. 370–3, see p. 371.

[73] A list of place names: Gyula Kristó, Ferenc Makk and László Szegfű, 'Adatok "korai" helyneveink ismeretéhez I', *AUSz Acta Historica* 44 (1973), see pp. 31–2 (twenty-four references); *ibid.*, p. 31 on the distortion of *séd*; 'Zsidóvár', in *KMTL*. Often, there is insufficient evidence to understand the relationship between a name and Jews, e.g. 'est via . . . usque ad monte, qui dicitur mons Iudeorum' (the names of the settlements there are St Ypolit and Curtoiz): Richard Marsina, ed., *Codex Diplomaticus et Epistolaris Slovaciae*, vol. I (Bratislava: Academiae Scientiarum Slovacae, 1971), p. 67, no. 69 (*RA*, no. 46).

[74] János Karácsonyi, *A magyar nemzetségek a XIV. század közepéig*, 3 vols. (Budapest: MTA, 1900–1), vol. III: pp. 160–1 a family named Zsidó ('Jew'); all known members from the thirteenth century are Christians; charters referring to a Christian warrior called Sydou (Zsidó), e.g. 1271: *HO*, vol. v: pp. 43–4, no. 35 (*RA*, no. 2103); 1289: *ibid.*, vol. vi: p. 343, no. 248.

Christians and non-Christians

Jewish population. There are few references to Jewish quarters in contemporary documents. In Esztergom, the *contrata Judeorum* was a part of the royal town. It occupied one corner, near one of the town gates.[75] In Buda, the 'Jewish street' was near the royal castle, inside – and very close to – the city walls, with the nearest city gate called 'Jew-Gate'.[76] The fact that we have few references to 'Jewish quarters' (or streets) is not surprising, because the internal arrangement of cities into districts in general was rare in Hungary.[77]

If we calculated the Jewish population on the basis that a quorum (מנין, ten adult males) was necessary to form a community, counting at least ten families for every known Jewish settlement, the total figure for the Jewish population of the thirteenth century would be several hundred to a thousand. Since, on the one hand, it is not certain that we know about every Jewish community, and, on the other, some of the Jewish population may well have lived in smaller groups in cities or villages without being able to form a quorum, relying on the services of a neighbouring community,[78] this calculation also remains tentative. Thus the Jewish population of medieval Hungary cannot be estimated with any precision. What is certain is the relatively small size of this population. Some western European towns had more Jewish inhabitants than the entire kingdom of Hungary; for example, at least 2,000–3,000 Jews lived in Rouen alone in the twelfth century.[79] Jews certainly constituted a tiny fraction (under 0.05 per cent) of Hungary's population (whose size is itself open to educated guesses).[80] It is also important to note that the Jewish settlements

---

[75] MOL DF 236350 (*MES*, vol. II: p. 360, no. 358; *MZsO*, vol. V, pt. 1: p. 12, no. 9; *RA*, no. 3986, in 1294). László Gerevich, ed., *Towns in Medieval Hungary* (Highland Lakes, N.J.: Atlantic Research and Publications and Budapest: Akadémiai Kiadó, 1990), pp. 29, 32.

[76] Büchler, *Zsidók története Budapesten*, pp. 36–7; László Zolnay, *Buda középkori zsidósága és zsinagógáik* (Budapest: Budapesti Történeti Múzeum, 1987), pp. 7–8; Géza Komoróczy, ed., *A zsidó Budapest* (Budapest: MTA Judaisztikai Kutatócsoport, 1995), pp. 13–14; now also available in English: *Jewish Budapest: Monuments, Rites, History* (Budapest: Central European University Press, 1999). *TF*, vol. IV: p. 617; György Györffy, *Pest-Buda kialakulása: Budapest története a honfoglalástól az Árpád-kor végi székvárossá alakulásig* (Budapest: Akadémiai Kiadó, 1997), pp. 147–8. During the fourteenth century, the Jewish street in Buda was moved to another location.

[77] László Gerevich, 'The Rise of Hungarian Towns along the Danube', in *Towns*, pp. 26–50, see p. 50.

[78] Examples: Emily Taitz, *The Jews of Medieval France: The Community of Champagne* (London and Westport, Conn.: Greenwood Press, 1994), p. 131; Irving A. Agus, *Rabbi Meir of Rothenburg: His Life and His Works as Sources for the Religious, Legal, and Social History of the Jews of Germany in the Thirteenth Century*, 2 vols. (Philadelphia: Jewish Publication Society, 1947), vol. I: p. 105; Robin R. Mundill, *England's Jewish Solution: Experiment and Expulsion, 1262–1290* (Cambridge: Cambridge University Press, 1998), pp. 17–25.

[79] Norman Golb, *The Jews in Medieval Normandy* (Cambridge: Cambridge University Press, 1998), p. 147. On figures elsewhere in medieval Europe: Kenneth R. Stow, *Alienated Minority: The Jews of Medieval Latin Europe* (Cambridge, Mass.: Harvard University Press, 1992), pp. 6–7.

[80] The population of thirteenth-century Hungary was estimated as at least 2 million by Györffy, 'Magyarország népessége', pp. 50–1. Widely accepted in Hungarian scholarship: e.g. Székely,

At the Gate of Christendom

were concentrated in western Hungary, reflecting immigration patterns from, and continuing ties to, German areas.

The sources relating to Jews in Hungary can be divided into two major groups: Hebrew and Latin sources. The narrative Hebrew sources consist of rabbinical *responsa* and a memorial poem. All of the *responsa* were produced outside Hungary by non-Hungarian Jews.[81] *Responsa*, being real answers to real questions, give insights into the life of Jewish communities. Given the small number of *responsa* concerning Hungary, however, their true significance cannot be fully determined. It is difficult to judge how characteristic or exceptional they were. Moreover, the interpretation of *responsa* raises questions about the motivations and reasons of those who sought an answer that led to the documentation of any one case, as well as about the agenda of the rabbis.[82] There are also archaeological finds: tombstones (with Hebrew inscriptions), synagogues, finds from Jewish streets, and coins with Hebrew letters. Latin sources were written about the Jews, but were not produced by them. They say very little about Jewish life within the community, and mainly reflect Christian concerns and contact between Jews and Christians. The Latin sources belong to various types: charters, laws, and royal and ecclesiastical correspondence.

MUSLIMS

The history of the Muslim settlement in Hungary is full of uncertainties due to a lack of sources. Scholars have taken different stands on the place(s) of origin of Hungary's Muslims, although many argue for a multiplicity of origins and/or times of arrival. They may have come from

---

footnote 80 (*cont.*)

Magyarország története, vol. 1, pt. 2: p. 1092; Erik Fügedi, 'A középkori Magyarország történeti demográfiája', in *Történeti Demográfiai Füzetek* 10 (Budapest: Központi Statisztikai Hivatal Népességtudományi Kutató Intézet, 1992, no. 1), pp. 7–60, see p. 23; Kovacsics, 'Történeti demográfia', p. 23 (1.5–2.3 million). Kristó, 'Magyarország lélekszáma' differs: 1 million at the beginning, 1.6 million at the end of the thirteenth century. These figures are no more precise than those mentioned above, but are none the less indicative of scale.

[81] Tadeusz Lewicki, 'Les sources hébraïques consacrées à l'histoire de l'Europe centrale et orientale et particulièrement à celle des pays slaves de la fin du IXe au milieu du XIIIe siècle', *Cahiers du Monde Russe et Soviétique* 2, no. 2 (1961): pp. 228–41; Franciszek Kupfer and Tadeusz Lewicki, eds., *Źródła Hebrajskie do Dziejów Słowian i niektórych innych ludów Środkowej i Wschodniej Europy* (Wrocław and Warsaw: Polska Akademia Nauk, 1956); Kohn, *Héber*; Shlomo Spitzer, ed., Hungarian tr. Andrea Strbik, 'Héber nyelvű források Magyarország és a magyarországi zsidók történetéhez', typescript. I thank A. Strbik for making the typescript available to me. I am indebted to Judith Bronstein for English translations of Hebrew texts.

[82] Peter J. Haas, 'The Modern Study of Responsa', in *Approaches to Judaism in Medieval Times*, 2 vols., ed. David R. Blumenthal, Brown Judaic Studies 57 (Chico, Calif.: Scholars Press, 1985), vol. II: pp. 35–71; 'Responsa', in *Encyclopaedia Judaica*, 16 vols. (Jerusalem and New York: Macmillan, 1971–2), vol. XIV: cols. 83–95.

the Khazar Empire,[83] Volga Bulgaria,[84] the Balkans,[85] or Khwarezm[86] with the Hungarians in the late ninth century, or during the rule of prince Taksony (? –c. 970), or during the tenth and eleventh centuries.[87] The evidence for these theories is often slight. The Chronicle of the Hungarian Anonymous (late twelfth or early thirteenth century), for example, relates that Muslims from the land of Bular arrived in Hungary during the reign of Taksony.[88] Nothing corroborates this text, and since the Anonymous's other stories and facts usually relate to his own time rather than to the periods he purportedly talks about, there is no reason to suppose this account to be reliable.

Medieval evidence is scarce and open to different interpretations, but it does point to a heterogeneous Muslim population, an indication that Muslims migrated into Hungary at different times and from different places during several centuries. From the only Muslim village that has been excavated, no find pre-dates the eleventh century.[89] Ibn Ya'qūb, however, mentions Muslims from Hungary travelling to Prague as early

---

[83] Pauler, *Magyar nemzet*, vol. I: p. 166; Charles D'Eszlary, 'Les Musulmans Hongrois du Moyen Age (VIIe–XIVe s.)', *IBLA. Revue de l'Institut des Belles Lettres Arabes* 19 (1956): pp. 375–86, see pp. 376–8; Károly Czeglédy, 'Az Árpád-kori mohamedánokról és neveikről', *Nyelvtudományi Értesítő* 70 (1970): pp. 254–9; repr. in *Magyar Őstörténeti tanulmányok*, Budapest Oriental Reprints Series, A2 (Budapest: Akadémiai Kiadó, 1985), pp. 99–104, p. 102.

[84] László Réthy, *Magyar pénzverő izmaeliták és Bessarábia* (Arad, 1880), pp. 13, 16; György Székely, 'Les contacts entre Hongrois et Musulmans aux IXe–XIIe siècles', in *The Muslim East. Studies in Honour of Julius Germanus*, ed. Gyula Káldy-Nagy (Budapest: ELTE, 1974), pp. 53–74, see p. 70; István Fodor, 'Archaeological traces of the Volga Bulgars in Hungary in the Árpád period', *AOASH* 33 (1979): pp. 315–25; *TF*, vol. IV: p. 500.

[85] Muslim mercenaries of the Byzantine Empire from Turkestan, settled in the Balkans, who came under Hungarian rule when László I conquered the Szerémség: János Karácsonyi, 'Kik voltak s mikor jöttek hazánkba a böszörmények vagy izmaeliták?' *Értekezések a történeti tudományok köréből a II. osztály rendeletéből*, no. 23, pt. 7 (Budapest, 1913), pp. 483–98. From Bulgaria (on the Danube): D'Eszlary, 'Musulmans', p. 379. Tadeusz Lewicki, 'Węgry i muzułmanie węgierscy w świetle relacji podróżnika arabskiego z XII w. Abū Hāmid al-Andalusī al-Ġarnatī'ego', *Rocznik Orjentalistyczny* 13 (1937): pp. 106–22, see p. 111.

[86] Czeglédy, 'Árpád-kori', p. 99; *TF*, vol. IV: p. 500. D'Eszlary, 'Musulmans', p. 380 also lists other places of origin including Spain that lack all foundation. Jenő Szűcs, 'Két történelmi', pp. 11–27 lists all the possible places of origin and times of arrival of these groups. See also H. T. Norris, *Islam in the Balkans: Religion and Society between Europe and the Arab World* (London: Hurst and Company, 1993), pp. 26–31, who lists various views.

[87] With the Hungarians: Pauler, *Magyar nemzet*, vol. I: p. 166; D'Eszlary, 'Musulmans', p. 376; Czeglédy, 'Árpád-kori', pp. 101–2. Under Taksony: D'Eszlary, 'Musulmans', p. 379, and, as a possibility, in several works. Tenth–eleventh c.: Karácsonyi, 'Kik voltak', p. 492; D'Eszlary, 'Musulmans', p. 380.

[88] 'Nam de terra Bular venerunt quidam nobilissimi domini cum magna multitudine Hismahelitarum, quorum nomina fuerunt Billa et Bocsu, quibus dux per diversa loca Hungarorum condonavit terras et insuper castrum, quod dicitur Pest, in perpetuum concessit.' Anonymous in *SRH*, vol. I: pp. 114–15.

[89] Ildikó M. Antalóczy, 'A nyíri izmaeliták központjának, Böszörmény falunak régészeti leletei I', *A Hajdúsági Múzeum Évkönyve*, 4 (Hajdúböszörmény: Hajdúsági Múzeum, 1980), pp. 131–70, see p. 164.

as the late tenth century (965).[90] Abū Hāmid in the twelfth century wrote of two different groups of Muslims in Hungary, and suggested different places of origin for them.[91] Contact with Muslims could in fact have taken place at different times. The Hungarians had lived within the Khazar Empire prior to their arrival in the Carpathian basin and Muslims played an important role there.[92] The Kavars who seceded from this empire and joined the Hungarian tribal alliance may have included Muslims. Hungarian documents talk about the Kaliz, a group of merchants originating from Khwarezm. The Khwarezmians, many of whom were Muslims, travelled and established trading colonies over the whole of the Turkic steppe and eastern Europe. They could have arrived in Hungary from the Khazar Empire, where Khwarezmians lived at the time of the secession of the Hungarian tribes, or during the tenth–twelfth centuries.[93] Perhaps there were Muslims among the Pechenegs as well, who arrived in Hungary in several waves.[94] Muslim mercenaries were also recruited to serve in Hungary. Scattered testimony suggests that Muslims continued to settle in the country at least until the late twelfth or maybe even until the mid-thirteenth century.[95] The Muslim population of Hungary, therefore, was far from homogeneous.

Medieval references to the number of Muslims in Hungary are vague and unreliable, and there are no modern calculations.[96] Abū Hāmid, who

[90] Ibn Ya'qūb, 'Relatio', p. 146.
[91] *Abu-Hámid Al-Garnáti utazása Kelet- és Közép-Európában 1131–1153*, ed. and tr. Tamás Iványi and György Bakcsi (Budapest: Gondolat Kiadó, 1985), p. 56. (Hungarian tr. of César E. Dubler, ed., *Abū Hāmid el Granadino y su relación de viaje por tierras eurasiáticas* (Madrid: Imprenta y Editorial Maestre, 1953) and parts of Gabriel Ferrand, ed., 'Le Tuhfat al-albāb de Abū Hāmid al-Andalusī al-Garnātī édité d'après les Mss. 2167, 2168, 2170 de la Bibliothèque Nationale et le Ms. d'Alger', *Journal Asiatique* 207 (July–December 1925): pp. 1–148, 193–303.) Partial German tr. in Ivan Hrbek, 'Ein Arabischer Bericht über Ungarn (Abū Hāmid al-Andalusī al-Garnātī, 1080–1170), *AOASH* 5 (1955): pp. 205–30, pp. 207–11. Attempts at identification of the two groups remain inconclusive: Hrbek, 'Ein Arabischer', pp. 214–22; Györffy, 'A csatlakozott népek', in *Magyarság*, pp. 58–9. Lewicki, 'Węgry i muzułmanie', pp. 110–12 maintains that Hungarian Muslims came from Bulgaria on the Danube. One of the groups, 'the Maghrebites', was identified with Muslim Pechenegs by some: Bolsakov, *Abu-Hámid*, p. 163, note 56; *Encyclopaedia of Islam*, new edn (Leiden: Brill, 1960–), vol. V: pp. 1016–17.
[92] Peter B. Golden, *Khazar Studies: An Historico-Philological Inquiry into the Origins of the Khazars*, 2 vols. (Budapest: Akadémiai Kiadó, 1980), vol. I: pp. 97–106; Golden, *Introduction*, pp. 241–2.
[93] Göckenjan, *Hilfsvölker*, pp. 44–89; 'kálizok', in *KMTL*.
[94] Hrbek, 'Ein Arabischer', pp. 219–22; Smail Balić, 'Der Islam im mittelalterlichen Ungarn', *Südost-Forschungen* 23 (1964): pp. 19–35.
[95] Abū-Hāmid says that the Hungarian king asked him to recruit Muslim soldiers: *Abu-Hámid*, p. 65; Muslim Pechenegs and perhaps even Cumans may have settled in Hungary. Islamic influences on Cumans: György Györffy, 'A kipcsaki kun társadalom a Codex Cumanicus alapján', in *Magyarság*, pp. 242–73, see p. 268. A papal letter mentions that Muslims hinder the conversion of Cumans to Christianity: ASV Reg. Vat. 15 f. 55v. (*Reg. Greg. IX* no. 561; *VMH*, p. 94, no. CLXVIII).
[96] André Miquel, *La géographie humaine du monde Musulman jusqu'au milieu du 11e siècle* (Paris: EHESS, 1988) does not mention Hungary. D'Eszlary, 'Musulmans', p. 385: 35,000 Muslims is a simple invention without any basis in the sources. Fügedi, 'A középkori Magyarország történeti demográfiája', pp. 15–16: the Muslim population cannot be calculated.

Christians and non-Christians

visited Hungary in the middle of the twelfth century, wrote about 'thousands' and 'innumerable masses' of Muslims in Hungary, but he wished to enhance the importance of Hungary's Muslim population in order to emphasize his own role as an 'apostle' of wayward Muslims (see chapter 7).[97] Yāqūt mentioned Muslims living in about thirty villages, each as large as a small city.[98] Yāqūt's source was a Hungarian Muslim who may have boasted about the size of the Muslim settlements in Hungary. More importantly, although Yāqūt's claim that there were many Muslim villages is corroborated by place names, it is impossible to estimate the size of these villages. Over forty place names based on a form of 'Ismaelita' or other designations for Muslims have been collected.[99] Apart from toponyms, other explicit references in laws and charters of Muslims living in medieval Hungary show that this population lived in both villages and cities in different parts of the country.[100] The size of villages in Hungary varied, some with fewer than thirty inhabitants, others containing hundreds.[101] Also, we cannot know how many of the Muslim villages existed at any one time. Thus estimates based on toponyms would range between a population of less than 2,000 to over 15,000. The only conclusion one can draw is similar to that in the case of the Jewish population: Muslims constituted a small minority in the kingdom.

There are both Arabic and Latin sources relating to the Muslims in Hungary. The Arabic sources were all written by Muslim authors, none of whom was an inhabitant of Hungary. They include materials from travel literature, geographical literature and encyclopedias. The interpretation of travel literature raises the problems generally linked to the genre. How much did the author know about the country? How much did he invent or base on other accounts (and were they reliable)? What hidden

---

[97] *Abu-Hámid*, p. 56. Abū Hāmid was born in 1080 in Granada. He travelled to study in Alexandria, Cairo and Baghdad. He lived and taught Islamic law in Saksin (on the Volga), and travelled from there to Volga Bulgaria, Kiev and Hungary (1150–3): Hrbek, 'Ein Arabischer', p. 206.

[98] Yāqūt, *Mu'djam al-buldān*, ed. Ferdinand Wüstenfeld (Leipzig, 1873), vol. I: pp. 469–70; I thank Patricia Crone for a translation of the Arabic text. French translation in *Géographie d'Aboulféda*, tr. Joseph Toussaint Reinaud, 3 vols. (Paris, 1848–83), vol. II: pp. 294–5. The Arab geographer Yāqūt encountered Hungarian Muslims in Aleppo *c.* 1220.

[99] Kristó *et al.*, 'Adatok', pp. 17 and 22–3; Gyula Kristó, 'Szempontok korai helyneveink történeti tipológiájához', *AUSz: Acta Historica* 55 (1976), p. 64. Szűcs, 'Két történelmi', p. 13 writes of eighty place names; he accepted Györffy's argument that the Alanian population of Hungary was Muslim and included all toponyms referring to them.

[100] E.g. 'ville hysmaelitarum': Bak, *Laws*, p. 29; 'villa hysmaelitarum de Opus': *ÁÚO*, vol. XI: p. 61, no. 40 (*RA*, no. 167), also mentioned as 'terre sarracenorum de villa Opus': *HO*, vol. VII: p. 3, no. 3 (*RA*, no. 222); *TF*, vol. I: p. 236 (Apos, county of Bodrog: *TF*, vol. I: p. 705); *TF*, vol. I: p. 217 (corrects *CD*, vol. IV, pt. I: p. 109) (1238); Szűcs, 'Két történelmi', p. 15. Györffy, *Pest-Buda*, pp. 112–15 speculates about the exact location of the Muslim settlement of Pest.

[101] Fügedi, 'A középkori Magyarország történeti demográfiája', p. 17; Attila Zsoldos, *Az Árpádok és alattvalóik* (Debrecen: Csokonai Kiadó, 1997), p. 221.

67

agenda determined his point of view?[102] In the case of authors who personally visited Hungary or drew their information from accounts by Hungarian Muslims, personal bias and misunderstandings could distort their testimony. Certain writers, repeating information culled from books, did not even have a clear knowledge of the geographical location of Hungary, let alone the details of Muslim life in the country. The Latin sources belong to the same genres and raise the same problems as those concerning the Jews. There is very little archaeological evidence; only one Muslim village has been excavated to date, and even the analysis of these finds has not been completed as yet.

CUMANS

The Cumans, called *Polovci* in Russian, *Valben* in German, *Comains* in French, and *Quibčāq* in Arabo-Persian sources (to cite but a few) emerged from Asia. Their origins and early history remain controversial. According to some scholars, there was continuity between the Cumans and the Qūn, a proto-Mongolian people. Others see the origin of the Cumans as being either from one of the tribes of the Oghuz union, the Türk Khaganate, or from other Turkic peoples. All these analyses are based on linguistic evidence and are inconclusive.[103] What is known is that various groupings coalesced into the Cuman (Quman)–Kipchak (Quipčaq) tribal union by the eleventh century. This included a variety of Turkic, Mongol and Iranian populations, combined over centuries of migrations initiated in northern China. Geographically distinct groupings made up the confederation whose territory at its peak extended from the Danube to the Irtys in western Siberia and Islamic central Asia.[104] This tribal confederation appeared in Rus' chronicles from the mid-eleventh century, and became the major power on the Eurasian steppe from then until the Mongol conquests in the early thirteenth century. The former

---

[102] Mary B. Campbell, *The Witness and the Other World: Exotic European Travel Writing 400–1600* (Ithaca and London: Cornell University Press, 1988), pp. 1–11.

[103] E.g. Joseph Marquart, 'Über das Volkstum der Komanen', chapter II of W. Bang and J. Marquart, *Osttürkische Dialektstudien*, Abhandlungen der Königlichen Gesellschaft der Wissenschaften zu Göttingen, Philologisch-Historische Klasse, n.s., 13, no. 1 (Berlin: Weidmannsche Buchhandlung, 1914), pp. 38–77; Gyula Németh, *Die Volksnamen quman und qūn*, Kőrösi Csoma Archivum 3 (1941–3); repr. Leiden: Brill, 1967), pp. 95–109; W. Barthold, 'Kipčak', in *The Encyclopaedia of Islam*, 5 vols. (Leiden: Brill and London: Luzac, 1913–38), vol. II: 1022–3; D. A. Rassovsky, 'Polovci I', *Seminarium Kondakovianum*, 7 (1935): pp. 245–62; Ligeti, *Magyar nyelv török kapcsolatai*, pp. 405–8. Overview: Golden, *Introduction*, pp. 270–7.

[104] D. A. Rassovsky, 'Polovci III', *Seminarium Kondakovianum* 9 (1937): pp. 71–85, and 10 (1938): pp. 155–77; Omeljan Pritsak, 'The Polovcians and Rus'', *AEMAe* 2 (1982): pp. 321–80, see pp. 342–68; Peter B. Golden, 'Cumanica IV: The Tribes of the Cuman-Qipčaqs', *AEMAe* 9 (1995–7): pp. 99–122.

Christians and non-Christians

population of the steppe, consisting of various nomadic tribes, accepted the rule of the Cuman–Kipchaks or escaped to neighbouring territories. The Cumans who migrated into Hungary when their power was superseded came from the western branch of this confederation.

The Cuman–Kipchaks (henceforth I shall refer to them as Cumans) played an important role in the history of the sedentary states of the region: first Khwarazm, Rus′, Byzantium and Georgia, then Bulgaria and Hungary. They conducted raids against their neighbours, and entered into various forms of alliances with them. Their settlement and assimilation took place in Georgia, Bulgaria and Hungary. From 1061 the Cumans engaged in skirmishes with the Rus′ians around the Dnieper. In the early twelfth century, Rus′ invasions weakened Cuman power, but with the decline of Rus′ unity, Cumans were drawn into the inheritance struggles and wars between the princes. Different subgroupings of the Cumans, each under their own leaders, established alliances with various Rus′ principalities from the middle of the twelfth century. From 1078 the Cumans fought on Byzantine territory as well. First conducting raids against the empire (chronicled in the works of Michael Attaleiates, Anna Comnena and the continuation of Skylitzes),[105] they wound up as the allies of Byzantium against the Pechenegs. On 29 April 1091 the Pechenegs were defeated, many killed, and the remnants scattered at the battle of Levunion. Cumans continued their alternately hostile and amicable relations with Byzantium and with the crusaders established on Byzantine lands. As a result of alliances, members of the Rus′ and crusader elite married daughters of Cuman chieftains. Cumans were called into Georgia in the early twelfth century, where they played a major part in the service of the ruler. They settled, converted to Orthodox Christianity, and were finally assimilated. The Cumans also participated in the second Bulgarian (Asenid) state, founded in 1187; the ruling dynasty itself may have been Cuman. When Cumans settled in the region between the Lower Dnieper and the Lower Danube and Carpathians is debated.[106] It is probable that from the late eleventh century Cumans started to raid Hungary as well. More sustained interaction between the Cumans and Hungary started only in the early thirteenth century.

[105] Byzantine sources on the Cumans: Gyula Moravcsik, *Byzantinoturcica*, 2 vols. (Berlin: Akademie Verlag, 1983), vol. I: pp. 91–4.
[106] László Makkai, *A Milkói (kún) püspökség és népei* (Debrecen: Pannonia Könyvnyomda, 1936), pp. 34–5; Petre Diaconu, *Les Coumans au Bas Danube aux XIe et XIIe siècles* (Bucharest: Editura Academiei Republicii Socialiste România, 1978); András Pálóczi Horváth, *Hagyományok, kapcsolatok és hatások a kunok régészeti kultúrájában* (Karcag: Karcag Város Önkormányzata, 1994), pp. 35–52; *TF*, vol. IV: pp. 114–16; András Pálóczi Horváth's model: 'Kunok a kelet-európai sztyeppén és Magyarországon', in *Az Alföld Társadalma*, ed. László Novák (Nagykőrös: Arany János Múzeum, 1998), pp. 109–46, pp. 122–3, 126; summary of recent Bulgarian works on the issue: Alexander Silayev, 'Frontier and Settlement: Cumans North of the Lower Danube in the First Half of the Thirteenth Century', MA thesis (Budapest: Central European University, 1998).

The Cumans established a nomadic society on the steppe, named Dešt-i-Qypčaq, the Kipchak plains, after them.[107] Their economy was based on tending animal herds and raiding. Captives, taken during the numerous raids against many countries, were sold into slavery. They had no central power and never formed a state. So far, no evidence has been uncovered to indicate that the Cumans had their own writing system. Their religion was animistic–shamanistic (see chapter 7). As a result of interaction with crusaders and travellers, by the thirteenth century there was a growing familiarity among Europeans with the Cumans and Cuman customs; this did not exclude portraying them as ferocious barbarians.[108] Soon, however, the steppe was subjugated by a new nomadic people, the Mongols.

Cuman power fell victim to this new, more organized and stronger tribal confederation. The Mongols fought many battles before extending their power to the entire steppe. After their first defeat, the Cumans sought a broad alliance involving the Rus' princes. Common danger and existing dynastic ties served as the basis of this alliance. The princes of Kiev, Chernigov, Galicia, Smolensk and Volynia joined the Cuman forces with their armies, but were defeated at the battle of Kalka in 1223. In 1239 the Cumans were defeated again, and this time the victorious Mongols pursued the conquest and pillage, devastating Kiev in 1240. Although some of the Cumans sought refuge in Hungary, most of them remained on the steppe, and integrated into the Mongol Empire of the Golden Horde. Because they outnumbered the Mongols, their language became dominant and they continued to observe many of their traditional customs while adapting some of those of the conquerors.[109] Cumans were also sold as slaves to many countries.[110] They achieved their greatest fame in Egypt, where the Cuman military slaves (*ghulams*) overthrew the ruling dynasty and founded a regime of their own: the Mamluks.

The Cumans arrived in Hungary prior to the Mongol invasion of the kingdom; the news of this event was even noted by Roger

---

[107] Peter B. Golden, 'The Quipčaqs of Medieval Eurasia: An Example of Stateless Adaptation in the Steppes', in *Rulers from the Steppe: State Formation on the Eurasian Periphery*, ed. Gary Seaman and Daniel Marks (Los Angeles: Ethnographics Press, 1991), pp. 132–57.

[108] Accounts: Geoffroy de Villehardouin, in *Un chevalier à la croisade. L'histoire de la conquête de Constantinople*, ed. Jean Longnon (Paris: Tallandier, 1981), pp. 135–68; Carpini, *Ystoria*, *passim*; William of Rubruck, 'Itinerarium Willelmi de Rubruc', in *Sinica Franciscana*, ed. Anastasius van den Wyngaert (Quarrachi: Collegio San Bonaventura, 1929), vol. I: pp. 164–339, *passim*. Jacques de Vitry wrote that they ate raw meat and drank the blood of horses: *Iacobi de Vitriaco libri duo quorum prior Orientalis sive Hierosolymitana, alter Occidentalis Historiae nomine inscribitur*, ed. Franciscus Moschus (Douai, 1597; facsimile repr. Westmead, Farnborough, 1971), p. 218.

[109] G. A. Fyodorov-Davidov, *Az Aranyhorda földjén*, Hungarian tr. of *Kurgani, idoli, moneti* (Moscow, 1968) (Budapest: Gondolat Kiadó, 1983).

[110] Charles Verlinden, 'Esclavage et ethnographie sur les bordes de la Mer Noir XIII–XIVe s.', in *Miscellanea Historica in Honorem Leonis van der Essen*, 2 vols. (Brussels and Paris, 1947), vol. I: pp. 287–98.

Bacon.[111] The local population came to see them as spies and the vanguard of the Mongols, and attacked the Cuman chieftain as King Béla IV of Hungary was preparing the defence against the Mongols. The Cuman chieftain Kötön and his family died and the Cumans left Hungary towards Bulgaria. They were soon invited back by King Béla and settled permanently in the kingdom. The size of the Cuman population in thirteenth-century Hungary has been the subject of several calculations, most based on a single figure in a medieval source. The canon Roger, who was present in Hungary at the time, stated in his narrative of the Mongol invasion that the Cumans entering the kingdom 'preter ipsorum familias circa quadraginta milia dicebantur'.[112] Because of the multiple meanings of the Latin word *familia*, this phrase was understood as indicating that the number of the Cumans was either 40,000, not including family members (women and children), or 40,000, not including servants. This figure, taken quite seriously, has been the basis of long debates as to whether 40,000 individuals or families moved into Hungary.[113] Medieval chroniclers are notorious for the imprecision of their figures; there is no reason to suppose the canon Roger to be a more reliable source of information than his contemporaries. The figure of 40,000 is suspicious for another reason: it is a topos used by many late antique authors when describing the 'barbarian' armies.[114] The same number was

---

[111] An anonymous Austrian author (Anonymous Leobiensis, probably a Dominican from Vienna or Krems, whose account covers the period until 1343) gave the date as Easter 1239: Hieronymus Pez, ed., in *Scriptores Rerum Austriacarum Veteres et Genuini*, 3 vols. (Leipzig, 1721–45), vol. I: cols. 750–972, see col. 815, repr. in Albinus Franciscus Gombos, *Catalogus Fontium Historiae Hungaricae*, 4 vols. (Budapest: Szent István Akadémia, 1937–43), vol. I: p. 270. Although Austrian annalists often used the same description of Cuman entry, they gave the date as 1241–2: 'Chronicon Austriacum', in Adrian Rauch, ed., *Rerum Austriacarum scriptores*, 3 vols. (Vienna, 1793–4), vol. II: pp. 213–300, partially repr. in Gombos, *Catalogus*, vol. I: pp. 504–18, see p. 506; Wilhelmus Wattenbach, ed., 'Annales Austriae, Continuatio Sancrucensis II', in *MGH SS*, vol. IX: p. 640; Juhász calculated autumn 1239: *SRH*, vol. II: p. 554. *The 'Opus Maius' of Roger Bacon*, ed. John Henry Bridges, 3 vols. (Oxford: Clarendon Press, 1897–1900), vol. I: p. 358.

[112] Rogerius, in *SRH*, vol. II: p. 554. A letter from Henry of Thuringia included in Matthew Paris gave the number 20,000: *Chronica Majora*, vol. VI: p. 77.

[113] *JK*, vol. II: p. 261: 40,000 families. Gyula Pauler, though he remarked that this figure was an exaggeration, did not try to correct it (*Magyar nemzet*, vol. II: p. 148, repeated in Székely, *Magyarország története*, vol. I, pt. 2: p. 1386). István Györffy, *Magyar nép, magyar föld* (Budapest: Turul, 1942), p. 28 accepted the figure uncritically, and counted six members per family, thus arriving at a total of 240,000. György Györffy, 'Magyarország népessége', p. 56, and 'Introduction', in Katona, *Tatárjárás*, p. 23 adopted the figure of 40,000 as indicative of the number of *individuals* moving into Hungary. Kovacsics, 'Történeti demográfia', p. 22: 40,000 individuals or families. Szűcs, *Utolsó Árpádok*, p. 18 without explanation took up this figure as the number of the Cumans who were recalled into Hungary after the Mongol invasion.

[114] 40,000 and 80,000: Walter Goffart, *Barbarians and Romans A.D. 418–584: The Techniques of Accommodation* (Princeton: Princeton University Press, 1980), pp. 231–4. I thank Mark Handley for drawing this analogy to my attention. See note 112 above for 20,000; this confirms that such statements were stereotypes and not reality.

used to describe the size of the Cuman population entering Georgia.[115] András Pálóczi Horváth has tried to provide a critical analysis of the number of Cumans in Hungary.[116] Discounting the information provided by Roger, he estimated the size of the Cuman population from the extent of their lands within the kingdom. On the basis of charters mentioning Cuman settlements, he calculated the territory inhabited by the Cumans at the beginning of the fourteenth century to have been 8,500 km^2. Drawing on medieval analogies, Pálóczi calculated a population density of 6–7 people/km^2. He arrived at a total Cuman population of 50–60,000 (or 10–12,000 families with five members per family). Estimating a 30 per cent population loss as a result of late thirteenth-century Cuman revolts and emigration, he advanced the figure of 70–80,000 as the number of Cumans who originally moved into Hungary. Although Pálóczi's method is more plausible than most, even this calculation rests on too many unsubstantiated and indeed unprovable suppositions (such as the 30 per cent population loss and the 6–7 people/km^2 population density) to provide an accurate estimate. All we can know is that the Cumans were certainly the largest of the three groups, and constituted perhaps up to 7–8 per cent of the population of Hungary in the second half of the thirteenth century. Their settlement was ultimately mostly concentrated in areas (the contours of which changed over time) in the central part of the kingdom, which to this day are known as 'Greater and Lesser Cumania' (Nagykunság and Kiskunság: see map 2).

The sources relating to the Cumans in Hungary are exclusively in Latin, written by Christians; there are no sources written (or dictated) by the Cumans themselves. Texts based on information supplied by Cumans do exist: the *Codex Cumanicus* written by missionaries and merchants in the Crimea and the Arabo-Kipchak glossaries.[117] They come from the period after the Mongol conquest, and no such sources exist concerning Hungary's Cuman population. The material which reflects the situation on the Cuman steppe is of limited value to the historian working on the Cumans in Hungary, who lived under very different circumstances. Christian sources include charters, letters, laws, chronicles and other nar-

---

[115] Golden, 'Cumanica I', p. 62.
[116] Pálóczi Horváth, *Besenyők*, pp. 52–3; András Pálóczi Horváth, 'A kunok megtelepedése Magyarországon', *Archaeologiai Értesítő* 101 (1974): pp. 244–59, see pp. 255–6.
[117] *Codex Cumanicus Cod. Marc. Lat. DXLIX.*, ed. Kaare Grønbech, facsimile edn (Copenhagen: Levin and Munksgaard, 1936). György Györffy, 'A Codex Cumanicus keletkezésének kérdéséhez', in *Magyarság*, pp. 220–41 and 'Kipcsaki'; Lajos Ligeti, *A Codex Cumanicus mai kérdései*, Keleti Értekezések, no. 1 (Budapest: Kőrösi Csoma Társaság, 1985); Peter B. Golden, 'The "Codex Cumanicus"', in *Central Asian Monuments*, ed. Hasan B. Paksoy (Istanbul: Isis Press, 1992), pp. 33–63.

rative sources, all in Latin, as well as representations in art. Their bias must be carefully appraised. The problems the historian faces are similar to those of other 'mute' groups in history, such as medieval peasants. The sources are more reliable witnesses to Christian sentiments towards the Cumans, but have to be scrutinized carefully when Cuman sentiments and actions are depicted. This lack of written material is to some extent counterbalanced by a large body of archaeological evidence, though this, of course, also raises problems of interpretation. Excavations still in progress have already uncovered many Cuman settlements and burials. Cuman graves in Hungary could be securely identified because the Hungarians themselves stopped practising horse burials in the eleventh century; this type of burial re-emerges in Hungary only with the settlement of the Cumans.[118] The types of objects in both solitary graves and mass cemeteries also differ from Hungarian grave finds. Finally, in many cases written evidence proves the burials were in Cuman areas. Written sources are also useful in the identification of Cuman settlements.

Non-Christians in Hungary constituted a minority in relation to the Christian population, the Cumans being the most numerous of the three groups. The following chapters analyse their treatment, position and fate in medieval Hungary.

[118] Pálóczi Horváth, *Hagyományok*, pp. 99–100.

Chapter 3

THE LEGAL POSITION OF HUNGARY'S NON-CHRISTIAN POPULATION

Laws are one of the major sources on the position of non-Christian groups in Hungary. Medieval definitions of a group's legal status are important indicators, although not necessarily a mirror, of that group's place in society. The first part of this chapter, therefore, analyses the laws and privileges defining the legal position of the non-Christian groups in Hungary. The second part of the chapter considers the degree to which non-Christian communities possessed internal autonomy. Finally, the third part is a comparison of the legal position of non-Christians and Christians. This then enables me to address questions concerning the legal foundation of non-Christian status in medieval Hungary. To what extent was the non-Christian population legally separated from the Christians? Did non-Christians have a different legal status from the other inhabitants of the country, and if so, of what did these differences consist?

THE LEGAL STATUS OF JEWS

Jews were consistently designated as *Judei* in Hungarian sources, as elsewhere in medieval Europe. The designation also signalled a legal category. It entailed certain privileges and certain restrictions, the content of which depended on the king of Hungary, who was at times pressured by nobles and ecclesiastics to increase restrictions. Two assertions concerning the Jews of Hungary have often been repeated: that Jews were serfs of the royal chamber according to the German model, and that prominent members of this group were nobles, elevated to that status by the king. As discussed in detail below, neither are accurate evaluations of Jewish status in medieval Hungary.

The main sources for that status are the laws promulgated by Hungarian kings, or synods where the king presided, concerning the kingdom's Jewish population. (Details of laws regulating trade, office-holding, and other aspects of Jewish participation in the kingdom are discussed in sub-

The legal position of Hungary's non-Christian population

sequent chapters.) The earliest such laws were either restrictive or aimed at regulating Christian–Jewish interaction. They endeavoured to prohibit or circumscribe certain behaviour or activities on the part of the Jews. Their aim was to avoid a clash of interests between Jews and Christians by preventing the former from engaging in activities deemed offensive. In the words of one such piece of legislation these measures were necessary 'in order not to bring scandal to Christianity'.[1] Thus László I and Kálmán prohibited Jews from trading in or holding Christian slaves, László decreed a heavy punishment for Jews who worked on Christian holy days, and Kálmán attempted to restrict Jewish settlement to episcopal centres.[2] The other aim of these decrees was to regulate Jewish–Christian dealings; Kálmán scrupulously set out the procedure to be followed in the case of sales or credit transactions between the two groups.[3] The clerical education of King Kálmán probably played a role in his obsessive interest in regulating every aspect of Jewish–Christian interaction; he was the only king from the Árpád dynasty to issue separate statutes concerning the Jews (*Capitula de Iudeis*).[4] The defence of the purity of Christians by interdictions against mingling with Jews plays a very minor role in medieval Hungarian legislation. Although the prohibition of Jewish–Christian intermarriage (explicitly forbidden only between Christian women and Jewish men) and the buying of non-*kasher* meat from Jews appears in synodal decisions during the reigns of László and Kálmán,[5] these stipulations were of slight importance in comparison with the regulations concerning Jews found in canon law during this period.

Canon law aimed at segregating Jews and Christians. Not only were intermarriage and concubinage between the two groups rigorously forbidden, but Christians were also not allowed to eat, drink, bathe or

---

[1] 'ne scandalizetur christianitas', the Synod of Szabolcs (1092), Bak, *Laws*, p. 59.
[2] *Ibid.*, pp. 31, 57, 59, 66, 68. Restricting Jewish settlement to episcopal sees did not come into effect; Jews settled in other towns as well. On dating and texts of early councils: Lothar Waldmüller, *Die Synoden in Dalmatien, Kroatien und Ungarn von der Völkwanderung bis zum Ende der Arpaden*, Konziliengeschichte 21 (Paderborn and Munich: F. Schöningh, 1987); Monika Jánosi, *Törvényalkotás a korai Árpád-korban*, Szegedi Középkortörténeti Könyvtár 9 (Szeged: Agapé, 1996); Monika Jánosi, 'A Szent László-kori zsinatok határozatainak keletkezéstörténete', *AUSz Acta Historica* 96 (1992): pp. 3–10; Monika Jánosi, 'Az első ún. esztergomi zsinati határozatok keletkezésének problémái', *AUSz Acta Historica* 83 (1986): pp. 23–9.
[3] Bak, *Laws*, p. 68.
[4] Salo W. Baron, *A Social and Religious History of the Jews*, 18 vols., 2nd edn (New York: Columbia University Press, 1967), vol. III: p. 212, and Bernát L. Kumorovitz, 'Szent László vásár-törvénye és Kálmán király pecsétes cartulája', in *Athleta Patriae: Tanulmányok Szent László történetéhez*, ed. László Mezey (Budapest: Szent István Társulat, 1980), pp. 85–109, see p. 89, have suggested that a large influx of Jews from the west necessitated legislation. There are no sources to prove this, except one mention by Cosmas, 'Chronicon', in *Fontes Rerum Bohemicarum*, vol. II: p. 140.
[5] 'De coniugio iudeorum et christianorum mulierum': Bak, *Laws*, p. 57. 'Nullus Christianus carnes ab eis spretas emere presumat': *ibid.*, p. 66. Meat 'despised by them [Jews]' is meat that does not satisfy the requirements of *kashrut*.

live with Jews, nor to accept medicine from them.[6] Pope Alexander III's decretal prohibited Jews from mingling with Christians on Good Friday; even their doors and windows were to be closed.[7] The very presence of the Jews, who were considered to be responsible for the death of Jesus and to have stubbornly resisted his teachings ever since, was not to be tolerated on that day. (The measure might also have served to protect the Jews, pre-empting any Christian hostility which was especially likely to erupt during the commemoration of Christ's death.) Jews were also prohibited from employing Christian nurses; it was feared that Jews would desecrate the host by pouring the nurse's milk into the latrine for three days after she had taken communion.[8]

This multitude of regulations had no impact in Hungary. The possibility remains that some of these stipulations were repeated in Hungarian synods whose decisions are now lost. None the less, surviving synodal and other legislation does not include any other mention of the necessity to defend Christian purity from pollution by Jews.

In the thirteenth century, Hungarian legislation concerning Jewish legal status was preoccupied with two issues: whether Jews could hold public offices and the regulation of everyday contacts and transactions between Jews and Christians. The former consisted of prohibitions following canonical stipulations by councils and popes, or modifications of these prohibitions, for which papal permission was sought.[9] The latter was inspired by a combination of economic and social realities, ecclesiastical pressure and Jewish desire for protection. The most important source for the legal status of Hungary's Jews is King Béla IV's privileges (1251) which set forth judicial procedures concerning the Jews.[10]

Béla used as his model the charter of privileges to Jews issued by Duke Frederick of Austria (1244).[11] Béla followed his model closely and has

---

[6] Examples of strict early legislation: José Vives, ed., *Concilios visigóticos e hispano-romanos* (Barcelona and Madrid: Instituto Enrique Flórez, 1963), pp. 27–30; Gratian, C. 28 q. 1 (esp. c. 10, c. 13, c. 14). On measures of separation in canon law in Gratian and later: Dahan, *Intellectuels*, pp. 160–79.

[7] Incorporated into Gregory IX's *Decretals*: X 5.6.4. Such curfews had been imposed earlier by local church councils, and repeated by popes after Alexander III: Simonsohn, *Apostolic See History*, pp. 130–2.   [8] X 5.6.13.

[9] Baron, *Social*, vol. IV: p. 9 on the beginning of canonical prohibitions; see chapter 5 for a discussion of Hungarian attempts at modifying these prohibitions.

[10] No surviving manuscripts prior to the fifteenth century are known. Originals of these MSS in Bratislava (first two) and Košic (third); photos in Budapest, Magyar Országos Levéltár (Hungarian National Archives, henceforth MOL) DF 239444 (1422); DF 240766 (1494); DF 270046 (1494; corrupt variant). Edition based on the two manuscripts in Bratislava: Alexander Büchler, 'Das Judenprivilegium Bélas IV. Vom Jahre 1251', in *Jubilee Volume in Honour of Prof. Bernhard Heller on the Occasion of his Seventieth Birthday*, ed. Alexander Scheiber (Budapest, 1941), pp. 139–46. Less reliable edition: *MZsO*, vol. I: pp. 27–30. *RA*, no. 962.

[11] Duke Frederick's privileges (1244) are edited in Johann Egid Scherer, *Die Rechtsverhältnisse der Juden in den deutsch-österreichischen Ländern*, Beiträge zur Geschichte des Judenrechtes im

The legal position of Hungary's non-Christian population

been accused of copying it slavishly without regard to local conditions.[12] Although King Béla did not show the same innovative spirit as, for example, Bolesław of Kalisz in the redrafting of the privileges, a detailed analysis shows that he did introduce certain modifications. It is a separate question, however, whether the emphasis expressed in these privileges reflected the role of the Jews in Hungarian economy and society. I believe the answer is no. The Jewish elite at the time of King Béla, who filled high positions and had contact with the king, came from and retained direct ties to Austria. The promulgation of the privileges was most probably prompted by their request. Their concerns are reflected in the text, and not those of all the Jews in the country.

Later transcriptions of the privileges recount the story of the manuscript tradition. In every known instance of the transmission of the privileges, copies were made at the request of Jews. The earliest surviving manuscript dates from 1422. This is not a simple copy, but a *transsumptum*: a verbatim transcription of an earlier charter inserted into the authentic royal charter of 1422. Thus the entire text of Béla's privileges as well as the story of repeated transcriptions were incorporated into the fifteenth-century document. After the original promulgation of the privileges, a copy was made in 1256 at the demand of the Jews living in Fehérvár (*Judei Albenses*). The privileges were then copied into the Register of the chapter of Fehérvár, which was one of the *loca credibilia*, an ecclesiastical body that had the right to issue charters at the demand of lay people or by royal order, and to record authenticated copies in its registers.[13] In 1396, at the initiative of a certain Solomon, a Jew from that city, King Sigismond ordered the chapter to search its archives for the letter of privileges. The copy in the Registers was then found and transcribed. In 1407 this was again copied at the request of two Jews (Saul from Buda and another Saul from Pest), and in 1422 King Sigismond had

---

Mittelalter 1 (Leipzig: Duncker und Humblot, 1901), pp. 179–84. These privileges were also adopted by Otakar II in Bohemia (1254) and Duke Bolesław the Pious in Great Poland (1264). On Frederick's policies: Klaus Lohrmann, *Judenrecht und Judenpolitik im mittelalterlichen Österreich*, Handbuch zur Geschichte der Juden in Österreich, 1 (Vienna and Cologne: Böhlau Verlag, 1990), pp. 53–84, *ibid.*, pp. 85–102 on Otakar II. On the Polish charter: Isaac Lewin, 'The Historical Background of the Statute of Kalisz', in *Studies in Polish Civilization*, ed. Damian S. Wandycz (New York: Institute on East Central Europe, Columbia University and The Polish Institute of Arts and Sciences in America, n.d. [1971?]), pp. 38–53.

[12] 'Béla IV copied the charter almost verbatim': Baron, *Social*, vol. x: p. 23; similarly Kubinyi, 'Zsidóság', pp. 20–1. Detailed comparisons between the two: Kohn, *Zsidók*, pp. 101–13 (maintains that they were adapted to suit the Hungarian circumstances); Ágost Helmár, *A magyar zsidótörvények az Árpádkorszakban*, Különlenyomat a pozsonyi kir. kath. főgymnasium 1878/9. évi értesítőjéből (Pozsony, 1879), pp. 13–24.

[13] On this institution: 'hiteleshely', in *KMTL*, with bibliography. Detailed study of one such institution: László Koszta, *A pécsi székeskáptalan hiteleshelyi tevékenysége (1214–1353)* (Pécs: Pécs Története Alapítvány, 1998).

this copied at the request of Joseph, a Jew from Buda.[14] Although we do not know how one of the Jewish residents in 1396 could know of the existence of the copy in the chapter's possession, whether it was via oral tradition, or through a tip from one of the canons, the authenticity of the document (and thus the text of Béla's privileges which we now possess) is ensured by a number of considerations. The method of *transsumptio* to ensure the continued validity of a charter was widespread in medieval Hungary, and the format of the charter as it exists today is in keeping with this tradition.[15] The practices of the *loca credibilia* are well known, and this instance fits into normal procedures. Finally, as Béla IV was one among several central European rulers who decided to adopt Duke Frederick's privileges, it is certain that the privileges had an important impact on the region in the mid- and late thirteenth century, and the story of the manuscript tradition was not the result of a fifteenth-century invention.[16]

Among the articles defining the status of Jews in the kingdom, certain provisions were purely protective, designed to deter Christians from harming Jews. It was decreed that if a Christian hurt a Jew, but without drawing blood, he had to pay damages to the king 'according to the custom of the kingdom' ('secundum consuetudinem regni'), as well as four silver marks to the Jew himself. If the perpetrator had no money, the king decided what his punishment was to be. Similarly, if a Christian wounded a Jew, he had to pay both the king and the Jew, this time giving twelve marks, as well as the sum necessary to cover doctor's fees, to the latter. If a Christian killed a Jew, he was to be punished (the form of punishment remained unspecified) in addition to losing all his possessions to the king. If a Jewish woman were raped by a Christian man, he was to be punished 'by a punishment equivalent to the cutting off of a hand' ('pena condigna, que quodammodo truncacioni manus correspondeat'). Jewish children came under special protection: their kidnappers were to be punished as thieves. This provision was presumably aimed at preventing the kidnapping and forced conversion of children; such a measure was often incorporated into both charters by secular rulers and papal bulls.[17] Royal protection extended to places as well as to people; those disturbing synagogues were to pay a fine. Jews were protected in court; no Jew

---

[14] MOL DF 239444; DF 240766; Büchler, 'Judenprivilegium', pp. 140–1, 145–6. (The manuscript codes remain the same for any quotations from Béla's charter; I shall not repeat them, but only give the page numbers of the edition.)

[15] Imre Szentpétery, *Magyar Oklevéltan* (Budapest: Magyar Történelmi Társulat, 1930, repr. Budapest: Hatágú Síp Alapítvány, 1995), pp. 7–8, 79–80, 245–6.

[16] A letter of privileges was forged for the Jews during the reign of Sigismond, but the forgery was discovered and the forger sent to the stake. Kubinyi, 'Magyarországi zsidóság', p. 15.

[17] Simonsohn, *Apostolic See History*, pp. 253–4.

was to be convicted if there were only Christian witnesses with the exception of cases when there could be no question about the truth of the charges.[18] Thus one of the characteristics of Jewish legal status was protection from Christians. Although the Jews were under royal protection, they were also in some sense treated as royal possessions. If a Jew was wounded or killed, the king was to receive compensation.

A series of stipulations provided protection for Jewish religious observance. Not only were synagogues protected (which was usual in papal bulls of protection as well[19]), but Jews were also exempt from swearing upon the Torah for insignificant matters, unless the king decided otherwise; they could not be forced to return pawned goods on their holy days; and they could transport their dead without having to pay customs.[20] This would be the first glimpse in the Hungarian sources of religious tolerance, indicating understanding and respect of those professing and practising another religion. It seems certain, however, that the origin of these stipulations lay on the Jewish and not the Christian side. Other articles covered Jewish economic activities (see chapter 4).

Finally, this text partially illuminates the position of the Jews within the general system of Hungarian jurisdiction. They had recourse to three means of proof: Jewish witnesses, an oath on the Torah, and the judicial duel. This last means of proof was mentioned for one type of case only in the privileges: if a Jew was killed in secret, but someone was suspected of having killed him, the case was to be solved by duel. It seems this was not the only type of case in which Jews (at least if they acted as part of a group that included Christians) had access to this means of proof. A late thirteenth-century charter describes a lawsuit in which Jews cooperated with Christians in negotiating a monetary settlement instead of the judicial duel.[21] These proofs combine contemporary practices in judging Christians with the form of proof that was applied to medieval Jews with increasing exclusivity elsewhere – the oath on holy scripture.

The Hungarian Jewish oath, moreover, remained devoid of degrading aspects for much longer (until the sixteenth century) than many of its counterparts. Jewish oath formulae existed already in the Visigothic period in Spain and the Carolingian Empire in Germanic lands, but became especially common from the late twelfth century. The belief in the effectiveness of oaths was impaired by suspicion of the Jews. How could Jews, routinely described as perfidious by Christian sources, be

---

[18] Büchler, 'Judenprivilegium', pp. 141–4. This was much more unusual than protective measures: although Pope Gregory X added a clause to the *Sicut Judeis* bull in 1272 that required the presence of Jewish witnesses as well in order to convict a Jew, this was deleted from later issues of the bull: Simonsohn, *Apostolic See History*, p. 119, and *Apostolic See Documents*, no. 234.

[19] Simonsohn, *Apostolic See History*, p. 122.   [20] *Ibid.*, pp. 143–4.

[21] Büchler, 'Judenprivilegium', p. 143. Charter: *MZsO*, vol. v, pt. 1: pp. 12–13, no. 11.

trusted if the validity of their oath depended solely on Jewish faith? In order to ensure that the oath was binding on Jews as well as acceptable to Christians, the text and rituals of oath-taking were elaborated.²² This could lead to the introduction of humiliating aspects as well: the Jewry oath in the second group of the Schwabenspiegel manuscripts, from the last two decades of the thirteenth century, included such measures; for example, the Jew was to stand on the skin of a sow.²³

It is in itself important that Jews were not barred from other means of proof (witnesses and duels) in Hungary. The thirteenth-century Jewry oath was probably just as simple and devoid of degrading aspects as surviving later versions from Hungary; it remained, together with the other two methods mentioned in King Béla's privileges, a true means of proof.²⁴ It was perhaps not a very well-known means in thirteenth-century Hungary, as King Béla expanded Duke Frederick's text in his privileges in order to explain *rodale* as 'the books of Moses'.²⁵ The sixteenth-century Hungarian Jewry oath which included humiliating aspects was influenced by German formulae.²⁶

In comparison with their model, Duke Frederick's charter, King Béla's privileges show two main tendencies. First, in some cases, Béla mitigated the punishment decreed for Christians who hurt Jews. This was true in terms of the monetary fine to be paid; these modifications may be purely a reflection of Hungary's weaker economy as compared to Austrian territories. For example, when Frederick would have the perpetrator pay in gold marks, Béla consistently substituted silver marks. It was also true in terms of the severity of the punishment prescribed. Thus while Frederick's

---

[22] Evelyne Patlagean, 'Contribution juridique à l'histoire des Juifs dans la Méditérranée médiévale: les formules grecques de serment', in Patlagean, *Structure sociale, famille, chrétienté à Byzance IVe–XIe siècle* (London: Variorum, 1981), no. XIV, pp. 137–56; Baron, *Social*, vol. IX: pp. 41–3, 259–60, vol. XI: pp. 106–10; Guido Kisch, *The Jews in Medieval Germany: A Study of their Legal and Social Status* (Chicago: University of Chicago Press, 1949), pp. 275–87; Ernő Winkler, *Adalékok a zsidó eskü középkori történetéhez* (Budapest: Pallas Nyomda, 1917); Walter Pakter, 'Did the Canonists Prescribe a Jewry-Oath?' *Bulletin of Medieval Canon Law* 6 (1976): pp. 81–7; Joseph Ziegler, 'Reflections on the Jewry Oath in the Middle Ages', in *Christianity and Judaism*, ed. Diana Wood, Studies in Church History 29 (Oxford: Blackwell, 1992), pp. 209–20.

[23] Kisch, *Jews*, pp. 278–9.

[24] Fourteenth-century Jewry oath in Pozsony: János Király, *Pozsony város joga a középkorban* (Budapest: MTA, 1894), pp. 342, 371. The fifteenth-century oath was still simple and not aimed at humiliation: Alexander [Sándor] Scheiber, 'Recent Additions to the Medieval History of Hungarian Jewry', *Historia Judaica* 14 (1952): pp. 145–58, see p. 154. Ernő Winkler, 'A zsidó eskü Magyarországon', *Magyar Zsidó Szemle* 44 (1927): pp. 29–47.

[25] 'super libris Moysi qui rodale appellatur' (supra librum in 1494) instead of 'super rodali' of the Austrian privileges: Büchler, 'Judenprivilegium', p. 143; Scherer, *Rechtsverhältnisse*, p. 182.

[26] In the *Tripartitum* of Werbőczy (1514, published in 1517), probably influenced by German law, in use by burghers of German origin in some Hungarian cities. Edition: *Werbőczy István Hármaskönyve* (Budapest: Franklin Társulat, 1897, repr. Pécs: Szikra Nyomda, 1989) pars III. tit. 36, p. 420.

law punished both the hitting of a Jew and the rape of a Jewish woman by mutilating the wrongdoer (his hand was to be cut off), Béla imposed an appropriate punishment, to be decided upon by the king: a 'punishment equivalent to the cutting off of a hand'. Second, in the case of the use of Christian witnesses, Béla's modification went in the direction of greater flexibility. While Frederick absolutely prohibited the use of Christian witnesses against Jewish defendants if the Christians were not backed by Jewish witnesses as well, Béla did allow such procedure if the facts were proven without a doubt. If a Jew was murdered and the perpetrator unknown, Frederick decreed that if there was a suspect, the case was to be decided by judicial duel. Béla added that fair and acceptable suspicion was the prerequisite for the case to pass to judicial duel. Moreover, while according to Frederick it was the ruler's task to produce the champion for the Jews, Béla omitted this phrase. Finally, Béla added a passage granting Jews the right to be judged according to these privileges even by the judge of the city where they lived, that is, not according to previous customs or town law. The judge who disobeyed this stipulation was to be removed from his position. Jews usually lived in cities in thirteenth-century Hungary; this additional clause in fact guaranteed the validity of the privileges for Jews living in the kingdom. Altogether, the modifications in Béla's privileges have been described as the reflection of the king's 'realistic approach', or as a proof that he was a just king.[27] These modifications meant that Jews were treated not as a specially privileged group, but as a group with its own privileges, one of many other groups in the kingdom.

The few references to the legal status of Jews surviving in other texts from the thirteenth century reflect such parallels between the treatment of Jews and other groups. Teka, having failed to prove his title to an estate by the necessary documents, lost the land. This was consistent with the policy of reclaiming royal donations, a policy that Hungarian kings equally used to benefit Jews.[28] In 1291, King András III granted certain privileges (exemptions from taxes and customs, the right to be judged by a twelve-member court and an elected judge from the city) to the city of Pozsony. Two groups are mentioned in the charter who are granted the 'same liberty as the burghers themselves': the Jews, though the rights of the archbishop of Esztergom and the local provost are upheld, and the fishermen.[29] In a case of litigation, the citizens and Jews of Körmend act

---

[27] Kohn, *Zsidók*, p. 111; Péter Újvári, ed., *Magyar Zsidó Lexikon* (Budapest: Pallas Nyomda, 1929), p. 104.

[28] *MZsO*, vol. I: pp. 8–10, no. 11 (*CD*, vol. III, pt. 2: p. 141; *RA*, no. 443); pp. 22–3, no. 21 (MOL DL 256; *CD*, vol. IV, pt. 1: pp. 272–4; *RA*, no. 731) for a case when an estate was taken away from a Christian lord to be given to Teka.

[29] MOL DF 238636 (original), DF 238715 (fourteenth-century copy) (*MZsO*, vol. I: pp. 55–8, no. 32; *RA*, no. 3837). 'Item iudei in ipsa ciuitate constituti habeant eandem libertatem, quam et ipsi

together.[30] Thus Jews were not considered to be citizens of towns, because in that case it would have been superfluous to include them explicitly, but they were not thereby disqualified from having the same rights as citizens.[31]

The king's grant of privileges raises the question of royal ennoblement of Jews. Lessees of revenues of the royal chamber (of the treasury, mint, etc.) were called *comites camere*. *Comes* (Hungarian *ispán*) has persistently been translated as 'count', and thus as a title a nobleman would hold. Indeed, both Hungarian and foreign scholars have claimed that Jewish *comites camere* were nobles,[32] though some scholars have speculated as to whether this nobility was revocable by the king, or perhaps granted for the duration of the office only.[33] I disagree with such an interpretation of the *comes camere* title; the *comes* in this case does not mean a noble, but simply an office, better understood if the meanings of *ispán* are explored.[34] The *ispán* was a layman who held power; the title was especially used for officials of the king appointed to oversee counties, castles or the treasury. Those appointed as heads of counties were normally recruited from the ranks of the nobility, but their noble status pre-dated their appointment, and was not contingent on it. The title *ispán/comes* itself referred only to the holder of such a position, and did not necessarily entail nobility. Therefore Jewish *comites camere*, similar to Christian burghers who held these positions, were *ispán*s, leasing royal offices, but they were not nobles; no revocable nobility existed in medieval Hungary. The king conferred a function, not noble rank, on them.

footnote 29 (*cont.*)
   ciues, salue [for saluo] iure archiepiscopi Strigoniensis et prepositi Posoniensis remanente.' It is unclear what these rights were; they may have been powers to judge and/or tax the Jews of the city, that were delegated by the king. There are several cases from medieval Europe where ecclesiastics obtained jurisdiction over Jews from the king: Simonsohn, *Apostolic See History*, p. 105. Charles I in 1324 granted royal protection to all freemen, both Jews and Christians, who wanted to settle in Sopron: *MZsO*, vol. I: p. 62, no. 35.

[30] 'cives ac Judei': *MZsO*, vol. v, pt. I: p. 12, no. 11.
[31] There are cases from medieval Europe when Jews were designated as citizens: Simonsohn, *Apostolic See History*, p. 95.
[32] For example, Kohn, *Zsidók, passim*; Pollák, *Zsidók története Sopronban*, p. 9; Daniel M. Friedenberg, *Medieval Jewish Seals from Europe* (Detroit: Wayne State University Press, 1987), pp. 316–25; Baron, *Social*, vol. X: pp. 20–1. Article 24 of the Golden Bull of 1222 has been interpreted as either prohibiting the ennoblement of Jews and Muslims, or restricting certain offices to nobles: 'Comites camere monetarii salinarii et tributarii nobiles regni, Ismaelite et Iudei fieri non possint.' Bak, *Laws*, p. 36 and note 32 on p. 101. Géza Érszegi, *Az Aranybulla* (Budapest: Helikon, 1990), pp. 32–3. The rewritten version in 1231 omits any mention of nobles, nor do other texts express concern over the ennoblement of non-Christians: Bak, *Laws*, p. 40, article 18.
[33] Friedenberg, *Medieval Jewish Seals*, p. 324 advances the hypothesis that 'these ranks of nobility were given and revoked at will by the king'.
[34] Székely, *Magyarország története*, vol. I, pt. 2: pp. 1175–6; Antonius Bartal, *Glossarium Mediae et Infimae Latinitatis Regni Hungariae* (Leipzig: Teubner and Budapest: Franklin Nyomda, 1901), p. 143; Steven Béla Várdy, *Historical Dictionary of Hungary* (Lanham, Md. and London: Scarecrow Press, 1997), p. 203.

The legal position of Hungary's non-Christian population

What, then, was the legal position of Jews in thirteenth-century Hungary? Can it be described as 'Jewish serfdom'? The term itself is not used in the Hungarian documents. It is true that the king claimed compensation if Jews were harmed; it is also true that he was their protector and highest judge. These are the arguments used by scholars to assert that the royal servitude of Jews, developed in German areas, is an adequate description of the situation of Jews in Hungary as well. Thus Béla's privileges have been seen as the adoption of the German principle according to which Jews were serfs of the imperial chamber, possessions of the crown.[35]

'Jewish serfdom' itself is a controversial issue.[36] It has been argued that it is not an adequate description of Jewish status everywhere in the Middle Ages, and blurs together theology, legal fiction, simile and legal definitions. In the case of German territories, where explicit use of the terminology existed, it is possible to dispute whether 'Jewish serfdom' was a legal fiction or not, whether it was a tool in the struggle between imperial and papal authority or a definition of Jewish status, and whether it made Jewish status unique or was designed to protect Jews. In contrast to usage in German territories, however, the only times when the royal chamber is mentioned in the sources in Hungary is in connection to *comites camere*, who were individuals bearing a title, not *servi camere*. Charters concerning Jews never talk of royal servitude. The fact that the king taxed, protected or judged the Jews is not an indication of chamber serfdom. He taxed, protected and judged many other groups as well. The assurance that he would not lodge at the houses of Jews, that Béla incorporated into his privileges for them, did not mean that he considered them royal property. In fact, the king assured other groups, notably the high-ranking *servientes regis*, who aspired to be included in the ranks of

---

[35] Kohn, *Zsidók*, pp. 114–15; Újvári, *Magyar Zsidó*, p. 104; Kubinyi, 'Zsidóság', p. 21; Lajos Venetianer, *A magyar zsidóság története a honfoglalástól a világháború kitöréséig, különös tekintettel gazdasági és művelődési fejlődésére* (Budapest, 1922; repr. Budapest: Könyvértékesítő Vállalat, 1986), p. 25; Szidónia Balog, *A magyarországi zsidók kamaraszolgasága és igazságszolgáltatása a középkorban*, Művelődéstörténeti Értekezések 28 (Budapest: Vasutas Szövetség, 1907), pp. 12–22, argues that royal serfdom was not 'fully' established in Hungary before the fourteenth century.

[36] Baron, '"Plenitude of Apostolic Powers"', argues that the main purpose was not to lower Jewish status, but to protect the Jews and establish imperial (over papal) authority over them. On German *Kammerknechtschaft*: Kisch, *Jews*, pp. 145–53, who argues that it brought a deterioration in Jewish status. Gavin I. Langmuir criticizes the validity of the concept and argues that 'Jewish serfdom' did not exist: '"Tanquam Servi": The Change in Jewish Status in French Law about 1200', chapter VII of *Toward a Definition*, pp. 167–94. J. A. Watt, 'The Jews, the Law, and the Church: The Concept of Jewish Serfdom in Thirteenth-Century England', in *The Church and Sovereignty c. 590–1918: Essays in Honour of Michael Wilks*, Studies in Church History Subsidia 9 (Oxford: Ecclesiastical History Society, 1991), pp. 153–72, asserted that *servicium* was not just an analogy, but a legal definition of the relationship of Jews to the king in England. Simonsohn, *Apostolic See History*, pp. 95–108.

the nobility, of the same privilege.[37] King Béla never claimed that the Jews belonged to his treasury as serfs, and there were numerous other groups under his protection. With Frederick's privileges, Béla adopted the system of payments to the treasury for harm done to Jews. This did not constitute royal servitude. Nor was Béla vying with the papacy or nobles for control over or income from Jews, a reason that could lead to the introduction of the terminology of royal servitude.[38] The Hungarian case resembled that of England in this respect: royal control over the kingdom's small Jewish population was not a contentious issue (although their office-holding was).[39] Jews enjoyed royal protection, but this remained within the framework of existing legal structures which were valid for other groups as well. As the last section of this chapter demonstrates, the king or his delegate was judge to many privileged groups in the kingdom.

Is Jewish status better described by the assertion that the position of the Jews of Hungary was 'almost unique in Europe at the time from a legal point of view'?[40] In Hungary, Jews were far from being the only group to have their own legal status linked to a group designation: *Latini*, *Saxones*, *servientes regis* and many others equally appear in the sources. The true context for the understanding of the Jewish legal position in Hungary is the Hungarian legal system, especially as it pertained to 'guests' (*hospites*), groups of immigrants who entered the kingdom or internal migrant settlers. After the analysis of each non-Christian group's legal status in the country, I shall return to this question of the uniqueness of Jewish legal status in the broader context of the legal status of immigrants in Hungary.

THE LEGAL POSITION OF MUSLIMS

In the thirteenth century, Muslims often appear together with the Jews in royal and ecclesiastical documents, with one major exception: King Béla IV's privileges concern only Jews, and no charter of privileges was ever promulgated (or has survived) for Muslims. Early laws on Muslims, however, differ significantly from those on Jews. Whereas very few prohibitions and coercive measures were enacted against Jews, especially as related to missionary efforts, eleventh- and early twelfth-century laws and

[37] Facsimile: Érszegi, *Aranybulla*. Bak, *Laws*, p. 34.
[38] Cf. Baron, '"Plenitude of Apostolic Powers"'; Agus, *Rabbi Meir of Rothenburg*, vol. I: pp. 132–50.
[39] Henry Gerald Richardson, *The English Jewry under Angevin Kings* (London: Methuen, 1960, repr. Westport, Conn.: Greenwood Press, 1983); Mundill, *England's Jewish Solution*. Langmuir 'Tanquam Servi' distinguished between France, where many lords had jurisdiction over Jews, and England, where a royal monopoly existed. See also note 29 above.
[40] Friedenberg, *Medieval Jewish Seals*, p. 313.

The legal position of Hungary's non-Christian population

synodal activity under Kings László I and Kálmán concerning Muslims dealt exclusively with their Christianization. In other words, their legal status as Muslims was not addressed; they were not supposed to survive as Muslims, but to convert (see chapter 6).

The mid-twelfth-century royal attitude was very different. The contrast between King Kálmán's laws and Abū Hāmid's description of the status of Muslims in Hungary in the 1150s could not be greater. This mid-twelfth-century traveller summed up his description with the emphatic remark: 'this king likes the Muslims'.[41] He spoke of exceptional goodwill and privileges; not only were Muslims not forced to become Christians, but they were also allowed to practise all the regulations of Islam openly. He added that King Géza II defended the Muslims' right to have concubines.[42] As there are no sources to compare with his account, the extent to which Abū Hāmid exaggerated remains a matter of conjecture. Yet this difference cannot be entirely ascribed to his imagination or boasting. He mentioned in two separate works that his son Hāmid married two Muslim women, daughters of two well-to-do Hungarian Muslims, while in Hungary. This son remained in the kingdom even after his father's departure.[43]

No royal laws concerning Muslims survive from the thirteenth century, except those which prohibited Muslims, together with Jews, from holding public offices. Some information on Muslim legal status can, however, be gleaned from charters, papal letters and the accounts of Muslim authors. In comparison with Muslims subject to Christian rule elsewhere, there was a major difference.[44] Muslims in Hungary did not come under Christian rule via conquest. No agreements (such as surrender agreements in the Iberian peninsula) were made, and there was no transfer of rule from a previous Muslim overlord. Both Abū Hāmid and Yāqūt describe Hungary's Muslims as soldiers of the king or serving him in other offices.[45] This seems to indicate that Muslims were under the jurisdiction and protection of the king. Muslims also paid taxes to the king. In one of the sources, this tax is likened to the *jizyah* that non-Muslims paid to the ruler in Muslim countries. This information was probably based on the account of a Hungarian Muslim religious scholar.[46] If this comparison is correct, it would suggest that Muslims paid this tax as a direct consequence of their status as protected non-Christians,

---

[41] *Abu-Hámid*, p. 62.   [42] *Ibid.*, pp. 60, 62.   [43] *Ibid.*, pp. 62, 83.
[44] Powell, ed., *Muslims under Latin Rule*.   [45] *Abu-Hámid*, p. 56; Yāqūt, pp. 469–70.
[46] *El-Cazwini's Kosmographie*, part 2: *Die Denkmäler der Länder*, ed. Ferdinand Wüstenfeld (Göttingen, 1848), p. 411. I thank Robert Morrison for translating this text from Arabic. The scholar's name is not recorded in the source, but he must have given his account in the second half of the thirteenth century, since he described the Mongol invasion of Hungary (1241–2).

because in Muslim countries this head tax was paid by those who were not followers of Islam, but were accepted as *dhimmi*. It is more likely that this description is a Muslim rendering of a legal status that meant dependence on the king. Hungarian sources do not specify the nature and reasons for this tax, except to show that King András II drew a constant revenue from the Muslims of Pest at the beginning of the thirteenth century.[47]

Some Muslims belonged to the queen of Hungary and paid annual taxes to her.[48] They were not slaves of the queen, as Pope Honorius III exhorted the queen to ensure that the Muslims did not hold Christian slaves; therefore this dependence must have been related to the legal status of these Muslims. Some of Hungary's Muslim population came under the queen's jurisdiction, protection and taxation. Socially, some Muslims seem to have belonged to the level of *iobagiones* (officers of an *ispán*) and *villani* (peasants), against whom they litigated for theft.[49]

Papal letters to thirteenth-century kings complained about Muslim office-holding; Muslims were no more excluded from such employment by their legal position than were Jews. There is one more telling detail in these papal letters. The popes asserted – based on information from the archbishop of Esztergom – that some peasants and common people converted to Islam of their own volition, because the Muslims' lot was better, since they had 'greater liberty' that the Christians wished to attain.[50] Mass, or even individual, conversion to Islam in thirteenth-century Hungary is a far-fetched idea; no documentation of any such case exists and Muslims themselves soon disappeared from the country. Were these allegations due to conscious fabrication, exaggeration or misunderstanding? I believe they

---

[47] 'proventus Sarracenorum de Pesth', which was one of the revenues that the king promised to the queen should he die while on a crusade to the Holy Land: ASV Reg. Vat. 9, f. 250v (1218) (*Reg. Hon. III*, no. 1320; Augustinus Theiner, *Vetera Monumenta Historica Hungariam Sacram Illustrantia*, vol. I: *1216–1352* [*VMH*] (Rome, 1859), p. 13, no. XXII).

[48] Honorius III: 'multitudo Sarracenorum Ungarie ad te pertinere dicatur', ASV Reg. Vat. 11, f. 113v (1221) (*Reg. Hon. III*, no. 3301; *VMH*, p. 30, no. LVIII). *Liber censuum*, ASV Misc. Arm. XV, no. 1, f. 354r on change from 'quasi servilis condicionis' to 'stipendarii' (*VMH*, p. 108, no. CLXXXVII).

[49] János Karácsonyi and Samu Borovszky, eds., *Az időrendbe szedett váradi tüzesvaspróba-lajstrom (Regestrum Varadinense)* (Budapest: A Váradi Káptalan Kiadása, 1903), nos. 209, 139. These Muslims may have been under the jurisdiction of Hungary's lay or ecclesiastical lords, but there is insufficient evidence to determine their legal status.

[50] 'nonnulli rustici christiani sponte se transferentes ad ipsos, et eorum ritum sectantes, Sarracenos se publice profitentur, ex eo quod in plurimis levior Sarracenorum condicio, quam christianorum existit'. ASV Reg. Vat. 13, f. 80r (1225) (*Reg. Hon. III*, no. 5611; *VMH*, p. 61, no. CXXVII); 'multi christianorum oneribus importabilium exactionem gravati, videntes Sarracenos melioris conditionis et maioris libertatis prerogativa gaudere, sponte se transferunt ad eosdem, et ritum suscipientes eorum, ut pari cum eis gaudeant libertate'. ASV Reg. Vat. 15, f. 55v (1231), (*Reg. Greg. IX*, no. 561; *VMH*, p. 94, no. CLXVIII). Cf. Archbishop Robert's accusations, *Liber censuum*, ASV Misc. Arm. XV, no. 1, f. 354–354v (*VMH*, p. 108, no. CLXXXVII).

The legal position of Hungary's non-Christian population

were partially fuelled by papal fears, arising out of the international situation of the time (this will be discussed in chapter 5), and out of Hungary's frontier position. But they rested at least in part on an observation of the Muslim legal position in Hungary.[51] The reference to the greater liberty of Muslims is anchored in thirteenth-century realities that were misinterpreted. Although no charter of privileges concerning Muslims survives, most or all came under the jurisdiction and protection of the king or the queen, and their rights and duties were probably defined. In this, in fact, they were in a more favourable position than the various peasant groups who were subject to their lords. This was not a sign of the Hungarian kings' special favour toward Muslims or neglect of Christians. The papal misconstruction of the situation lay in taking the legal position of the Muslims as the manifestation of just such favours, instead of appreciating its real significance. In truth, the Muslims, just like the Jews, were one of the many status groups of medieval Hungary who possessed their own privileges.

THE LEGAL STATUS OF CUMANS

The Cumans' legal status in Hungary is known through charters, chronicles, papal letters and laws promulgated in order to regulate the behaviour, rights and duties of the Cumans. From the beginning, the Cumans had a collective legal status. But this legal status was not stable; it consisted of an intricate web of changing details. Prior to the Mongol invasion, it was the king himself who welcomed the Cumans into the country and served as the godfather of the Cuman chieftain Köten (see chapter 6). This displayed on a symbolic plane the Cumans' dependence on royal protection, and created personal ties between Hungarian and Cuman elites. Roger described the Cumans' need for this protection by emphasizing the hatred they inspired among the general population. 'If the king had not favoured them, they would not have stayed in Hungary.'[52] He also mentioned that the king swore an oath to protect the Cumans and that royal dignity dictated the honouring of 'guests' (*hospites*, the term used for immigrants and new settlers, implying liberties and privileges) who had no protector but the king.[53] He added that since the Cumans 'did not know submission', they were settled in one bloc in the middle

---

[51] Nineteenth- and early twentieth-century authors often uncritically adopted or even exaggerated the view of the advantageous standing of Muslims in Hungary: e.g. Albin Csinos, *Az izmaeliták Magyarországon* (Esztergom: Laiszky János Könyvnyomdája, 1913).

[52] 'Si rex eis favorabilis non fuisset, ipsi in Hungaria non stetissent': *SRH*, vol. II: p. 559.

[53] *Ibid.*, 'Nam dicebat regiam dignitatem introductos hospites honorare maxime, cum hoc eis promiserit iuramento et ipsum sit in fide sua ceperint imitari, et cum essent eis Hungari odiosi, solum regem habebant in Hungariam protectorem.'

of the country.⁵⁴ We can detect the presence of legal issues beneath Roger's moralizing tone. The Cumans, as a group, came under direct royal protection as 'guests' from the time of their entry into Hungary, and their community was exempt from the jurisdiction of Hungarian landlords, unless they had voluntarily settled on the land of these lords and engaged themselves as servants.⁵⁵

The legal status of the Cumans did not deteriorate after their second settlement in the country after the Mongol invasion, but some of its particulars were soon modified. Some time after his marriage to the daughter of the Cuman chieftain (perhaps Zeyhan), the younger king István assumed the title 'dominus Cumanorum', lord of the Cumans.⁵⁶ He certainly used the title from 1262 until his succession to the throne in 1270.⁵⁷ Thus, for the period when he was younger king, this new arrangement, intertwined with internal politics concerning the relative power of the king in the realm, gave him the highest authority over the Cumans. Legal structure and personal ties were combined in this system as well. Upon István's becoming king, the Cumans again came directly under royal protection. This remained a constant, though the most important person of the realm after the king, the palatine (*comes palatinus*), assumed the title 'judex Cumanorum', judge of the Cumans, from at least 1270.⁵⁸ This change may well have been linked to István V's accession. The Cumans were not deprived of royal protection or the possibility of appeal, but from then and with short interruptions into the modern period, the palatine was *ex officio* the 'judge of the Cumans', who interceded on their behalf with the king.⁵⁹

---

⁵⁴ *Ibid.*, p. 554: 'erat gens dura et aspera subdi nescia'.
⁵⁵ This is mentioned by Rogerius, *ibid.*, p. 557.
⁵⁶ István took the title 'younger king' (*iunior rex*) and ruled over the eastern part of the kingdom (1262–70), sharing power with his father Béla IV. Earlier scholars identified Erzsébet, István's wife, as Köten's daughter (*JK*, vol. II: p. 286). This opinion is untenable: Köten and his family died in 1241, and Erzsébet's parents were mentioned as having received baptism after that date. Györffy ('A Nagykunság és Karcag a középkorban', in *Magyarság*, pp. 305–11, see p. 307) identified Erzsébet's father with Zeyhan. Zeyhan is mentioned as King Béla's relative and as chief of the Cumans in this period (*cognatus noster* and *dux cumanorum* in a charter in 1255 by King Béla IV: MOL DL 97856; *HO*, vol. VIII: p. 62, no. 48; *RA*, no. 1054).

The marriage is dated to 1254 by Pauler, *Magyar nemzet*, vol. II: p. 205 on the basis of the date of the Dominican General Chapter held at Buda, where Erzsébet's parents were baptized, and to 1246 on the basis of a text concerning messengers that King Béla sent to the Mongols that year (see below).
⁵⁷ Imre Szentpétery, 'V. István ifjabb királysága', *Századok* 55–56 (1921–2): pp. 77–87, see pp. 82–6; concluded that the only occurrence prior to 1262 was in a forged charter (p. 82).
⁵⁸ *CD*, vol. V, pt. 1: p. 43 (*RA*, no. 1989). *JK*, vol. II, p. 424. From then many occurrences, e.g. *ÁÚO*, vol. III: p. 253 (*RA*, no. 2094); *HO*, vol. I: p. 58, no. 46, vol. IV: p. 209, no. 153, p. 408, no. 290, vol. V: p. 63, no. 51; Ferenc Kubinyi, *Árpádkori oklevelek, 1095–1301* (Pest, 1867), p. 125, no. 149. The first and perhaps second palatine to fill this role also had marriage ties to the Cumans: Emil Jakubovich, 'Kún Erzsébet nőtestvére', *Turul* 37 (1922–3): pp. 14–27; *TF*, vol. II: p. 527.
⁵⁹ In the eighteenth century, when the territory called As-Cumania within Hungary was pawned, the palatine was at the head of a movement to prevent, and then to invalidate this act (see below).

The legal position of Hungary's non-Christian population

The most elaborate set of regulations concerning the Cumans are the so-called Cuman laws of 1279. Two texts exist, their contents displaying significant differences. Scholars have called the two texts the 'first' and 'second' Cuman law, or 'draft' or 'agreement' and 'law', thus maintaining that either both laws were binding, or that the second text was the final version of the law, and therefore the only one that was legally binding.[60] Suspicion about eighteenth-century interpolations into this text was voiced by two scholars, but their views have not been accepted.[61] In fact, the first text is the only authentic medieval document; the 'second Cuman law' is an eighteenth-century forgery. Therefore the assertions of the second text should not be accepted as characteristic of thirteenth-century conditions unless there is corroborating medieval evidence. Consequently many of the generally accepted conclusions regarding Cuman status must be modified.

It is necessary to delve into the history of the manuscript tradition, as well as into eighteenth-century history, in order both to explain the authentic, binding character of the 'first Cuman law', and to prove that the second text is a forgery. According to the accepted view, both were issued by King László IV. The first text is a charter promulgated by King László on 23 June 1279, incorporating the demands of the papal legate Philip concerning the Cumans in five articles. The second text is dated seven weeks after the first, on 10 August. At the end of the first charter, the king promised to hold a general congregation and issue its decrees, together with the text of the first charter, under a golden bull. The second text, therefore, has been taken to be the result of this promise. The reason for the textual differences between the two texts has been explained in various ways. According to some scholars, there were two Cuman laws, both governing the life of the Cumans in Hungary.[62] Others think that, after the promulgation of the first text, the king and the Cumans managed

---

[60] 'First' and 'second' laws is the most usual, e.g.: György Györffy, 'A magyarországi kun társadalom a XIII–XIV. században (a kunok feudalizálódása)', in *Magyarság*, pp. 274–304, see p. 281 and Pálóczi Horváth, *Besenyők*, p. 68; draft: Erzsébet S. Kiss, 'A királyi generális kongregáció kialakulásának történetéhez', *AUSz Acta Historica* 39 (1971): pp. 1–56, see pp. 35–7. Szűcs, *Utolsó Árpádok*, p. 303: first text as the legate's dictate, second text as the only binding law.

[61] Miklós Kring, 'Kun és jász társadalomelemek a középkorban', *Századok* 66 (1932): pp. 35–63, 169–88; Borsa, in *RA*, no. 3000. Against these views, Györffy asserted that the document is authentic ('Magyarországi kun', p. 282). Mária Frick claimed there was a uniformity of the rhythmic text (this, however, is not true) and concluded that the document was authentic in 'A kun törvények és a budai zsinat határozatai' (unpublished dissertation, József Attila Tudományegyetem, Szeged, 1966. The copy in the University Library is missing, and the author could not furnish a copy of the manuscript. It is cited in S. Kiss, 'Királyi', pp. 36–7, n. 184). I thank Patrick Zutshi for his opinion on the style of the text.

[62] Henrik Marczali, *A magyar történet kútfőinek kézikönyve* (Budapest: Atheneum, 1901), pp. 174–83; Pálóczi Horváth, *Besenyők*, p. 68; János Botka, 'A jogállás és a katonai szolgálat kapcsolata a kunok és a jászok török hódítás előtti történetében', *Zounok: A Jász- Nagykun- Szolnok megyei Levéltár évkönyve* 11 (1996): pp. 65–75, pp. 69–70.

to persuade the legate to change some of its requirements, and so the second text was promulgated, superseding the first.[63] According to another group of scholars, however, the first text was a simple agreement, made either at the legate's dictate or as a draft for the law. According to them, the second text was the only Cuman law, promulgated at the general congregation.[64]

There are other cases where Hungarian kings issued the same charter twice, first under a wax seal, then under a golden bull; the contents of the charter did not necessarily change.[65] Thus King László's promise to promulgate the 'Cuman law' under a golden bull does not in itself mean that the second charter needed to be textually different from the first. An analysis of the manuscript tradition yields conclusive results about the first text, and proves that the 'second Cuman law' is a forgery. The text of the 'first Cuman law' survives in a fourteenth-century transcription, whereas there are only eighteenth-century manuscripts of the second.[66] The first charter regulating Cuman status cannot be called a draft; an examination of the document which rehearsed it in 1339 proves this beyond any doubt. Pope Benedict XII sent Johannes de Amelio to search out and copy documents from the papal archives then kept at Assisi.[67] Johannes chose documents that were privileges given to the Church by various rulers, or that touched on other important ecclesiastical affairs. He had the selected documents transcribed verbatim, and the subscription of notaries public attested to the faithfulness of the copies. Clearly, he selected the most authoritative version of each document to copy. Had there been a 'second Cuman law' in a charter of László IV under a golden bull, Johannes would have chosen that. Nor is there mention of such a document in the inventory of 1339, which listed the charters bearing a golden bull in the papal archives.[68] In 1339,

---

[63] Pauler, *Magyar nemzet*, vol. II: pp. 353–7; *JK*, vol. II: p. 337; Gyula Kristó, *A magyar nemzet megszületése* (Szeged: Szegedi Középkorász Műhely, 1997), p. 237.

[64] Szűcs, *Utolsó Árpádok*, p. 303; Zsoldos, *Árpádok*, p. 174.

[65] E.g. the oath of Bereg: Knauz, *Esztergomi főegyháznak okmánytára*, vol. I: p. 26, no. 32 (*RA*, no. 500); p. 34, no. 46 (*RA*, no. 902). *A Frangepán család oklevéltára*, ed. Lajos Thallóczi and Samu Barabás, Monumenta Hungariae Historica Diplomataria 35 (Budapest: MTA, 1910), vol. I: p. 30, no. 54.

[66] First text: ASV AA Arm. I-XVIII-595; ed. (only László's charter) *VMH*, pp. 339–41, no. DLVI; *RA*, no. 2962. Second text: e.g. Budapest, Országos Széchenyi Könyvtár [OSzK] Quart. Lat. 1280, ff. 59r–64v; Budapest, Egyetemi Könyvtár Coll. Pray. tom. XVI, pp. 56–9; MOL DL 56727; ed. Marczali, *Magyar történet*, pp. 178–83; *RA*, no. 3000.

[67] Franz Ehrle, 'Zur Geschichte des Schatzes, der Bibliothek und des Archivs der Päpste im vierzehnten Jahrhundert', *Archiv für Litteratur- und Kirchen-Geschichte des Mittelalters* I (1885): pp. 1–48, 228–364. I thank Patrick Zutshi for this reference.

[68] Ed. in Pietro Sella, *Le Bolle d'Oro dell'Archivio Vaticano* (Vatican City: Biblioteca Apostolica Vaticana, 1934), pp. 3–7.

The legal position of Hungary's non-Christian population

then, there was no other version of the Cuman law available to Johannes than the 'first'.

Johannes described the charter of King László as letters patent (*litterae patentes*), with a white wax seal suspended on red silk thread. The front of the seal bore the image of King László, seated on a royal throne, holding an orb surmounted by a double cross in his left hand. The back of the seal bore a shield with a double cross. This is clearly the king's *sigillum duplex*.[69] By the second half of the thirteenth century, the Hungarian royal chancery consistently used the suspended *sigillum duplex* for charters of privileges, whereas charters of a temporary character were sealed with the *sigillum simplex*.[70] Thus there can be no question about the nature of this charter: it was not a draft, and even if it was promulgated due to pressure by the papal legate, it was a binding royal document.

The second text surfaced in suspicious circumstances, during the eighteenth-century movement to have Cuman privileges restored. In 1702 Leopold I sold the Jász-Kun (As-Cuman) territory. This more or less corresponded to the area where the Cumans lived in the Middle Ages. By the fifteenth century, 'Cuman' legal status and privileges were linked to a territorial organization, which came to include the As (see chapter 2). Subsequently, inhabitants of this area, known by the eighteenth century as 'As-Cumans', continued to have a privileged legal status within Hungary. As the kingdom became part of the Habsburg Empire, the emperor disregarded previous privileges and treated the territory as 'newly acquired' land. After 1702, the inhabitants were fighting for redemption and the restoration of their privileged status. Their struggle lasted for many decades, during which various documents were collected as proofs of As-Cuman legal standing. That is when copies of the 'second Cuman law' started to surface. They are simple transcriptions by hand, without any attempt to forge a 'thirteenth-century' charter.[71] These eighteenth-century manuscripts claimed to be exact copies of the text of King László IV's original charter, without giving precise information as to the location of that original. When György Pray published the text in 1774 in his *Dissertationes historico-criticae in annales veteres Hunnorum,*

---

[69] Imre Szentpétery, 'IV. László király pecsétváltoztatásai', *Levéltári Közlemények* 1 (1923): pp. 310–20.

[70] Bernát Kumorovitz, *A magyar pecséthasználat története a középkorban* (Budapest: Magyar Nemzeti Múzeum, 1993): pp. 53–4. Johannes's usage (*litterae patentes*) did not conform to the vocabulary of diplomatic used in Hungary, where the document would have been described as *litterae privilegiales*.

[71] I am working on an article that provides a detailed analysis of the eighteenth-century forgery of the 'second Cuman law'. On the eighteenth-century emergence of the document, see *JK*, vol. II: p. 337; *CD*, vol. V, pt. 2: p. 519.

Avarum, et Hungarorum, a note indicated that it was 'from the original'. In the manuscript of the *Dissertationes*, however, Pray gave more precise information, claiming that 'F. Subich, secretary to Prince Albert', gave him a transcript (*copia*) of the document.[72] The alleged original in the Habsburg archives proves elusive even in this case. Subsequent editions refer back to this early edition, or to eighteenth-century manuscripts. There are no data about any authentic witness to a thirteenth-century document on which the eighteenth-century copy might have been based. Moreover, research in the archives of Vienna, although renewed by several scholars, has produced no evidence that any medieval copy of the Cuman law (that could have been communicated to Pray) was ever held there.[73] The copies of the Cuman law that were held in these archives are themselves eighteenth-century manuscripts. In other words, there is no original medieval charter, or even medieval copy; no text or authentic account of such a text exists prior to the eighteenth century. The 'second Cuman law' incorporated most of the text of the 'first', with additions culled from other medieval texts and statements about the noble status of the Cumans. None of the contents of this 'second law' can be accepted, unless there is independent corroboration from authentic medieval sources.

The authentic text regulating Cuman status is thus a royal charter, containing the promises and oath of King László IV to the legate. The king swore to observe the articles dictated by Philip (incorporated into the royal charter). These were above all concerned with their conversion and settlement (see chapters 4 and 6). Cuman legal status was defined collectively, just as it had been at the time of their entry into the kingdom. Cumans constituted an *universitas*, which could delegate two chiefs (*principales*) to represent them.[74] As a group, they came under royal jurisdiction. The importance of the Cumans is clearly reflected in their participation at the general congregation. This precursor of parliament was developing in the second half of the thirteenth century. Together with prelates and nobles, the Cumans also attended. At the congregation of 1298, two communities were represented apart from the nobles and

---

[72] György Pray, *Dissertationes historico-criticae in annales veteres Hunnorum, Avarum, et Hungarorum* (Vienna, 1774), p. 117; Egyetemi Könyvtár, Coll. Pray. tom. XVI, p. 56.

[73] *JK*, vol. II: p. 443 on previous research. I thank István Fazekas, Hungarian delegate to the Viennese archives, for communicating to me that there is no trace in the records of the Haus- Hof- und Staatsarchiv of any manuscripts of the Cuman law. The copies in the collection of Ferenc Kollár, originally held there, now in the Hungarian National Archives (MOL I 7, vol. 18: pp. 408–13, vol. 52: pp. 515–19, vol. 54: pp. 439–48) are themselves eighteenth-century copies.

[74] 'pro se et universitate Comanorum': ASV AA Arm. I-XVIII-595 (*VMH*, p. 340). Botka, 'A jogállás' linked the collective legal status to their military role. See Kristó, *Magyar nemzet megszületése*, pp. 237–40 on collective rights.

ecclesiastics: the Saxons and the Cumans. The mention of these groups together in the charters shows once again that Cumans enjoyed collective legal status.[75]

THE JUDICIAL AUTONOMY OF NON-CHRISTIANS

Any analysis of the legal status of Hungary's non-Christian groups would be incomplete without a consideration of their autonomy in internal judicial matters. This issue cannot be fully explored for lack of documentation, but there are some indications as to whether these communities depended on the Hungarian judicial system or had their own procedures for the resolution of internal affairs. Almost nothing is known about what issues led to internal litigation within these communities. With the exception of the recorded rabbinical *responsa* no documentation survives concerning intra-communal judicial issues. Even the results based on the surviving *responsa* are meagre; they provide only a glimpse into the life of the Jewish community. This lack of documentation can be explained by the loss of medieval texts and/or the primarily oral judicial procedures of the communities in question. The hypothesis of a loss of documents is a feasible one, considering not only the general circumstances (especially a series of invasions and wars from the thirteenth century on), but also the ruptures in the life of the non-Christian communities concerned. For example, no one could have had an interest in preserving a document dealing with a dispute between two members of a long-extinct Muslim community after the thirteenth century; and the expulsion of the Jews in the fourteenth century must have led to the loss of property, including documents. The original existence but subsequent loss of such documents is corroborated by the fact that rabbinical *responsa* of the period were preserved in foreign compilations in the case of the Jewish community, although there remains no record of the existence of these *responsa* within Hungary. Overall very few private documents survive from the period; texts that were less likely to fall into oblivion were those that retained their value over time: titles to land, royal donations and the like. The oral nature of juridical procedure is an especially viable hypothesis in the case of the Cumans, who had no written culture and left no written records. The information from laws, charters and other texts provides no more than the skeletal framework of non-Christian judicial autonomy. The true day-to-day functioning of internal procedures remains shrouded in silence.

---

[75] *ÁÚO*, vol. IV: p. 176, no. 107 (*RA*, no. 2999), pp. 181–2, no. 110 (*JK*, vol. II: p. 444, no. 71; *RA*, no. 2997, in 1279). In 1298: Bak, *Laws*, p. 48; *CD*, vol. VI, pt. 2: pp. 130–47. In 1277: S. Kiss, 'Királyi', p. 30.

At the Gate of Christendom

King Béla IV, following Duke Frederick's charter, granted a large degree of autonomy in internal judicial matters to the Jews of Hungary in his charter of privileges. The king retained important powers; it was to him that the Jews could appeal, and he remained their highest judge, with a royal official as his substitute.[76] Rulers in Poland similarly had supreme judicial authority over Jews.[77] Béla's privileges repeatedly mention the judge of the Jews (*iudex iudeorum* or *iudex suus*), who was the organ of justice in cases between Jews. This judge could not interfere of his own accord, however, but only upon request by one of the parties. After an accusation was made, he was to follow a prescribed procedure, calling upon the parties to appear before him; there were fines for not complying with his summons. He had to announce the final judgement in front of the synagogue; the maximum amount that the judge could impose as punishment was fixed. It is not clear who these judges were in Hungary. In Austria they were Christians appointed by the duke.[78] The existence of a 'judge of the Jews of the realm' (*országos zsidóbíró*), is documented in Hungary from the late fourteenth century. This judge was the appointed leader of all the Hungarian Jewish communities, in charge of cases between Jews and Christians.[79]

Hebrew documents reveal another aspect of autonomy, the procedure for seeking justice from rabbis. Jewish law encompassed religious and civil law (*halakha*). In Hungary as well, not only religious matters, but also other types of litigation were taken before rabbis. No decisions of Hungarian rabbis have come down to us, although such decisions had probably existed, as we see in a case of appeal, where the two litigants mentioned a previous decision. This probably refers to a Hungarian *beth-din*.[80] The existing documents show that Hungarian Jews turned to

---

[76] In appeals concerning cases between Jews, the king could delegate judgement to a royal official ('camerarius'); in capital crimes, only the king was to judge: Büchler, 'Judenprivilegium', p. 142. The 'camerarius' is interpreted by Balog, *Magyarországi zsidók*, p. 73, as the *tárnokmester* (high royal official with economic and juridical functions); by Kohn, *Zsidók*, p. 105, as the chancellor (the head of the royal chancery, always a high-ranking ecclesiastic).

[77] Maurycy Horn, 'Jewish Jurisdiction's Dependence on Royal Power in Poland and Lithuania up to 1548', *Acta Poloniae Historica* 76 (1997): pp. 5–17.

[78] Lohrmann, *Judenrecht*, pp. 70–1. Western European patterns: Stow, *Alienated Minority*, pp. 159–64. According to Balog, *Magyarországi zsidók*, pp. 58–62, Christian judges in Hungary; according to Imre Hajnik, *A magyar bírósági szervezet és perjog az Árpád- és vegyesházi királyok alatt* (Budapest, 1899), p. 110, the judge was elected by Christian and Jewish city-dwellers; according to Kubinyi, 'Magyarországi', p. 9, no such judges existed prior to the late fourteenth century in Hungary.

[79] This position was created by Louis the Great (first mentioned in 1371). Circa 1467, this office was replaced by that of the prefect, himself a Jew, and appointed by the king. Kohn, *Zsidók*, pp. 162, 211–12; Baron, *Social*, vol. x: p. 28; Balog, *Magyarországi zsidók*, pp. 65–8; Kubinyi, 'Magyarországi zsidóság', pp. 11, 17; András Kubinyi, 'Mendel', in *Encyclopaedia Judaica*, vol. xi: col. 1316 and 'Praefectus Judaeorum', in *ibid.*, vol. xiii: col. 963.

[80] Spitzer, 'Héber', no. 16d. Kupfer and Lewicki, *Źródła*, p. 213.

The legal position of Hungary's non-Christian population

foreign rabbis, either in writing or in person when the latter travelled through the country, to seek a solution to contested questions. Two types of issues appear in these *responsa*: either a matter of principle had to be clarified, or two individuals brought their litigation before the rabbi. The rabbis acted independently of Hungarian royal jurisdiction, and at the same time provided an international network of advice, assuring a link between Jewish communities in different countries. During the thirteenth century, rabbi Isaac ben Moses, the author of *Sefer Or Zaru'a*, travelled through Hungary, and recorded the cases brought before him. Rabbi Isaac was born in Bohemia, studied with German and French rabbis, travelled widely, and wrote the *Or Zaru'a*, a compilation including *responsa*.[81] The most detailed case concerning Hungary that he recounted provides information on the legal procedure itself, which conformed to medieval Jewish practice throughout Europe.[82] The two litigants first appeared in court (*beth-din*), with witnesses. The decision was given in writing. Either party could appeal to another rabbi. Thus the whole procedure remained within the structures of the Jewish community, and was completely independent of the Hungarian legal system and the king. The Jews themselves felt secure that the procedures of the *beth-din* would not be revealed to Christian authorities, as the case discussed in this *responsum* attests. The case involved two men who claimed ownership of a Jewish slave-girl, who converted to Christianity, then reverted to Judaism. She had to hide, because canon law prohibited such 'apostasy'. None the less the rabbi was not afraid to have all the details of the case recorded.[83] This shows the complete separation of Jewish and Christian judicial authorities; to reveal the story of the maid's repeated conversions and her hiding among the Jews to Christian authorities would have invited reprisals upon the Jewish community. The dangers such revelations could bring are demonstrated by cases elsewhere in Europe, where those who converted to Christianity and then reverted to Judaism had to move away to distant locations where their story was not known to Christians.[84]

[81] *Encyclopaedia Judaica*, vol. IX: cols. 25–7; I. Elbogen, A. Freiman and H. Tykocinski, eds., *Germania Judaica*, vol. I (Tübingen: Mohr, 1963), p. 402.
[82] Spitzer, 'Héber', no. 16d; Kupfer and Lewicki, *Źródła*, p. 213; Isaac ben Moses, *Sefer Or Zaru'a*, vol. I, ed. H. Lipa and J. Höschel (Zhitomir, 1862), p. 223.
[83] I disagree with Gyula Wellesz, 'Izsák b. Mózes Ór Zarua és az üreghi zsidók', *Magyar Zsidó Szemle* 21, no. 4 (1904): pp. 370–3 that before 1233 (András II's oath concerning the treatment of non-Christians) Jews could hold Christian slaves, and therefore the conversion of the Jewish girl did not prevent her returning to Jewish employment. Laws against such practices appeared much earlier (see chapter 4).
[84] Irving A. Agus, *Urban Civilization in Pre-Crusade Europe: A Study of Organized Town-Life in North-Western Europe during the Tenth and Eleventh Centuries Based on the Responsa Literature*, 2 vols. (Leiden: Brill, 1965), vol. II: pp. 690–1. Joseph Shatzmiller, 'Jewish Conversion to Christianity in Medieval Europe 1200–1500', in *Cross Cultural Convergences in the Crusader Period*, ed. Michael Goodich, Sophia Menache and Sylvia Schein (New York: Peter Lang, 1995), pp. 297–318, see pp. 314–15.

No direct source illuminates the legal practices within the Muslim community. Abū Hāmid claims to have educated Hungary's Muslims in several religious matters. Among these, he mentions some that are of a juridical nature: the law of inheritance and polygamy.[85] According to his account, his teachings on both issues were effective, and the Hungarian Muslims conformed to them. The Muslims in Hungary may have welcomed Abū Hāmid's teachings, and they may also have turned to him for clarification on religious issues, but there is no evidence of his having arbitrated in litigation between Muslims. Therefore his role only partially resembles the one filled by itinerant rabbis for the Jewish community. Abū Hāmid himself was a religious scholar and law teacher, as well as a merchant, and he travelled to different parts of the world teaching Muslim law.[86] It is impossible to determine whether Abū Hāmid's involvement in the internal affairs of Hungarian Muslims is an isolated case, due to his long stay in Hungary, or whether the country's Muslims, like the Jews, turned to outside authorities more regularly. In any case, the chances of Hungarian Muslims being able to consult such travellers grew increasingly slimmer, because by the thirteenth century Hungary was off the trade or other main routes frequented by Muslims. If not before, by that time Hungary's Muslims had to devise ways of being self-reliant in internal legal matters.

Self-reliance necessitated the training of legal experts. Religious scholars (who were trained in law) were well respected by Muslims in Hungary, as Yāqūt's account shows. He encountered Hungarian Muslims who went to study Muslim law in Aleppo in the early thirteenth century, and was told that the Muslim community in Hungary would honour them as a consequence of their knowledge.[87] Al-Kazwīnī probably drew his information from such a Muslim religious scholar (*faqīh*) from Hungary.[88] It seems that the Muslims had their own structures and autonomy to deal with juridical problems within the community, although (as discussed in chapter 7) this ultimately did not prevent their assimilation.

Hungary's Muslims also relied on Christian legal structures, more specifically in their litigation with the kingdom's Christian population. The source for this is the famous Register of Várad, a list of the ordeals performed under the auspices of the canons of Várad.[89] Three of the ordeals

---

[85] *Abu-Hámid*, pp. 56, 61.
[86] O. G. Bolsakov, 'Abu-Hámid al-Garnáti és művei', in *Abu-Hámid*, pp. 11–28; Hrbek, 'Ein Arabischer', p. 206.   [87] Yāqūt, p. 470; in Reinaud, *Géographie*, p. 295.
[88] *El-Cazwini*, p. 411.
[89] Hot-iron ordeals from 1208 to 1235. A printed edition was prepared in 1550 and subsequently the manuscripts disappeared. The best critical edition to date is Karácsonyi and Borovszky, eds., *Időrendbe szedett váradi*. On the Register: Imre Zajtay, 'Le Registre de Varad: Un monument judiciaire du début du XIIIe siècle', *Revue Historique de Droit Français et Étranger*, ser. 4, 32 (1954): pp.

concern Muslims. The description of each case is very succinct. In all three cases it was Muslims who accused Christians – twice of theft, while the nature of the third complaint is not specified – and asked that the case be decided by ordeal. Once the accusation was brought by an individual, twice by groups. In two cases, the accusation was followed by the ordeal (carrying hot iron); in the third case a settlement was reached before a judge who was delegated by the king. In one case, the accused were cleared of the charges, in another, they were burnt, and thus declared guilty, and in the third instance, that of the agreement, the Muslim accuser received a payment of five marks (instead of the twelve that he had claimed).[90] There was thus no prejudice against Muslims. Indeed, the lack of attention to the religion of the parties is remarkable in these histories. Bartlett's study of ordeals indicates that, generally, trial by ordeal was not applied to Jews and non-Christians.[91] Yet, in these cases, although the Muslims are designated as 'Ysmaelitae', their presence at a Christian ceremony generated no surprise. The ordeals of Várad were performed in the presence of the relics of St László, with priests playing a major role even after the prohibitions that were enacted by the Fourth Lateran Council. The Muslims may have had Christian oath-helpers with them. Although in one case the Muslim accuser acted alone, this is the one that ends in an agreement rather than an ordeal. In the two other cases the Muslims were supported by others: 'coadiuvantibus aliis'.

The Cumans, who reached Hungary in a group organized according to their own social structure, differed greatly from both the Jews and the Muslims, who arrived in many waves from different countries, and whose communities had to be forged in Hungary. Although these Cumans were the remnants or parts of several tribes and therefore their traditional tribal structures had been disrupted, they were the most coherently organized of Hungary's non-Christian groups at the time of their entry. They possessed their own social and juridical organization under their own chieftains. The Cumans, like other steppe peoples, were able to attach themselves to empires of various kinds, whilst preserving their own internal structures. The main characteristic of political formations on the steppe was invariably the integration of groups that had different internal organizations and legal systems, spoke different languages, and

527–62; Robert Bartlett, *Trial by Fire and Water: The Medieval Judicial Ordeal* (Oxford: Clarendon Press, 1986), pp. 63, 128; Dominique Barthélemy, 'Présence de l'aveu dans le déroulement des ordalies (9–13e s.)', in *L'Aveu: Antiquité et Moyen-Age*, Collection de l'Ecole Française de Rome 88 (Rome: Ecole Française de Rome, 1986), pp. 191–214, see pp. 204–7.

[90] Karácsonyi and Borovszky, *Időrendbe szedett váradi*, pp. 203, 229, 276, no. 139 (old no. 192), no. 209 (41), no. 326 (38).

[91] Bartlett, *Trial*, pp. 53–4. Concerning Jews, also Ziegler, 'Reflections on the Jewry Oath', p. 213.

At the Gate of Christendom

professed a variety of religions.[92] These groups kept their own unity and identity intact, attaching themselves to the ruler through their own chiefs. The ties existed only at the highest level between the ruler and subordinate peoples. Steppe nomads were loosely integrated under a common military and political leadership, performing military service but not assimilated into one political and cultural unit. This, for example, is exactly how the Hungarian tribes formed a part of the Khazar Empire. When the Cumans first moved into Hungary, they relied on the pattern to which they were accustomed: keeping their internal organization and independence intact, they became members of the kingdom by coming under royal power. The inherent flexibility of their organization allowed subjection to a ruler governing a kingdom whose customs and religion were largely alien to the Cumans. The king ensured their loyalty by personal ties as well; King Béla became the godfather of a Cuman chieftain, his son István the husband of a chieftain's daughter. Already by the early thirteenth century, when missionaries were sent to Cumania, the extension of Hungarian sovereignty and baptism were linked (see chapter 6).

The Cumans' own conception of the ties that were henceforth to bind them to the Hungarian king and of their own legal position in the country is reflected in a description of the wedding ceremony of István. The description survives in a unique manuscript appended to Plano Carpini's account of his voyage to the Mongols.[93] It depicts King Béla listening to the report of papal messengers about the life and habits of the Tartars in 1246 – thus after the Mongol invasion, but still amid constant fear of a new attack. The papal messenger is called Brother John in the text; Denis Sinor identified him with John of Plano Carpini, who, he concluded, returned from his mission via Hungary, to give intelligence to the king about what he saw during his trip to the Mongols.[94] The note goes on to say that King Béla, alarmed by the reports of both the papal messenger and his own, feared an onslaught of Mongols. As a result, he had his son (already crowned, and ruling over a part of the country as 'younger king'), marry the daughter of the Cuman king. During the wedding feast, ten Cuman lords swore over a dog 'cut into two by a sword, as is their custom, that they would hold the land of the Hungarians, as men faithful to the king, against the Tartars and barbar-

---

[92] Seaman and Marks, *Rulers from the Steppe*; Sinor, ed., *Cambridge History of Early Inner Asia*; Golden, *Introduction, passim*; Khazanov, *Nomads*, chapter V on a variety of nomad states. On the adaptability of the Cumans: Golden, 'Qipčaqs'.

[93] Luxembourg, BN cod. 110, f. 187r, ed. Henrik Marczali, *Magyar Történelmi Tár* (1878), p. 376, and with slight differences by Géza Istványi, 'XIII. századi följegyzés IV. Bélának 1246-ban a tatárokhoz küldött követségéről', *Századok* 72 (1938): pp. 270–2.

[94] Denis Sinor, 'John of Plano Carpini's Return from the Mongols: New Light from a Luxemburg Manuscript', in *Inner Asia*, no. XII.

The legal position of Hungary's non-Christian population

ous nations'.[95] That swearing an oath while cutting a dog to pieces was a Cuman custom is confirmed by Jean de Joinville's account, whose source, the eyewitness Philippe de Toucy, recounted a similar ceremony.[96] The significance of the ritual is explained there as well: 'this is how they should be cut in pieces if they failed [i.e. did not keep their oath to] each other'.[97] This description thus shows that the Cumans relied on their own customs and religious tradition in defining their relationship to the Hungarian king – a precious piece of information because ordinarily the sources are mute on the Cumans' point of view. The Cumans thus probably saw their integration into Hungary as allegiance to the king, established by a marriage alliance and an oath. This was completely in keeping with steppe traditions of loose integration by ties to the ruler of an empire. It did not entail total submission.

The Cumans certainly seem to have retained a large degree of autonomy in internal matters in the second half of the thirteenth century. If the argument that the As arrived in Hungary together with the Cumans is correct, then it would affirm the hypothesis that the Cumans enjoyed full internal autonomy; if the Hungarians made no distinction whatsoever between Cumans and As, peoples who certainly differed in language and perhaps in religion, it was because they dealt exclusively with the representatives of the Cumans and did not engage at all in their internal affairs. There is also more positive evidence for Cuman autonomy and ties to the king via the Cuman elite. Cuman society was hierarchical and produced its own representatives. Two Cuman lords promised that the Cumans would obey the Cuman articles. They are said to have 'acted in the name of and with the consent of' the Cumans.[98] This did not mean

---

[95] 'In his autem nuptiis(1) X(2) Comanorum convenerunt iurantes super canem gladio bipartitum(3) iuxta eorum consuetudinem, quod terram Hungarorum(4) tamquam regis fideles contra Tharthoros et(5) barbaras nationes obtinebunt'. Marczali, *Történelmi Tár*, p. 376. The following are variations in Istványi's edition ('XIII. századi', p. 271): (1) nuptys, (2) principes *add*. (3) bipertitum, (4) Hungarum, (5) et *om*. On these oaths and the role of dogs in Cuman religion, Denis Sinor, 'Taking an Oath over a Dog Cut in Two', in *Altaic Religious Beliefs and Practices*, ed. Géza Bethlenfalvy *et al.* (Budapest: Research Group for Altaic Studies, Hungarian Academy of Sciences and Department of Inner Asiatic Studies, ELTE, 1992), pp. 301–5; Peter B. Golden, 'The Dogs of the Medieval Qüipčaqs', in *Varia Eurasiatica: Festschrift für Professor András Róna-Tas* (Szeged: Department of Altaic Studies, 1991), pp. 45–55; Peter B. Golden, 'Wolves, Dogs and Quipčaq Religion', *AOASH* 50 (1997): pp. 87–97. Similar oaths 'per canem seu lupum' among the Hungarians of the ninth–tenth centuries: Gyula Pauler and Sándor Szilágyi, eds., *A Magyar Honfoglalás Kútföi* (Budapest: MTA, 1900; repr. Budapest: Nap Kiadó, 1995), p. 326; Csanád Bálint, 'A kutya a X–XII. századi magyar hitvilágban', *Móra Ferenc Múzeum Évkönyve 1971/1* (Szeged: Szegedi Nyomda, 1971), pp. 295–315, see p. 308.

[96] Jean Sire de Joinville, *Histoire de Saint Louis*, ed. Natalis de Wailly (Paris: Firmin Didot, 1874), pp. 270–2.

[97] 'Que ainsi fussent-il decopei se il failloient li uns à l'autre', *ibid.*, p. 272.

[98] 'Uzuz et Tolon principales Comanorum, pro se et universitate Comanorum, quorum vicem et consensum se habere dicebant', ASV AA Arm. I-XVIII-595; *VMH*, p. 340. (Marczali, *Magyar*

modern representation, but that probably two of the highest-ranking Cumans acted as a liaison between their people and the king.

The charter that regulated Cuman status in 1279 provides a rudimentary description of the internal judicial procedures of the Cuman community. Cuman society was organized into extended families, and those into branches; judicial investigation was to proceed within these units.[99] Cumans had their servants and dependants who were fully subject to the jurisdiction of their lords, to the extent that the charter of 1279 stipulated that the Cumans were responsible for ensuring that their own servants kept the law.[100] This charter shows that the Cumans retained their social organization and internal judicial procedures, and that in the negotiations between king and Cumans a large degree of legal autonomy was codified. They were subject as a group to the king of Hungary, with the palatine as intermediary. The whole community was exempt from the jurisdiction of local authorities. The king dealt with the Cumans, if it came to matters pertaining to the whole community, mainly through their representatives.

The legal status of the Cumans was transformed into territorial privileges in the later Middle Ages. As Cuman society evolved away from the system of clans and chieftains, the so-called Cuman captains taking the place of chiefs, Cuman clans gave way to a territorial organization ('seats', *sedes*, *szék*) in the fifteenth century. These territorial units had their own taxation, privileges and judicial system.[101]

Certain similarities have emerged in the discussion of the legal status of Hungary's three non-Christian groups. In each case, non-Christians had some sort of group status and autonomy in internal juridical matters. The most serious hindrance to creating a fuller picture of the legal procedure of the communities, that is, the lack of documents produced by these communities in resolving their internal affairs, is perhaps at the same time an eloquent testimony to their legal autonomy. The lack of royal charters dealing with such litigation is at least partially indicative of the legal status of these non-Christian communities. As royal charters were a category of documents more likely to survive than other texts, and the king was always the judge or at least the highest possible recourse for non-

---

footnote 98 (*cont.*)
történet, p. 176 distorts the first name as 'Usacus'; he uses 'Cumanorum', and the words 'pro se et universitate Comanorum' are omitted.)
[99] ASV AA Arm. I-XVIII-595 (*VMH*, p. 340): ecclesiastical investigation intended to ensure compliance with the law was to proceed 'per singulas generationes eorum et generationum gradus sibi in invicem quacumque linea attinentes'.
[100] *Ibid.* 'nec pacientur fieri . . . per suos famulos et subiectos' (concerning hurting or killing Christians). [101] Györffy, 'Magyarországi kun', pp. 299–304; 'kun székek', in *KMTL*.

The legal position of Hungary's non-Christian population

Christians in Hungary, the fact that royal charters did *not* deal with cases internal to non-Christian communities may indicate that issues involving members of the community were usually solved within it, without recourse to outside (even royal) intervention. This possibility is strengthened by a comparison with other parts of the medieval world. Elsewhere, Christian authorities became involved in juridical procedures between members of non-Christian communities at the demand of non-Christians themselves. For example, *mudejars* of Valencia took cases to the Christian monarch to appeal, and local jurisdiction passed increasingly into the hands of nobles.[102] As rabbis had no coercive powers over members of the Jewish community, Jews sometimes turned to Christian authorities to enforce punishment; the prohibitions against informing attest to intra-communal tensions.[103] Hungary's non-Christians perhaps did not resort to Christian authorities in purely intra-communal affairs.

THE HUNGARIAN LEGAL SYSTEM AND THE NON-CHRISTIANS

To assess fully the legal status of Hungary's non-Christian groups, their position has to be compared to that of the Christian inhabitants of the kingdom. The following pages draw on a number of studies in order to outline the main characteristics of the medieval Hungarian legal system, so that the status of non-Christian groups can be placed in context.

Society in thirteenth-century Hungary consisted of many groups, each with its own legal position. I shall differentiate between two types of groups: those who were called *hospites*, 'guests' (that is, immigrants, though not necessarily from other countries; they could be Hungarians who were newcomers to a particular village or area) on the one hand, and all the other groups who were designated by their social rank, on the other. The period after the foundation of the Christian kingdom was characterized by an increasing differentiation of social strata. The simple social structure of the warrior elite, free and unfree, gave way to a diversity of status groups. Groups according to social rank were in a state of flux in the thirteenth century. In charters the scribe would note whether someone was a royal *serviens*, a nobleman, an *ispán*, and so forth. Both Hungarians and foreigners were included in these groups. Thus the groups were not divided on an ethnic basis, though the question of origins was important for the nobility, as attested by a thirteenth-century text. A list of 'immigrant nobles' was composed and subsequently

[102] Harvey, *Islamic Spain*, pp. 128–33.
[103] Agus, *Rabbi Meir of Rothenburg*; Elena Lourie, 'Mafiosi and Malsines: Violence, Fear and Faction in the Jewish Aljamas of Valencia in the Fourteenth Century', in Lourie, *Crusade and Colonisation*, no. XII.

incorporated into the chronicle of Simon of Kéza, László IV's cleric, as well as into the fourteenth-century Hungarian chronicle compositions.[104] This was a list of names of noble families who came from foreign lands. It should be noted that the line of admissibility into the ranks of the nobility was drawn not between 'Hungarians' and 'foreigners', but between 'old' and 'new'; what the nobles objected to was the ennobling of recent newcomers by the king, seeing this process as harmful to their own privileged status. There was an effort to codify, to create a 'canon' of noble families, excluding the claims of others. Not just nobles, but other social groups would have their own 'freedoms' and obligations, made up of taxes they had to pay, forms of landholding and military service, and the nature of the authority under whose jurisdiction they belonged. These groups had special names (such as the *szepesi lándzsások*, 'lance-bearers from Szepes'), or simply lived in a community which constituted the legal framework for their existence. During the thirteenth century, some of these groups were integrated into a unified nobility, as attested by numerous royal charters that lifted individuals and families out of their former, lower status and elevated them to the ranks of the nobility.[105] Lower down the social scale, there existed a multitude of free, semi-free and slave groups. A process of unification was taking place in the ranks of the peasantry during the thirteenth century.[106] Until the late thirteenth and fourteenth centuries, when a socially and legally defined nobility and peasantry largely replaced a myriad of smaller groupings, Hungarian society had many levels of 'freedoms', duties and privileges. Thus, even without considering immigrants, the nature of society was one of complex stratification, the legal status of each individual being dependent on the group to which he belonged.

'Guests' should be treated separately for two reasons. First, they were

---

[104] *SRH*, vol. I: pp. 187–92 (Kézai 'De nobilibus advenis') and 294–304. Dated *c.* 1270 by some scholars, to the 1240s by others: Sándor Domanovszky, *Kézai Simon mester krónikája* (Budapest: MTA, 1906), pp. 120, 128–30; Elemér Mályusz, *Az V. István-kori Gesta*, Értekezések a történeti tudományok köréből n.s. 58 (Budapest: Akadémiai Kiadó, 1971), pp. 62–83; Gyula Kristó, 'Magyar öntudat és idegenellenesség az Árpád-kori Magyarországon', *Irodalomtörténeti Közlemények* 94 (1990): pp. 425–43, with a summary of interpretations on pp. 438–42. László Veszprémy, 'Kézai Simon a "fajtiszta" Magyarországról', *Magyar Könyvszemle* 109, no. 4 (1993): pp. 430–3 against racial interpretation. New edition with English tr.: László Veszprémy and Frank Schaer, eds. and trs., *Simon of Kéza: The Deeds of the Hungarians* (Budapest: Central European University Press, 1999).

[105] E.g. MOL DL 40177 (*ÁÚO*, vol. IV: pp. 276–8, no. 174; *RA*, no. 3368). On the process: Székely, *Magyarország története*, vol. I, pt. 2: pp. 1320–32; Erik Fügedi, *Ispánok, bárók, kiskirályok: a közép-kori magyar arisztokrácia fejlődése* (Budapest: Magvető Kiadó, 1986); Erik Fügedi, 'The Aristocracy in Medieval Hungary', in *Kings, Bishops, Nobles and Burghers in Medieval Hungary*, tr. János M. Bak (London: Variorum Reprints, 1986), no. IV.

[106] Ilona Bolla, *A jogilag egységes jobbágyosztály kialakulása Magyarországon*, Értekezések a történeti tudományok köréből, n.s. 100 (Budapest: Akadémiai Kiadó, 1983).

The legal position of Hungary's non-Christian population

always clearly designated as such in the documents, implying special legal status, which was precisely defined by the thirteenth century. Second, the non-Christian groups, as immigrants themselves, can be more readily compared to *hospites*.[107] None the less, I wish to insist on one basic feature that pervaded the whole of society irrespective of who was a 'guest' and who was not: this society could be defined as 'cellular', that is, built up of many small groups, each in its own niche, with specific obligations and privileges. The emphasis here is on the large number of existing and possible groups that constituted this society. 'Guests' were internal or foreign migrants of different social standing. At the lower end of the social scale, newly created peasant communities enjoyed certain privileges. Whereas initially the king had a monopoly in settling 'guests' on his lands, during the course of the thirteenth century ecclesiastical and lay landowners also gained this right. The example of one village shows that the settlers were exempt from taxes for a certain number of years, and the amount of their tax was fixed for the subsequent years. They could leave if they wished and they had the right to bequeath their property to whomever they chose if they had no heir.[108] At the top, immigrants could be knights, who received large landed estates and became members of the nobility.

'Guests' from other countries appear in documents under names such as *Saxones*, *Theutonici* and *Latini*. 'Guest' status always entailed possessing privileges.[109] For the sake of comparison, leaving aside the issue of internal migration, I shall concentrate on these groups of foreign *hospites* and their legal status in the country. They are best known from the thirteenth century, when the privileges were granted in writing. By then, the history of dealings with other peoples was a long one. The experiences of the 'Hungarians' (themselves, let us not forget, a mixed population) prior to founding a kingdom were of multi-ethnic empires, whose

---

[107] Szűcs mentioned that the legal status of Jews resembled that of *hospites*: *Utolsó Árpádok*, p. 69.
[108] E.g. *HO*, vol. v: p. 40, no. 32 (*RA*, no. 1799). László Solymosi, *A földesúri járadékok új rendszere a 13. századi Magyarországon* (Budapest: Argumentum, 1998), pp. 7–18.
[109] Places of origin and areas of settlement of immigrants in twelfth- to thirteenth-century Hungary: Pauler, *Magyar nemzet*, vol. I: pp. 341–5; Székely, *Magyarország története*, vol. I, pt. 2: pp. 1092–1105. On *hospes* privileges: Emma Lederer, 'A legrégebbi magyar iparososztály kialakulása', *Századok* (1927–8), pp. 510–28; Bolla, *Jogilag egységes*, pp. 87–8; Fügedi, 'Középkori magyar városprivilégiumok', pp. 43–73; Szűcs, *Utolsó Árpádok*, pp. 34–5, 174–6, 272–3; Gyula Kristó, 'Öt pondust fizetők és várhospesek', *AUSz Acta Historica* 92 (1991): pp. 25–35; András Kubinyi, 'A királyi várospolitika tükröződése a magyar királyi oklevelek arengáiban', in *Eszmetörténeti Tanulmányok a Magyar Középkorról*, ed. György Székely (Budapest: Akadémiai Kiadó, 1984), pp. 275–91; Erik Fügedi, *Koldúló barátok, polgárok, nemesek: tanulmányok a magyar középkorról* (Budapest: Magvető Kiadó, 1981), pp. 398–418; László Solymosi, 'Hospeskiváltság 1275-ből', in *Tanulmányok Veszprém megye múltjából*, ed. László Kredics (Veszprém: Veszprém megyei levéltár, 1984), pp. 17–100; Jenő Szűcs, 'The Peoples of Medieval Hungary', in *Ethnicity and Society in Hungary*, ed. Ferenc Glatz (Budapest: Institute of History of the Hungarian Academy of Sciences, 1990), pp. 11–20.

At the Gate of Christendom

groups preserved their own customs and laws. This practice was continued after the settlement of the tribal alliance in Hungary, where they mingled with a local population of Slavs. In the first centuries of the Hungarian settlement, the old nomad momentum was still prevalent.

From the eleventh century it was coupled with a new Christian rhetoric of welcoming foreigners.[110] Immigrants did not receive charters of privileges, but retained their laws and customs. It was from the late twelfth century that written guarantees were given to immigrants. Numerous privileges survive from the thirteenth century, allowing for a comparison of *hospes* privileges. Erik Fügedi called medieval Hungary 'a land of guests',[111] and it has often been emphasized that a flow of foreigners into the kingdom characterized the Hungarian Middle Ages. A text incorporated into the fourteenth-century Hungarian chronicle lists the foreigners who arrived in Hungary this way: 'Czechs, Poles, Greeks, Spaniards, Ishmaelites or Saracens, Pechenegs, Armenians, Saxons, Thuringians, those from Meissen and the Rhine, Cumans and Latins'.[112] Immigrants included knights, city-dwellers and peasants; the process of their immigration and their eventual legal position differed.

Knights usually arrived either alone or in the retinue of a queen, as Hungarian kings almost always married foreign princesses who arrived with their own servants, attendants and courtiers. Many of them established families and were assimilated into the nobility. Out of approximately fifty aristocratic clans of the thirteenth to fifteenth centuries, about fifteen originated as descendants of foreign knights. Usually, by the third generation, these families could claim membership amongst the highest nobility, the barons, who were appointed to the highest public offices.[113] Their legal status thus became one with the group into which they were assimilated, the nobility. They arrived individually, and did not find a group of their countrymen endowed with privileges to join. Nor had they any incentive to try to form such a group; as it was impossible to attain a higher status than that of a noble, they did not aspire to a special legal status. For example, an Aragonese knight, Simon, showed his valour in the defence of Hungary against the Mongols. He received several estates from the king in recognition of his service. He himself was sometimes called Hispanus in the documents, denoting his Iberian back-

---

[110] Examples in the *Libellus* attributed to St István and the *Lives* of Sts István and László I: *SRH*, vol. II: pp. 624–5, 378–9, 387, 396, 398–9, 518.

[111] Erik Fügedi, 'Das mittelalterliche Königreich Ungarn als Gastland', in *Kings, Bishops*, no. VIII; Erik Fügedi, 'A befogadó: a középkori magyar királyság', *Történelmi Szemle* (1979, no. 2): pp. 355–76.

[112] Mályusz, *V. István-kori Gesta*, p. 63; *SRH*, vol. I: p. 303 (based on a mid-thirteenth-century text): 'Bohemi, Poloni, Greci, Ispani, Hismahelite seu Saraceni, Bessi, Armeni, Saxones, Turingi, Misnenses et Renenses, Cumani, Latini'. [113] Fügedi, 'A befogadó', pp. 367–8.

ground. His sons, however, lost this designation; it did not become the label of a legal group. Instead, they were simply called nobles.[114] Simon and his descendants were absorbed into the group whose social rank they shared.

Masses of settlers came from many lands: Moravian, Polish, Czech and other Slavic immigrants, who were often not distinguished from one another in charters but called *Sclavi*,[115] arrived as well as people from French, Walloon, German and Italian areas. Numerically the most important groups were of German origin, called *Saxones* if they came from southern German areas or *Theutonici* if they came from northern territories, and the so-called *Latini*.[116] *Latinus* was a collective term, designating people who came from Flanders, from French or from Italian territories.[117] The immigration of *Latini* began with the arrival of French monks at the end of the eleventh century, and continued with the settlement of knights and then of larger masses of people. These immigrants arrived in several waves, and their ultimate destiny in terms of legal status depended on whether or not they constituted lasting groups. Those who did retained a defined legal position. Others were assimilated into the group corresponding to their social rank. *Latini*, *Saxones* and *Theutonici* retained these designations and the corresponding legal status for generations because they arrived *en masse* and could settle down together. Their communities took diverse forms: they moved into villages and cities or settled in territorial units.

Peasants were often recruited by appointed settlers to create villages and till the land. They were given *hospes* privileges that granted them freedom of movement, determined their dues, and in 'lesser' (civil) cases allowed them juridical autonomy, although they remained under the jurisdiction of their lord. City-dwellers were often attracted in organized groups, for example by contracts to mine. Germans either moved into already existing cities, in some cases eventually taking over the leading role, such as in Buda, or founded new towns, especially in the north of the country, where German merchants used the capital they had accumulated through trade to finance mining operations. These German towns, unlike those established in Slavic lands, where a German city remained the court of appeal for the new foundation, did not adopt the laws of a city from their mother country, nor did they

---

[114] *MZsO*, vol. I: pp. 8–10, no. 11 (*RA*, no. 443); *CD* vol. IV, pt. 1: pp. 274–5 (MOL DL 255; *RA*, no. 732); vol. VI, pt. 2: p. 229.
[115] József Szalay, 'Városaink nemzetiségi viszonyai a XIII. században', *Századok* 14 (1880): pp. 533–57, see p. 555.   [116] Fügedi, 'A befogadó', p. 376.
[117] Mihály Auner, 'Latinus', *Századok* 50 (1916): pp. 28–41; Erik Fügedi, 'Városok kialakulása Magyarországon', in *Kolduló barátok*, pp. 311–35, see pp. 324–5.

keep their legal connections to such a city. In Hungary, their rights were set out in the charter of privileges given by the king, and they had right of appeal to the king. Rights such as paying taxes 'more theutonicorum' were received by non-Germans as well.[118] Communities of *Latini* lived in separate quarters of existing towns. They did not keep a filiation to the place of their origin either, but lived according to the legal framework provided by their local charter of privileges. Again, they received their privileges from the Hungarian kings. Although they did have well-defined duties and obligations, their communities were not isolated from the rest of the population, but allowed others to settle in their midst.[119]

During the thirteenth century, there was a tendency to create territorial units out of privileged groups or create one collective legal category for scattered groups. Thus privileges of the city-dwelling *hospites* of Fehérvár were granted to other cities. The formation of geographical areas with their own privileges in Transylvania and the county of Szepes was linked to German settlement. Excellent source material survives in the form of charters of privileges, the most famous being King András II's charter to the *Saxones* of Szeben in 1224 (the so-called *Andreanum*). The privileges of these territorial communities consisted of economic and legal rights. Of the former, free landholding, exemption from customs, and the payment of a set amount of tax are the most notable. The *hospites* also received immunity from the jurisdiction of the county's *ispán*, could elect their own judges, and were under the jurisdiction of the king or his representative. They could even choose their own priests and practise Christianity in their own language.[120]

Hospes privileges to immigrants who formed their own communities or geographical units under royal jurisdiction included several or all of the following elements: they had a separate jurisdiction, independent of the county; they were under the authority of judges elected from their own ranks on the lower levels, and of a royal dignitary appointed for this purpose, or sometimes of the king himself, on a higher level. They lived in their own territories under their own administration; they usually had a separate system of taxation, sometimes paying unique types of taxes, and they often had ecclesiastical autonomy at a lower level, through the

---

[118] Szalay, 'Városaink', p. 534. András Kubinyi, 'Németek és nem-németek a középkori magyar királyság városaiban', *Internationales Kulturhistorisches Symposion Mogersdorf 1994* (Eisenstadt, 1996), pp. 145–58. [119] Fügedi, 'Városok kialakulása'; Szalay, 'Városaink', p. 555.
[120] On territorial *hospes* privileges: József Deér, *Pogány magyarság, keresztény magyarság* (Budapest: Királyi Magyar Egyetemi Nyomda, 1938; repr. Budapest: Holnap, 1993), pp. 187–218; Kristó, *Magyar nemzet*, pp. 232–7. The *Andreanum*: RA, no. 413. Cf. on territorial/personal law in the early Middle Ages: Patrick Amory, 'The Meaning and Purpose of Ethnic Terminology in the Burgundian Laws', *Early Medieval Europe* 2 (1993): pp. 1–28.

The legal position of Hungary's non-Christian population

election of their priests. Finally, they sent their own military units to serve the king.[121]

This cursory examination of the legal structures of Hungarian society shows that even though society began to be more hierarchically stratified – several groups dissolving into the unifying categories of 'nobility' or 'peasantry' – it was still largely cellular in the thirteenth century, with a diversity of groups having their own duties and privileges. This was true for the whole of society, but 'guests' were even more likely to form communities that had a distinct legal status. Nevertheless, this legal structure is not to be confused with the fluidity of social categories that characterized early medieval western Europe; in thirteenth-century Hungary, group statuses were highly defined, usually by written privileges. Many Christian groups, whether they lived in villages and cities or had their own territorial units, had *hospes* status, and their duties and rights were put into writing and guaranteed by the king. Thus these communities had both their internal legal autonomy and a well-defined legal position compared to the rest of the population.

It is clear, then, that the legal status of Hungary's non-Christians was not extraordinary, but in keeping with the status of many other groups. Indeed, in some instances they were referred to as *hospites* in the sources: the Cumans are said to be welcomed by King Béla because kings have to honour *hospites*, and *hospes* status is evoked in relation to Teka when he sells land.[122] Moreover, although Jews were designated as *Judei*, Muslims as *Ismaelite* or *Sarraceni* and Cumans as *Cumani*, the legal categories thereby created were not distinctive, but fit in with the usage of *Latini* or

---

[121] E.g. *HO*, vol. v: pp. 60–2, no. 49 (*RA*, no. 2973). Gyula Szekfű, 'A magyarság és kisebbségei a középkorban: Vázlatok egy hazai kisebbségtörténethez'; 'Még egyszer középkori kisebbségeinkről'; and 'A nemzetiségi kérdés rövid története', in *Állam és nemzet: Tanulmányok a nemzetiségi kérdésről* (Budapest: Magyar Szemle Társaság, 1942), pp. 39–53, 54–68, 85–177 respectively. Elemér Mályusz asserted that, prior to the thirteenth century, Hungarian kings wished to scatter immigrants, forcing them to settle in small groups in different places, in order to create a unified country whose inhabitants spoke one language. According to him, this was replaced in the thirteenth century by a conscious royal policy of settling large groups together, which was the kings' response to the breaking up of royal domains, in order to keep these groups under royal (instead of noble) rule. It should be noted that Mályusz was writing in 1939, at the height of Hungarian nationalism and territorial revisionism, and his essay constitutes part of the debate of his times. Elemér Mályusz, 'A középkori magyar nemzetiségi politika', *Századok* 73 (1939): pp. 257–94, 385–448; Elemér Mályusz, 'Le problème de l'assimilation au moyen âge', *Nouvelle Revue de Hongrie* 64 (1941): pp. 291–301. Also his lectures, published posthumously: *Népiségtörténet* (Budapest: MTA Történettudományi Intézete, 1994). Mályusz based his explanation of early royal policy on the fact that the names of non-Hungarian communities are attested in the names of many villages scattered throughout various parts of the kingdom. As Szekfű pointed out, this phenomenon was simply the result of different waves of immigration, not of conscious royal policy of settlement. Szekfű, 'Még egyszer', pp. 58–9.

[122] *SRH*, vol. II: p. 559 (see above for text); *MZsO*, vol. I: p. 13, no. 14 (*CD*, vol. III, pt. 2: p. 271; *RA*, no. 495) 'dictus Theha sicut hospes in revocacione predicte terre . . . interesse non potest'.

Theutonici. Non-Christian status could differ in some details from that of other groups, but the fact itself that non-Christian groups had their own privileges did not distinguish them from the rest of the *hospes* groups. That is, they did not have a separate legal status *because* they were non-Christians. In such a cellular society non-Christians could easily have their own niche, their legal status allowing them protection by the king (although authority in matters of justice and taxation could, it seems, be delegated in some cases) as well as internal legal autonomy. The legal frameworks were the same as for Christians. In the case of Jews and Muslims, this automatically had religious connotations, because both Jewish and Muslim law was inseparable from religion. Jews and Muslims can be compared with the category of distinct and privileged village or town communities, which had a collective status, while the Cumans soon gained a territorial status. The papacy could not accept the legal status accorded to these non-Christian groups (see chapter 5). From the papal point of view, only integration via conversion or separation of non-Christians was acceptable. Thus from this perspective the legal position of Hungary's non-Christians was inadmissible in a Christian kingdom, because it did not fit into either category. The real difference, therefore, in the development of the legal position of Hungary's non-Christian groups, as compared to other privileged inhabitants of the kingdom, was determined by their religion and the ensuing ecclesiastical intervention.

Chapter 4

NON-CHRISTIANS IN HUNGARIAN ECONOMY AND SOCIETY

Non-Christians living within Christendom played a variety of economic and social roles in medieval Europe. Well-known examples include Jewish participation in trade and money-lending, and Muslim involvement in agriculture. 'Pagan' populations rarely existed within Christian kingdoms by the Central Middle Ages, but those neighbouring Christian countries were sometimes drawn into other than hostile relationships with the Christian world: these took the form of trade and military help. Non-Christian roles within Christendom were largely determined by the possibilities and restrictions created by the Christian majority. They were partially linked to Christian views of what was and was not a proper role for those of another religion, and partly connected to local social and economic development. Ideology and economic conditions did not necessarily form a coherent whole. Tensions and conflict were resolved in a variety of ways. Similarly, the roles non-Christians played in Hungary are indicators of the social and economic life of the kingdom, not simply of royal or ecclesiastical policy. They are one key to the understanding of the position of these groups in Christian society. This position was not determined solely by Christian ideological arguments for exclusion and separation, but manifested itself in, and was influenced by, the concrete roles of each group.[1]

To some extent social and economic roles depended on numbers. In some areas of conquest, the Christian elite depended on peasant labour provided by local non-Christians. Thus early Reconquest Valencia relied heavily on its Muslim population to farm the land and keep the irrigation system functioning; resettled Muslims on Mallorca also cultivated the soil. Elsewhere, small minorities could fill important cultural roles, like the Jews in Iberia. Non-Christian military service for Christian lords

---

[1] On the differences of socio-cultural and socio-economic integration: Bronislaw Geremek, *Les marginaux parisiens aux XIVe et XVe siècles* (Paris: Flammarion, 1976).

could involve a small group, like the Muslims of Lucera under Frederick II, or a large one, like the native population in Livonia fighting on the side of the Sword-Brothers against the bishop of Leal.[2] In Hungary, non-Christians had primarily non-agricultural functions in society. Their roles can be divided into two major groups: those related to the economic functioning of the kingdom and those related to military matters. Jews and some Muslims were primarily involved in the former, while other Muslims and the Cumans were prominent in the latter. There was no cultural 'golden age' in Hungary, produced by Christian–non-Christian interaction. Nor, contrary to prevalent views, were non-Christian roles economically so essential as to produce a royal policy of toleration.

TRADE

Both Muslim and Jewish merchants were active in Hungary from the foundation of the kingdom. The first signs of their activity refer to long-distance trade. Chasdai ibn Shaprut (mid-tenth century) mentioned Jews in Hungary who were in contact with Rus'.[3] Ibrāhīm ibn Ya'qūb mentioned Jews and Muslims from Hungary in his account about traders in Prague (c. 965).[4] From the same period, evidence for such Jewish trade survives from Bohemia and Poland as well.[5] These merchants traded in slaves, which gave rise to ecclesiastical and papal objections and prohibitions, especially because it gave immediate power to non-Christians over Christians – a situation unacceptable to an establishment that stressed the divinely ordained submission of 'infidels' to Christians.[6]

The first king to prohibit Jewish trading in Christian slaves in Hungary was King Kálmán.[7] A document concerning slaves bought from Jews in

---

[2] Thomas F. Glick, *Irrigation and Society in Medieval Valencia* (Cambridge, Mass.: Belknap Press, 1970). Abulafia, *Mediterranean Emporium*, pp. 57–60; Abulafia, 'Monarchs and Minorities'; Christiansen, *Northern Crusades*, p. 123.

[3] Golb and Pritsak, *Khazarian Hebrew Documents*, p. 92; Aleksander Gieysztor, 'Les Juifs et leurs activités économiques en Europe orientale', in *Gli Ebrei nell'Alto Medioevo*, 2 vols., Settimane di Studio del Centro Italiano di Studi sull'Alto Medioevo 26 (Spoleto, 1980), vol. I: pp. 489–522, p. 507.

[4] Ibn Ya'qūb, 'Relatio', p. 146. See also *Encyclopaedia of Islam*, vol. V: pp. 1013–14.

[5] Marsina, *Codex Diplomaticus*, vol. I: p. 38, no. 41; Gieysztor 'Juifs', p. 509; Lewicki, 'Sources hébraïques', p. 232.

[6] Baron, *Social*, vol. IV: p. 9 (eighth century); *ibid.*, vol. IX: p. 25 (twelfth–thirteenth centuries). Papal letters against Jews holding Christian slaves survive from the sixth century: Simonsohn, *Apostolic See Documents*, nos. 10, 11, 12, 15, 22, 24. Göckenjan, *Hilfsvölker*, pp. 72–6, on Jewish and Muslim slave-merchants as well as on slave-holding in Hungary. On papal injunctions against Jews trading in Christian slaves during the Middle Ages: Simonsohn, *Apostolic See History*, pp. 158–63.

[7] About 1100: 'Nullus Judeus Christianum mancipium emere vel vendere audeat': Bak, *Laws*, p. 31. The king repeated the same stipulation in his statutes concerning Jews with the addition that all Christian slaves, whatever their language or place of origin (that is, not only Hungarian Christians), were to be included in this prohibition; *ibid.*, p. 68. He did not mention Muslim slave-merchants.

Non-Christians in Hungarian economy and society

Hungary survives in the form of the copy of a will written around 1150. The testator left manumitted slaves to the family monastery. That he had bought these slaves from Jews was proven by the names of Jewish witnesses to the sale, listed in the will. The date of the sale itself (though obviously prior to 1150) is unknown.[8] Scholars who analysed this document all agreed that the sale of these slaves had been carried out according to the law of King Kálmán, who ordered that trade transactions between Jews and Christians be recorded in a charter (see below).[9] Yet they remained curiously silent on the irony of such a hypothesis: if the parties in question obeyed Kálmán's law in setting their transaction into writing, how is it that they disregarded the king's injunction that no Jew should dare to buy or sell a slave? There are two possible explanations. Either the Jewish seller was obeying Kálmán's law that 'no Jew should . . . retain any [Christian slaves] in his service; and he shall lose those which he has now, if he does not sell them in the allotted time',[10] that is, he was selling his own Christian slaves instead of being a slave-merchant; or the law of Kálmán was disregarded and the sale of the slaves was recorded not out of a spirit of submission to royal decrees but out of other considerations, perhaps in the interest of the monastery to which they were donated.

In 1233 the prohibition of slave-holding still figured among the papal demands to the Hungarian king; Muslims were mentioned together with Jews as having Christian slaves.[11] Slave-holding itself was only gradually disappearing in Hungary from the end of the thirteenth century onwards, so Jews and Muslims may have still held Christian slaves in 1233 (Abū Hāmid in the mid-twelfth century recorded that he bought slaves in Hungary for his own use); yet this reference is no longer connected with the organized trade of slaves by non-Christians.[12] The consolidation of new kingdoms in central and eastern Europe during the eleventh century

---

[8] László Fejérpataky, 'A Gutkeled-Biblia', *Magyar Könyvszemle* n.s. 1 (1892–3): pp. 15–16; *MZsO*, vol. X: p. 43, analysed by Sándor Scheiber, *MZsO*, vol. IX: pp. 7–8; Bernát L. Kumorovitz, 'A középkori magyar "magánjogi" írásbeliség első korszaka (XI–XII. század)', *Századok* 97 (1963): pp. 1–31; German version: 'Die erste Epoche der ungarischen privatrechtlichen Schriftlichkeit im Mittelalter', *Etudes Historiques* (Budapest: Akadémiai Kiadó, 1960), pp. 253–90. These manumitted slaves became bondsmen.

[9] Scheiber, in *MZsO*, vol. IX: p. 8; and László Mezey, 'A latin írás magyarországi történetéből', *Magyar Könyvszemle* 82 (1966): pp. 1–9, 205–16, 285–304, see p. 8; Kumorovitz, 'Középkori', pp. 7–8. Bernát Kumorovitz, 'A Kálmán kori "cartula sigillata"', *Turul* 58–60 (1944–6): pp. 29–33; Kumorovitz, 'Szent László vásár-törvénye'.

[10] 'Nullus Judeus . . . [Christianum mancipium] in suo servitio tenere sinatur; nunc vero qui habet, si interea datis sibi induciis non vendat, amittat'. Bak, *Laws*, p. 31.

[11] MOL DF 248771 (Marsina, *Codex Diplomaticus*, vol. I: pp. 295–58, no. 407) and confirmation in *VMH*, p. 117, no. CXCVIII. See chapter 5 on King András II's oath of Bereg (1233).

[12] Lajos Tardy, *A tatárországi rabszolgakereskedelem és a magyarok a XIII–XV. században*, Kőrösi Csoma Kiskönyvtár 17 (Budapest: Akadémiai Kiadó, 1980), p. 69; Simonsohn, *Apostolic See History*, p. 167; *Abu-Hámid*, p. 58.

led to a decline of a supply of slaves from the region; the later medieval slave-trade shifted to other areas.[13] The emerging kingdoms offered other occupations in trade and finance.[14] Even in the tenth century, slaves had not been the only merchandise traded by Jewish and Muslim merchants; ibn Yaʿqūb mentioned fur and lead as well. Jewish merchants mentioned in the customs tariff of Raffelstetten (on the Bavarian–Bohemian border) in the early tenth century may have traded in eastern goods as well as in slaves.[15] Muslim trade was important in the earlier Middle Ages. One branch of the trade between the Muslim east and the west probably linked Hungary to Prague and Kiev until about the late tenth century, as attested by Arab *dirhems* and works of art found in Hungarian tombs.[16]

Later on, Jews continued to participate in developing international trade, while Muslims were active within Hungary. From the mid-eleventh century on, the long-distance trade route connecting the German Empire to Kiev passed through Hungary. Jewish merchants were active in this trade. Jewish merchants returning to Regensburg from Kiev travelled through Esztergom in the late eleventh century. These merchants employed non-Jews as well, who travelled with them.[17] Trade between German territories and Hungary was also carried on by Jewish merchants travelling between the two areas. The *responsa* of Yehudah ha-Kohen, rabbi of Mainz (d. *c.* 1070), mention Jews trading between Mainz and Hungary. They bought goods in German territories for sale in Hungary, and vice versa.[18] Several Jewish settlements in Hungary were established on twelfth-century trade routes between Austria and

---

[13] Olivia Remie Constable, *Trade and Traders in Muslim Spain: The Commercial Realignment of the Iberian Peninsula 900–1500* (Cambridge: Cambridge University Press, 1994), pp. 204–6; Verlinden, 'Esclavage et ethnographie'; for the origin of slaves see Charles Verlinden, *L'esclavage dans l'Europe médiévale*, 2 vols. (Bruges: Rijksuniversiteit te Gent, 1955–77); Tardy, *Tatárországi rabszolgakereskedelem*, chapters III–IV.   [14] Gieysztor, 'Juifs', p. 522.

[15] Marsina, *Codex Diplomaticus*, vol. I: p. 38, no. 41: 'theloneum solvant tam de mancipiis, quam de aliis rebus'; Zsigmond Pál Pach, 'The Transcarpathian Routes of Levantine Trade in the Middle Ages', in *Quand la montagne aussi a une histoire: mélanges offerts à Jean-François Bergier*, ed. Martin Körner and François Walter (Bern, Stuttgart and Vienna: Paul Haupt, 1996), pp. 237–46, esp. pp. 237–8.

[16] Székely, 'Contacts', pp. 60–9 analyses the evidence for this early medieval trade. István Gedai, 'A magyar numizmatika keleti vonatkozásai', *Magyar Numizmatikai Társaság Évkönyve* (1972): pp. 189–93; Csanád Bálint, 'Az európai dirhem-forgalom néhány kérdése', *Századok* 116 (1982): pp. 3–32.

[17] Kohn, *Zsidók*, pp. 405–8; Kupfer and Lewicki, *Źródła*, pp. 65, 69; dating to the end of the eleventh c. by Sándor Scheiber, *Héber kódexmaradványok magyarországi kötéstáblákban: A középkori magyar zsidóság könyvkultúrája* (Budapest: A Magyar Izraeliták Országos Képviselete, 1969), p. 104. Gieysztor, 'Juifs'; Pach 'Transcarpathian Routes'.

[18] Kohn, *Héber*, pp. 47–8, documents V/2–3. Lewicki, 'Sources hébraïques', p. 232; Kupfer and Lewicki, *Źródła*, pp. 39–40; Irving A. Agus, *The Heroic Age of Franco-German Jewry: The Jews of Germany and France of the Tenth and Eleventh Centuries, the Pioneers and Builders of Town-Life, Town-Government and Institutions* (New York: Yeshiva University Press, 1969), pp. 27, 102–3, 115; Agus, *Urban Civilization*, vol. II: pp. 88–93.

Hungary. This indicates trading with Austrian Jews of Völkermarkt, Judenburg and Pettau.[19] It seems from the *responsa* that the Jewish trade between Hungary and neighbouring areas was based on informal partnerships or 'friendships', a form of Jewish trade association also known from the Cairo Genizah and western European *responsa*.[20]

Muslim merchants continued to participate in Hungary's economic life after their early medieval international trade routes ceased to function. The Synod of Szabolcs in 1092 mentioned 'merchants whom they call Ishmaelites', and a trade route leading from Szeged to Bátmonostor was named after them.[21] The name of the road, 'Calizutu', is a combination of 'káliz', that is, Khwarezmien Muslims, and the Old Hungarian form of 'út', road. It was probably related to the role Muslims played in the administration of salt production and sale, as Szeged was a royal salt depot.[22] Many of the known Muslim settlements were close to internal trade routes of the kingdom.[23] A late-twelfth-century charter explicitly mentioned Ishmaelites among those having to pay market and port customs duties, presumably because they carried on internal trade; a thirteenth-century charter referred to the market of a Muslim village.[24] The Muslim community of Pest, which provided King András II with important revenues, most likely did so by its involvement in trade; Pest was a port for Danubian trade.[25]

Policies implemented by eleventh-century Hungarian kings and synods to strengthen the newly implanted Christian religion in the country, such as moving the weekly market day from Sunday to Saturday when observant Jews could not work, and prohibiting Jews from working on Sundays, may have adversely affected Jewish activities.[26] Yet the first

---

[19] Kubinyi, 'Magyarországi zsidóság', pp. 4–5; Kubinyi, 'Németek és nem-németek', p. 146, n. 8; Joseph Babad, 'The Jews in Medieval Carinthia: A Contribution to the History of the Jews in the Alpine Countries of Europe', *Historia Judaica* 7 (1945): pp. 13–28, 193–204, see pp. 16–17; Wilhelm Wadl, *Geschichte der Juden in Kärnten im Mittelalter*, 2nd edn (Klagenfurt: Kärtner Landesarchiv, 1992), pp. 18–20.

[20] S. D. Goitein, *A Mediterranean Society: The Jewish Communities of the Arab World as Portrayed in the Documents of the Cairo Geniza*, vol. I: *Economic Foundations* (Berkeley and Los Angeles: University of California Press, 1967), pp. 164–6; Agus, *Heroic Age*, pp. 121–31.

[21] 'De negotiatoribus quos ysmaelitas appellant': Bak, *Laws*, p. 57; 'Caluzwt' (1185) and 'viam que vocatur Caluzutu' (1208) cited by Györffy, 'A csatlakozott népek', p. 53; Székely, 'Contacts', p. 59.

[22] András Kubinyi, 'Urbanisation in the East-Central Parts of Medieval Hungary', in *Towns*, pp. 103–49, see pp. 112–13; Göckenjan, *Hilfsvölker*, pp. 59–66.

[23] Szűcs, 'Két történelmi', p. 15.

[24] *CD*, vol. II: pp. 303–4 (*RA*, no. 168, survives in a fifteenth-century copy); 'forum de villa Sarachenorum que vocatur Curlach' (Curlach, Bács county): *TF*, vol. I: p. 217 (corrects the text of *CD*, vol. IV, pt. 1: p. 109; *RA*, no. 637).   [25] Gerevich, *Towns*, p. 27.

[26] The change in the weekly market day took place during the reign of Béla I (1060–3). It was recorded in the Hungarian chronicle and the text was incorporated into fourteenth-century chronicle versions: Domanovszky, 'Chronici Hungarici', in *SRH*, vol. I: p. 358. Synod of Szabolcs (1092): 'Si in die dominico aut aliis maioribus festivitatibus iudeum laborantem aliquis invenerit . . . cum quibus instrumentis laboraverit, illa amittat.' Bak, *Laws*, p. 59.

extensive regulation of local trade transactions between Jews and Christians appeared under King Kálmán (1095–1116). It was not supplanted, at least by any explicit set of rules, until the mid-thirteenth century. These remarkable regulations stipulated, in a country where both literacy and its uses were very limited, that every sale between a Jew and a Christian should be recorded in a charter and sealed with the seals of both buyer and seller (*cartula sigillata*).[27] This document was to be produced in the event of later questions about the validity of the sale. Both Jewish and Christian witnesses were to be present at the sale, and their names had to be included in the document.[28] To what extent this law was put into practice is impossible to determine: if they were drawn up, these documents intended for private use not only perished through war and other disasters but were also destroyed when they ceased to have any importance to their owners. It is also clear that these rules aimed at the sale of goods of significant value and not everyday local market transactions.

The important mid-thirteenth-century privileges granted to the Jews by Béla IV regulated Jewish–Christian trade as well. Across the kingdom, Jews were granted unimpeded travel, and Jewish merchants were to pay the same customs as citizens of the city where the merchant resided.[29] This meant that Jewish trade was not hindered by any special duties or customs. Moreover, the privilege granted protection to the Jews travelling in the country. This guaranteed equality to Jewish merchants living in or passing through Hungary, engaged in internal or external trade. In 1279 the papal legate tried to force Jews to wear distinguishing signs and prohibited the Christians from trading with Jews who did not wear this sign, but this prohibition was not enforced.[30] Thus the legal setting was favourable to Jewish trade within the kingdom. Hungarian Jewish merchants also continued to trade in Czech and German lands. For example, a mid-thirteenth-century *responsum* mentioned salted fish transported from Hungary to Austria.[31] No thirteenth-century regulations of Muslim trade exist, although Muslims may have continued to participate in local trade.

---

[27] On literacy in Hungary: Székely, *Magyarország története*, vol. 1: part 2: pp. 1392–1406. In England, financial transactions involving Jews were to be put into writing only from the end of the twelfth century: Mundill, *England's Jewish Solution*, pp. 5–8.

[28] Bak, *Laws*, p. 68; MZsO, vol. 1: p. 4, no. 7; Kumorovitz, 'Középkori'; see also note 8 above; Ladislaus Mezey, 'Anfänge der Privaturkunde in Ungarn und der Glaubwürdige Orte', *Archiv für Diplomatik* 18 (1972): pp. 290–302.

[29] Büchler, 'Judenprivilegium', p. 143; Béla used *tributum*, the word used in Hungary for 'tax', 'toll', 'customs', instead of Frederick's *muta*.

[30] Romualdus Hube, ed., *Antiquissimae Constitutiones Synodales Provinciae Gneznensis* (St Petersburg, 1856), p. 160. See chapter 5 on clothing regulations.

[31] Kupfer and Lewicki, *Źródła*, p. 212; Isaac ben Moses, *Sefer Or Zaru'a*, vol. 1: p. 141; Büchler, *Zsidók*, p. 24. Gyula Wellesz, 'Izsák B. Mózes Or Zarua és az esztergomi zsidók', *Magyar Zsidó Szemle* 20, no. 2 (1903): pp. 148–50, see p. 150.

Non-Christians in Hungarian economy and society

No documents exist as to the volume of Jewish or Muslim trade in Hungary, nor do we know much about the nature of the merchandise they traded in the thirteenth century. There are some indications that Jews in medieval Poland were engaged in both long-distance trade of luxury goods, and retail trade of textiles, minerals and animals during this period; the situation in Hungary may have been similar.[32] There is a text concerning a merchant in the employment of the younger king István in 1264.[33] It is an account written for the king to show the merchandise delivered, the payments made, and the balance of 749.5 marks that the king owed the merchant. The latter supplied a great variety of luxury goods: textiles, including cloth from Flanders, silk from Italy and purple from Asia, jewels, and ecclesiastical vessels. The last editor and commentator of this text, László Zolnay, maintained that the merchant can be identified with Welven, one of the known Jewish lessees of the treasury. No means of identification of the merchant other than his name are related in the text. The name in the document, however, is 'Syr Wullam' or 'Wilamus/Wylamus', and while corrupted, all the variations of this particular name point to its bearer as a William (or one of its equivalents), and not to the Jewish 'Voluelinus, Welven, Velvin' (probably 'Wolf').[34] Whether Wilamus was a foreign or a Hungarian merchant cannot be known. It is certain that he resided for long periods in Hungary, since payments to him were made in several places in Hungary, and that he must have known the king and had previous transactions with him.[35] He must also have been rich enough to provide credit to the king. He also loaned money to Hungarian barons in return for pawns. Jews often made such loans, but they were by no means the only ones to do so, and therefore this cannot be a decisive argument in favour of Wilamus's Jewish origin.[36] For these reasons Zolnay's identification is very dubious; it remains an open question whether Wilamus was Jewish.

---

[32] Bernard D. Weinryb, *The Jews of Poland: A Social and Economic History of the Jewish Community in Poland from 1100 to 1800* (Philadelphia: Jewish Publication Society of America, 1973), pp. 64–5.

[33] First published by Giovanni Soranzo, 'Acquisti e debiti di Bela IV. Re d'Ungheria', *Aevum. Rassegna di scienze storiche, linguistiche e filologiche publicata per cura della Facoltà di Lettere dell'Università Cattolica del Sacro Cuore*, anno 8, fasc. 2–3 (Milan, 1934), pp. 343–56. László Zolnay, 'István ifjabb király számadása 1264-ből', in *Budapest Régiségei*, no. 21 (Budapest: Budapesti Történeti Múzeum, 1964), pp. 79–111, re-published Dénes Huszti's corrected version of the text, dated it, and analysed the personal and topographical names.

[34] Zolnay, 'István', pp. 108–10. Other identification of 'syr Wilamus': Guillaume de Saint Omer (1209–42), son-in-law of Béla IV (Soranzo, cited in Zolnay, 'István', p. 83; impossible if Zolnay's dating is correct); a Venetian merchant (Huszti, cited in *ibid.*, p. 108).

[35] *Ibid.*, pp. 80–2, 103–6. Analysis of information on 'Syr Wilamus' from the document: pp. 108–11.

[36] Zolnay argued that only Jews made such loans, but he disregarded the evidence to the contrary. See Emma Lederer, *A középkori pénzüzletek története Magyarországon (1000–1458)* (Budapest: Kovács Nyomda, 1932), p. 74.

FINANCIAL FUNCTIONS AND OFFICE-HOLDING

The best-documented economic role of non-Christians in thirteenth-century Hungary is the financial one. Specific functions included money-lending and leasing positions connected with the royal treasury such as money-minting and tax-collecting.

Money-lending

Money-lending, a medieval occupation traditionally associated with the Jews of Europe, was practised in Hungary as well. Just as elsewhere in Europe, however, Jews were not the only ones engaged in this occupation: Christians, and especially monasteries, also lent money, often against land as security.[37] Loans between Jews and Christians were first regulated by King Kálmán. Whether a Jew lent to a Christian or a Christian to a Jew, they were to have witnesses, and the borrower was to have a pledge. For a value over 3 *pensae* they were also to put the deal in writing and affix their seals to the charter.[38] The formulation is telling: the loan was described not as a sum of money, but as 'the value of' over 120 denars, and there was no mention of a rate of interest or conditions of repayment. Given the small volume of charter production and the mostly agricultural economy in early twelfth-century Hungary, it is certain that this was not a regulation necessitated by a money economy. It was not money-lending with which the king was concerned, but the interaction between Jews and Christians. The law aimed at minimizing the possibility of conflict and ensuring that eventual disputes would be settled.

Jewish money-lending at a rate of interest in return for sureties was regulated by the mid-thirteenth-century charter of privileges granted to the Jews by Béla IV. It specified the terms of money-lending between Jews and Christians. A Jew could clear himself by oath if the Christian borrower asserted that the sum of money lent to him was smaller than that claimed by the Jewish money-lender, or if the Christian, despite denials by the Jew, maintained that he had given a surety. If it was a Jewish lender who claimed that a Christian owed him money, lent against a surety, and the Christian denied this, the Christian could clear himself by taking an oath. Jewish money-lenders were allowed to accept any object as a pawn except blood-stained clothes. This permission even included

---

[37] E.g. *Hazai Oklevéltár*, p. 74, no. 65, p. 94, no. 87; *Budapest történetének okleveles emlékei*, vol. 1: *1148–1301*, ed. Dezső Csánki and Albert Gárdonyi (Budapest: A Székesfőváros Kiadása, 1936), p. 176, no. 160. Lederer, *Középkori pénzüzletek*, pp. 15–17, 52.

[38] Bak, *Laws*, p. 68. *Pensa* was a money of account, 1 pensa was equivalent to 40 denars: 'pénzverés', in *KMTL*.

Non-Christians in Hungarian economy and society

estates of nobles and ecclesiastical clothes, but with the stipulation that the latter had to be pawned by the prelate of the church. This went against ecclesiastical prohibitions of Jews trading in Church property.[39] Jewish money-lenders were protected from unjust claims. If a Christian wanted to reclaim a pawned object saying that it had been stolen from him, but the Jew swore that he had not known this, the sum of money loaned against this object had to be repaid. Likewise, if the Jewish money-lender lost a surety by fire or theft 'known to everyone', he was cleared from further claims upon taking an oath. The privileges allowed for an interest to be charged on the interest itself, provided the borrower repaid the capital but not the interest when he redeemed the pawn. In the case of non-payment for a full year, the Jewish money-lender could sell the pawned object after bringing it to the judge and proving that the surety was not more valuable than the capital and interest combined. If the pawn was not claimed within a year after the expiration of the agreement, it became the property of the Jewish money-lender. The Jewish lender could not be forced to give the surety back on one of his holy days ('in sua feriali die'), and if the surety was taken back by force the perpetrator was to be punished.[40]

These stipulations followed with slight modifications the privileges granted to Austrian Jews by Duke Frederick in 1244. The restriction that Jewish money-lenders could accept ecclesiastical clothes as sureties only if these were pawned by the prelate did not appear in the Austrian privileges. Frederick specified that stolen property pawned to an unsuspecting Jewish money-lender could only be reclaimed upon the payment of the capital and the accrued interest. Béla demanded only the repayment of the capital. Frederick set the maximum amount of interest that could be charged; Béla omitted to regulate it. Certain variations in vocabulary also distinguished the passages in Béla's privileges from Frederick's: for example, we consistently find *pena* (*poena*) in Béla's text for *usura* in Frederick's.

The king did not blindly copy his model, but how much in the section on economic roles and privileges reflected Hungarian conditions? As

---

[39] Simonsohn, *Apostolic See History*, pp. 185–8. In Frederick's privileges 'iudeus recipere poterit ... omnia ... exceptis sanguinolentis et malefactis': Scherer, *Rechtsverhältnisse*, p. 180, who emends 'malefactis' to 'madefactis', and interprets the text as meaning bloody and wet garments: pp. 201–4. King Béla added 'vestibus': Büchler, 'Judenprivilegium', p. 142. According to Iogna-Prat, *Ordonner et exclure*, p. 280, bloody cloth mentioned in such regulations meant 'reliques eucharistiques'. The prohibition of accepting blood-stained or wet clothes as pawns appeared frequently in German laws: Kisch, *Jews*, p. 219.

[40] Büchler, 'Judenprivilegium', pp. 143–4. The clause on Jews clearing themselves from charges of accepting stolen objects occurred in privileges from the late eleventh century: Kisch, *Jews*, pp. 212–13.

discussed in chapter 3, the promulgation of the privileges was most probably prompted by Jews who arrived from Austria who formed the elite of the Hungarian Jewish communities, and the text showed their concerns and not the general situation of Jews in Hungary. None the less, the modifications point to differences in local conditions between Austria and Hungary. Thus the use of *pena* instead of *usura* as well as a lack of regulation of the maximum interest reveal different attitudes due to a less developed money economy. *Pena* was used in a type of loan secured by land. If the borrower did not repay the sum by a fixed date, he was to pay a punishment (*pena*) which replaced interest.[41] In comparison, a widespread practice of money-lending, such as in Germany, led to significantly more detailed regulations.[42] In Hungary, the activities of Jewish financiers involved with kings and nobles were much more important than urban money-lending. For example, Fredman received two villages from King László IV in lieu of payment for the loan he had provided to the king, and Teka was the guarantor in an agreement of payment between the Hungarian king and the Austrian duke in 1225.[43] Similarly, Béla's stipulation that Jews were to accept ecclesiastical clothes only if pawned by prelates may have been based on the fear that lay noble patrons of monasteries and churches would pawn ecclesiastical goods when in financial difficulties.

A well-documented and fascinating case-history of such a transaction survives from Hungary. Wid, the head of a prominent noble family, the Gutkeled, pawned the Bible of the family monastery at Csatár under his patronage to Farkas, a Jew from Vasvár, in exchange for a loan. The conditions of the loan were put into writing. It was agreed that if Wid did not repay this loan in several instalments by the dates agreed upon, Farkas could dispose of the Bible as he wished. Wid indeed failed to pay, and Farkas must have sold the valuable book, which ended up as one of the prized possessions of the monastery at Admont. Wid donated land to the monastery of Csatár in 1263 as a compensation for the lost Bible. The inner binding of the Bible preserved the inscriptions through which its history is known, a story corroborated by Wid's charter of donation.[44] Wid's charter gives the sum lent to him as 70 marks, whereas an inscription in the Bible, giving details of the terms of repayment, indicated the sum of 24.5 marks. Whether it was accrued interest that raised the original 24.5 marks to 70, or additional loans, cannot be determined. Seventy marks was a very large sum. In comparison, the average yearly revenue

[41] Lederer, *Középkori pénzüzletek*, pp. 19–21. [42] Kisch, *Jews*, pp. 217–41.
[43] Fredman: *MZsO*, vol. I: pp. 54–5, no. 31; MOL DL 105378 (*HO*, vol. VIII: p. 206, no. 162). Teka: *MZsO*, vol. I: p. 5, no. 9. Similar Jewish financiers: Babad, 'Jews in Medieval Carinthia', pp. 20–4.
[44] *MZsO*, vol. I: p. 33, no. 25; *MZsO*, vol. V, pt. 1: p. 11, no. 7. Fejérpataky, 'Gutkeled-Biblia'; *MZsO*, vol. IX: pp. 8–10. The Bible is now in Vienna, Österreichische Nationalbibliothek ser. nov. 2701–2702. Lohrmann, *Judenrecht*, p. 89.

from one unit of land (*ekeföld*) in the thirteenth century was 2.5 marks, the price of a warhorse between 10 and 15 marks.[45] The case aroused such interest that it was even used as a model in a fourteenth-century compilation for teaching purposes (only fragments survive of this codex). Whether constructed purely for didactic reasons, or based on a now lost charter of King András III, this text has the king intervening in the case many years later.[46] In this compilation, however, the Bible was pawned to a Jew not by a lay patron, but by the abbot of the monastery. This conforms to the pawning of ecclesiastical objects to Jews by clerics elsewhere in Europe: for example, in medieval London and France.[47] It should be noted that by the fourteenth century the pawning of ecclesiastical objects to Jews was not accepted by all. For example, in the mid-fourteenth century, a parish priest was accused of pawning sacerdotal dress and chalices to Jews.[48]

Money-lending on a smaller scale to people other than members of the high nobility, for example to townsmen, may have started in the thirteenth century, but no evidence of it survives prior to 1300. Even then, the first example is a loan disguised as a sale of land: the Christian seller had the option of buying the land back within a year.[49] On the other hand, a cursory investigation of fourteenth- and fifteenth-century sources reveals a growing occurrence of such money-lending, already described in unambiguous terms.[50] It is possible that more documentation of this practice survived from this period, but the rise of money-lending is not simply an impression due to an increased number of available documents. Jews were forced out of royal employment; there were no non-Christian lessees of high offices in the fourteenth and fifteenth centuries except converts.[51] At the same time they were allowed

---

[45] Bálint Hóman, *Magyar pénztörténet 1000–1325* (Budapest: MTA, 1916, repr. Budapest: Maecenas Könyvkiadó, 1991), pp. 540, 542, and 501 on price of land. Various views exist concerning the size of one *ekeföld*; 1 royal *ekeföld* (or *ekealja*, *aratrum*) was 150 royal *hold* (*iuger*), about 126 hectares: István Bogdán, 'mértékek', in *KMTL*.

[46] Géza Érszegi and László N. Szelestei, 'Fogalmazásmintákat tartalmazó tankönyv töredékei a 14. század első feléből', in *Tanulmányok a középkori magyarországi könyvkultúráról*, ed. L. N. Szelestei (Budapest: Országos Széchényi Könyvtár, 1989), pp. 297–326, see p. 318 (text; also in *MZsO*, vol. XVIII: p. 457, no. 803), and p. 302 (comments).

[47] Joe Hillaby, 'The London Jewry: William I to John', *Jewish Historical Studies* 32 (1990–2): pp. 1–44, p. 9; Jordan, *French Monarchy*, p. 31. Simonsohn, *Apostolic See History*, pp. 186–7.

[48] Jenő Házi, *Sopron szabad királyi város története*, pt 1, vol. 1 (Sopron: Székely Nyomda, 1921), pp. 102–4, no. 168.   [49] MOL DF 283482 (*MZsO*, vol. I: pp. 60–1, no. 34).

[50] *MZsO*, vol. I: pp. 66–75, 84–6, nos. 39, 40, 41, 42, 43, 44, 54, 55; Elemér Mályusz, ed., *Zsigmondkori oklevéltár*, vols. I and II (Budapest, 1951–8), nos. 1177, 1461, 2653, 3041, 3847, 4022, 4642, 4833, 4851, 4959.

[51] The most famous case is that of Imre Szerencsés (Fortunatus), *MZsO*, vol. I: pp. 330, 332–3, nos. 279, 281–2; Kohn, *Zsidók*, pp. 271–86, 387–93; Kohn, *Héber*, pp. 75–81; Kubinyi, 'Magyarországi zsidóság', pp. 23–5.

to fill necessary but despised economic roles, which was quite consistent with north-western European patterns.⁵² Moreover, as the money economy developed under the Angevins, more opportunities opened up for money-lending at the local level. This trend characterized the entire region; even in Poland, where Jews retained their positions as lessees of tolls and taxes in the fourteenth and fifteenth centuries, 'the city burgher replaced the nobleman as the main borrower'.⁵³ In thirteenth-century Hungary, however, lending to kings and nobles, and even more importantly the activity of financiers connected to the royal mint and the treasury, characterized Jewish involvement in the money economy, rather than urban money-lending.

'Public office': roles connected to the mint and treasury

A system of farming out revenues was introduced in thirteenth-century Hungary, creating possibilities for non-Christians. The traditional view, still repeated occasionally, has attributed the change to the personal whim of a spendthrift king, András II, who is said to have had recourse to the farming out of revenues as an additional source of quick income upon finding the treasury empty.⁵⁴ In fact, the system was part of the reform initiated by King András's chief treasurer and later palatine, Denis, son of Apod, who undertook to transform the system of royal finances from one based on natural economy to one based on monetary income. He was ahead of his time; the system only triumphed with the fourteenth-century Angevin king of Hungary, Charles Robert.⁵⁵ Denis was excommunicated in 1232 by the archbishop of Esztergom for promoting Muslim and Jewish office-holding, and he was blinded on the orders of Béla IV upon Béla's accession to the throne in 1235. As kings gave up being the most important landlord of the realm, and thus relinquished a large portion of their revenues from their extensive domains, they searched for new ways of administration and new sources of revenue. The farming out of taxes, customs and the mint to '*ispán*s of the treasury' (*comites camere*) was among these innovations.⁵⁶ Taxes and customs were

---

⁵² Even in the later Middle Ages Hungarian Jews were not 'exclusively or even primarily . . . moneylenders': Baron, *Social*, vol. x: p. 27. Similar shift towards money-lending by the Jews of southern Italy: David Abulafia, 'Il Mezzogiorno peninsulare dai bizantini all'espulsione (1541)', in *Storia d'Italia Annali*, vol. XI: *Gli ebrei in Italia dall'alto medioevo all'età dei ghetti*, ed. Corrado Vivanti (Torino: Einaudi, 1996), pt 1: pp. 5–44, see pp. 16–17.   ⁵³ Weinryb, *Jews of Poland*, p. 60.
⁵⁴ Hóman, *Magyar pénztörténet*, p. 465; Scheiber, *Jewish Inscriptions*, p. 77.
⁵⁵ Bálint Hóman, *A magyar királyság pénzügyei és gazdaságpolitikája Károly Róbert korában* (Budapest: Budavár tudományos társaság, 1921), chapter IX; Lajos Huszár, 'A középkori magyar pénztörténet okleveles forrásai', *Numizmatikai Közlöny* 70–1 (1971–2): pp. 39–49, see pp. 45–7.
⁵⁶ Zsigmond Pál Pach, 'A harmincadvám eredete' (Budapest: Akadémiai Kiadó, 1990), pp. 29–32, 38. On the *comes camere* see also chapter 3 above.

Non-Christians in Hungarian economy and society

collected by the lessees. Minting became decentralized. Until the early thirteenth century, there was one mint, most likely in Esztergom. From the 1220s on, several mints were established in Csanád, Szerém, Buda and Zagreb. Nevertheless, money-minting remained a royal monopoly throughout the Middle Ages, controlled by the king or his delegates.[57] Royal mints were farmed out to individuals through leasing contracts from the king.[58]

Jewish, and to a much lesser extent Muslim, financial roles were linked to these changes in the organization of collecting royal revenues. Although in modern terms they were not officials, at the time the *comes camere* were seen as occupying public office and exercising power over Christians. Muslims are mentioned as office-holders only in papal letters and laws. Individual Muslim *comites camere* are, with one exception, not documented, while Jewish ones are.[59] Charters primarily used only the general denomination *comes camere*, *ispán* of the royal treasury. The *camera* refers to the treasury without identifying which one of a subset of functions was meant. The Golden Bull of 1222 and the oath of Bereg of 1233 gave a list of offices not to be granted to non-Christians in the future, a promise that was honoured more in the breach than in the observance: *comites camere* of the mint, of salt and of tolls.[60] The *comes camere* could then be a lessee of one type of revenue (the mint, or taxes or customs and so forth), or could fill more than one function simultaneously.

Royal employment of non-Christians in administrative functions was not without precedent in Hungary. Muslim administrators were certainly employed at least periodically; a royal charter of 1111 mentions the 'agents of the royal fisc, who are called *káliz* [Khwarezmian Muslims] in Hungarian'.[61] Abū Hāmid also mentioned Muslims in royal service,

---

[57] On the structure of mints: Hóman, *Magyar pénztörténet*, pp. 456–73. The mint was probably in Esztergom from the earliest times, though data about its location exists only from the thirteenth century, when Esztergom was the main mint. Lajos Huszár, 'Az esztergomi középkori pénzverde', *Komárom megyei múzeumok közleményei*, I (1968): pp. 207–20. Lajos Huszár, *A budai pénzverés története a középkorban* (Budapest: Akadémiai Kiadó, 1958), pp. 23–6.

[58] Hóman, *Magyar pénztörténet*, p. 461; Huszár, 'Esztergomi középkori', pp. 214–15.

[59] References to Muslim office-holders: Bak, *Laws*, p. 36 (1222); p. 40 (1231); MOL DF 248771 (Marsina, *Codex Diplomaticus*, vol. I: pp. 295–8, no. 407) and *VMH*, p. 117, no. CXCVIII (*RA*, no. 500, in 1233), *Liber censuum*, ASV Misc. Arm. XV, no. 1, f. 353v (*VMH*, p. 108, no. CLXXXVII). Jewish lessees are enumerated in n. 95. Daniel M. Friedenberg, *Jewish Minters and Medalists* (Philadelphia: Jewish Publication Society of America, 1976), p. 15, and 'Jewish Mint Masters of Medieval Hungary', *The Shekel*, 24, no. 4 (1991): pp. 20–5 gives a distorted and simplistic image of a quasi-pagan kingdom in thirteenth-century Hungary, where there was no objection to using Jewish mint-masters.

[60] Bak, *Laws*, pp. 36, 40. András III also promised not to confer positions on 'pagans': *CD*, vol. VII, pt. 2: p. 140, no. CCCCII (*RA*, no. 3705).

[61] 'institores regii fisci, quod hungarice caliz vocant': László Fejérpataky, ed., *Kálmán király oklevelei* (Budapest, 1892), p. 42 (*RA*, no. 43); the Muslim *monetarii* mentioned here may be mint-masters, ibid., pp. 42–3. Göckenjan, *Hilfsvölker*, chapter VI on the *káliz*, pp. 66–71 on financial functions.

At the Gate of Christendom

without specifying the nature of this service.[62] As discussed above, Muslims were probably also involved in the sale of salt, and salt production was under royal control.

According to the traditional view in Hungarian historiography, Muslims were also involved in minting. Some scholars have asserted that Muslims had been minters since the eleventh century.[63] This position, however, is not supported by the numismatic evidence. The basis of this theory is a royal charter from 1111 and certain Hungarian coins. The charter mentioned Muslim *monetarii*, and scholars, taking the existence of Muslim minters for granted, have usually understood this as a reference to minters. The context, however, was a debate between Muslim custom-collectors and the local community. Thus these *monetarii* were royal agents, maybe mint-masters (this usage still occurred in the thirteenth century[64]), but the text is not evidence for the existence of Muslim minters.

A group of Hungarian silver and copper coins bear pseudo-Arabic inscriptions.[65] Their dating, on the basis of hoard and technical evidence, is the middle or late twelfth century. They are usually explained as the work of Muslim minters. One hypothesis would have Muslim merchants minting the coins for their own use, at a time of coin shortage due to political upheavals.[66] Strict royal control over minting, the fact that minters lived in one community the known members of which were

---

[62] *Abu-Hámid*, p. 56.
[63] Réthy, *Magyar pénzverő izmaeliták*; Hóman, *Magyar pénztörténet*, pp. 239–40, 463, 472. (In twelfth century: Göckenjan, *Hilfsvölker*, p. 67.)
[64] HO, vol. V: p. 62, no. 49 (RA, no. 2973): the *monetarii* are charged to travel around in order to carry out the yearly exchange of coins. See 'monetarius', in *Novum Glossarium Mediae Latinitatis ab anno DCCC usque ad annum MCC*, ed. Franz Blatt et al. (Copenhagen: Ejnar Munksgaard, 1957–).
[65] László Réthy, *Corpus Nummorum Hungariae*, vol. I: *Az Árpádházi királyok kora* (Budapest: MTA, 1899), nos. 101–3, 109, 117–26, 166, 167 (including coins with Cufic ornaments), also see p. 19; Lajos Zimmermann, *Árpádházi királyok pénzei: Pótlék a Corpus nummorum Hungariae 1. füzetéhez* (Budapest: MTA, 1907) (Additions to Réthy), nos. 16, 23–5, 31; both incorporated in László Réthy and Günther Probszt, *Corpus Nummorum Hungariae* (Graz: Akademische Druck- und Verlagsanstalt, 1958). Emil Unger, *Magyar Éremhatározó*, 2nd edn (Budapest: Magyar Éremgyűjtők Egyesülete, 1974), nos. 65, 78, 97, 98, 119, 123. Lajos Huszár, *Münzkatalog Ungarn, von 1000 bis Heute* (Budapest: Corvina, 1979), nos. 73, 111, 112, 138, 139, 185, 186, 187. Réthy included no. 102 as a gold coin; it is in fact gilded, and probably a modern forgery: Géza Jeszenszky, 'Az első magyar rézpénzek', *Numizmatikai Közlöny* 34–5 (1935–6): pp. 35–47, see pp. 46–7; Huszár, *Münzkatalog*, no. 73. Philip Grierson, *The Coins of Medieval Europe* (London: Seaby, 1991), p. 100. I have seen the examples in the Hungarian National Museum and the Fitzwilliam Museum, Cambridge.
[66] Artúr Pohl, 'Hozzászólás középkori rézpénzeink kérdéseihez I', *Érem* 29, no. 2 (1973): pp. 56–7; Artúr Pohl, Hozzászólás középkori rézpénzeink kérdéseihez II', *Érem* 31, no. 2 (1974): pp. 5–7; Artúr Pohl, 'A kovarezmiai mohamedánok szerepe a magyar középkori pénzverésben', *A Magyar Numizmatikai Társulat Évkönyve* (1975), pp. 79–85; Artúr Pohl, 'Der Islamische Einfluss auf die Münzprägung Ungarns im 12. Jahrhundert', *Hamburger Beiträge zur Numismatik* 27–9 (1973–5): pp. 163–8.

Christians, the short period of time these coins circulated, their lack of value, and the relative unimportance of the Muslim trading community in Hungary by the mid- and late twelfth century all render these explanations implausible.

These coins belong to a rare group of medieval imitation coins: copper coins imitated for local use, not the more usual example of gold or silver imitations, valuable and widely recognized, which were probably used in trade.[67] Copper coinage itself was rare in medieval Europe: the available models were Byzantine and Islamic. Indeed, in twelfth-century Sicily and the crusader states where copper coins were struck, both of these models were used.[68] Similarly, two types of copper coins were minted in Hungary: the pseudo-Arabic ones and another type imitating Byzantine models.[69] Many questions remain that could only be solved by a numismatic evaluation of possible models, classes of coins, design and legend, that has not, so far, been undertaken. The myth of Muslim minters should be laid to rest; the explanation may lie in the enterprising spirit of Béla III. It was possibly a monetary experiment that did not last.[70] The Hungarian case would then resemble other instances of the use of copper coins, where reliance on outside models and monetary reform were linked.

In the thirteenth century, however, non-Christians were not simply employed by the king in administrative functions; the *comites camere* leased royal revenues and possessed great wealth. Non-Christians also gained new visibility, due to the controversies their employment as *comites camere*

---

[67] E.g., Offa's gold coin has been explained this way: C. E. Blunt, 'The Coinage of Offa', in *Anglo-Saxon Coins: Studies Presented to F. M. Stenton*, ed. R. H. M. Dolley (London: Methuen, 1961), pp. 50–1. The inscriptions often became nonsensical as direct contact with Muslims ceased: Domenico Spinelli, *Monete Cufiche battute da Principi Longobardi Normanni e Svevi nel regno delle due Sicilie* (Naples, 1844), pp. 228–36; Antonio Vives y Escudero, *Monedas de las dinastías Arábigo-españolas* (Madrid, 1893), pp. lxxviii–lxxx; Rodolfo Spahr, *Le Monete Siciliane dai Bizantini a Carlo I d'Angiò (582–1282)* (Zurich and Graz: Association Internationale des Numismates Professionnels, 1976), pp. 135–88; Michael L. Bates and D. M. Metcalf, 'Crusader Coinage With Arabic Inscriptions', in *The Impact of the Crusades on Europe*, ed. Harry W. Hazard and Norman P. Zacour, vol. VI of *A History of the Crusades*, ed. Kenneth M. Setton (Madison: University of Wisconsin Press, 1989), pp. 421–82; Paul Balog and Jacques Yvon, 'Monnaies à légendes arabes de l'orient latin', Revue Numismatique, 6th ser., 1 (1958): pp. 133–68. Peter Spufford, *Money and its Use in Medieval Europe* (Cambridge: Cambridge University Press, 1988), pp. 174–5.

[68] Lucia Travaini, 'Entre Byzance et l'Islam: le système monétaire du royaume normand de Sicile en 1140', Bulletin de la Société Française de Numismatique 46, no. 9 (1991): pp. 200–4; Lucia Travaini, 'A Neglected Cufic Copper Coin of Roger II in Sicily', Numismatic Circular 98, no. 9 (1990): pp. 312–13; Bates and Metcalf, 'Crusader coinage', pp. 438–9.

[69] Réthy, *Corpus*, nos. 98–100; Unger, *Magyar Éremhatározó*, no. 122; Huszár, *Münzkatalog*, no. 72.

[70] Gedai thought Béla ordered the minting of these coins to counterbalance the influx of Byzantine copper coins: 'Magyar numizmatika', p. 192. I examine this problem in more detail in my 'Imitation Coins and Frontier Societies: The Case of Medieval Hungary', *AEMAe* 10 (1998–9): pp. 5–14. If numismatists established what the model used for the Hungarian coins was, it would help us understand the reasons for the issue of the coinage.

sparked at the time. Opposition partly drew on resistance to the new economic forms, partly on Christian theology about the role of non-Christians, and partly on noble and ecclesiastical aims to secure the high offices and revenues. There was no inherent necessity for Jews and Muslims to occupy these positions, and they did not always do so. Many *ispáns* of the treasury such as the Venetian Archinus (1249) and a burgher of Buda, Walter (c. 1265–73), who may have been German, were Christians.[71] The kings probably chose to lease revenues to people with sufficient financial reserves and guarantees. Those Jews who were involved in international finance and trade were good candidates. Jews and Muslims also depended on royal protection, and were, for that reason, more reliable.

Although normative texts mention Jews as *comites camere* in all the possible functions, charter evidence often includes only references to the management of the treasury or the royal fisc in general. Some charters, however, specify Jewish roles in the collection of taxes and customs, and minting. Welven, Nekkul and Altman leased the collection of the 'thirtieth' customs duty (*tricesima*) from the queen prior to 1268.[72] References in written texts as well as coins with Hebrew letters on them attest to Jewish involvement in minting in the thirteenth century.[73] Coins inscribed with Hebrew letters have prompted the opinion that Jews were minters.[74] But, just as in the case of Muslims, texts contain explicit references only to mint lessees. Also, as mentioned above, surviving evidence shows that minters lived in an organized community near Esztergom, first as royal servants, then as citizens.[75] There is no evidence for the existence of Jewish minters. The coins were minted in the royal mints, and bear Latin legends and the name of the king. Their design includes typical patterns such as royal busts and various animals. Apart from the Hebrew letter, they do not differ from other royal coinage in style.[76]

---

[71] Archinus: *MES*, vol. I: p. 379, no. 488 (*RA*, no. 914). Walter: *MES*, vol. I: pp. 520–1, no. 678 (*MZsO*, vol. I: p. 34, no. 26; *RA*, no. 1439), vol. II: p. 25, no. 7 (*RA*, no. 2418); *MZsO*, vol. I: p. 36, no. 27 (MOL DF 248542; *MES*, vol. I: p. 550, no. 721; *CD*, vol. IV, pt. 3: pp. 443–57; *RA*, no. 1577); *ÁÚO*, vol. IX: pp. 551–2, no. 401 (*RA*, no. 2619); Huszár, *Budai pénzverés*, p. 24. Tibor Horváth and Lajos Huszár, 'Kamaragrófok a középkorban', *Numizmatikai Közlöny* 54–5 (1955–6): pp. 21–33, see p. 22.

[72] *MZsO*, vol. I: p. 36, no. 27 (*RA*, no. 1577). Pach, *Harmincadvám*, pp. 38–9.

[73] According to an eleventh-century *responsum* a Jew asked permission from the Hungarian queen to have his own coins minted in the royal mint; this concerns a private deal, not Jewish involvement in official minting. Kohn, *Héber*, pp. 45–6; Kupfer and Lewicki, *Źródła*, p. 39; Agus, *Urban Civilization*, pp. 232–5.

[74] Kohn, *Zsidók*, p. 100; Hóman, *Magyar pénztörténet*, p. 463.

[75] Huszár, 'Esztergomi középkori pénzverde', pp. 212–14.

[76] The coins as catalogued in Huszár, *Münzkatalog* (H), Réthy, *Corpus* (C), Zimmermann's additions to Réthy (CP), and Unger, *Magyar Éremhatározó* (U) are as follows: H no. 266 (C 1: no. 226; U no. 158; Huszár's var. *a* of this is CP no. 45); H no. 267 (obulus; C 1: no. 227; U no. 159); H no.

Non-Christians in Hungarian economy and society

The identification of the Hebrew letters is disputed. There are no inscriptions of texts on the coins, only individual letters. The letters have been identified by Gyula Rádóczy and Sándor Scheiber as *aleph* (א), *pey* (פ), *chet* (ח), *tet* (ט), and *shin* (ש);[77] by Daniel Friedenberg as *tet* (ט), *tsadi* (צ), *aleph* (א) *shin* (ש); by Géza Komoróczy as *alef* (א), *chet* (ח), *kaf* (כ), *mem* (מ), *pey* (פ).[78] This diversity is due to the inherent difficulties of identification. The obverse and reverse of medieval coins do not necessarily coincide in their orientation, and even the circular legend on the rim and the Hebrew letter in the middle need not have the same orientation. In many cases we have no guide at all as to the direction from which we should be looking at the letters; and some letters can be identified differently depending on what is considered to be the top and bottom; thus one of the letters can be *tet* (ט) or *pey* (פ), and *mem* (מ) can be mistakenly identified as a *tsadi* (צ).

There is more of a consensus over the significance of the Hebrew letters.[79] Scholars have pointed out that only certain letters were used, and have claimed that these corresponded to the names of Jewish *ispán*s of the treasury known from documents: the letters were used to distinguish coins made during the office of these men.[80] The Hebrew letters are best explained as initials or identifying marks linked to Jewish *ispán*s

---

306 (C 1: no. 241; U no. 238); H no. 307 (obulus; C 1: no. 242; U no. 239); H no. 310 (C 1: no. 244; U no. 243); H no. 311 (obulus; CP no. 46; U no. 244); H no. 312 (Vs. is that of no. 310); H no. 352 (C 1: no. 292; U no. 274); H no. 353 (obulus; C 1: no. 293; U no. 275); H no. 357 (C 1: no. 297; U no. 278); H no. 358 (obulus; C 1: no. 298; U no. 279); H no. 359 (C 1: no. 347; U no. 283); H no. 399 (C 1: no. 349; U no. 319); H no. 400 (C 1: no. 350; U no. 320); H no. 401 (C 1: no. 348; U no. 284); H no. 404 (C 1: no. 352; U no. 285); H no. 405 (C 1: no. 353; U no. 322). I have seen the coins kept in the Department of Coins of the Hungarian National Museum and the Fitzwilliam Museum, Cambridge.

Numbers in hoards: Gyula Rádóczy, 'Héber betűjeles Árpád-házi pénzek', *Numizmatikai Közlöny* 70–1 (1971–2): pp. 33–7, see p. 36. The small silver obols are *c.* 11 mm. No work has analysed the weights, sizes, classes and circulation patterns of the coins.

[77] Rádóczy, 'Héber betűjeles'; Sándor Scheiber, 'A héber betűjeles Árpád-házi pénzekhez', *Numizmatikai Közlöny* 72–3 (1973–4): p. 91.

[78] Friedenberg, *Jewish Minters*, p. 17. In his *Medieval Jewish Seals*, pp. 321–5, he adopted Rádóczy's scheme, and identified *tet* (ט), *chet* (ח), *aleph* (א), *pey* (פ) and maybe *shin* (ש). Mel Wacks, 'Medieval Hungarian Silver Coins with Hebrew Letters', *The Shekel*, 22, no. 5 (1989): pp. 10–11, identified *aleph* (א) and *tsadi* (צ) on certain coins of these series. Komoróczy, ed., *Zsidó Budapest*, p. 12. Kohn, *Zsidók*, p. 100 is unreliable (identifies *shin* (ש), *lamed* (ל), and *khuf* (ק)). Many mistakes in Saul and Sondra Needleman, 'Medieval Coins with Hebrew Letters', *The Shekel* 16, no. 5 (1983): pp. 11–15.

[79] Except Zolnay who has maintained that the letters were serial markings, signifying coins made during the same minting: *Buda középkori zsidósága*, p. 27. But the letters were not consecutive according to the Hebrew alphabet, and serial markings were not used at all on thirteenth-century Hungarian coins. Horváth and Huszár, 'Kamaragrófok', see p. 21.

[80] Rádóczy, 'Héber betűjeles'; Loránt Nagy, 'Adatok a késő Árpád-kori pénzek kormeghatározásához', *Numizmatikai Közlöny* 72–3 (1973–4): pp. 43–7; Scheiber, *Jewish Inscriptions*, p. 77 (photographs of the coins on p. 78); Scheiber, 'Héber betűjeles'; Friedenberg, *Medieval Jewish Seals*, pp. 317–25.

of the treasury. None the less, the complete identification of the *ispáns* of the treasury responsible for these coins with those known from the documents is far from proven. It has been called into question on the basis of numismatic evidence itself; coins bearing a *tet*, attributed to the *ispán* of the treasury Teka by Rádóczy, have been identified by Loránt Nagy as coins from the late 1260s, whereas Teka disappeared from the texts by 1243.[81] The uncertain identification of the Hebrew letters themselves frustrates attempts to match each name signalled by a Hebrew letter with an *ispán* of the treasury known from the documents.

The practice of identifying marks did not reflect personal pride; rather it facilitated control. Hungary was not unique: there are many medieval examples of Jewish minters and mint-masters in other areas of medieval Europe, such as Aragon–Catalonia, Castile, Austria, the German Empire, Bohemia and Poland.[82] Often in these cases Hebrew letters and even inscriptions were used on coins. For example, during the reign of Mieszko III in the twelfth century, Jews were heads of the mint, and coins were minted with the names of both the prince and the Jewish official in Hebrew letters. Polish coins with Hebrew inscriptions also appeared in the mid- and late thirteenth century.[83] There are also Czech (Moravian) examples from the thirteenth century.[84]

As mentioned in chapter 3, the Jewish elite in Hungary came from or had links with Austria. It seems that most of the Jews known to have filled the position of *comites camere* belonged to this group. Teka came to Hungary from the duchy of Austria, and he kept his ties with the latter. He was the guarantor of loans between the Austrian duke and the Hungarian king; he returned to Austria after several years in Hungary and then moved back to Hungary.[85] Henel and his three sons, who performed

---

[81] Rádóczy, 'Héber betűjeles', p. 34; Nagy, 'Adatok', pp. 44–5. Nagy's conclusions are not accepted by Friedenberg, *Medieval Jewish Seals*, p. 321.

[82] Friedenberg, *Jewish Minters*, pp. 8–19. Friedenberg, *Medieval Jewish Seals*, p. 325; Baron, *Social*, vol. XI: p. 125 and vol. XII: pp. 90–4; Wadl, *Geschichte der Juden*, pp. 22, 110, 127. Examples of farming out minting in the late Middle Ages: N. J. Mayhew and Peter Spufford, eds., *Later Medieval Mints: Organisation, Administration and Techniques*, British Archaeological Reports, International Series 389 (Oxford: BAR, 1988), pp. 17, 49–50.

[83] Gieysztor, 'Juifs', p. 512; Marian Gumowski, *Hebräische Münzen im mittelalterlichen Polen* (Graz: Akademische Druck, 1975), with a table of all types on pp. 133–4.

[84] Jadwiga Zakrzewska-Kleczkowska, 'Brakteaty z napisami hebrajskimi ze Střelic', in *Sborník II. Numismatického Symposia 1969*, ed. Jiří Sejbal (Brno: Moravské Museum, 1976): pp. 182–97, with English summary.

[85] *MZsO*, vol. I: pp. 5–6, no. 9 (1225); pp. 8–10, no. 11 (*RA*, no. 443, in 1228). Bernát Mandl, 'Adalék néhány Magyarországban szereplő középkori zsidó történetéhez', *Magyar Zsidó Szemle* 35 (1918): pp. 58–65, see pp. 59–61. His lands in Hungary were near Austria: Pollák, *Zsidók története Sopronban*, p. 9. His name appears in other forms, such as Teha and Techa. Apart from Teka's Austrian origins, there are hypotheses of Teka's origins relating to Tachau, Bohemia, and to the river Tajo, Spain (Scheiber 'Héber betűjeles', p. 91), although there are several examples of individuals in Hungary bearing the name Teka (Katalin Fehértói, *Árpád-kori kis személynévtár*

Non-Christians in Hungarian economy and society

the functions of *comites camere* in the royal fisc and of customs collectors for the queen before and around 1265, were equally connected with Austria. Henel may have come from Austria. Two of his sons, Welven and Nekkul, were *comites camere* in Austria as well.[86] This is an example of what Weinreich has described as 'Jewish geography': the way medieval Jews constructed their world did not necessarily correspond to European political boundaries.[87] The Jewish elite of thirteenth-century Hungary moved with ease between the kingdom and the Duchy of Austria.

Papal letters and Hungarian laws continued to mention Muslims in public office in the thirteenth century without identifying individuals; usually Muslims and Jews appeared together in these sources as lessees.[88] Muslims, or at least converts, were sometimes employed in these positions. Samuel, *ispán* of the treasury under András II, was a 'false Christian', who seems to have been a convert from Islam.[89] Muslims may have been employed as lesser officials in connection with salt production and sale, continuing earlier roles, but no evidence of this survives. In the early thirteenth century Muslims owed service (*servitia*) to the king, who complained about its disruption due to ecclesiastical investigations, without describing what the service consisted of.[90]

(Budapest: Akadémiai Kiadó, 1983), p. 332). Hugo Gold, *Gedenkbuch der Untergegangenen Judengemeinden des Burgenlandes* (Tel Aviv: Olamenu, 1970), pp. 7–8. His activities tied him to Austria and Hungary: Lohrmann, *Judenrecht*, pp. 50–1.

[86] *MZsO*, vol. I: pp. 34–45, nos. 26–7 (*RA*, nos. 1439 and 1577, in 1265 and 1268). Coins with an aleph (א) have been attributed to Altman, Henel's third son: Ródóczy, 'Héber betűjeles', p. 35. The names appear in many (corrupted) forms in the Latin texts. Friedenberg, *Medieval Jewish Seals*, p. 324; Zolnay, *Buda középkori zsidósága*, pp. 26–7; Lohrmann, *Judenrecht*, pp. 83, 87–90 on Austrian connection.

[87] Max Weinreich, *History of the Yiddish Language*, tr. Shlomo Noble (Chicago and London: University of Chicago Press, 1980), p. 47.

[88] Bak, *Laws*, pp. 36, 40 (1222, 1231); *Liber censuum*, ASV Misc. Arm. XV, no. 1, f. 353v (*VMH*, p. 108, no. CLXXXVII; 1232); MOL DF 248771 (Marsina, *Codex Diplomaticus*, vol. I: pp. 295–98, no. 407); *VMH*, p. 117, no. CXCVIII (1233); Solomon Grayzel, *The Church and the Jews in the XIIIth Century*, 2 vols., rev. edn (New York: Hermon Press, 1966 and Detroit: Wayne State University Press, 1989), vol. II: no. 17 (Simonsohn, *Apostolic See Documents*, no. 216; *MZsO*, vol. I: p. 32, no. 24; *MES*, vol. I: pp. 487–8, no. 629) (1263). Jewish, Muslim and pagan office-holding: ASV Reg. Vat. 19, f. 139v [previously 133v] (*Reg. Greg. IX*, no. 5000; *VMH*, p. 173, no. CCCXIII; 1239); *CD*, vol. VII, pt. 2: p. 140, no. CCCCII (*RA*, no. 3705, in 1291).

[89] *Liber censuum*, ASV Misc. Arm. XV, no. 1, f. 355r (*VMH*, p. 109, no. CLXXXVII). The fourteenth-century mint-masters Jacob and John 'Saracen' were also thought to be converted descendants of Muslims (they used the head of a Saracen as their mint mark): Réthy, *Magyar pénzverő*, pp. 21–2. Elemér Mályusz, 'Az izmaelita pénzverőjegyek kérdéséhez', *Budapest Régiségei: A Budapesti Történeti Múzeum Évkönyve* 18 (1958): pp. 301–11, proved that they were Italians (though he did not question the existence of Muslim minters for an earlier period). See also István Gedai, *Magyar Nemzeti Múzeum, A Magyar aranypénzverés története: vezető* (Budapest: Népművelési Propaganda Iroda, 1982), p. 9. Hóman, *Magyar pénztörténet*, p. 467; Artúr Pohl, 'A középkori magyar verdejegyrendszer kialakulásának kora', *Érem* 30, no. 1 (1974): pp. 6–7.

[90] ASV Reg. Vat. 18, f. 68v (*Reg. Greg. IX*, no. 2758; *VMH*, p. 136, no. CCXXXVII).

Papal letters routinely complained not only about Jews but also Muslims and pagans in public offices, depicting a virtual 'take-over' by non-Christians of high royal offices. Accusations came from the lay and ecclesiastical elites, with the aim of securing the positions and income for themselves. This is clear from the Golden Bull (1222, 1231) and the oath of Bereg (1233), which aimed to restrict access to these positions, and to ensure ecclesiastical rights to the sale of salt. The claim, accepted by the popes and many modern scholars, that non-Christians were preferred to Christians in Hungarian royal offices, was exaggerated.[91] The assertion that András III praised a Jewish overseer of the mint, often repeated in scholarship as a proof of this traditional view, is based on a mistranslation; the king does not talk about a Jew at all, but a man in the service of a local judge (*homo iudicis*).[92] It is certain that when non-Christians filled *high* official positions, these were invariably linked to certain economic functions, and especially the renting of royal monopolies and revenues. As for the Cumans, only their military role is documented (see below). This, especially as they served the king as military guard, may have been confused with other forms of service by the papacy, and thus included in letters of complaint. Lists of holders of high political offices such as the palatine, senechal (*országbíró*), master of the horse (*lovászmester*) and others, show that all of these positions were held by members of noble families and not by non-Christians.[93] One exception is Mizse, a newly converted Christian from Islam, who was László IV's palatine (*comes palatinus, nádor*). Whether or not sincere in his new religion, even he was at least a convert.[94] In fact, non-Christians were in a minority even as *comites camere*. We know of a minimum of twenty Christian *ispán*s of the treasury as opposed to one 'false Christian' (Muslim) and six Jewish ones from the thirteenth century.[95] Non-Christians had no monopoly in Hungarian finances.

---

[91] Modern scholars holding this view: e.g., Hóman, *Magyar pénztörténet*, pp. 462–7; Pohl, 'Kovarezmiai', p. 80.

[92] MOL DF 238636 (1291; *MZsO*, vol. I: p. 57, no. 32; *RA*, no. 3837), copies: MOL DF 238715 (1317) and 238737 (1352).

[93] Hóman and Szekfű, *Magyar történet*, vol. II: tables between pp. 512–13, 520–1, 608–9, 616–17.

[94] Mizse: *SRH*, vol. I: p. 474; *Seifried Helbling*, ed. Joseph Seemüller (Halle, 1886), pp. 177, 180, 182; Pauler, *Magyar nemzet*, vol. II: p. 413.

[95] Jewish *ispán*s of the treasury: Teka (1228, 1232): *MZsO*, vol. I: pp. 8–10, 13, nos. 11, 14 (*RA*, nos. 443, 495). Henel (1250, certainly not a *comes camere* by 1265): *MZsO*, vol. I: pp. 34–5, no. 26 (*RA*, no. 1439). Welven, Altman and Nekkul (before 1265 and 1265–8): *MZsO*, vol. I: pp. 34–45, nos. 26, 27 (*RA*, nos. 1439, 1577). Fredman (1280–2): MOL DL 105378, DL 50148 (*HO*, vol. VIII: p. 206, no. 162; p. 221, no. 178; *MZsO*, vol. IX: p. 27, no. 1; *RA*, no. 3189). These dates reflect the periods for which the activity of these *comites camere* is documented, but they probably all served for a longer time. There may have been other Jewish *comites camere* whose activity is not recorded. Complete list of known *ispán*s of the treasury: Horváth and Huszár, 'Kamaragrófok'. Sometimes a Christian name occurs several times in the list; I counted these instances as the repetition of the same name, but if they denote different individuals, then the number of Christian *ispán*s of the treasury is above twenty.

Non-Christians in Hungarian economy and society

The Hungarian kingdom was not the only one where non-Christians were employed by the king during the Middle Ages. In newly conquered Iberian lands Jews were welcome both as intermediaries between Muslims and Christians and as royal functionaries. They were transmitters of knowledge, translators and middlemen, as well as courtiers and tax-collectors.[96] Even Muslims were sometimes employed by the kings in high offices.[97] Jews in German and eastern European areas, which had no Muslim population, were also in royal service; evidence of them as tax-collectors and agents of the mint survives in Poland from the mid-twelfth century onwards, in the Duchy of Austria, and in the German Empire.[98]

Despite different institutional backgrounds, there are structural similarities between the Hungarian case and that of the Iberian peninsula. In both frontier societies economic development opened up positions that non-Christian office-holders filled. In both, monarchs found it useful to rely on non-Christian groups. But Jews and Muslims did not monopolize these positions, nor did they control the financial matters of the kingdom. Although highly visible in the sources, they had no exclusive hold over finances; we always find Christians filling similar roles. Burns has warned that the documented existence of Jewish financiers has been turned into the unjustifiable stereotype of Jews controlling the finances of the crown.[99] His remark has implications beyond Spain. Ideology, medieval and modern, distorted the significance of non-Christian economic roles.

NON-CHRISTIAN PRESENCE IN AGRICULTURE

To say that the agricultural function of non-Christians was not important in Hungary is not to deny that they held land. They were able to hold landed property. They often did so as a consequence of their other economic and military functions.

Jewish landholding has often been seen as having disappeared by the High Middle Ages, but even the western European case was not so straightforward.[100] In Hungary, there is evidence of Jewish landholding

---

[96] E.g. Baer, *History*, vol. I: chapters II–IV; Baron, *Social*, vol. XII: pp. 92–4; Jerome Lee Shneidman, 'Jews in the Royal Administration of Thirteenth Century Aragon', *Historia Judaica* 21 (1959): pp. 37–52; Shneidman, 'Jews as Royal Bailiffs in Thirteenth Century Aragon', *Historia Judaica* 19 (1957): pp. 55–66.   [97] Harvey, *Islamic Spain*, p. 139; Boswell, *Royal Treasure*, p. 86.
[98] Jerzy Kłoczowski, ed., *Histoire religieuse de la Pologne* (Paris: Le Centurion, 1987), pp. 82–3, 86; Baron, *Social*, vol. XII: p. 91. Also above, p. 126, on minting.
[99] Burns, 'King Jaume's', pp. 132–4; Roberto Bonfil, *Tra due mondi: cultura ebraica e cultura cristiana nel Medioevo* (Naples: Liguori, 1996), pp. 177–80 also argues that Jews were not economically indispensable.
[100] Baron, *Social*, vol. XII: pp. 34–5; Stow, *Alienated Minority*, pp. 213–24.

as late as the fourteenth century. Early laws prohibiting Jewish ownership of Christian slaves did not put an end to Jewish landholding. King Kálmán allowed Jews to buy and own land, and to use 'pagan' slaves, affirming that 'Jews, if they can buy it, are permitted to hold' land.[101] Moreover, Jews may have owned land without using slaves. Toponyms based on the word 'Jew' (*zsidó* in Hungarian) such as Sydov, Sydou and Sydouar, as well as the Latin *Mons Iudeorum, castrum Iudeorum*, are sometimes interpreted as a sign of Jewish ownership.[102] Even if this far-from-uncontroversial hypothesis were accepted, toponyms provide no clues as to the time and nature of Jewish ownership, as discussed in chapter 2. Luckily, we need not rely exclusively on such precarious evidence. Thirteenth-century charters provide some idea of the modalities of Jewish landholding.

Most of the sources on Jewish landholders pertain to individuals who filled the role of '*ispán* of the treasury' (*comes camere*). These landholders are highly visible in the documentation, but they are not necessarily representative of thirteenth-century Jewish landholding patterns in Hungary. Royal charters only deal with specific cases in question, without setting out the judicial framework of Jewish landholding. Thus we learn that the Jewish *comes camere* Teka could not prove his title to an estate by showing a charter of donation; he was ordered to give up this property so that the king could donate it to someone else.[103] Another piece of land initially granted by King András II to Simon, then reclaimed by Béla IV (in his campaign of revoking land prior to the Mongol invasion) and given to Teka, was donated again to Simon.[104] The sons of the Jewish *comes camere* Henel, mentioned above, gave the king the castle of Komárom and surrounding areas which they had inherited from their father, who himself had held the property from the king, in lieu of their debt. The king sold these to his *comes camere* Walter as perpetual heredi-

---

[101] Law of Kálmán (between 1095 and 1116) c. LXXIV–LXXV: 'Nullus Judeus Christianum mancipium emere vel vendere audeat, aut in suo servitio tenere sinatur; nunc vero qui habet, si interea datis sibi induciis non vendat, amittat.' 'Agriculturam autem si quis eorum habet, paganis hanc mancipiis exerceat. Possessiones quidem Judei, qui possunt emere, habeant, sed ipsi nusquam, nisi ubi sedes episcopalis est, manere sinantur.' Bak, *Laws*, p. 31. Synod of Esztergom, c. LXII (between 1105 and 1116) also against Jews holding Christian slaves: Bak, *Laws*, p. 66. Synod of Szabolcs (1092), c. X: 'Si iudei . . . aliquam personam christianam in servitio aput [sic!] se detinuerint, ab eis libertati reddantur, venditoribus earum pretium tollatur et in sumptum episcoporum veniat.' Bak, *Laws*, p. 57.

[102] Kristó et al., 'Adatok', p. 32; Kubinyi, 'Magyarországi zsidóság', pp. 5–6. On problems of interpretation, see chapter 2 above. In France and Spain *Mons Judaeorum* designated especially Jewish cemeteries: Golb, *Jews in Medieval Normandy*, pp. 145–6.

[103] *MZsO*, vol. I: pp. 8–10, no. 11 (*RA*, no. 443) 1228.

[104] MOL DL 256 (*CD*, vol. IV, pt. 1: pp. 272–4; *MZsO*, vol. I: pp. 22–3, no. 21; *RA*, no. 731) (1243). Example of revoking land from a Christian owner: Iván Borsa, ed., *A Justh család levéltára 1274–1525* (Budapest: Akadémiai Kiadó, 1991), p. 14, no. 8 (*RA*, no. 4013).

Non-Christians in Hungarian economy and society

tary possessions. The same brothers, this time in lieu of paying their debt to the queen, gave her the same castle of Komárom as well as the mill of Tata; she in turn gave them to Walter.[105] Finally Fredman, financier of King László (Ladislas) IV, received two villages as his hereditary possessions because the king could not repay his debt. Fredman proceeded to sell one of the villages for 299 silver marks to one of his neighbours.

The modalities of land sale conform to those between Christians. Fredman obtained royal permission for the sale;[106] similarly Teka sold a piece of land that had been given to his father by the king with explicit royal permission.[107] Fredman also promised to deal with any eventual opposition to the sale, should it arise; this clause appears in other charters of sale, assigning sole responsibility for having acted legally to the seller.[108] The land involved in these sales was originally obtained by royal donation.[109] Sometimes the land in question had previously belonged to serving-people of the king (*conditionarii*).[110] Twice their rights to the land were explicitly annulled in the new donation. Another time the new owner is said to possess the land in the same way as the serving-people had done. In the second half of the century, Hungarian kings donated lands of royal *conditionarii* to individuals and to the Church with or without the population on it, and these cases were examples of that practice.

Jewish landownership meant the ability to use, inherit and buy land. Using land could include major building projects; a certain Scechtinus, about whom nothing is known apart from his religion, built a castle in Vasvár.[111] We learn that Teka inherited land from his father and Henel

---

[105] *MZsO*, vol. 1: pp. 34–5, no. 26 (*Budapest történetének oklevéles*, pp. 82–3, no. 67; *CD*, vol. IV, pt. 3: p. 283, 1 April 1265; *RA*, no. 1439), pp. 35–45, no. 27 (*CD*, vol. IV, pt. 3: pp. 443–57, 1268; *RA*, no. 1577). The explanation of these two transactions is unclear. Three years separate the two charters; the first describes the Jews giving the land to the king, the second, to the queen. Kohn, *Zsidók*, p. 118, maintained that Henel's sons first gave their estate to the king but then bought it back, thus being able to give it up again three years later. This lacks any documentary basis. It is possible that Henel's sons gave the estates to the king and queen for their debts at the same time, but the second royal charter, which ratified the queen's actions, was given later than the actual events. See *RA*, no. 1577.

[106] *MZsO*, vol. 1: pp. 54–5, no. 31 (*HO*, vol. VIII: p. 206, no. 162, 7 Feb. 1280, copied in 1291); MOL DL 50148 (*HO*, vol. VIII: pp. 221–2, no. 178; *RA*, no. 3189). Zsigárd, Nyitra county. Royal approval of sale between Christians: e.g. *ÁÚO*, vol. II: p. 191, no. 119 (*RA*, no. 686).

[107] *MZsO*, vol. 1: p. 13, no. 14 (*RA*, no. 495) 1232.

[108] In cases of sale between Christians: e.g. *ÁÚO*, vol. IV: p. 207, no. 123.

[109] The rights of the owners of such lands were in principle restricted, although these restrictions were not necessarily accepted in practice: 'adomány', in *KMTL*.

[110] MOL DL 50148 (*HO*, vol. VIII: pp. 221–2, no. 178; *RA*, no. 3189, in 1282) on the new owner possessing land in the same way as *retiferi* (fishermen) had; MOL DL 256 (*MZsO*, vol. 1: p. 23, no. 21; *RA*, no. 731) annulled rights of *odvornici* (royal serving-people who produced food and goods).

[111] *MZsO*, vol. VIII: p. 27, no. 2 (*RA*, no. 2732). There is no information on who built other 'castles of the Jews': *CD*, vol. IV, pt. 2: p. 459 (*RA*, no. 885); Kubinyi, 'Magyarországi zsidóság', p. 6.

passed on his estates to his sons, who inherited together, and not on the basis of primogeniture.[112] Fredman and Teka sold land, and, in 1300, Daniel, a Jew from Trencsén, bought a piece of land and garden from a Christian couple, inhabitants of the city.[113] Although this was a transaction of money-lending disguised as a sale, with the sellers retaining the option to 'buy' their land back within a year, the charter envisaged the possibility of the land remaining in Daniel's possession. It is also noteworthy that this is an example of Jewish ownership of a plot of land, as opposed to previous cases of large estates. Charter evidence for transactions in cities, where plots of land and houses were pawned to Jewish money-lenders, survived only from the fourteenth century onwards, though the practice may already have existed in the thirteenth century.[114] Jewish landholding could entail the payment of tithe.[115]

The thirteenth century brought fundamental changes in royal power over land; the king increasingly lost his rights as the ultimate 'owner' of all lands. King Béla IV tried to revoke his father's donations on a large scale prior to the Mongol invasion; the ultimate failure of this policy signalled the end of the old system. The king did, however, retain the right to reclaim land in certain cases, such as treason, and all land without heirs escheated to him.[116] Moreover, certain lands remained directly under his power, inhabited by serving-people, although many of the previously

---

[112] Teka: *MZsO*, vol. I: p. 13, no. 14 (*RA*, no. 495); Henel: MOL DF 248542 (*MZsO*, vol. I: p. 36, no. 27 as Henuk; *MES*, vol. I: p. 550, no. 721; *RA*, no. 1577).

[113] Teka: *MZsO*, vol. I: p. 13, no. 14 (*RA*, no. 495). Fredmann: MOL DL 105378 (copy: 50148) (*HO*, vol. VIII: pp. 205–6, no. 162; *MZsO*, vol. I: pp. 54–5, no. 31), *HO*, vol. VIII: pp. 221–2, no. 178 (MOL DL 50148; *RA*, no. 3189), pp. 302–3, no. 249 (*RA*, no. 3831). Daniel: MOL DF 283482, 30 March 1300 (*MZsO*, vol. I: pp. 60–1, no. 34).

[114] After the case in 1300, *MZsO*, vol. I: pp. 66–7, no. 39 (1349) and pp. 73–5, no. 44 (1367); *MZsO*, vol. V: pp. 19–20, no. 32 (1384). Similar transactions between Christians: e.g. *HO*, vol. III: pp. 39–40, no. 30 (1291); *ibid.*, vol. VIII: p. 278, no. 226 (1290). Lederer, *Középkori pénzüzletek*, pp. 14–29.

[115] In Hungary, the first evidence of this is in a fourteenth-century forgery: *MZsO*, vol. I: pp. 19–20, no. 18 (*CD*, vol. III, pt. 2: p. 426; *RA*, no. 544), but it is probable that the practice started earlier in the kingdom. Popes demanded that Jews pay tithes from the twelfth century on (some local synods did so already in the late eleventh century); the demand was also extended to Muslims living under Christian rule: Simonsohn, *Apostolic See History*, pp. 180–5; Simonsohn, *Apostolic See Documents*, nos. 54, 66, 81, 85, 86, 88. The bishop of Wrocław insisted on the Jewish payment of tithes in the thirteenth century: *ibid.*, no. 119.

[116] József Gerics, 'Nemesi jog – királyi jog a középkori magyarországi birtoklásban', in Gerics, *Egyház, állam és gondolkodás Magyarországon a középkorban* (Budapest: METEM, 1995), pp. 275–94; József Gerics, 'Az "új adomány" jogintézménye a 13. századi magyar okleveles gyakorlatban', *Levéltári Szemle* 36, no. 1 (1986): pp. 21–30; István Rákos, 'IV. Béla birtokrestaurációs politikája', *AUSz, Acta Historica* 47 (1974): pp. 3–29. On one type of debate: Attila Zsoldos, 'Terra hereditaria és szabad rendelkezésű birtok (Szempontok a várjobbágyi birtoklás egyes kérdéseinek megítéléséhez)', in *Unger Mátyás Emlékkönyv*, ed. Péter E. Kovács, et al. (Budapest: MTA Történettudományi Intézet, 1991), pp. 23–37. In the thirteenth century the *várjobbágyok*, the military elite of royal castellanies, claimed they had a right to freely sell or possess all their land, while the kings endeavoured to assert their ultimate right over these lands.

royal lands were transformed into estates held by nobles.[117] Jewish landholding mirrored these changes. Jews, like Christians, were asked to prove ownership by a charter of donation. The type of land was specified, just as in the case of Christian owners; lands that once belonged to *conditionarii* became personal possessions. Jews also inherited and sold land according to the same laws as Christians did and used Latin sale documents. Overall, the cases of Jewish landholding conformed to the general patterns of Hungarian landownership.

The modalities characterizing Jewish ownership were not unique to Jews with one important exception: the power Jews could exercise over the Christian inhabitants of estates. Land use was described in a passage of King Béla IV's privileges. The passage concerned estates pawned by nobles to Jewish money-lenders. Such estates could rightfully be used by the Jews only in the following manner: they were not allowed to exercise any power (jurisdiction) over the Christian inhabitants of the estate and were to collect revenues from it only until a Christian, who need not be the original borrower, redeemed it.[118] These conditions did not appear in the Austrian model for Béla's privileges, but were added by the king; this indicates their relevance in Hungary. Thus Christian efforts to control Jewish participation in the use of land were directed not at prohibiting access to land, but at circumscribing the extent of Jewish power over Christians.[119]

Muslim landownership is not well documented, but the evidence that Muslims lived in compact villages implies that they owned and farmed land.[120] Iron ploughshares among the archaeological finds in a Muslim village provide additional evidence that Muslims were involved in agriculture.[121] Post-1241 references are rare; István V donated land that he qualified as a 'village of the Ishmaelites' to his mother.[122] Other land

---

[117] Szűcs, *Utolsó Árpádok*, pp. 61–6. On the serving-people: Bolla, *Jogilag egységes*, chapter III.

[118] Büchler, 'Judenprivilegium', p. 144. A case in the mid-fourteenth century, when land was pawned to a Jewish money-lender, then redeemed: *Anjoukori Okmánytár*, vol. VI: pp. 45–6, 84, nos. 21, 47.

[119] One additional text would throw new light on the question of Jewish landownership, provided that the men involved in this donation were proven to be Jews. This text sets forth a donation of land by a Christian lord to several brothers to reward their faithful service. The donation was made according to Austrian vassalage laws, and included the right to sell the land. The editors of the text maintain that the brothers were Jewish, on the sole evidence of the name of their father, Ebron Mendel. But both the lack of the designation 'Judeus' and the type of donation are unusual compared to other surviving evidence. It is possible that the individuals mentioned in the charter were Jewish, but it seems to me that they were at least converts from Judaism. Their names (Wolfgerus, Nycolaus, Andreas, Mychael) may be indications of such conversion, although not necessarily (see Chapter 7 for a discussion of names). *MZsO*, vol. XIII: p. 47, no. 1 (13 July 1296). Cf. Zvi Avneri, ed., *Germania Judaica*, 2 vols. (Tübingen, 1968), vol. I: p. 199.

[120] See chapter 2. Göckenjan, *Hilfsvölker*, pp. 71–2.   [121] Antalóczy, 'Nyíri', p. 133.

[122] (1266) ASV Reg. Vat. 32, f. 84v (*Reg. Clem. IV*, no. 333; *VMH*, p. 283, no. DXVII; *CD*, vol. IV, pt. 3: p. 366; *RA*, no. 1849).

grants made after 1241, however, occasionally specified that the land had been in the possession of Muslims prior to the invasion, but was now deserted.[123] The Mongol invasion destroyed many of the Muslim villages. The features of Muslim landownership – village communities engaged in agriculture – albeit different from most known cases of Jewish landholding – individual ownership of estates – thus also conformed to Christian patterns. Individual ownership of small domains existed as well; in one instance the land of a Muslim who died without heirs escheated to the king.[124]

Cuman ownership of land is a more complicated issue. First, Cuman settlement in the country had to become consolidated. Following initial Cuman immigration came the exodus of the Cumans upon the murder of their chieftain Köten, their second settlement in Hungary, and then the gradual transformation of their way of life. The acquisition of landed estates became increasingly important in that process. Therefore in speaking of the Cumans' relationship to land, chronology is especially important. An initial report portrayed them as roaming around the kingdom with their cattle, not respecting the peasants' planted fields, and thereby arousing the hostility of the population.[125] According to its author, the canon Roger, the Cumans wandered aimlessly; a misperception of the nomadic life.[126] What the text shows is the clash between the

---

[123] 'antea per Saracenos possidebatur': MOL DF 263904 (CD, vol. IV, pt. 2: p. 425; RA, no. 1146, in 1257, transcribed in 1279); Bő, county of Heves: TF, vol. III: pp. 74–5.

[124] JK, vol. II: p. 418, no. 53 (CD, vol. IV, pt. 3: p. 343; RA, no. 1856); Mikelaka, county of Arad: TF, vol. I: p. 181 (1266).

[125] Rogerius, SRH, vol. II: p. 554: 'Cum autem rex Comanorum cum suis nobilibus et rusticis cepit Hungariam peragrare, quia iumentorum habebant armenta infinita, in pascuis, segetibus, ortis, virgultis, vineis et aliis Hungaros graviter offendebant.' Uncritically adopted by JK, vol. II: p. 262. Pauler, Magyar nemzet, vol. II: p. 149, presented it as a problem only while the Cumans were led to the areas assigned to them in the country. Rus' chronicles also compared Cuman and ninth-century Hungarian nomadism: Hodinka, Orosz évkönyvek, p. 41.

[126] On Cuman nomadism: Golden, 'Nomads and their Sedentary Neighbors'; Cambridge History of Early Inner Asia; Rásonyi, Hidak a Dunán, p. 121; Sinor, 'Introduction', in Inner Asia, pp. 1–13. Examples from the Codex Cumanicus: Györffy, 'Kipcsaki', pp. 244, 246, 254. Evidence from Byzantium, Rus' and Golden Horde: Robert de Cléry, 'De ceux qui se croisèrent', in Un chevalier à la croisade. L'histoire de la conquête de Constantinople, ed. Jean Longnon (Paris: Tallandier, 1981), pp. 229–30; Dimitri A. Rassovsky, 'Les Comans et Byzance', in Actes du IVe Congrès International des Etudes Byzantines, Bulletin de l'Institut Archéologique Bulgare 9 (1935): pp. 346–54; Carpini Ystoria on seasonal migrations: in Wyngaert, ed., p. 108; Daffinà et al., p. 309. László Selmeczi, 'A kunok nomadizmusának kérdéséhez', in Régészeti-néprajzi tanulmányok, pp. 87–99, especially pp. 94–6, Cumans as semi-nomads; see also Gábor Hatházi, 'A perkátai kun szállástemető (előzetes beszámoló az 1986–88. évi feltárásokról)', in A Móra Ferenc Múzeum Évkönyve 1984–85/2 (Szeged: Szegedi Nyomda, 1991): pp. 651–74. On definitions of nomadism: Rhoads Murphey, 'An Ecological History of Central Asian Nomadism', in Ecology and Empire: Nomads in the Cultural Evolution of the Old World, ed. Gary Seaman, Proceedings of the Soviet–American Academic Symposia, vol. I (Los Angeles: University of Southern California and Ethnographics Press, 1989), pp. 41–58; Barfield, Perilous Frontier, pp. 20–4; Khazanov, Nomads, chapter I; János Matolcsi, 'A középkori nomád állattenyésztés kelet-európai

Non-Christians in Hungarian economy and society

Cumans' need for pasture and the peasants' need for cultivation and animal farming. The king attempted to rectify this problem by breaking up the block of Cuman settlement and dispersing them across the country.[127]

After their second arrival, the Cuman way of life changed from a nomadic to a settled one. Hungarian historiography has unanimously maintained that certain areas were immediately designated for their settlement, parts of which still bear their name to this day (Nagykunság, Kiskunság; Greater and Lesser Cumania). These areas were between the rivers Duna and Tisza, and on the eastern side of the Tisza around the Körös and between the Maros and Temes rivers. According to one calculation, Cumans were allocated regions where up to 50–80 per cent of the villages were destroyed by the Mongol invasion.[128] Noting Cuman landholding outside this area, scholars have tried to find explanations for what they saw as 'atypical' landholding, outside the designated Cuman regions, such as to the west of the Danube.[129] One author has noted that he found no adequate answer to the puzzling issue of archaeological and toponymic evidence for early Cuman presence in an area that lay outside the 'designated territory'.[130]

The sole source of the idea that from the time of Béla IV Cumans were assigned these specific territories is the so-called second Cuman law, which I have shown in the previous chapter to be untrustworthy. The text emphasized that Béla IV gave the Cumans these lands to inhabit; the purpose of the eighteenth-century forger was to establish the Cumans' right to this area of the country by claiming royal donation. The Cumans certainly settled in this area, as archaeological finds testify,[131] but the notion that these alone were 'Cuman lands', and that this area belonged to the Cumans alone (along with certain rights) was a modern invention in order to aid Cuman redemption in the eighteenth century. Cumans in the thirteenth century did not have to own land within this area, and landholding outside it was not atypical.

Cumans were organized into clans, which were based on kin groups, but incorporated non-relatives as well. Four clans and their territories have been identified: the Borchol clan between the rivers Maros and

---

jellegzetességei', in *Nomád társadalmak és államalakulatok*, ed. Ferenc Tőkei, Kőrösi Csoma Kiskönyvtár 18 (Budapest: Akadémiai Kiadó, 1983), pp. 281–306. Cf. Gyula Kristó, 'A X. század közepi magyarság "nomadizmusának" kérdéséhez', in *Tanulmányok az Árpád-korról* (Budapest: Magvető Kiadó, 1983), pp. 51–76.

[127] Rogerius, in *SRH*, vol. II: p. 557; Pálóczi Horváth, *Besenyők*, p. 42.

[128] Györffy, 'Magyarország népessége', p. 53. His calculations about the destruction are exaggerated: see chapter 1 above, pp. 36–7.

[129] According to Györffy, 'Magyarországi kun', p. 280, it was a measure to avoid the establishment of feudal dependence among the Cumans. [130] Hatházi, 'Perkátai', p. 655.

[131] Map of finds: Pálóczi Horváth, 'Hagyományok', p. 104; Pálóczi Horváth, *Besenyők*, p. 49.

Temes; Cherthan in an area covering parts of the counties Pest, Fejér, Szolnok, Csongrád and Bodrog; Olaas between the rivers Tisza and Körös; and Kool (or Koor) south of the Maros.[132] The often-repeated assumption about seven Cuman clans who divided among themselves the lands granted by King Béla is based on the 'second' Cuman law. While the authentic text speaks about clans or kin groups (*generationes*), only the interpolated version includes the number seven. Given the eighteenth-century Cuman quest for privileges equalling those of nobles, it is no surprise that they modelled themselves on the Hungarian tradition which told of seven tribes who conquered Hungary. The forger may also have relied on the Hungarian chronicler Anonymous, who related that seven leaders of the 'Cumani' ('duces Cumanorum'; understood as Cuman in pre-twentieth-century Hungarian historiography) and their followers joined the Hungarians in the ninth century.[133]

The permanent settlement of the Cumans figured prominently in legislation based on papal demands. In 1279, the articles regulating Cuman status, promulgated under the pressure of a papal legate, decreed: '[the Cumans] will leave and abandon their tents and houses made of felt [i.e. yurts], and they had specifically taken it on themselves to live and stay in villages, in buildings and houses built upon the ground'.[134] A charter of László IV mentioned the exchange of vacant noble lands in areas of Cuman settlement in order to promote the consolidation of large blocks of Cuman territory.[135] The consensus among historians has been that Cumans received completely deserted lands, or territories around the areas populated by the Hungarians, and continued to be nomads for about a century, relying primarily on animal herding. It was taken for granted that the Cumans had to be forced to adopt a settled way of life

---

[132] Györffy, 'Magyarországi kun', pp. 274–5, 299–304. Pálóczi Horváth, *Besenyők*, pp. 48–52; Lajos Horváth, 'Adatok az alánok és a kunok történetéhez', in *A Jászkunság kutatása 1985*, ed. István Fazekas, László Szabó and István Sztrinkó (Kecskemét and Szolnok: Szolnoki Damjanich János Múzeum, 1987), pp. 187–214, see pp. 193–204. There are debates whether the names Ilonchuk and Kuncheg were those of clans or families.

[133] *SRH*, vol. I: pp. 46–7. The chronicle was known at least from the mid-seventeenth century: *SRH*, vol. I: p. 16. Identified with the Cumans: *JK*, vol. II: pp. 25–7; with those who joined the Hungarians in Khazaria: György Györffy, *Krónikáink és a magyar őstörténet* (Budapest: Balassi Kiadó, 1993), pp. 124–5; Loránd Benkő, 'Anonymus kunjairól', in *Kelet és Nyugat között: Történeti Tanulmányok Kristó Gyula tiszteletére*, ed. László Koszta (Szeged: Szegedi Középkorász Műhely, 1995), pp. 39–67 argued that they were an invention of Anonymous as part of the story of eastern origins; see also Loránd Benkő, 'Anonymus "kunjainak" személynevei', in Benkő *Név és történelem: tanulmányok az Árpád-korról* (Budapest: Akadémiai Kiadó, 1998), pp. 40–57.

[134] 'Et quod descendent et recedent a tabernaculis suis et domibus filtrinis, et habitare et morari in villis . . . in edificiis et domibus solo fixis expressius assumpserunt.' ASV AA Arm I-XVIII-595 (*VMH*, p. 340, no. DLVI; *RA*, no. 2962).

[135] *RA*, no. 3004; there is a slight suspicion concerning the authenticity of the charter.

as opposed to a nomadic one, and that the earliest permanent settlements appeared in the 1330s.[136]

Archaeological excavations, however, reveal a different story. The areas where Cumans lived were interspersed with the estates of other landowners; moreover, the lands of each *aul* were separate. The territory that any one group, consisting of several extended families, had at their disposal, was 40–50 km^2, certainly not enough to continue a nomadic life.[137] Full-scale nomadism had to be abandoned in the thirteenth century. Relinquishing nomadism and settling in established villages, however, is not necessarily the same. How long various groups retained a limited mobility before they settled in permanent villages is still debated. According to archaeologists, two types of settlements emerged: those that developed from Cuman camps and villages planted from the fourteenth century on. At issue is whether the Cuman camps already represent a fixed settlement structure. Previous villages, destroyed during the Mongol invasion, influenced the settlement patterns of the Cumans, who chose these ruined villages as the bases for their winter camps. Some archaeologists propose that winter camps gradually evolved into villages in the late fourteenth and fifteenth centuries. Others maintain that winter camps themselves were already stable, and not annually changing, and by the end of the thirteenth and beginning of the fourteenth century, Cuman settlements were permanently fixed.[138]

---

[136] Kring, 'Kun és jász társadalomelemek', p. 46; László Marjai Szabó, 'A kunok betelepítése és az állandó szállások kialakulása a Nagykúnság területén', *Az Alföldi Tudományos Intézet Évkönyve* I (1944–5): pp. 97–106, see pp. 100–1. Györffy, 'Magyarországi kun', p. 277; on p. 274 he claimed that the Cumans were 'approximately on the level of social development of the conquering Hungarians [that is of the ninth century]'. Cf. Selmeczi, *Régészeti-néprajzi tanulmányok*, pp. 61–2.

[137] Gábor Hatházi, 'A kunok régészeti és történeti emlékei a Kelet-Dunántúlon', Ph.D. Dissertation (Budapest: ELTE, 1996), p. 57; Gábor Hatházi,'Megjegyzések a kun településhálózat megszilárdulásának kérdéséhez', in *Internationales Kulturhistorisches Symposion Mogersdorf 1994* (Eisenstadt: Amt des Bürgenlandischen Landesregierung, 1996), pp. 27–33; there was even less territory at their disposal in the XIV–XVth c.: Pálóczi Horváth, 'Kunok megtelepedése', p. 257.

[138] Ferenc Horváth, 'Régészeti adatok a kunok Dél-Alföldi történetéhez', in *Jászkunság kutatása*, pp. 66–74, see pp. 69–70; permanent villages from mid XIVth c.: András Pálóczi Horváth, 'Steppe Traditions and Cultural Assimilation of a Nomadic People: The Cumanians in Hungary in the 13th–14th Century', in *Archaeological Approaches to Cultural Identity*, ed. Stephen J. Shennan (London: Unwin Hyman, 1989; repr. London: Routledge, 1994), pp. 291–302; András Pálóczi Horváth, 'Keleti népek bevándorlása és letelepedése a középkori Magyarországon: a kunok példája', in *Internationales Kulturhistorisches Symposion Mogersdorf 1994*, pp. 17–20; András Pálóczi Horváth, 'Situation des recherches archéologiques sur les Comans en Hongrie', *AOASH* 22, no. 2 (1973): pp. 201–9; András Pálóczi Horváth, 'L'immigration et l'établissement des Comans en Hongrie', *AOASH* 29 (1975): pp. 313–33. Late XIV–XVth c: Ferenc Horváth, 'Csengele középkori temploma', *Móra Ferenc Múzeum Évkönyve 1976–77 / 1* (Szeged: Szegedi Nyomda, 1978), pp. 91–126. By XIIIth–XIVth c.: László Selmeczi, 'A szállástól a faluig: adatok a magyarországi kunok településtörténetéhez', in *Régészeti-néprajzi tanulmányok*, pp. 61–85; Selmeczi, 'Kunok nomadizmusának', pp. 87–99. (However, Selmeczi's 'The Settlement Structure of the Cumanian Settlers in the Nagykunság', in *Hungaro-Turcica: Studies in Honour of Julius Németh*, ed. Gyula Káldy-Nagy (Budapest: Eötvös Loránd University, 1976), pp. 255–62, advocated the view of

The nature of the evidence itself is problematic. No excavations of Cuman settlements have as yet produced an authentically dated thirteenth-century stratum. Cuman mass cemeteries attest to a certain stability of the Cuman population, but both the exact beginnings of such cemeteries and their relations to permanent settlements are debated.[139] Scholars also had recourse to toponyms; the names of Cuman settlements were often compounds of a personal name and the word 'dwelling' (*descensus*). Some of the personal names used were traditional Turkic ones, that is, those settlements may have been named before the stock of names changed – in the thirteenth or early fourteenth centuries.[140] On the other hand, some individuals retained their Turkic names much longer, so this is not an infallible method for dating settlements. The interpretation of charter evidence is controversial as well. Traditionally, fourteenth-century charters that describe Cumans as living 'in circuitu villarum', 'circa ecclesiam', 'iuxta locum', or mention Cuman *descensus* whose names change or are uncertain, were seen as proof of still mobile camps. According to Gábor Hatházi, however, the settlements were fixed, but their names changed in every generation, to correspond to the name of their leader, and this led to such designations in charters.[141] Finally, perhaps some groups retained their mobility longer than others, even into the fifteenth century, as the excavations of one area suggest.[142] The outcome of the process of settlement, however, is clear; by the fifteenth and sixteenth centuries Cumans lived in villages whose structures resembled those of Hungarian villages with the exception of the presence of a yurt near the house.[143]

Thirteenth-century charter evidence yields important information on Cuman landownership. Early signs of integration coincided with a disruptive Cuman presence. Cumans occupied land by force, looting and

footnote 138 (*cont.*)
fourteenth–fifteenth century settlement.) Hatházi, 'Megjegyzések'; Hatházi, 'Perkátai'. On the difficulties of the sedentarization of subject nomads: Khazanov, *Nomads*, pp. 198–202, 221.
[139] Selmeczi, *Régészeti-néprajzi tanulmányok*, pp. 24, 32; Hatházi, 'Perkátai', p. 656; Hatházi, 'Megjegyzések', pp. 27–30; Horváth, 'Csengele', pp. 118–24.
[140] László Rásonyi, 'Les noms toponymiques du Kiskunság', *Acta Linguistica Academiae Scientiarum Hungaricae* 7 (1958): pp. 73–146; Hatházi, 'Perkátai', p. 655, Pálóczi Horváth, *Besenyők*, pp. 96–7.
[141] *JK*, vol. III: p. 486, no. 33 (1349), p. 511, no. 56 (1389); Imre Nagy et al., eds., *Codex diplomaticus domus senioris comitum Zichy de Zich et Vásonkő* [*CDZ*], 12 vols. (Pest: Magyar Történelmi Társulat, 1871–1931), vol. II: pp. 268–9, no. 190. Pálóczi Horváth, 'Kunok megtelepedése', p. 256; Hatházi, 'Kunok régészeti', p. 57.
[142] Sixteenth century: István Méri, 'Beszámoló a Tiszalök-Rázompusztai és Túrkeve-Mórici ásatások eredményéről II', *Archaeologiai Értesítő* 81 (1954): pp. 138–54, see p. 139.
[143] László Selmeczi, 'Nomád települési struktúra a Nagykunságban', in *Régészeti-néprajzi tanulmányok*, pp. 49–59; Selmeczi, 'Settlement Structure'. On Cuman settlement in one area: András Pálóczi Horváth, 'A kun betelepedés Kiskunfélegyháza környékén és a város korai története', *Múzeumi Kutatások Bács-Kiskun megyében 1995–1996* (Kecskemét, 1997), pp. 25–33. On other characteristics of the Cuman villages: Selmeczi, *Régészeti-néprajzi tanulmányok*, p. 76; p. 93 on the types of animals. Méri, 'Beszámoló a Tiszalök-Rázompusztai'.

burning; they devastated villages, especially when they participated in Hungarian civil wars in the 1260s and during the reign of László IV.[144] Cumans also received grants of land from the king in many areas of the kingdom, very often to win or keep their allegiance.[145] Cumans were given estates for faithful service to the king, especially during the civil war that raged between Béla IV and his son István in the 1260s, but they often lost these holdings. Sometimes Cumans deserted their lands; more often, their possessions were revoked by the kings as Cuman political loyalties changed, thus obstructing the development of stable Cuman ownership. Cumans similarly gained and lost lands during the rule of László IV.[146] During the thirteenth century, the Cuman extended family often retained communal ownership. When they initiated certain transactions, such as the sale of land, the charters carefully specified that all the 'cognati' were present, or at least gave their consent through representatives; sometimes the portion of a non-consenting relative was exempted from the transaction.[147] This conformed to local practice; there are similar examples among Christian inhabitants of the kingdom.[148] Once, when the relatives' consent was not included in the charter, the text confirmed that the sale was none the less valid, and nobody from the kin group ('per aliquem cognatorum vel consanguineorum') could challenge its validity.[149] Cumans bought and sold land, sometimes paying in money instead of goods. There are examples of seeking royal approval for the sale of land.[150] Land was inherited by all the sons, and when a Cuman

---

[144] See the section on military roles below, p. 146.
[145] *JK*, vol. II: p. 416, no. 50 (*CD*, vol. IV, pt. 3: p. 183; *RA*, no. 1417), p. 418, no. 53 (*RA*, no. 1856); *CDZ*, vol. I: pp. 214–15, no. 247; MOL DL 975 (*ÁÚO*, vol. IV: pp. 76–7, no. 37; *JK*, vol. II: p. 429, no. 64; *Budapest történetének oklevelés*, p. 166, no. 150; *RA*, no. 2821); *HO*, vol. VIII: p. 80, no. 64 (*RA*, no. 1246).
[146] E.g. MOL DF 248407 (Knauz, *Esztergomi főegyháznak okmánytára*, vol. I: p. 52, no. 78; *MES*, vol. I: pp. 514–17, no. 670; *JK*, vol. II: p. 414, no. 49; *RA*, no. 1416); *JK*, vol. II: p. 420, no. 54 (*CD*, vol. IV, pt. 3: pp. 407–9; *RA*, no. 1869); MOL DL 1170 (*JK*, vol. II: pp. 448–9, no. 77; *CD*, vol. V, pt. 3: p. 260; *RA*, no. 3348); *HO*, vol. VIII: p. 80, no. 64 (*RA*, no. 1246); MOL DL 975 (*ÁÚO*, vol. IV: pp. 76–7, no. 37 gives the name of the Cuman as Torzol instead of Torzok; *RA*, no. 2821).
[147] *ÁÚO*, vol. XII: p. 534, no. 436; MOL DL 40166 (*ÁÚO*, vol. XII: p. 389, no. 320; *JK*, vol. II: p. 447, no. 75; *CD*, vol. VII, pt. 5: p. 595, no. CCCXCVI; *RA*, no. 3213); *JK*, vol. II: pp. 418–19, no. 53 (*RA*, no. 1856); Knauz, *Esztergomi főegyháznak okmánytára*, vol. II: p. 144, no. 165 (*JK*, vol. II: p. 450, no. 78).
[148] E.g., *ÁÚO*, vol. IV: p. 228, no. 138, p. 277, no. 174 (MOL DL 40177; *RA*, no. 3368); *Hazai Okleveltár*, pp. 86–7, no. 79. Cf. Gerics, 'Nemesi jog'.
[149] *JK*, vol. II: p. 456, no. 85 (*ÁÚO*, vol. IX: p. 486, no. 347).
[150] *JK*, vol. II: p. 418, no. 53 (*RA*, no. 1856); MOL DL 86854 (*ÁÚO*, vol. XII: p. 313, no. 261; the name of the land is 'Gyopol' correctly); *JK*, vol. II: p. 456, no. 85 (*ÁÚO*, vol. IX: p. 486, no. 347); MOL DF 235968 (*JK*, vol. II: p. 450, no. 78; *CD*, vol. V, pt. 3: p. 273; Knauz, *Esztergomi főegyháznak okmánytára*, vol. II: p. 144, no. 165; *MES*, vol. II: pp. 179–80, no. 159; *ÁÚO*, vol. IX: p. 405, no. 288); *MES*, vol. II: pp. 333–4, no. 333. A Cuman buying land and then selling it: *Anjoukori Okmánytár*, vol. II: pp. 508, 512–13, nos. 435, 440, 441 (1330). MOL DL 40166 (*ÁÚO*, vol. XII: p. 389, no. 320; *RA*, no. 3213; the name of the land is Rohosnicha correctly).

died without heirs his land escheated to the king, according to the custom of the kingdom.[151]

Already in the thirteenth century some Cumans behaved as Christian landlords of the period did, and possessed lands cultivated by peasants. In one instance Cumans exchanged their land, which was deserted, for lands inhabited by peasants.[152] Cuman landowners established border markers on their estates; one family maintained a water-mill.[153] Some of these Cumans were Christians, while others were not converted. There were Cuman landowners who integrated into the ranks of the nobility.[154] During the fourteenth and fifteenth centuries landed estates developed under the power of Cuman lords.[155] On the other end of the scale were those Cumans who became members of the peasantry. The Cumans are the only non-Christian group for whom we possess references to their supplying agricultural labour for Christian lords in the thirteenth and fourteenth centuries.[156] Integration as a minority into an already settled society provided patterns for the development of settlement and land use.

MILITARY ROLE

Non-Christians played a major role in Hungary in providing military power. Both Muslims, especially until the mid-thirteenth century, and Cumans, especially in the second half of the thirteenth century, served the king as soldiers, along with other Hungarian or non-Hungarian peoples.

Muslims entered the army in organized units and not on an individual basis, although nobles occasionally also employed Muslims in attacks against their neighbours within Hungary.[157] Muslim participation in the Hungarian army is documented by several sources. Abū Hāmid, who lived in Hungary for three years in the middle of the twelfth century,

---

[151] *JK*, vol. II: p. 456, no. 85 (*ÁÚO*, vol. IX: p. 486, no. 347); MOL DL 1170 (*CD*, vol. V, pt. 3: p. 260, corrected in *JK*, vol. II: pp. 448–9, no. 77; *RA*, no. 3348); *JK*, vol. II: p. 416, no. 50 (*RA*, no. 1417); *JK*, vol. II: p. 461, no. 92 (*CD*, vol. VI, pt. 2: pp. 25–7; *RA*, no. 4090). Examples of lands of Christians who died without an heir escheating to the king: *Hazai Oklevéltár*, p. 84, no. 76 (*RA*, no. 2868), p. 105, no. 99 (*RA*, no. 3450). József Gerics and Erzsébet Ladányi, 'A magyarországi birtokjog kérdései a középkorban', *Levéltári Szemle* 41, no. 4 (1991): pp. 3–19, see p. 3.

[152] MOL DL 1343 (*ÁÚO*, vol. XII: p. 534, no. 436; *JK*, vol. II: pp. 459–60, no. 90) (1292).

[153] *HO*, vol. VIII: p. 80, no. 64 (*RA*, no. 1246); MOL DF 248407 (Knauz, *Esztergomi főegyháznak okmánytára*, vol. I: p. 52, no. 78; *MES*, vol. I: pp. 514–17, no. 670; *JK*, vol. II: p. 414, no. 49; *RA*, no. 1416); *JK*, vol. II: p. 450, no. 78. [154] Györffy, 'Magyarországi kun', p. 280.

[155] *Ibid.*, pp. 291–304; Pálóczi Horváth, *Besenyők*, pp. 96–104; agriculture: László Selmeczi, 'Régészeti ásatások a Nagykunságban', in *Tanulmányok a 700 éves Kunhegyesről*, ed. Ernő Szurmay (Kunhegyes: Kunhegyesi Nagyközségi Tanács, 1989), pp. 5–16, p. 9.

[156] Rogerius, in *SRH*, vol. II: p. 557; Györffy, 'Magyarországi kun', p. 281; Pálóczi Horváth, *Besenyők*, p. 99.

[157] ASV Reg. Vat. 12, ff. 25v–26r, 34v, 35v–36r (*Reg. Hon. III*, nos. 4233, 4299, 4300; *VMH*, pp. 37, 39–40, nos. LXXVII, LXXXI, LXXXII).

described Muslims in Hungary serving the king in war, and he himself witnessed a war against Byzantium where Hungary's Muslims played an active role.[158] This is corroborated by the Byzantine Ioannes Kinnamos, who recorded that a contingent of Muslims living in Hungary was sent by Géza II to fight against Byzantium on the side of the Serbs in 1150.[159] King Géza II must have been pleased with his Muslim soldiers, for he charged Abū Hāmid to recruit more of these Muslims 'who, although poor and weak, excel in bowmanship'.[160] Another report referred to Hungarian Muslim soldiers sent when the bishop of Prague requested military aid in the twelfth century.[161] Yāqūt encountered Hungarian Muslims in Aleppo in the early thirteenth century, who told him that they served the king in war, fighting together with the Hungarians, who, according to them, only fought opponents of Islam.[162] Roger's account of the Mongol invasion mentioned the Muslim soldiers captured by the Mongols.[163] As late as 1260 there is a mention of Muslim soldiers in Béla IV's army, in his campaign against Otakar II of Bohemia.[164]

The Muslim military element was important to the kings of Hungary, but it was equally a source of some anxiety according to two Muslim sources. Yāqūt mentions that the kings prohibited the Muslims from erecting walls around their settlements, and were on the watch for any possible sign of revolt.[165] Abū Hāmid relates that when he planned a trip to Rumiyya the Hungarian Muslims dissuaded him by saying that the Hungarian king would suspect them of a conspiracy with his brother, who was married to the princess of Rumiyya. They feared that the king might misconstrue Abū Hāmid's visit as the beginning of an alliance between that brother and Hungary's Muslims, and consequently destroy the latter.[166] A Muslim revolt, however, never erupted.

Muslims were employed as soldiers by other kings as well, for example in Navarre, in southern Italy and by the Byzantine emperors.[167] The

---

[158] *Abu-Hámid*, pp. 56, 59–60.
[159] Moravcsik, *Fontes Byzantini*, p. 202, Greek text and Hungarian tr.
[160] *Abu-Hámid*, p. 65 (from the Hungarian tr.).
[161] Wilhelmus Wattenbach, ed., 'Vincentii Pragensis annales', in *MGH SS*, vol. XVII: pp. 658–83, see p. 667.   [162] Yāqūt, p. 470 (Reinaud, *Géographie*, p. 294).
[163] Rogerius, in *SRH*, vol. II: p. 582.
[164] Rudolf Köpke, ed., 'Annales Otakariani', in *MGH SS*, vol. IX: pp. 181–94, see p. 185.
[165] Yāqūt, p. 469 (Reinaud, *Géographie*, p. 294).
[166] *Abu-Hámid*, p. 82. Scholars are debating whether he planned to go to Constantinople (Lewicki, 'Węgry i muzulmanie', pp. 117–18), or Rus' (*Abu-Hámid*, p. 82): the ruler of either could have been suspected of a plot against the king.
[167] Harvey, *Islamic Spain*, pp. 139, 145; Christoph T. Maier, 'Crusade and Rhetoric against the Muslim Colony of Lucera', *Journal of Medieval History* 21 (1995): pp. 343–85, esp. p. 344, with further bibliography. In Byzantium they served as allied troops (auxiliaries): Mark C. Bartusis, *The Late Byzantine Army: Arms and Society, 1204–1453* (Philadelphia: University of Pennsylvania Press, 1992), pp. 50–3, 93–4.

Hungarians themselves probably became familiar with this practice while they were a part of the Khazar Empire, where Muslims had an important military role. They were employed there as soldiers in the royal army and even the *wazîr* (chief military commander) had been a Muslim.[168] It is possible that at the beginning, Hungarian kings had adopted this model. In any case, they continued to employ Muslim soldiers until well into the thirteenth century.

Cumans were the most important military element employed as nomadic light cavalry in thirteenth-century Hungary. The Hungarian army included some heavy mounted cavalry (knights), large units of light cavalry, and nomadic-style light cavalry fighting with bows and arrows according to eastern modes of warfare.[169] That is, the mounted vanguard attacked the enemy with arrows, then turned back as if in flight, luring the enemy into a trap. Their armament was also specially adapted to this type of warfare. For example, a Cuman grave in Hungary yielded four different sorts of arrow-heads, suited for killing horses, and piercing leather or metal armours.[170] Although the Hungarians themselves had originally used the same battle tactics, they lost these skills during centuries of settled life. It took constant practice, easily obtained in a nomadic way of life, but not in an agricultural one, to retain the ability to fight in this manner. Thus it was constantly necessary to replenish the ranks of these soldiers, and, over the centuries, Hungarian kings integrated several different groups into their armies who were capable of performing nomadic light cavalry service. Various elements of Hungary's population constituted these units over time, such as the *székely* and the Pecheneg. (In addition to being integrated into the army these groups were also settled as border guards.[171]) Each group gradually lost its effectiveness; prior to Cuman immigration nomadic light cavalry was diminishing.[172]

---

[168] Golden, *Introduction*, p. 242; Miquel, *Géographie*, p. 521.

[169] András Borosy, 'A lovagi haditechnika és a lovagság Magyarországon az Árpád-korban', *Társadalom- és Művelődéstörténeti tanulmányok. Mályusz Elemér Emlékkönyv*, ed. Éva H. Balázs, Erik Fügedi and Ferenc Maksay (Budapest: Akadémiai Kiadó, 1984), pp. 47–57.

[170] On techniques, strategy and weapons: Katalin U. Kőhalmi, *A steppék nomádja lóháton, fegyverben*, Kőrösi Csoma Kiskönyvtár 12 (Budapest: Akadémiai Kiadó, 1972); Denis Sinor, 'Quelques passages relatifs aux Comans, tirés des chroniques françaises de l'époque des croisades', in *Silver Jubilee Volume of the Zinbun-Kagaku-Kenkyusyo, Kyoto University*, ed. Shigeki Kaizuka (Kyoto: Nissha, 1954), pp. 370–5, see p. 374; András Borosy, 'A XI–XIV. sz. magyar lovasságról', *Hadtörténelmi közlemények* 9, no. 2 (1962): pp. 119–74, see pp. 137–55; arrow-heads: András Pálóczi Horváth, 'A csólyosi kun sírlelet hadtörténeti vonatkozásai', *A Móra Ferenc Múzeum Évkönyve 1969/1* (Szeged: Szegedi Nyomda, 1969), pp. 115–21, see pp. 118–20.

[171] György Györffy, 'A székelyek eredete és településük története', in *Magyarság*, pp. 11–42; Györffy, 'Besenyők és magyarok'; Göckenjan, *Hilfsvölker*; Pauler, 'Néhány szó hadi viszonyainkról', pp. 508–13; D. A. Rassovsky, 'Péchénègues, Torks et Béréndés en Russie et en Hongrie', *Seminarium Kondakovianum* 6 (1933), pp. 1–66.

[172] Borosy, 'XI–XIV. sz. magyar lovasságról', pp. 137–55.

Non-Christians in Hungarian economy and society

The Cumans were welcomed into the country initially with the view of providing additional military power against enemies.[173] Drawing on nomad military power by a sedentary society in this way was a typical pattern of nomad–sedentary interaction. The Cumans performed military service in a variety of capacities and societies: for example, as Mamluk slave-soldiers in Egypt, as allied troops of Byzantium against other nomads, as mercenaries in Rus' domestic wars, and as immigrants in royal service, as was the case in Hungary.[174] The nomad-style light cavalry of Hungary was reborn with the Cumans. But the Cumans, numerically more important and under their own leaders, were not as easily manageable as the Muslim contingents. The Muslims, despite being a potential source of revolt, never turned against the king. The Cumans from the beginning proved to be a much graver source of danger to the kingdom: when the Cumans left Hungary after the murder of their chief Kötöny, they devastated the lands on their way. None the less King Béla invited them back to Hungary by 1246. Hungarian kings found Cuman military potential too tempting to resist, yet repeatedly had to face the menace posed by the Cumans; consequently they both courted and feared them.

Originally the explicit reason for establishing a Cuman military contingent was that they should protect the country against Mongol attacks. As King Béla wrote to the pope, 'for shame, today we defend our country with pagans'.[175] In fact, however, the potential of the Cuman military force was used for other ends. From the time of their re-entry into the kingdom, they were employed in wars waged against Hungary's neighbours. It has been calculated that between 1246 and 1278 the Cumans participated in ten wars against Austria, Moravia, Carinthia and Styria.[176] Protests against the 'un-Christian' behaviour of a Christian king, using pagans in his raids against other Christian countries, and allegations of the cruelty of the pagans appear repeatedly in sources from these lands.[177]

---

[173] Rogerius, in *SRH*, vol. II: p. 559.

[174] Golden, 'Nomads and their Sedentary Neighbors', pp. 68, 72–4; Peter B. Golden, 'The Polovcii Dikii', *Harvard Ukrainian Studies* 3–4 (1979–80): pp. 296–309. Sinor, *Cambridge History of Early Inner Asia*, pp. 282–3; Hodinka, *Orosz évkönyvek*, pp. 304–7, 318–19, 340–1, 358–9, 360–1, 368–9, 392–5; Simon Franklin and Jonathan Shepard, *The Emergence of Rus 750–1200* (London and New York: Longman, 1996), pp. 260–72; Pritsak, 'Polovcians and Rus''; Reuven Amitai-Preiss, *Mongols and Mamluks: The Mamluk–Īlkhānid War, 1260–1281* (Cambridge: Cambridge University Press, 1995), pp. 17–19. Khazanov, *Nomads*, p. 212.

[175] 'prohdolor per paganos hodie regnum nostrum defendimus': ASV AA Arm. I-XVIII-605 (*VMH*, p. 231, no. CCCCXL; *RA*, no. 933a).

[176] Györffy, 'Magyarországi kun', p. 278 (wars in 1246, 1250, 1252, 1253, 1260, 1270, 1271, 1273, 1276 and 1278).

[177] For example: 'In prefatis nempe terris nunquam fecit tot horribilia rex christianus' (as Béla IV): Wilhelmus Wattenbach, ed., 'Annales Austriae, Historia annorum 1264–1279', in *MGH SS*, vol. IX: pp. 649–54, p. 651. See also the *Chronica* of Johannes of Marignola on Hungarian attacks against Bohemia, with the use of Cumans: *Fontes Rerum Bohemicarum*, 8 vols. (Prague: Musea

This was a recurring complaint in the Middle Ages against Christian kings who resorted to the help of 'pagan' armies.[178] The Cumans were still employed in foreign wars during the reign of Louis the Great in the fourteenth century, but Cuman light cavalry had disappeared by the fifteenth century.[179]

Cumans, however, had yet another military function: kings sought to turn them into the military basis for royal power within the kingdom at the time of growing noble strife and anarchy. Cumans played a similar role in Khwarazm, Rus' and Georgia.[180] From the time of their re-entry the Cumans participated in internal as well as external wars. During the reign of Béla IV civil war broke out between the king and his heir István, who ruled over the eastern part of the kingdom from 1257 (king of Hungary 1270–2). Some nobles sided with the king, others with the prince, gaining estates and privileges for their support. During the wars that continued intermittently for several years, István and Béla tried to keep or sought to win Cuman backing, both giving land grants to their supporters. István, although *dominus Cumanorum* and husband to a Cuman chieftain's daughter, did not securely command Cuman fidelity. Their support was so important that István spent large sums on procuring presents for prominent Cumans, hoping to retain their loyalty. He gave them clothes embroidered with golden thread, scarlet textiles and silks, and clothes from Ghent. In one instance, he spent 134 marks on such presents, out of a total expenditure of 1,485.5 marks.[181] (Cumans

footnote 177 (*cont.*)
Království Českého, Nakladem Nadáni Františka Palackého, 1873–1932), vol. III: pp. 492–604, see p. 568. Bruno of Olomouc complained about the Cuman danger to Gregory X: AA Arm. I-XVIII-3104 (*VMH*, pp. 307–8, no. DXXXV). Some other texts: *JK*, vol. II: p. 406, no. 38; 'Annales Otakariani', *MGH SS*, vol. IX: pp. 182–3, 185; Wilhelmus Wattenbach, ed., 'Annales Sancti Rudberti Salisburgenses', in *MGH SS*, vol. IX: pp. 758–810, see pp. 792, 798, 800; Wilhelmus Wattenbach, ed., 'Annales Austriae, Continuatio Vindobonensis', in *MGH SS*, vol. IX: pp. 698–722, see p. 710; Philip Jaffé, ed., 'Hermanni Altahensis annales', in *MGH SS*, vol. XVII: pp. 381–407, see p. 393; 'Cronica Przibiconis dicti Pulkaua', in *Fontes Rerum Bohemicarum*, vol. V: pp. 3–207, see p. 143; Wilhelmus Wattenbach, ed., 'Annales Austriae, Continuatio Praedicatorum Vindobonensium', in *MGH SS*, vol. IX: pp. 724–32, see p. 731; 'Paltramus seu Vatzo, consul Viennensis: Chronicon Austriacum ad a. 1301', in *Scriptores Rerum Austriacum*, 3 vols., ed. Hieronymus Pez (Leipzig, 1721–45), vol. I: cols. 707–24, see cols. 717–18, repr. in Gombos, *Catalogus*, vol. III: pp. 1958–9; Ottokar of Steier, *Österreichische Reimchronik*, ed. Joseph Seemüller, in *MGH DC*, vol. V, pt. 1: pp. 204–5, 227–8. Similar views in a letter of Pope Innocent IV: *CD*, vol. IV, pt. 2: pp. 198–200.

[178] E.g. Francis Dvornik, *The Making of Central and Eastern Europe* (London: Polish Research Centre, 1949), p. 185 (Henry II); Norman Daniel, 'The Legal and Political Theory of the Crusade', in *The Impact of the Crusades on Europe*, ed. Harry W. Hazard and Norman P. Zacour, vol. VI of *A History of the Crusades*, ed. Setton, pp. 3–38, see p. 4; Rowell, *Lithuania*, pp. 234–7.

[179] Pálóczi Horváth 'Csólyosi kun sírlelet hadtörténeti vonatkozásai', p. 116; Borosy, 'XI–XIV. sz. magyar lovasságról', pp. 153–5 (cites sources).

[180] Serzhan M. Akhinazov, 'Kipcaks and Khwarazm', in *Rulers from the Steppe*, pp. 126–31; Golden, 'Cumanica I'; also note 174 above.   [181] Zolnay, 'István', pp. 81–2.

Non-Christians in Hungarian economy and society

were courted in a similar manner in Byzantium and Rus'; nomads attached great importance to silks and fine textiles.[182] He also involved them in decision-making; in the peace treaty of 1262, István mentioned that he was ready to declare peace, having asked the advice and gained the assent of the Cuman leaders.[183] For all his efforts, István could not keep the loyalty of all 'his' Cumans. King Béla employed Cuman troops several times against his son, and sought to win the allegiance of others by the persuasion of intermediaries.[184] István described those who changed sides as rebelling against him.[185] In the peace treaty of 1266, Béla agreed not to entice István's Cumans into his own service.[186] Pope Urban IV condemned the civil war, and especially this reliance on non-Christians.[187]

During the reign of István's son, László IV (1272–90), the Cumans gained unprecedented importance. László himself was half Cuman, and, more importantly, political anarchy was reaching its zenith. László succeeded to the throne as a minor, with his Cuman mother Queen Erzsébet (Elizabeth) as regent. Nobles did not fail to exploit this occasion to increase their power. László had been abducted by Joachim, the viceroy (*bán*) of Croatia and Slavonia, before István's death. At the time of his succession, László was a prisoner of Joachim, who gained the support of the queen-regent, while another faction of the nobility plotted to take power. This group attempted to capture the queen, and having been defeated, turned to Otakar II, the Czech king, for support. It is unnecessary to describe all the details of the intrigues and wars that followed; the young king had almost no reliable supporters from among his nobles. The Cumans were much more dependent on the king; they seemed to be a firmer basis of royal power. Jenő Szűcs has even argued that László wished to establish an autocratic rule using Cuman support.[188]

Cumans constituted the elite military bodyguard of King László, called *neugerii* in Latin documents. This name misled scholars to identify the *neugerii* as members of a separate ethnic group until the true explanation

---

[182] Rassovsky, 'Comans et Byzance', pp. 350–1; Thomas T. Allsen, *Commodity and Exchange in the Mongol Empire: A Cultural History of Islamic Textiles* (Cambridge: Cambridge University Press, 1997), esp. pp. 11–12, 22, 28–9, 46–7, 50–1.
[183] *CD*, vol. IV, pt. 3: p. 70 (*MES*, vol. I: p. 476, no. 619; *RA*, no. 1791).
[184] *JK*, vol. II: p. 420, no. 54 (*RA*, no. 1869); *ÁÚO*, vol. IV: p. 24, no. 9 (*RA*, no. 2364); *HO*, vol. VI: pp. 240–3, no. 172 (*RA*, no. 2990); Pauler, *Magyar nemzet*, pp. 256–7. *MES*, vol. I: pp. 560–1, no. 722 (intermediaries). On land grants see above, p. 139.
[185] 'contra nos insurrexerant': *JK*, vol. II: p. 421, no. 54 (*RA*, no. 1869).
[186] 'Promisimus insuper predicto filio nostro . . . quod nec nos, nec domina regina . . . alliciemus, sollicitabimus, aut recipiemus Cumanos.' ASV Reg. Vat. 32, f. 83r (*Reg. Clem. IV*, no. 332; *VMH*, p. 285, no. DXVIII; *RA*, no. 1481).
[187] ASV Reg. Vat. 29, f. 100r (*Reg. Urb. IV*, no. 1243; *VMH*, p. 265, no. CCCCLXXXV; see pp. 167–8).
[188] Szűcs, *Utolsó Árpádok*, pp. 310–21.

was furnished by Gyula Németh.[189] The institution had parallels among the Mongols; *nökers* left their tribes in order to serve a chieftain. This *comitatus*-type organization provided a seemingly reliable personal guard and standing army for the lord. Such military support must have been highly desirable for László, given the uncertain fidelity of his nobles.

Yet the Cumans turned out to be a two-edged weapon. Their military power, fostered by the kings, allowed the Cumans to act independently. Many examples show this before and during László's reign. During the civil war of the 1260s, the Cumans did not simply obey royal orders, but also devastated Hungarian villages, plundered, and assaulted the population. During the reign of István V, the bishop of Nyitra was returning from an embassy to the duke of Austria when Cumans captured him and his men. The Cumans murdered eighteen members of the bishop's retinue, and took their possessions. A certain Mark damaged a charter concerning his rights to an estate when he had to wade through water to escape from the Cumans; a village was destroyed when Cumans, led by a local Christian, attacked, taking the property of the inhabitants, ruining the church, and killing three of the *ispán*'s men. The bishop of Vác rented a stone tower in 1285 in order to ensure that his dependants had a place of refuge in case of an attack: the list of potential attackers included the Cumans. Thirty-seven men died during the defence of the church of St Lawrence at Haj (Bodrog county) against the Cumans.[190] Finally, it was Cuman discontent, probably linked to the pressures of settlement and Christianization (see chapter 6) that brought about László's end. This discontent led first to attempted emigration, then to a large-scale revolt. In 1280 the Cumans tried to leave Hungary, but László led a military campaign to force them back.[191] In 1282 the Cumans turned against King

---

[189] Summary of attempts to identify the 'neugar people' in *JK*, vol. II: pp. 362–3; he identifies them as Cumans, but from the erroneous etymology of the name of the Mongol ruler Nogai. Gyula Németh, 'Kun László király nyőgérei', *Magyar Nyelv* 49 (1953): pp. 304–18; Gyula Németh,'Wanderungen des Mongolischen wortes *nökür* "genosse"', *AOASH* 3 (1953): pp. 1–23. The word was adopted into Hungarian via the Cuman language and not directly from Mongol: Ligeti, *Magyar nyelv török kapcsolatai*, p. 541. Cf. Turkic slave bodyguards: C. I. Beckwith, 'Aspects of the Early History of the Central Asian Guard Corps in Islam', *AEMAe* 4 (1984): pp. 29–43.

[190] The above-mentioned cases respectively: MOL DL 1146 (*ÁÚO*, vol. XII: p. 388, no. 319; *RA*, no. 3227); *CD*, vol. V, pt. 3: pp. 417–18 (*RA*, no. 3489), p. 442; MOL DF 251667 (*HO*, vol. VI: p. 309, no. 224); *HO*, vol. VII: p. 199, no. 157; Knauz, *Esztergomi főegyháznak okmánytára*, vol. I: p. 91, no. 127 (*CD*, vol. V, pt. 3: p. 288, *Budapest történetének okleveles*, p. 220, no. 205; *RA*, no. 3375); Kubinyi, *Árpádkori oklevelek*, p. 133, no. 155 (*ÁÚO*, vol. IX: pp. 381, no. 271; *RA*, no. 3284). Another charter mentions the many and great excesses of the Cumans ('propter plurimos et enormes excessus'): MOL DF 248407 (*CD*, vol. IV, pt. 3: p. 184; *RA*, no. 1416). On Cumans in Hungarian civil wars e.g. *JK*, vol. II: pp. 419–20, no. 54 (*RA*, no. 1869); *HO*, vol. VI: pp. 240–3, no. 172 (*RA*, no. 2990). Cuman looting and attacks against estates and churches: *CD*, vol. VII, pt. 5: pp. 464–5, no. CCXCI; *HO*, vol. VI: pp. 190–1, no. 136 (*RA*, no. 2410).

[191] Esp. *JK*, vol. II: pp. 454–5, no. 84 (*CD*, vol. V, pt. 3: pp. 409–12; *RA*, no. 3499); *Hazai Oklevéltár*, pp. 116–17, no. 110 (*RA*, no. 3544); *HO*, vol. VI: p. 316, no. 229 (*RA*, no. 3410), p. 317, no. 230

Non-Christians in Hungarian economy and society

László in open rebellion. László won the battle of Hód (1282), which earned him the praise of his chronicler Simon of Kéza.[192] He was able to subjugate the Cumans, but could not quell their dissatisfaction. This eventually led to his assassination in 1290.[193] László's successors continued to use Cuman military power in their campaigns during the fourteenth century, but none relied so extensively on their support as he had done.[194]

Non-Christians played several economic roles, and had an important part in the military system of medieval Hungary. They neither occupied positions available only to them, entirely different from those occupied by Christians, nor were they marginalized, or set completely apart by restrictions. Their contribution was not negligible, and at times, such as during the early thirteenth-century reform of royal finances, and after the Mongol invasion, it was very important to the kings of Hungary, but it was not irreplaceable. Venetian and German burghers filled the same economic roles as Jews and Muslims. Thus the recurrent thesis that Béla IV promulgated his privileges of 1251 for the Jews because he had to rely on them as part of the programme to rebuild the economy of the kingdom after the Mongol invasion is unfounded. Jewish involvement with royal revenues started well before the Mongol invasion of 1241, and King Béla IV himself had already asked the pope for permission to employ non-Christians in 1239.[195] The traditional argument of 'toleration' arising from sheer economic necessity is untenable.[196] Hungarian kings were not forced to rely on non-Christians for lack of alternative economic possibilities; they employed them because these rulers used all available resources. The most important non-Christian contribution from the point of view of building royal power was military. The Cumans were the least replaceable in their military capacity, but also the most dangerous element. Although a number of groups, among them Christianized ones, filled military roles as border guards and light cavalry, the Cumans

---

(*RA*, nos. 3079, 3413). Attila Zsoldos, 'Tétényről a Hód-tóig', *Történelmi Szemle* 39 (1997): pp. 69–98; p. 89 and notes 117–22 with references to all the texts.

[192] *SRH*, vol. I: p. 187. The dating of this battle has been debated (1280 or 1282): János Karácsonyi, 'A Hód-tavi csata éve', *Századok* 35 (1901): pp. 626–36; László Blazovich, 'IV. László harca a kunok ellen', *Századok* 111 (1977): pp. 941–5; Zsoldos, 'Tétényről', notes to pp. 88, 95–6 on the charter evidence.

[193] Claims that László was killed by a jealous relative of his Cuman concubine (Pauler, *Magyar nemzet*, vol. II: p. 573) or that the Cuman assassins were instigated by Hungarian nobles (Károly Szabó, *Kun László 1272–1290* (Budapest: Franklin Társulat, 1886; repr. Budapest: Maecenas Könyvkiadó, 1988), p. 179) were refuted by Györffy 'Magyarországi kun', pp. 286–7.

[194] Borosy, 'XI–XIV. századi magyar lovasságról', pp. 153–5; Ágnes Kurcz, *A lovagi kultúra Magyarországon a 13–14. században* (Budapest: Akadémiai Kiadó, 1988), pp. 45–7.

[195] See chapter 5, p. 160.   [196] See K. Stow's remark in Grayzel, *Church*, vol. II: p. 79.

presented an unprecedented opportunity for the kings of Hungary to strengthen their power. At the same time, they were no mere tools of royal power, but also constituted a threat to it. They also clashed with the population of the kingdom because of their radically different way of life: the thirteenth century brought about only the beginning of economic and social integration. From a social and economic perspective, Jews and Muslims were much better integrated than Cumans.

Non-Christian opportunities were in part determined by the economic context, and the one Hungary provided was in many ways similar to that of other frontier regions of Europe. The Jews of Hungary, like those of Poland, Sicily or the Iberian peninsula, were not primarily money-lenders in the thirteenth century; landownership and leasing royal revenues presented different possibilities. The situation of Muslims and, to some extent, of the Cumans, closely controlled by and serving the kings of Hungary, resembled that of the dependent Muslim communities of Lucera and Valencia. The presence of a large mass of newly arrived 'pagans', although unique compared with other thirteenth-century European kingdoms, is not at all unusual in comparison with yet another frontier, that between sedentary societies and the nomad world. Thus, striking similarities exist between the Cuman military roles in Hungary and Georgia.

To say that the situation of Hungary's non-Christian population can fruitfully be compared with that of other frontier societies is not to claim that all frontier regions were the same in economic and social possibilities. It is crucial to evaluate each situation separately, but it is equally important to show that the received opinion about the non-Christian, and especially Jewish, economic position in medieval Christendom has been formulated on the basis of north-western European patterns. Once economic and social roles in frontier regions of Christendom are scrutinized, we are left with a richer picture than that of marginalized and outcast groups on the fringe of society.

Chapter 5

CONFLICTS BETWEEN THE PAPACY AND THE KINGS

Non-Christians in Hungary, as elsewhere in medieval Europe, were subject to local lay and ecclesiastical legislation, as well as to the papacy via Church councils and decretals. This chapter investigates the points of contention between Hungarian kings and the popes over the kingdom's non-Christians, the arguments and the vocabulary used by each side, and the role of local nobles and ecclesiastics in these conflicts. Policies over non-Christians (regulating, for example, usury or dress) were not the only controversial topics of concern to medieval kings and popes; debate erupted over many issues after the late eleventh century. The immediate causes varied, from the question of who could invest a bishop with the ring and staff, to whether a king could repudiate his wife, but they were all part of the underlying power politics between the pontiffs and the monarchs. By the thirteenth century issues of sovereignty played an important part in these power struggles.

To place papal conflicts with Hungarian kings in context, one should keep in mind that during the Middle Ages both ecclesiastical and royal policies contained elements of protection of and discrimination against non-Christians. Nor were ecclesiastical views uniform on this issue: popes, theologians or religious orders would at times adopt different approaches. The thirteenth-century papacy as a whole, as well as individual popes, often pursued the contradictory goals of ensuring the physical safety of Jews, while enforcing their separation from Christians, relegating them to a position of inferiority and condemning them as depraved, obstinate, treacherous, false and harmful to Christians. For example, Pope Martin IV intervened in Portugal to ensure that the king did not employ Jews in positions and offices with power over Christians and enforced the wearing of distinguishing clothing. But he also reissued *Sicut Judaeis*, a bull of protection for the Jews.[1] Innocent IV included the

---

[1] Grayzel, *Church*, vol. II: nos. 48 and 45 (Simonsohn, *Apostolic See Documents*, nos. 251, 248); Simonsohn, *Apostolic See History*, pp. 42–5.

protection of Jews against the ritual murder libel in the *Sicut Judaeis* and other bulls, but at the same time upheld the decision to burn the Talmud.² Similar examples could be cited.³ Certain popes went even further in offering protection to individuals: Pope Nicholas IV asked Rudolph I of Habsburg to release Rabbi Meir of Rothenburg from prison, although his intervention remained ineffective.⁴ The case of the Jews was to some extent a special one, as a consequence of both their physical presence as scattered minorities and the historical and doctrinal relations between Judaism and Christianity. Jews lived in small communities within Christian Europe, and were not military foes such as Muslims or Mongols, although a Christian myth increasingly turned them into an enemy intent on killing Christian children and poisoning the rest of the population. On the doctrinal level, Christianity's development from and subsequent attempt entirely to supplant Judaism posed the question of a continued Jewish presence. Attempts to refute and to eradicate that presence intensified in the central Middle Ages. Ecclesiastical policies towards Muslims and pagans were no less complex. 'Saracens' were enemies to be exterminated, or, as some hoped, converted. However, Muslims who lived peacefully in Christian countries were to be tolerated.⁵ 'Pagans' were sometimes seen as the enemies of Christendom, or even eschatological figures, and at other times as awaiting conversion.⁶

Royal policies also included measures of both protection and separation toward non-Christian subjects. For example, even King Louis IX of France, who was certainly no friend of the Jews, and who promulgated one harsh measure after another against them, including enforcing the wearing of distinguishing signs and the burning of the Talmud, ordered

---

² Simonsohn, *Apostolic See History*, pp. 52–4, 304–6; Simonsohn, *Apostolic See Documents*, nos. 171, 183, 185, 188.
³ Grayzel, *Church*, vol. II: nos. 50, 51 (nos. 2, 11, 31, 38, 41, 45 for the various versions of the *Sicut Judaeis* bull of protection; Simonsohn, *Apostolic See Documents*, nos. 255, 206, 213, 234, 238, 242, 248). Simonsohn, *Apostolic See History*, pp. 16–17, 23–5, 39–93 on the ambivalence of papal politics, and pp. 28–30 on the variety of views among theologians. Clerical behaviour also ranged from protection to inciting Christians to pogroms, e.g. Robert Chazan, ed., *Church, State, and Jew in the Middle Ages* (New York: Behrman House, 1980), chapter VII; Langmuir, *Toward a Definition*, part 4.
⁴ Grayzel, *Church*, vol. II: no. 54; Simonsohn, *Apostolic See Documents*, no. 259.
⁵ Henri Gilles, 'Législation et doctrine canoniques sur les Sarrasins', in *Islam et chrétiens du Midi (XIIe–XIVe s.)*, Cahiers de Fanjeaux 18 (Fanjeaux: Edouard Privat, 1983), pp. 195–213; Norman Zacour, *Jews and Saracens in the Consilia of Oldradus de Ponte* (Toronto: Pontifical Institute of Mediaeval Studies, 1990), pp. 22–6; Southern, *Western Views*, esp. pp. 34–72; Daniel, *Islam*, pp. 131–45; Kedar, *Crusade and Mission*.
⁶ Richard, *Papauté*, esp. pp. 13–16, 63–85; Jean Richard, 'Les Mongols et l'Occident: deux siècles de contacts', and 'Discussion', in *1274: Année charnière*, pp. 85–96 and 97–102 respectively. Schmieder, *Europa*.

that goods wrongly taken from the Jews be returned to them.[7] The *Siete Partidas* granted protection to Jews and Muslims while also heavily circumscribing their activities.[8] Kings of Aragon protected 'their' Muslims, but also took some of them hostage for ransom.[9]

Neither popes nor kings conformed to one set of ideas and behaviour concerning non-Christians. None the less, non-Christians sometimes became pawns in the power struggle between the two, and the problem was more acute in areas that incorporated large non-Christian populations. Countries on the frontiers of Christendom (for example, Spain and Sicily) were especially on the receiving end of papal admonitions. Kings of Leon, Castile and Navarre were urged not to employ Jewish envoys to the Muslim authorities, but to keep the laws concerning the proper place of Jews in a Christian society. Clement IV warned Jaime of Aragon that the argument of usefulness could not warrant the retention of Saracens in his realm; they were to be expelled. Prominent in the charges against Frederick II was his alleged preference for Islam.[10]

The Hungarian case shows similar papal interventions. While there is no indication among the surviving texts and registers that papal letters were written urging Hungarian kings to moderate their policies against non-Christians, many were sent to force reluctant kings to conform to articles of canon law disadvantageous to non-Christians. Some of the issues in these controversies were ones general to medieval Europe, others were linked to Hungary's position on Christendom's frontier. Incursions and a heterogeneous population set the scene for papal fears and the possibility of manipulating them. The Mongol invasion was a dividing line in several respects. With the arrival and settlement of the Cumans, new issues and problems came into existence. The sudden large-scale intrusion of the non-Christian world into the Christian one altered the view and policies of the Hungarian king and influenced the pope as well. Did Hungarian kings have more favourable, or more lenient, ideas about non-Christians than other rulers? Was Hungarian royal policy a late survival of religious tolerance (or lack of interest in religious issues) often seen as a characteristic of steppe nomads? Were the popes the friendly

---

[7] Jordan, *French Monarchy*, p. 148; Le Goff, *Saint Louis*, pp. 793–814.
[8] Part VII tit. XXIV–XXV *Las Siete Partidas*, tr. Samuel Parsons Scott (Chicago, New York and Washington: Commerce Clearing House, 1931); Dwayne E. Carpenter, *Alfonso X and the Jews: An Edition of and Commentary on Siete Partidas 7.24 'De los judíos'* (Berkeley and Los Angeles: University of California Press, 1986); Baer, *History*, vol. I: pp. 115–17.
[9] Boswell, *Royal Treasure*, chapters VI, VII (p. 337 ransom).
[10] Edward A. Synan, *The Popes and the Jews in the Middle Ages* (New York: Macmillan, 1965), pp. 107, 109, 117, 121; Peter Linehan, *The Spanish Church and the Papacy in the Thirteenth Century* (Cambridge: Cambridge University Press, 1971), pp. 178–9; Abulafia, *Frederick II*, pp. 314, 319; analysis: pp. 244–8, 252, 256, 334–6. On papal–royal conflicts over Jews: Simonsohn, *Apostolic See History*, pp. 462–9.

benefactors of the kingdom of Hungary, as several scholars have claimed,[11] or main actors in the formulation and propagation of policies that made crusades and persecution of non-Christians an essential element of Christian society?[12]

'SINCE IT IS QUITE ABSURD THAT ANY WHO BLASPHEME AGAINST CHRIST SHOULD HAVE POWER OVER CHRISTIANS'[13]

The popes' conflict with the rulers over non-Christians in Hungary began in the 1220s. It centred on the employment of non-Christians in positions of power over Christians, on the issue of separating the former from the latter, and on the alleged attraction that non-Christian life had for the Christian inhabitants of the country. The earliest papal interventions in Hungary concerned Christian slaves and servants of Muslims. Pope Honorius III admonished both the king and queen of Hungary in separate letters to encourage the removal of both enslaved and free Christians (presumably servants) from the Muslims (1221).[14] Two justifications were given: first, that it was unworthy for those marked with Christ's sign (that is, baptized) to be subject to the enemies of the Christian faith (an argument used already by Gregory the Great[15]) and, second, that cohabitation would lead many to slip into 'pagan error'. Neither replies nor actions from the king are known, but the pope was certainly not satisfied, because in 1225 he blamed the archbishop of Kalocsa for tolerating such matters in the kingdom, and even in his own diocese.[16] This papal letter also condemned the holding of public offices

---

[11] Lajos Balics, *A római katolikus egyház története Magyarországban*, 2 vols. (Budapest: Szent István Társulat, 1888–90); Vilmos Fraknói, *Magyarország egyházi és politikai összeköttetései a római Szent-Székkel*, 2 vols. (Budapest: Szent István Társulat, 1901–2). Sweeney, 'Papal–Hungarian' posits a traditional papal–Hungarian cooperation.

[12] Moore, *Formation*; Cohen, *Under Crescent*, pp. 36–40.

[13] 'Cum sit nimis absurdum, ut blasphemus Christi in Christianos vim potestatis exerceat'. Lateran IV c. 69: Joseph Alberigo, Joseph Dossetti Perikle, P. Joannou, Claudio Leonardi and Paul Prodi, eds., *Conciliorum Oecumenicorum Decreta*, 3rd edn (Bologna: Istituto per le Scienze Religiose, 1973), p. 266; on variations in different manuscripts: Antonius Garcia y Garcia, ed., *Constitutiones Concilii quarti Lateranensis una cum commentariis glossatorum* (Vatican City: Biblioteca Apostolica Vaticana, 1981), p. 108.

[14] ASV Reg. Vat. 11, f. 113v (*Reg. Hon. III*, nos. 3301, 3296; *VMH*, p. 30, nos. LVIII, LIX). On such papal concern elsewhere from the twelfth century: Simonsohn, *Apostolic See History*, pp. 163–71.

[15] Baron, *Social*, vol. III: p. 30; this, in turn, went back to the prohibition of Jews owning Christian slaves beginning in the fourth century. Synan, *Popes*, pp. 26–8; Simonsohn, *Apostolic See History*, pp. 158–63. The idea that the Christian religion would be polluted recurs from the early Middle Ages: Simonsohn, *Apostolic See Documents*, no. 10 (593).

[16] ASV Reg. Vat. 13, f. 80r (*Reg. Hon. III*, no. 5611; *VMH*, pp. 60–1, no. CXXVII). In the Register, the addressee is added in the margin by a different hand, as the appropriate line in the text was left blank and never filled in by the rubricator. The archbishop was Ugrin from the Csák family, who played an important role in politics.

and of Christian slaves by Muslims and Jews. The pope referred to the Council of Toledo, and its confirmation by the Fourth Lateran Council that non-Christians were prohibited from holding public office. Gregory IX also continued to intervene in these matters.[17]

These letters give the impression that Hungary was on the verge of becoming a Muslim country. Honorius III and Gregory IX deplored an intolerable co-mingling of Muslims and Christians, due to slave-holding and marriage. They claimed that the Muslims held Christian slaves, used them as concubines, forcibly converted them to Islam, and did not allow the baptism of their sons; that they married Christian women often by pretending to be Christians and then compelled them to apostasy. Muslims were also accused of preventing the conversion of Cuman slaves to Christianity. Moreover, Muslims were presented as acquiring an increasing hold over Christians, who were forced to sell their children to the Muslims as slaves due to their poverty, 'and thus freemen become slaves and Christians in a certain manner Saracens'.[18] Adults, according to the pope, being poor and aspiring to a better life, spontaneously converted to Islam. As already indicated in chapter 3, Hungary can hardly be said to have been submerged under the influence of Muslims. In addition, although in the mid-twelfth century Abū Hāmid described Muslim slave-ownership and concubinage (which may have continued, but we have no later Muslim references to it),[19] there is no evidence of previous papal anxiety. What was responsible for this sudden interest on the part of the pope?

Papal concerns were based on two foundations: information from within the country and the popes' own view of urgent issues in Christendom. Both need to be explored in order to explain this diatribe against Hungary's Muslims. With respect to the former, not only did Hungarian bishops and archbishops communicate information to the pope, they were often the ones to initiate papal intervention. Their reliance on papal help to pressure the king can be understood in the context of controversies over royal power and ecclesiastical rights in Hungary. In the 1220s and 1230s, prelates, together with the emerging lower nobility, were involved in the movements against King András II's policies, which led to the promulgation of their privileges, the Golden Bull of 1222 and its rewriting in 1231. Papal interest in Hungary's non-Christians was linked to these events. The Registers of Innocent III contain numerous

---

[17] ASV Reg. Vat. 13, f. 80r; 15, ff. 55r–56r; 17, ff. 77r–78r (*Reg. Hon. III*, no. 5611, *Reg. Greg. IX*, nos. 561, 1498; *VMH*, p. 60, no. CXXVII, p. 94, no. CLXVIII, pp. 114–15, no. CXCV; Simonsohn, *Apostolic See Documents*, nos. 117, 126). Toledo III (589) c. 14 already prohibited the employment of Jews in public offices: Vives, *Concilios visigóticos*, p. 129.
[18] 'et sic liberi fiunt servi et christiani quodammodo sarraceni', ASV Reg. Vat. 15, f. 55v (*Reg. Greg. IX*, no. 561; *VMH*, p. 94, no. CLXVIII).   [19] *Abu-Hámid*, pp. 58–9.

letters to Hungary, but this pope, who otherwise turned his attention to the issue of non-Christians, did not do so regarding Hungary. The reason for this was that Hungarian prelates themselves showed no interest in this topic. Non-Christians only became a point of contention in the context of new forms of employment by the king. This was linked to economic reform following the alienation of royal lands. Ecclesiastics and the *servientes regis*, who wished to attain noble status, resisted both this policy of alienation, an issue in which Pope Honorius III intervened with the decretal *Intellecto*; and the farming out of revenues.[20] The Muslim communities of southern Hungary perhaps played an especially important role in royal service, hence a letter to the archbishop of Kalocsa. Ecclesiastical efforts to facilitate conversion, of both Muslims and Cumans, probably also played a part (see chapter 6). Despite medieval and modern assertions, it was not an especially disruptive non-Christian presence that evoked ecclesiastical reactions.[21] As discussed in chapter 4, non-Christians were not the only ones to fill these positions, but their role was the easiest one to challenge on the basis of canonical regulations.

Connections between local protest and papal interventions appear in several texts. One article of the Golden Bull concerned non-Christians: Jews and Muslims were prohibited from holding public offices.[22] Similar admonitions appeared in papal letters from 1225. Subsequently, the Golden Bull was renewed in a modified form, and among the changes in the 1231 version some were in favour of prelates.[23] Most importantly, the

---

[20] James Ross Sweeney, 'The Decretal Intellecto and the Hungarian Golden Bull of 1222', in *Album Elemér Mályusz* (Brussels: Les Editions de la Librairie Encyclopédique, 1976): pp. 91–6; James Ross Sweeney, 'The Problem of Inalienability in Innocent III's Correspondence with Hungary: A Contribution to the Study of the Historical Genesis of Intellecto', *Mediaeval Studies* 37 (1975): pp. 235–51. See chapter 4, p. 120 on the economic reforms; new royal revenues from c. 1215: Pach, *Harmincadvám*, p. 38.

[21] Some modern authors assume non-Christian financial abuses: 'We would not be wrong if we connected the . . . abuses of the Jewish and Saracen (Ismaelite) counts of the treasury, of these unscrupulous profiteers of the medieval monetary administration, to the establishment of the system of lease'. Hóman, *Magyar pénztörténet*, p. 462. Cf. Frigyes Kahler, 'Das Pizetum-Recht', *A Debreceni Déri Múzeum Évkönyve 1986* (Debrecen: Déri Múzeum, 1987): pp. 179–91, see pp. 185–6. Göckenjan, *Hilfsvölker*, pp. 76–82 also stresses the dominant position of non-Christians in these functions.

[22] 'Comites camere monetarii salinarii et tributarii nobiles regni, Ismaelite et Iudei fieri non possint': Bak, *Laws*, p. 36. On *servientes regis*: Bolla, *Jogilag egységes*, pp. 62–6. The Golden Bull of 1222 derived its name from the pendant seal. It included articles that guaranteed the status and military, economic and juridical rights of the *servientes regis*. It also gave them and the bishops the right to resist any future king who disregarded these privileges. Bak, *Laws*, pp. 97–106; Érszegi, *Aranybulla* (*RA*, no. 379).

[23] It guaranteed ecclesiastical privileges in Hungary (e.g. clerics and cases concerning marriage were not to be judged in lay courts), and gave prelates a measure of control over the palatine, who held the highest lay position in the kingdom after the king. ASV Misc. Arm. XV, no. 1, ff. 355–356v (*VMH*, pp. 109–10, no. CLXXXVII); Bak, *Laws*, pp. 38–41 (*RA*, no. 479). In subsequent centuries until 1916, kings of Hungary confirmed the 1222 version of the Golden Bull. On ecclesiastical privileges see *VMH*, pp. 111–12, no. CXC.

right of resistance by bishops and nobles incorporated into the Golden Bull of 1222 was replaced by the right given to the archbishop of Esztergom to excommunicate the king if he did not act according to the articles of the Golden Bull.[24] The 1231 redaction retained the article prohibiting non-Christian office-holding, although the wording was somewhat different. Among other changes, *Sarraceni*, more in line with papal usage, replaced *Ismaelite*.[25]

Archbishop Robert of Esztergom was clearly leading the attack on non-Christian status. 'The news reached us from the report made by you [i.e. the archbishop of Esztergom] and by various others', states one of Gregory IX's letters demanding a change in the position of Hungary's non-Christians.[26] As Gregory's letter shows marked similarities to Honorius III's from 1225, it is probable that Robert, then bishop of Veszprém, was already in the background of the charges in 1225. The similarities between the 'abuses' attributed to Muslims by the two popes and those described by Robert himself in 1232 (see below) also confirm Robert's role in supplying information not only to Gregory IX but earlier to Honorius III. Robert's close relationship to Honorius III is manifest in his election to the archbishopric in 1226; after the chapter of Esztergom failed to agree, the pope appointed Robert.[27] Both versions of the Golden Bull specifically included minting among the public offices forbidden to Jews and Muslims. It is noteworthy that the royal mint was in Esztergom, the seat of the archbishop who was himself actively involved in the supervision of minting and drew revenues from it.[28] Robert was one of the medieval churchmen whose efforts to build clerical power led to clashes with rulers. In addition to leading clerical opposition to King András II in these years, he initiated the (failed) process of canonization for Archbishop Lucas, one of his twelfth-century predecessors in the see of Esztergom, who himself was embroiled in controversies

---

[24] Bak, *Laws*, p. 41.
[25] 'Monete et salibus et aliis publicis officiis Iudei et Sarraceni non preficiantur.' Bak, *Laws*, p. 40.
[26] 'ex tua et quamplurium aliorum relatione ad nos rumor ascendit', 3 March 1231, ASV Reg. Vat. 15, f. 55r (*Reg. Greg. IX*, no. 561; *VMH*, p. 94, no. CLXVIII). The original letters sent to the pope do not survive. Archbishop John of Esztergom had been one of the leaders of the movement against King András's policies until his death in 1222; he may have been the informant of the pope before Robert. 'János' in *KMTL*.
[27] Robert was born near Liège, began his Hungarian ecclesiastical career in 1207, and was the archbishop of Esztergom from 1226 until his death in 1239. He backed Prince Béla (later Béla IV) against King András II. *Monumenta Romana*, vol. I: pp. lxxxii–lxxxvii; László Koszta, 'Róbert', in *KMTL*, p. 576. He may already have been the pope's informant in 1221: the pope claims it is said ('dicatur') that the Muslims commit abuses.
[28] Hóman, *Magyar pénztörténet*, pp. 457, 468–70. Huszár, 'Esztergomi középkori pénzverde', pp. 208–9. Kahler, 'Pizetum', argued that the archbishop's right to supervise started in 1239, although he had regularly received a tithe from the revenues prior to that date. Since 1221 some other mints existed as well, but the main one remained that of Esztergom.

with several Hungarian kings. Robert was also active in missionary activity to the Cumans.[29]

Part of the explanation for papal interest in Hungary's non-Christians is therefore found in the opposition to King András II's policies, especially by Robert. Requesting conformity to canonical norms was used to pressure the king. It was not non-Christian subversive activity, but politics that lay at the root of the first papal letters concerning non-Christians addressed to the Hungarian king. The wider context – the preoccupations of the pope – made him receptive to accusations (especially against Muslims) emanating from Hungary. Crusading was a recurring concern in the first third of the century. King András II himself was finally pressed into participation in the crusade of 1217, and there was a renewed effort to recruit crusaders in Hungary.[30] In 1220–1, the crusaders first captured Damietta, and then suffered a complete defeat. Pope Gregory IX strove to send Frederick II on crusade, then after 1229 to discredit his peace treaty with the Muslims in the east. The early thirteenth century was also a period when papal attention focused on the Muslims of Sicily. In response to a Muslim revolt that started in 1220, in 1222 Frederick II destroyed the Muslim leadership there, and continued his policy of deporting Sicilian Muslims to Lucera for several years from 1223. The creation of this Muslim colony itself, however, played a role in conflicts with Gregory IX, who protested against it.[31] In the same years that Pope Honorius III took note of the Muslims in Hungary, he wrote to those fighting the Muslims in the Iberian peninsula: at the end of 1220, and in 1221, he gave indulgences to those who fought; in 1225 he expressed his joy that fighting was resumed.[32] That is, the popes advocated an antagonistic approach to Muslims in a variety of countries in these decades; the Muslims of Hungary seemed more of a menace as part of a larger picture.

The first, drawn-out conflict over the office-holding and influence of Muslims and Jews in Hungary culminated in 1232–3. In 1232 Archbishop

---

[29] György Györffy, 'Thomas à Becket and Hungary', *Angol Filológiai Tanulmányok* 4 (1969): pp. 45–52. Papal order to investigate Lucas's sanctity: 1231, ASV Reg. Vat. 15, f. 125r-v (*Reg. Greg. IX*, no. 714; *VMH*, p. 99, no. CLXXIII); 1233, Reg. Vat. 16, f. 88v (*Reg. Greg. IX*, no. 1098, *VMH*, p. 111, no. CLXXXIX). On mission see chapter 6.

[30] E.g. 1226, *VMH*, pp. 70–1, nos. CXLVI, CXLVII. This continued after the death of Honorius III as well: 1231–2, *Reg. Greg. IX*, nos. 657, 774 (*VMH*, p. 97, no. CLXXI, pp. 102–3, no. CLXXVII). András Borosy, 'A keresztesháborúk és Magyarország', *Hadtörténelmi Közlemények* 109, no. 1 (1996): pp. 3–41; 109, no. 2 (1996): pp. 11–53.

[31] Abulafia, *Frederick II*, pp. 144–8; John Phillip Lomax, 'Frederick II, his Saracens, and the Papacy', in *Medieval Christian Perceptions of Islam*, ed. John Victor Tolan (New York: Garland, 1996), pp. 175–97. Honorius III: J. N. D. Kelly, *The Oxford Dictionary of Popes* (Oxford and New York: Oxford University Press, 1986; repr. 1990), pp. 188–9.

[32] Demetrio Mansilla, *La documentación pontificia de Honorius III (1216–1227)*, Monumenta Hispaniae Vaticana 2 (Rome: Instituto Español de Historia Eclesiastica, 1965), pp. 251, 274–5, 416, 421, 429–31.

Robert excommunicated several of the king's advisers, though he refrained from excommunicating the king himself, and placed the kingdom under an interdict because the articles of the Golden Bull of 1231, and, as he emphasized, especially the articles concerning non-Christians, were not put into effect.[33] Robert claimed that the employment of Jews and Muslims in public offices continued and the situation of the Muslims had even improved so dramatically that the poor flocked by thousands ('infinita milia') to espouse Islam. He accused Saracens of influencing the king to withdraw donations from the churches and of affecting the country negatively. Among those excommunicated for favouring the continued employment of Muslims was the highest royal dignitary, the palatine; the chief treasurer (*camerarius et magister tavernicorum*) was threatened with excommunication unless he changed his ways. The third person mentioned by name was a former *comes camere*, Samuel. The archbishop recounted that Samuel had already been convicted of heresy and ordered to take the cross and go to the Holy Land, yet he failed to comply. He patronized and supported Muslims and false Christians. He himself was a 'false Christian', that is, a convert from Islam, whose 'heresy' was presumably a continued secret adherence to his original religion.[34] Finally, the archbishop forbade everyone to have any relations with Muslims until the latter let go 'all Saracens who were baptized, wished to be baptized, or were the children of those who were baptized' living with them, whether they were slaves or freemen.

Although the archbishop laid a strong emphasis on the continued employment of Muslims and Jews, and the 'unjust privileges' of Muslims, as the reasons for the interdict, other ecclesiastical interests played an important part. The palatine is said to have despoiled many clerics of their benefices and goods, and to have injured many of them. In general, Robert bemoaned the situation of the Church in Hungary. The reasons behind the archbishop's anger can also be deduced from King András's reactions. He restored landed properties that he had taken away from the archbishop and granted him other privileges without changing the status of non-Christians in Hungary.[35]

King András persuaded the archbishop to suspend the interdict and at the same time appealed to the pope. Gregory IX, at the king's request,

---

[33] ASV Misc. Arm. XV, no. 1, ff. 353r–356v (*VMH*, pp. 107–11, no. CLXXXVII).

[34] 'ymo Sarracenos et falsos Christianos similes sui substinet', in *ibid.*, f. 355r (*VMH*, p. 109, no. CLXXXVII). In his discussion of coins with Hebrew letters Rádóczy ('Héber betűjeles', p. 35) identifies one of the letters as a ש (shin) and hypothetically links it to Samuel as a *comes camere* of Jewish origin; Scheiber ('Héber betűjeles', p. 91) confirms this on the basis of photographs. The identification of the Hebrew letter is problematic, however, and Robert's account suggests that Samuel, supporting Muslims and false Christians who are 'similar' to him, was a convert from Islam. [35] *MES*, vol. I: pp. 286–8, nos. 333–6; *RA*, nos. 488–91.

sent a legate to Hungary. Jacob (Giacomo) of Pecorara, cardinal bishop of Palestrina, had the task of mediating between the Church and the king.[36] Jacob of Pecorara arrived in Hungary toward the end of 1232, and the ensuing negotiations led to the oath of Bereg. The king could not resist the simultaneous pressure of prelates and nobles and the threat of papal sanctions. The pope reproached the king for reneging on his previous promises, repeated Archbishop Robert's accusations, and admonished András to obey the legate.[37] At the same time, he empowered the legate to renew the interdict and excommunication of members of the king's entourage if necessary in order to enforce the compliance of the king, but expressly forbade him to excommunicate the king himself or his sons.[38] This right he reserved to himself, thus circumscribing the field of legatine authority.[39]

The oath of Bereg (20 August 1233) was formulated according to the legate's demands; it consisted of two main sections, one concerning non-Christians, the other ecclesiastical privileges, especially salt revenues.[40] The legate endeavoured to ensure that neither the king nor his nobles appropriated ecclesiastical revenues. The king promised not to impair ecclesiastical privileges, and to pay 10,000 marks in five years as compensation for revenues already appropriated.[41] Articles relative to non-

---

[36] Heinrich Zimmermann, *Die päpstliche Legation in der ersten Hälfte des 13. Jahrhunderts* (Paderborn: F. Schöningh, 1913), pp. 109–13. Paravicini Bagliani, *Cardinali*, vol. I: pp. 114–27, esp. p. 120; Tibor Almási, 'Egy ciszterci bíboros a pápai világuralom szolgálatában: Pecorari Jakab', *Magyar Egyháztörténeti Vázlatok* (1993, nos. 1–2): pp. 129–41.

[37] ASV Reg. Vat. 17, ff. 77r–78r (*Reg. Greg. IX*, no. 1498; *VMH*, pp. 114–15, no. cxcv). Almási has suggested that although this and the following letters, dated 12 August 1233 in the Registers, probably did not arrive prior to the oath of Bereg, the legate used threats similar to those expressed by the pope, and convinced András that the pope would back the legatine decisions: Tibor Almási, 'A beregi egyezmény megkötésének diplomáciai mozzanatai', *AUSz Acta Historica* 83 (1986): pp. 31–9.

[38] ASV Reg. Vat. 17, f. 78r–v (*Reg. Greg. IX*, nos. 1499, 1500; *VMH*, pp. 115–16, nos. cxcvi, cxcvii).

[39] The pope could determine in each case what powers he committed to a legate and what he reserved for himself: Robert C. Figueira, '"Legatus apostolice sedis": The Pope's "alter ego" According to Thirteenth-Century Canon Law', *Studi Medievali*, 3rd ser., 27, no. 2 (1986): pp. 527–74, see pp. 539, 543–50.

[40] Originals in the archives of the archbishopric of Esztergom: Knauz, *Esztergomi főegyháznak okmánytára*, vol. I: pp. 26–7, no. 32; photo reproduction MOL DF 248771; *RA*, no. 500; edition: Marsina, *Codex Diplomaticus*, vol. I: pp. 295–8, no. 407. A subsequent oath confirmed the agreement in Esztergom (the text was incorporated into the *Liber censuum*): *VMH*, vol. I: pp. 116–19, no. cxcviii (Marsina, *Codex Diplomaticus*, pp. 299–300, no. 409; *RA*, no. 501). On the sources and the sequence of events: Almási, 'A beregi egyezmény'; Almási, 'Egy ciszterci bíboros'.

[41] This was the equivalent of the salt revenues that the king had withheld from the Church in Hungary. Among the public offices Jews and Muslims held was the position of collector of salt revenues. The king promised that church officials would be able to buy the salt for a fixed price at the salt mines and could oversee the transportation and sale of the salt (including Hungarian and foreign trade). Clerics were also exempt from taxation and they were to be under the exclusive jurisdiction of ecclesiastical judges; and marriage cases were reserved to the jurisdiction of ecclesiastical courts.

Christians were prominent; the king swore again not to employ Jews and Muslims as officers of the treasury and of the mint, or as money-changers, salt intendants and tax-collectors, not even by subjecting them to Christian superiors. The king also had to swear that Jews and Muslims would not only be forbidden to own Christian slaves but would also be effectively prevented from such ownership and from cohabitation with Christians by the following means: every year the palatine or another royal servant would be dispatched to see that the law was not violated; all violators, whether Jews, Muslims or Christians, would lose their property and become slaves for life.

Jacob also obtained separate oaths on the agreement from the princes and the high dignitaries of the royal court.[42] Moreover, in 1234 Prince Béla (the future Béla IV) took an oath to compel the inhabitants of his lands and territories to obey the Roman Church if they had been disobedient, and to extirpate heretics, false Christians, and Christians who had deserted their faith in order to adopt that of the Muslims or Jews.[43] The inclusion in the oath of these last two groups of Christians, brought together in the heading of the *Liber censuum* entry as those 'contra fidem Catholicam', indicates the success of Robert's accusations.[44] His insistence that non-Christians posed a danger in enticing Christians away from the true faith as well as in 'infiltrating' Christian families by false pretences clearly influenced the legate.[45] Archbishop Robert's accounts of the rise of Muslim influence in Hungary certainly fuelled papal fears, but the underlying issue was not a danger to the position of Christians in Hungary. Instead, King András's reforms, ecclesiastical privileges and revenues in Hungary and the enforcement of ecclesiastical norms in the exercise of royal power were at stake. One element of this was the subjection of non-Christians to Christian power.

Papal–royal controversy continued along the same lines even after the legate's departure from Hungary. The archbishop of Esztergom and the bishop of Bosnia (the Dominican John of Wildeshausen) were charged with the task of proclaiming a new interdict if the king did not fulfil his promises. And this was, indeed, the case; in 1234 the interdict was promulgated once again. Yet the controversy was not simply over the position

---

András was unable to pay the 10,000 marks (an important sum; in 1235, his daughter Yoles, betrothed to the king of Aragon, was to receive a dowry of 12,000 silver marks; *RA*, no. 537) and in 1235 Pope Gregory IX permitted him to pay within ten (instead of five) years. *Reg. Greg. IX*, no. 2755; *VMH*, p. 135, no. CCXXXIV.

[42] From the *Liber censuum*: *VMH*, pp. 119–20, no. CXCIX, pp. 123–4, no. CCVIII; *RA*, no. 599.

[43] 'Universos hereticos et alios christianos, qui relicta fide christianitatis ad superstitionem Ysmahelytarum vel Iudeorum pervertuntur . . . et falsos christianos . . . extirpare': *Liber censuum*, ASV Misc. Arm. XV, no. 1, ff. 358v–359 (*VMH*, p. 124, no. CCIX; *RA*, no. 604).

[44] 'Iuramentum regis Bele de hereticis et aliis contra fidem catholicam de terra sua extirpandis', *ibid.*, f. 358v. [45] See also pp. 186–7, 199.

of non-Christians; the power struggle between the papacy, Hungarian prelates and the king was complex, as Archbishop Robert sided with the king this time.[46] The pope was willing to compromise partially over the question of non-Christians in 1235. At King András's request he permitted a modification in the system of yearly control the papal legate Jacob had wished to institute. Yearly investigation was to ensure that Muslims did not have Christians living with them. András complained that the investigation would in fact be continuous, and would prevent Muslims from fulfilling their obligations to the king. The pope allowed the investigation to take place once every two years.[47] Negotiations, threats and punitive measures failed to produce any material change in the royal policy towards non-Christians. King András died in 1235 without obeying papal wishes concerning non-Christians. He never resisted openly; he promised to obey and took several oaths to that effect. But his promises and vows were never fulfilled.

Throughout the thirteenth century, non-Christians continued in royal employment, and so did expressions of papal discontent; this type of controversy was a common one in medieval Europe.[48] King Béla IV had the novel idea of submitting a well-researched petition (known from the subsequent papal response) to Pope Gregory IX in 1239, asking for permission to farm out royal revenues to non-Christians. This document was certainly prepared by someone familiar with canon law. The argument in favour of the petition was Pope Gregory IX's own decretal concerning the granting of this privilege to the King of Portugal, Sancho II. This bull had been incorporated into Gregory's *Decretales*, and was therefore easily accessible to a canonist.[49] This is one example of how some of the most 'modern' intellectuals of the thirteenth century, clerics trained at Bologna, Padua or Paris, then served royal interests. There was no obvious split between Roman lawyers in the service of royal power and canonists in that of the popes; we find the latter in the 'royal camp' as well.[50] The pope responded by advising King Béla to employ Christians

---

[46] ASV Reg. Vat. 17, f 197v (*Reg. Greg. IX*, no. 2036; *VMH*, p. 126, no. CCXIII).
[47] ASV Reg. Vat. 18, f. 68v (*Reg. Greg. IX*, no. 2758; *VMH*, p. 136, no. CCXXXVII). No evidence survives about the procedure in Hungary. In the same year, the pope canonized Erzsébet (Elizabeth) of Thüringia-Hungary, daughter of King András. André Vauchez, *La sainteté en Occident aux derniers siècles du Moyen Age* (Rome: Ecole Française de Rome, 1988), pp. 49, 657.
[48] Baron, *Social*, vol. XI: pp. 117–18, vol. XII: pp. 90–100. Grayzel, *Church*, vol. II: pp. 246, 257, 259 (Polish, English and German synods); Simonsohn, *Apostolic See Documents*, no. 55; Simonsohn, *Apostolic See History*, pp. 147–54 (pp. 150–1 on Hungary).
[49] Pope Gregory's bull about the farming out of revenues in Portugal: X 5.6.18; *Reg. Greg. IX*, no. 733; Grayzel, *Church*, vol. I: no. 64 (1231). See also *ibid.*, vol. II: no. 57 (Simonsohn, *Apostolic See Documents*, nos. 130, 261).
[50] Links between Roman law and kingship: Walter Ullmann, *Principles of Government and Politics in the Middle Ages*, 4th edn (London: Methuen, 1978), pp. 159–72, 194–200; József Gerics, 'Adalékok

Conflicts between the papacy and the kings

whenever possible, and reminded him that his permission to do otherwise (as in the case of the authorization to King Sancho) was contingent upon the employment of Christian overseers.[51] In 1263 Urban IV reproached Béla IV for still employing Jewish and Muslim officials. Bruno, bishop of Olomouc, complained of the same in his report to the pope in 1272. The Synod of Buda in 1279 decreed that non-Christians should not be employed, and stipulated that prelates should not rely on the services of non-Christians in collecting revenues. A Jewish *comes camere* is still known from 1280. Kings László IV in the 1280s and András III in 1291 promised not to employ non-Christians.[52]

As the popes were drawn into conflict over local issues, they increasingly wanted to enforce a variety of canonical norms through their legates. Some of these, like efforts to exclude non-Christians from public offices, matched the demand of certain local groups. But papal policy did not stop there. The papacy advocated a more thorough separation of Christians and non-Christians, for which no initiative or even support was found in the kingdom. Legates tried to introduce distinguishing signs to Hungary, in accordance with canon 68 of the Fourth Lateran Council (1215) which decreed that in order to avoid a confusion between Christians on the one hand, and Jews and Saracens on the other, these non-Christians should wear distinguishing clothing. This rapidly became a standard requirement throughout Christendom, although there was an evolution from distinguishing clothing to distinguishing signs, and the time of their introduction varied greatly.[53] In Hungary, legislation on

---

a Kézai-krónika problémájának megoldásához', *Annales Universitatis Scientiarum Budapestinensis de R. Eötvös nominatae, Sectio Historica* 1 (1957): pp. 106–34, see pp. 117–19. Other cases: György Bónis, *A jogtudó értelmiség a Mohács előtti Magyarországon* (Budapest: Akadémiai Kiadó, 1971), pp. 19–25; Jenő Szűcs, 'A kereszténység belső politikuma a XIII. század derekán: IV. Béla király és az egyház', *Történelmi Szemle* 21 (1978): pp. 158–81.

[51] Reg. Vat. 19, f. 139v [previously f. 133v] (*Reg. Greg. IX*, no. 5000; *VMH*, p. 173, no. CCCXIII; Simonsohn, *Apostolic See Documents*, no. 167).

[52] Urban IV: Knauz, *Esztergomi főegyháznak okmánytára*, vol. II: p. 84, no. 106; also *MES*, vol. I: p. 487, no. 629 (Grayzel, *Church*, vol. II: no. 17; Simonsohn, *Apostolic See Documents*, no. 216). Géza Érszegi, 'Eredeti pápai oklevelek Magyarországon (1199–1417)', Ph.D. dissertation (Budapest, 1989), p. 248, no. 142. Bruno: ASV AA Arm. I-XVIII-3104 (*VMH*, pp. 307–8, no. DXXXV). Synod of 1279: Hube, *Constitutiones*, p. 161. On *comites camere* see chapter 4. László IV: János Karácsonyi, 'A mérges vipera és az antimonialis: korkép Kún László idejéből', *Századok* 44 (1910): pp. 1–24, see pp. 4, 8; András III's promise was linked to the protection of the nobility's interests, and mentioned 'pagani' only: *CD*, vol. VII, pt. 2: p. 140, no. CCCCII (*RA*, no. 3705). Charles Robert was still urged not to employ non-Christians around 1319: Simonsohn, *Apostolic See Documents*, no. 298a.

[53] Garcia y Garcia, ed., *Constitutiones Concilii quarti Lateranensis*, pp. 107–8; Ulysse Robert, *Les signes de l'infamie au Moyen Age: Juifs, Sarrasins, hérétiques, lépreux, gagots et filles publiques* (Paris, 1891), pp. 114–15; Dahan, *Intellectuels*, pp. 36–7, 159–76; Simonsohn, *Apostolic See History*, pp. 135–8. On early regulation: Benjamin Z. Kedar, 'The Subjected Muslims of the Frankish Levant', in *Muslims under Latin Rule*, ed. James M. Powell (Princeton: Princeton University Press, 1990), pp. 135–74, see p. 166. Cf. S. D. Goitein, *Mediterranean Society*, vol. II: *The Community* (Berkeley and Los

distinguishing signs first appeared in the oath of Bereg (1233), the agenda of which was determined by a papal legate; the king was to ensure that Jews and Muslims were distinguished from Christians by evident signs (no precise description of the required signs was given).[54] Clearly, this measure did not go into effect, because another papal legate, Philip of Fermo, decreed the wearing of such signs in 1279. Philip, whose role is discussed in the third section of this chapter, introduced legislation at the Synod of Buda: Jews were ordered to wear a red circular patch over their breast on the left side of their outer garment, Muslims a similar sign in yellow.[55] Those who did not obey were to be punished; no Christian was to associate in any way with those not wearing the sign. The relevant section of the synod stipulated punishment for disobedient Jews and Muslims, but also excommunication for Christians who willingly associated with them; such 'ecclesiastical excommunication in reverse' was a standard measure employed by the papacy, in order to bring pressure on the Jews.[56] This attempt also failed; the dates by which the signs were to be introduced were left blank or erased from the manuscripts.[57] Once papal attention was turned to the non-Christians in Hungary, the regulation of their status was envisaged according to ecclesiastical ideas that no longer corresponded to local concerns. The legates endeavoured to implement an ecclesiastical policy that found no favour in Hungary.

The separation of non-Christians from Christians was a recurring theme in thirteenth-century Europe, manifest among other issues in injunctions concerning distinguishing clothing and signs or repeated prohibitions against employing non-Christians. As rulers of frontier areas of Christendom benefited from the services of varied non-Christian populations, prolonged and bitter conflicts could emerge with the papacy over appropriate policies towards these groups. In the Hungarian case, popes argued that they wished to enforce universal canonical norms. They expressed fear of non-Christian pollution and falsehood, and maintained that it was in the interest of all Christians to conform to regulations of

footnote 53 (cont.)
Angeles: University of California Press, 1971), pp. 285–8 on Muslim laws to distinguish non-Muslims. For detailed discussion of the Hungarian case see Nora Berend, 'Medieval Patterns of Social Exclusion and Integration: The Regulation of Non-Christian Clothing in Thirteenth-Century Hungary', *Revue Mabillon* n.s. 8 (69) (1997): pp. 155–76.

[54] Cf. note 40; MOL DF 248771 (Marsina, *Codex Diplomaticus*, vol. 1: pp. 295–8, no. 407); *VMH*, p. 117, no. CXCVIII.

[55] Hube, *Constitutiones*, pp. 159–60. On the synod see Waldmüller, *Synoden*, pp. 188–200. On the overall importance of legatine activity in Hungarian synods, *ibid.*, pp. 220–4. On the manuscript tradition of the text, see appendix 3.

[56] Hube, *Constitutiones*, pp. 159–60. Simonsohn, *Apostolic See History*, p. 103.

[57] Hube, *Constitutiones*, p. 160, note. I am grateful to the late Aleksander Gieysztor for his help in trying to locate the manuscripts. So far, the search has been unsuccessful; the manuscripts may have been among those destroyed in the Second World War.

Conflicts between the papacy and the kings

separation and to keep non-Christians from 'positions of power' over Christians. They protested that the situation of the non-Christians in Hungary harmed both the Church and royal dignity.[58] The kings evidently had a different approach; far from adopting the view that non-Christians constituted a menace, they resisted papal and ecclesiastical pressure. Although defiance was followed by an effort to appear to comply, in reality the kings continued old practices: a royal response by no means unique to Hungary.[59]

HUNGARY, THE GATE OF CHRISTENDOM: BIRTH OF A FRONTIER IDEOLOGY

The Mongol invasion, the only major incursion of 'pagans' into the territory of thirteenth-century Christendom, was a turning point in the history of papal–royal conflicts, and led to the development of a frontier ideology used by King Béla IV to secure concessions from the pope.[60] The real experience of the Mongol destruction and danger lay at the basis of this ideology. By 1241, prior to the invasion, King Béla was already uneasy about the approaching Mongols. Messengers like Brother Julian (who set out to find and convert the Hungarians who remained in 'Magna Hungaria' during the migrations) returned with news of destruction. Julian also brought a letter from the Mongol khan warning King Béla of an imminent attack, and alerting the king to the approaching danger.[61] After the invasion, Béla continued to seek information about the Mongols' movements and plans through his own spies and Hungary's eastern connections.[62] The trauma of the invasion, as well as the continued fear of another attack after 1241, are well documented.[63] Mongol attacks did indeed recur in Poland and in Hungary in the second half of

---

[58] 'libertas conculcatur, ecclesie et dignitati regie non modicum derogatur': ASV Reg. Vat. 15, f. 55v (Reg. Greg. IX, no. 561; VMH, p. 94, no. CLXVIII).

[59] Partially similar patterns prevailed when the popes set out to enforce the indissolubility of marriage in the face of the resistance of the kings of France. The kings first refused to obey; they then endeavoured to receive papal dispensation to separate from their wives, manipulating the new rules to achieve their aim (for example, referring to a suddenly discovered blood relationship with their wives). Georges Duby, *Medieval Marriage: Two Models from Twelfth-Century France* (Baltimore: Johns Hopkins University Press, 1978).

[60] On relations between Béla IV and the Church see note 11 above; Szűcs, 'Kereszténység belső politikuma'; László Solymosi, 'Egyházi-politikai viszonyok a pápai hegemónia idején (13. század)', in *Magyarország és a Szentszék*, pp. 47–54.

[61] Dörrie, *Drei Texte*, pp. 162–82; Sinor, 'Relations entre les Mongols', pp. 40–4. On impending Mongol attack in Hungary, also Paulus Scheffer-Boichorst, ed., 'Albrici monachi Triumfontium Chronicon', in *MGH SS*, vol. XXIII: pp. 631–950, see p. 946. About Mongol spies captured in Galicia and sent to Béla IV, and the spies sent by Béla to the Mongols: Matthew Paris, *Chronica Majora*, vol. VI: pp. 75–6.

[62] Sinor, 'Mongols and Western Europe', pp. 525–6; Tardy, *Tatárországi rabszolgakereskedelem*, p. 16 on diplomatic relations with Mongols. [63] See chapter 1, pp. 37–8.

the thirteenth century, but these resembled nomad raids long familiar to these countries, rather than conquest.

Letters from King Béla during the invasion reflected need and despair. After his escape to Zagreb, Béla addressed a letter to the pope, asking him to send help speedily, lest once 'the wolf has torn the lamb asunder, it should be impossible to find anyone who could be helped'.[64] He also stressed the importance of the Mongol invasion as affecting the safety of the whole Christian world, saying that the Mongols were especially eager to subjugate Christians.[65] In another letter he reported that the Mongols were preparing to conquer every Christian country. He asked for a crusade, specifically demanding Venetian catapults to prevent the Mongols from crossing the Danube. Christendom, he thought, should be united against the common enemy.[66] The king sent letters to the German emperor and other kings; Hungarian ecclesiastics were equally active in soliciting help.[67]

Popes responded to the Mongol danger in a variety of ways. Papal policies in relation to Hungary were only one part of a complex of attitudes, comprising eschatological fears as well as pragmatic attempts at a military alliance.[68] Gregory IX exhorted King Béla to fight against the enemy and to pray to God who, he hoped, would not allow a Christian kingdom to be destroyed. The pope also took the royal family under the protection of the apostolic see and granted the same indulgence to those taking the cross for the Hungarian cause as to those fighting for the Holy Land.[69] None of these measures had any practical consequences. Despite preaching the cross in Germany, a crusade to help Hungary did not materialize.[70] Papal protection was not effective either; Duke Frederick of Austria forced King Béla to cede three western Hungarian counties to him. As the pope himself acknowledged, his controversy with Emperor Frederick was of the utmost importance at the time, and he was unable to provide help.[71] The conflict with the empire, the death of Pope Gregory IX just

---

[64] 'Ne, interveniente paululum mora, lupo agnum frustratim comedente, inveniri nequeat, cui valeat subveniri': ASV AA Arm. I-XVIII-104 and Instr. Misc. 4809 (*VMH*, p. 182, no. CCCXXXV; *RA*, no. 706).

[65] 'Omnes et maxime christianos suo dominio subiugare gloriantes', *ibid.*.

[66] J. L. A. Huillard-Bréholles, ed., *Historia Diplomatica Friderici Secundi*, 7 vols. (Paris: Henri Plon, 1852–61), vol. VI, pt. 2: pp. 902–4; *RA*, no. 712.

[67] E.g., *CD*, vol. IV, pt. 1: pp. 212–13; *ÁÚO*, vol. II: p. 126, no. 71 (*RA*, no. 707); *RA*, no. 708; György Györffy, 'Újabb adatok a tatárjárás történetéhez', *Történelmi Szemle* 33, nos. 1–2 (1991): pp. 84–8.

[68] See chapter 1, p. 38. Paravicini Bagliani, *Trono di Pietro*, pp. 240–3, bibliography on p. 247.

[69] ASV Reg. Vat. 20, ff. 81v–82v (*Reg. Greg. IX*, nos. 6057, 6058, 6059, 6060, 6061; *VMH*, pp. 183–4, nos. CCCXXXVII–CCCXXXIX).

[70] Peter Jackson, 'The Crusade Against the Mongols (1241)', *Journal of Ecclesiastical History* 42 (1991): pp. 1–18; Christoph T. Maier, *Preaching the Crusades: Mendicant Friars and the Cross in the Thirteenth Century*, paperback edn (Cambridge: Cambridge University Press, 1998), pp. 59–60.

[71] ASV Reg. Vat. 20, f. 90r (*Reg. Greg. IX*, no. 6094; *VMH*, p. 185, no. CCCXLII).

at the time of the invasion, the vacancies, and the short span of Celestine IV's reign did not favour efficient papal intervention.[72] Innocent IV took steps to counter the Mongol threat. In 1243 he appointed Berthold of Aquileia to recruit crusaders in German lands against the Mongols. By that time the Mongol armies had withdrawn from Hungary, but everyone feared their return. The First Council of Lyons (1245) also dealt with the problem. The rulers of countries in the line of possible Mongol attacks were advised to fortify their borders with walls and castles; the pope promised monetary aid for this purpose (without specifying the dates of its delivery).[73] Innocent also wrote to the Hungarian archbishops separately, encouraging them to seek out and fortify suitable places that would shelter them from future Mongol attacks.[74] He also promised aid in 1247 in case the Mongols returned.[75] The pope tried in yet another way to counteract the Mongol danger. With him began the age of missions to the Mongols in the hope of their conversion.[76] Clement IV also acknowledged the necessity to defend Hungary against the Mongols.[77]

The Mongol invasion, however, precipitated a new phase of papal–royal conflict that surpassed the issue of practical help against the Mongols. What started as *Realpolitik* quickly turned into the reinterpretation of Christian ideology, which became a political weapon in Béla's hands. Royal and papal rhetoric reveal a growing gap between two interpretations of rule on Christendom's frontiers. Popes had been advocating a territorial view of Christendom, whose frontiers had to be defended and expanded.[78] The Mongol attack endangered this Christian territory, and, as Pope Innocent IV wrote to Béla IV, he would help because the 'cause of the Tartars is not yours alone, but a common one, and concerns any Christian'.[79] It was this line of thought

---

[72] The Mongols began the invasion of Hungary on 12 March 1241 and won the battle of Muhi on 11 April. King Béla was writing from Zagreb on 18 May. Gregory IX died on 22 August 1241. The most common view in Hungarian historiography is that the pope preferred to focus on the struggle with Frederick II rather than to help against the Mongols: e.g. Lederer, 'Tatárjárás', Szűcs, *Utolsó Árpádok*, p. 78; Gyula Kristó, *A Kárpát-medence és a magyarság régmúltja (1301-ig)* (Szeged: Szegedi Középkorász Műhely, 1993), p. 254; though some say the pope was unable to help: Ilona Pálfy, *A tatárok és a XIII. századi Európa* (Budapest: Királyi Magyar Egyetemi Nyomda, 1928) p. 36. Cf. Jackson, 'Crusade against the Mongols'; Schmieder, *Europa*, pp. 30, 73–5.
[73] Alberigo et al., *Conciliorum Oecumenicorum Decreta*, p. 297, c. 4.
[74] *Reg. Inn. IV*, no. 2958; *VMH*, p. 204, no. CCCLXXX.
[75] *Reg. Inn. IV*, nos. 30, 2957, 4000; *VMH*, pp. 187–8, no. CCCXLVIII, pp. 203–4, no. CCCLXXIX, p. 206, no. CCCLXXXVIII. Maier, *Preaching*, pp. 84–5.
[76] Richard, *Papauté*, pp. 70–83; Jean Richard, 'Le discours missionnaire: l'exposition de la foi chrétienne dans les lettres des papes aux Mongols', in Richard, *Croisés, missionnaires et voyageurs: les perspectives orientales du monde latin médiéval* (London: Variorum, 1983), no. XVII.
[77] *Reg. Clem. IV*, no. 113; *VMH*, p. 280, no. DXIII. [78] See chapter 2, p. 43.
[79] ' in facto . . . Tartarorum, quod non est proprium, sed commune, ac tangit quemlibet christianum, te toto posse iuvare intendimus'. *Reg. Inn. IV*, no. 2957; *VMH*, p. 203, no. CCCLXXIX.

that was used to argue for Hungary's special position in one of Béla's letters (*c.* 1250), the precise dating of which has been debated.[80] The king complained that the pope and all Christian kings had abandoned him and Hungary.

When the Tartars fought against us in our kingdom, we put our request over this matter before the three principal courts of Christendom, that is Yours, which is thought and believed to be the mistress and superior of all courts by Christians, the imperial one, to which we were ready to submit ourselves because of this, if at the time of the said pestilence it had given us efficient aid and help; and we had our request laid before the court of the Franks, but from all these we received neither consolation nor help, but only words.[81]

Traditionally understood as the desperate cry of a Christian king for help, even the physical form of the letter, surviving in the Vatican Archives, contradicts that analysis. Sealed with a golden bull, the letter was carefully crafted in both form and content.[82] It expounded a frontier ideology in the service of royal power.

Béla expressed his astonishment that Louis IX was allowed to leave Europe, and that the pope and kings expended money and effort to save the Latin east and the Latin Empire of Constantinople; their fall would not affect Christendom in the way the loss of Hungary would. Béla warned the pope that Hungary, having already suffered through a Mongol onslaught, could not successfully resist another comparable attack. The inhabitants would not even try to fight; rather they would surrender out of fear. Béla made two points that were the cornerstone of his new ideology. First he argued that Hungary was the key point on the Christian frontier, the gate of Christendom; if it fell, the road to conquer the rest of the Christian world would be open. Hungary, 'if it is possessed by the Tartars, will be for them an open gate to other regions of the

---

[80] ASV AA Arm. I-XVIII-605; facsimile: Aldo Martini, *I sigilli d'Oro dell'Archivio Segreto Vaticano* (Milan: Franco Maria Ricci, 1984), plate 9E (*VMH*, pp. 230–2, no. CCCCXL); *RA*, no. 933a. The original only provides the month and day (11 November). The dating has been most thoroughly discussed by Toru Senga, 'IV. Béla külpolitikája és IV. Ince pápához intézett "tatár-levele"', *Századok* 121 (1987): pp. 584–612. He dates it to 1247. Previous opinions included 1254 (Pauler, *Magyar nemzet*, vol. II: p. 521 and *CD*, vol. IV, pt. 2: p. 218); 1253 (János Karácsonyi, 'Magyar Sibilla', *Turul* 37, no. 1 (1922–3): pp. 3–13, see pp. 9–10); 1250 (*RA*, no. 933a); 1248 (Mór Wertner, *IV. Béla király története okirati kútfők nyomán* (Temesvár, 1893), p. 120, note 3).

[81] 'Requisivimus enim, adhuc Thartharis in regno nostro dimicantibus contra nos, super condicto negocio tres tocius christianitatis principaliores Curias, scilicet vestram, que domina et magistra omnis Curie a christicolis creditur et habetur, et imperialem, cui eciam propter hoc nos submittere decreveramus, si tempore predicte pestilencie nobis competens auxilium impenderet et iuvamen; Francorum eciam Curiam requiri fecimus: de quibus omnibus nichil consolacionis vel subsidii recepimus, nisi verba.' Martini, *Sigilli*, plate 9E; *VMH*, p. 231.

[82] It is one out of eight letters sealed with a golden bull that were sent by Béla IV and are still conserved in the Vatican Archives. Martini, *Sigilli*, pp. 50–2, nos. 9A–H; *Bibliografia dell'Archivio Vaticano* (Vatican City, 1992), vol. v: pp. 58–9; Sella, *Bolle d'Oro*, pp. 4–5.

Catholic faith'.[83] Second, he maintained that, if he received no help, he would have to resort to any policy that helped avoid a second Mongol attack in the future.

Béla turned Christian ideology to his advantage; he put pressure on the popes to get concessions by arousing their anxiety with an insistence on impending danger. In this view, Hungary played a special role for Christendom, and therefore its ruler should enjoy special rights. Béla maintained that since Christians would not help, he had to resort to the help of 'pagans', going as far as the creation of personal ties via marriage. 'For the good of Christendom . . . we defend our kingdom today by pagans, humiliating our royal majesty, and we tread the enemies of the church underfoot with the aid of pagans.'[84] The king benefited both from the presence of the Cumans' military power, and from blackmailing the pope by presenting the alliance with the Cumans as a deed of last resort. This way, Béla also claimed that without violating his commitment as a Christian king, he could use 'pagan' or other non-Christian help – an idea that, as we have seen, was not readily acceptable.

King Béla used the argument about Hungary's precarious position over the years to press the pope not to give benefices in Hungary to foreign clerics, and to accept a royal candidate to the archbishopric of Esztergom.[85] Béla presented these issues as necessary for the functioning of the kingdom, and thus in the interest of Christendom, protected by Hungary.[86] The king kept papal interest alive by reporting to Pope Alexander IV that the Mongols proposed a marriage alliance between either Béla's son and a Mongol princess, or Béla's daughter and a Mongol prince. Again, the fragility of the kingdom and its possible detachment from Christendom was emphasized.[87]

Béla also used similar rhetoric to secure papal sympathies for himself in the prolonged wars with his son István. Early in 1264 Urban IV reproved both Béla and István for relying on the help of infidels: 'he [István] intends to call on the help of the Cumans against you [Béla], and you on that of the pagans of Livonia and other neighbouring infidels

---

[83] 'si possideretur a Thartharis, esset pro ipsis apertum hostium alias fidei catholice regiones'. Martini, *Sigilli*, plate 9E; *VMH*, p. 231.

[84] 'Propter bonum christianitatis maiestatem regiam humiliando . . . per paganos hodie regnum nostrum defendimus et per paganos infideles ecclesie conculcamus.' *Ibid.*

[85] ASV AA Arm. I-XVIII-608 (*VMH*, pp. 232–3, no. CCCCXLII); ASV Reg. Vat. 25, f. 224v (*Reg. Alex. IV*, no. 2963; *VMH*, p. 241, no. CCCCLIV).

[86] This was part of Béla's post-invasion policies, on which see Szűcs, 'Kereszténység belső politikuma'; Fügedi, *Vár és társadalom*, pp. 18–32; Fügedi, *Castle and Society*, pp. 50–64; Szűcs, *Utolsó Árpádok*, pp. 3–95; Béla also had plans to marry one of his sons to Pope Innocent IV's niece: Fraknói, *Magyarország egyházi*, p. 72.

[87] Béla's message is known from Pope Alexander IV's response: ASV Reg. Vat. 25, f. 224r (*Reg. Alex. IV*, no. 2963; *VMH*, p. 240, no. CCCCLIV).

against him'.[88] Yet when, later on in the same year, the pope wrote to prelates in Hungary, he only concentrated on the danger the Cumans posed to the kingdom. He referred to information from ambassadors of King Béla, and urged the prelates to deal with the Cuman problem. The heinous deeds of the Cumans and their 'contagious presence' endanger the existence of Christianity in the kingdom: it is to be feared that the kingdom would lose its claim to be Catholic if 'gentile superstition' grew.[89] As I show in chapter 6, the king gave widely differing accounts of the success of Cuman conversion depending on his political aims. Béla thus evoked the same fear of Hungary being separated from Christendom, this time not by outside attack, but the internal activity of 'pagans'.

Despite King Béla's success at generating papal fears, the popes did not accept his views about the rights of a ruler on the frontier. The idea of a precarious, endangered Christianity in Hungary, however, proved to be a lasting one. Pope Alexander IV formulated the most extensive papal response (echoed by Urban IV) to Béla's frontier ideology. He disputed King Béla's basic premise that he was acting as a Christian king in the interest of a Christian kingdom. The pope presented all dealings with non-Christians other than efforts at conversion as potentially harmful to King Béla, and claimed that Christianity in Hungary would be endangered by the actions of the king. Alexander rebuked Béla for having suggested that the Church failed to help him in his need, pointing out that his predecessors were unable to help because of the fight with Emperor Frederick.

Pope Alexander IV and then Urban IV were sufficiently alarmed at the news of Mongol marriage proposals to send letters to the king and to Hungarian prelates to prevent Béla from entering into any treaty or marriage alliance with the Mongols.[90] The existing marriage alliance with the Cumans made Béla's threat of entering into such an agreement with the Mongols effective. The pope asserted that this alliance would entail helping the Mongols in war even against Christians. He emphasized that a truly Christian king would never resort to such means for the preser-

---

[88] 2 February 1264: 'ipse contra te Cumanorum, tuque contra eum paganorum de Livonia et aliorum infidelium vicinorum auxilium intenditis invocare': Reg. Vat. 29, f. 100r (*Reg. Urb. IV*, no. 1243; *VMH*, p. 265, no. CCCCLXXXV mistakenly 'fidelium' instead of 'infidelium').

[89] 'de ipsorum contagiosa presentia maculatur' 'propter quod imminet non immerito formidandum, ne prefatum regnum processu temporis caderet a titulo catholice claritatis, si quod absit, spurcitia gentilium ibi ... susciperet incrementum'. Reg. Vat. 29, f. 337v (*Reg. Urb. IV*, no. 2769; *VMH*, p. 270, no. CCCCXCIII).

[90] *Reg. Alex. IV*, no. 2963; *Reg. Urb. IV*, no. 1242; *VMH*, : pp. 239–41, no. CCCCLIV, pp. 264–5, nos. CCCCLXXXIII–CCCCLXXXIV. Different interpretation in Muldoon, *Popes, Lawyers*, pp. 59–60. Also see Schmieder, *Europa*, pp. 85–6 on Alexander IV's letter.

vation of his earthly kingdom.[91] The pope warned Béla that such a 'shameful alliance' would be a break from the community of believers and would turn Béla 'from the protector of the Christian name into a persecutor of believers'.[92] The pope also gave more practical reasons for his position. Drawing his information from such missionaries/spies as John of Plano Carpini, Alexander pointed out that the Mongols, pretending to enter into alliances, in fact trapped their 'allies'; they were treacherous and never kept their word.[93] It was a matter of definition to the pope that unbelievers did not keep their word. He also maintained that marriage between Christians and unbelievers was not a true, binding marriage.[94]

Alexander IV's final arguments were moral and ideological. As a Christian, Béla should know that God was both just and merciful. While he allowed epidemics and tribulations such as the Mongol invasion to take place for the sins of Christians, he would listen to true believers. Steadfast faith and prayer would help overcome these dangers. The pope thus shifted the blame to Béla and the Hungarians, implying that the invasion was, in the final analysis, a consequence of their own sins: a common explanation for Christian defeat, already used for the first failures of crusaders.[95] The solution, therefore, was a thorough reform of their morals and behaviour. At this point, moralizing shifted to a pursuit of ecclesiastical aims. Among the necessary reforms, the pope emphasized the honour due to the Church, and the safeguarding

---

[91] 'abhorrere tamen deberet christianissimus princeps, etiam regna quelibet mundi, etiam denique vitam propriam et suorum regnis temporalibus preferendam sibi tam detestabilibus, tamque probrosis compendiis preservare'. ASV Reg. Vat. 25, f. 224r (*Reg. Alex. IV*, no. 2963; *VMH*, p. 240, no. CCCCLIV).

[92] 'ab[a]ruptus a corpore fidelium et fedo federe infidelibus nationibus copulatus fias de propugnatore christiani nominis fidelium impugnator': *ibid*. On similar papal attitude to Bohemond VI of Antioch who became a Mongol tributary: Peter Jackson, 'The Crisis in the Holy Land in 1260', *English Historical Review* 95 (1980): pp. 481–513.

[93] Carpini, *Ystoria*, ed. Wyngaert, pp. 47, 83–5, 94 (ed. Daffinà *et al*., pp. 247, 283–5, 294–5) on Mongol treachery. Similarly Simon of Saint-Quentin:*Simon de Saint-Quentin: Histoire des Tartares*, ed. Jean Richard (Paris: P. Geuther, 1965), p. 38. Roger's account about the invasion of Hungary also included such instances: *SRH*, vol. II: pp. 580–1.

[94] 'gaudere non poteris, ut tibi promissorum conventorumque suorum servent constantiam, quam aliis non observant. Certo nempe fidei vinculo teneri nequeunt, cum veram fidem non habeant infideles . . . Matrimonii quoque nexus nec christiano paganum, nec christianum pagano coniungit . . . Si ergo . . . filium vel filiam tuam contingat gentilis conubii contagio maculari . . . [this deed] non iuris effectum, sed solam creatoris tuam contumeliam continebit . . . et sic cum non nisi domino lex christiana permittat nubere christiano, filius vel filia tua cum infideli uxore, vel viro execrabilium nuptiarum infame ac captiosum contubernium sortietur, et peribit . . . in obsceno adulterini thori volutabro lugenda eo tempore soboles principis christiani.' ASV Reg. Vat. 25, f. 224r–v (*VMH*, p. 240). Canon law on marriage between Christians and 'infidels': James A. Brundage, *Law, Sex and Christian Society in Medieval Europe* (Chicago: University of Chicago Press, 1987), pp. 244, 267–8, 340.

[95] Jonathan Riley-Smith, *The First Crusade and the Idea of Crusading*, 2nd paperback printing (Philadelphia: University of Pennsylvania Press, 1994), p. 133.

of ecclesiastical liberties such as canonical elections. Refusing all the help Béla had requested – sending archers and reducing the number of prebends given to foreigners in Hungary – Alexander IV claimed that he had provided what he was able to and what the king could expect without arrogance.

The Mongol invasion led to a royal ideology that built on the pre-existing notion of a territorial Christendom, whose frontiers had to be defended and expanded ('defence' often stood for territorial expansion) by lay rulers. Rulers on the frontiers could turn this rhetoric to their benefit; by claiming special status on the Christian frontier, it was possible to pressure the popes for concessions on a variety of issues. Frederick III of Castile used very similar justifications as the defender of Christendom against Muslims to argue that he had a right to use ecclesiastical taxes, influence the appointment of the archbishop, and even get away with adultery.[96] King Béla tried to benefit both from the opportunities provided by Hungary's frontier position, and from an ideology of Hungary as the 'gate' of Christendom. Thus he invited the Cumans to settle in the kingdom, and initiated a marriage alliance with them. He deployed them in internal wars as well as in campaigns against Christian countries. At the same time he complained about the necessity of relying on the Cumans, of the precarious position of Hungary on the frontier of Christian Europe, and of the danger that it might fall prey to the Mongols. He used Hungary's frontier position to justify his policy towards non-Christians, and to buttress royal interest in controversies with the popes. King Béla maintained that he was attentive to the good of Hungary and Christendom. The popes countered that deviation from the ecclesiastical view necessarily meant a straying from the path of Christianity; Béla would be acting against the good of Christendom if he acquiesced to any form of alliance with the Mongols, and therefore his argument could not be accepted. The debate was part of the power politics between the king and the popes. Papal arguments were calculated to ensure ecclesiastical privileges in Hungary; Béla's were designed to enlarge the sphere of royal power. In these exchanges, issues of sovereignty were attached to notions of Christendom.

Subsequently, the idea of a Christian frontier had a long career in the region. It had great success in fifteenth- and sixteenth-century Poland and Hungary in the form of the 'bulwark' or 'shield' of Christendom, in the context of the Turkish wars. As the Ottoman danger and conquests in this region were much more lasting than the Mongol one, popes and humanists took up the royal formula of Poland and Hungary being

[96] Linehan, *Spanish Church and the Papacy*, pp. 103–12. More broadly in Spain: Linehan, 'Religion, Nationalism', esp. p. 189.

Conflicts between the papacy and the kings

Christendom's defenders. Ultimately, the notion became part of the national identity of both countries, lasting to the present day.[97]

POLITICAL FRAGMENTATION AND THE CUMANS

Controversy in the later thirteenth century shifted from the position of non-Christians in a Christian kingdom to the position of Hungary itself. The Mongol invasion, the subsequent arguments of King Béla, and the settlement of the Cumans in the kingdom fed the fear of Hungary's detachment from Christendom. These fears culminated during the reign of King László IV the Cuman (1272–90). At that time, conflict focused on whether it was possible to integrate the Cumans, or whether the king and the kingdom of Hungary would fall into 'paganism'.[98]

László is one of the most fascinating figures of Hungarian history, sparking many debates about the correct interpretation of his role and personality. He has been alternately seen as an evil king, a weak youngster under bad influence, an inexperienced youth struggling with too many political difficulties, and an aspiring autocrat.[99] Son of István V and Erzsébet, daughter of a Cuman chieftain, László acceded to the throne as a minor, ruled amidst growing political strife and fragmentation, and was assassinated by the Cumans. Ecclesiastical persecution began in his lifetime, and after his death he was transformed into a wholly negative figure. While András II did not carry out his promises and Béla IV wanted to turn current Christian ideology to his advantage, László broke openly with the ecclesiastical concept of a Christian king to such an extent that he was not only accused of being a bad king, but also came to be seen as not a Christian. This image was constructed during his lifetime by prelates and nobles who opposed László; after his death it was perpetuated under the Angevin kings of Hungary.[100]

---

[97] Casimir the Great in the fourteenth century: Rhode, *Ostgrenze Polens*, chapter VI; Knoll, 'Stabilization of the Polish Western Frontier'; Lajos Terbe, 'Egy európai szállóige életrajza (Magyarország a kereszténység védőbástyája)', *Egyetemes Philológiai Közlöny* 60 (1936): pp. 297–351; Sándor Őze, '"A kereszténység védőpajzsa" vagy "üllő és verő közé szorult ország": A nemzettudat átformálódása a 16. század közepén a dél-dunántúli végvári katonaságnál', in *Magyarok Nyugat és Kelet között*, ed. Tamás Hofer (Budapest: Balassi, 1996), pp. 99–107.

[98] László III or IV; in the list of Hungary's kings, he is the fourth to bear the name László, but since László III was an infant who never ruled (he was crowned in August 1204 and died in May 1205, at the age of five), he was often called, especially by his contemporaries, László III. Biography: Szabó, *Kun László*.

[99] Deér, *Pogány magyarság*, pp. 235–6; Pauler, *Magyar nemzet*, vol. II: esp. p. 333; Szabó, *Kun László*, and Engel, *Beilleszkedés*, pp. 237–8; Szűcs, *Utolsó Árpádok*, pp. 310–21.

[100] Concepts of kingship and of the good king changed not only over time, but even between different groups. Medieval kingship has been the subject of numerous studies. A recent overview with bibliography: Jacques Le Goff, 'Le roi dans l'Occident médiéval: caractères originaux', in *Kings and Kingship in Medieval Europe*, ed. Anne J. Duggan (London: King's College, 1993), pp. 1–40.

Although in the latter part of László's reign, ecclesiastical attacks against him reached a scale unknown under previous kings of Hungary, the relations between the papacy and László started amicably. Upon the death of his father in 1272, László succeeded to the throne at the age of ten. Pope Gregory X wrote to assure the young king of his support, and asked the prelates and nobles to help him.[101] By 1278 Pope Nicholas III thought it necessary to send a legate, Philip, bishop of Fermo, to Hungary, due to chaotic conditions there.[102] In letters addressed to Hungarian prelates and to foreign princes, the pope emphasized that the legate was to help King László.[103] Therefore, the opinion, first stated by medieval chronicles, and repeated by some historians, that Philip was sent to Hungary with the object of disciplining the king and his Cumans is mistaken.[104]

The pope was informed by Hungarian nobles about the situation in the kingdom; and in the letter addressed to the legate he listed issues such as the disregard of the liberty of the Church and the oppression of the royal throne that necessitated the legatine mission.[105] Although Philip was appointed as legate to Poland, Galicia, Croatia, Serbia and other territories as well as Hungary, he was instructed to use the insignia of *de latere* legates 'who cross the sea' in Hungary only, in order to ensure the efficacy of his intervention.[106] Philip was authorized to use such insignia even though he was not a cardinal; this shows the importance that the pope attached to the legation.[107] Indeed, a fourteenth-century illustration of the *Illuminated Chronicle* depicts Philip with a cardinal's insignia; the illuminator could not conceive of such an important legation without

---

[101] *VMH*, pp. 304–6, nos. DXXXII–DXXXIII; *Reg. Greg. X*, nos. 764–5.
[102] Augustin Demski, *Papst Nikolaus III*, Kirchengeschichtliche Studien 6 (Münster: H. Schöning, 1903), pp. 226–34. On the legate: Kasimir Golab, 'De Philippo Firmano Episcopo eiusque statutis legativis a. 1279', *Revista Española de Derecho Canonico* 16 (1961): pp. 187–200.
[103] ASV Reg. Vat. 39, ff. 89v–90r (*Reg. Nic. III*, nos. 312–14; *VMH*, pp. 328–30, nos. DXLV–DXLVII).
[104] *SRH*, vol. I: p. 473; Ottokar of Steier, in *MGH DC*, vol. V, pt. I: pp. 322–3; 'Annales Austriae Continuatio Vindobonensis', in *MGH SS*, vol. IX: p. 711; Hóman and Szekfű, *Magyar történet*, pp. 601–2; Fraknói, *Magyarország egyházi*, pp. 82–3; Györffy, 'Magyarországi kun', p. 281. This view was already criticized by Szűcs, *Utolsó Árpádok*, pp. 301–2.
[105] ASV Reg. Vat. 39, ff. 88v–89v (*Reg. Nic. III*, no. 312; *VMH*, pp. 327–8, no. DXLIV).
[106] 'qui missi de latere mare transeunt': ASV Reg. Vat. 39, f. 89v (*VMH*, p. 328, no. DXLIV). On the special status of legates going on missions overseas: Figueira, 'Legatus apostolice sedis', pp. 566, 570.
[107] In thirteenth-century canon law usually only cardinal legates were characterized as *de latere*: Robert C. Figueira, 'The Classification of Medieval Papal Legates in the Liber Extra', *Archivum Historiae Pontificiae* 21 (1983): pp. 211–28. On the development of the legal status of legates: Karl Ruess, *Die Rechtliche Stellung der Päpstlichen Legaten bis Bonifaz VIII* (Paderborn: F. Schöningh, 1912). On legatine insignia: Figueira, 'Legatus apostolice sedis', pp. 565–72, and Ruess, *Rechtliche*, pp. 185–210. The wording of the papal commission to Philip was copied in the 1307 appointment of Cardinal Gentilis as legate to Hungary: *Monumenta Vaticana Historiam Regni Hungariae Illustrantia* (Budapest, 1884), ser. I, vol. II: p. 3.

Conflicts between the papacy and the kings

the legate being a cardinal.[108] The legate's powers included the authorization to excommunicate anyone (even the king), to absolve from excommunication, to punish the clerics who accompanied him on his journey, to oversee the goods of the archbishopric of Esztergom during the see's vacancy, and to distribute prebends and benefices.[109] Nicholas III thus gave more extensive powers to his legate than Gregory IX had given to Jacob of Pecorara. The pope delegated his authority more fully in order to enable the legate to act according to the needs he would perceive once in Hungary. Philip was not just to carry out one task, but to bring order to Hungary. The most immediate issue awaiting resolution was the vacancy of the archbishopric of Esztergom, but Philip was also to ensure that ecclesiastical privileges and royal authority would be restored.[110]

Late thirteenth-century Hungary was characterized by growing forces of anarchy. Factionalism was manifest in the struggle for positions (twenty-two men took turns to fill the office of palatine during the reign of László[111]) and in the civil wars. Political fragmentation culminated soon after László's death in the period of 'kinglets', *kiskirályok*, when the most powerful magnates ruled over extensive territories, disregarding royal authority.[112] Seeking a basis for monarchical power, László turned to the Cumans, who constituted his guard and retinue reminiscent of nomadic empires. Other rulers also relied on Cumans to fight against internal enemies. The closest parallel to László's use of them is the case of King Davit' II Ağmašenebeli (1089–1125) who invited the Cumans into Georgia and relied on them against his own aristocracy.[113]

After his arrival, the papal legate quickly came to see Hungary's non-Christians as the crux of the problem. His hostility was directed in particular at the Cumans, although, as described above, he legislated on the status of Jews and Muslims as well. With the appointment of Lodomer

---

[108] László Mezey and László Geréb, eds., *Képes Krónika* (Illuminated Chronicle), 2 vols, facsimile edition (Budapest: Helikon, 1964), f. 65, p. 129.

[109] ASV Reg. Vat. 39, ff. 90r–92v (*Reg. Nic. III*, nos. 315–42; *VMH*, pp. 330–6, nos. DXLVIII–DXLIX).

[110] ASV Reg. Vat. 39, ff. 166v–167r, f. 89r–v (*Reg. Nic. III*, nos. 1037, 312; *VMH*, p. 339, no. DLV and p. 328, no. DXLIV respectively).

[111] Jenő Gutheil, *Az Árpád-kori Veszprém*, 2nd edn (Veszprém: Veszprém Megyei Levéltár, 1979), p. 226.

[112] Events in all standard handbooks, analyses include Gyula Kristó, *A feudális széttagolódás Magyarországon* (Budapest: Akadémiai Kiadó, 1979), pp. 80–3; Gyula Kristó, *Az Aranybullák évszázada*, 2nd edn (Budapest: Gondolat Kiadó, 1981), pp. 154–86; Szűcs, *Utolsó Árpádok*, pp. 322–47.

[113] Golden, 'Qipčaqs'. Within Hungary, King István II perhaps relied on the Pechenegs in the early twelfth century in a similar way: Ferenc Makk, 'Megjegyzések II. István történetéhez', in *Középkori kútfőink kritikus kérdései*, ed. János Horváth and György Székely (Budapest: Akadémiai Kiadó, 1974), pp. 253–9.

as archbishop of Esztergom, moreover, Philip promoted an ardent enemy of King László to be head of the Hungarian Church. Thus when the legate began to focus his activities on the Cumans, conflict between him and King László became inevitable. For László, the Cumans represented his only power-base and dependable military support; he could not afford to alienate them.[114]

As a consequence of the legate's activity, in 1279 King László took an oath to observe the articles drawn up by Philip concerning ecclesiastical liberties and the Cumans. The Cumans were to be Christianized, if necessary even by force, settled, and compelled to conform to ecclesiastical regulations.[115] Although László IV complied with the wishes of the papal legate in decreeing that war would be organized against the Cumans if they did not obey,[116] he was not eager to implement these stipulations. The war he later had to undertake against the rebellious Cumans was not an effort to ensure their conversion, but a war against disobedient subjects. When László attempted to resist Philip's demands on policy toward the Cumans, the legate excommunicated him. A cycle of penitence, papal admonitions, periods of amicable relations with the papacy, further resistance, including the imprisonment of the legate, and excommunication followed.[117] László's behaviour, the reports of prelates and nobles who opposed attempts to establish strong royal power, and ensuing papal intervention shifted the focus from Hungary's non-Christians to the king himself. To the issue of the role of the Cumans in Hungary and their forced integration, was added the query whether László himself was a Christian.

Most of the Cumans in Hungary either were not baptized or did not conform in their way of life to Christian norms; they were not settled, they did not observe marriage laws, they destroyed churches. Therefore the king's close association with them was used by his opponents, who included prelates as well as nobles, to accuse him of being not simply a Cuman by origin, but a 'pagan' by choice. Popes Nicholas III, Honorius IV and Nicholas IV remonstrated with the king for not keeping his promises. They exhorted him to conform to Christian costume and hairstyle, to leave the company and example of 'Tartars, Saracens, nökers and pagans', and threatened to proclaim a crusade against them and against

[114] Szűcs, *Utolsó Árpádok*, p. 306.   [115] See chapter 6, pp. 219–22.
[116] 'faciemus exercitum generalem', ASV AA Arm. I-XVIII-595 (*VMH*, p. 341, no. DLVI).
[117] Detailed accounts: Fraknói, *Magyarország egyházi*, pp. 84–90; Szabó, *Kun László*, pp. 85–109; Pauler, *Magyar nemzet*, pp. 357–76; Zsoldos, 'Téténytől', p. 82–6. Papal letters attesting the fluctuations in papal–royal relations from 1279: *Reg. Nic. III*, nos. 607–11, *Reg. Martin IV*, nos. 215–16, *Reg. Hon. IV*, nos. 761–2; *VMH*, pp. 341–6, nos. DLVII–DLXI, pp. 350–1, nos. DLXIX–DLXX, pp. 353–6, nos. DLXXIII–DLXXVI. László attempted to obstruct the synod of Buda: AA Arm. I-XVIII-592 (*VMH*, p. 347, no. DLXIV; *RA*, no. 3066).

Conflicts between the papacy and the kings

the king himself if necessary.[118] That László's behaviour was condemned by the Church comes as no surprise. First he refused to carry out the dispositions of the legate; then he defied well-established canonical regulations relating to the indissolubility of marriage and the validity of religious vows.

László repudiated his wife Isabella, daughter of the Angevin King Charles of Sicily, and took a Cuman mistress. László was not the only medieval king to have repudiated his wife, nor alone in disregarding ecclesiastical disapproval.[119] Because László's mistress was a Cuman woman, however, the case was exploited as additional proof of his having turned 'pagan'.[120] Archbishop Lodomer called the king's Cuman concubine Aydua a 'poisonous viper', accused them of copulating in public, and demanded that Aydua be exiled into the farthest territory of the kingdom to keep her from meeting the king.[121] He complained that László gave Aydua the revenues and honour due to the queen of Hungary, while keeping the queen herself imprisoned in a convent. Isabella was held in a convent, whose superior at the time was László's sister Erzsébet, on the island of the Blessed Virgin (made famous by its former inhabitant Margit (Margaret) of Hungary, aunt of King László, whose canonization process started soon after her death in 1270).[122]

---

[118] Nicholas III had already threatened him by 'temporalibus correctionibus' and an 'insurrectio': ASV Reg. Vat. 39, f. 220r (*Reg. Nic. III*, no. 607; *VMH*, p. 343, no. DLVII). The threat 'proponere verbum crucis' appears in the letter of Honorius IV on 12 March 1287 (Reg. Vat. 43, f. 119r; *Reg. Hon. IV*, no. 761, *VMH*, p. 354, no. DLXXIII), repeated in a letter to the archbishop of Esztergom, but not in those to prelates and other rulers: f. 119v; *VMH*, pp. 354–5, nos. DLXXIV–DLXXV, no separate number in *Reg. Hon. IV*) A marginal note in the Register refers to unusual direct papal intervention: after copying the letter into the Register, it was returned to the pope who changed it, but the new form was not recorded. Nicholas IV's letter copies the version that appears in the Register: Reg. Vat. 44, ff. 25v–26r (*Reg. Nic. IV*, no. 194; *VMH*, pp. 357–9, no. DLXXVII). The threat of crusade was renewed in 1290: ASV Reg. Vat. 45, ff. 167r–168v (*Reg. Nic. IV*, nos. 4313–22; *VMH*, pp. 361–4, nos. DLXXXII–DLXXXIV). These papal letters list 'Tartaros, Sarracenos, Neugerios et Paganos'.

[119] Royal repudiation and resistance, especially frequent in the early Middle Ages, continued into the thirteenth century, e.g. the case of Philip Augustus of France: Jean Gaudemet, 'Le dossier canonique du mariage de Philippe Auguste et d'Ingeburge de Danemark (1193–1213)', *Revue Historique de Droit Français et Etranger* 62 (1984): pp. 15–29, repr. in Gaudemet, *Droit de l'Eglise et vie sociale au Moyen Age* (Northampton: Variorum Reprints, 1989), no. XIV.

[120] Other concubines: Pope Honorius IV wrote that László 'infidelibus . . . se copulavit mulieribus' Reg. Vat. 43, f. 119v (*Reg. Hon. IV*, no. 762; *VMH*, p. 355, no. DLXXVI), so did the cardinals: *CD*, vol. V, pt. 3: p. 363. Similarly in many chronicles, for example: *SRH*, vol. 1: pp. 472–3. Ottokar of Steier, in *MGH DC*, vol. V, pt. 1: p. 322; Philip Jaffé, ed., 'Annales Colmarienses maiores 1277–1472', in *MGH SS*, vol. XVII: pp. 202–32, see p. 207.

[121] Karácsonyi, 'Mérges vipera', p. 5: 'venenosa vipera'. Lodomer's two letters survived only in thirteenth-century copies. They have been accepted as letters sent to the pope, except by György Györffy, who has proposed that they were only exercises in style, and toned-down versions were sent: 'Még egyszer Szűcs Jenő: Az utolsó Árpádok c. művéről', *Századok* 130 (1996): pp. 999–1007. Papal responses show that Lodomer did send accusations against László to the popes.

[122] *CD*, vol. V, pt. 3: pp. 461–3; MOL DF 200719 (*CD*, vol. VII, pt. 2: pp. 127–9, no. CCCLXXXVIII); *ÁÚO*, vol. IV: pp. 341–2, no. 218; *HO*, vol. VI: pp. 343–4, no. 248. The island was originally

The king was also instrumental in removing this same sister from the convent of the Blessed Virgin. Erzsébet abandoned her life as a nun in order to marry a Czech noble.[123] This was one of László's most violently anti-ecclesiastical deeds. Lodomer claimed that, in answer to ecclesiastical remonstration, László exploded: 'If I had fifteen or more sisters in as many cloistered communities as you like, I would snatch them from there to marry them off licitly or illicitly; in order to procure through them a kin-group who will support me by all their power in the fulfilment of my will . . . I am the law over myself and I will not suffer to be confined by the laws of some priests.'[124]

Archbishop Lodomer also reported to the pope László's alleged threat that 'beginning with the archbishop of Esztergom and his suffragans I shall exterminate the whole lot right up to Rome with the aid of Tartar swords'.[125] By 1288, then, László was represented not simply as a bad king and suspect Christian, but as a menace to Christendom, indeed as an ally of the Mongols. László 'endeavours with unceasing efforts to bring Tartar barbarity into the country and to tear asunder and consume . . . Christ's flock'.[126] It became routine to play upon the fear generated by the Mongols in order to impress on the pope the magnitude of the danger. Fear of a Mongol alliance, first exploited by King Béla IV, and disapproval of the Cumans and King László were thus combined. Lodomer's reports and papal letters envisaged the loss of Hungary to the Christian world through joint external and internal causes. Recurring Mongol raids in Poland and Hungary were reminders of the external danger. The pres-

footnote 122 (cont.)
called Insula Leporum; from 1265 Insula Beatae Virginis; from the fourteenth century Insula Beatae Margarethae; the Dominican convent there was built for Margit after her parents, King Béla IV and his wife, offered her as an oblate: 'Margit-sziget', in *KMTL*.

[123] In the canonization process of Margit (1276) there are glimpses of Erzsébet's life in the convent and her own beliefs. She was an oblate. Although bored by the living Margit's prolonged prayers, she believed in her miraculous powers after death, and recounted several cures from various illnesses that Margit accomplished for her: *Monumenta Romana*, vol. I: pp. 185–6.

[124] 'Si quindecim, inquiens, vel plures in quantumlibet claustris religiosis haberem sorores, extractas licitis vel illicitis copularem conjugiis, per quas ad explendas voluntates meas totis mihi viribus assistentes acquirerem parentelas . . . ipse enim mihi sum lex nec aliquorum astringi patiar legibus sacerdotum'. Karácsonyi, 'Mérges vipera', p. 7. Lodomer called Erzsébet not a 'sancti- but an antimonialis,' *ibid.*, p. 6.

[125] 'Ab archiepiscopo, inquit, Strigoniensi suffraganeisque incipiens gladiis Tartaricis amputari faciam omnem obertam usque Romam'. Karácsonyi, 'Mérges vipera', p. 7. Even Szűcs, who otherwise trusts Lodomer's account, advises caution with regard to accepting this statement: *Utolsó Árpádok*, p. 318. Papal letters also refer to a Mongol alliance, see note 118 above.

[126] 'Tartaricam barbariem . . . in hoc regnum inducere continuatis procuravit studiis et procurat dilaniari crudeliter et consumi . . . oves Christi', Karácsonyi, 'Mérges vipera', p. 8. Also accusations that László was an ally of the Mongols, offered to marry the Mongol khan's daughter, and became a pagan (pp. 3, 4, 9, 10). Similar accusations about László living like a Mongol and his marriage alliance with Mongols: 'Annales Sancti Rudberti Salisburgenses', in *MGH SS*, vol. IX: p. 806.

Conflicts between the papacy and the kings

ence of the un-Christianized Cumans was construed by many as an internal peril to Christianity.[127] Linking the two through the person of the Hungarian king set the scene for threats of a crusade against László. László's alleged alliance with the Mongols cannot, however, be substantiated at all. In fact, between 1285 and 1288 László rewarded his men for having repelled the Mongols; some of them also helped Poland against a Mongol attack.[128] Severed Mongol heads were sent to the king as a sign of victory.[129]

Finally there was no need for ecclesiastical opposition to foil László's plans; he was assassinated by the Cumans.[130] With his death, the idea of a crusade also vanished. The archbishop's previous propaganda made such a strong impression on Pope Nicholas IV, however, that he ordered an enquiry after László's death to determine 'whether at the time of his death the king kept and served the Christian faith . . . whether the king died as a Catholic Christian'.[131] The results of this investigation are not known, but evidence from both the time of his death and after it shows that László was not generally considered to have died as a 'pagan'. When his mother Erzsébet gave donations for the salvation of several members of the Hungarian dynasty just prior to László's death in 1290, László's name was on the list.[132] According to a chronicle tradition, he was buried in the cathedral of Csanád.[133] His successors on the throne and even Pope Boniface VIII referred to him as 'of renowned memory'.[134]

None the less, László went down in history as a bad or possibly evil king. The fourteenth-century Hungarian chronicle composition portrays László as the root of all evil: corrupted by his Cuman concubines, he led the whole population astray into paganism, until meeting his well-deserved

---

[127] See chapter 6, pp. 201–3.
[128] 1285: *Székely oklevéltár*, vol. IV: pp. 2–3, no. 657 (*RA*, no. 3362); MOL DL 40177 (*ÁÚO*, vol. IV: pp. 276–8, no. 174; *RA*, no. 3368); 1287: *RA*, no. 3444; 1288: MOL DL 1229 (*CD*, vol. V, pt. 3: pp. 398–400; *RA*, no. 3503); MOL DL 1230 (*ÁÚO*, vol. IX: pp. 465–7, no. 334; *RA*, no. 3504); MOL DL 28502 (*CD*, vol. V, pt. 3: pp. 452–4; *RA*, no. 3534). Reward for service on the border of the Mongol empire (1286): *HO*, vol. VI: pp. 315–16, no. 229 (*RA*, no. 3410). Szabó, *Kun László*, pp. 117–21; Pauler, *Magyar nemzet*, vol. II: pp. 386–8.
[129] MOL DL 57222 (*CD*, vol. V, pt. 3: pp. 393–7; *RA*, no. 3502); MOL DL 1298 (*ÁÚO*, vol. V, p. 3: no. 2; *RA*, no. 3686). [130] See chapter 4, note 193.
[131] 'utrum prefatus Rex . . . mortis sue tempore fidem teneret catholicam et servaret . . . utrum Rex ipse decesserit tanquam catholicus Christianus'. ASV Reg. Vat. 45, f. 172r (*Reg. Nic. IV*, no. 4377; *VMH*, p. 369, no. DXCII).
[132] MOL DF 219422 (*HO*, vol. VIII: pp. 279–80, no. 227; *ÁÚO*, vol. IX: pp. 524–5, no. 380). This was in the tradition of such donations, e.g. *HO*, vol. V: pp. 12–14, no. 9 (*RA*, no. 511); *HO*, vol. VIII: p. 171, no. 133 (*RA*, no. 2591).
[133] *Chronicon Budense*, ed. József Podhradczky (Buda, 1838), p. 212. Kálmán Juhász, *A csanádi püspökség története 1243–1307* (Makó: Makói Nyomda, 1933), pp. 16–23.
[134] András III's reference to the charter of 'regis Ladizlai inclite recordationis fratris nostri karissimi patruelis', *RA*, no. 4243; also nos. 3951, 3662. *Reg. Bon. VIII*, no. 5025; *VMH*, p. 393, no. DCXXVIII ('clare memorie').

end at the hands of his assassins. In this version, Philip of Fermo was sent to Hungary because László lived 'according to Cuman, not Catholic, custom', and the Hungarians adopted Cuman hairstyle and dress. Hungary's decline, symbolized by 'King László's cart', is attributed to him. The chronicle claimed that carts had to be drawn by people, because of a shortage of animals due to incessant wars and robbery.[135] The *Illuminated Chronicle* reinforces this negative judgement through visual means. László's portrait is strikingly different from that of his predecessors; he wears the traditional Cuman attire of a caftan and conical hat. This visual message is especially powerful, since the image contrasts with that of other kings; even Attila the Hun is portrayed as king in western-style clothes, sitting on a throne.[136] The only scenes that the illuminator chose to illustrate in the story of King László, furthermore, were the portrait of the king (in Cuman costume), the second Mongol invasion, the arrival of the papal legate Philip, and László's assassination by the Cumans, with the king himself again in Cuman clothing.[137] These images definitely convey the condemnation of László as a pagan, dying a death that would lead to damnation.

Modern scholars have adopted this view in varying degrees. The question whether László's was a 'pagan' court and rule needs to be explored here, in order to analyse the significance of Cuman presence in the development of kingship in Hungary. Disregarding the unusual element in László's case (compared with other thirteenth-century monarchs), his reliance on 'pagan' Cumans, László's opposition to the papacy has been seen as the upholding of strong royal power, even drawing on Roman law.[138] Alternatively, placing the emphasis on the king's reliance on the Cumans, several historians have interpreted László's reign as a complete reversal of previous trends, a return to 'paganism'. Discounting Catholic or romanticizing approaches based on László's alleged character, the most important such view is that of Jenő Szűcs. He has seen László's policy after 1286 as an autocratic attempt at rulership. According to Szűcs, László wished to place himself out of the Christian–feudal matrix, to rely on neither the Church nor the nobility, and to rule purely with the aid of Cuman military force. Szűcs also suggests that László was influenced by Cuman experience and ideas of rulership.[139]

[135] *SRH*, vol. I: pp. 471–4. Written during the Angevin period.
[136] László: *Képes Krónika*, f. 64v, p. 128. Attila: f. 5v, p. 10, f. 7, p. 13. Other kings: e.g. f. 19v, p. 38; f. 20, p. 39; f. 57v, p. 114; f. 61v, p. 122. Berend, 'Medieval Patterns'.
[137] *Képes Krónika*, ff. 64v–65v, pp. 128–9.
[138] Emma Lederer, 'Az egyház szerepe az Árpádkori Magyarországon', *Századok* 83 (1949): pp. 79–105; József Gerics, 'Az államszuverenitás védelme és a "két jog" alkalmazásának szempontjai XII–XIII. századi krónikáinkban', *Történelmi Szemle* 18 (1975): pp. 353–72; Gerics, 'Adalékok a Kézai-krónika', pp. 117–19.
[139] Szűcs, *Utolsó Árpádok*, pp. 310–21; he quotes the passages attributed to László by Lodomer as an example of 'blind will', and denies the influence of Roman law: p. 318.

Conflicts between the papacy and the kings

Did László indeed place himself out of a Christian matrix? Both certain contemporaries and later historians had doubts about László's adherence to Christianity from 1279 on, and for the period following 1286 there is a consensus about László's un-Christian behaviour. Yet despite his violent confrontation with the papacy and Archbishop Lodomer, László continued to rely on certain Christian institutions. Prior to 1286 László donated lands, revenues and rights to various ecclesiastical institutions and refounded a dilapidated monastery.[140] One charter mentions the king's visit to a church, and he was keen to promote the canonization of his aunt Margit.[141] He defeated the Cumans in 1282 and rewarded those who repulsed the Mongols.[142] His cleric Simon of Kéza described László as a son of the Church, born under the sign of Mars, and victorious over the rebellious Cumans.[143] Even in the period following 1286, at the height of Lodomer's accusations against him, the king continued his donations to certain Hungarian churches and prelates.[144] After removing his sister Erzsébet from the convent, he returned all the properties of the nuns at her demand.[145] According to the tradition of the hermits of the order of St Paul (founded in Hungary during the thirteenth century), László gave them land.[146] He also gave lands and revenues to monasteries to ensure the salvation of his soul, as well as the souls of his father and grandfather.[147] He sent Paul, a *legum doctor*, to Rome as his ambassador.[148] Until his death, he continued to have recourse to *loca*

---

[140] E.g., *CD*, vol. V, pt. 3: pp. 231–3 (*RA*, no. 3302); *MES*, vol. II: pp. 204–6, no. 184 (*RA*, no. 3376); *CD*, vol. V, pt. 2: pp. 333–4 (*RA*, no. 2700); *CD*, vol. V, pt. 2: pp. 328–30 (*RA*, no. 2733); *ÁÚO*, vol. XII: pp. 193–6, no. 162 (*RA*, no. 2769) *CD*, vol. V, pt. 2: pp. 378–80 (*RA*, no. 2797); *RA*, nos. 2806, 2882; *MES*, vol. II: p. 87, no. 71 (*RA*, no. 2924); *RA*, no. 3259; *MES*, vol. II: p. 199, no. 179 (*RA*, no. 3385); *RA*, no. 3394; donated estates to the church of Veszprém for the salvation of his father István V's soul: *HO*, vol. V: pp. 65–6, no. 53 (*RA*, no. 3141).

[141] MOL DL 30583 (*HO*, vol. VIII: p. 237, no. 191; *RA*, no. 3361): 'cum nos . . . ad ecclesiam beati Mychaelis archangeli causa devocionis accessissemus'. *Monumenta Romana*, vol. I: p. cxii.

[142] See note 128 above. [143] *SRH*, vol. I: pp. 185–7.

[144] MOL DL 1221 (*Budapest történetének oklevéles*, vol. I: p. 241, no. 222; *ÁÚO*, vol. IX: p. 471, no. 338; *RA*, no. 3490). *CD*, 5, pt. 3: p. 517 (*RA*, no. 3424); *CD*, vol. V, pt. 3: p. 349 (*RA*, no. 3452); *CD*, vol. V, pt. 3: p. 402 (*RA*, no. 3473); *CD*, vol. V, pt. 3: p. 417 (*RA*, no. 3489); *Budapest történetének oklevéles*, vol. I: p. 242, no. 224 (*RA*, no. 3495); Franz Zimmermann and Carl Werner, *Urkundenbuch zur Geschichte des Deutschen in Siebenbürgen*, 3 vols. (Hermannstadt, 1892–1902), vol. I: p. 159 (*RA*, no. 3509); *CD*, vol. VII, pt. 5: p. 472, no. CCC (*RA*, no. 3510); *RA*, no. 3542; Zimmermann and Werner, *Urkundenbuch*, vol. I: p. 161 (*RA*, no. 3547); *MES*, vol. II: pp. 217–18, no. 193 (*RA*, no. 3419); *RA*, nos. 3525, 3550. I have not included the donations and restitutions to churches in Esztergom made under pressure from Archbishop Lodomer (a series of charters dated 18 April 1288: *RA*, nos. 3483–6).

[145] MOL DL 1221 (from a transcript of King Sigismond in 1428; *Budapest történetének oklevéles*, vol. I: p. 241, no. 222; *RA*, no. 3490).

[146] In the Order's Inventory of Privileges: MOL DF 286489, pp. 81–2; Gregorius Gyöngyösi, *Vitae fratrum eremitarum ordinis sancti Pauli primi eremitae*, ed. Ferenc L. Hervay (Budapest: Akadémiai Kiadó, 1988), pp. 49–50.

[147] *CD*, vol. VII, pt. 5: pp. 472–4, no. CCC (*RA*, no. 3510); *RA*, no. 3525 (1289).

[148] *MES*, vol. II: pp. 217–18, no. 193 (*RA*, no. 3419).

credibilia, in order to verify that all details concerning royal land donations were in order, and to draw up charters to this effect.[149] Thereby he relied on a Christian institution that began to fill this role during the reign of László's predecessors. One of László's last dated charters was issued to ensure that the nuns of the island of the Blessed Virgin received the customs revenues due to them.[150]

Despite his reliance on Christian institutions, László did not accept ecclesiastical norms or the Church's power over the king. 'It is not up to your lord [i.e. the archbishop of Esztergom] to set laws for us, but rather to follow those set by us; his lot is to comply, not the authority to govern.'[151] Archbishop Lodomer attributed these words to László and interpreted the refusal to obey the Church as a sign of László's demented fury; the historian Szűcs saw them as the 'manifesto' of an autocrat. This sentence, as well as the one quoted above ('I am the law over myself and I will not suffer to be confined by the laws of some priests'), convey the idea that royal power is not merely equal to but above that of the Church. Whether or not Roman law influenced László in formulating these notions, they were not part of a Cuman-inspired bid for absolute power. Indeed, these statements could not have been borrowed from the Cumans, who had no central authority on the steppe. Nor is there any resonance here of Mongol ideas of rulership, which were not autocratic.[152] Instead of construing Cuman influence as a stimulus to aspire to absolute power and tyranny, it is more fruitful to search for the source of these ideas in either the entourage of Archbishop Lodomer, or that of King László. It is impossible to tell whether the king made such a speech, or the archbishop composed it, attributing it to the king in order to mobilize papal support for himself. Clerics with legal training, capable of constructing such arguments, could be found in the entourage of either. The king could have been advised by one of the lawyers at the court how to claim authority even over the Church. The archbishop could rely on one of the clerics whose legal education he had financed, or perhaps he himself (he may have studied law at Bologna) supplied the material to turn László's insubordination into a legally formulated challenge to papal power.[153]

---

[149] Such a charter was drawn up on 28 May 1290 (László died in July of the same year); *ÁÚO*, vol. IX: pp. 559–60, no. 411 (*RA*, no. 3560).   [150] *ÁÚO*, vol. IX: p. 522, no. 377 (*RA*, no. 3563).

[151] 'Non est, inquit, domini vestri legem nobis imponere, sed impositam per nos sequi, obsequendi eum manere debet necessitas, non auctoritas imperandi'. Karácsonyi, 'Mérges vipera', p. 7.

[152] Golden, *Introduction*, pp. 279–80, 286–91; Golden, 'Qipčaqs'; Morgan, *Mongols*, pp. 38–40, 61–3, 108–11.

[153] 'Lodomér', in *KMTL*. Two entries regarding a 'Lodomerius' from Hungary at Bologna were identified with the archbishop, although no proof for this identification was provided: Rabán Gerézdi, 'Veress Endre: Olasz egyetemeken járt magyarországi tanulók anyakönyve és iratai 1221–1864', *Századok* 76 (1942): pp. 338–44, see p. 340. He certainly sent one of his nephews

Conflicts between the papacy and the kings

In either case, however László himself justified his resistance to ecclesiastical pressure, certain Christian institutional arrangements in Hungary may have contributed to his disobedience. The *Eigenkirche* (proprietary church) organization survived in thirteenth-century central Europe, where lay proprietors often controlled the possessions of monasteries or churches and the election of the priest.[154] Such rights were donated by László to his faithful nobles.[155] One of Pope Martin IV's letters attests to the importance László attached to this prerogative.[156] The king complained that the legate Philip had filled some of the vacancies in Hungarian churches which belonged under the king's patronage. The pope reassured him that this would not prejudice László's rights of *ius patronatus* – though the pope certainly understood the term in the sense prevalent in the west by the late thirteenth century, and not as rights to a proprietary church. The first synod to legislate against these customs in Hungary was that of Buda in 1279, the agenda for which was dictated by the papal legate Philip. It defined lay rights as *ius patronatus* (according to the regulations that had been elaborated in canon law), and prohibited previous practices.[157] During the thirteenth century it was also customary canonically to elect royal candidates to bishoprics in Hungary, and the kings guarded this right.[158] Thus László was able to draw on well-established custom to see royal power as above that of the Church.

Archbishop Lodomer certainly feared the subordination of ecclesiastics to royal power. He knew how to whip up papal anxiety by the image of László turned pagan leading a Mongol attack against the Church. That he was not entirely selfless in his pursuit of King László is clear from a letter of Pope Nicholas IV written after László's death.[159] The pope reproved Lodomer for no longer sending information of Hungarian

to study in Padua: Bónis, *Jogtudó*, p. 24. On Lodomer's letters as legal constructs see note 138 above and Kornél Szovák, 'Lodomér érsek leveleiről', in *Egyházak a változó világban*, ed. István Bárdos and Margit Beke (Tatabánya: Komárom-Esztergom Megye Önkormányzata és József Attila Megyei Könyvtár, 1992), pp. 141–3; József Gerics, 'Krónikáink és a III. András-kori rendi intézmények friauli-aquileiai kapcsolatairól', *Filológiai Közlöny* 21 (1975): pp. 309–25, see pp. 310–11.

[154] Ferenc Kollányi, *A magánkegyúri jog hazánkban a középkorban* (Budapest: MTA, 1906); Solymosi, 'Egyházi-politikai viszonyok'; Elemér Mályusz, 'Die Eigenkirche in Ungarn', *Wiener Archiv für Geschichte des Slawentums und Osteuropas* 5 (1966): pp. 76–95. On royal rights: Vilmos Fraknói, *A magyar királyi kegyúri jog* (Budapest, 1895). In other central European countries: Jerzy Kłoczowski, 'L'Europe centrale et orientale à l'époque de Lyon II', in *1274: Année charnière*, pp. 503–15, esp. p. 510.

[155] E.g., *CD*, vol. v, pt. 3: p. 487 (*RA*, no. 3553); *ÁÚO*, vol. ix: pp. 558–9, no. 410 (*RA*, no. 3554).

[156] ASV Reg. Vat. 41, f. 70v (*Reg. Martin IV*, no. 215; *VMH*, pp. 350–1, no. DLXIX).

[157] Hube, *Constitutiones*, pp. 107–12 (articles 53–6). Peter Landau, *Jus patronatus: Studien zur Entwincklung des Patronats im Dekretalenrecht und der Kanonistik des 12. und 13. Jahrhunderts* (Cologne and Vienna: Böhlau Verlag, 1975).

[158] Solymosi, 'Egyházi-politikai viszonyok', pp. 47–8; Fraknói, *Magyar királyi kegyúri*, pp. 17–34.

[159] ASV Reg. Vat. 45, f. 178r–v (*Reg. Nic. IV*, no. 4429; *VMH*, p. 374, no. DCIII).

events following the king's death, while during the reign of László, the archbishop had constantly complained about how the king's evil ways endangered the realm. Yet the pope thought that the state of the kingdom (a disputed succession) warranted anxiety. Lodomer ceased to complain probably because he was satisfied. He was instrumental in the choice of King András III as László's successor and filled an important position in the royal council.[160]

Lodomer and the popes condemned László by using the already established means of recasting political enemies as enemies of Christians. This idea had strong roots in the eleventh and twelfth centuries, and crusading against Christian political enemies emerged fully at the end of the twelfth and the beginning of the thirteenth centuries.[161] Many of the charges against László fit into this framework. More specifically, the ecclesiastical image of László had many similarities to that of the Emperor Frederick II. Both rulers were accused of aping their non-Christian subjects: László of adopting Cuman food, dress and hairstyle,[162] Frederick of wearing Muslim garb.[163] Both were rebuked for immoral conduct and rejection of Christian belief.[164] As the news concerning László spread, there was even confusion about the accusations: the annals of the monastery of Waverly wrote of László as having turned Muslim.[165] Lodomer endeavoured to present László as the arch-enemy of the Church, just as Frederick had been; justifying a crusade with the rhetoric that László posed a danger to Christendom was reminiscent of the conflict between Pope Innocent IV and Frederick II. In 1279, another ruler came under similar attack. On the complaints of local prelates, Pope Nicholas III protested against Alfonso X of Castile's offences against the Church. Among these was the charge of a dangerous Jewish impact on public life; his accusers represented Alfonso X as barely Christian, and under the influ-

---

[160] Pauler, *Magyar nemzet*, vol. II: pp. 414–21.

[161] Joseph Strayer, 'The Political Crusades of the Thirteenth Century', in *The Later Crusades 1189–1311*, ed. Robert Lee Wolff and Harry W. Hazard, vol. II of *A History of the Crusades*, ed. Kenneth M. Setton (Madison, Wis.: University of Wisconsin Press, 1969), pp. 343–75; Norman Housley, 'Crusades against Christians: Their Origins and Early Development, c. 1000–1216', in *Crusade and Settlement*, ed. Peter W. Edbury (Cardiff: University College Press, 1985): pp. 17–36. Abulafia, *Frederick II*, pp. 380–9, on crusade first used against a ruler.

[162] ASV Reg. Vat. 39, f. 219r (*Reg. Nic. III*, no. 607; *VMH*, p. 342, no. DLVII); Karácsonyi, 'Mérges vipera', p. 4.

[163] D'Alverny, 'La connaissance de l'Islam au temps de Saint Louis', p. 236.

[164] On the charges against Frederick: Ernst Kantorowicz, *Frederick the Second 1194–1250*, Eng. tr. E. O. Lorimer (New York: Richard R. Smith, 1931), pp. 190–7; Ernst Kantorowicz, *Kaiser Friedrich der Zweite: Ergänzungsband* (Berlin: Georg Bondi, 1931), pp. 68–70. Abulafia, *Frederick II*, p. 372; he refutes the traditional opinion about Frederick as an 'oriental prince' (p. 439).

[165] Henry Richards Luard, ed., *Rerum Britannicarum Medii Aevi Scriptores*, Rolls Series 36 (*Annales Monastici*), pt. 2 (London, 1865, repr. Nendeln and Liechtenstein: Kraus Reprint, 1971), pp. 406–7.

Conflicts between the papacy and the kings

ence of Jews.[166] There existed a pattern to present Christian kings, whose policies aroused ecclesiastical opposition, not simply as enemies of the Church, but of Christianity.

King László tried to fight the growing power of the nobility. His reliance on the Cumans stands out in comparison to western neighbours, but fits in well with patterns in Christian countries to the east of Hungary, such as Georgia and Rus' principalities, whose rulers often had recourse to the help of Cumans.[167] These rulers had marriage alliances with these nomads, or even invited them into their territories, without becoming 'pagans' themselves. The availability of the Cumans led László to take advantage of their presence, but this in turn brought him into conflict with the Church. Yet he also relied on Christian institutions and personnel, and even continued to claim to be the head of the Hungarian Church. Neither an evil 'pagan' tyrant, nor simply an upholder of royal power, László combined a frequent medieval royal attitude with novel means to achieve his aims: resistance to ecclesiastical and papal pressures with the opportunities presented by Hungary's frontier position. It was this position that made the incorporation of the Cumans, and reliance on their military force, possible. Thirteenth-century fears of the detachment of Hungary from Christendom were to some extent taken up by modern scholars who have seen the reign of King László as an 'alternative' to western Christian patterns. If we consider that 'pagan' nomads had similar roles in countries such as Georgia and Rus', and that the ecclesiastical pattern of attacking political enemies was to accuse them of being non-Christians, this image has to be modified. The ecclesiastical and monarchical *structure* of the Hungarian kingdom did not come under attack; but the means that this frontier society provided for the building of royal power in the late thirteenth century were unique in a western perspective.

PAPAL AND ROYAL ATTITUDES: THE ROLE OF NON-CHRISTIANS IN CHRISTIAN SOCIETY

As discussed above, papal–royal controversy over non-Christians was connected to conflicts within Hungary and to questions of sovereignty.

[166] Peter Linehan, 'The Spanish Church Revisited: The Episcopal *gravamina* of 1279', in *Authority and Power: Studies on Medieval Law and Government Presented to Walter Ullmann on his Seventieth Birthday*, ed. Brian Tierney and Peter Linehan (Cambridge: Cambridge University Press, 1980), pp. 127–47, repr. as no. IV in Linehan, *Spanish Church and Society 1150–1300* (London: Variorum Reprints, 1983); Linehan, *Spanish Church and the Papacy*, p. 176, n. 1; p. 219 (similar charges in 1267). Attempts to brand Pedro the Cruel as pro-Jewish: Elena Lourie, 'A Jewish Mercenary in the Service of the King of Aragon', *Revue des Etudes Juives* 137 (1978): pp. 367–73, repr. as no. VIII in Lourie, *Crusade and Colonisation: Muslims, Christians and Jews in Medieval Aragon* (Aldershot: Variorum, 1990), see p. 373.

[167] Golden, 'Cumanica I'; Golden, 'Nomads and their Sedentary Neighbors', pp. 72–3.

Were the exchanges about the place of non-Christians in a Christian kingdom also due to a difference between papal (or ecclesiastical) and royal perceptions of the nature and role of non-Christians themselves?

The first step in royal policies was the admission of non-Christians. Jews and probably Muslims had lived in the kingdom from its beginnings, but also continued to migrate to the country, where they were allowed to settle. Occasionally kings took an active part in soliciting the entry of non-Christians: King Géza II sought to recruit Muslim soldiers and King Béla IV invited the Cumans back after they had left the kingdom. Yet in the late eleventh and twelfth centuries the Muslims, and in the thirteenth century the Cumans, were the targets of missionary policy; they were regarded as potential Christians. The king even made the baptism of the Cumans the explicit condition of their gaining entry prior to the Mongol invasion. None the less, thirteenth-century royal policies did not conform to papal expectations or canon law. The kings failed to implement restrictions and exclusionist measures; they employed, protected, and thus contributed to the peaceful existence of non-Christians in the country. The kings of Hungary employed non-Christians to ensure royal revenues, to improve the defence of the country and to strengthen royal power; their interpretation of being a 'Christian king' often departed radically from ecclesiastical notions. Royal letters and charters, themselves drawn up by clerics who served in the royal chancery, do not give ideological statements about the role of non-Christians. The latter usually appear in a matter-of-fact way, a *Iudeus*, *Ismaelita* or *Cumanus* rendering services, receiving rewards, or losing a piece of land. These texts are more expressive only when Cumans are condemned for their infidelity to the king. Then sometimes they are accused of deceit and insincere adherence to Christianity, at other times of *lèse majesté*.[168]

Were royal attitudes a result of a policy of tolerance or pragmatic toleration, perhaps of 'steppe tolerance', or religious indifference?[169] The notion of 'steppe tolerance' has been brandished as an explanation of multireligious political formations in Eurasia, where no religious conformity was expected. Such a description of the non-exclusive nature of belief systems on the steppe has been justly challenged,[170] and its applic-

---

[168] See chapter 6, p. 198.

[169] For debates on the meaning and possibility of medieval tolerance: Powell, ed., *Muslims under Latin Rule*; Cohen, *Under Crescent*, chapter 1; G. R. Elton, 'Introduction', in W. J. Sheils, ed., *Persecution and Toleration* (Oxford: Blackwell, 1984), pp. xiii–xv.

[170] On steppe tolerance: Denis Sinor, 'Central Eurasia', in Sinor, *Inner Asia*, no. I; Sinor, *Cambridge History of Early Inner Asia*, p. 15; Jean-Paul Roux, 'Les religions dans les sociétés turco-mongoles', *Revue de l'Histoire des Religions* 201 (1984): pp. 393–420; Pritsak, 'The Polovcians and Rus'', p. 370. Criticism: Devin DeWeese, *Islamization and Native Religion in the Golden Horde* (Philadelphia: Pennsylvania State University Press, 1994), chapter I and p. 67, n. 1. On medieval Christian views

ability within a Christian kingdom is even more questionable. Although expressions of tolerance can be found in some medieval texts, there is no evidence from Hungary of explicit royal views on the appropriateness of allowing adherents of different religions to exist side by side with Christians.[171] Contrary views on the pernicious nature of non-Christians do exist, even from such 'tolerant' rulers as Béla IV who admitted the Cumans, but also wrote about their treachery.[172] These instances correspond entirely to ecclesiastical pronouncements. The monarchs' attitude to their non-Christian subjects was rarely unequivocal. As analysed in chapter 4, the argument of toleration for economic necessity is untenable. The kings often did benefit from the services of non-Christians, and thus a degree of *de facto* acceptance for pragmatic reasons did exist, but was only one part of a web of considerations to increase royal power. It was one tool in the power struggles with nobles, popes and other political foes. Nor does the theory of an 'ideology of silence' provide an adequate explanation. This theory argues that coexistence lasted only as long as neither side could completely prevail, and was unwillingly accepted by Christians. While coexistence was not openly attacked, nor was peaceful interaction with non-Christians explicitly discussed; the tension between religious belief (religious exclusivism) and reality was resolved by an 'ideology of silence'.[173] In Hungary, however, coexistence was not forced upon the Christian side. Nor should we forget that royal policies towards non-Christians were not necessarily the reflection of the personal piety of kings. András II collected relics during his crusade, while in Hungary he stubbornly resisted demands to exclude non-Christians from public offices.[174] Béla IV was a patron of the mendicant orders, while he introduced the privileges for Jews.[175] Instead of assuming a forced suspension of religious zeal, or a genuine lack of religiosity and indifference, it is perhaps more fruitful to see royal attitudes to non-Christians as one means of building royal

---

on Mongol indifference to religious issues: chapter 2 above, note 47, and the letter of Johanca, a missionary to the Mongols (1320): ed. A. C. Moule in *Archivum Franciscanum Historicum* 17 (1924): pp. 65–70.

[171] Cary J. Nederman and John Christian Laursen, eds., *Difference and Dissent: Theories of Toleration in Medieval and Early Modern Europe* (Lanham: Rowman and Littlefield, 1996); Cary J. Nederman and John Christian Laursen, eds., *Beyond the Persecuting Society: Religious Toleration Before the Enlightenment* (Philadelphia: University of Pennsylvania Press, 1998).

[172] See note 89 above and chapter 6, p. 220.

[173] Halperin, 'Ideology of Silence'. He developed his argument especially concerning Christians and Muslims in the frontier society of Valencia, but claimed that the 'ideology of silence' model fits other examples of the medieval religious frontier (p. 449).

[174] *SRH*, vol. I: p. 466, vol. II: p. 42; Mályusz, *V. István-kori Gesta*, pp. 113–14.

[175] Erik Fügedi, 'La formation des villes et les ordres mendiants en Hongrie', in Fügedi, *Kings, Bishops, Nobles*, no. XII; Szűcs, 'Kereszténység belső politikuma', p. 181.

power. Moreover, it was the legal and social structure of the kingdom that made a place for non-Christian groups; royal policies were not the exclusive basis of their existence. Political imperatives, the kingdom's structures and its position on the Christian frontier combined in shaping non-Christian status.

Papal response to Hungarian royal policies concerning non-Christians ranged from occasional dispensation through insistent urging to conform to ecclesiastical norms to accusations and intervention. An analysis of the vocabulary of papal letters concerning non-Christians in Hungary shows that they projected a schematic and basically negative image of these groups. These letters often drew on the ones received by the popes from prelates in Hungary. There is, however, no striking change between the vocabulary of the narrations (based on the letters sent by ecclesiastics from Hungary) and that of the papal dispositions; these letters convey an ecclesiastical–papal ideology.[176] Even if we do not consider letters concerning the Mongols after the invasion of 1241–2, which naturally emphasized the 'Tartar' danger, non-Christians emerge as the 'enemy within'. They were referred to as enemies of the Christian name and faith, blasphemers of Christ, and infidels who wallow in error.[177] We encounter the stock accusations that Jews are perfidious and the murderers of Christ, and that 'pagans' are cruel and kill Christians.[178] Even the recognition of their religion as a coherent system of belief was sometimes denied to them; the word 'pagan' was occasionally used interchangeably with 'Saracen', and both Judaism and Islam appear as 'superstition'.[179] Jews and Muslims were often grouped together without distinction.[180] According to these texts, non-Christians pollute by their presence and, worse, intentionally deceive Christians in order to divert them from the true faith and lead them into error: Cumans gain the trust of Christians undeservedly by their fraudulent conversion, Muslims marry Christian women under the false pretence of being Christians themselves, and then

---

[176] Most of the letters survive in the papal registers, instead of the copy that was sent. On the differences and the characteristics of such documents: Thomas Frenz (tr. Sergio Pagano), *I documenti pontifici nel Medioevo e nell'età moderna* (Vatican City: Scuola vaticana di paleografia, diplomatica e archivistica, 1989). On originals in Hungary: Érszegi, 'Eredeti pápai oklevelek'.

[177] 'inimici fidei christianae': ASV Reg. Vat. 11, f. 113v; 'Christi blasphemus': Reg. Vat. 13, f. 80r and Reg. Vat. 15, f. 55v; 'de gentilitatis errore revocare': Reg. Vat. 14, f. 26r and f. 137v (*Reg. Hon. III*, nos. 3301, 5611, *Reg. Greg. IX*, nos. 561, 139, 344; *VMH*, p. 30, no. LVIII, pp. 60–1, no. CXXVII, p. 94, no. CLXVIII, p. 86, no. CLIV, p. 91, no. CLXII respectively).

[178] ASV Reg. Vat. 18, f. 353v (*Reg. Greg. IX*, no. 4056; *VMH*, p. 160, no. CCLXXXIII).

[179] 'pagani' and 'sarraceni' or 'Ismaelitae' used interchangeably: ASV Reg. Vat. 12, ff. 26r, 34v, 35v; Reg. Vat. 18, f. 68v (*Reg. Hon. III*, nos. 4233, 4299, 4300, *Reg. Greg. IX*, no. 2758; *VMH*, p. 37, no. LXXVII, p. 40, no. LXXXII, p. 39, no. LXXXI, p. 136, no. CCXXXVII respectively). 'ad superstitionem Ysmahelytarum vel Iudeorum pervertuntur': *Liber censuum*, ASV Misc. Arm. XV, no. 1, f. 359 (*VMH*, p. 124, no. CCIX).

[180] Also in the Golden Bull and the oath of Bereg (chapter 4, p. 121 and above pp. 154–9).

Conflicts between the papacy and the kings

coerce them to apostatize.[181] Their malicious intent was emphasized: 'some among them, though in fact they are Saracens, mendaciously pretending to be Christians . . . in order secretly to send their arrows into the innocent, under cover of the appearance of piety, deceive many simple Christians, and seduce not a few of the astute ones, attracting them vilely to the error of infidelity'.[182] Because the Cumans sided with István in his war against his father Béla IV, they were described as cunning and receiving baptism deceitfully.[183]

Papal letters to Hungary, projecting a preoccupation with a combined non-Christian threat to Christendom, fitted into a trend in the thirteenth century. James Muldoon has pointed out that, in the second half of that century, Jews and Muslims were seen by the papacy as forming a 'joint threat' to Christendom, and the lines distinguishing Jews and Muslims blurred.[184] Papal ideas in this respect were often not formed on the basis of Hungarian realities, but drew on a long ecclesiastical tradition. What is striking, however, is that only one aspect of the available tradition is represented in these letters; the other, protective, side is absent.

In these letters, 'pagans' are alternately characterized as impious, cruel, ferocious, evil, cunning, dangerous, treacherous, ruining and devastating Christian lands,[185] and as ignorant and wandering in spiritual darkness, but receptive to conversion.[186] This ambivalence had deep roots in medieval ecclesiastical sources, and was applied to the Hungarian

---

[181] ASV Reg. Vat. 11, f. 113v, Reg. Vat. 13, f 80r, Reg. Vat. 15, f. 55v, Reg. Vat. 17, f. 77r–v, Reg. Vat. 29, f. 337v (*Reg. Hon. III*, nos. 3301, 3296, 5611, *Reg. Greg. IX*, nos. 561, 1498, *Reg. Urb. IV*, no. 2769; *VMH*, p. 30, nos. LVIII, LIX, p. 61, no. CXXVII, p. 94, no. CLXVIII, pp. 114–15, no. CXCV, pp. 269–70, no. CCCCXCIII).

[182] 'quidam eorum, cum revera sint Sarraceni, se christianos mendaciter confingentes . . . ut sagittent innoxios in occultis sub palliata specie pietatis, multos christianorum decipiunt simplices et nonnullos seducunt astutos, illos ad infidelitatis errorem nequiter attrahendo'. Reg. Vat. 15, f. 55v (*Reg. Greg. IX*, no. 561; *VMH*, p. 94, no. CLXVIII). See also Reg. Vat. 17, f. 77v (*Reg. Greg. IX*, no. 1498; *VMH*, pp. 114–15, no. CXCV).

[183] 'cum austutia [sic] multe fraudis'; 'fidem . . . fallaciter susceperunt': ASV Reg. Vat. 29, f. 337v (*Reg. Urb. IV*, no. 2769; *VMH*, p. 270, no. CCCCXCIII).

[184] Muldoon, *Popes*, esp. p. 52. See also Nirenberg, *Communities*, chapters II and IV (early fourteenth century). Saracens were seen as a category of pagans and represented pagans in canon law according to Benjamin Z. Kedar, 'De Iudeis et Sarracenis: On the Categorization of Muslims in Medieval Canon Law', in Kedar, *The Franks in the Levant, 11th to 14th Centuries* (Aldershot: Variorum, 1993), no. XIII.

[185] ASV Reg. Vat. 12, f. 18r; Reg. Vat. 20, ff. 81v–82v, 89v–90r; Reg. Vat. 22, f. 75r; Reg. Vat. 25, ff. 223v–225r; Reg. Vat. 29, ff. 99v–100r, f. 337v (*Reg. Hon. III*, no. 4187; *Reg. Greg. IX*, nos. 6057, 6059, 6060, 6094; *Reg. Inn. IV*, no. 5266; *Reg. Alex. IV*, no. 2963; *Reg. Urb. IV*, nos. 1242, 2769; *VMH*, p. 37, no. LXXVI, pp. 183–5, nos. CCCXXXVII–CCCXXXIX, CCCXLI, p. 209, no. CCCXCIII, pp. 239–41, no. CCCCLIV, pp. 264–5, nos. CCCCLXXXIII–CCCCLXXXIV, p. 270, no. CCCCXCIII), *Reg. Inn. IV*, nos. 35, 4000; *Reg. Clem. IV*, no. 113 (*VMH*, p. 188, no. CCCXLVIII, p. 206, no. CCCLXXXVIII, p. 280, no. DXIII).

[186] ASV Reg. Vat. 14, f. 26r–v (*Reg. Greg. IX*, no. 139; *VMH*, pp. 86–7, no. CLIV); *Reg. Inn. IV*, nos. 1362, 6275 (*VMH*, pp. 193–4, no. CCCLXII, p. 217, no. CCCCX); *Reg. Inn. IV*, no. 6273.

situation.[187] In these papal letters, the first image is applied to the Mongols and those Cumans who disappoint expectations of conversion and integration, while the second is applied to the Cumans in the perspective of missionary efforts. Overall, a negative image of 'pagans' dominates, except when they are thought to be willing to convert. Although popes supported efforts to form alliances with the Mongols against the Muslims (often linked to hopes of Mongol conversion), no echo of such support found its way into letters addressed to Hungarian kings, which expounded the pernicious effects of alliances with 'pagans'. Thus, for example, Louis IX of France, a king canonized soon after his death, planned an alliance with the Mongols, linked to the attempt to reconquer the Holy Land. Preparing for the Second Council of Lyons (1274), Humbert de Romans even disclaimed a comparison between the barbarians of the ancient world and the Mongols, who 'even though they persecute the Hungarians (but only them), nevertheless provide help against the Saracens', and are thus potential allies.[188] At the same time, popes warned Béla IV and László IV that reliance on or alliance with the Mongols or the 'pagan' Cumans was a breach of royal duties, and kings resorting to such measures could not be good Christian kings.

Although these letters drew on a stock of traditional views and vocabulary, they used a very restricted selection, and conveyed a conventional image of the adherents of non-Christian religions. This view was schematic and wholly negative, unless the issue was conversion, as in the case of the Cumans. Overall, even the vocabulary reinforced an image of non-Christians that corresponded to the policies required of the kings, and conveyed the message that employing or relying on these treacherous infidels was incompatible with the office of a Christian king. What motivated this choice? Hungary's position on the frontier of Christendom generated fear and led the popes to focus on a non-Christian threat. The Mongol invasion, the subsequent rhetoric of King Béla IV who emphasized the danger in order to gain concessions from the popes, and the incorporation of the Cumans strengthened this view. Indeed, it became something of a cliché to apply to Hungary whenever trouble arose: during the succession dispute of 1301 papal letters reverted to the notion of Hungary as prey to 'Cuman, Tartar, schismatic and pagan' enemies,

---

[187] Richard E. Sullivan, *Christian Missionary Activity in the Early Middle Ages* (Aldershot: Variorum Reprints, 1994); Fletcher, *Conversion*, chapters XII and XIV; Edward A. Synan, 'The Popes' Other Sheep', in *The Religious Roles of the Papacy: Ideals and Realities 1150–1300*, ed. Christopher Ryan (Toronto: Pontifical Institute of Mediaeval Studies, 1989), pp. 389–411; Richard, *Papauté*, pp. 12–15, 65–165. Cf. Rowell, *Lithuania*, chapter VII.

[188] 'Si solos Hungaros persequantur, contra tamen Saracenos praebent auxilium'. Cited in Jean Richard, 'Chrétiens et Mongols au concile: la papauté et les Mongols de Perse dans la seconde moitié du XIIIe siècle', in *1274: Année charnière*, pp. 31–44, see p. 32.

although in fact the disorder was caused by Christian pretenders.[189] Popes intervened in a similar manner in the politics of the Iberian peninsula. This suggests an interplay between stereotype, local situation, local information and fears about the possible loss of Christian lands on the frontier of Christendom in shaping papal attitudes. The conflicts between popes and Hungary's rulers, and the issues of sovereignty involved, were in many respects similar to controversies elsewhere in medieval Europe, but took on novel aspects, because some of the means available to Hungarian kings differed from the ones at the disposal of other rulers.

Papal–royal controversy over non-Christians in Hungary arose from a number of roots: conflicts of interest within the kingdom; power struggles over sovereignty; clashes between ecclesiastical ideology and norms on the one hand, and policies of kings adapted to their own interests on the other; and the frontier position of Hungary. Real dangers gave rise to anxieties that could then be manipulated by monarchs and prelates alike.

[189] 'Regnum . . . est collapsum, et quasi datum in predam, et per Cumanorum, Tartarorum, Scismaticorum et paganorum hostiles incursus fere ad nichilum est deductum.' *VMH*, p. 387, no. DCXXI (*Reg. Bon. VIII*, no. 4400). Similar texts: *Reg. Bon. VIII*, nos. 4401, 5025 (*VMH*, p. 388, no. DCXXII, p. 392, no. DCXXVIII).

Chapter 6

CHRISTIAN PERCEPTIONS AND ATTITUDES

Neither a 'tolerant', nor a 'persecuting' society, medieval Hungary was home to a range of attitudes towards the non-Christian groups that it incorporated. From matter-of-fact acceptance to fear, to a wish to incorporate through conversion, perceptions and expectations were varied, sometimes ambivalent. Episodes of persecution as well as different forms of incorporation occurred, with occasional attempts to introduce policies of separation and exclusion, often initiated by the papacy. Papal views on Hungary's non-Christians were discussed in the previous chapter; together with ecclesiastical traditions they obviously shaped Christian views within the kingdom, and greatly contributed to creating the framework within which non-Christian status could be imagined and discussed. Non-Christian presence in Hungary also generated negative images outside Hungary about the character of the entire kingdom and its inhabitants.

CHRISTIAN CATEGORIZATION OF NON-CHRISTIANS

In Hungary, the Latin terminology used to describe the three non-Christian groups was uniform across genres; charters, laws and chronicles, for example, employed the same designations: *Judeus, Cumanus, Ismaelita* and *Saracenus*. Thus it was not the tradition of the genre in question that governed the use of these terms. Two changes happened in the period. Besides the traditional *Ismaelita, Saracenus* was increasingly used in Hungary from the mid-twelfth century.[1] Also, *Cunus* was replaced by *Cumanus* in the late twelfth and early thirteenth centuries. Latin *Cunus* was used to designate mounted nomads from the east in early Hungarian chronicles, regardless of their background: this collective term was

[1] Czeglédy, 'Árpád-kori', p. 99. According to Göckenjan, *Hilfsvölker*, p. 56, the toponym Scerecin (1138) was already a variant of Saracen.

Christian perceptions and attitudes

applied to Pechenegs, Oghuz and others. Due to western influences, such as papal letters, *Cumanus* supplanted *Cunus*, and became the only Latin term to designate the Cumans.[2]

Parallel to the Latin terminology, a vernacular one existed as well, manifest in toponyms mentioned in medieval written sources. Some form of the modern Hungarian word *zsidó*, 'Jew' (a loan-word from Slavic languages) must have been used by the population, since mentions of place names based on 'sydo' appear in thirteenth-century charters.[3] The Hungarian form *böszörmény* (derived from the Arabo-Persian word for Muslim), a synonym of *Ismaelita* and *Saracenus*, is attested by place names from the thirteenth century onwards.[4] Whereas *Cumanus* replaced the original *Cunus* in Latin terminology in the late twelfth century, the vernacular *kun*, originally also a generic term for eastern nomads, which appears in place names from the twelfth century onwards, came to indicate exclusively the Cumans, and has remained the Hungarian designation for them to this day.[5]

What is the significance of these terms? Jews were called *Judei* all over Christian Europe; *Ismaelita*, *Saracenus*, *Cumanus* are also names that were in use in many different areas. When used to describe the kingdom's non-Christian population, *Judeus*, *Ismaelita* and *Saracenus* had a legal and religious content. In charters designating a person's status, or in the Register of Várad which lists cases of ordeal where Muslims participated, the usage of the term is matter-of-fact and linked to legal position.[6] Chronicles describing the immigration of different groups mention Ishmaelites along with Saxons and Spaniards among those who entered the country, intermarried and even rose to the ranks of the nobility.[7] In these texts, there is no explicit reference to the different religious background of the *Ismaelite*. They are treated on a par with other, including Christian, immigrants who had their own legal status. The religious context, and the primarily negative connotations well known from thirteenth-century Europe, predominate in such texts as letters to and from the pope complaining about Muslim influence (see chapter 5) and sermons containing

---

[2] György Györffy, 'A kun és komán népnév eredetének kérdéséhez', in *Magyarság*, pp. 200–19, see pp. 210–17.

[3] Sydovpothok (1247): *CD*, vol. VI, pt. 2: p. 377 (*RA*, no. 864); Sydofelde (1294): *MZsO*, vol. V, pt. 1: p. 12, no. 10; Kristó *et al.*, 'Adatok', pp. 31–2. On the etymology: Benkő, *Magyar nyelv történeti-etimológiai szótára*, vol. III: pp. 1217–18.

[4] Czeglédy, 'Árpád-kori', p. 99. First mention: 1275, *CD*, vol. V, pt. 2: p. 305. Kristó *et al.*, 'Adatok', pp. 22–3. It may have been borrowed from Pecheneg or Cuman: Benkő, *Magyar nyelv történeti-etimológiai szótára*, vol. I: pp. 365–66.

[5] Kristó *et al.*, 'Adatok', p. 22; Györffy, 'Kun és komán népnév', p. 216.

[6] See also chapters 3 (pp. 96–7), 4 and 7.   [7] *SRH*, vol. I: pp. 114–16, 303–4.

references to Jews (see below). Hungarian laws also contrast Jews and Muslims with Christians, rather than with Hungarians or any other 'ethnic' group.[8] It has been suggested that *Ismaelita* and *Saracenus* can be understood as a reference to places of origin, and that *böszörmény* denoted a specific ethnic group; yet the inconsistent usage of these was pointed out half a century ago.[9] Religion and biological connotations are occasionally combined: Ishmaelites are called a *genus*, a convert from Judaism to Christianity, 'iudeus baptizatus'.[10]

There is more material relevant to the connotations of *Cumanus*. Following Patrick Geary, one can look at usages concerning groups and individuals separately.[11] As a group, Cumans were designated as *Cumani* or as *gens* or *populus Cumanorum*, their leaders as *nobiles* or *duces Cumanorum*. These terms were used in the following contexts: as a group to be converted, as an enemy, as an army, as recipients of collective privileges, as a constituent of the general congregation (the precursor of parliament), and as inhabitants of the kingdom. The term that is used the most frequently is *Cumani* alone; this can function in any of the abovementioned meanings. *Gens Cumanorum* usually had negative connotations – either that Cumans were 'infidels', that is, not Christians, or that they were perfidious traitors, rebels against the king of Hungary.[12] *Gens* was a word that could be used to condemn in Christian vocabulary, although it could also designate a people with positive implications.[13] *Populus* and *duces* (or *principales*) *Cumanorum*, on the other hand, had positive connotations; they were applied to the newly converted Cumans, in

---

[8] Bak, *Laws*, pp. 29–30, 57, 66.

[9] Réthy, *Magyar pénzverő* (Ishmaelites were Volga-Bulgarians); Karácsonyi, 'Kik voltak' (Ishmaelites were Caliz from Turkestan); Hrbek, 'Ein Arabischer', pp. 214–23; Göckenjan, *Hilfsvölker*, p. 57. Béla Kossányi, 'A XI–XII. századi "ismaelita" és "saracenus" elnevezésekről', in *Emlékkönyv Károlyi Árpád születése nyolcvanadik fordulójának ünnepére*, ed. Sándor Domanovszky (Budapest: Sárkány Nyomda, 1933), pp. 308–16.

[10] Bak, *Laws*, p. 30; MOL DL 40049 (*ÁÚO*, vol. II: p. 319, no. 220; *RA*, no. 1235).

[11] Patrick Geary, 'Ethnic Identity as a Situational Construct in the Early Middle Ages', *Medieval Perspectives* 3, no. 2 (1988): pp. 1–17, see p. 6.

[12] MOL DL 1170 (*CD*, vol. V, pt. 3: pp. 258–61, corrected in *JK*, vol. II: pp. 448–9, no. 77; *RA*, no. 3348); ASV Reg. Vat. 14, f. 64v (*Reg. Greg. IX*, no. 187; *VMH*, p. 88, no. CLVII); Rogerius, in *SRH*, vol. II: p. 554 ('gens dura et aspera subdi nescia'). 'Gens Tartarorum' in a negative sense from the same period, e.g. MOL DL 57222 (*CD*, vol. V, pt. 3: pp. 393–7; *RA*, no. 3502); *CD*, vol. V, pt. 3: pp. 398–40 (*RA*, no. 3503).

[13] Already used by the Romans to designate barbarians, it was often used by Christian writers from the earliest times to designate pagans, infidels and adversaries of God. It was also a neutral or positive term to designate any people: *Thesaurus Linguae Latinae* (Stuttgart and Leipzig: Teubner, 1900–), vol. VI, pt 2: cols. 1842–65. Negative usage in the early Middle Ages: Walter Pohl, 'Telling the Difference: Signs of Ethnic Identity', in *Strategies of Distinction: The Construction of Ethnic Communities, 300–800*, ed. Walter Pohl and Helmut Reimitz (Leiden: Brill, 1998), pp. 17–69, see p. 68. On positive meanings of *gens Ungarorum*: Kristó, *Magyar nemzet*, pp. 157–78; Jenő Szűcs, *A magyar nemzeti tudat kialakulása* (Szeged: József Attila Tudományegyetem Magyar Őstörténeti Kutatócsoport, 1992), *passim*.

laudatory contexts.[14] *Populus* had strong Christian resonances (*populus dei*), and the use of *duces* implied a higher degree of Cuman social organization. From the many contemporary examples for this shift of vocabulary, one can cite the case of the Mongols. For example, Pope Innocent IV, in a letter to Hospitallers in Hungary, contrasted 'gens impia Tartarorum' with 'christianus populus'. The same pope, when he was writing to the Mongols in order to encourage their conversion, addressed them as 'rex et populus Tartarorum'.[15] Although these usages were not completely consistent, and *Cumani* alone fulfilled negative, positive or value-neutral functions, *populus* seems to have denoted a higher status in these texts than *gens*.[16] It was conversion to Christianity that bestowed this more elevated position and the concomitant vocabulary on the Cumans.

When *Cumani* was used in parallel structures, it was contrasted with a variety of groups: *Hungari*,[17] *Christiani*,[18] *nobiles*,[19] *Tartari*.[20] That is, *Cumani* was seen as an equivalent, from a modern point of view, of an indistinct selection of categories: 'ethnic' (alongside Hungarians or Mongols), religious (contrasted to Christians, a synonym of 'pagans'), and as a status group (as in the structure 'Cumans and nobles'). Cumans, then, were far from being systematically or exclusively characterized and categorized as an 'ethnic group'. There was no distinct vocabulary to designate Cumans as 'pagans', as members of a social stratum, or as a politically organized people.

If we turn to the designation of individuals, *Cumanus* usually appeared in charters after the name of the person, such as 'Koncha Cumanus' or

---

[14] *Reg. Greg. IX*, no. 344 (*VMH*, pp. 90–1, no. CLXII); *Magyar diplomáciai emlékek az Anjou korból*, 3 vols., ed. Gusztáv Wenzel, (Budapest, 1874–6), vol. I: p. 34, a letter by Charles, king of Sicily, father-in-law of László IV to the Cumans to help the young king (1272). ASV AA Arm. I-XVIII-595 (*VMH*, p. 340, no. DLVI).

[15] *Reg. Inn. IV*, nos. 4000, 1364–5 (*VMH*, p. 206, no. CCCLXXXVIII; pp. 194–6, nos. CCCLXIII–CCCLXIV) respectively.

[16] On similar use of *populus* and *gens* by Augustine and Jerome, that is, *populus* denoting a higher degree of organization and/or closer relationship to God, see Jeremy duQuesnay Adams, *The Populus of Augustine and Jerome: A Study in the Patristic Sense of Community* (New Haven and London: Yale University Press, 1971).

[17] E.g. 'nullus tam de Hungaris, quam de Comanis . . . audeat molestare'. MOL DL 975 (*ÁÚO*, vol. IV: pp. 76–7, no. 37; *RA*, no. 2821); 'exercitum Hungaricum et Comanicum': *HO*, vol. VI: p. 241, no. 172 (*RA*, no. 2990); Rogerius, in *SRH*, vol. II: pp. 554, 557, 559, 567, 568. (Roger was from southern Italy and arrived in Hungary with the papal legate Jacob. He did not speak of the Hungarians as 'us'); 'insultus Tartarorum et Cumanorum, tum etiam Ungarorum': *Budapest történetének oklevelei*, p. 220, no. 205 (*RA*, no. 3375).

[18] E.g. *CD*, vol. IV, pt. 1: pp. 212–13; ASV AA Arm. I-XVIII-595 (*VMH*, p. 340). Similar structures (Christians as synonym of Poles, and pagans as Pomeranians): Robert Bartlett, 'The Conversion of a Pagan Society in the Middle Ages', *History* 70 (1985): pp. 185–201, see p. 191.

[19] E.g. *ÁÚO*, vol. IV: pp. 181–2, no. 110 (*RA*, no. 2997); *CD*, vol. VI, pt. 2: pp. 130–47 (at the general congregation of 1298). [20] Rogerius, in *SRH*, vol. II: pp. 566, 568.

'Bachkolda Cumanus'.²¹ Even when the Cumans were mentioned together with non-Cumans, the 'ethnicity' of the latter was not mentioned. There was no 'Stephanus Hungarus' to match 'Bachkolda Cumanus' in these contexts. This is already an indication that it is not primarily ethnic identity that is at issue here. The charters in which these designations appear concern privileges or land transactions such as donations, sale and exchange. In documents of land transaction, the identity of the persons involved was important in vouching for the validity of the transaction, in order to ascertain which other members of the family could have claims, or to prove that the person could indeed sell the land.

The designation was usually not qualified in any way. In rare instances, *Christianus Cumanus* took the place of simple *Cumanus*.²² Sometimes an individual who was known to be a Cuman from other sources appeared in a charter *without* being designated as a Cuman. This always happened when other indications of individual status were given, such as *comes* or the name of the clan (family), for example 'de genere Borchol'.²³ These alternative designations were in keeping with those used by the Hungarian nobility.²⁴ This indicates that when individuals exchanged their designation as *Cumanus* – either at their own initiative or by scribal decision due to the perceptions about them – it was not to embrace another 'ethnic' (e.g. Hungarian) identity, but to show their higher social status. Cuman in the sense of 'origins' was used a few times, but not in Hungarian sources. Bruno, bishop of Olomouc (Moravia), wrote that the queen of Hungary herself was a Cuman; Queen Erzsébet's Cuman 'origins' were emphasized by other authors as well.²⁵ Charles I of Sicily (the father-in-law of László IV) appealed to the Cumans to support the young László because 'the identity of origin ties you [to him]'.²⁶ Even though *Cumania* appeared very frequently in later thirteenth-century Hungarian sources – it was still a part of the royal title despite the emptiness of this claim – this territory was not explicitly mentioned as some sort of 'homeland' for Hungary's Cumans.

Cumanus in individual designations in Hungary therefore was not pri-

---

[21] *JK*, vol. II: p. 416, no. 50 (*RA*, no. 1417), p. 420, no. 54 (*RA*, no. 1869).

[22] I found only three instances: MOL DL 40166 (*ÁÚO*, vol. XII: p. 389, no. 320; *RA*, no. 3213); Knauz, *Esztergomi főegyháznak okmánytára*, vol. II: pp. 144–5, no. 165; *ÁÚO*, vol. XII: pp. 534–5, no. 436 (*JK*, vol. II: p. 447, no. 75, p. 450, no. 78, pp. 459–60, no. 90). The first and second charters concern the same individuals.

[23] *JK*, vol. II: pp. 418–19, no. 53 (*RA*, no. 1856), p. 456, no. 85.

[24] Fügedi, *Ispánok*, p. 79: 'de genere' designations appear from the early thirteenth century; Fügedi, 'Aristocracy'.

[25] ASV AA Arm. I-XVIII-3104 (*VMH*, p. 308); Johannes Marignola in *Fontes Rerum Bohemicarum*, vol. III: p. 568; 'Continuatio Cosmae Pragensis', in *Fontes Rerum Bohemicarum*, vol. II: p. 311. See also chapter 7, p. 262.

[26] 'eidem iuniori Regi nationis identitas vos astringit', *Magyar diplomáciai*, p. 34.

marily a marker of ethnicity, but of legal status.[27] It signalled the adherence of the individual to the group that, as Cumans, had privileges and a collective legal status.[28] The only possibly contradictory evidence is found in the use of *Christianus Cumanus*. The term, however, appeared very rarely. Neither did it gain a wider currency in later periods, when more or even all the Cumans were Christianized.[29] Perhaps it served to distinguish Christian family members from still 'pagan' ones, as the designations *Christianus Cumanus* and *Cumanus* were used within the same charter in reference to different members of the same kin group.

We cannot know how the Cumans themselves formulated their own identity. It would be misleading to call the identity attributed to them by others 'ethnic identity', as perceptions of the Cumans in medieval Hungary were very fluid. Contrary to this fluidity, in modern ethnic consciousness or identity, whether professed or imposed, the main building block of the 'imagined communities' is the alleged fixed content of ethnicity, similar to national identities.[30] The medieval evidence does not support any meaningful imposition of the modern category of 'ethnicity'.[31]

CHRISTIAN PERCEPTIONS OF NON-CHRISTIANS

The idea that Hungary, and other central European countries in the Middle Ages, were characterized by 'tolerance' holds no more true for society than for the kings.[32] Although we have only glimpses of popular

---

[27] Cf. Patrick Amory, *People and Identity in Ostrogothic Italy* (Cambridge: Cambridge University Press, 1997), esp. introduction. Patrick Amory, 'The Meaning and Purpose of Ethnic Terminology'.

[28] This was similar to the usage concerning other groups, see Fügedi, 'Befogadó', and chapter 3 above pp. 88, 92.

[29] Documents in *JK*, vol. III: pp. 459–770 (1301–1537). Even individuals with obviously Christian names such as John or Paul are not designated as 'Christianus Cumanus', but simply 'Cumanus'. It should be noted, however, that the name *Kun* (Cuman) started to appear in the fourteenth century, and eventually became a family name; it could designate origin from a family or from a place: Katalin Fehértói, *A XIV. századi magyar megkülönböztető nevek* (Budapest: Akadémiai Kiadó, 1969), pp. 14–16.

[30] Of the growing literature, see especially Thomas Hylland Eriksen, *Ethnicity and Nationalism: Anthropological Perspectives* (London and Boulder, Colo.: Pluto Press, 1993); Fredrik Barth, ed., *Ethnic Groups and Boundaries: The Social Organization of Cultural Difference* (Bergen and Oslo: Universitets Forlaget and London: George Allen and Unwin, 1969); Benedict Anderson, *Imagined Communities: Reflections on the Origin and Spread of Nationalism*, rev. edn (London and New York: Verso, 1993).

[31] Similar results for the early Middle Ages: e.g. Geary, 'Ethnic Identity'; Amory, *People and Identity*; Pohl and Reimitz, *Strategies of Distinction*.

[32] Szekfű, 'Magyarság és kisebbségei', in *Állam és nemzet*, pp. 39–53; Fügedi, 'Befogadó'. According to Kristó, *Magyar nemzet*, xenophobia in Hungary started in the thirteenth century. Similar views for Poland: Benedykt Zientara, 'Nationality Conflicts in the German–Slavic Borderland in the 13th–14th Centuries and their Social Scope', *Acta Poloniae Historica* 22 (1970): pp. 207–25; Benedykt Zientara, 'Foreigners in Poland in the 10th–15th Centuries: Their Role in the Opinion of the Polish Medieval Community', *Acta Poloniae Historica* 29 (1974): pp. 5–28.

views and behaviour toward non-Christians in Hungary, these glimpses show that the local population was no more intrinsically 'tolerant' than were its western counterparts. Similarly, no aspect of local ecclesiastical attitudes, although they were by no means homogeneous, could be described as 'tolerant' towards non-Christians. It is also necessary to emphasize at the outset that documents refer to views and attitudes of only certain segments of society and only during certain periods.

Fear of and contempt for non-Christians surfaced in various circumstances. Immediately after the arrival of the Cumans, strife erupted. Discontent with the Cuman presence manifested itself in a variety of ways. Popular accusations that the Cumans took every opportunity to rape the daughters and wives of their Christian neighbours and defile the beds of the mighty, fall into the well-known category of anxiety over sexual contamination; the casual violation of Cuman women by Hungarians did not give rise to such fears.[33] The idea that the Cumans were spies of the Mongols, come to prepare the conquest of the kingdom, resembles to some extent beliefs concerning Jewish conspiracy with Muslims for the conquest of medieval Iberia.[34] Nobles and courtiers, discontented with the policies of Béla IV, who wished to establish a strong royal power at their expense, blamed the Cumans, accusing them of being favourites of the king, and of influencing him in his decisions; the king was seen as willing to serve justice if it was in the interest of the Cumans, but not if it was against them.[35] The accusations led to the massacre of the Cuman chieftain Köten and his family by the crowds of Pest. The lynch mob is described by the canon Roger: 'all the people were shouting against him: he should die, he should die! He is the one who brought about the destruction of Hungary!'[36] The subsequent massacres and pillage perpetrated by Hungarian peasants against the Cumans also show deep-seated hostility. As the Cumans left Hungary, they burnt villages and looted, and murdered those who tried to resist,[37] which served to confirm the popular suspicions that the Cumans were enemies as much

---

[33] Rogerius, in *SRH*, vol. II: p. 554. Cf. Nirenberg, *Communities*, chapter V, esp. pp. 136–56; anxieties concerned pollution of the social group via the bodies of women, not the behaviour of its men.

[34] Rogerius, in *SRH*, vol. II: p. 560. Spies of the 'Rutheni', according to the surviving text (an early edition, the manuscript having been lost), but as the editor remarked, it was a mistake for 'Tartari', as it occurs in the description of the Mongol conquest. Nirenberg, *Communities*, pp. 64–7.

[35] *SRH*, vol. II: pp. 556, 554.

[36] *Ibid.*, p. 566: 'clamabat totus populus contra eum: Moriatur, moriatur! ipse est, qui destructionem Hungarie procuravit!' Roger recorded that some people imputed the murder to the duke of Austria, and some to the orders of King Béla himself. Another account by a fourteenth-century Austrian chronicler: 'Anonymous Leobiensis', in Pez, *Scriptores Rerum Austriacarum*, col. 815, reprinted in Gombos, *Catalogus*, vol. I: p. 270. Here Köten kills his family and himself before the people can break in. [37] *SRH*, vol. II: pp. 567–8.

as the Mongols. A marginal notation written in 1241 in the calendar of the Benedictine monastery of Boldva identified the enemies as Cumans, not as Mongols: 'John's wife is killed and Chucar's wife is captured by the Cumans.'[38]

After their settlement in Hungary, ecclesiastical disapproval of the Cumans was quickly added to popular suspicion. This attitude was not without foundation: as described in chapter 4, the Cumans were often unruly. They participated in the civil war between King Béla IV and his son István, and rebelled against King László IV. During the course of these wars, the Cumans took captives from the population of the kingdom of Hungary and destroyed or appropriated houses and fields. The violent behaviour of the Cumans, however, often did not differ from the violence of Christians who also attacked churches and killed ecclesiastics.[39] Yet, in the case of the Cumans, their violence was directly attributed to their being 'pagans'. That is why the regulation of Cuman status in 1279 placed so much emphasis on ending Cuman violence against Christians and churches: it stipulated that Cumans cease killing Christians, and restore all the estates belonging to churches and Christian inhabitants that they held by force.[40]

Distrust and fear of the Cumans were not restricted to the population and ecclesiastics. Even the kings, who relied on them, doubted their fidelity; this was often justified. As discussed in chapter 4, István V gave them lavish gifts to ensure their loyalty (in vain) in his fight against his father King Béla IV, and in the peace treaty with Béla he stipulated that his father not entice away 'his' Cumans. King László IV faced the rebellion of the Cumans and was assassinated by them. Although the cause of Cuman revolt is unclear, and the regulation of Cuman status imposed by the papal legate Philip may have triggered Cuman discontent,[41] the explanation

---

[38] 'Uxor Johannis occiditur et uxor Chucar a cumanis captiuatur', *Sacramentarium*, (*Codex Prayanus*) OSzK, MNy 1, f. 15. The codex was in use in Pozsony (Bratislava) at the time: Polycarpus Radó, *Libri liturgici manuscripti bibliothecarum Hungariae et limitropharum regionum* (Budapest: Akadémiai Kiadó, 1973), pp. 40–4. Some Hungarian proverbs also reflect distrust of the Cumans: if something is 'secure as a Cuman bond', then it is false ('Biztos, mint a kunkötés': Margalits, *Magyar közmondások*, p. 479).

[39] E.g. *RA*, nos. 2747, 2750, 3416; Pauler, *Magyar nemzet*, vol. II: pp. 322–4, 411; Gutheil, *Árpád-kori Veszprém*, pp. 228–9, 231–5; *ÁÚO*, vol. I: p. 246, no. 144; László Erdélyi, ed., *A Pannonhalmi Szent-Benedek-rend története*, 12 vols. (Budapest: Stephaneum, 1902–16), vol. I: p. 743, no. 155, p. 745, no. 157; *ÁÚO*, vol. XI: pp. 269–70, no. 184.

[40] ASV AA Arm. I-XVIII-595 (*VMH*, p. 340, no. DLVI). A fifteenth-century forged charter, purporting to be from 1284, was made more 'authentic' by adding a detailed description concerning the destruction of properties and a church by Cumans: *ÁÚO*, vol. IX: p. 385, no. 274 (*RA*, no. 3343; János Karácsonyi, *A hamis, hibáskeltű és keltezetlen oklevelek jegyzéke 1400-ig* (Szeged: JATE, 1988), no. 159).

[41] See chapter 4 on war. Pauler, *Magyar nemzet*, vol. II: p. 370, and Szabó, *Kun László*, p. 99; Györffy, 'Magyarországi kun', p. 285, and Blazovich, 'IV. László', p. 945. Györffy, *ibid.*, pp. 286–7, also attributes the revolt to economic reasons (the lack of foreign wars and consequent lack of booty and slaves).

At the Gate of Christendom

offered by thirteenth-century sources themselves laid the blame wholly on the Cumans. Royal charters which mention the battles against the Cumans and the concordant testimony of the chronicler Simon of Kéza refer to Cuman infidelity and treason against the person of the king. These sources present the Cumans as rebels, unfaithful to the king and enemies of the kingdom. The 'motive' attributed to them for rising against the king was their heedless daring. Their treason was defined as *lèse majesté* ('crimen lese maiestatis'); they were seen as breaking their loyalty to the king, not to Christianity.[42] Fourteenth-century chronicles elaborated this theme and gave an account of a Cuman attempt to conquer Hungary, supposedly with the help of Cumans from the steppe under a certain Oldamur.[43] Later exaggerations notwithstanding, even the court cleric and ecclesiastics in the chancery of László IV, the king who was the most closely associated with the Cumans, linked Cuman revolt to a fundamental deficiency and unreliability of the Cumans themselves.

The basic incompatibility of a settled, Christian population and a nomadic 'pagan' one, coupled with Cuman military power, may have given a more substantial basis to popular hatred and fear of the Cumans. But there was no more 'tolerance' of other non-Christians. Lack of documentation precludes the exploration of popular attitudes to Muslims, but the kings of Hungary did not completely trust them and were anxious about the possibility of revolt.[44] To the distrust of Muslims

---

[42] *CD*, vol. v, pt. 3: pp. 215–16, 223–6, 249–51 (MOL DL 57217, *RA*, no. 3332, 'versi in perfidiam'), p. 452 (DL 28502; *RA*, no. 3534; *Székely oklevéltár*, 8 vols., ed. Károly Szabó and Lajos Szádeczky (Kolozsvár, 1872–98 and Budapest: MTA, 1934), vol. I: pp. 21–3, no. XVIII, 'crimen lese maiestatis'); *JK*, vol. II: pp. 448–9, no. 77 (DL 1170, *RA*, no. 3348); Kubinyi, *Árpádkori oklevelek*, pp. 125–6, no. 150 (*RA*, no. 3220). Simon of Kéza, in *SRH*, vol. I: p. 187. (War against the king by Christians is also 'crimen lese maiestatis': MOL DL 86840; *ÁÚO*, vol. XII: p. 112, no. 102; *RA*, no. 2564.) Many other charters on the Cuman revolts: *JK*, vol. II: pp. 448–9, no. 77 (*RA*, no. 3348); *ÁÚO*, vol. XII: pp. 453–4, no. 379 (*CD*, vol. v, pt. 3: p. 354; *RA*, no. 3433); Hazai Okleveltár, pp. 99–100, no. 94 (*RA*, no. 3266), pp. 116–17, no. 110 (*RA*, no. 3544); Kubinyi, *Árpádkori oklevéltár*, p. 126, no. 150 (*RA*, no. 3220); *HO*, vol. VI: pp. 325–7, no. 236 (*RA*, no. 3447); MOL DL 1298 (*ÁÚO*, vol. v: pp. 2–3, no. 2; *RA*, no. 3686); *HO*, vol. VI: pp. 416–17, no. 310 (*RA*, no. 4013); MOL DL 1142 (*HO*, vol. VI: p. 291, no. 209; *RA*, no. 3212) *HO*, vol. VI: pp. 311–12, no. 226, p. 332, no. 239 (*RA*, no. 3505), p. 416, no. 310 (*RA*, no. 4013); *CD*, vol. v, pt. 3: pp. 223–4. Although the charter MOL DL 57217 (*RA*, no. 3332) has been damaged, some lines that have been omitted in the edition can be read partially: 'strenue dimicantes . . . [vi]riliter . . . [. . .]nentes ea triumphaliter superata et . . . duos Cumanos bene armatos in area belli'. References to Cuman revolt were even used in later medieval forged charters: *JK*, vol. II: pp. 446–8, nos. 74, 76 (*CD*, vol. v, pt. 3: pp. 165–7; *RA*, nos. 3171, 3238); *CD*, vol. v, pt. 3: pp. 353–4 (*RA*, no. 3070).

[43] *SRH*, vol. I: p. 471. Two charters give similar accounts, but they are not authentic: *CD*, vol. v, pt. 3: pp. 122–4 (*RA*, no. 3200) is forged ('non solum regnum nostrum sibi subiugare, verum etiam coronam nostram Regiam subripere conabantur', p. 124); *HO*, vol. VIII: pp. 450–2, no. 371 (*RA*, no. 3179, see also no. 4306), is suspect. See also Blazovich, 'IV László', p. 944, Zsoldos, 'Tétenytől', p. 95.

[44] *Abu-Hámid*, p. 82; Yāqūt, p. 469 (in Reinaud, *Géographie*, p. 294). See chapter 4, p. 141.

because of their military potential was added the ecclesiastical fears of pollution of Christians by insincere converts, 'false Christians'. As we have seen, popes, on the basis of information from prelates in Hungary, wrote of a massive infiltration by Muslims pretending to be Christians, marrying Christian women and then dragging them into error. The deception ascribed to these converts was especially abhorred, their influence to pervert Christians feared. Moreover, according to Christian theology and canon law by the thirteenth century, it was a much graver sin to have seen the truth (according to canon law, even having been baptized by force) and then fall into 'error', than never having been converted at all.[45] The fear and hate surrounding 'false Christians' can be fully appreciated if one considers the *conversos* (*Marranos*) of Spain.[46]

It is tempting to contrast the persecution of Jews in the west with their peaceful existence in Hungary (and in east-central Europe in general).[47] Although instances of persecution may have been rarer in Hungary, they did exist; there was no basic difference in popular attitudes that would have prevented such outbreaks. Around the mid-thirteenth century, Pozsony was the scene of accusations that prove there was no prevalent 'tolerance' protecting Jews in Hungary. The case is known from a commemorative prayer written, it seems, by a member of the Jewish community of Pozsony.[48] The accusation centred on a host.[49] Accusations against Jews for blaspheming the host were being formulated in medieval Europe at the time, linked to developments in Christian theology. Miracle stories and other texts progressively created a negative link between Jews and the consecrated host throughout the thirteenth century, prior to the emergence of the full-blown accusation of violent host desecration in 1290.[50] The inhabitants of Pozsony were receptive to

---

[45] Pope Gregory IX accordingly wrote to King Béla IV that although pagans are cruel, they only torment and punish Christians in their body; Jews are perfidious and killed Christ, but they do believe in their erroneous way in God the Father; heretics, schismatics and those leaving the fold of the true faith are more of a danger to Christians than pagans and Jews: ASV Reg. Vat. 18, f. 353v (*Reg. Greg. IX*, no. 4056; *VMH*, p. 160, no. CCLXXXIII).

[46] *Marranos* (converted Jews) present an analogous problem, but with much more extensive documentation. Baer, *History*, vol. II: pp. 270–92; Cecil Roth, *A History of the Marranos*, 4th edn (New York: Schocken Books, 1975), pp. 29–53, 74–98; Benzion Netanyahu, *The Origins of the Inquisition in Fifteenth-Century Spain* (New York: Random House, 1995); Yosef H. Yerushalmi, 'Assimilation and Racial Anti-Semitism: The Iberian and the German Models', *The Leo Baeck Memorial Lecture no. 26* (New York: Leo Baeck Institute, 1982), see pp. 7–16.

[47] Kohn, *Zsidók*, pp. 68, 101, 128; Baron, *Social*, vol. X: chapter 42, esp. pp. 50–1.

[48] Siegmund Salfeld, ed. and German tr., *Das Martyrologium des Nürnberger Memorbuches* (Berlin, 1898), pp. 334–7. The account is written in the first person singular. A. Neubauer, 'Le Memorbuch de Mayence', *Revue des Etudes Juives* 4 (1882): pp. 1–30. I thank Anna Abulafia for her help with this text. [49] Salfeld, *Martyrologium*, p. 154.

[50] Peter Browe, *Die Eucharistischen Wunder des Mittelalters* (Breslau: Müller and Seiffert, 1938), pp. 128–38; Peter Browe, 'Die Hostienschändungen der Juden im Mittelalter', *Römische Quartalschrift für Christliche Altertumskunde und für Kirchengeschichte* 34 (1926): pp. 167–97; Miri Rubin,

these new trends; the town had links to German areas, as it was in the immediate vicinity of Austria, with a sizeable German settlement. A Jewish man, Jonah, who had tried to escape dressed as a woman when the accusations emerged, was arrested and condemned as a 'blasphemer'. Taken to his execution, Jonah prayed to avoid the forced baptism that he feared was to be his fate, and then rejected the crucifix offered to him.[51] The author described his death using biblical images of stoning, and added the *topos* that his body, mutilated beyond recognition, was not given back to the community to be buried. This murder and the looting of Jewish property that followed it reflects an easily aroused popular prejudice and hatred. Jewish martyrs are also listed in 1298.[52] The memorial list shows that the persecution of Jews that swept through many German towns at the time extended into Hungary, though no details are known.

International orders carried the negative ecclesiastical views of the Jews to Hungary, as attested by a collection of Latin university sermons composed in Pécs by a Hungarian Dominican between 1255 and 1275.[53] The image it projects conforms closely to thirteenth-century models.[54] Although there is no systematic description of the Jews in these sermons, they are mentioned many times. The composite picture that emerges is that of the Jews as 'the people of darkness', unbelievers, who are responsible for the death of Jesus.[55] For this crime they are punished by the torments of Hell.[56] The Jews are depicted not simply as non-believers, but

footnote 50 (*cont.*)
'Desecration of the Host: The Birth of an Accusation', *Studies in Church History* 29 (1992): pp. 169–85; Miri Rubin, *Gentile Tales: The Narrative Assault on Late Medieval Jews* (New Haven and London: Yale University Press, 1999), esp. pp. 27–37; Langmuir, *Toward a Definition*, pp. 61–2; Simonsohn, *Apostolic See History*, pp. 58–60. There is no reliable evidence for the alleged first case from 1243 or 1247 in the German Beelitz (Dahan, *Intellectuels*, pp. 27–8): Rubin, *Gentile Tales*, p. 213, note 1. On such accusations in fourteenth- and fifteenth-century Germany and Hungary: József Sümegi, 'Az oltáriszentség és a Szent Vér tisztelete a középkori Magyarországon', *Magyar Egyháztörténeti Vázlatok* 3 (1991): pp. 107–19.

[51] The Hebrew text was censored; its editor interprets the sentence as referring to a crucifix: Salfeld, *Martyrologium*, pp. 335, 337.

[52] *Ibid.*, p. 67. On alleged host desecration at the start of these massacres: Simonsohn, *Apostolic See History*, p. 60.

[53] Eduardus Petrovich and Paulus Ladislaus Timkovics, eds., *Sermones compilati in studio generali Quinqueecclesiensi in regno Ungarie* (Budapest: Akadémiai Kiadó, 1993). The editors determined the dating and provenance of the collection on the basis of internal evidence. St István of Hungary is called 'rex noster' and Hungarian saints are well represented, which points to a Hungarian composition. The mention of St Dominic as 'pater noster Dominicus' and other characteristics led to the identification of the author as a Dominican: pp. 14–19. Confirmed by Edit Madas, 'A "Pécsi Egyetemi Beszédek"', *BUKSZ* 8, no. 4 (1996): pp. 415–19.

[54] Jeremy Cohen, *The Friars and the Jews: The Evolution of Medieval Anti-Judaism* (Ithaca and London: Cornell University Press, 1982), pp. 226–41; Robert Chazan, *Medieval Stereotypes and Modern Antisemitism* (Berkeley, Los Angeles and London: University of California Press, 1997), chapter IV.

[55] Petrovich and Timkovics, *Sermones*: 'Gens tenebrarum', p. 52; Jews do not believe in Christ: pp. 70, 91; Jews responsible for the death of Christ: pp. 125, 246, 368, 388.   [56] *Ibid.*, p. 388.

Christian perceptions and attitudes

even as Christ haters.[57] In addition, Jews are described as infidels who have *no* faith; their religion is designated as *cultus*, as opposed to Christian faith (*fides*).[58] Moreover, they are stupid and foolish.[59] When Jews provide a positive example, the reference is to biblical times; the distinction is driven home even by a change in terminology: *Hebreus* is used instead of *Judeus*.[60] Finally, in an *exemplum* that is mentioned to illustrate the power of the sign of the cross, the devil is shown powerless against a Jew who is thus protected. The gesture alone is enough to save him, even though 'the vessel is empty', that is, the Jew's soul does not contain the faith of Christ.[61]

The presence of non-Christians also generated negative views outside Hungary about the whole kingdom and its population. In the previous chapter, I discussed the early thirteenth-century papal concern with Muslim 'influence' over Hungary, and the controversy over László IV's alleged 'pagan' orientation. The popes were not alone in forming an unfavourable opinion of the Cuman impact on Hungary. There were two main reasons for this. First, the Cumans participated in military expeditions outside the kingdom as part of the royal army. Second, their presence revived the traditional identification, present in western European sources since the tenth century, of Hungarians with Scythians and then with Huns, eastern nomads who attack Christian countries.[62] In the thirteenth and early fourteenth centuries, some chroniclers related (and condemned) the spread of Mongol, Cuman or 'barbarian' fashion in Hungary. The pope exhorted László IV to return to wearing 'Christian' clothing.[63] Perhaps at his court, or if Ottokar of Steier is correct even earlier, Cuman costume may have influenced the attire of the nobility. If this was the case, it would fit into the explanatory model of Georg Simmel, who emphasized the necessity for the upper classes to find ever-changing new forms of fashion to differentiate themselves from the rest of the population.[64] Ottokar of Steier (or of Horneck; died between 1312 and 1318), who treated Hungarian affairs at length in his *Reimchronik*,

---

[57] Ibid., p. 353.   [58] 'Cultus': *ibid*., p. 26; 'infidel': p. 378.
[59] 'Stultus', 'insipiens': *ibid*., p. 368.   [60] Ibid., p. 250.
[61] 'Vas vacuum sed bene signatum': *ibid*., p. 247. Frederic C. Tubach, *Index Exemplorum: A Handbook of Medieval Religious Tales* (Helsinki: Akademia Scientiarum Fennica, 1969) does not list any exact equivalent. The closest *exemplum* type is no. 1346, where the sign of the cross made by a repentent sinner on his deathbed banishes the devil. On the belief in the efficacy of the sign of the cross: Jean-Claude Schmitt, *La raison des gestes dans l'Occident médiéval* (Paris: Gallimard, 1990), pp. 321–2.
[62] Györffy, *Krónikáink*, pp. 48–9; Bálint Hóman, *A magyar hún-hagyomány és hún-monda* (Budapest: Egyetemi Nyomda, 1925), pp. 33–42; Elemér Mályusz, *A Thuróczy-krónika és forrásai*, Tudománytörténeti Tanulmányok 5 (Budapest: Akadémiai Kiadó, 1967), pp. 51–2; Róna-Tas, *Hungarians*, pp. 423–7.   [63] See chapter 5, pp. 174, 182.
[64] Georg Simmel, 'Fashion', *International Quarterly* 10 (1904): pp. 130–55, see pp. 133–8.

described the wedding of Prince Béla of Hungary (son of Béla IV) to a niece of Otakar II of Bohemia. According to Ottokar of Steier, the hairstyle of Hungarian nobles was similar to that of Mongols. They used pearls and precious stones to adorn their beards and wore braids.[65] Ottokar cast the Hungarians as the opposite of courtliness, using traditional stereotyping.[66] Other chroniclers in Bohemia and German lands recorded that men there started to wear braids 'like Hungarians' and 'barbarians'.[67] These reports were also not independent of a condemnation of Hungarians as the enemy. The evidence is elusive: very few such references exist, and some may be descriptions of the Cumans themselves – simply mentioned as 'Hungarians' or 'barbarians' by these chroniclers – rather than of any adoption of Cuman customs by the Hungarian population. Moreover, the chroniclers' purpose in using these descriptions, the function of these episodes in the overall structure of the works, and the effects of a general interest in orientalism at the time on their views remain insufficiently explored. Whether the Hungarians themselves started to dress according to Cuman style is therefore uncertain. What is clear is that some chroniclers in neighbouring countries often inimical to Hungary depicted Hungarians as 'barbarians'.

Many of these sources from neighbouring countries interpreted Cuman influence over Hungarians as affecting the very essence of the kingdom not only external signals like clothing and hair. In these accounts Hungarians themselves were becoming 'pagans'. Since there were recurring wars between Hungary and its neighbours, these authors had political reasons to show the depravity of Hungary, an enemy kingdom. An anonymous Dominican author from Austria recorded one of the Hungarian attacks against Otakar of Bohemia in these terms: '[Bohemia was attacked] by Cuman unbelievers and semi-Christian Hungarians.'[68] The bishop of Olomouc urged Gregory IX (in 1272) to turn his attention to the problems in central Europe, emphasizing that the Cumans of Hungary were killing Christians and spreading paganism,

---

[65] *MGH DC*, vol. v, pt. 1: pp. 105–6, lines 7980–8010. Tr. and analysis: András Vízkelety, 'Béla hercegnek, IV. Béla király fiának menyegzője', *Irodalomtörténeti Közlemények* 97 (1993): pp. 571–84. On the importance of hair in accusations: Robert Bartlett, 'Symbolic Meanings of Hair in the Middle Ages', *Transactions of the Royal Historical Society*, 6th ser., 4 (1994): pp. 43–60.

[66] Vízkelety, 'Béla hercegnek'.

[67] 'Chronicon Francisci Pragensis', (1320s) in *Fontes Rerum Bohemicarum*, ed. Josef Emler, vol. IV (Prague, 1884), pp. 347–456, see p. 404; Pez, *Scriptores Rerum Austriacarum*, vol. I: col. 948 (Anonymus Leobiensis). Zsuzsa Lovag, 'A magyar viselet a 11–13. században', *Ars Hungarica* 2 (1974): pp. 381–408, see p. 383, p. 399, n. 2. Gábor Klaniczay, 'Daily Life and the Elites in the Later Middle Ages: The Civilized and the Barbarians', in *Environment and Society in Hungary*, ed. Ferenc Glatz (Budapest: MTA Történettudományi Intézet, 1990), pp. 75–90, accepts these statements as facts.

[68] 'ab incredulis Comanis et a semichristianis Hungaris': Pez, *Scriptores Rerum Austriacarum*, vol. I: col. 849, reprinted in Gombos, *Catalogus*, vol. I: p. 276.

Christian perceptions and attitudes

endangering the existence of Christianity in the region.[69] An Austrian annalist wrote that the papal legate Philip went to Hungary not just to convert the Cumans but to 'recall the Christian Hungarians, who had nearly forgotten the Christian life . . . to the catholic faith'.[70] He added that the Hungarians did not wish to obey. Ottokar of Steier put words in the mouth of the legate Philip, according to which he would rather see the king and all his men turn pagan than set foot in the kingdom again.[71] The annals of the canons of St Rudbert from Salzburg spoke of the inhabitants of Hungary having polluted the purity of Christian faith through their association with the Cumans.[72] The controversy between King László IV and the papacy, analysed in the previous chapter, gave fuel to the accusation that the Hungarians were 'pagans'. The actual behaviour and role of the Cumans, their possible influence on fashion, and the strategy to fit them into an anti-Hungarian image by political enemies perpetuated a negative attitude towards the Cumans themselves, and revived the identification of Hungarians with eastern nomads and/or barbarians.

Modern historians have also interpreted the Cuman presence in Hungary as exercising an attraction or a fascination on the local population who 'rediscovered' their 'pagan' roots by the agency of the Cumans. According to this argument, a 'pagan resurgence', or, in Gábor Klaniczay's words, an 'ideal of deliberate barbarism' (in opposition to western norms and ideals) was born, inspired by the Cumans.[73] Did Cuman presence generate an alternative 'norm' or ideal? In other words, did resistance to western models lead to an emphasis on the eastern origins of the Hungarians and a wider identification with the Cumans?[74] The evidence used for this hypothesis consists of references to the adoption of Cuman costume in Hungary, cited above, and the chronicle of Simon of Kéza. Simon, court cleric of King László IV, wrote (or adapted) a version of the history of the Hungarians in which the Huns and the Hungarians

---

[69] ASV AA Arm. I-XVIII-3104 (*VMH*, pp. 307–8, no. DXXXV). On the background: Kłoczowski, 'L'Europe Centrale', p. 508.

[70] 'Philippus . . . Ungariam venit; Ungaros christianos, qui christianam vitam fere obliti fuerant, et Comanos ad fidem catholicam studuit revocare.' 'Annalium Austriae Continuatio Vindobonensis', in *MGH SS*, vol. IX: pp. 698–722, see p. 711. Similarly 'Chronicon Austriacum anonymi', in *Rerum Austriacarum scriptores*, 3 vols., ed. Adrian Rauch (Vienna, 1793–4), vol. II: pp. 213–300, see p. 275, reprinted in Gombos, *Catalogus*, vol. I: pp. 504–18, see p. 514.

[71] *MGH DC*, vol. V, pt. 1: p. 329, lines 24945–8.

[72] 'terra illa [Ungaria], que fedis ritibus Comanorum puritatem fidei christiane fedavit': 'Annales Sancti Rudberti Salisburgenses', in *MGH SS*, vol. IX: p. 805.

[73] Deér, *Pogány magyarság*, pp. 235–6; Klaniczay, 'Daily Life', p. 85, describes Simon of Kéza as the initiator of this ideal.

[74] Also see my 'How Many Medieval Europes? The "pagans" of Hungary and Regional Diversity in Christendom', in *The Medieval World*, ed. Janet Nelson and Peter Linehan (London: Routledge, forthcoming).

descended from a common ancestor.⁷⁵ The interpretation that Simon provided an alternative to western norms rests on the long-held assumption that his choice to incorporate the history of the Huns into the history of the Hungarians was due to romantic–pagan tendencies prevalent at the court of László, an assumption that has already been refuted by Jenő Szűcs.⁷⁶ Simon of Kéza constructed the thesis of Hun–Hungarian continuity from a series of western ecclesiastical sources.⁷⁷ As Szűcs has proved, the pervading ideology is not 'pagan–barbarian' but what he called a budding medieval 'nationalism'.⁷⁸ Simon may have drawn on his knowledge of Cuman customs to lend verisimilitude to his description of ancient Hun–Hungarian practices, but he never shows any sympathy for 'pagans' in general or the Cumans living in the kingdom in particular; indeed he gloats over their defeat at the hands of László IV.⁷⁹ Simon was not a propagandist of an 'ideal of deliberate barbarism'.

---

[75] The authorship of the 'History of the Huns', part of the Hungarian chronicle, has been debated:
  1. Simon of Kéza wrote this section of the chronicle himself: Bálint Hóman, *A Szt. László-korabeli Gesta Ungarorum és XII–XIII. századi leszármazói* (Budapest: MTA, 1925); Imre Madzsar, 'A hún krónika szerzője', *Történeti Szemle* 11 (1922): pp. 75–103; László Erdélyi, *Krónikáink atyja Kézai* (Szeged: Prometheus Nyomda, 1933); Jenő Szűcs, 'Társadalomelmélet, politikai teória és történetszemlélet Kézai Gesta Hungarorumában', in Szűcs, *Nemzet és történelem* (Budapest: Gondolat Kiadó, 1974), pp. 415–555, first published in *Századok* 107 (1973): pp. 569–643, 823–78 with a long appendix that was not included in *Nemzet és történelem* (see pp. 870–2); in German in Szűcs, *Nation und Geschichte: Studien* (Budapest, 1981), pp. 263–328; shorter English version 'Theoretical Elements in Master Simon of Kéza's *Gesta Hungarorum* (1282–1285)', in *Simon of Kéza: The Deeds of the Hungarians*, ed. and tr. László Veszprémy and Frank Schaer (Budapest: Central European University Press, 1999), pp. xxix–civ; unless indicated otherwise, I refer to the *Nemzet és történelem* version of this article. János Horváth, 'A hun-történet és szerzője', *Irodalomtörténeti Közlemények* (1963): pp. 446–76; Mályusz, *Thuróczy-krónika*; Mályusz, *Az V. István kori Gesta*.
  2. Simon used an already existing version: Domanovszky, *Kézai Simon mester krónikája*; Sándor Domanovszky, 'Kézai és a hun-krónika', in Domanovszky, ed. *Károlyi Emlékkönyv*, pp. 110–32; György Györffy, 'A hun-magyar krónika szerzője', in Györffy, *Krónikáink és a magyar őstörténet*, pp. 152–80. The manuscripts of previous chronicle compositions that Simon may have used have not survived and Simon's own work exists in various later copies and reworked versions only. (On the manuscript tradition see the preface of Domanovszky's edition, *SRH*, vol. 1: pp. 131–9.)

[76] László Mezey, 'Szent István XIII. századi verses históriája', in *Magyar Századok: Irodalmi műveltségünk történetéhez* (Budapest: Egyetemi Nyomda, 1948), pp. 41–51; János Horváth, *A magyar irodalmi műveltség kezdetei* (Budapest: Magyar Szemle Társaság, 1931, repr. Akadémiai Kiadó, 1988) p. 44; Mályusz, *Thuróczy-krónika*, p. 52; Gyula Németh, ed., *Attila és hunjai* (Budapest: Magyar Szemle Társaság, 1940, repr. Budapest: Akadémiai Kiadó, 1986). Szűcs, 'Társadalomelmélet'.

[77] Szűcs, 'Társadalomelmélet', pp. 420–7. Also Gyula Kristó, 'Volt-e a magyaroknak ősi hun hagyományuk?' in *Mítosz és történelem*, ed. Mihály Hoppál and Márton Istvánovits (Budapest: MTA Néprajzi Kutatócsoport, 1978), pp. 55–64; László Veszprémy, 'A Hun-magyar hagyomány alakulása és a tatárjárás', *Hadtörténelmi Közlemények* 104 (1991): pp. 22–33.

[78] Szűcs, 'Társadalomelmélet', esp. pp. 458–9.

[79] Ibid., p. 436. On Cumans: *SRH*, vol. 1: pp. 186–7. Simon mentions the Cumans living in Hungary during his own times only twice. They participate in the royal army and loot the enemy's baggage during battle; they also plot against and are defeated by the king.

Christian perceptions and attitudes

The nascent self-identification with Scythians and Huns in the construction of 'Hungarian' identity was part of the search for illustrious ancestors rather than a turn towards 'paganism' or barbarity. Such 'ancestors' were becoming necessary at the time, in order to emphasize the prestige of peoples and kingdoms. Competition for Trojan ancestry was accompanied by the proliferation of myths of origin especially from the twelfth century onwards.[80] Simon of Kéza used what western chronicles had been repeating for centuries – the descent of Hungarians (and Huns) from Scythians – but advocated a different interpretation. He explained in his preface that he gave the 'true' version of this descent, and wanted to refute the lies of western authors.[81] Simon had a western education and ample opportunity to acquaint himself with western views of Scythian–Hungarian kinship.[82] As Attila the Hun had indeed ruled over an area that later became part of Hungary, the notion of Hun–Hungarian continuity had a 'historical' basis. Simon revised these views by assigning a more positive role to the Huns. He emphasized Attila's power: he was the scourge of God, feared by the whole world.[83] Moreover, he was the head of an empire, elected 'Romano more'.[84] Attila's empire was at the origin of the Hungarian kingdom, to match the prestige of the Trojans who 'founded' France. Yet Simon did not depict Attila as a model ruler. A lecherous tyrant, who suffocated on his own blood on his wedding night (his nose started to bleed while he was asleep after an excess of drink and sex), was hardly an 'ideal' for Hungarian kings to follow.[85] Moreover, the conscious incorporation of a real or imagined pre-Christian past had already started in the early thirteenth century, and not with Simon. Ecclesiastical authors of the previous two centuries saw the conversion of the Hungarians and the reign of St István as the foundation of the kingdom but, beginning in the early thirteenth century, some clerics reintegrated the 'pagan' Hungarian past in a more positive light, and

---

[80] Colette Beaune, *Naissance de la nation France* (Paris: Gallimard, 1985), pp. 22–74; Susan Reynolds, *Kingdoms and Communities in Western Europe 900–1300*, 2nd edn (Oxford: Clarendon Press, 1997), pp. 213, 258, 272–3, 296–7; Susan Reynolds, 'Medieval *Origines Gentium* and the Community of the Realm', *History* 68 (1983): pp. 375–90; Lars Boje Mortensen, 'Saxo Grammaticus' View of the Origin of the Danes and his Historiographical Models', *Cahiers de l'Institut du Moyen Age Grec et Latin* 55 (1987): pp. 169–83. I thank Kurt Villads Jensen for directing my attention to Mortensen's article.   [81] *SRH*, vol. I: pp. 141–2.
[82] Szűcs, 'Társadalomelmélet', pp. 420–7. The analysis is based on the text itself; the issue of authorship therefore does not alter it. See also the appendix of 'Társadalomelmélet', in *Századok*, pp. 829–73.
[83] *SRH*, vol. I: p. 151. Simon also drew on the medieval legends of Alexander the Great, especially in his description of Attila: István Borzsák, 'A Nagy Sándor-hagyomány Magyarországon', *Antik Tanulmányok* 30, no. 1 (1983): pp. 1–18. On various medieval Attila legends: Sándor Eckhardt, 'Attila a mondában', in *Attila és hunjai*, pp. 143–216.   [84] *SRH*, vol. I: p. 150.
[85] *SRH*, vol. I: pp. 160–1.

Attila was linked to Hungarian history.[86] Simon's chronicle was a learned creation of identity, due precisely to a Latin Christian education. Its aim was not the assumption of a barbarian identity in opposition to western culture. Quite the contrary, it was to procure an ancient and illustrious ancestry, equal to the Romans, thereby elevating the Hungarians to the rank of other 'ancient' peoples.

Not all contemporaries accepted this version of Hungarian origins. King László IV's ecclesiastical opposition, crystallized around Archbishop Lodomer, insisted on the radical break between a 'pagan' and a Christian past. For them, István I, the first Christian king of the kingdom, rather than Attila, was the key figure of Hungary's past. A new rhyming liturgical office for St István was composed between 1270 and 1290, probably by an author in the entourage of Lodomer; while incorporating earlier (notably twelfth-century) pieces, it was largely an original creation.[87] It did not replace the older István office everywhere, but it was used from the late thirteenth century onwards in the diocese of Esztergom and other churches. While the old liturgical office portrayed István primarily as an ascetic saint, in the new office István's role as the apostle of Hungary was emphasized. This representation of István is not a thirteenth-century invention; it is an important element in his *Vitae* and even in earlier masses.[88] But the parts of the

[86] Mályusz, *Thuróczy-krónika*, pp. 26–45; Kristó, 'Magyar öntudat', pp. 431–2; Szűcs, 'Társadalomelmélet', pp. 491–2; Kristó, *Magyar nemzet*, pp. 218–21; Veszprémy, 'A Hun-magyar hagyomány alakulása'. The name Attila was already used in Hungary in the twelfth century: Németh, ed., *Attila és hunjai*, p. 191.

[87] On date, authorship, composition: Mezey, 'Szent István', (hypothetically identified the author as Nicholas, Augustinian prior of Esztergom); József Török, 'A középkori magyarországi liturgia története', in *Kódexek a középkori Magyarországon* (Budapest: Országos Széchenyi Könyvtár, 1985), pp. 49–66; József Török, 'Szent István tisztelete a középkori magyar liturgiában', in *Szent István és kora*, pp. 197–201; Robert Folz, *Les saints rois du Moyen Age en Occident VIe–XIIIe siècles* (Brussels: Société des Bollandistes, 1984), pp. 198–9; Benjamin Rajecky, *Magyarország zenetörténete* (Budapest: Akadémiai Kiadó, 1988), vol. I: pp. 335–8. On the significance of the new office: Folz, *Saints rois*, pp. 210, 212–13; Szűcs, 'Társadalomelmélet', p. 494.

Editions: József Dankó, *Vetus hymnarium ecclesiasticum Hungariae* (Budapest, 1893), pp. 194–204; Clemens Blume and Guido Maria Dreves, *Analecta Hymnica Medii Aevi*, 55 vols. (Leipzig: O. R. Reisland, 1886–1922), vol. XXVIII: pp. 195–9. The corpus of antiphons making up the thirteenth-century office of István consisted of unique compositions, and not copies from the liturgy of other saints: *Corpus Antiphonalium Officii*, ed. Renatus-Joannus Hesbert, vol. III: *Invitatoria et Antiphonae* (Rome: Herder, 1968), nos. 402, 6866, 7115, 9277, 17665, 18844, 24516, 26579, 24891, 30978. The *lectiones* are included in the edition based on the oldest (thirteenth-century) manuscript: Károly Kniewald, 'A zágrábi érseki könyvtár MR 126 (XI. szd.) jelzésű Sacramentariumának magyar rétege a MR 67. sz. zágrábi Breviarium (XIII. szd.) megvilágításában', *Pannonhalmi Szemle* (1938), pp. 36–54. The new office was in use in Esztergom and many other churches: Paris, BN, lat. 8879, ff. 400v–402; Radó, *Libri liturgici* nos. 91, 93, 104, 115, 122, 180, 181. In the archbishopric of Kalocsa a different office was used in the fourteenth century: Budapest, OSzK, Clmae 33, ff. 312v–315.

[88] The *Vitae* are edited by Emma Bartoniek, in *SRH*, vol. II: pp. 363–440. A twelfth-century sermon emphasizing the role of István in the Christianization of Hungary: OSzK, MNy 1 (*Codex Prayanus*), ff. 84v–85.

Christian perceptions and attitudes

new office that were composed in the thirteenth century (as opposed to those taken over from earlier versions of the office) emphasize that only István, a strong king chosen by God, could overcome the stubbornness and cruelty of the pagan Hungarians and bring about their conversion. The *lectiones* selected from the *Life* also recounted the pagan past of the Hungarians who were the 'scourge of Christendom', and highlighted István's predestined role to convert them. Although the motif of Christianization appears in liturgical offices of other royal saints (St Olaf, St Wenceslas of Bohemia), it is not their main theme.[89] István's office is described by Folz as singular in its insistence on the pagan errors of the Hungarians.[90] As Mezey has argued, the singularity is due to the motivation to go beyond honouring the saint and create a propaganda piece. The office upheld István's example as the apostle to the pagan Hungarians and at the same time condemned pagans, who were represented as cruel enemies of Christendom.

None the less, the incorporation of Attila into Hungarian history became part of the 'historical' tradition, open to new interpretations. Hungary's Renaissance King Matthias (1443–90) was called a second Attila by his chronicler Thuróczy, a theme elaborated upon by the king's Italian humanist courtier Antonio Bonfini.[91] This same king had one of the largest collections of books in Europe at the time, and was a patron of Italian humanist scholars, sculptors and architects. Clearly, Thuróczy's description was no more a sign of an 'ideal of deliberate barbarism', a rejection of 'western models' than Simon's chronicle. An anti-western and anti-Christian reinterpretation of 'Scythian' identity is a modern phenomenon.

The pictorial representation of the Cumans in medieval Hungary incorporated both a negative, even demonized, image and a positive one, linked to the construction of Hungarian identity. Based on the thirteenth-century legends of St László, fourteenth-century murals depicted the fight of the saint against a Cuman who abducted a woman during a raid.[92] The painters often represented Cuman clothing and weapons in detail. The Cumans in these frescoes are enemies of the saint, and by this fact alone negative figures. Moreover, they are often demonized; for example, fire or an evil spirit escapes from the mouth of the Cuman at

---

[89] Folz, *Saints rois*, pp. 207–9, 211–18. Martyrdom and penitence are important themes.
[90] *Ibid.*, pp. 210, 212–13.
[91] Deér, *Pogány magyarság*, pp. 241–2. Mályusz, *Thuróczy-krónika*, pp. 110–21.
[92] Klaniczay and Madas, 'Hongrie', pp. 117–20, 135–7. Photographs: László, *Szent-László legenda*. Zsuzsa Lukács, 'A Szent László legenda a középkori magyar falképfestészetben', in *Athleta Patriae: Tanulmányok Szent László történetéhez*, ed. László Mezey (Budapest: Szent István Társulat, 1980), pp. 161–204. A version of the story in Rus' chronicles: Hodinka, *Orosz évkönyvek*, pp. 463–7, 473–81.

Székelyderzs, Kakaslomnic, Szepesmindszent and Karaszkó.[93] The elaborations of the story in the Angevin Legendary served to further the contrast between the saint and the Cuman. A final scene was added, in which after the saint rests his head on the lap of the maiden he has saved, the Virgin Mary appears to heal his wounds.[94] This suggests an interpretation that turns the episode into a fight between a Christian saint and the Infidel. It has been proposed that the frescoes served the Church in its fight against tenacious pagan customs and pagan groups, or expressed the anti-Cuman sentiment of particular groups.[95] They were found in churches mainly near the borders of medieval Hungary.[96] The origin of the motifs in these paintings has been debated – that is, whether they go back to eastern, Asian prototypes (thus representing an ancient layer of Hungarian tradition), to Byzantine precedents such as the *Digenis Akritas*, or to western courtly ideals.[97] The textual basis of these paintings, the legend of the saint including the story of the fight with the Cuman, was certainly completed by the early thirteenth century, yet the representations in churches do not begin until the late thirteenth and early fourteenth centuries. The royal court, nobles – including someone whose ancestor received his lands from King László IV after the battle against the Cumans – and communities of monks figure prominently among the donors in the early fourteenth century. In the case of the frescoes at Bántornya, the motivation of the family who commissioned them can be linked to the Angevin court.[98] The frescoes cannot be connected with Esztergom or other episcopal centres, and do not seem to be part of an ecclesiastical programme, although a lingering fear and hatred of the Cumans probably influenced their genesis.

Yet in Hungarian art Cuman costume was not only the sign of the infidel and evil. The same fourteenth-century *Illuminated Chronicle* that represented King László IV as a 'Cuman' in order to condemn him (see chapter 5), also included many images of groups in costumes similar to or identical with that of the Cumans in both negative and positive con-

---

[93] László, *Szent László-legenda*, pp. 98, 112, 136, 150, respectively.
[94] Ferenc Levárdy, *Magyar Anjou Legendárium*, facsimile edn (Budapest: Magyar Helikon, 1973), pp. 135–36; Lukács, 'Szent László legenda', p. 169. It is perhaps the maiden László has saved who reveals herself as the Virgin.
[95] Terézia Kerny, 'Keresztény lovagoknak oszlopa', in László, *Szent László-legenda*, pp. 213–23, see p. 213; Lukács, 'Szent László', pp. 176–7.
[96] Map in László, *Szent László-legenda* (inner cover); Lukács, 'Szent László legenda', p. 173.
[97] Asian precedents: László, *Szent László-legenda*, pp. 24–34, 186–7, 191–3. Byzantine: Vlasta Dvoráková, Vasile Dragut and Jan Bakoš, cited in *ibid.*, pp. 38–41, 226. Western: András Vízkelety, 'Nomád kori hagyományok vagy udvari-lovagi toposzok?', *Irodalomtörténeti Közlemények* 85 (1981): pp. 243–75.
[98] Kerny, 'Keresztény lovagoknak', pp. 213–15; Lukács, 'Szent László legenda', p. 178; Tamás Bogyay, 'A bántornyai falképek donátorairól', *Ars Hungarica* 14, no. 2 (1986): pp. 147–58.

texts. Indeed, the ancestors of the Hungarians, Mongols, Cumans and a variety of eastern nomads were depicted in the same attire. Ernő Marosi has drawn attention to layers of meaning associated with the representations of eastern nomads (he based his argument primarily on the *Illuminated Chronicle*), analysing learned 'orientalism' and ideology.[99] Discounting notions that the miniatures contain accurate representations of the Cumans, he argued that they were connected with the self-representation of a people wishing to emphasize its descent from the Scythians. Marosi and his critics raised the issue of the reality of these depictions of costume and hairstyle. That they are linked to historical reality is confirmed by archaeological finds from Cuman graves in Hungary, research into steppe armament and clothing, as well as the analysis of the costumes of other figures depicted in the same images.[100] It is significant therefore that in order to represent the Scythian–Hun–Hungarian identity, the artist depicted the ancestors of the Hungarians in the same way as eastern nomads, and used many elements of the Cuman costume as his prototype. Again, there was an interplay between reality and its ideological uses. On the level of representation, the Cumans came to embody both the contemptible, demonized enemy, in accordance with medieval stereotyping of, for example, Muslims,[101] and the 'Hungarians' themselves, in the form of their Scythian ancestors. It is noteworthy that there was no comparable interest in representing Hungary's other non-Christians.

Explicitly expressed opinions about non-Christians were predominantly negative. Even the learned creation of identity that gave a prominent role to eastern nomads as the ancestors of Hungarians did not mean

---

[99] Ernő Marosi, 'Zur Frage des Quellenwertes mittelalterlicher Darstellungen: 'Orientalismus' in der Ungarischen Bilderchronik', in *Alltag und materielle Kultur im mittelalterlichen Ungarn*, ed. András Kubinyi and József Laszlovszky, Medium Aevum Quotidianum 22 (Krems, 1991), pp. 74–107; Ernő Marosi, 'Magyarok középkori ábrázolásai és az orientalizmus a középkori művészetben', in *Magyarok Kelet és Nyugat közt* (Budapest: Balassi, 1996), pp. 77–97; Ernő Marosi, *Kép és Hasonmás: művészet és valóság a 14–15. századi Magyarországon* (Budapest: Akadémiai Kiadó, 1995), chapter I. Reviews: János Bak, *BUKSZ* (1993, no. 2): pp. 218–21; János Végh, Tünde Wehli, János Bak and Sándor Tóth, *BUKSZ* (1998, no. 1): pp. 58–66.

[100] Pálóczi Horváth, *Hagyományok*, pp. 105–37, 177–86; László Selmeczi, 'A magyarországi kunok temetkezése a XIII–XVI. században', in *Régészeti-néprajzi tanulmányok*, pp. 21–47, see p. 24. Kőhalmi, *Steppék nomádja*, pp. 52–4, 104–6, 133–4, 195; Gyula László, 'Adatok a kunok tegezéről', *A Néprajzi Múzeum Értesítője* 32 (1940): pp. 51–9. István Zichy, 'A Képes Krónika miniatűrjei viselettörténeti szempontból', in *Petrovics Elek Emlékkönyv* (Budapest: Az Országos Magyar Szépművészeti Múzeum barátai és tisztviselői, 1934), pp. 59–70; Annamária Kovács at the Central European University, Budapest, is working on the costumes of László, the maiden he saved and the warriors in the same images where the Cumans are portrayed; these represented the latest fashions.

[101] Sénac, *L'image de l'autre*; Ruth Mellinkoff, *Outcasts: Signs of Otherness in Northern European Art of the Late Middle Ages* (Berkeley, Los Angeles and Oxford: University of California Press, 1993).

a 'rehabilitation' of the Cumans then living in the kingdom. Attila became firmly established as the ancestor of the Hungarians: his name is still a popular choice for boys. Yet the Cumans did not get a more sympathetic treatment. Simon of Kéza, the same chronicler who propagated Hun–Hungarian continuity, exulted over the crushing of the Cuman revolt that happened during his own life.

CHRISTIAN MISSIONARY EFFORTS

Missionary activity has been a characteristic drive within Christianity from the earliest period of its existence. There are, however, different methods of Christianization, as well as a variety of motivations for propagating Christianity. In Hungary, the choice between peaceful methods and force differed with regard to missions within and outside the kingdom. Inside Hungary, even without resorting to forced baptism, laws could create a hostile environment to 'encourage' conversion. Attempts to convert and integrate the entire community affected only two groups: the Muslims (in the late eleventh and early twelfth centuries) and the Cumans (in the thirteenth century).

There was never any comparable effort to convert the Jews. Perhaps because of the larger harvest to be had from Cuman souls, the mendicants showed no great interest in Jewish ones.[102] While an increasingly aggressive missionary effort was directed at the Cumans, there was no organized preaching to the Jews and Muslims in the thirteenth century, and no Jewish–Christian debates. This was perhaps also linked to the fact that neither Christians, Jews or Muslims in thirteenth-century Hungary had a flourishing intellectual life. In the Dominican sermon collection of Pécs, there is only one sermon 'dirigitur . . . ad Judeos'.[103] This is a university sermon for learned Christians, one of three in honour of Christ; the other two mention idolaters and the faithful. It is a short and formulaic outline, rather than a full text, and there is no information about whether it was ever used to preach, and the details that would have been added in the course of delivery as an actual sermon. Its focus is the incarnation of Christ, calling on Jews to abandon ignorance. Just as religious disputations did not seem to have taken place in thirteenth-century Hungary, no compulsory attendance at Christian sermons was introduced either, unlike in many western European kingdoms.[104] Only the personal initiative of ecclesiastics, such as the abbot of Pannonhalma, the

---

[102] In contrast to western Europe: Cohen, *Friars and the Jews*; Chazan, *Daggers of Faith*; Simonsohn, *Apostolic See History*, pp. 238–62.   [103] Petrovich and Timkovics, *Sermones*, p. 381.
[104] Chazan, *Church, State and Jew*, pp. 255–63; Chazan, *Daggers of Faith*, pp. 38–47; Dahan, *Intellectuels*, pp. 220–6; Jordan, *French Monarchy*, pp. 150, 161; Simonsohn, *Apostolic See History*, pp. 257–8.

Christian perceptions and attitudes

most important Hungarian Benedictine monastery, resulted in the conversion of some individuals.[105] Two of these converts established a house for further Jewish converts.[106]

Aggressive legislation aimed at the eradication of the Muslim presence from Hungary in the late eleventh and early twelfth centuries. The Synod of Szabolcs in 1092 decreed that those Ishmaelites who, having been baptized, return to their old religion 'through circumcision' will be forced to leave their village and move into a new one, unless they prove their innocence.[107] Such an article from a Hungarian synod suggests that there were a considerable number of Muslims who had been converted to Christianity, possibly even as children (if they had not been circumcised), whose return to Islam was feared. Forced relocation was introduced as the means of conversion and integration in Kálmán's laws in the early twelfth century. Each Muslim village was to build a church and endow it, and then half of the population of the village was to move to another place to live with Christians. Even intermarriage was decreed; Ishmaelites were to marry their daughters to Christians. Some of the measures were to prevent Muslims from observing their religious customs of fasting, abstaining from pork, and ablutions in their own homes. Finally, Ishmaelites, when receiving guests, were to eat only pork for meat. Those who accused the Ishmaelites of infractions were to receive a part of the property of those denounced.[108]

Although we have no evidence whether or not forced baptism of Muslims took place, these measures, primarily at royal initiative (the Synod of Szabolcs was also convoked and presided over by the king), belong to an approach to conversion that also characterized Charlemagne

---

[105] The source is a papal letter; the original survives in the Archives of Pannonhalma: Érszegi, 'Eredeti pápai oklevelek', no. 69. Edition: *MZsO*, vol. I: p. 20, no. 19; Augustus Potthast, *Regesta Pontificum Romanorum*, 2 vols. (Graz: Akademische Druck- und Verlagsanstalt, 1957), no. 9897. See also chapter 7, pp. 235–6.

[106] ASV Reg. Vat. 18, f. 154v (*Reg. Greg. IX*, no. 3144). See chapter 7, p. 236.

[107] 'De negotiatoribus, quos appellant ismahelitas, si post baptismum ad legem suam antiquam per circumcisionem rediisse inventi fuerint, a sedibus suis separati ad alias villas removeantur. Illi vero, qui inculpabiles per iudicium apparuerint, in propriis sedibus remaneant.' Bak, *Laws*, p. 57.

[108] 'Si quis ysmahelitas in ieiunio seu comestione porcineque carnis abstinentia vel in ablutione aut in quolibet sue facinore deprehenderint, ysmahelite regi deputentur. Qui vero eos accusabat, de substantia eorum partem accipiat.

'Unicuique ville hysmaelitarum ecclesiam edifficare, de eademque villa dotem dare precipimus. Que postquam edificata fuerit, media pars ville ysmahelitarum villam emigret, sicque altrinescus sedeant, et quasi unius moris in domo, nunc nobiscum, una eademque ecclesia Christi in divina unanimiter consistant.

'Ysmahelitarum vero nullus audeat filiam suam iungere matrimonio alicuius de genere sua, sed nostra.

'Si quis ysmahelitarum hospites habuerit, vel aliquem in convivium vocaverit, tam ipse, quam convive eius de porcina tantum carne vescantur.' (*Decretum Colomanni*, based on the decisions of the assembly of prelates and lay lords at Tarcal): Bak, *Laws*, pp. 29–30.

and late medieval Spain.[109] The context was a concern for Christian purity and unity: in this case, that of the kingdom of Hungary. The same laws that tried to ensure Muslim conversion also dealt with enforcing church attendance and burial in churchyard cemeteries for the Christian population. There was a great emphasis on the *Christian* nature of the kingdom, and, by the time of King Kálmán, an insistence that 'mature faith' and 'perfect religion' had been achieved.[110] This should include the Muslims, too: 'as in a house of one way of life, let them thenceforth reside together with us and of one mind in the one and same divine Church of Christ'.[111] As early canon law did not define the position of Muslims within Christian countries (Muslims subjected to Christian rule began to be treated in the same way as Jews only gradually after Gratian),[112] there was no ready framework for policies concerning Hungary's Muslims. Moreover, the ideas that fuelled the first crusade may have provided additional impetus for anti-Muslim legislation during King Kálmán's reign.[113] It is impossible to know to what extent such laws, calculated to disrupt and destroy the Muslim communities of Hungary, were implemented. There is no evidence of a missionary activity, and indeed, prior to the development of mendicant orders, the means to complement laws by proselytizing were not as readily available. Abū Hāmid signalled the presence of both secret adherents to Islam, who pretended to be Christians, in twelfth-century Hungary, and those who openly professed their faith.[114] Some converts who were suspected of being 'false Christians' are known from the thirteenth century as well.[115] The existence of these clandestine Muslims may point to the partial efficacy of earlier laws. These laws themselves have no counterparts in the thirteenth century. Yet conversions to Christianity may have continued, as in 1232 Archbishop

---

[109] Lawrence G. Duggan, ' "For Force is not of God"? Compulsion and Conversion from Yahweh to Charlemagne', in *Varieties of Religious Conversion*, pp. 49–62; Fletcher, *Conversion*, pp. 213–22; Peter Brown, *The Rise of Western Christendom* (Oxford: Blackwell, 1997), chapter 16; Rosamond McKitterick, *The Frankish Kingdoms under the Carolingians, 751–987* (London and New York: Longman, 1983), pp. 61–3; Maurice Kriegel, 'La prise d'une décision: l'expulsion des Juifs d'Espagne en 1492', in *Chrétiens, Musulmans et Juifs dans l'Espagne médiévale*, ed. Ron Barkaï (Paris: Cerf, 1994), pp. 253–300; Henry Kamen, *Spain 1469–1714: A Society of Conflict*, 2nd edn (London and New York: Longman, 1991), pp. 38–44; Meyerson, *Muslims of Valencia*.

[110] Kálmán 'vidit adultam fidem perfecte religionis robor accepisse': Bak, *Laws*, p. 25.

[111] For the quotation see note 108 above; Bak, *Laws*, p. 29 (I disagree with the translation proposed there).

[112] Zacour, *Jews and Saracens*, pp. 22–6; Peter Herde, 'Christians and Saracens at the Time of the Crusades: Some Comments of Contemporary Medieval Canonists', *Studia Gratiana* 12 (1969): pp. 359–76.

[113] E.g. Norman Daniel, 'Crusade Propaganda', in *A History of the Crusades*, ed. Kenneth Setton, vol. VI: pp. 39–97; Riley-Smith, *The First Crusade and the Idea of Crusading*.

[114] Abu-Hámid, p. 56.

[115] ASV Misc. Arm. XV, no. 1, f. 355r (*VMH*, p. 109, no. CLXXXVII); *SRH*, vol. I: p. 474; Pauler, *Magyar nemzet*, vol. II: p. 413.

Christian perceptions and attitudes

Robert demanded that Muslim who converted or wished to convert (whether free or slaves) be separated from their old coreligionists.[116] Whether the public investigation of Muslim ownership of Christian slaves in the thirteenth century led to religious disputation or missionary activity is not known.

By the thirteenth century, ecclesiastical policies aimed at separating Jews and Muslims from Christians in Hungary; organized missionary activity focused only on the Cumans. Missions to the Cumans living in the neighbourhood of Hungary and within the kingdom were part of thirteenth-century missionary activity both in methods and agents. The Mongol invasion constitutes an important dividing line: a stage of missionary activity linked to policies of expansion was followed by a stage of internal missions. This is not to say that no missionary travelled to foreign lands from Hungary after the Mongol attack. None the less, the main thrust of missionary activity turned inwards. Dominicans and later Franciscans played the major role in these missions – members of these new orders that specialized in preaching and learning languages for missionary purposes in medieval Europe.[117]

Prior to the Mongol invasion, the Cumans, the eastern neighbours of the kingdom, were a major source of concern for the king of Hungary, and quickly became a prime target of missionary activity.[118] Cumans were raiding Hungary as Pechenegs and other nomads had done before them. In 1211, King András II invited the Teutonic Knights to defend his territories against the Cumans ('ad munimen regni contra Cumanos').[119] He settled the Knights in the region called Barcaság (Burzenland) in Transylvania, an area lying in the way of Cuman attacks. The Knights built first wooden, then stone castles with royal permission, provided defence, and even started an offensive and conquered parts of Cumania. They also began converting the Cumans, some of whom were willing to be baptized after military defeats.[120] Another result of the early phase of

---

[116] ASV Misc. Arm. XV, no. 1, f. 355r (*VMH*, p. 109, no. CLXXXVII).

[117] Jean Richard, 'L'enseignement des langues orientales en Occident au Moyen Age', in *Croisés, missionnaires et voyageurs* (London: Variorum, 1983), no. XVIII; Berthold Altaner, *Die Dominikanermissionen des 13. Jahrhunderts: Forschungen zur Geschichte der Kirchlichen Unionen und der Mohammedaner- und Heidenmission des Mittelalters* (Habelschwerdt: Frankes Buchhandlung, 1924); Richard, *Papauté*; E. Randolph Daniel, *The Franciscan Concept of Mission in the High Middle Ages*, 2nd edn (St Bonaventure, N.Y.: Franciscan Institute, 1992).

[118] Studies on Danish crusades and mission will offer interesting comparisons: Alan Murray, ed., *Crusade and Conversion on the Baltic Frontier 1140–1500* (Aldershot, forthcoming).

[119] Documents are collected in Zimmermann and Werner, *Urkundenbuch*, vol. I: pp. 11–60. András II's donation: pp. 11–12 (*RA*, no. 261). See also Hartmut Boockmann, *Der Deutsche Orden* (Munich: Beck, 1981), pp. 68–9.

[120] 'quidam ex illis [Cumans] dictis fratribus [Teutonic Knights] se reddentes cum uxoribus et parvulis ad baptismi gratiam convolarunt'. ASV Reg. Vat. 16, f. 88r (*Reg. Greg. IX*, no. 1096; *VMH*, p. 106, no. CLXXXV).

contacts was that Cuman slaves and Cuman horses were brought into the kingdom.[121] In 1225 King András ousted the Knights, after they wanted the territory to come directly under papal power.[122] This, however, did not affect the process of missionary activity that was set off by Teutonic success; Dominicans undertook the conversion of the Cumans.

This missionary movement served many functions. First, it furthered political interests. It was sponsored by Prince Béla (future Béla IV) for purposes of territorial expansion. He was present, with the archbishop of Esztergom, at the baptism of the Cuman chieftain Bortz. According to the Dominican account King András II himself was the godfather of Membrok. The conversions were tied to political submission; Bortz took an oath of fidelity to the Hungarian king.[123] To convert the Cumans offered the hope of not only peace on the eastern borders, but the extension of the kingdom itself; the kings of Hungary adopted the title 'rex Cumanie' from 1233. Mission and conquest were intertwined.

Second, the missions to Cumania combined missionary impulse with the interests of the Hungarian Church, especially those of the archbishop of Esztergom. After being contacted in 1227 by Dominicans who had prepared the conversion of one of the Cuman chieftains, Archbishop Robert asked for and received dispensation from the pope for his previously taken crusading vow. Conducting missions to Cumania was an acceptable alternative because 'a larger good should be preferred to a smaller merit'.[124] The case of Robert's vow was clearly treated by the pope according to one of the established categories of dispensation: 'when a greater obligation than that involved in the vow was assumed'.[125] He was also appointed as papal legate to Cumania. He bap-

---

[121] ASV Reg. Vat. 15, f. 55v (*Reg. Greg. IX*, no. 561; *VMH*, p. 94, no. CLXVIII); *CD*, vol. III, pt. 1: p. 303. On communication with Cumans: Jean Richard, 'The *Relatio de Davide* as a Source for Mongol History and the Legend of Prester John', in *Prester John*, pp. 139–58, see pp. 148, 154.

[122] Zimmermann and Werner, *Urkundenbuch*, pp. 29–31, 35–6. Honorius III and Gregory IX intervened, writing letters for years to persuade the king to change his mind, but in vain. See also chapter 1 above, p. 33.

[123] ASV Reg. Vat. 14, f. 64r (*Reg. Greg. IX*, no. 186; *VMH*, p. 87, no. CLVI; *Commentariolum de provinciae Hungariae originibus*, in *Monumenta Ordinis Fratrum Praedicatorum Historica* [*MOPH*], vol. 1: pp. 305–9, repr. in Nicolas Pfeiffer, *Die Ungarische Dominikanerordensprovinz von ihrer Gründung 1221 bis zur Tatarenwüstung 1241–2* (Zurich, 1913), pp. 143–6, see p. 145 (on the source: M. H. Vicaire, *Saint Dominique et ses frères: évangile ou croisade?* (Paris: Cerf, 1967), p. 40); Albericus of Trois-Fontaines, in *MGH SS*, vol. XXIII: p. 920; Ludevicus Weiland, ed., 'Emonis Chronicon', in *MGH SS*, vol. XXIII: pp. 454–523, see p. 511.

[124] ASV Reg. Vat. 14, f. 26r–v (*Reg. Greg. IX*, no. 139; *VMH*, pp. 86–7, no. CLIV). Papal confirmation of complete absolution from this vow, 'cum igitur maius bonum minori sit merito preferendum . . . accedendi ad dictas provincias licentiam tibi concedimus': ASV Reg. Vat. 15, ff. 53v–54 (*Reg. Greg. IX*, no. 556, *VMH*, p. 93, CLXVII).

[125] James A. Brundage, *Medieval Canon Law and the Crusader* (Madison and London: University of Wisconsin Press, 1969), Chapter II, 'The Crusade Vow to the Early Thirteenth Century', pp. 30–65 (see p. 65).

Christian perceptions and attitudes

tized Bortz and his men and he appointed (in 1227 or 1228) the bishop of the newly founded Cuman bishopric: Theodoric, Dominican provincial of Hungary.[126] For a brief period the bishop may have been a suffragan of Esztergom, but in 1229 Pope Gregory IX exempted the bishopric from the archbishop's power and took it directly under his own jurisdiction.[127] The papacy similarly wished to ensure the independence of newly created bishoprics from those who had helped found them in other areas, for example the Baltic and Lithuania.[128] Yet the archbishop of Esztergom continued to play an important role as papal legate to Cumania (1227–31/2).[129] Dominicans who went to Cumania from Hungary established ties to the kingdom; these were reinforced by the political relations between the king of Hungary and the newly converted Cumans. At the same time, the bishop of the Cumans participated in Hungarian ecclesiastical politics, much like Hungarian bishops; for example in adjudicating a case between a monastery and a bishopric.[130] Even though the Cuman bishopric was supposedly under direct papal jurisdiction, in practice its ties to Hungary remained strong until the Mongol invasion.[131]

Third, the mission was dear to the Dominicans and was presented as fulfilling an old dream of St Dominic himself. The Cumans, the nearest 'pagans' on the eastern border of Christendom, seem to have attracted his attention, though it is not clear to what extent he interested himself

---

[126] *Commentariolum*; *Magnum Chronicon Belgicum*, in Pfeiffer, *Ungarische*, pp. 178–9; ASV Reg. Vat. 14, f. 64r–v (*Reg. Greg. IX*, nos. 185, 187; *VMH*, pp. 87–8, nos. CLV, CLVII). The history of the Cuman bishopric: Makkai, *Milkói (kún) püspökség*; Ioan Ferenţ, *A kunok és püspökségük*, tr. Péter Pál Domokos (Budapest: Szent István Társulat, 1981; tr. of *Cumanii şi episcopia lor* (Baj, 1933)); also Altaner, *Dominikanermissionen*, pp. 141–8. There was competition from Orthodox priests: *Reg. Greg. IX*, no. 2198 (*VMH*, p. 131, no. CCXXV).

[127] ASV Reg. Vat. 14, f. 137v (*Reg. Greg. IX*, no. 345); *VMH*, p. 90, no. CLXI: 'te ac successores tuos a cuiuslibet subiectione preterquam Romani Pontificis liberos esse decernimus et immediate ad iurisdictionem sedis apostolice pertinere'. Gregory IX also mentions the Cuman bishopric as 'ad nos nullo medio pertinentem': ASV Reg. Vat. 17, f. 220r (*Reg. Greg. IX*, no. 2156; *VMH*, p. 131, no. CCXXIV). See also Makkai, *Milkói (kún) püspökség*, p. 40.

[128] Christiansen, *Northern Crusades*, pp. 122–6 for mostly unsuccessful papal attempts. For the short Lithuanian experiment in the mid-thirteenth century: Paulius Rabikauskas, 'La cristianizzazione della Lituania (XIII e XIV secolo)', in *L'Eglise et le peuple chrétien*, pp. 3–11. Pomerania: Lotter, 'Crusading Idea', p. 281. See also Richard, *Papauté*, p. 15.

[129] Zimmermann, *Päpstliche*, p. 135.

[130] *Reg. Greg. IX*, no. 2882 (*VMH*, pp. 141–2, no. CCL). The bishop is mentioned with Hungarian ecclesiastics: ASV Misc. Arm. XV, no. 1, f. 353r (*VMH*, p. 107, no. CLXXXVII).

[131] Ioan Ferenţ has argued that the Cuman bishopric was always independent of the jurisdiction of the archbishopric of Esztergom. According to him, earlier papal protection to the Cumans was against the Hungarians: Ferenţ, *Kunok és püspökségük*, esp. pp. 140–4.

[132] According to the second version of the *Libellus* (written by Jordan of Saxony in preparation for the canonization of Dominic in 1233–4), Diego bishop of Osma wished to consecrate himself to the conversion of the Cumans and to resign his episcopal obligations, but the pope prevented his resignation. The first version of the *Libellus* has Saracens instead of Cumans, and Peter of Cernai only writes 'pagans' without any specifications. If Diego indeed wanted to convert the

in their conversion.¹³² The Hungarian Dominicans, however, represented themselves as carrying out St Dominic's wishes, leaving no room for ambiguity. The account of their missionary activity, written in 1259 by a Hungarian Dominican, asserts that the friars acted according to the wishes of the saint when they set out to convert the Cumans.¹³³ The Hungarian Dominican province, established after the second General Chapter of the Order of the Preachers in 1221, was the basis of the Dominicans' Cuman mission; the friars travelled from Hungary to the Cumans.¹³⁴

The missions themselves yielded nothing but failure and martyrs at first. When they were finally crowned with success, it was more political necessity than Christian fervour that made the Cumans receptive to Christian teaching. The Cumans needed allies and protection against several enemies.¹³⁵ The ruler of Khwarazm began extending his territory to the detriment of the Cumans in 1208. In 1223, the Mongols defeated the Rus'–Cuman army at the river Kalka; this was the first in a series of encounters that led to the Mongol conquest of Cumania. Conversion, or the promise of conversion, was a powerful gambit when negotiating for political support with Christian powers: in this respect the case of the Cumans resembles that of early medieval Bulgaria and thirteenth- and fourteenth-century Lithuania.¹³⁶ It is impossible to say how many

footnote 132 (cont.)
Cumans, this was probably the origin of Dominic's idea of missions to them. Jordan of Saxony, 'Libellus de principiis ordinis praedicatorum', ed. H. Ch. Scheeben, in *MOPH*, vol. XVI: pp. 34–5 (n. 17); Pierre des Vaux-de-Cernai, *Historia Albigensis*, 3 vols., ed. Pascal Guébin and Ernest Lyon (Paris: Champion, 1926), vol. I: p. 42.

St Dominic's wish to convert the Cumans: testimonies at the canonization process at Bologna, Frater Rodolph (no. 32) and Fr Paul of Venice (no. 43) spoke of plans to convert the Cumans, while William of Montferrat (no. 12) spoke about Dominic's wish to evangelize Prussia (*MOPH*, vol. XVI, pp. 149–50, 162, 133–4). Peter Ferrand, *Legenda Sancti Dominici*, ed. M.-H. Laurent, in *MOPH*, vol. XVI, p. 232 (n. 32) wrote that Dominic wished to convert the Saracens. Kedar, *Crusade and Mission*, p. 120, follows this view. M. H. Vicaire, *Histoire de Saint Dominique*, 2 vols. (Paris: Cerf, 1957), vol. I: pp. 131–2, vol. II: pp. 199–200 on gradual shift of interest to Cumans. See also Altaner, *Dominikanermissionen*, p. 4.

[133] *Commentariolum*, p. 144. Also according to 'Brevissima chronica magistrorum generalium ordinis Praedicatorum', in *Veterum scriptorum et monumentorum historicorum, dogmaticorum, moralium amplissima collectio*, 9 vols., ed. Edmond Martène and Ursin Durand (Paris, 1724–33), vol. VI: cols. 350–1.

[134] The Order sent one of its members, Paulus Hungarus, a canon lawyer, formerly a student at Bologna, to Hungary. Paul and four Dominicans set out in 1221; a Hungarian province was founded and by 1241 there were thirteen Dominican convents in Hungary. Pfeiffer, *Ungarische* (pp. 75–88 on Cuman mission); Miklós Pfeiffer, *A Domonkosrend magyar zárdáinak vázlatos története* (Kassa: Szent Erzsébet Nyomda, 1917); András Harsányi, *A Domonkos-rend Magyarországon a reformáció előtt* (Debrecen, 1938; repr. Budapest: Kairosz, 1999), pp. 19–28 on the Order in Hungary in the thirteenth century.

[135] ASV Reg. Vat. 14, f. 64v (*Reg. Greg. IX*, no. 187; *VMH*, p. 88, no. CLVII). Ferenţ, *Kunok és püspökségük*, pp. 138–41, argued that Asen II of Bulgaria was among these enemies.

[136] Richard E. Sullivan, 'Khan Boris and the Conversion of Bulgaria: A Case Study of the Impact of Christianity on a Barbarian Society', in *Christian Missionary Activity*, no. IV; Jonathan Shepard,

Christian perceptions and attitudes

Cumans were involved in the conversions beginning from 1227. Dominican sources name two Cuman chieftains, Bortz (or Burch) and Membrok, who converted with their families and followers – Membrok supposedly with about a thousand Cumans. A papal letter mentions a multitude of Cuman converts, but ultimately, as the Dominican author commented, the number of converts could be calculated by Jesus Christ alone.[137] Once the Cumans were baptized, Pope Gregory IX wished to ensure that they persisted in their new faith. Conforming to well-established traditions of leniency to neophytes, the pope allowed some flexibility in their treatment.[138] The new converts were likened to children; and 'as milk is preferable for tender infancy to wine', they were not to be discouraged by the strict enforcement of every canonical regulation. The bishop of the Cumans was directed to absolve new converts from such offences as 'sacrilege' and minor cases of violence against priests.[139] A hundred-day indulgence was granted to all those who helped construct churches for the Cumans. The Cumans themselves – this 'new plantation' of faith – were taken under the protection of the Apostolic See.[140]

'Slavs and Bulgars', in *The New Cambridge Medieval History*, vol. II, ed. Rosamond McKitterick (Cambridge: Cambridge University Press, 1995), pp. 228–48, see pp. 238–44; Henry Mayr-Harting, *Two Conversions to Christianity: The Bulgarians and the Anglo-Saxons*, The Stenton Lecture 1993 (Reading: University of Reading, 1994); Rowell, *Lithuania*, chapter VII; Mažeika, 'Bargaining for Baptism'.

[137] ASV Reg. Vat. 14, f. 64r (*Reg. Greg. IX*, no. 186; *VMH*, p. 87, no. CLVI). *Commentariolum*, p. 144; 'Numerum autem eorum, qui ad fidem domini nostri Ihesu Christi de die in diem convertebantur, ipsius solius est computare', p. 145. Albericus of Trois-Fontaines, in *MGH SS*, vol. XXIII: p. 920 mentions 'fifteen thousand' converts.

The names and identities of these Cuman chieftains are debated. Ferenț, *Kunok és püspökségük*, pp. 125–6, thought Burch was the son of Bortz, and Bortz and Membrok were the same person. Richard, *Papauté*, p. 24, and Györffy, 'Kipcsaki kun társadalom', p. 269, argue that they were father and son, based on *Reg. Greg. IX*, no. 139 (*VMH*, pp. 86–7, no. CLIV). In *MOPH*, vol. I: p. 306, Burch is understood to be a corruption of Borics; Györffy proposes that 'Bortz' is Bey-bars; László Rásonyi ('Les anthroponymes comans de Hongrie', *AOASH* 20 (1967): pp. 135–49, see p. 138; and 'Kuman Özel Adlari', *Türk Kültürü Araştırmalari* 3–6 (1966–9): pp. 71–144, see p. 95) identifies the name as Borč or Burč. On the disagreement over whether the baptisms took place in Cumania or Transylvania: István Petrovics, '"Új" források a kunok kereszténységre térítéséről?' *AUSz Acta Historica* 86 (1988): pp. 3–7.

[138] Muldoon, *Popes*, pp. 33, 37–8, 93–4; Lucien Musset, 'La pénétration chrétienne dans l'Europe du Nord et son influence sur la civilisation Scandinave', in *La conversione al cristianesimo nell'Europa dell'alto medioevo*, Settimane di Studio del Centro Italiano di Studi sull'Alto Medioevo 14 (Spoleto, 1967), vol. I: pp. 263–325, see pp. 300–5; Sullivan, *Christian Missionary*, p. 94; Fletcher, *Conversion*, pp. 220–2.

[139] 'quoniam infantia tenera potius est lacte quam vino', ASV Reg. Vat. 14, f. 137v (*Reg. Greg. IX*, no. 345; *VMH*, p. 90, no. CLXI). In 1245, after the fall of the Cuman bishopric, Pope Innocent IV directed Franciscan missionaries that new converts could remain even in those marriages that were not valid according to canon law, and could be absolved from minor sins: *Reg. Inn. IV*, no. 1362; *VMH*, pp. 193–4, no. CCCLXII.

[140] ASV Reg. Vat. 14, ff. 64v, 137v, Reg. Vat. 17, f. 220r (*Reg. Greg. IX*, nos. 187, 344, 2156); *VMH*, p. 88, no. CLVII, p. 91, no. CLXII ('novella plantatio'), p. 131, no. CCXXIV. Makkai, *Milkói (kún) püspökség*, pp. 38–9.

The Cuman bishopric, however, was short-lived. The Mongol attack in 1241 wiped it out (producing many Dominican martyrs), and the subsequent Mongol conquest made its planned re-establishment impossible.[141]

The Mongol invasion of Hungary and occupation of Cumania put an end to Hungarian royal involvement in the conversion of that land. Dominicans and Franciscans continued their missionary efforts in the east, and Hungarian members of the orders joined the ranks of missionaries who endeavoured to convert the Mongols and those Cumans who were integrated into the Golden Horde.[142] Hungarian kings and ecclesiastics, however, now turned their attention towards the interior: their aim was to convert the newly settled Cumans in Hungary.[143]

When the Cumans first moved into Hungary, they were baptized, King Béla IV himself serving as the godfather of the Cuman chieftain Köten.[144] When the Cumans were invited back after the Mongol invasion, missionary activity had to start anew. Baptism and dynastic marriage were linked, with István's marriage to Erzsébet the Cuman. Baptism was of great symbolic importance, but the distance between baptism and 'conversion' proved to be much larger than initially supposed. Scholarship has increasingly come to see conversion as gradual, rather than linked to one event, and far from being a simple exchange of an old faith for the new.[145] In Hungary, a similar process of recognition took place in the thirteenth century. There was a recurrent notion during the period that

---

[141] *Commentariolum*, p. 145: 90 or 190 martyrs. Plans to re-establish the bishopric failed: Makkai, *Milkói (kún) püspökség*, pp. 45–7.

[142] On the role of Hungarian Franciscans in the Mongol missions of the late thirteenth and fourteenth centuries: György Balanyi, 'Adatok a ferencrendiek tatárországi missziós működésének történetéhez', *Katholikus Szemle* 39 (1925): pp. 70–84; János Karácsonyi, *Szent-Ferenc rendjének története Magyarországon 1711-ig*, 2 vols. (Budapest: MTA, 1923–4), vol. I: pp. 37–8; Ligeti, *Magyar nyelv török kapcsolatai*, pp. 416–17. The letter of a Hungarian Franciscan missionary among the Mongols, frater Johanca (1320) in *Archivum Franciscanum Historicum* 17 (1924), pp. 65–70. Johanca described the missionary work the Franciscans were doing among the Mongols and other peoples of the Golden Horde, mentioned other Hungarian missionaries there, and requested more missionaries, especially Germans, Englishmen and Hungarians because, he claimed, they learned the language of the Mongols with greater ease than others. Papal letters on Franciscans from Hungary converting Cumans and Mongols (1278): *Reg. Nic. III*, nos. 182, 183 (*VMH*, p. 337, nos. DLI, DLII). On Dominicans in these missions: Richard, *Papauté*, pp. 66, 71, 77–8, 83, 88–9. On the diminishing importance of Hungary as a 'base' for the missions: Tardy, *Tatárországi*, chapter II.

[143] Prior to the immigration of the Cumans, Cuman slaves in Hungary may already have been converting to Christianity, perhaps even from Islam. In 1232 Archbishop Robert mentioned Cumans in the list of converts and potential converts who should be separated from the Muslim community: ASV Misc. Arm. XV, no. 1, f. 355r (*VMH*, p. 109, no. CLXXXVII). In 1233, Muslims were also accused of buying Cumans who had recently converted or wished to convert, and preventing them from becoming Christians: ASV Reg. Vat. 17, f. 77v (*VMH*, p. 115, no. CXCV; *Reg. Greg. IX*, no. 1498). [144] Rogerius, in *SRH*, vol. II: pp. 559, 567.

[145] Karl F. Morrison, *Understanding Conversion* (Charlottesville and London: University Press of Virginia, 1992), chapter I; Muldoon, *Varieties of Religious Conversion*.

Christian perceptions and attitudes

'pagans' were not hampered by religious belief, which lent itself to the interpretation that once the true faith was shown to them, they would follow it whole-heartedly.[146] In this vein, initially missionary enthusiasm continued, fostered by a belief in the quick voluntary conversion of the Cumans. After a while it gave way to a view that baptism was not sufficient and that 'pagans' were deceitful in their conversion. Eventually, this led to the conviction that conversion should be imposed by force if necessary. Since the Cumans formed a minority within Hungary, such measures could be put into practice.

After the second entry of the Cumans to Hungary, Dominicans continued to engage in missionary activity among them, seeing it as the direct continuation of their work in Cumania; Franciscans also joined in this work.[147] The Dominican account of 1259 described the work of Christianization as still incomplete but proceeding successfully at the time of the writing. Ten brothers were designated (with royal backing) to preach to and baptize the Cumans; the author estimated the number of those already converted by 1259 to be several thousand.[148] What methods did the Dominicans use? Maybe they preached through interpreters as did the Christian missionaries to the Cumans in the vicinity of the Black Sea; maybe they learned the language of the Cumans, as some of the missionaries sent to the Golden Horde learned the language of the Mongols.[149] It is also impossible to know whether the missionaries followed the Cumans – a faint echo of the long journeys with the nomadic Mongols – or obliged them to congregate in certain places, build churches and listen to preaching, a method that was encouraged in Cumania.[150]

---

[146] 'Vita Innocentii IV', in Melloni, *Innocenzo IV*, p. 270; Ricoldo of Montecroce, 'Libellus fratris Ricoldi ad nationes orientales', in Antoine Dondaine, ed., 'Ricoldiana. Notes sur les oeuvres de Ricoldo da Montecroce', *Archivum Fratrum Praedicatorum* 37 (1967): pp. 119–79, see pp. 162–3; R. Lull, cited by Richard, *Papauté*, p. 119; Altaner, *Dominikanermissionen*, p. 165.

[147] Altaner, *Dominikanermissionen*, pp. 149–50; Karácsonyi, *Szent-Ferenc rendjének története*, vol. I: pp. 24–6, 41–2. The Franciscan Berthold of Regensburg perhaps preached to the Cumans and those associating with them in Hungary: *Analecta Franciscana*, vol. II (Quaracchi: Collegio San Bonaventura, 1887), p. 84 (sixteenth-century source); *Berthold von Regensburg. Vollständige Ausgabe Seiner Predigten*, 2 vols., ed. Franz Pfeiffer (Vienna: Braumüller, 1862–80), vol. I: pp. xvi, xxi, xxvii.

[148] *Commentariolum*, pp. 145–6. Accounts of baptism without much instruction in Asia: James D. Ryan, 'Conversion vs. Baptism? European Missionaries in Asia in the Thirteenth and Fourteenth Centuries', in *Varieties of Religious Conversion*, pp. 146–67.

[149] The *Codex Cumanicus* includes sentences in Cuman, to be memorized by the missionaries, one expressing regret that no interpreter is at hand, therefore the missionary cannot deliver a sermon, the other reassuring the faithful that the interpreter is bound by secrecy just as much as the confessor: cited by Györffy, 'A Codex Cumanicus', pp. 234–5. On Dominican methods elsewhere: Altaner, *Dominikanermissionen*, pp. 43, 83, 91–5, 166–7, 229–37.

[150] Johanca's letter, see note 142 above; ASV Reg. Vat. 14, f. 64v (*Reg. Greg. IX*, no. 187; *VMH*, p. 88, no. CLVII).

At the Gate of Christendom

The optimistic expectations of a speedy and full success of the conversions seemed to have been fulfilled in the 1250s. Again, we find papal leniency to the new converts. In 1253, Innocent IV authorized the Hungarian archbishops to absolve newly converted Cumans in cases when they infringed Christian canon law.[151] In 1254, Béla IV reported daily successes to the pope in the conversion of the Cumans and in 1260 he announced that all the Cumans were converted.[152] Far from signalling the end of the process of Cuman conversion, this news heralded the end of the first, optimistic phase of Christian expectations.

In 1264 King Béla turned to the pope for help against the Cumans, whom he represented as a danger to Christianity.[153] The Cumans, whose successful incorporation into the Church he had reported a few years previously, now became enemies. From Pope Urban IV's answer it seems that Béla did not explicitly link his change of opinion to the role of the Cumans in the civil war, but presented it as an independent concern. Béla's change of opinion, however, was a result of this war; the Cumans sided with his son István. The same year Urban IV had expressed his discontent that István used the Cumans against Béla.[154] Béla IV accused the Cumans of only pretending to convert, and reproached them that their baptism did not bring about a true respect for Christianity. He claimed that the Cumans ridiculed the consecrated host and priests, made stables out of churches and continued raping Christian women and killing Christians. As a result of Béla's initiative, Pope Urban IV urged the archbishops of Esztergom and Kalocsa to ensure the baptism of all the Cumans, and to set a date by which all those not yet baptized were to convert.[155] He also ordered the archbishops to compel those already baptized to keep the faith and lead a Christian life. Finally, they were to organize a crusade if necessary against recalcitrant Cumans, so that those

---

[151] ASV Reg. Vat. 22, f. 237r (*Reg. Inn. IV*, no. 6275; *VMH*, p. 217, no. cccx). It is unclear whether the Dominicans converting the Cumans in Hungary had the same extensive powers of dispensation as those granted to Dominicans 'in terris . . . Cumanorum' and other infidels in the same year: *Reg. Inn. IV*, no. 7753 (*VMH*, pp. 223–4, no. ccccxxv). Although the 'in Cumanie' may be understood to mean missions in the Cuman territories now under Mongol rule, the letter was addressed to Hungarian archbishops which suggests the pope meant the Cumans living in Hungary. There may also have been some confusion at the papal curia concerning the extent of the mission. Also see *Reg. Inn. IV*, no. 6273.

[152] ASV AA Arm. I-XVIII-608 (*VMH*, p. 233, no. ccccxlii). *CD*, vol. iv, pt. 3: pp. 30–3 (*RA*, no. 1241): 'Cumani . . . accedentes ad veram lucem fidei orthodoxae, in sacro fonte lavacri baptismatis, ad quod universi indifferenter confluxerunt, aliquo non excepto, ipsius fidei charactere insigniri, et romanae Ecclesiae . . . incorporari salubriter meruerunt' (p. 31).

[153] Béla sent emissaries to the pope, with complaints known from the papal response: ASV Reg. Vat. 29, f. 337v (*Reg. Urb. IV*, no. 2769; *VMH*, pp. 269–70, no. ccccxciii).

[154] ASV Reg. Vat. 29, f. 100r (*Reg. Urb. IV*, no. 1243; *VMH*, p. 265, no. ccccLxxxv), dated 2 February 1264; see chapter 5, pp. 167–8.

[155] ASV Reg. Vat. 29, f. 337v (*Reg. Urb. IV*, no. 2769; *VMH*, pp. 269–70, no. ccccxciii), dated 14 July 1264.

Christian perceptions and attitudes

baptized would obey Christian precepts, and those refusing baptism would be expelled.

The change from almost boundless optimism in the quick success of Christianization to its opposite – a view that even those who accepted baptism only pretended to convert – highlights more than the political opportunism of King Béla. It also reflects the fundamental differences between Christian and Cuman perceptions of Christianization. Initially, the fact of conversion (baptism) was taken by king, missionaries and ecclesiastics alike as a sign of the end of the battle for the souls of the Cumans. Therefore, the continued 'un-Christian' behaviour of the converted Cumans seemed to signal an insincerity of conversion.[156] The Cumans, however, as was characteristic of steppe people, easily integrated new beliefs but did not commit themselves to one religion exclusively. Once this 'treacherous' behaviour became the centre of attention, the emphasis shifted to enforcing conversion and conformity to Christian norms, relying on that long-time complement to missionary persuasion, the force of arms. This was also urged by clerics from neighbouring countries which experienced military confrontations with Hungary; they explained Cuman violence by the 'paganism' of the perpetrators, and used it as leverage for papal backing (see above, pp. 202–3).

By 1279 when the papal legate Philip imposed the Cuman articles on the king, there was no question about even a temporary choice between conversion and Cuman religious practices. The text stipulated that each and every Cuman be baptized, cease to observe all pagan customs and rituals, and adopt the Christian way of life. Although this was presented as the 'wish' of the Cumans themselves, several provisions were included to ensure that they complied. The legate was to appoint and send suitable investigators regularly to enquire into the affairs of each kin group, its servants included; both royal and ecclesiastical punishment was to follow non-compliance with the regulations.[157] Moreover, the king was to keep Cumans as hostages to ensure cooperation. Finally, the text explicitly stated that the Cumans were to be forced to submit if necessary. The king promised that if the Cumans were not to be induced by persuasion to observe and implement all of the articles, he would wage war against them in order to force them to obey. These regulations aimed at the conversion of all the Cumans with the threat of force.[158] The complex

---

[156] 'qui ad baptismale lavacrum pervenerunt, fidem dampnabiliter respuunt, quam in sacramento huiusmodi fallaciter susceperunt': *ibid.*

[157] ASV AA Arm. I-XVIII-595 (*VMH*, pp. 339–41): 'universi Comani et singuli cuiuscumque etatis et sexus, qui nondum sunt baptisati, volunt et desiderant recipere baptismatis sacramentum'.

[158] *Ibid.*, 'Quod si prefatos Comanos ad predicta et singula observanda et implenda exhortacionibus, persuasionibus, racionibus et precibus forsitan inducere non possumus, recepimus, promisimus et iuravimus, quod . . . contra dictos Comanos indicemus et faciemus exercitum generalem . . . ad

procedure of Cuman integration was presented in religious terms, and the motivation as a wish to 'enlarge the tents of the faith of the Lord'.[159] The stipulations can be divided into two main groups: one addressing strictly religious issues, and the other attempting to change the Cuman way of life. The first required baptism, obedience to the Church, and giving up pagan practices; the second called for permanent settlement in houses, refraining from killing within the kingdom, and relinquishing ecclesiastical and other lands and buildings occupied by Cumans. Thus Christianization was to include the enforced acceptance of social norms. A papal letter referred to one alleviation only: Cumans were to be allowed to retain their traditional hairstyles.[160]

That at least some continued to see the process of voluntary conversion as a viable alternative is shown in a miracle story. In one of her posthumous miracles, Margit of Hungary (d. 1270) procured the conversion of a 'pagan' Cuman, Zeicze.[161] When he heard Christians talk about the miracles of Margit, he ridiculed them and said that if Margit could indeed work miracles, she should restore the sight of his horse, which had been blind in one eye for three years. 'I would believe in your God, would receive your faith and will be baptized with my whole family.'[162] The miracle was immediately accomplished and the Cuman kept his word. The story assumes daily interaction between Christians and unbaptized Cumans, portraying the latter as able to communicate with the Hungarian population, presumably in the vernacular. It throws light on the expectation that the head of the family would decide about the conversion of the whole family. It is also a testimony that the existence of unbaptized Cumans was taken for granted in the late thirteenth century; the writer described Zeicze as a well-known man. Peaceful everyday interaction between an unbaptized Cuman and his Christian neighbours

---

footnote 158 (cont.)
  compellendum eos per dictum exercitum et alios quolibet utiles modos brachio regie potestatis ad recipienda, facienda, ac etiam observanda omnia et singula supradicta.'

[159] Ibid.: 'cupientes toto mentis annisu tentoria fidei dominice ampliare'.

[160] ASV Reg. Vat. 39, f. 219r (Reg. Nic. III, no. 607; VMH, p. 342, no. DLVII): 'Cumanorum nuntii . . . recepissent . . . articulos, uno excepto videlicet de barbis radendis et crinibus breviandis.'

[161] Princess Margaret was offered as an oblate when she was a child, became a Dominican nun, refused to leave the convent despite parental pressure and lived an ascetic life. Testimonies for canonization were written down in 1276, and miracles were collected, but she was canonized only in 1943. Elemér Mályusz, 'Árpádházi Boldog Margit', in Domanovszky, Károlyi Emlékkönyv, pp. 341–84; Tibor Klaniczay and Gábor Klaniczay, Szent Margit legendái és stigmái (Budapest: Argumentum Kiadó, 1994). The miracle: Nándor Knauz, A nápolyi Margitlegenda (Esztergom, 1868), pp. 140–1, reprinted in Gombos, Catalogus, vol. III: pp. 2526–7. This is a version of the legend written in 1340 on the basis of the original depositions in 1276. In the depositions, the account of the miracle is now lost: Monumenta Romana, vol. I: p. cxxx.

[162] 'credam in Deum vestrum, fidem vestram recipiam et cum tota familia mea babtizabor', Knauz, Nápolyi, p. 141; Gombos, Catalogus, vol. III: p. 2527.

Christian perceptions and attitudes

was represented as not miraculous at all.[163] Papal–royal correspondence about the 'Cuman problem' shows the slow process of Christianization. In the early fourteenth century Pope John XXII still exhorted the prelates not to collect tithes too soon from recent converts.[164] In 1399 the Franciscans received papal authorization to carry out pastoral duties among the Cumans who 'for the most part' have converted.[165]

Integration through conversion was the main aim of Christian policies towards the Cumans, although its forms changed from an optimistic expectation of quick voluntary conversion to more interventionist and aggressive methods. Jews did not become targets for similar missionary activity. Individual initiatives did lead to conversions, but there was no systematic effort to assimilate them. After a brief period of legislation to ensure the conversion of the Muslim population, there was little interest in converting Muslims during most of the twelfth and thirteenth centuries. At the same time, papal intervention increasingly sought to impose clear-cut guidelines: Jews and Muslims were to be separated from Christians and 'pagans' either converted, or, if they stubbornly resisted, expelled.

Christian perceptions and attitudes ranged from the matter-of-fact to fear and even an ambivalent attraction. Fear of non-Christians moved between reality and stereotype. Royal apprehension about Muslim or Cuman treachery was linked to their military potential. In the case of the Cumans, their revolt proved that the fears were not groundless. Anxiety and hostility evoked by imagined threats – such as a Cuman–Mongol alliance or the desecration of the host by Jews – which led to Christian violence against non-Christians, may have been less prevalent in thirteenth-century Hungary than in western areas of Europe, but they were by no means absent. The most remarkable feature of Christian attitudes was the ambivalence towards the Cumans. There were great expectations of their conversion and integration; yet they were also negatively stereotyped as the enemy. Moreover, while the Cumans were demonized, they also came to stand for a more abstract type: the 'eastern nomad', and thus the ancestors of the Hungarians.

---

[163] Zeicze was 'inter christianos Ungarie satis notus': Knauz, *Nápolyi*, p. 140; Gombos, *Catalogus*, vol. III: p. 2526.
[164] *Reg. Ioh. XXII*, no. 41127; *VMH*, pp. 519–20, no. DCCCII (1328).
[165] On fourteenth-century developments: *JK*, vol. II: pp. 35, 164–6; Karácsonyi, *Szent-Ferenc rendjének története*, vol. I: pp. 41–2. A papal letter of 1351 (*VMH*, p. 797, no. MCCXVIII) and a royal charter of 1354 (*JK*, vol. III: p. 489) are still concerned with the Christianization of the Cumans. In 1364 Urban V demanded that the Cumans pay tithes: *VMH*, pp. 59–60, no. CVIII. A papal letter of 1399 (*JK*, vol. III: pp. 531–4; *CD*, vol. X, pt. 2: pp. 670–5) describes the difficulties of conversion in the past, and adds: 'nationes ipsae iam ex per magna parte ad fidem Catholicam sunt conuersae' (pp. 532, 672).

Chapter 7

NON-CHRISTIAN COMMUNITIES: CONTINUITY, TRANSFORMATION, CONVERSION AND ASSIMILATION

The coexistence of different groups entails interaction. Interaction can lead to widely different results: clashes, assimilation, changes in the customs of one or both sides, and the subjugation or even extermination of one of the groups. Among the possible outcomes are various forms of acculturation, from the incorporation of selected cultural (including religious) practices and beliefs to the adoption of a whole cultural–religious system. Such influences can be mutual, affecting both sides, or unidirectional, where elements of the dominant culture are adopted by the dominated one. This process can take place peacefully or by violent means. Acculturation can result in syncretism, in the reinterpretation of adopted elements, in the coexistence of two systems, or the replacement of one system by another.[1] This chapter analyses these trends in relation to the three non-Christian groups of Hungary.

An explanation of the sustained existence or assimilation of a group requires the analysis of both Christian and non-Christian attitudes. Declared Christian policies aiming at exclusion or conversion, the subject of previous chapters, were only part of the forces at play. The context of living in a Christian society, the cohesion of non-Christian communities, the degree and means of their resistance all contributed to the preservation or assimilation of these groups. The Jews, Muslims and Cumans of Hungary constituted a small minority within a Christian world. There

---

[1] Urs Bitterli, *Die 'Wilden' und die 'Zivilisierten': Grundzüge einer Geistes- und Kulturgeschichte der europäisch-überseeischen Begegnung* (Munich: Beck, 1976); Michel Meslin, 'Rencontres des religions et acculturation', in *Rencontres de Religions. Actes du Colloque du Collège des Irlandais tenu sous les auspices de l'Académie Royale Irlandaise*, ed. Proinsias Mac Cana and Michel Meslin (Paris: Les Belles Lettres, 1986), pp. 15–24; Thomas F. Glick and Oriol Pi-Sunyer, 'Acculturation as an Explanatory Concept in Spanish History', *Comparative Studies in Society and History* 11 (1969): pp. 136–54; MacKay, *Spain*, pp. 79–94; Jerry H. Bentley, *Old World Encounters: Cross-Cultural Contacts and Exchanges in Pre-Modern Times* (Oxford: Oxford University Press, 1993); Ivan G. Marcus, *Rituals of Childhood: Jewish Acculturation in Medieval Europe* (New Haven and London: Yale University Press, 1996), pp. 8–13.

Non-Christian communities

was a shared space of life and daily activities between Christians and non-Christians. Jews often lived in the walled city centres, and Christians lived among Jews even in areas called Jewish 'quarter' or 'street'.[2] 'Pagan' Cumans could listen to stories about Christian saints from their neighbours. Muslims took cases of litigation against Christians to be decided by ordeal. Non-Christian acculturation, either in the form of borrowing cultural elements such as names, architectural styles or village patterns, or even ultimately the adoption of Christianity, was often the result of continuous interaction. In this process, the structure of the non-Christian communities, the roles they filled in Hungarian society, and their ties to coreligionists abroad all played a role in the shaping of their response to the Christian environment. These non-Christian responses – continuity, transformation and assimilation – are the subject of this chapter. Non-Christian influence on Christians is almost impossible to trace: very few sources show the process and forms of Christian borrowing and acculturation.

THE JEWS

Jewish communities survived in Hungary throughout the Middle Ages, though waves of immigrants and perhaps the brief expulsion in the 1350s changed the composition and location of many communities.[3] Later medieval Jews themselves emphasized continuity. Their successful efforts to have the privileges of Béla IV (1251) renewed from 1396 (renewals were granted in 1396, 1406, 1422, 1431, 1436, 1438, 1453, 1464, 1493) were based on the assumption that Jewish communities of the fifteenth century were descendants of the thirteenth-century community, inheriting their privileges. What accounts for the survival of Jewish life in Hungary throughout the Middle Ages, and is 'continuity' an adequate description for the non-assimilation of Hungary's Jewish population?

Jewish religious life, including contacts with Jews in other areas, is the first element of the answer. The sources for the religious life of Jews in Hungary are the *responsa*, rabbinical decisions concerning problems raised

---

[2] Gerevich, *Towns*, pp. 29, 32, 100. Canons had houses in the Jewish section of Esztergom: MOL DF 236350 (*MES*, vol. II: p. 360, no. 358; this part of the text also in *MZsO*, vol. V, pt. 1: no. 9, p. 12; *RA*, no. 3986); Christian houses stood among Jewish ones on the 'Jewish street' of Sopron in the late Middle Ages: Dávid, *Soproni*, pp. 9, 14–23. The current excavations of the Jewish street of thirteenth-century Buda have unearthed a Christian pilgrim's badge. I am grateful to András Végh for communicating to me the results of excavations prior to the publication of the material.

[3] Róbert Dán, 'Mikor űzte ki I. Lajos a zsidókat?' *Tanulmányok Budapest Múltjából*, 24, A Budapesti Történeti Múzeum Évkönyve 1991, pp. 9–15. Previously the dislocation of the Jewish street was thought to have been the result of the short-lived expulsion and subsequent resettlement of the Jews (Zolnay, *Buda*, pp. 8–14), but excavations currently under way suggest it may have been linked to the building of a church under the reign of King Zsigmond (Sigismond).

At the Gate of Christendom

by these communities, and archaeological finds. Traditional interpretations of the texts have pointed to signs of lax religious observance. Reconsidering texts and contexts often yields different results. They show, moreover, the religious and legal networks that tied Hungary's Jews to their coreligionists. The earliest *responsa* concerning Hungary survive from the eleventh century.[4] They reveal how trade relations created not only business dealings but a network of access to religious authorities. The Jews mentioned in the three earliest texts, decisions by Rabbi Yehudah ha-Kohen, traded between Hungary and Mainz; they took their dispute before a rabbi in Mainz. There is no consensus as to whether these were 'German' Jews who went to Hungary temporarily, or 'Hungarian' Jews.[5] One of the Jewish litigants is described as travelling on business in the service of the Hungarian queen, as well as interceding with her concerning money-minting. The phrase 'in the land of Hagar' that appears in this text is proof neither of the place of origin nor place of residence of the Jewish litigants.[6] Rather than providing an answer to the 'national origin' of the Jewish merchants, the *responsa* are significant for showing regular contact and mobility between the two areas (Mainz and Hungary): clearly these Jewish merchants spent time in both.

Another *responsum* from the late eleventh century throws more light on the condition of Hungarian Jewish communities as well as on the ties that bound them to coreligionists abroad.[7] Two Jews from Regensburg were travelling through Hungary, returning from Rus' (Galicia). On a Friday evening, one of the wheels of their wagon broke, and they had to stop to repair it. When they finally reached the nearest community, Esztergom, the Jews were already coming out of the synagogue. The travellers were not greeted, nor allowed to enter the synagogue the following day, for having broken the Sabbath. On the following Sunday, the community gathered to listen to the punishment decreed by two rabbis, who were not locals, but were probably travelling through the country.[8] This punish-

---

[4] They were included in Rabbi Yehudah ha-Kohen's (d. Mainz *c.* 1070) *Sefer HaDinim*, parts of which were incorporated into an edition of Meir of Rothenburg's *responsa*: Agus, *Rabbi Meir of Rothenburg*, p. 73; Kupfer and Lewicki, *Źródła*, pp. 38–40. Lewicki, 'Sources hébraïques', p. 236. These texts are also on the *responsa* database on CD-Rom developed at the Bar-Ilan University. Hungarian tr. Kohn, *Héber*, pp. 45–8; Eng. tr. Agus, *Urban Civilization*, pp. 88–93, 232–5.

[5] German: Kohn, *Héber*, p. 48, based on the wording 'Ruben and Simon were in the land of Hagar [Hungary]':

ראובן ושמעון היו בארץ הגר

Hungarian: Agus, *Heroic Age*, pp. 103, 249.

[6] Kupfer and Lewicki, *Źródła*, pp. 38–9, 59; Kohn, *Héber*, pp. 45–46. בארץ הגר.

[7] Kupfer and Lewicki, *Źródła*, p. 65; Kohn, *Zsidók*, pp. 405–8 (ed. and tr.), pp. 359–66 (analysis). On the correct dating: Scheiber, *Héber kódexmaradványok*, p. 104.

[8] Scheiber, *Jewish Inscriptions*, p. 81; Kohn, *Zsidók*, pp. 360–1, argued that there was a scribal error in the text, and it was only one rabbi who sat in judgement.

ment was threefold, comprised of whipping, fasting and monetary payment. In the text, the community's behaviour toward the merchants is justified by the claim that it was necessary in order to prevent members of the community from following a bad example, and to avoid a more serious deterioration of the faith. The traditional explanation, based on this statement, is that the Hungarian Jews were very lax in their observance, and the harsh punishment was intended to deter them from infractions of the religious laws.[9] This interpretation is contradicted by the text itself, which says that the Jews of Esztergom observed the Sabbath and were outraged at the foreigners' behaviour. It was the community, not the rabbis, who initiated the condemnation of the merchants from Regensburg. The statement described above, rather than a condemnation of the community's standards, was more likely a moral warning, a didactic device both for the Jews at the time and later readers; *responsa* were written down and collected to serve later generations, not just the immediate participants of a case. The community turned to foreign rabbis for the solution of this case. Scheiber drew the conclusion from this that 'there was no rabbi in Hungary at that time'.[10] Although it is possible that there was no rabbi in Esztergom at the time, or that he was temporarily absent, many other reasons could have led to the involvement of foreign rabbis. The local rabbi may have referred the case to them; it is even possible that, while the names of the foreign rabbis were included in the text of the decision, that of the local one was left out, because the former were more prestigious or better known, at least to the final editor of the *responsum*. (The *responsum* survives in the thirteenth-century collection of a Roman Jewish compiler, and not in manuscripts related to Hungary.[11])

A later text complains about the level of religious life of the Jews in Hungary. According to Rabbi Eliezer ben Isaac, writing to a rabbi in Paris at the end of the twelfth century, most Jewish communities in Hungary, as well as in Poland and Rus', were so poor that they could not hire religious scholars. They had to make do with any intelligent man to be their cantor, rabbi and the teacher of their children, who then supplemented his meagre wages with donations during various feasts.[12] Taking the author's background into consideration, it is clear that he probably had access to quite accurate information about the communities he described. Eliezer was born in Bohemia and lived in Speier. He was,

---

[9] Kohn, *Zsidók*, pp. 364–5.
[10] Scheiber, *Jewish Inscriptions*, p. 81. Professional rabbis did not exist even in many large communities in German areas: Agus, *Heroic Age*, pp. 254–7.
[11] In the collection of Abraham of Rome: Lewicki, 'Sources hébraïques', p. 237; Kohn, *Zsidók*, p. 359.
[12] Kupfer and Lewicki, *Źródła*, p. 159; Kohn, *Héber*, p. 55. Rabbi Eliezer wrote this letter around 1190. See the remarks of Weinreich, *History of the Yiddish Language*, p. 90.

however, not an unbiased observer. Rabbi Eliezer's aim was to convince his correspondent of the necessity of keeping the custom of donations; he argued that by abolishing them these communities would remain without religious study, prayer or rabbi. Therefore the information he provides should not be taken as a reflection on the general decline of religious knowledge. Indeed, Rashi mentioned the opinion of a Jew from Hungary on the question of the name of Sabbath Ha-Gadol; Isaac ben Moses Or Zarua sent an answer to a certain Jacob ben Isaac, who was perhaps living in Hungary, and described him as a scholar.[13] Clearly there were some learned men in the community. Moreover, Rashi's Jewish informant from Hungary described how the Jewish community stayed late in the synagogue on the Sabbath before Passover to discuss issues related to the festival, showing their interest in religious matters.[14]

Other texts contribute to the assessment of the standards of Jewish religious practice in Hungary. A divorce letter was identified in twelfth-century France as having been written in Hungary because, among other characteristic traits, it was written in an easy, and rather careless Hebrew.[15] The thirteenth-century *responsa* of Rabbi Isaac provide varied information about the religious observance of Hungarian Jews. The communities of Buda and Esztergom were concerned about the possibility of using hot springs for the purposes of a *mikvah* (ritual bath).[16] The *Or Zaru'a* also cites the case of a man in voluntary exile for inadvertently killing a child, who can lead prayers in the community of Esztergom after having repented, as an example of the correct attitude in such circumstances.[17] The validity of an engagement in Nyitra was the topic of another *responsum*; the girl refused to accept a belt and ring sent by her husband-to-be and his mother with a messenger from Ureg. Although these were accepted by another woman in her name and the girl was thereafter treated as betrothed, both her refusal and the lack of legal authorization for a third party to act in the name of the fiancé rendered the engagement invalid.[18] There was a litigation over a slave-girl, and one text

---

[13] H. L. Ehrenreich, ed., *Sepher Ha-Pardes and Liturgical and Ritual Work, Attributed to Rashi* (Deva: bi-Defus ha-Ahim Kattsburg, 1924), p. שמו (p. 343); Kohn, *Héber*, p. 154. Wellesz, 'Esztergomi zsidók', p. 150; Isaac ben Moses, *Sefer Or Zaru'a*, vol. 1: p. 40. Jacob may have been Jacob ben Isaac ha-Laban of Prague who moved to Hungary: Avneri *et al.*, *Germania Judaica*, vol. 1: pp. 38, 405. That the case concerns Esztergom has been argued by Wellesz and accepted in *Germania Judaica*, vol. 1: p. 406.
[14] Ehrenreich, *Sepher Ha-Pardes*, p. שמו (p. 343).
[15] Spitzer, 'Héber', no. 14.
[16] On this and the following *responsa* of R. Isaac: Lewicki, 'Sources hébraïques', p. 140. Kupfer and Lewicki, *Źródła*, p. 212; Spitzer, 'Héber', no. 16a; Isaac ben Moses, *Sefer Or Zaru'a*, vol. 1: p. 101.
[17] Spitzer, 'Héber', no. 16b (only a short section of the text); Isaac ben Moses, *Sefer Or Zaru'a*, vol. 1: p. 40.
[18] Spitzer, 'Héber', no. 16c and Kupfer and Lewicki, *Źródła*, p. 214 contain only part of the text; Isaac ben Moses, *Sefer Or Zaru'a*, vol. 1: p. 226.

Non-Christian communities

mentioned that salted fish exported from Hungary was *kasher*.[19] The descriptions are usually succinct, but the rabbis, in their decisions, never indicated that Hungary's Jews deliberately departed from Jewish religious tenets or disregarded religious laws. At the same time, no famous rabbi or halakhist came from Hungary during this period, and Hebrew manuscripts produced in Hungary are known only from the fourteenth or later centuries.[20] No centres of Jewish scholarship existed in Hungary comparable with those that flourished in thirteenth-century German and French areas.[21] Most Jews in the Hungarian kingdom, though observant, did not attain high standards of learning; they lacked the education and/or means to become scholars.

Jewish observance left material, as well as textual, traces. Synagogues, cemeteries, and thirteenth-century gravestones attest to the performance of religious duties. The earliest synagogue whose remains survive today is that of Sopron built in the early 1300s.[22] It was discovered in 1967, excavated and reconstructed, revealing that the synagogue included a prayer hall for women, a ritual bath and a hospice, according to Jewish custom. The synagogue was built in thirteenth-century Gothic style, incorporating some of the latest stylistic developments, and shows south German influence.[23] A cornerstone, with what are probably the names of the founders, was discovered, but the now fragmentary inscription does not yield enough information to allow the identification of the founders. Synagogues in Esztergom and Buda are also mentioned in thirteenth-century texts.[24]

Cemeteries are recorded from Buda, Vasvár and Esztergom (though the earliest reference to the last is from the early fourteenth century).[25] Gravestones provide information about naming and dating practices as

---

[19] Spitzer, 'Héber', no. 16d; Kupfer and Lewicki, *Źródła*, p. 213; Isaac ben Moses, *Sefer Or Zaru'a*, vol. I: p. 223. Analysed by Wellesz, 'Izsák b. Mózes Ór Zarua és az üreghi zsidók'. See also *Germania Judaica*, vol. I: p. 406. Fish: Kupfer and Lewicki, *Źródła*, p. 212; Isaac ben Moses, *Sefer Or Zaru'a*, vol. I: p. 141.

[20] There is an exception, a Jewish scholar who immigrated from France with his family at the end of the eleventh century: Scheiber, *Héber kódexmaradványok*, p. 147. According to Kohn, *Zsidók*, pp. 149, 383, Yehuda (Liebermann), a Jewish scholar who emigrated from Germany to Hungary, lived in Pozsony between 1250 and 1275. This dating has been proven wrong; Yehuda lived in the late fifteenth century: Miksa Pollák, *A zsidók Bécsujhelyen: Tanulmány a zsidók történetéhez Alsó-Ausztriában és Magyarországon* (Budapest: Athenaeum, 1892), p. 75. On Hebrew manuscripts: Scheiber, *Héber kódexmaradványok*, already listing a late eleventh-century 'Hebrew psalter' (p. 95) in the possession of a Hungarian monastery. This, however, need not have been a product of Hungarian Jews. On fourteenth-century fragments: Scheiber, 'Recent additions', pp. 157–8. Baron, *Social*, vol. X: p. 30.

[21] Stow, *Alienated Minority*, pp. 147–50.

[22] Scheiber, *Jewish Inscriptions*, pp. 87–93; Dávid, *Soproni*. Both include photographs.

[23] Dávid, *Soproni*, pp. 67–9, 75–81.

[24] *Ibid.*, pp. 34, 102; Scheiber, *Jewish Inscriptions*, pp. 81–7.

[25] Scheiber, *Jewish Inscriptions*, pp. 103–6.

well as about the Hebrew script used. No complete gravestones survive from the thirteenth century; of the existing pieces, two have the dates intact. The gravestone inscriptions were transcribed, translated and analysed by Sándor Scheiber.[26] The inscriptions are in Hebrew, but with grammatical mistakes. This is another indication that Jews living in Hungary knew the language of religion and ritual, but lacked a sophisticated and thorough knowledge. Gravestone inscriptions show that Jewish names were also recorded according to custom, giving the name of the deceased as well as that of the father. The year of death, moreover, was calculated according to the millennia; that is, Hungarian Jews did not adopt the way of calculating time from their Christian neighbours, but kept – at least for ritual purposes – their own, based on the time of the Creation.

In summary, Hungarian Jewry throughout the Árpád age belonged to the Slavic–Germanic Jewish cultural group that by the late Middle Ages merged as the Ashkenazim.[27] The existing evidence concerning their religious practices shows that the halakhic rules were observed, or advice was sought in case of questions. Issues that appear in *responsa* resemble those raised by communities in German or French areas.[28] The recorded answers do not condemn the Jewish communities of Hungary for a lack of observance. Certain mistakes were committed, but these concerned especially Hebrew, indicating not so much negligence but the low level of written culture.

Ties between the Jews of Hungary and their coreligionists abroad contributed to the formation and survival of the Jewish communities of Hungary. The influx of Austrian, Czech and other Jews, which continued throughout the Middle Ages, meant a growth in numbers, as well as a steady means of contact. Even when no new immigrants arrived, individuals provided a link, although not a constant or uniform one, with many other communities. Jewish merchants, financiers and others travelled to and from Hungary. Jews from Hungary travelled most frequently to German and Slav areas, where they had contacts with local Jewish communities.[29] One such encounter is alluded to by Rashi, who, around 1090, probably in one of the German cities, met a Jew from Hungary, an important person in the community (קָצִין) who talked to him about relig-

---

[26] *Ibid.*, pp. 110–55 (with photographs).
[27] Büchler, *Zsidók*, p. 24. In the fifteenth century Spanish Jews also settled in Hungary: András Kubinyi, 'Spanyol zsidók a középkori Budán', in *MZsO*, vol. XII: pp. 19–26; Kubinyi, 'Magyarországi zsidóság', p. 23.
[28] E.g. Agus, *Rabbi Meir of Rothenburg*.
[29] On the contacts between travelling Jewish merchants and local Jewish communities, see Weinreich, *History of the Yiddish Language*, pp. 51, 83, 333. On such contacts in the Mediterranean, see Goitein, *Mediterranean Society*, vol. I: p. 350; vol. II: pp. 135–6.

Non-Christian communities

ious issues.³⁰ Foreign rabbis also travelled through Hungary occasionally, but trade routes probably provided a more established means of contact. Accounts of Jewish visitors to Hungary appear in rabbinical *responsa*, and also on the inscription of an Austrian tombstone.³¹ One of the elders of a Jewish community in Carinthia was murdered while he was staying in Hungary in 1130. The circumstances of the case are unknown, but he was not a permanent settler in Hungary, because his body was taken back to his home and buried there. Merchants, settlers and rabbis maintained contacts between Jewish communities in Hungary and those in Austrian, German and Slav territories, facilitating the flow of information, advice and rabbinical decisions.

To what extent were Jews in Hungary influenced by the Christian community around them? Several indicators provide the answer, such as the adoption of local customs, dress codes and naming patterns, the structure of the Jewish communities, and, finally, the importance of conversion. We do not have sufficient information about Jewish attitudes to the Christian inhabitants of the kingdom. One of the Jewish litigants from Hungary is quoted in a *responsum* as calling Christians 'star- and constellation-worshippers', a somewhat denigrating term describing those who do not believe in God.³²

The possibilities provided by the surrounding Christian society influenced the formation of the Jewish elite. This elite consisted of those, mostly Austrian (and at least in Sopron, southern German³³), Jews who settled more or less permanently in Hungary and became lessees of the treasury. They had large estates where they may have stayed for periods of time, and presumably they had to spend some of their time at the royal court as well as travelling. As several of these men moved back and forth between Austria and Hungary, and some finally went back to Austria, it is possible that their ties with local Austrian communities were stronger than those linking them with Hungarian ones. Information on the life and organization of Jewish communities in Hungary is scarce. Jewish long-distance merchants must have been among the rich members of the community. One *responsum* mentions Jews having Jewish domestic

---

[30] Ehrenreich, *Sepher Ha-Pardes*, p. שמו (p. 343); Kohn, *Héber*, pp. 49–50, 153–4.
[31] Scheiber, *Jewish Inscriptions*, pp. 107–10.
[32] עבו"ם Spitzer, 'Héber', no. 16d; Kupfer and Lewicki, *Źródła*, p. 213. The original and modern Hebrew meaning of the word is 'pagans'. It was not the only term applied to Christians by Jews; some of the other designations were much more denigrating: see Goitein, *Mediterranean Society*, vol. II: p. 278; Mikel de Epalza, *Jésus otage: Juifs, Chrétiens et Musulmans en Espagne (VI–XVII siècles)* (Paris: Cerf, 1987), pp. 63–128 (as idol worshippers: p. 106); Anna Sapir Abulafia, 'Invectives Against Christianity in the Hebrew Chronicles of the First Crusade', in *Christians and Jews in Dispute* (Aldershot: Ashgate, 1998), no. XVIII.
[33] On the basis of the style of the synagogue, Dávid suggests that those who commissioned the building (certainly among the elite of the community) had southern German origins: *Soproni*, p. 80.

231

slaves.[34] The existence of the synagogue in Sopron, described above, also contradicts the notion that Hungarian Jewish communities were impoverished, indicating that at least certain members of the community were rich enough to pay for the construction of a Gothic synagogue.[35] But if the report of Rabbi Eliezer is to be trusted, other Jews in Hungary were poor. What their means of subsistence was, whether tilling the soil or selling merchandise locally, as in Poland, cannot be known.[36] If there was indeed a communal structure of a wealthy elite and poorer members in menial occupations, this would reflect a pattern prevalent in the early Middle Ages among Jewish communities in German lands.[37] Living in a Christian kingdom provided possibilities especially for the elite, which in turn had consequences within the Jewish communities.

Christian influences also affected everyday life. Building styles, as elsewhere in Europe, were adopted from local (in this case Christian) architecture. The Gothic window of the synagogue in Sopron corresponds to that of the local Franciscan monastery, and other parallels have been noted between the synagogue and Christian buildings.[38] Current excavations of the thirteenth-century Jewish street in Buda have revealed that the ground-plan of the houses corresponded to those of Christian buildings. This is also true for the pottery that was discovered there.[39] Whether Jewish attire resembled that of local Christians remains an open question. No pictorial representation of Jews from the period survives from Hungary, nor any description of their costume. They may have worn a distinctive type of hat as in German areas, but there is no reference to it prior to the fifteenth century.[40] Then the *Judenhut*, Jewish hat, and distinctive clothing were prescribed by German urban law in Hungary.[41]

The analysis of naming patterns is a well-known method of probing religious and cultural influences. Of the medieval Jewish names from

---

[34] Kupfer and Lewicki, *Źródła*, p. 213; Spitzer, 'Héber', no. 16d.
[35] Dávid, *Soproni*, pp. 34, 102; Scheiber, *Jewish Inscriptions*, p. 87.
[36] Weinryb, *Jews of Poland*, chapter III. On poverty of Jewish communities, see also Stow, *Alienated Minority*, p. 90.   [37] Stow, *Alienated Minority*, pp. 90, 164–72.
[38] Dávid, *Soproni*, pp. 80–1. Cf. 'Synagogue', *Encyclopaedia Judaica*, vol. xv: cols. 579–629; Jerrilynn D. Dodds, 'Mudejar Tradition and the Synagogues of Medieval Spain: Cultural Identity and Cultural Hegemony', in *Convivencia: Jews, Muslims, and Christians in Medieval Spain*, ed. Vivian B. Mann, Thomas F. Glick and Jerrilynn D. Dodds (New York: George Braziller, 1992), pp. 113–31.
[39] I thank András Végh and Károly Magyar for this information.
[40] Thérèse and Mendel Metzger, *Jewish Life in the Middle Ages* (Secaucus, N.J.: Chartwell Books, 1982), pp. 115–16; Alfred Rubens, *A History of Jewish Costume*, 2nd edn (London: Vallentine, Mitchell, 1973), pp. 97, 106–7; Berend, 'Medieval Patterns', p. 160.
[41] *MZsO*, vol. I: pp. 161–2, no. 122, p. 164, no. 127, from the German lawbook of Buda (1421). The hat and distinctive clothing are mentioned several times in the sixteenth century: *ibid.*, p. 289, no. 240 (1514), pp. 306–7, no. 257 (1520, the king prohibits anyone from forcing the Jews of Pozsony to wear Jewish clothing), pp. 308–9, no. 259 (only the king is to determine Jewish clothing).

Non-Christian communities

Hungary, many are German in origin, others are biblical; Farkas, meaning wolf in Hungarian, and Peter also appear.[42] Farkas may be a translation from German or Yiddish, although it was a common Hungarian name as well.[43] Peter appears on a tombstone in Hebrew as פטר. The reading 'Pater' has been suggested, backed by the assertion that Peter, 'the name of a renegade', was 'objectionable from the religious point of view'.[44] Scheiber convincingly argued that the name was indeed Peter, which sometimes occurred among medieval Jews.[45] The most striking aspect of this list is the prevalence of German names. They belonged to the Jewish elite, whose names were the most often recorded, and who were of Austrian or other Germanic background. It is known that scribes in later periods were prone to change or even translate names into Latin or the vernacular language of the society they lived in, thus changing the forms actually used by the Jews.[46] Similar tendencies may have affected the forms of names in thirteenth-century Latin documents. It seems, however, that the explanation is more complex than scribal agency. Peter, which appears on a Jewish tombstone, is certainly not the result of translation. The occurrence of German and some Hungarian Jewish names indicates that at least some Jews adopted a name that fitted the local naming patterns for everyday use; medieval Jews had such a practice in other parts of Europe.[47] Those who came from German areas conformed to German and not Hungarian naming patterns. As we do not have enough data from Hebrew sources about the names individuals used in Hungary, in most cases it is impossible to know whether the local name was assumed parallel to a Hebrew name for public and business life, as is recorded, for example, in the case of Persian and Valencian Jews, or

---

[42] Yitzchak (Isaac), c. 1050; Teka,★ c. 1225; Henuk or Henel,★ 1242; Voluelinus★ (Wolflin), Neklinus★ (Nickel) and Oltmannus★ (Altmann) 1242–68; Farkas, 1263; Jonah, between 1250 and 1280; Daniel, 1300: Kohn, Zsidók, pp. 377–83 (erroneously lists Yehuda 1250–75 as well). (★ denotes Jews of Austrian/German origin.)

Pesah, 1278; Peter, 1278: Scheiber, *Jewish Inscriptions*, pp. 113–15. Abraham and Meir, 1300s: Scheiber, *Jewish Inscriptions*, p. 93. Friedman, 1280–2: HO, vol. VIII: p. 206, no. 162, p. 221, no. 178 (MOL DL 50148; RA, no. 3189). Schechtinus: MZsO, vol. VIII: no. 2, p. 27 (RA, no. 2732). This was also a German name, derived from Schechtlein: Scheiber, *Héber kódexmaradványok*, p. 91.

The use of biblical names was popular in Hungary among the Christian population; therefore such names do not necessarily designate their bearer as Jewish (or a convert): Lóránd Benkő, *A régi magyar személynévadás* (Budapest: Néptudományi Intézet, 1949), pp. 6, 8.

[43] Scheiber, 'Recent additions', p. 155, n. 5. According to Lohrmann, Lublinus (Volvlinus) and Farkas is the same person: *Judenrecht*, p. 89. Fehértói, *Árpád-kori*, pp. 123–5.

[44] The opinion of Zimmels, cited by Scheiber, *Jewish Inscriptions*, p. 114.

[45] Scheiber, *Jewish Inscriptions*, pp. 114–15.

[46] Lívia Bernáth Scheiberné, *A magyarországi zsidóság személy- és családnevei II. József névadó rendeletéig*, A Magyarországi Zsidó Hitközségek Monográfiái 10 (Budapest: A Magyar Izraeliták Országos Képviselete, 1981), pp. 16–17.

[47] E.g. Jews in Muslim Spain sometimes adopted names used by the Muslims: Roth, *Jews, Visigoths*, p. 181; Jews translated their names into French: Richardson, *English Jewry*, p. 129.

as the only name to be used even in Hebrew documents (like the 'Peter' mentioned above).[48]

Comparison of usages of Jewish names in Latin and Hebrew texts (the only ones produced in Hungary being the inscriptions in stone) reveals a consistent discrepancy between the two. Latin documents give only one name, whereas the Hebrew ones employ the traditional 'X, son of Y' formula. Since the Latin documents were produced by many different scribes, this concordance is not a scribal error, but must be due to conformity to the customary use and recording of names, either by Jews when dealing with non-Jews, or by the scribes. The use of the full name occurred only within the Jewish community.

To what extent did Jews adopt Christian names for the kingdom and its inhabitants, or designate them by their own terminology? Hungary itself had a Hebrew name, in conformity with the medieval Jewish custom of imposing geographic names from the Bible upon the countries where Jews lived. '[T]his transposition should be seen as an endeavor on the part of a dislocated and scattered people to somehow rationalize the medieval world at least imaginatively; a kind of continuity was established.'[49] Hungary received the name 'the land of Hagar'.[50] The similarity of the words Hungaria and Hagar doubtless helped to establish this transposition of names; whether there was any other reason for the choice of this Hebrew name remains a question. It should be noted that the naming is unusual in that it involves the name of a biblical person instead of a topographical name. Jews used both the Hebrew and the local vernacular forms of the kingdom's name in the eleventh–thirteenth centuries: Eliezer ben Isaac from Speier used 'Ungaria'; one of Rabbi Kalonymos of Worms's disciples 'Hungaria'; Benjamin of Tudela 'Ungaria' and its derivatives; Isaac ben Moses 'Or Zarua' who visited Hungary, mostly the Hebrew name but also 'Ungaria'; Rashi, who had a Hungarian informant, and the authors of several *responsa* mentioned in this chapter used the Hebrew name.[51] Place names appearing in the *Sefer Or Zarua* resemble Slavic forms of these names, such as Bud(e)n and Ostrigom.[52] This may

---

[48] Tadeusz Lewicki, 'Les commerçants Juifs dans l'Orient Islamique non méditerranéen aux IXe–XIe siècles', in *Gli Ebrei nell'Alto Medioevo*, 2 vols., Settimane di Studio del Centro Italiano di Studi sull'Alto Medioevo 26 (Spoleto, 1980), vol. I: pp. 375–99, see p. 382. Burns, *Crusader Kingdom of Valencia*, p. 138.

[49] Weinreich, *History of the Yiddish Language*, pp. 79–80.   [50] Kohn, *Héber*, pp. 150–9.

[51] See the *responsa* cited above and Kohn, *Héber*, p. 51; Marcus Nathan Adler, *The Itinerary of Benjamin of Tudela* (London: Oxford University Press, 1907), pp. 20, 106. On Or Zarua see Wellesz, 'Esztergomi zsidók', p. 150.

[52] Spitzer, 'Héber', no. 16a; Kupfer and Lewicki, *Źródła*, p. 212; Isaac ben Moses, *Sefer Or Zaru'a*, p. 101. Buda: בודן Esztergom: אוסטריגום. See the remarks of Scheiber, *Héber kódexmaradványok*, p. 107; and Kupfer and Lewicki *Źródła*, pp. 224–5 on the relationship between Slavic forms and the Hebrew name.

be due either to the usage that Jews adopted from the local Christian population, or to the background of the author himself: Isaac was born and partly educated in Bohemia. It also raises the question of what language the Jews in Hungary spoke; toponyms and personal names (analysed above) indicate that they may have spoken any combination of Hungarian, Slavic, German and Yiddish.

Several indicators show that the local Christian environment influenced the everyday lives of Jews, from architectural styles to naming patterns; this growth of a common cultural framework, the merging of Christian (or Muslim) elements into Jewish culture, while retaining religious difference, has been described as a pattern of pre-modern Jewish life.[53] Christian influence led not only to this 'inward acculturation' of borrowed elements, but sometimes to 'outward acculturation': conversion. A few examples of Jewish conversion to Christianity survive from the thirteenth century. They attest to voluntary conversions without outside pressure albeit not without outside incentives (the one known attempt to forcibly convert a Jewish man, described in the previous chapter, failed). Real or imagined positive incentives seem to have played a major role in the conversion of three individuals whose stories are known from thirteenth-century sources: a category not very common in the typology of voluntary Jewish conversions established by Shatzmiller.[54]

A Jewish slave-girl found her burdens too hard and, according to the text of a *responsum* that deals with the litigation between her former and new owner, sought to alleviate them by leaving her master (stealing some of his money) and converting to Christianity.[55] She imagined that her situation would be ameliorated by this action, but subsequently her life in the service of a Christian master seemed even harder to her. Therefore she reverted to Judaism and went into hiding in a Jewish community. She was then sold by two members of that community to her second (Jewish) master. This story indicates that Jews in Hungary, as in other Christian countries, could not legally revert to Judaism once they converted to Christianity.[56] That is why the girl had to hide, and why her former owner claimed that he could not keep her.

Two converted Jews of Hungary appear in a papal letter written in

---

[53] Bonfil, *Tra due mondi*, pp. 3–64; Marcus, *Rituals of Childhood* (inward and outward acculturation); Goitein, *Mediterranean Society*, vol. II: esp. p. 407.

[54] Shatzmiller, 'Jewish Conversion', p. 311. See also chapter 4 above, note 51 on a late medieval convert who rose to a high position.

[55] Spitzer, 'Héber', no. 16d; Kupfer and Lewicki, *Źródła*, p. 213.

[56] Canon law: Gratian, D. 4 *De consecratione*, c. 94; VI 5.2.13. Even forced baptism was binding for life: Gratian, D. 45, c. 5. On the decretists: Dahan, *Intellectuels*, pp. 143–52. He cites cases from western Europe that prove the question was not purely an academic one: pp. 191–4, and above, chapter 3, note 84. On papal policy: Simonsohn, *Apostolic See History*, pp. 345–8.

answer to their appeal.⁵⁷ Pope Gregory IX intervened on behalf of two laymen, converted Jews, Nevronius and Anselmus (these were presumably their new names received upon baptism). He wanted to ensure that they got the yearly sum of money and other, unspecified benefits that the abbot of the Benedictine monastery of Pannonhalma had promised to allot to them as long as they lived if they converted to Christianity. Once they did convert, however, he refused to pay.⁵⁸ The papal response ordered the abbot to fulfil his promise, to show both his devotion and that he did not regret having encouraged their conversion. Although it seems that it was primarily this promise that influenced the two men to convert, we do not know why the abbot made the promise in the first place. These two converts were also allowed to retain the goods they had acquired licitly prior to their conversion. They established a house in Esztergom for the use of other Jews who converted or wished to convert to Christianity. The pope took the two converts and the house under the protection of St Peter.⁵⁹ Such *domus conversorum* were established elsewhere by monarchs, in order to lodge and feed converts who lost their material possessions due to their conversion.⁶⁰ We do not have any indications about how readily converts were accepted by local society; one glimpse reveals how long the memory of such conversions lasted. In a charter concerning landownership, the deceased vendor, Pouca, was described as the son-in-law of a baptized Jew ('iudeus baptizatus').⁶¹

Despite changes, conversion and discontinuity, the Jews of late medieval Hungary sought to construct a continuity between themselves and their coreligionists in thirteenth-century Hungary, primarily as a legal fiction. The continuous petitions for the renewal of the thirteenth-century privileges to the kings from Jewish communities of many cities show that Jews saw the thirteenth-century charter as defining their rights and privileges. Despite ruptures in the life of the communities – expulsion, relocation of Jewish neighbourhoods, influx of new immigrants – continuity was emphasized. Jewish insistence on separateness from non-Jews and the importance attributed to continuity have been identified as basic

---

⁵⁷ *MZsO*, vol. I: p. 20, no. 19; Érszegi, 'Eredeti pápai oklevelek', no. 69; Potthast, *Regesta*, no. 9897; Simonsohn, *Apostolic See Documents*, no. 145 and *Apostolic See History*, pp. 249–51. It does not appear in the Registers of Gregory IX.

⁵⁸ Abbeys and chapters supporting new converts elsewhere: Simonsohn, *Apostolic See Documents*, nos. 50, 72 (Grayzel, *Church*, vol. I: no. 6). On the policy of promising material advantages to bring about conversion: Simonsohn, *Apostolic See History*, pp. 244–51.

⁵⁹ ASV Reg. Vat. 18, f. 154v; *Reg. Greg. IX*, no. 3144. The names are given as Nivellonus and Anselmus. Simonsohn, *Apostolic See Documents*, no. 150.

⁶⁰ Shatzmiller, 'Jewish Conversion', p. 312.

⁶¹ MOL DL 40049 (*ÁÚO*, vol. II: p. 319, no. 220; *RA*, no. 1235). On identification of Jewish converts in western Europe: Jonathan Elukin, 'From Jew to Christian? Conversion and Immutability in Medieval Europe', in *Varieties of Religious Conversion*, pp. 171–89.

Non-Christian communities

techniques of keeping Jewish identity.[62] Out of the three groups Jews were certainly the only ones to have retained their religious and communal structures throughout the centuries. 'Continuity', however, is a partially misleading description of Jewish survival. Acculturation, through the gradual adoption of such elements as building styles and names from the surrounding society, started in the Middle Ages. This did not mean assimilation into Christian society; the framework for Jewish life was that of 'two worlds': Jewish traditions in the local context. Jews were part of and outside Christian society.[63]

THE MUSLIMS

In sharp contrast to Jewish survival, Hungary's Muslims had disappeared by the fourteenth century. In other medieval kingdoms Muslim populations were eradicated by Christian coercion. For example, Frederick II relocated the Sicilian Muslims by force to Lucera, and the colony was suppressed in 1300; forced baptism and expulsion ended Muslim life in Spain in the late medieval period.[64] The Hungarian case was to some extent different. Evidence of measures to force Muslims to convert comes only from the late eleventh and early twelfth centuries. At least some Muslim communities obviously survived this period of forced integration, although conversions resulted from it. Few individual converts are known, but both Christian and Muslim sources indicate the presence of converts from Islam.[65] As Muslims became the target of forcible integration, suspicions surfaced against 'false Christians': converts who secretly practised Islam or were suspected of doing so. According to legislation during the reigns of Kings László and Kálmán, Ishmaelites caught fasting or refusing to eat pork, and those who 'after having been baptized return to their old religion' were to be punished. The account of Abū Hāmid in the mid-twelfth century also mentioned converted Muslims who secretly adhered to the rituals of Islam.[66] During the early thirteenth-century controversy over non-Christian office-holding, accusations concerning deceitful Muslim converts abounded.[67] After the early twelfth

---

[62] Jacob Katz, *Exclusiveness and Tolerance: Studies in Jewish–Gentile Relations in Medieval and Modern Times* (Oxford: Oxford University Press, 1961, repr. Westport, Conn.: Greenwood Press, 1980), p. 46.   [63] Cf. Bonfil, *Tra due mondi*; Marcus, *Rituals of Childhood*.
[64] Abulafia, *Frederick II*, p. 146; Abulafia, 'Monarchs and Minorities'; Bernard Lewis, *Cultures in Conflict: Christians, Muslims, and Jews in the Age of Discovery* (Oxford: Oxford University Press, 1995), pp. 47–8.
[65] Samuel: *Liber censuum*, ASV Misc. Arm. XV, no. 1, f. 355r (*VMH*, p. 109, no. CLXXXVII); Mizse: *SRH*, vol. I: p. 474.
[66] Bak, *Laws*, pp. 29, 57: 'post baptismum ad legem suam antiquam . . . rediisse inventi fuerint'. *Abu-Hámid*, p. 56.   [67] See chapter 5, pp. 153–7, 186–7.

century, ecclesiastical pressure to restrict Muslim activities was strong at times, and, at least according to Archbishop Robert, the conversion of Muslims continued, but there is no evidence of forced conversion or relocation.

The most detailed picture of the life of these communities is Abū Hāmid's account from the middle of the twelfth century.[68] He wrote of two categories of Muslims on the basis of religious affiliation (professing Islam openly or secretly), tying these categories to places of origin.[69] He also described these two groups as determined in their occupation: those who openly professed Islam were soldiers, whereas the secret adherents who pretended to be Christians 'served' the king (Abū Hāmid did not specify the type of service). These groups may have been in a hierarchical position in relation to each other within the Muslim communities, as the 'soldiers' were set apart according to Yāqūt's account as well.[70] The Muslim from Hungary who was Yāqūt's informant, though he spoke of himself as one of the Muslim soldiers serving the Hungarian king, went to study in Aleppo. He was probably long absent from Hungary and he clearly did not participate in any wars in the service of the Hungarian king while studying; yet he belonged to the 'class' of soldiers. It seems, therefore, that the status of soldier designated a social rank as well. It may have constituted the highest rank in the Muslim social hierarchy of the kingdom.

Abū Hāmid also talked about the religious observance of the Muslims, but we should keep in mind that he clearly aggrandized his own importance as bringing Islam to the Muslims of Hungary. Interestingly, he never claims to have tried to 'convert' those who pretended to be Christians, but portrayed himself as the teacher of those who professed Islam openly. According to Abū Hāmid, although they had practised Islam prior to his arrival, these Muslims were ignorant of many important religious rules. He specifically mentioned that the Muslims knew neither Arabic nor the custom of preaching and praying on Friday.[71] He claimed to have taught them marital and inheritance laws and regulations about eating; he allowed them to have concubines as well as up to four wives, but forbade them to drink wine. At least in his immediate circle, his teachings were carried out unhindered; Abū Hāmid himself kept several concubines while in Hungary, and his son married two Muslim

---

[68] The relevant part of his account for the following paragraph is *Abu-Hámid*, pp. 56–7.
[69] What he meant by the two categories has been debated, see chapter 2, p. 66.
[70] Yāqūt, p. 470; in Reinaud, *Géographie*, p. 295.
[71] Nirenberg, 'The Current State of Mudejar Studies', has argued that Muslim authors routinely characterized mudejars in Spain as falling away from normative Islamic practices; living under Christian rule was equated with decline and corruption regardless of the level of knowledge and practice. Similar attitudes may have coloured Abū Hāmid's views.

Non-Christian communities

women from Hungary.[72] The extent of his alleged successes is more questionable when it comes to his account of how he convinced the king of Hungary about the wisdom of Muslim tenets. Abū Hāmid records a conversation he supposedly had with the king through an interpreter. He argued that Christians could drink wine without negative effects, but it was harmful for Muslims, so it was in the king's interest too that they abstained, as they would be more efficient soldiers. Muslim polygyny would also benefit the ruler, as more children would be born, eventually to serve in his army. Abū Hāmid related that the king, as a result, defended these Muslim customs even against Christian priests.[73] In another episode, he portrayed the Byzantine emperor as having been convinced by a Muslim from Hungary to allow his own Muslim subjects to practise Islam and even build mosques for them.[74] Abū Hāmid boasted of having taught Arabic to the Muslims of Hungary, of having ensured that they practised their prayers and other religious obligations, and of having instructed them on the duty of pilgrimage to Mecca. Finally he congratulated himself that, as a result of his teaching, Friday preaching was carried on in more than ten thousand places. Abū Hāmid chose a somewhat inflated way of saying 'many', flaunting the efficacy of his actions and preaching.

Although Abū Hāmid's account in general is to be used with caution, the overall loss of religious tradition of Muslims, especially a lack of Arabic learning, is quite plausible.[75] Other accounts confirm that the Muslims of Hungary did not conform to all the precepts of Islam. Yāqūt, in the 1220s, was surprised to see that even those Hungarian Muslims who went to study religious law did not observe the prescriptions of Islam in their clothing and even shaved their beards.[76] Defining themselves as Muslims, they were not at all ashamed of conforming to Christian customs in their appearance, and explained that those Muslims who served the king as soldiers all adopted that attire. Theirs was a conformism of the elite; although they aspired to higher status within the Muslim community by studying Muslim religious law (Yāqūt's informant talked about the prestige awaiting them in the Muslim community of

---

[72] *Abu-Hámid*, pp. 56, 61, 62, 83.   [73] *Ibid.*, pp. 61–2.   [74] *Ibid.*, p. 60.
[75] Réthy, *Corpus Nummorum*, p. 19, and following him, Szűcs, 'Két történelmi példa', p. 17, Göckenjan, *Hilfsvölker*, p. 67, mistakenly stated that the inscriptions of the pseudo-Arabic coins (discussed in chapter 4) included the Arabic 'illahi', thus believing that Hungary's Muslims spoke Arabic. Arabic manuscripts were listed among the possessions of the Benedictine monastery of Corvey in Saxony (in 1094 and 1379) as having been taken from Hungary: Erdélyi, *Pannonhalmi Szent Benedek-rend*, vol. I: p. 360. There is no mention about their place of production. Neither the coins (bearing only nonsensical ornamental script), nor the manuscripts warrant the conclusion that the Muslim population of Hungary spoke Arabic.
[76] Yāqūt, p. 470; in Reinaud, *Géographie*, p. 295.

Hungary, once they return as trained scholars[77]), they willingly conformed to some Christian customs. Some individuals even chose to convert. Both alleged crypto-Muslims known by name in the thirteenth century occupied high positions (*comes camere, comes palatinus*), and thus their conversion may have been a 'career move'.[78] Many Muslims in Hungary, however, identified themselves as Muslims in the thirteenth century, and did not convert to Christianity: the excavations of a Muslim village yielded no ruins of a church.[79] According to thirteenth-century information, Hungary's Muslims belonged to the school of Abū Hanifa, a Sunnite branch of Islam.[80] But Abū Hāmid, much as he liked to present himself as a prophet, had been unable to reverse the process of integration.

Despite their religion, these Muslims were more a part of the kingdom of Hungary than of the world of Islam. They served Christian kings without any apparent anxiety about a possible clash between their own and the kings' interest in foreign wars, explaining that the enemies of Hungary were also the enemies of Islam.[81] Allegiance to the Hungarian king, however, seems to have overridden that to Islam; Hungarian Muslims fought against Byzantium, although Muslims who served in the Byzantine army were captured in those wars.[82] A further episode sheds light on the relations of Muslims to the kingdom of Hungary. In 1217, a Hungarian noble, taken captive by Muslims in the Holy Land, was freed with the help of 'Hungarian Saracens' studying in Jerusalem, whom he sent for, and who greeted him very amicably and engineered his release.[83] These Muslim students identified more with the Hungarian captive than with his Muslim captors.

Very few names of Muslims survive.[84] They include Hungarian, Latin and Christian names, such as Péntek, Hungarian for 'Friday', perhaps conforming to the Christian practice in the kingdom of naming people

---

[77] Ibid.   [78] See chapter 4, pp. 127–8 and note 65 above.   [79] Antalóczy, 'Nyíri', p. 166.

[80] *El-Cazwini*, p. 411; Yāqūt, p. 469; in Reinaud, *Géographie*, p. 294. It is uncertain whether other branches of Islam were represented as well. Without knowing of the existence of these sources, Karácsonyi has speculated that Hungarian Muslims were Shi'ites: 'Kik voltak', p. 487.

[81] According to Yāqūt, Hungarian Muslims had no qualms about fighting for the Hungarian king because his enemies were also those of Islam: p. 470; in Reinaud, *Géographie*, p. 294.

[82] *Abu-Hámid*, p. 59.

[83] The text is cited in the article by Benjamin Z. Kedar, 'Ungarische Muslime in Jerusalem im Jahre 1217', *AOASH* 40, nos. 2–3 (1986): pp. 325–7, p. 325, repr. as no. XV in Kedar, *The Franks in the Levant, 11th to 14th Centuries* (Aldershot: Variorum, 1993).

[84] Texa, Iliaz (<Arabic Ilyās), Pentek, Elias, Peter, in Karácsonyi and Borovszky, *Időrendbe szedett váradi*, pp. 203, 229, 276, early thirteenth century; Ismail ibn Hassan, in *Abu-Hámid*, p. 65; Billa, Bocsu, Ethey, Heten in Anonymus, in *SRH*, vol. 1: pp. 114–15; Porcus, Etheius, Markus, Magiug (<Arabic and Iranian Mādzūdz), 1111, in Fejérpataky, *Kálmán király oklevelei*, pp. 42–3 (*RA*, no. 43); Györffy, 'Csatlakozott népek', p. 52. See also Fehértói, *Árpád-kori*, pp. 53, 154, 214, 272–4, 336. See the remarks of Richard W. Bulliet, 'Conversion to Islam and the Emergence of a Muslim Society in Iran', in *Conversion to Islam*, ed. Nehemia Levtzion (New York and London: Holmes and Meier, 1979), pp. 30–51, esp. pp. 46–7 on how undesirable it was to show off adhesion to Islam in a non-Muslim environment by the adoption of clearly Muslim names.

Non-Christian communities

after days, or a nickname based on Muslim religious practice; Porcus, perhaps a sobriquet; and Peter.[85] There are, however, no texts, such as tombstones in the case of Jews, that would reflect the naming patterns used by the Muslims themselves. Sources mention few Arabic names, and classical Arabic naming patterns are only represented once in Abū Hāmid's account. He took a man called Ismail ibn Hassan with him from Hungary on his recruiting trip east.[86] Ismail was one of Abū Hāmid's students, and he may have received this name from Abū Hāmid himself. Otherwise, Hungary's Muslims, like other inhabitants, are designated by only one name in the sources, and most of these names do not appear to be specifically related to Islam.

An obvious reason for both ignorance of Islamic tenets and conformism to local ways was isolation from other Muslim communities. It has been demonstrated that the persistence of Muslim colonies in the early Middle Ages was due to regular contacts with the Muslim world.[87] In the case of Hungary's Muslims, contacts with coreligionists abroad must have been very rare. According to Abū Hāmid, in the mid-twelfth century, Muslims in the Byzantine army had no idea about the existence of Muslims in Hungary.[88] By this period it was exceptional for a Muslim to travel to Hungary. In the early thirteenth century, Muslim communities from Hungary sent some of their members to centres of learning to acquire sufficient knowledge of Islam to serve the communities of their origin. We know of such students in Aleppo and Jerusalem, and of a Muslim scholar from Hungary who travelled abroad after 1241.[89] Links of this kind seem to have been insufficient. Already Yāqūt's informant was acutely aware of the isolation of Hungary's Muslims: 'we are surrounded by Christian lands'.[90] Although seeing their own isolation, these Muslims did not complain about either Christian pressure to convert, or oppressive laws. Neither did Muslim authors, recording their conversations with coreligionists from Hungary, report animosity towards the Christian population of the kingdom; they employed matter-of-fact designations such as Franks, Hungarians, Bashgirds and Christians.[91]

---

[85] Péntek was a not uncommon Christian name: Fehértói, *Árpád-kori*, pp. 269–70; Ferenc Terestyéni, *Magyar közszói eredetű személynevek az 1211-i tihanyi összeírásban* (Budapest: Magyar Nyelvtudományi Társaság, 1941), p. 45; Loránd Benkő, *Hungarian Proper Names* (Budapest: Akadémiai Kiadó, 1972), p. 231; 'Péntek' in Benkő, ed., *Magyar nyelv történeti-etimológiai szótára*, vol. III: p. 156. Porc: Fehértói, *Árpád-kori*, p. 282.   [86] *Abu-Hámid*, p. 65.
[87] Miquel, *Géographie humaine du monde Musulman*, pp. 515–24. Similarly, contacts with the Islamic world were important for the Muslims of late medieval Valencia: Meyerson, *Muslims of Valencia*, pp. 258–69.   [88] *Abu-Hámid*, p. 60.
[89] Yāqūt, p. 470; in Reinaud, *Géographie*, p. 295; Kedar, 'Ungarische Muslime'; *El-Cazwini*, p. 411.
[90] Yāqūt, p. 469 ('Les chrétiens nous environnent de toute part' in Reinaud, *Géographie*, p. 294).
[91] Yāqūt, pp. 469–70, in Reinaud, *Géographie*, pp. 294–5; *El-Cazwini*, pp. 411–12. Cf. the often negative medieval (esp. Spanish) Muslim views of Christians discussed by Epalza, *Jésus*, pp. 129–226.

It is worthwhile to deal here with the 'founding myth' of Muslim life in Hungary as it was known in the twelfth and thirteenth centuries, for it sheds light on contemporary notions about the place of the kingdom's Muslims in the world of Islam. With some variations, this story is incorporated into the accounts of Yāqūt and Ibn Saʿīd (whose narrative is cited in the work of Abū-'l-Fidā').[92] Both versions relate that in the distant past Muslim scholars travelled to the area of Hungary and converted the ancestors of Hungary's Muslims to the true faith. Yāqūt mentions seven, Ibn Saʿīd only one such scholar. The Hungarian Anonymous, in the late twelfth or early thirteenth century, wrote that the ancestors of the Muslims (Ishmaelites) migrated from Bulgaria to Hungary.[93] This may be a version of the same story, because the Anonymous often based his chronicle on information received from people he knew; alternatively, it may simply reflect a wave of Muslim immigration to Hungary, because the Anonymous was also prone to misdating events.[94] It seems that, by the thirteenth century, the isolation of Hungary's Muslims from the world of Islam made it inconceivable for Muslim authors that they had once constituted an integral part of that world. Instead, their origins were seen as the result of a conversion to Islam within Hungary initiated from abroad.

The only catastrophe that was described in Muslim sources as putting an end to Islam in Hungary was the Mongol invasion; this was even depicted as having completely eradicated the Muslim inhabitants of the country.[95] The invasion probably caused heavy losses in the ranks of Muslims who served in the royal army, but it did not wipe out the entire Muslim population; sporadic references to Muslims survive from the later part of the thirteenth century. Muslims are mentioned as serving in the army even in the 1260s.[96] Yet Muslims soon disappeared from Hungary. By the fourteenth century, sources in Hungary do not mention their existence, except for converts, such as Jacob, himself a Christian, but son of a Muslim.[97] It seems that the already partly converted and decimated

---

[92] Yāqūt, p. 470; in Reinaud, *Géographie*, p. 294. Referring to Ibn Saʿīd, Abū-'l-Fidā' wrote of two neighbouring countries, the Bashkirs who converted to Islam, and the Hungarians who converted to Christianity: Reinaud, *Géographie*, pp. 294–5.

[93] *SRH*, vol. I: p. 114.

[94] See, for example, György Györffy, *Anonymus: rejtély vagy történeti forrás?* (Budapest: Akadémiai Kiadó, 1988), pp. 7–26.

[95] Ibn Saʿīd, in Reinaud, *Géographie*, p. 294; *El-Cazwini*, pp. 411–12. Distorted version in al-Dimashkī, *Manuel de la Cosmographie du Moyen Age*, tr. M. A. F. Mehren (Paris, 1874), p. 256.

[96] 'Annales Otakariani', in *MGH SS*, vol. IX: p. 185.

[97] *Anjoukori Okmánytár*, vol. I: p. 537, no. 485: 'Jacobus filius comitis Misce sarraceni' (in 1319); perhaps son of Mizse, *comes palatinus* of László IV. The name Ibrahim also occurs in a variety of forms among Christians (including the official of a church) in the thirteenth century; they are perhaps converts from Islam: Erdélyi, *Pannonhalmi Szent Benedek rend*, vol. I: pp. 222–3, 261, 780, no. 185 (*RA*, no. 635); *ÁÚO*, vol. VIII: p. 174, no. 121 (*RA*, no. 1871); *HO*, vol. VI: pp. 113–14,

Muslim population finally integrated into Christian society; a case of 'conversion by assimilation'.[98]

Hungary's Muslims, or at least those studying in Aleppo in the thirteenth century, conceived of themselves as the followers of the true faith, converted by foreigners. Aggressive Christianization led to a wave of conversion in the eleventh and early twelfth centuries, with a number of 'false converts' in its wake.[99] Although accusations portrayed intermarriage as a scheme to deceive (see chapter 5), marriages between converts and local Christians would have been a natural product of the process of integration. Conversion, although not under duress, seems to have continued in the thirteenth century. Even those who kept their religion openly held tenuous ties to the world of Islam. They sent members of their communities to study *sharī'a*, but they were slipping away from the observance of rituals and regulations prescribed by Islam. Isolation from the Muslim world and Christian influence led to the disregard of many religious tenets and a willingness to adopt the customs of the local population. After presumably heavy losses during the Mongol invasion, the process of acculturation finally ended for the remaining groups (which must have been very small, as even prior to the invasion the Muslims constituted probably less than 1 per cent of the population) in assimilation and conversion. Such trends due to Christian influence were important in changing Muslim life even for larger communities, such as the Muslims of Iberia. The late medieval al-Wansharīshī warned that 'one has to beware of the pervasive effect of their [the Christians'] way of life, their language, their dress, their objectionable habits, and influence on the people living with them over a long period of time, as has occurred in the case of the inhabitants of Avila and other places'.[100] He used some rhetorical exaggeration to claim that no full Muslim life can be led under Christian domination. None the less, independent evidence confirms the process of acculturation in Iberia.[101] Also, due to their isolation, Muslims in China assimilated to the point of complete rejection of Islam.[102] As

---

no. 75 (*RA*, no. 1364); Fehértói, *Árpád-kori*, p. 166. A papal letter *c.* 1319 mentions Muslims in Hungary: they are not to be appointed to public offices and not to have mosques, nor be allowed a public call to prayer: Simonsohn, *Apostolic See Documents*, no. 298a. This injunction is so different from previous papal letters about Hungarian Muslims, that maybe it was not inspired by conditions in Hungary, but those in Iberia.

[98] Bentley, *Old World Encounters*, p. 9. Balić, 'Der Islam', mistakenly attributed the laws of Kálmán (see chapter 6 above, note 108) to Charles Robert in the fourteenth century, and thought that forced conversion put an end to Muslim life in Hungary.

[99] Szűcs, 'Két történelmi', argued that Muslims assimilated peacefully. He ignored earlier laws aiming at conversion, the end of further immigration, and the effects of the Mongol invasion.

[100] Harvey, *Islamic Spain*, p. 58, see also pp. 55–60, 118–20.

[101] Powell, ed. *Muslims under Latin Rule*, pp. 62, 66.

[102] Raphael Israeli, 'Islamization and Sinicization in Chinese Islam', in *Conversion to Islam*, pp. 159–76.

these examples show, it is not surprising that the small and isolated Muslim population of Hungary experienced a loss of tradition.

THE CUMANS

The fate of the Cumans differed from that of both the Jews and the Muslims. Under persistent and strong Christian pressure, they converted and were integrated by the fifteenth century. None the less, during the eighteenth and even the twentieth centuries, the inhabitants of what used to be the medieval Cuman territories in Hungary have claimed continuity with the Cumans of the thirteenth century by a series of reinventions of identity. After the entry of the Cumans into Hungary, Christian expectations centred on a speedy conversion of these 'pagans'. The process was in reality more gradual, and affected different groups at different rates. It was a manifold process, including baptism, a change of habits, permanent settlement, and the adoption of local customs, names and attire. Cuman resistance did not aim at the conservation of a 'pagan religion'; indeed, their belief system was closely linked to their way of life and social system. Therefore Cuman revolts and resistance were triggered by changes in their way of life, partly enforced by Christians, partly brought on by the change of circumstances. Thus nomadism had to be discontinued for lack of sufficient territory, a limited possibility of raiding, and Christian pressure on the Cumans to settle. None the less, 'pagan' religious practice was tenacious, despite its lack of codification, creating a syncretism among baptized Cumans. Graves often provide evidence for the continuity of some elements of traditional burial customs even among the converted.

A brief description of Cuman religious belief and practice, not as familiar to historians of medieval Europe as Judaism or Islam, is in order.[103] Medieval written accounts of Cuman practices by those who encountered them, compilations of texts and word lists based on information from Cumans, merchants and missionaries, and archaeological excavations reveal much about Cuman religion in the steppe. The Cumans brought these practices with them to Hungary, where over time they were transformed and lost due to the changed circumstances and outside pressure.

Characteristics of Cuman burial practices on the steppe included burial with a horse – either the whole animal, or certain parts, or the stuffed skin – in graves oriented towards the east, with large mounds

---

[103] For detailed analyses: Jean-Paul Roux, *La religion des Turcs et des Mongols* (Paris: Payot, 1984); Peter B. Golden, 'Religion among the Qipčaqs of Medieval Eurasia', *Central Asiatic Journal* 42, no. 2 (1998): pp. 180–237.

Non-Christian communities

(*kurgans*) erected over them.[104] Written sources indicate the custom of burying servants with their masters.[105] Jean de Joinville described the burial of a Cuman chieftain or other leader.[106] One of his faithful men followed him into the grave, and was given messages to carry to an ancestor ('the first king' of the Cumans according to Joinville) in the other world. He was also given gold and silver by Cuman lords, to be repaid to these lords after their death. This practice may have been reserved for the leaders alone. Yet, although not in such radical form, the needs of the dead were always attended to, as objects found in the graves show.[107] The Cumans provided the departed with saddle, harness and other accoutrements, with arms, jewelry, clothing and objects of everyday use. Metal cauldrons were also placed in the graves of the Cuman aristocracy. The archaeological finds correspond to written accounts that point to Cuman beliefs in an afterlife where the dead continued to have material needs.

The so-called *kamennye baby* direct attention to another aspect of Cuman religious practices.[108] These stone statues of men and women were placed on the *kurgans*. Several types of statues exist: stele, and sitting or standing figures. The divergent forms may simply reflect chronological differences, but they may also signal social hierarchy. Around 3,000 of these statues have been catalogued by Russian scholars. They were connected with the Cuman elite; the practice of putting up such statues declined as the Cuman social hierarchy disintegrated and the old elite disappeared under Mongol rule in the second half of the thirteenth and in the fourteenth centuries. By the thirteenth century, these statues did not stand over the grave of the people they represented: on the south Russian steppe several of them were placed in close proximity to one another on earlier mounds, surrounded by a stone hedge. The statues held cups in their hands, and animal bones were found near them. These areas were probably sanctuaries where animal sacrifices were performed. From the original notion of appeasing the spirit of the departed until it reached its final destination, a cult of ancestors developed. Each clan venerated a number of dead men and women whose spirits, they hoped, would aid the living.

Abū 'l-Fidā', writing in the early fourteenth century, attributed an

---

[104] Pálóczi Horváth, *Hagyományok*, pp. 53–8, synthesizing the results of previous scholarship.
[105] 'Albrici monachi Triumfontium Chronicon', in *MGH SS*, vol. XXIII: p. 950. Joinville, *Histoire*, p. 272. Archaeological evidence and Byzantine and Islamic sources on such human sacrifice in Turkic steppe societies: Golden, 'Religion among the Qipčaqs', p. 195.
[106] Joinville, *Histoire*, pp. 272–4, using the term 'chevaliers': knight. On background: Sinor, 'Quelques passages', pp. 370–2.
[107] Pálóczi Horváth, *Hagyományok*, pp. 53–72 (with illustrations), describing and analysing the results of Russian scholars.
[108] *Ibid.*, pp. 71–95, synthesizing the results of previous scholarship. William of Rubruck described these statues: 'Itinerarium', p. 186.

interest in astrology to the Cumans; according to him they believed in celestial influences and worshipped the stars.[109] Some Cuman names are indeed derived from words such as 'moon' (Aydua) and 'full moon' (Tolon).[110]

Descriptions also indicate shamanistic practices. The Russian chronicle attributed to Nestor recounts how Boniak, the chief of the Cuman army, started to howl like a wolf at midnight in order to ascertain the outcome of an approaching battle. When several wolves answered him, he was assured of victory for the following day.[111] This story probably reflects the shamanic divination practice of communing with the ancestral spirit. The idea of descent from a wolf, and the wolf–warrior association had long Turkic traditions.[112] A close relative of the wolf, the dog, was also of prime importance in the Cuman belief system. Dog sacrifices at Cuman graves, taking an oath while cutting a dog to pieces, and personal names based on the word 'dog' attest to the importance of dogs in Cuman beliefs as an agent of purification or scapegoat.[113] Shamans played a central role in the lives of the Turkic steppe people; they had contacts with the other world, and could foretell the future, heal the sick and influence the weather. The missionary William of Rubruck described the shamans of the Mongols, enumerating their practices.[114] The ancient beliefs of the Hungarians also centred on shamanism.[115] Cuman shamans themselves are not depicted in any of the sources, although the word itself crops up. The *Codex Cumanicus* contains references to 'fortune-tellers' and female 'enchanters'.[116] John of Plano Carpini misunderstood the

---

[109] Reinaud, *Géographie*, p. 291, based on Ibn Saʿīd. Roux, *Religion*, pp. 92–3, 124–32 on Turkic astronomy and astrology.

[110] László Rásonyi, 'Anthroponymes comans de Hongrie', *AOASH* 20 (1967): pp. 135–49, see pp. 136, 146. Györffy, 'Kipcsaki kun', p. 268, argues that the name Könček was derived from the word 'sun', but according to Rásonyi, 'Anthroponymes comans', p. 143, from 'trousers'.

[111] *Chronique dite de Nestor*, tr. Louis Leger, Publications de l'Ecole des langues orientales vivantes, ser. 2, vol. XIII (Paris: Ernst Leroux, 1884), p. 212.

[112] Golden, *Introduction*, p. 280; Golden, 'Religion among the Qipčaqs'; Golden, 'Wolves, Dogs'.

[113] Golden 'Wolves, Dogs', pp. 93–7; Mircea Eliade, *Shamanism: Archaic Techniques of Ecstasy*, Bollingen Series, no. 76 (Princeton: Princeton University Press, 1964), pp. 466–7. Prior to their Christianization, the Hungarians also adopted steppe beliefs and the dog played similar roles: Bálint, 'Kutya'.

[114] Rubruck, 'Itinerarium', pp. 300–5.

[115] Vilmos Diószegi, ed., *Az ősi magyar hitvilág* (Budapest: Gondolat Kiadó, 1971); Vilmos Diószegi, *A pogány magyarok hitvilága*, Kőrösi Csoma Kiskönyvtár 4 (Budapest: Akadémiai Kiadó, 1967); István Dienes, *A honfoglaló magyarok* (Budapest: Corvina Kiadó, 1972), pp. 47–57. Shamanistic practices of the Hungarians prior to Christianization were reconstructed by ethnographers largely on the basis of folklore, folk-tales and surviving practices, comparing these data to other, contemporary shamanistic practices. See also Eliade, *Shamanism*.

[116] Kaare Grønbech, *Komanisches Wörterbuch: Türkischer Wortindex zu Codex Cumanicus* (Copenhagen: Munksgaard, 1942) p. 191. Clauson, *Etymological Dictionary*, p. 625 (*ka:m*). Qam also in the Mamlūk-Quipčaq glossary: Golden, 'Religion among the Qipčaqs', p. 206.

Non-Christian communities

Cuman *qam* (shaman) as the name of a god.[117] Moreover, several practices reported in Muslim and Christian sources were shamanistic. Apart from the episode of Boniak's divination with wolves, they include Robert de Cléry's assertion that the Cumans 'venerate' animals, probably misunderstanding the role of animals as psychopomps who conducted the soul to the underworld, and Rashīd al-Dīn's account of rain-making with the help of magical stones.[118]

Cumans also practised the blood-oath. As described by Joinville, they mingled their own blood in a cup with that of their sworn companions, mixed it with wine and water and drank it to create a blood-bond ('et lors si distrent que il estoient frere de sanc'; they were now 'blood brothers'). This emulated the biological ties of brotherhood that were recognized as binding each party to fidelity.[119] The blood-oath was an ancient form of creating alliances between equals; the Hungarians also practised it prior to their Christianization.[120]

This, then, was the religious background of the Cumans when they arrived in Hungary. By then they had also encountered Christianity and Islam and sporadic individual or group conversion had taken place.[121] Written as well as archaeological sources relate to Cuman religious practices in Hungary and the process of religious change due to Christianization. Christian influences, whether imposed or through everyday interaction, led to a transformation of Cuman life. Conversion, in the sense of baptism, was the easiest to force on the Cumans, but it was only one element, and although symbolically key, in practice by far the least important in the process of integration. Some medieval awareness of the complexity of this process appears occasionally in the texts. A 'Christian' way of life means not only baptism, but also settlement, the adoption of local customs, dress, and so forth.[122] Christianization left its mark on many aspects of Cuman life, from burial practices to naming

---

[117] Carpini, *Ystoria*, ed. Wyngaert, p. 41; ed. Daffinà *et al.*, p. 240.
[118] Robert de Cléry, 'De ceux qui se croisèrent', in *Un chevalier à la croisade. L'histoire de la conquête de Constantinople*, p. 230; Eliade, *Shamanism*, pp. 93–4, 97–9, 156–7 (ornaments of the shaman which provided him with a magical body in animal form). Rashīd al-Dīn, *Successors*, pp. 36–7. Other Muslim authors also referred to such rain-making by Turkic shamans: Golden, 'Religion among the Qipčaqs', pp. 207–9. On Turkic shamanism: Roux, *Religion*, pp. 59–98; Jean-Paul Roux, 'La religion des peuples de la steppe', in *Popoli delle Steppe: Unni, Avari, Ungari*, Settimane di Studio del Centro Italiano di Studi sull'Alto Medioevo, 2 vols. (Spoleto, 1988), vol. II: pp. 513–32.
[119] The description of this ceremony as practised by the Cumans: Joinville, *Histoire*, p. 272. Also see A. Benisch, ed., *Travels of Rabbi Petachia of Ratisbon*, 2nd edn (London: Longman, 1861), pp. 4–5.
[120] On the significance of the blood-oath: 'Serment de sang', in Yves Bonnefoy, ed., *Dictionnaire des Mythologies*, 2 vols. (Paris: Flammarion, 1993), vol. II: pp. 420–1. Golden, 'Religion among the Qipčaqs', pp. 192–3; Roux, *Religion*, pp. 227–30. Hungarian–Cuman comparison: Sándor Eckhardt, 'Kun analógiák a magyar ősvalláshoz', *Magyar Nyelv* 34 (1938): pp. 242–4.
[121] Golden, 'Religion among the Qipčaqs', pp. 217–26.   [122] See chapter 6, pp. 221–2.

patterns, permanent settlement, clothing, and Cuman social structure. By analysing the trends and chronology of these changes, it is possible to clarify the process of Christianization and integration. The following pages address the continuities and modifications in these various areas of Cuman life.

To what extent did the Cumans retain their traditional beliefs once they migrated into Hungary? Cuman religious practice is never described in Hungarian sources. Usually Cumans are described as 'pagans', a catch-all term that hides the specificity of religious practice. Written sources mention the 'worship of idols' and 'pagan rites'; these descriptions reflect Christian views of 'paganism' even though the former may be based on Cuman ancestor worship.[123] Archaeological finds in Hungary provide more information. The richest sources are the burial places of the elite: the solitary graves of chieftains, heads of clans and other high-ranking individuals. Mass cemeteries contain fewer objects; they were used for centuries, some probably starting from the thirteenth century.[124] Their identification as Cuman cemeteries was facilitated by the types of objects, which in both mass cemeteries and solitary graves differ from Hungarian grave finds. In many cases written evidence corroborates that the burials were in Cuman areas.

The Cumans kept practising traditional burials into the fourteenth century. Eleven solitary graves of the thirteenth and early fourteenth centuries have been excavated to date, yielding over 300 objects.[125] Of these graves, seven belonged to men, four to women. They were buried far away from cemeteries and settlements. The burial rites and finds in Hungary correspond to those in the steppe regions. The graves were oriented toward the east, and contained remains of horses, harnesses and other objects. The distribution of the grave finds by place of origin also indicates the still important hold of steppe influences. These objects can be associated to three different cultural zones, reflecting the impact of

[123] The regulation of Cuman status in 1279: 'ydolorum cultura' and 'paganorum ritus': ASV AA Arm. I-XVIII-595; *VMH*, p. 340, no. DLVI. 'Ydolorum cultura' as a characteristic of 'paganism' in general was already used in the *Codex Prayanus*: OSzK, MNy 1, f. 122. The Cuman practice of erecting statues (*kamennye baby*) over burial mounds may have been understood by Christian commentators as an instance of idol worship, but they may equally have simply drawn on stock Christian images of 'pagans'.

[124] László Selmeczi, 'A kunok és a jászok régészeti kutatásának néhány problémája', in *Régészeti-néprajzi tanulmányok*, pp. 101–13.

[125] Pálóczi Horváth, *Hagyományok*, pp. 104–23, 132–5. Some of these graves were unearthed using unscientific methods, and some of the objects have been lost since their discovery. In addition, finds from seven other sites have been attributed to the Cumans but, according to Pálóczi Horváth, insufficient evidence precludes secure identification of some, while he refutes the Cuman origin of others (*ibid.*, pp. 124–37). Recently, Ferenc Horváth has discovered another grave, attributing it to a member of the Cuman elite, but no published information is as yet available on the discovery.

Non-Christian communities

each on the Cuman elite of late thirteenth-century Hungary. About 40 per cent of the finds are of an eastern steppe origin, about 24 per cent Byzantine and about 16 per cent Hungarian or western European.[126] Steppe-type burial mounds do not characterize these graves, although sometimes they are near small mounds. This fact may be due to soil conditions (sand) that facilitated erosion, or more likely to the Cumans' effort to make their traditional burials less conspicuous under Christian pressure.[127] No stone statues were found in Hungary, but István Fodor has argued that wooden statues similar to the *kamennye baby* of the steppe probably existed but have since disintegrated.[128] He has resorted to data provided by toponyms and descriptions of boundary markers. According to him, 'idol' and 'Cuman portrait' that appear among them can be identified with the *kamennye baby*. He has explained the change in material – exclusively wood instead of stone – by the disruptive effect of the Cuman flight from the Mongols. It is faster to make wooden statues, and it requires less preparation and fewer specialized implements. By the time workshops producing stone statues could have been established, Christian pressure to convert already made such practices impossible. It seems, then, that the Cumans originally practised their ancestor cult in Hungary, too.

Solitary burials themselves indicate that those buried were not Christians, as the latter would have been interred in cemeteries around a church. Other aspects of the burial practice, present in the Cuman mass cemeteries as well, show the continuity of traditional beliefs. Placing food in the grave is one such custom. The food was to nourish the departed until they reached their destination.[129] Arms, jewelry, knives and clothes were also buried with the dead to equip them for everyday needs. Again, a comparison with Christian graves in Hungary demonstrates that these are 'pagan' practices.[130]

Perhaps the main characteristic of traditional Cuman graves was burial with a horse, or part of a horse. Full horses were interred in only three of the solitary graves in Hungary; no graves included parts of horses, but

---

[126] Pálóczi Horváth, *Hagyományok*, pp. 139–75. The total does not add up to 100 per cent because some of the objects could not be identified or categorized.
[127] The mounds called 'Cuman mounds' (*kunhalmok*) in Hungary were remains from prehistoric times and had no connections to the Cumans: Györffy, *Magyar nép*, pp. 46–9; Pálóczi Horváth, *Besenyők*, p. 90. Missionaries, though tolerating many social customs, were determined to extirpate burial under a tumulus in early medieval Scandinavia as well: Musset, 'Pénétration chrétienne', pp. 299–305.
[128] István Fodor, 'Lehettek-e kun sírszobrok Magyarországon?' in *Jászkunság kutatása*, pp. 3–10. Wooden statues existed on the steppe as well, but those made of stone were better preserved.
[129] Horváth, 'Régészeti adatok a kunok Dél-alföldi történetéhez', p. 67.
[130] András Pálóczi Horváth, 'A Balota pusztai középkori sírlelet', *Cumania: A Bács-Kiskun megyei múzeumok évkönyve* 11 (1989): pp. 95–148, see p. 123.

most contained harnesses or other horse accoutrements.[131] Different explanations have been advanced to account for this phenomenon. It could have been due to a scarcity of horses, or to tribal custom, since even on the steppe, differences existed between the burial practices of various Cuman tribes.[132] The horse was maybe buried in a separate grave (as sometimes happened on the steppe[133]) which was never found or has since been destroyed. It may also be a sign of the slow phasing out of the custom.

There is evidence for the survival of some 'pagan' practices in graves of commoners, in cemeteries for an already converted population, throughout the fourteenth century. William of Rubruck also noted the conservation of 'pagan' burial practices in the case of a baptized Cuman on the steppe.[134] In Hungary, in one grave, the head of the deceased rested on a dog; dogs were also buried on the edge of another Cuman settlement.[135] The importance of dogs in the Cuman belief system explains the presence of these animals. Certain graves in mass cemeteries showed signs of fire. The fire was either lit in the grave just prior to burial, or next to it, and then the remains of the pyre were placed in the pit under the body. These were purificatory practices linked to beliefs in the life of the spirit after death. They served to chase away the evil spirits before the deceased could be placed in the grave.[136] Objects linked to Cuman beliefs also continued to be placed in graves in mass cemeteries throughout the fourteenth century. These included amulets: crystals, horse teeth and animal bones;[137] eggs (an ancient symbol of fecundity) in graves of women;[138] mirrors;[139] and artemisia, placed under the head of the deceased.[140] A sharp (in general, iron) knife is also usually found in

[131] Pálóczi Horváth, *Hagyományok*, pp. 140–1.   [132] Ibid., pp. 54–7.   [133] Ibid., p. 55.
[134] Rubruck, 'Itinerarium', p. 187.
[135] Selmeczi, 'Magyarországi kunok temetkezése', p. 39. András Pálóczi Horváth, 'A Lászlófalván 1969–74-ben végzett ásatások eredményei', *Cumania: A Bács-Kiskun megyei múzeumok évkönyve* 4 (1976): pp. 275–309, see p. 293.
[136] Selmeczi, 'Magyarországi kunok temetkezése', p. 43; Horváth, 'Csengele', p. 111. On the purificatory value of fire: Jean-Paul Roux, 'Fonctions chamaniques et valeurs du feu chez les peuples altaïques', *Revue de l'Histoire des Religions* 189 (1976): pp. 67–101.
[137] Pálóczi Horváth, 'Balota pusztai', p. 124; László Selmeczi, 'Adatok és szempontok a kunok régészeti kutatásához Szolnok megyében', in *Régészeti-néprajzi tanulmányok*, pp. 5–20, see p. 16; Pálóczi Horváth, *Besenyők*, p. 93; Hatházi, 'Perkátai', p. 661. The horse teeth may have been a token for horse sacrifice. Some of these practices are attested in graves identified by Selmeczi as belonging to the As: the remains of a fire, the presence of tools, arms and amulets (fish vertebrae, rabbit feet, and shells): László Selmeczi, 'Régészeti adatok a jászok szokásaihoz és hiedelemvilágához', in *Régészeti-néprajzi tanulmányok*, pp. 185–211; on amulets also Selmeczi, *Négyszállási I. számú jász temető*, p. 87.
[138] Ferenc Móra, 'Ásatás a Szeged-Öttömösi Anjou-kori temetőben', *Archeológiai értesítő* 26 (1906): pp. 18–27, see pp. 21–4. These data are from fourteenth-century graves.
[139] Pálóczi Horváth, 'Situation des recherches', p. 206.
[140] Selmeczi, 'Adatok és szempontok', p. 111. This practice occurs in mass cemeteries, and there is not enough comparative archaeological material to prove that it was an exclusively Cuman custom.

Non-Christian communities

these graves; Selmeczi has argued that the purpose of this was not simply to serve its owner in the other world, but to ward off the evil eye.[141] Jewels and remains of food placed in the grave were also common.[142]

The exact reconstruction of Cuman religious practices remains open to interpretation, but it is certain that for two or three generations after their arrival, the Cumans retained their traditional burial practices especially for the elite, although modifications had already started to occur. Christian prohibitions and influences, present from the moment of the Cumans' entry, brought about the abandoning of the most conspicuous elements (such as *kurgans*). The practice of providing the deceased with food and everyday objects continued. Ancestor cult and shamanism, although no conclusive evidence survives from Hungary, probably existed at least during the early period of Cuman settlement in the kingdom.[143]

Archaeological evidence also sheds light on the process of the Christianization of the Cumans. How fast and to what extent did Cuman religious belief and practice change after their immigration? Only 16 per cent of the objects found in thirteenth-century solitary graves are western Christian or Hungarian in origin; the rest pertain to the previous spheres of Cuman life, the steppe and Byzantium.[144] Even some of those objects associated with western Christendom may in fact come from the Latin empire of Constantinople and reflect political ties, rather than integration into the new area of Cuman life. The objects that originate in the Roman Christian world are primarily swords and pieces of armament or jewelry with no explicit Christian connotations. The only exception is a belt with metal studs, bearing inscriptions of prayers to four saints.[145] We cannot determine whether its Cuman owner used the belt, perhaps received as a gift, perhaps bought, for the purpose of enhancing his prestige or whether it was an article of Christian devotion. The adoption of Christian objects is not necessarily an indication of conversion: the baptism (as a magical protection) of otherwise 'pagan'

---

[141] Selmeczi, 'Magyarországi kunok temetkezése', p. 42; Hatházi, 'Perkátai', p. 660; Pálóczi Horváth, 'Balota pusztai', p. 128.
[142] Hatházi, 'Perkátai', p. 659; Selmeczi 'Magyarországi kunok temetkezése', p. 39.
[143] Jenő M. Fehér, *Középkori magyar inkvizíció* (Buenos Aires: Editorial Transsylvania, 1968), described trials of Cuman shamans in thirteenth- to fourteenth-century Hungary, but his source, a copy of an alleged medieval manuscript that 'disappeared', is probably a modern forgery: Ferenc Schram: 'A középkori sámánperekről', *Ethnographia* 79 (1968): pp. 281–4; János Horváth, 'Anonymous és a kassai kódex', in *Középkori kútfőink kritikus kérdései*, ed. János Horváth and György Székely (Budapest: Akadémiai Kiadó, 1974), pp. 81–110, see pp. 102–6; Gedeon Borsa, 'A kassai kódex hitelességéről', *Magyar Könyvszemle* 88 (1972), pp. 88–90.
[144] Pálóczi Horváth, *Hagyományok*, pp. 160–75.
[145] 'S. Stephane ora pro me, S. Bartholome ora pro me, S. Margareta ora pro me, S. Iacobe ora pro me': *ibid.*, p. 111.

northerners led to their interring Christian crosses, used as charms or amulets, in graves.[146]

The methodology used to establish correlations between conversion and change in naming patterns applies to the Christianization of the Cumans as well.[147] Changes in naming practices were slower than the conversion rate. In other words, the appearance of a large stock of Christian names is a clear indication that the population in question had been converted for some time and was willing to give up traditional names for their children in favour of Christian ones. A multitude of Cuman names from Hungary survive in documents. László Rásonyi has compiled lists of these traditional Turkic anthroponyms and toponyms.[148] His analysis shows that the Cuman names of Hungary are representative of Turkic anthroponyms in general, falling into the following categories: totemistic names, names indicative of parental desire, protection or a wish for the child's life, and names due to chance happenings, such as the first word the parents uttered or the first object the mother saw after giving birth. Thus the most common names in the traditional stock referred to animals (such as Alpra, <Al-bura, male camel of reddish colour; Ityk, <itük, young dog), qualities (for example Alpar, <alper, man-hero; Tác, <taz, bald), and objects (like Kemenche, <kämänće, a little archery bow), or were designed to protect from evil spirits by misguiding or confusing them (for example Bolmaz, non-existent; Tepremez <täprä, don't move). These traditional names reveal the magical ways of thinking characteristic of Turkic nomads. They were replaced by Christian ones gradually. The turning point was the period between roughly 1330 and 1360, when Cumans whose father still bore a traditional name appear in large numbers with Christian names. Christian names outnumber traditional Turkic ones by the last third of the fourteenth century in the stock of names, although the latter still existed in the sixteenth century.[149]

The pace of the process of Christianization was not uniform among various Cuman groups within Hungary. Although some members of the elite were close to the royal court and Christian influences, at the same time others retained their traditional form of burial (solitary graves, rich grave goods) until the mid-fourteenth century. This signalled social status

---

[146] Musset, 'Pénétration chrétienne', pp. 276–7, 286–7.
[147] Benkő, *Régi magyar személynévadás*, on early medieval Hungary. Bulliet's general model: 'Conversion'.
[148] Rásonyi, 'Noms toponymiques'; Rásonyi, 'Anthroponyms comans'; Rásonyi, 'Kuman Özel Adlari'.
[149] Pálóczi Horváth, 'Kunok megtelepedése Magyarországon', p. 257; Pálóczi Horváth, 'Immigration', p. 331; Pálóczi Horváth, 'Steppe traditions', p. 296. A similar process of name change in Kosovo: István Schütz, 'Les contacts médiévaux albano-comans reflétés par l'onomastique de Kosovo', *AOASH* 40 (1986): pp. 293–300.

to their people that burial in a Christian cemetery did not replace for a few generations. Some of the Cuman mass cemeteries were located around churches that already existed in the thirteenth century, whereas in other cases a church was built only in the fifteenth century. The thirteenth- to fifteenth-century strata of Cuman mass cemeteries show a mixture of traditional and Christian customs; the last elements of the 'pagan' traditions had disappeared by the sixteenth century.[150] Cuman conversion, in the sense of the baptism of the Cuman population, was completed during the fourteenth century.[151] The process of Christianization was gradual and proceeded through a stage when the Cumans mixed Christian and traditional practices; thus objects linked to 'pagan' traditions were still placed into graves in fourteenth-century Christian mass cemeteries around churches. The process of Christianization was faster for some of the Cuman groups than others; in some areas of Cuman settlement churches were built only in the fifteenth, or even in the late sixteenth century, sometimes over previous 'pagan' cemeteries.[152]

Bartlett's analysis of the 'partial but permanent conversion' of the Pomeranians to some extent fits the first phase of the Cuman conversion process as well: the destruction of a 'pagan' cult was irreversible even if it was not immediately accompanied by a thorough Christianization of the people.[153] Christian missions and pressure, life within a Christian environment and the disintegration of traditional Cuman society destroyed the 'pagan' belief system as a functioning whole. Christianization, however, was not simply a matter of coercion from the Christian side, although force and threats did play an important role. The infiltration of Christianity was facilitated by Cuman attitudes. Political expediency, considerations of prestige, and a willingness, characteristic of steppe nomads, to integrate new elements of belief, made baptism initially acceptable to many of them. Increasingly thereafter, Cumans lived among a Christian population, intermarried with them, and listened to their stories. This led to religious integration; every Cuman village eventually had a church, complaints regarding continued 'pagan' practices ceased.

[150] László Selmeczi, 'A kunok és jászok emlékanyagának kutatása', in *Középkori régészetünk ujabb eredményei és időszerű feladatai*, eds. István Fodor and László Selmeczi (Budapest: Magyar Nemzeti Múzeum, 1985), pp. 79–92; Selmeczi, 'Magyarországi kunok temetkezése', pp. 31–45; Selmeczi, 'Kunok és a jászok régészeti'; Horváth, 'Csengele', pp. 113–15; Méri, 'Beszámoló a Tiszalök-Rázompusztai', p. 142.
[151] *JK*, vol. II: pp. 35, 164–6 and vol. III: pp. 531–4. See chapter 6, p. 223.
[152] Selmeczi, 'Adatok és szempontok', p. 19 (Homokszállás still had no church in 1571: p. 12); Selmeczi, 'Régészeti ásatások', p. 12; Horváth, 'Csengele'; László Selmeczi, 'A magyarországi "jászkunok" és a tételes vallások', *A Szolnok megyei múzeumok évkönyve* 7 (1990): pp. 207–11. Sometimes a pre-existing church was rebuilt as early as the end of the thirteenth century: Hatházi, 'Perkátai', p. 656.   [153] Bartlett, 'Conversion of a Pagan Society'.

None the less, it was perhaps the component of constraint in their Christianization that contributed to Cuman enthusiasm for Calvinism in the sixteenth century, similar to the 'heretic' Bosnian population that was open to Islamization under Ottoman rule.[154]

Changed circumstances and outright pressure for social and religious adaptation in the thirteenth century led to Cuman dissatisfaction and revolt. This resembled the pattern of 'pagan' resistance in the first period of Christianization, such as can be seen in Sweden, Poland and Hungary in the eleventh century. It also raises the question whether contacts between the Cumans who migrated to Hungary and those who remained on the steppe could contribute to a persistence of Cuman traditions in Hungary. The Cumans who did not flee from the steppe were subjugated by the Mongols, and eventually incorporated into the Empire of the Golden Horde. According to a Mongol source, the Cumans fell under Mongol power by the right of conquest, and the Hungarian king's harbouring of the fugitive Cumans caused the attack against Hungary in 1241.[155] This attitude did not promise flourishing contacts between the Cumans of Hungary and the steppe. Cuman community life, unlike that of Muslims and Jews, neither provided an impetus for seeking regular outside contacts with coreligionists, nor was dependent on such contacts. Desire for arbitration in legal cases and the need to train religious and legal experts played no role. Therefore religious motivations for such contacts were non-existent, as opposed to Muslims who sent students to study Islamic law and Jews who turned to foreign rabbis. Intermittent contacts fed not by Cuman aspirations but by Hungarian royal and ecclesiastical aims may have existed. King Béla IV sent spies to the Mongols.[156] Cumans who travelled abroad in royal service may have participated in these diplomatic missions, but there is no information on their destinations.[157] None the less, Cuman dissatisfaction and military defeat within Hungary pushed the Cumans to re-establish contacts and flee to their previous territories now under Mongol rule. Charters and a contemporary chronicle mention Cumans who left the kingdom and had to be brought back from the 'boundaries and limits' of the Mongols.[158] This attempted Cuman flight back to the steppe became, in fourteenth-century chronicle compositions and forged charters based on the chronicle accounts, an accusation that the

---

[154] Rásonyi, *Hidak*, p. 123.   [155] See chapter 1, note 107.
[156] Marczali, *Magyar Történelmi Tár*, p. 376; Sinor, 'Relations entre les Mongols', pp. 39–62.
[157] Parabuch, receiving a donation of land for such service in 1266: *JK*, vol. II: pp. 418–19, no. 53 (*RA*, no. 1856). See also *ÁÚO*, vol. VIII: p. 203, no. 136 (*RA*, no. 1876).
[158] 'de finibus et terminis Tartarorum': *CD*, vol. V, pt. 3: p. 410 (*JK*, vol. II: p. 454, no. 84; *RA*, no. 3499); *Hazai Oklevéltár*, pp. 116–17, no. 110 (*RA*, no. 3544); *HO*, vol. VI: p. 317, no. 230 (*RA*, no. 3413); Simon of Kéza, in *SRH*, vol. I: p. 187 'ad populos barbaros fugierunt'.

Non-Christian communities

Cumans of Hungary called in their relatives under the leadership of Oldamur to conquer the kingdom.[159]

Costume is an important indicator of social status, including the degree of integration into the surrounding society. Cuman attire and armaments in Hungary have been reconstructed from archaeological finds and fourteenth-century pictorial representations.[160] A comparison between this reconstruction and the *kamennye baby* of the Russian steppe (which represent the details of Cuman clothing and have been interpreted in the light of archaeological finds) demonstrates the process of change in Hungary.[161] These statues portray both men and women wearing a caftan fastened by a belt; the clothing under the caftan is not visible. Their long boots are attached to their belts at the front by a strap (rarely represented on statues of women). Men wear leather armour, strengthened by leather or felt disks attached to the chest and back, and conical or dome-shaped helmets. Suspended from their belts are various objects, including a bow-case with bow, a quiver, a knife and a comb. Women wear a large variety of head-dresses, often with a veil hanging at the back covering the hair, though sometimes one or two braids are visible. They also exhibit a variety of jewelry, including two typical of the steppe: torques, a type of neck-ornament that usually consisted of one or several metal strands attached to a ribbon or necklace and hung around the neck, and a head-dress made of a series of silver rings on a solid, cylindrically shaped material which was fastened at the temples, producing a horn-shaped ornament.

In their attire and armament the Cumans combined traditions and certain new elements during the thirteenth and early fourteenth centuries in Hungary. Most of the evidence comes from burials of the elite. Cuman men (in solitary graves) were buried in their warrior's outfit. Some wore dome-shaped helmets characteristic of the nomad military elite and chain-mail. Their armament consisted of a bow and arrows, a sword and sometimes a mace, which appeared in Hungary with the Cumans in the thirteenth century: arms typical of light cavalry units.[162] The adoption of Hungarian swords was not unknown.[163] A few wore studded belts of a western European type; these may have been gifts from

---

[159] See chapter 6, note 43.
[160] Pálóczi Horváth, *Hagyományok*, pp. 105–37, 177–86 (*passim* for a list of the objects found in graves); Pálóczi Horváth, *Besenyők*, pp. 75–83; András Pálóczi Horváth, 'Le costume coman au Moyen Âge', *Acta Archaeologica Academiae Scientiarum Hungaricae* 32 (1980): pp. 403–27; András Pálóczi Horváth, 'Régészeti adatok a kunok viseletéhez', *Archaeologiai Értesítő* 109 (1982): pp. 89–107; also see chapter 6 above, pp. 207–9.
[161] On Cuman dress and weapons as represented on the *kamennye baby*, see the synthesis of Pálóczi Horváth, *Hagyományok*, pp. 80–5.
[162] János Kalmár, *Régi magyar fegyverek* (Budapest: Natura Szegedi Nyomda, 1971), pp. 19–20.
[163] Selmeczi, 'Adatok és szempontok', p. 8.

At the Gate of Christendom

the king of Hungary or from the rulers of the Latin empire of Constantinople with whom the Cumans were allied.[164] Some graves contain two buckles over the skeleton. Although the textiles have completely disintegrated, these buckles indicate that their owner wore trousers and a caftan, the traditional costume worn by the Cumans on the steppe.[165] In addition to these archaeological finds, fourteenth-century images depict Cuman men: manuscript illuminations (the *Illuminated Chronicle*, and the Angevin *Legendary*), and murals that represent the fight of St László and the Cuman.[166] As discussed in chapter 6, the symbolic use of Cuman representations did not exclude the realistic portrayal of elements of Cuman attire. Cuman men appear in long caftans, fastened by a belt, wearing high conical hats, occasionally chain-mail and a helmet. They are armed with bows, bow-cases, arrows, quiver and sword. Cuman attire was different from that of the local population, who usually wore long tight trousers and tunics, which in the thirteenth century came just below the knee. Over the tunic, a cloak or mantle was worn.[167]

Archaeological finds from the thirteenth and early fourteenth centuries show that Cuman women equally retained their traditional attire. Two buckles found in graves indicate the wearing of caftan and trousers. Women also continued to wear torques; the characteristic horn-shaped Cuman female head-dress of the steppe, as well as mirrors, have also been found in Cuman graves in Hungary.[168] Other jewelry used by Cuman women (especially finds from mass cemeteries) was partly similar to apparel worn by Hungarian women at the time, such as rings, buttons and hairpins, and partly identifiable with those widespread in the Balkans, for example, a type of earring.[169] The Cumans brought these latter with

---

[164] István Éri, 'Adatok a kígyóspusztai csat értékeléséhez', *Folia Archaeologica* 8 (1956): pp. 137–52; Pálóczi Horváth, 'Situation des recherches', p. 203; András Pálóczi Horváth, 'A Felsőszentkirályi kun sírlelet', *Cumania: A Bács-Kiskun megyei múzeumok évkönyve* 1 (1972): pp. 177–204, see pp. 189–90, 196; András Pálóczi Horváth, 'A csólyosi kun sírlelet', *Folia Archaeologica* 20 (1969): pp. 107–34; Pálóczi Horváth, *Hagyományok*, pp. 161–9.

[165] Pálóczi Horváth, 'Régészeti adatok', p. 103; Selmeczi, 'Adatok és szempontok', p. 16; Hatházi, 'Perkátai', p. 659.

[166] The *Képes Krónika* (Illuminated Chronicle) was written on the basis of earlier Hungarian chronicles in the second half of the fourteenth century, and illuminated with 147 miniatures. The *Magyar Anjou Legendárium* (Angevin Legendary) is a manuscript of saints' *Vitae*, produced for the Angevins of Hungary. László, *Szent László-legenda*, includes colour reproductions of all surviving wall-paintings of the fight of László and the Cuman.

[167] Lovag, 'Magyar viselet', pp. 397–8.

[168] Pálóczi Horváth, *Hagyományok*, pp. 145–8.

[169] Two detailed case-studies with photographs: Pálóczi Horváth, 'Balota pusztai'; Gábor Hatházi, '14. századi ruhakorongpár Sárosdról és viselettörténeti kapcsolatai', *Archeológiai Értesítő* 114, no. 1 (1987–8): pp. 106–20. István Fazekas and András Pálóczi Horváth, *A kunok emléke Magyarországon* (Kiskunfélegyháza: Kiskun Múzeum, 1985), pp. 11–13, on fourteenth- and fifteenth-century ornaments. By the beginning of the fourteenth century most jewelry already belonged to local types in one area: Gábor Hatházi, 'A kunok régészeti és történeti emlékei a Kelet-Dunántúlon' (Ph.D. dissertation, Budapest: ELTE, 1996), p. 58.

Non-Christian communities

them from their previous home. There are no representations of Cuman women in Hungary.

Thus the costume of the first few generations of Cumans in Hungary (and especially of the Cuman elite in the thirteenth and early fourteenth centuries) shows a continuity of essential elements, with some changes, in comparison to the *kamennye baby* of the steppe. The most characteristic parts of male and female Cuman clothing remained traditional. They continued to wear caftans and long boots, and men retained the habit of hanging a knife, bow and other objects from their belts. Objects from the steppe and Byzantium, including Byzantine coins placed in graves (maybe as provision for the journey the soul of the deceased had to take) brought by the Cumans to Hungary, were also used.[170] It seems that changes and adaptations to local styles first affected two areas: articles especially associated with prestige and armour. Belts adorned with studding and an elaborate clasp found in Cuman graves in Hungary started to replace the simple belts of the Russian steppe; belts were an important symbol of social status for nomads of the thirteenth-century steppe.[171] The use of jewelry and ornaments corresponding to local styles was also already significant in the thirteenth century. The most important change was related to weapons and armour; the Cumans adopted western-type swords and the chain-mail that protected them better than the traditional leather armour. Chain-mail was used not only in Hungary, but on the steppe as well by the military elite.[172] Some Cumans also adopted the straight stirrup, suitable for hard-soled shoes as opposed to the traditional soft boots, and (in the fourteenth century) spurs.[173] None the less, their most important form of arms, the bow, was represented in the same way on the *kamennye baby* and on the Hungarian murals of the fourteenth century. The Cuman bow was permanently drawn, kept in a bow-case hanging from the belt, and accompanied by a quiver whose upper part opened out, in which the arrows were stacked pointing upwards.[174]

Cumans adopted local articles, first Byzantine ones in the Balkans, then Hungarian products, either for practical reasons (such as in the case of chain-mail) or for prestige (studded belts, jewelry). At the same time, they retained important elements of their traditional attire (caftan, bow

---

[170] Pálóczi Horváth, 'Balota pusztai', p. 131; Pálóczi Horváth, *Hagyományok*, pp. 144–60.
[171] Rásonyi, *Hidak*, pp. 133–4; Mark G. Kramarovsky, 'The Culture of the Golden Horde and the Problem of the "Mongol Legacy"', in *Rulers from the Steppe*, pp. 255–73, see p. 261.
[172] Swords: Kalmár, *Régi magyar fegyverek*, pp. 58–9. Chain-mail: Pálóczi Horváth, 'Csólyosi kun sírlelet hadtörténeti vonatkozásai', pp. 116–17.
[173] Fazekas and Pálóczi Horváth, *Kunok emléke*, p. 11; rounded stirrups were preserved in other Cuman graves: *ibid.*, p. 14; István Fodor, 'Az osztrogozsszki lelet', *Cumania: A Bács-Kiskun megyei múzeumok közleményei* 4 (1976): pp. 255–63.
[174] László, 'Adatok a kunok tegezéről'; Gyula Kristó, *Az Árpád-kor háborúi* (Budapest: Zrínyi Kiadó, 1986), pp. 216–79; Kőhalmi, *Steppék*, pp. 194–200.

and arrows). Mixture characterized the first phase of integration, with new elements incorporated into the Cuman attire; during the fourteenth century, and in some areas as early as the beginning of that century, they were assimilated into the local population in their attire and ornaments.[175]

Cumans also had a distinctive way of wearing their hair that differed from the Hungarian custom. As both *kamennye baby* and Hungarian sources show, Cuman men had no beards, wore a narrow moustache and braided their hair into one or three tresses that fell onto their backs.[176] The top of the head was shaved. This was not a specifically Cuman, but a nomad hairstyle, common on the steppe.[177] The Hungarians, at the time of their arrival in the Carpathian basin, wore similar plaits and shaved the rest of their heads. This hairstyle was branded as 'pagan' and its eradication was linked to the Christianization of the country in the eleventh century. The shaving of the head became a punishment for criminals.[178] New hairstyles resembled western ones and men grew beards.[179] The frescoes depicting the fight of King László I and the Cuman portrayed the king wearing western hairstyle and a beard, in sharp contrast to his Cuman opponent's moustache and braids.[180]

The Cumans resisted demands to relinquish their hairstyle and costume more than baptism. King László IV, while he acquiesced in the regulation of Cuman status demanded by the papal legate, and made the conversion of all Cumans obligatory, asked the legate's permission to allow the Cumans to retain their traditional hairstyle.[181] László himself promised to give up Cuman attire and hairstyle; these highly symbolic markers of identity were essential parts of the accusation that he had become a 'pagan'.[182] As in every culture, throughout the Middle Ages both clothing and hair had special significance in distinguishing personal

---

[175] Gábor Hatházi, 'A Hantos-széki kunok településtörténete' (M.A. thesis, Budapest: ELTE, 1985), p. 140; Hatházi, 'Kunok régészeti', pp. 39–50; Horváth, 'Régészeti adatok a kunok Dél-Alföldi történetéhez', pp. 66–7.

[176] Pálóczi Horváth, *Hagyományok*, pp. 80, 177; László, *Szent László-legenda*, pp. 47, 49, 51, 96–8 (they are also sometimes depicted wearing a beard: see, for example p. 180).

[177] Descriptions of Mongol hair: Carpini, *Ystoria*, ed. Wyngaert, pp. 32–3 (ed. Daffinà et al., pp. 232–3); Rubruck, 'Itinerarium', p. 182; Simon de Saint-Quentin, p. 31. See the remarks of Jean Dauvillier in Paul Pelliot, *Recherches sur les chrétiens d'Asie Centrale et d'Extrême-Orient: Oeuvres post-humes de Paul Pelliot* (Paris: Imp. Nationale, 1973), p. 17.

[178] On pagan Hungarians shaving their head: Pauler and Szilágyi, *Magyar Honfoglalás Kútfői*, p. 327. As punishment: Bak, *Laws*, p. 14; Erdélyi, *Pannonhalmi Szent-Benedek-rend*, vol. I: p. 753, no. 166 (1237). [179] Lovag, 'Magyar viselet', p. 383.

[180] See the photographic reproduction in László, *Szent László-legenda*, pp. 97–8, 112.

[181] ASV Reg. Vat. 39, f. 219 (*VMH*, p. 342, no. DLVII).

[182] *Ibid.*: 'dimisso paganorum abusu, resumeres christianorum habitum, tam in vestibus quam capillis'. The *Illuminated Chronicle* expanded this: according to its author, the legate exhorted the Hungarians to stop shaving their beards, cutting off their hair, and wearing Cuman hats: *SRH*, vol. I: p. 473.

Non-Christian communities

status in the social hierarchy by making it immediately visible.[183] It is meaningful that this external aspect of Cuman life – an appearance that evoked the steppe and 'pagan' beliefs – could initially be safeguarded in the Christian kingdom of Hungary. Regulations on clothing and hair had two intertwined aspects: real or desired control by those in power over a subjected group, and the self-defined identity of the group itself. Thus the element of control and external definitions of identity can be seen, for example, in Christian relations to Muslims in Iberia and the attitude of the English to the Irish. Subject Muslims were to wear their hair cut in a round style.[184] Irish hairstyle and Irish clothing were not to be adopted by Englishmen; regarded as a sign of barbarity they were markers of legal status as well.[185] Hair and clothing were also significant in the self-definitions of identity.[186] Conversion raised the problem of whether or not attire had to be changed.

The conversion process, during which identity was in transition, and was expected to change, focused attention on these markers of identity. Abū Zayd (Saʿīd), a Muslim who converted to Christianity in conquered Valencia, retained his Islamic costume after his conversion.[187] The conversion of the 'pagan' Bulgars and Mongols to Christianity also raised the issue of clothing and hair. The Bulgars and the Mongols, like the Cumans, were troubled by the idea of relinquishing their traditional attire. In both cases, like that of the Cumans in Hungary, ecclesiastical response was initial leniency. In 866, Pope Nicholas I wrote to Khan Boris of Bulgaria about a variety of questions raised by conversion to Christianity, including the problem of traditional clothing.[188] In 1291 Pope Nicholas IV wrote to a converted Mongol, a son of Arghun, in

---

[183] Roland Barthes, 'Histoire et sociologie du vêtement', *Annales ESC* (1957, no. 3): pp. 430–41; Simmel, 'Fashion'; Michel Pastoureau, *Couleurs, images, symboles. Etudes d'histoire et d'anthropologie* (Paris: Le Léopard d'Or, 1989), see chapter III, 'Les codes vestimentaires', pp. 31–9; Gábor Klaniczay, 'Fashionable Beards and Heretic Rags', in Klaniczay, *The Uses of Supernatural Power* (Cambridge: Polity Press, 1990), pp. 51–78; Michel Pastoureau, ed., *Le vêtement: Histoire, archéologie et symbolique vestimentaires au Moyen Age*, Cahiers du Léopard d'Or 1 (Paris: Le Léopard d'Or, 1989); Mellinkoff, *Outcasts*; Bartlett, 'Symbolic Meanings of Hair'.

[184] Bartlett, 'Symbolic Meanings of Hair', p. 47.

[185] Ibid., pp. 45–6; Boivin, *Irlande*, p. 114.

[186] The Irish were critical of those who followed English ways; thus elements of self-definition mingled with those of external regulation (see previous note). When the Muslims of Granada capitulated in the late fifteenth century, the treaty with the victors allowed them to retain their own dress among other concessions: Bishko, 'Spanish and Portuguese Reconquest', p. 453. Not necessarily every member of a group conformed to the same costume and hairstyle; moreover, these could be changed over time: Pohl, 'Telling the Difference', esp. pp. 64–5.

[187] Robert I. Burns, *Society and Documentation in Crusader Valencia* (Princeton: Princeton University Press, 1985), p. 186.

[188] Sullivan, 'Khan Boris'; Shepard, 'Slavs and Bulgars'; Mayr-Harting, *Two Conversions*; Fletcher, *Conversion*, p. 367; *MGH Epp.*, vol. VI: pp. 568–600, see p. 588.

answer to his query, advising him not to change his traditional costume, in order to avoid conflict with his people.[189] Measures like these were meant to be temporary and ease the transition of newly converted people to full Christianization.[190] For the populations involved, like the Cumans in Hungary, however, clothing and hair remained central to their identity.

Another important aspect of integration was the changing structure of Cuman society. On the steppe, the Cumans were organized into clans and tribes, led by khans. Some of these clans had higher status than others. Studies have shown that nomad societies developed through contacts and interaction with sedentary states, even without being integrated as a subject minority. Cuman society was changing – through contacts with sedentary neighbours – by the mid-thirteenth century. Some chieftains became more important than others, certain clans gained more respect than the rest, and Rus' sources refer to an emerging clan aristocracy. Immediately preceding the Mongol invasions, Cuman society was perhaps moving towards a more centralized organization under Könchek's son Yur'i. This development, however, was arrested by the Mongol conquest.[191]

Cuman social structure upon their arrival in Hungary was determined by previous events. Cuman tribal organization was disturbed by losses and the flight from the Mongols. Fragments of tribes from several clans entered the kingdom of Hungary and never recombined into new tribes.[192] Perhaps these immigrants were firmly associated under the leadership of one chief, Köten. The canon Roger certainly thought so, and called him king.[193] This may, however, represent a Christian understanding of Cuman society; other texts suggest that more fluidity may have characterized their social organization, and they had more than one leader.[194] Clan organization already coexisted with social differentiation

---

[189] *Reg. Nic. IV*, no. 6833; Lucas Wadding, *Annales Minorum*, 5 vols. (Rome, 1731–3), vol. V: p. 258. Muldoon, *Popes*, pp. 67–9; Berend 'Medieval Patterns', p. 170.

[190] See chapter 6, pp. 207–9 on symbolic meanings of the representation of Cuman-style attire in art.

[191] Golden, 'Polovcii Dikii', pp. 305–9; Golden, 'Nomads and their Sedentary Neighbors', pp. 61–8; Peter B. Golden, 'Cumanica II: The Ölberli (Ölperli): The Fortunes and Misfortunes of an Inner Asian Nomadic Clan', *AEMAe* 6 (1986): pp. 5–29. On the differentiation of Cuman society in the late thirteenth century around the Black Sea (under Mongol rule): Györffy, 'Kipcsaki kun', pp. 257–8. Boris I. Vladimirtsov, *Le régime social des mongols: Le féodalisme nomade* (Paris: Adrien Maisonneuve, 1948), claimed that nomadic society developed its own 'feudalism', as clans were falling apart with the emergence of vassal–lord relationships.

[192] Described as 'generationes', 'generationum gradus' belonging to 'linea' in the Cuman articles of 1279: ASV AA Arm. I-XVIII-595 (*VMH*, p. 340, no. DLVI). The forged second Cuman law mentions 'septem generaciones Comanorum': Marczali, *Magyar történet kútföinek*, p. 181. See chapter 4 above, text and notes 132–3.   [193] *SRH*, vol. II: pp. 553–4.

[194] Two 'principales Comanorum' negotiated the acceptance of the Cuman articles of 1279: ASV AA Arm. I-XVIII-595 (*VMH*, p. 340, no. DLVI). King Charles of Sicily addressed his letter to

Non-Christian communities

between the elite, called nobles by the canon Roger, and commoners, called peasants or 'poor'.[195] At the time of their arrival in Hungary, the poor members of Cuman clans were willing to serve Hungarian lords.[196]

The Hungarian context and integration as a minority further influenced Cuman social transformation. Cuman leadership and the Hungarian royal family became linked through a marriage alliance. The union of István (the future István V), Béla IV's son, and Erzsébet, the daughter of a Cuman chieftain, opened the way for the quick integration of a part of the Cuman elite. Erzsébet was baptized prior to her marriage, which was clearly a dynastic one.[197] Béla IV justified it as contracted for the defence of the country.[198] The Cuman elite related to Erzsébet found itself incorporated into the highest stratum of Hungarian society: other female members of her family married Hungarian nobles, King Béla IV called the Cuman Zeyhan 'dux' and his relative, and Erzsébet's son became king of Hungary.[199] This was not the only road to integration into the nobility. The formation of a Cuman landed elite in Hungary was also possible through obtaining hereditary landholdings and legal rights over the inhabitants of the land. Yet in the first generation there was a lot of fluidity; the acquisition and loss of lands was linked to political fortunes, as explored in chapter 4. Thus social differentiation preceded the development of a stable nobility.[200] By the end of the

the Cumans of Hungary to 'Magnifico viro Albret et aliis nobilibus Cumanis': *Magyar diplomáciai*, p. 34.

[195] 'Nobiles': Rogerius, in *SRH*, vol. II: pp. 554, 557. (The eighteenth-century version of the Cuman law insisted on 'nobiles', but for the very specific purpose of proving Cuman privileged status: Marczali, *Magyar történet kútfőinek*, pp. 179–83.) High-ranking individuals also appear as 'dominus' in charters, for example *JK*, vol. II: pp. 418–19, no. 53 (*RA*, 1856). Rogerius, in *SRH*, vol. II: p. 554, 'rustici'; p. 557, 'pauperes'. Cumans mentioned as 'depauperati': MOL DL 40166 (*ÁÚO*, vol. XII: p. 389, no. 320; *RA*, no. 3213). Kring, 'Kun és jász', p. 47 interprets this stratification as purely a difference in wealth, but not in social rank.

[196] *SRH*, vol. II: p. 557.

[197] Erzsébet's conversion: 'Cumana nacione, licet baptizata', (Johannes of Marignola) in *Fontes Rerum Bohemicarum*, vol. III: p. 568; 'natione Comana, sacramentis tamen fidei initiata', in ibid., vol. II: p. 311. Her father and his followers were baptized in 1254: 'Gerardi de Fracheto Vitae Fratrum Ordinis Praedicatorum necnon cronica ordinis ab anno MCCIII usque ad MCCLIV', ed. Benedictus Maria Reichert, in *MOPH*, vol. I: p. 338. The marriage has been dated to 1247 on the basis of a note concerning the wedding ceremony (see chapter 3, pp. 98–9), and to 1254 on the basis of the General Chapter of the Dominican Order where Erzsébet's father was baptized. Such dynastic marriages with Cumans elsewhere: Golden, 'Nomads and their Sedentary Neighbors', p. 72; Sinor, 'Quelques passages'; A. Longnon, 'Les Toucy en Orient et en Italie au 13e siècle', *Bulletin de la Société des Sciences Historiques et Naturelles de l'Yonne* 96 (1957): pp. 33–43.

[198] 'Propter defensionem fidei christiane filio nostro primogenito Cumanam quandam thoro coniunximus maritali': ASV AA Arm. I-XVIII-605; Martini, *Sigilli*, plate 9E (*VMH*, p. 231, no. CCCCXI; *RA*, no. 933a).

[199] 'Zeyhanus karissimus cognatus noster' (1255): MOL DL 97856 (*HO*, vol. VIII: p. 62, no. 48; *RA*, no. 1054). On marriages between Elizabeth's relatives and the local elite: *RA*, no. 2524; Jakubovich, 'Kún Erzsébet nőtestvére'.

[200] Kring, 'Kun és jász', pp. 44, 48. See also Györffy, 'Magyarországi kun', p. 280.

thirteenth century the Chertan clan rose to an important position. Their territory was the largest; the richest solitary graves were also found in this area.[201]

The rapid integration of part of the Cuman elite aroused fears and criticisms in some quarters. This was true of István and Erzsébet's marriage itself, and especially of Erzsébet's suitability as queen and then regent of Hungary. King Béla's apology to the pope, referred to above, tried to neutralize opposition by presenting the alliance as necessary for the defence of Hungary and of Christendom. Political opponents, however, could capitalize on the notion that 'pagans' controlled power in Hungary. Bruno, bishop of Olomouc, complained that the queen of Hungary was a Cuman and her close relatives were 'pagans'; he argued that this threatened the survival of Christianity in the country.[202] His agenda was linked to the political aspirations of Otakar of Bohemia. A Byzantine author described the wife of the Hungarian king as a Cuman prisoner whom the king married for her beauty; he interpreted the marriage according to a pattern more familiar in Byzantium.[203]

Modern scholars were quick to draw conclusions about the insincerity of Erzsébet's conversion, and attributed various negative traits to her based on evidence that she took ecclesiastical property and promoted her favourites, and that her seal bore the inscription 'daughter of the emperor of the Cumans'.[204] All this, however, adds up to proof of her wild temperament and insincerity only when mixed with a generous dollop of prejudice. During one of the periods of disagreement between Erzsébet and King László, the king accused her of wishing to attack, destroy and occupy ecclesiastical property. She indeed held ecclesiastical lands under her control for a while.[205] Yet the explanation does not lie in Erzsébet's

---

[201] Pálóczi Horváth, 'Kunok megtelepedése', pp. 254–5; Pálóczi Horváth, 'Immigration', see p. 325. The history of this clan will be analysed in more detail by Gábor Hatházi, in his article on Halas, 'Két világ határán: A kun székközpont és magyar mezőváros a középkorban' (manuscript; I thank the author for allowing me to read the article prior to publication).

[202] 'Ipsa Regina Ungarie est Cumana, proximi parentes eius gentiles sunt', ASV AA Arm. I-XVIII-3104 (*VMH*, p. 308, no. DXXXV), and *MGH, Leges*, vol. IV, pt. 3: pp. 589–94, p. 590.

[203] Georges Pachymérès, *Relations historiques*, ed. and French tr. Albert Failler and Vitalien Laurent, 2 vols., Corpus Fontium Historiae Byzantinae 24, pts. 1 and 2 (Paris: Les Belles Lettres, 1984), vol. II: p. 412.

[204] Szabó, *Kun László*, pp. 23, 38; Pauler, *Magyar nemzet*, vol. II: pp. 333, 412; Szűcs, *Utolsó Árpádok*, pp. 281–2. On the variety of views about medieval queens: John Carmi Parsons, ed., *Medieval Queenship* (New York: St Martin's, 1993); Anne J. Duggan, ed., *Queens and Queenship in Medieval Europe* (Woodbridge: Boydell Press, 1997); this collection includes an article on medieval ambiguity about powerful queens (Karen Pratt, 'The Image of the Queen in Old French Literature', pp. 235–59) and the situation in Hungary: János M. Bak, 'Queens as Scapegoats in Medieval Hungary', pp. 223–33.

[205] László's accusation: *CD*, vol. v, pt. 3: pp. 245–6 (*RA*, no. 3155). Erzsébet appropriated tithes and occupied a village belonging to the bishop of Zagreb: *AÚO*, vol. XII: pp. 392–3, no. 323, pp. 414–15, no. 344 (*RA*, no. 3311); *CD*, vol. v, pt. 3: pp. 222–3, 228–31 (*RA*, no. 3310).

Non-Christian communities

'pagan' spirit, as cases of the destruction of ecclesiastical property or the expropriation of ecclesiastical revenues by Christians show.[206] She wished to promote her protégés to various positions, and backed Miklós (Nicholas) Kán, her candidate to the archbishopric, who had the doors locked on the chapter of Esztergom to force them to elect him.[207] Medieval monarchs, however, often wished to impose their own candidates. Finally, the inscription on her seal, seen as evidence of her 'pagan' pride, is much better explained by a Christian–imperial frame of reference. This inscription identifies Erzsébet as 'by the grace of God, queen of Hungary and daughter of the emperor of the Cumans'.[208] The seal therefore represents Erzsébet's claim to rulership simultaneously as conferred on her by her birth (descent from an emperor), and her position as a Christian queen. The seal was produced in 1273, at the time of Erzsébet's regency, her power precarious amidst growing anarchy. The idea of descent from an 'emperor' did not originate in Cuman pride; the Cumans never had emperors. Rather, it indicates Christian references and an attempt to assert authority. A later seal (from 1280) no longer bears the inscription, but reverts to the usual phraseology.[209] Moreover, whether or not personally devout, Erzsébet acted like a Christian queen. Her court was staffed by clerics and she used all the usual channels to issue charters and conduct diplomatic affairs. She donated revenues to monasteries and churches.[210] One of these donations was explicitly for her own salvation and that of her son László IV, her husband István V, Béla IV, and his wife Maria. In this charter she thanked God for having 'recalled [her] from pagan error and led [her] to the recognition of the true light'.[211] She also had a godson ('filius spiritualis').[212] Immediate integration on the highest level was therefore possible, despite some doubts and criticisms. It was easier to turn a 'pagan' chieftain's daughter into the queen of a Christian kingdom than some medieval and modern authors would have us believe.

The entire Cuman society in Hungary underwent a profound transformation. These changes eventually culminated in complete integration and assimilation: the loss of their original belief system, language,

---

[206] E.g. *HO*, vol. VII: p. 170, no. 129; *ÁÚO*, vol. I: pp. 310–12, no. 189, pp. 317–18, no. 194.
[207] *Reg. Nic. III*, no. 70; *VMH*, pp. 324–6, no. DXLII.
[208] 'Elisabet dei gratia regina Ungarie et filia imperatoris Cumanorum', MOL V8, box 1162, no. 844; reproduction in Szabó, *Kun László*, p. 131.   [209] MOL V8 box 375, no. 63612.
[210] For example, *HO*, vol. VI: pp. 261–2, no. 187; Gutheil, *Árpád-kori Veszprém*, no. 39.
[211] 'nos in signum retribucionis seu reconpensacionis donorum nostri creatoris, quibus nos a gentilitatis errore reuocatam, et ad agnicionem ueri luminis perductam, multiplici effectu gracie sue decorauit . . . aliquibus operibus pietatis uolentes occurrere et respondere . . . [donations follow]' MOL DF 219422 (*HO*, vol. VIII: p. 279, no. 227; *ÁÚO*, vol. IX: pp. 524–5, no. 380). There is no basis for seeing this as an expression of repentence for her ways, contrary to what some authors have suggested. Rather, it refers to her baptism.
[212] *CD*, vol. V, pt. 3: p. 22 (*RA*, no. 3053).

customs. In the fourteenth century, clans – at least theoretically organized along the lines of blood relationship – began to evolve into a hierarchy based on the ownership of land. Clan structure eventually broke up due to the development of a nobility and peasantry. The disintegration of Cuman clan-based social structure and the development of a new hierarchy of lords and peasants was the result of integration into the surrounding society.[213] According to György Györffy, clan leaders (captains) became landowning lords and their families hereditary nobility, while the status of the rest of the Cumans deteriorated. Previously communal Cuman lands became private estates, and the captains obtained even more land through royal donation, the settlement of previously uninhabited land, or purchase. Many were also ennobled by the king. By the late fourteenth century some Cuman clan members became royal serfs, others populated the lands of clan captains, and some became serfs on the lands of other nobles.[214] In the fifteenth century the territorial organization of *székek* (*sedes*) developed. Whereas the heads of clans who became captains (*szálláskapitányok*) in the fourteenth century owed their position to the ownership of landed estates, the captains of the *sedes* (*székkapitányok*) were officials.[215] According to Györffy, social integration was accomplished by the late fifteenth century.[216] In comparison, the Cumans who immigrated to Georgia in the twelfth century, and provided military service for the king against external enemies and his own nobles, integrated rapidly into Georgian society. Their Christianization and 'Georgianization' were fast and very thorough.[217]

The Cumans were integrated into the kingdom. However slowly for some, complete acculturation was the result of their incorporation. They progressively adopted the Christian religion, naming patterns, local social and settlement structures, attire and customs. They lost their own language and spoke Hungarian.[218] By the modern period, the Cumans were indistinguishable from Hungarians. Population movements, both into and away from the areas settled by the Cumans, and the Ottoman conquest and

---

[213] Kring, 'Kun és jász', pp. 53–5. During this time some Cumans fled from their homes to escape from the power of their lords. Kring interpreted this movement as the sign of the recent subjugation of the previously free clan commoners, who tried to escape the deterioration of their status and loss of their liberty.

[214] Györffy, 'Magyarországi kun'; Házházi, 'Két világ határán', pp. 37–8, argues that the majority of Cumans perhaps had a similar status to royal free warriors (*várjobbágy*) during the fourteenth and fifteenth centuries.   [215] Rásonyi, *Hidak*, p. 128.

[216] Györffy, 'Magyarországi kun', pp. 289–90. Also see András Pálóczi Horváth, 'A kunok feudalizálódása és a régészet', in *Középkori régészetünk*, pp. 93–104; on the stages of integration, Pálóczi Horváth, 'Kunok a kelet-európai sztyeppén', pp. 115–16.

[217] Golden, 'Cumanica I'.

[218] István Mándoky Kongur, *A kun nyelv magyarországi emlékei* (Karcag: Karcag Város Önkormányzata, 1993), pp. 12, 30, 38 (in the sixteenth and seventeenth centuries). On the patterns of subject nomad–sedentary interaction: Khazanov, *Nomads*, pp. 212–21.

destruction, all led to a thorough mixing of inhabitants in 'Greater and Lesser Cumania' (names given to the two main areas of Cuman settlement in Hungary). At the same time, the construction of a separate Cuman consciousness and identity began. It emerged from the eighteenth-century fight for rights to a territory and a legal status (presented as granted in the thirteenth century).[219] The movement led to the forging of the 'second Cuman law'. In addition, during the 1740s, when Cuman was no longer a living language, a Cuman version of the Lord's Prayer suddenly surfaced. It was a translation from Hungarian of the Protestant version of the prayer, abundant in mistakes.[220] It was taught in schools in 'Cumania' until the mid-twentieth century, and became a cornerstone of Cuman identity. In the twentieth century, enthusiastic self-styled Cumans, some of whom came from families that had migrated to the 'Cuman' area recently, collected 'Cuman folklore'. This consisted of a mixture of early modern and modern elements, for example a type of 'traditional Cuman' dance adapted from Transylvanian dances, 'Cuman characteristics' such as pride, and a staunch Calvinism. This folklore was by no means a survival of medieval Cuman culture. Just as the population of 'Greater and Lesser Cumania' was mixed beyond a possibility of identifying the 'descendants' of the thirteenth-century Cumans, the identity they now claimed was not the revival of an old tradition, but a newly invented one presented as an unbroken continuum. This 'ethnic' consciousness was not based on the survival of traditional Cuman customs, but on legal privileges attached to a territory.

Although interaction between the Cuman minority and the rest of the population resulted in the final assimilation of the Cumans, Cuman influence left some traces in Hungary as well, especially in the form of loanwords in Hungarian. The impact was strongest in the areas of Cuman settlement, where local dialect incorporates words adopted from the Cuman not used in other parts of the country, but even there the number of such words is small. Cuman loan-words attest Cuman influence especially in the domains of horse-breeding, hunting, eating and fighting.[221]

---

[219] See chapter 3, pp. 89–92. Their privileges and legal position were the same as those of the As: Szabó, *Jász etnikai csoport*, vol. II: p. 5.
[220] István Mándoky Kongur, 'A kun miatyánk', *Szolnok Megyei Múzeumi Évkönyv* (1973): pp. 117–25; Golden, '"Codex Cumanicus"', p. 56.
[221] E.g. *tőzeg* (dried manure of cattle), *kantár* (bridle), *árkány* (a type of horse accoutrement), *balta* (axe), *buzogány* (war-club), *bicsak* and *bicska* (pocket-knife), *csákány* (as armament; hatchet); names of animals and plants: Ligeti, *Magyar nyelv*, pp. 244–50, 287, 305–16, 538–44; Lajos Ligeti, 'Tőzeg', *Magyar Nyelv* 34 (1938): pp. 207–10; István Mándoky Kongur, 'A kun nyelv magyarországi emlékei', in *Kelet-Kutatás. Tanulmányok az orientalisztika köréből*, ed. György Kara and József Terjék (Budapest: Kőrösi Csoma Társaság, 1976), pp. 143–51. On Cuman loan-words used only locally (in the areas of Cuman settlement): István Mándoky Kongur, 'Néhány kún eredetű nagykunsági tájszó', *Nyelvtudományi Közlemények* 73 (1971): pp. 365–85; Mándoky Kongur, *Kun nyelv*, pp. 93–129.

A breed of dog (*komondor*) used by shepherds was probably also introduced by the Cumans.[222] Certain features in this region were also identified as 'Cuman'. Thus the most popular type of hat in the sixteenth to eighteenth centuries in the Alföld (Hungarian plains) was called a 'Cuman hat', and a village pattern in the same area (houses built in groups without any order, with meandering paths between them) was associated with the Cumans. Extensive animal husbandry on the Hungarian plains and the shepherds' way of life away from the villages with their animals has also been understood as a Cuman legacy. As Greater and Lesser Cumania are part of the Hungarian plains, many of the modern practices and customs prevalent on the plains have been associated with the Cumans.[223] They are, however, early modern in origin, and do not represent a continuity of medieval Cuman tradition.

Non-Christians in Hungary followed different paths. Continued Jewish survival contrasted with the disappearance of Muslims and the gradual but eventually complete religious and social integration of Cumans. Christian objectives were not the sole determinants of the ultimate fate of these communities. Thirteenth-century ecclesiastical policies aimed at the integration of the Cumans and at the separation of Jews and Muslims from Christians both by restrictions on roles and behaviour and by distinguishing signs. Two partial successes of these policies were Cuman integration and the fourteenth-century expulsion of the Jews. None the less, the integration was accomplished more slowly than foreseen; the expulsion did not last long and Jews returned to Hungary. The Christian society of the kingdom provided a context that differed from the ecclesiastical formulations. Hungarian society influenced non-Christian micro-societies by the occupations it offered to non-Christians, and the degrees of social and economic integration it afforded. Fiscal functions, trade and military service helped form elites within these communities and provided a measure of incorporation.

The determining factors on the non-Christian side were complex. Social and economic roles, social structure and relations with coreligionists abroad all played a role in the ultimate outcome: assimilation or continuity. Both the Jewish and Muslim populations were heterogeneous, consisting of several immigrant groups who arrived in different waves. Yet their respective distance from coreligionists was different. By the thirteenth century, the Muslims of Hungary became an isolated outpost of the world of Islam. In contrast, religious tradition and contacts with core-

---

[222] Benkő, *Magyar nyelv*, vol. II: p. 540.
[223] István Györffy and Károly Viski, *A magyarság tárgyi néprajza*, 2 vols. (Budapest: Királyi Magyar Egyetemi Nyomda, n.d. (before 1934)), vol. I: pp. 126, 385–98; vol. II: pp. 179–80, 194–5.

ligionists, as well as new immigrants, ensured that despite individual conversions Jewish communities not only survived but even grew after the thirteenth century. For the majority, 'inward acculturation' did not lead to complete assimilation. Conversion for the Muslims was the end of the process of social integration, whereas for the Cumans it was only the beginning. Cumans lived in territories assigned to them, and had their own social structure and judicial system. Their way of life differed greatly from that of other inhabitants of the kingdom. The road from baptism, accepted by many members of the first generation, to integration was a long one, that entailed various transformations. Conversion was followed by a more thorough Christianization and adaptation to local customs from the second and third generations, and ended in complete assimilation. It was a curious paradox of their 'paganism' that although it had no independent uniting power, its elements survived for a long period. Once the social fabric was destroyed or transformed, the traditional belief system could be replaced by Christianity. Yet various practices tenaciously continued, even among Christianized Cumans.

The rich and varied interplay between royal and ecclesiastical policies, social and economic possibilities, non-Christian social structure and religious cohesion, resulted in several possible outcomes: survival, transformation or assimilation. The diverse roads taken by Hungary's non-Christian groups show that they should not be lumped together as 'other'.

CONCLUSION

The analysis of the economic, social, legal and religious position of non-Christians in Hungary has implications for the study of medieval frontier societies, minorities, identity and the nature of exclusion from and integration into society.

The situation of non-Christians in Hungary was unique within contemporary Latin Christendom in two respects. First, three groups of non-Christians were present as late as the thirteenth century: Jews, Muslims and 'pagans'. Second, they did not become part of the kingdom through conquest. Hungary was a frontier kingdom, but not primarily a conquest kingdom in the eleventh to thirteenth centuries. The non-Christian population migrated to Hungary, rather than being forced to become a part of it, as was the case (with minor exceptions) in Iberia, Prussia and other medieval frontier areas.

Keeping this singularity in mind, a brief summary of the results of this study is necessary before drawing more general conclusions. In order to gain a satisfactory picture, we need to consider the interplay between the economic, social, legal, political and religious realities. Hungary was not a case of 'tolerance due to economic necessity'. Non-Christians certainly played economic roles, even important ones, but they were not irreplaceable. They did not exclusively fill any occupation or role. The same monetary functions were held by Jews, Muslims and Christians, and there was no need for middlemen between Christians and another culture (as opposed to Reconquest Iberia). Therefore, despite the existence of non-Christian social and economic roles, their status cannot simply be attributed to their economic importance and a concomitant royal 'tolerance'.

Political reasons were prominent in contributing to policies protecting non-Christians; kings, in order to build their military and financial power, were facilitating the settlement and survival of groups they believed would be dependent and thus loyal. In their endeavour to build strong royal power, kings of Hungary relied on and gave privileges to

Conclusion

non-Christian groups. Thus attempts to construct central power in Hungary did not lead to discrimination and persecution.

In the Hungarian case, royal policies concerning non-Christians triggered royal–ecclesiastical conflicts. Information supplied by clerics within Hungary was often the basis of papal intervention. Yet the course of these conflicts was partly shaped by papal concerns; popes demanded the regulation of non-Christian status according to ecclesiastical norms. Although the role of the papacy elsewhere was more ambivalent (sometimes protecting non-Christians and sometimes militating for harsh measures against them), in Hungary the popes advocated a strict choice between integration by conversion or measures of exclusion. This was largely due to fears about Hungary's detachment from Christendom. Yet a purely religious explanation of Christian policies towards non-Christians is not satisfactory.

In Hungary non-Christian legal status was not fundamentally different from the pattern of legal statuses of Christians (especially of *hospites*) prevalent at the time. Non-Christian legal status was not a unique category. It seems that as long as Hungarian society remained 'cellular', that is, while a multitude of small corporate groups made up the fabric of society, non-Christians were not separated by their legal status from the rest of society. As the social structure crystallized into more homogeneous strata of nobles and peasants, the status of non-Christians became distinctive.

The exploration of Christian policies towards non-Christians has to be complemented by the examination of the processes within Hungary's non-Christian groups. They were a definite minority in a Christian kingdom, and their divergent paths of integration and survival point to the criteria of assimilation and/or its avoidance. Religious cohesion and a recognized communal legal status facilitated the survival of these groups, but these alone could not ensure the non-assimilation of the group. Both the preservation of continuous contact (via immigration and other means) with coreligionists and the structure of the non-Christian community were key factors. Isolation ultimately led to assimilation, however great the original difference was between the culture, language and religion of the minority and majority groups.

This study also shows that rather than being mutually exclusive alternatives, peaceful coexistence and enmity occurred together. At times, different elements of the majority group displayed discrepant behaviour towards the minority. Popular animosity, for example, coexisted with a royal policy that encouraged the presence of non-Christians. Interaction between the Christian and non-Christian population, moreover, was both peaceful and violent. Christians lived together with Jews on streets called 'Jewish Street', a clear example that they did not seek to separate their location of everyday life. Yet there was also popular persecution of Jews. Cumans were feared and hated, yet they also came to be depicted in the same way as the ancestors of the Hungarians. The question, therefore, is not whether a country was tolerant or not to its non-Christian minorities during the Middle Ages. Instead, we should ask what interconnected forms of acceptance and rejection existed regarding groups outside Christianity in each specific case. In Hungary, policies towards the three groups differed; we do not witness the birth of a 'persecuting society' that was equally oppressive to all marginal groups, but rather we can observe the varieties of attitudes toward these groups.

Hungary's frontier situation influenced many of the policies towards non-Christians. The kingdom's origins on the periphery of Christendom, its not-too-distant pagan past, its traditions barely or not yet extinct, and the constant proximity of the non-Christian world all provided a context very different from the areas of long-standing Christianization. The position of non-Christians in this frontier kingdom aroused deeper fears and sharper reactions than in the core of Europe. The fact that Hungary continued on the frontier of Christendom throughout the Middle Ages meant that the kingdom was both accustomed to an influx of immigrants of all kinds from east and west and was geared to defend itself (and Christendom) against intruders. Hungary developed its own frontier ideology in the thirteenth century, centring on the claim that the kingdom was essential to the defence of Christendom. This ideology culminated in the concept of Hungary (just like Poland and other countries on the eastern frontier) as 'the bulwark of Christendom' during the Ottoman wars of the fifteenth and sixteenth centuries, when the frontier cut across the kingdom itself, and became highly militarized. But the country also continued to incorporate new settlers; it remained a 'guest-land', a meeting point of cultures and religions. As King Béla IV had characterized it, Hungary was a gate that could give or restrict access.[1]

These results have implications for the study of medieval history beyond their immediate Hungarian significance. First, they show the necessity for a complex analysis of the status of non-Christians (and other minority groups) in Christian society. As non-Christians were a complex part of medieval society so were there multiple causes behind integration and exclusion (this terminology is more relevant to the Middle Ages than tolerance and intolerance). Neither ecclesiastical ideology, nor royal

---

[1] 'Hostium ad alias fidei catholice regiones', ASV AA Arm. I-XVIII-605; Martini, *Sigilli*, plate 9E (*VMH*, p. 231, no. CCCCXL).

policy, nor any one ingredient alone determined non-Christian status. Christian theology and devotion played a role in attitudes towards non-Christians, but so did social, economic and legal structures.

Second, the case of Hungary as a frontier society calls attention not only to the importance of distinguishing between the concept and the reality of 'frontiers', but to the fact that there are multiple concepts and realities. This entails the analysis of medieval definitions of frontiers, and of the types of relations that existed across, as well as within, the societies that developed along such frontiers. It also means the study of both real interaction and medieval frontier rhetoric as ideological construct.

Third, this research furthers the understanding of the processes of the 'making' of Europe. Christianity was a major organizational factor; from the Church's point of view, conversion to Christianity was *the* prerequisite and sign of integration into society. At the same time, the forces of expansion were not the only ones at work, as Bartlett's model would have it.[2] There was a fluidity at the borders of Europe; not only could conquerors from the core push further outwards, but non-Christians and non-Europeans were also able to penetrate Europe and become integrated into frontier areas.

Fourth, my results confirm the constructed nature of individual and group identity. Identity can be based on a combination of any number of elements; religious belief or hairstyle can have equal importance in signalling a certain identity. The group itself may place a higher value on certain aspects and relinquish others; this does not necessarily coincide with outsiders' perceptions of the importance of these markers of identity. For example, Cumans were willing to be baptized, but wished to retain their hairstyles and customs; while from a Christian point of view baptism was the most important step in changing identities from 'pagan' to 'Christian'. Furthermore, 'objective' markers of identity (such as language, law, religion, etc.) do not necessarily match the consciousness of a special identity. Even in the case of total assimilation, when markers of identity do not differ from those of the surrounding society, a group may invent a special identity.

The Hungarian material also raises questions about the study of formations of medieval 'ethnic' identity. Modern ethnic identity centres around the myth of the primacy of a fixed 'ethnic content', in contrast to the fluidity of medieval 'ethnicity'. In the medieval context *group* identity should be investigated without labelling it ethnic. Group identity, formed from the inside or enforced from the outside, was a relevant factor of medieval life. Ethnicity, it seems to me, is a modern invention that does

---

[2] Bartlett, *Making of Europe*.

more to muddle the issue than to clarify it when applied to the Middle Ages.

Finally, as indicated above, I should like to suggest a shifting of analysis from the issue of tolerance and intolerance to that of integration and exclusion. In order for tolerance to exist, there has to be a recognition of other religions (or of 'otherness' in a more general sense) as valid alternatives – a criterion that was lacking in medieval Europe when Christianity was seen as the only possibility for salvation. If 'toleration' is used in a loose sense, that is, as allowing the presence of certain groups, its meaning is so vague that it cannot be a useful analytical tool. Moreover, the terminology of exclusion and integration highlights the ambiguities and shadowy areas that characterize life. Social exclusion and integration are not mutually exclusive; rather, groups can be integrated in some respects, while excluded in others. Official policy is not necessarily indicative of social realities; for example, religious exclusion can coincide with economic integration. In addition, groups themselves can adopt some aspects of the culture of the surrounding society while rejecting others. Non-Christian status was not a monolithic construct of exclusion, victimization and 'otherness'; economic, social and legal positions did not necessarily correspond, nor in turn conform to religious ideology. These non-Christian groups were 'inside' and 'outside' Christian society at the same time, that is, they were part of society although not converted and assimilated, and thus not completely integrated into it. Adapting Norbert Elias's terminology, they were established outsiders.[3] Clear-cut 'us' and 'them', or the opposite, a harmonious 'we' group, exist only in exceptional circumstances. The true query, relevant not only to the study of the past but to our own times and very selves, concerns the ways in which individuals or groups participate in society.

---

[3] Norbert Elias and John L. Scotson, *The Established and the Outsiders*, 2nd edn (London: Sage, 1994).

APPENDIX 1: HUNGARIAN KINGS OF THE HOUSE OF ÁRPÁD

István I (Stephen) (Saint) 997–1038 (crowned king 1000/1001)
Péter (Peter) 1038–41; 1044–6
Aba Sámuel (Samuel Aba) 1041–4
András (Endre) I (Andrew) 1046–60
Béla I 1060–3
Salamon (Solomon) 1063–74
Géza I 1074–7
László I (Ladislas) (Saint) 1077–95
(Könyves) Kálmán (Coloman the Learned) 1095–1116
István II (Stephen) 1116–31
(Vak) Béla II (the Blind) 1131–41
Géza II 1141–62
István III (Stephen) 1162–72
László II (Ladislas) 1162–3
István IV (Stephen) 1163
Béla III 1172–96
Imre (Emeric or Henry) 1196–1204
László III (Ladislas) 1204–5
András (Endre) II (Andrew) 1205–35
Béla IV 1235–70
István V (Stephen) 1270–2
(Kun) László IV (Ladislas the Cuman) 1272–90
András (Endre) III (Andrew) 1290–1301

APPENDIX 2: TOPONYMS, WITH LATIN AND GERMAN EQUIVALENTS

Bécsújhely (today Wiener-Neustadt in Austria): Nova Civitas
Bereg (today Beregi in the Ukraine)
Buda (today part of Budapest): Ofen
Csanád (today Cenad in Rumania): Tschanad
Esztergom: Strigonium, Gran
Fehérvár (now Székesfehérvár): Alba Regalis and Alba Regia, Stuhlweissenburg
Fehérvár, Gyulafehérvár (today Alba Iulia in Rumania): Alba, Weissburg, Karlsburg
Kakaslomnic (today Vel'ká Lomnica in Slovakia): Grosslomnitz
Kalocsa: Colotsa
Karaszkó (today Kraskovo in Slovakia)
Komárom (today Komárno in Slovakia): Comaromium, Kamarun, Komorn
Nagyszombat (today Trnava in Slovakia): Tyrnavia, Tyrnau
Nagyvárad or Várad (today Oradea in Rumania): Varadinum, Grosswardein
Nyitra (today Nitra in Slovakia): Nitria, Neutra
Pannonhalma: Mons Pannonie, Martinsberg
Pécs: Quinqueecclesiae, Fünfkirchen
Pest (today part of Budapest): Pestinum
Pozsony (today Bratislava in Slovakia): Posonium, Pressburg
Sopron: Sopronium, Suprun, Ödenburg
Szeben (today Sibiu in Rumania): Cibinium, Hermannstadt
Szeged: Szegedinum, Segedin
Székelyderzs (today Dârjiu in Rumania)
Szepesmindszent (today Bijacovce in Slovakia)
Szerém (today Mitrovica in Serbia): Sirmium
Trencsén (today Trenčín in Slovakia): Trentsinium, Trentschin
Üreg (today Jarok in Slovakia near Nitra): also Ireg
Vác: Vaczium, Waitzen
Vasvár: Castrum Ferreum, Eisenburg
Zágráb (today Zagreb in Croatia): Zagrabia, Agram

APPENDIX 3: THE MANUSCRIPT TRADITION OF THE SYNOD OF BUDA (1279)

There has been a consensus among scholars that two manuscript traditions exist of the synodal canons.[1] These are supposedly the following.

1. Two manuscripts in Rome, which contain only the first 75 of the synodal canons (indeed, end in the middle of a sentence, that is, the text of canon 75 itself is incomplete in these manuscripts):
   Bibliotheca Vallicellana B12 ff. 520v–534r
   ASV, AA Arm. I-XVIII-594.
   This version was the basis of the edition of Raynald and others.[2]
2. Manuscripts in Poland (of which the oldest was transferred to St Petersburg and has since disappeared), edited by Hube, containing all of the canons.[3]

One explanation even claimed that the reason for this discrepancy was that László IV interrupted the synod, dispersing those gathered, and thus the synod's work was not completed.[4] The basis of this theory is a charter of King László, in which he promises compensation for having attempted to hinder the work of the synod.[5] The charter, however, does not indicate that the synod was dispersed by László.

In fact, the two Roman manuscripts do not represent a separate manuscript tradition. The one in the Vatican Archives is incomplete, and the other is a copy of an incomplete manuscript. The text as it exists today in the Vatican Archives is clearly a fragment of a longer manuscript (which thus presumably originally included the entire text of the synodal decisions). The manuscript is a gathering of four double leaves (quaternio); the leaves are ruled and pricked. At some point this gathering was separated from the rest of the manuscript, as in the bottom right-hand corner of the last folio under the last line there is a catchword that indicates the first words of the first page of the next gathering – the gathering that is now missing from the manuscript. Therefore this manuscript originally probably contained all the canons

---

[1] Waldmüller, *Synoden*, p. 193; Péter Erdő, 'A részleges egyházjog forrásszövegei a Magyarországon őrzött középkori kódexekben', *Magyar Könyvszemle* 108, no. 2 (1992): pp. 301–11, see p. 305.
[2] Odoricus Raynaldus, *Annales Ecclesiastici ab anno MCXCVIII ubi desinit Cardinalis Baronius*, vol. III (Lucca, 1748), pp. 623–36. [3] Hube, *Antiquissimae Constitutiones*.
[4] Raynaldus, *Annales Ecclesiastici*, p. 636; Sámuel Kohn, '1279. budai zsinat végzései', *Történelmi Tár* (1881): pp. 543–50. Already refuted by Pauler, *Magyar nemzet*, vol. II: p. 559, note 249.
[5] ASV, AA Arm. I-XVIII-592 (*VMH* p. 347, no. DLXIV; *RA*, no. 3066).

of the synod. The other partial text of the synodal canons is included in a codex in the Bibliotheca Vallicellana that contains a collection of copies of various papal, legatine, imperial and royal documents. The text of the Synod of Buda ends with exactly the catchwords of the Vatican manuscript, in mid-sentence. Among other texts, the codex also contains copies of royal letters from Hungary, the originals of which were in the Vatican Archives; it seems probable that the copy of the synodal canons in the Vallicellana codex was based on the incomplete Vatican manuscript. Therefore there are no distinct manuscript traditions in central Europe and in Rome; the text is incomplete in the Roman manuscripts simply because part of the manuscript held in the Vatican was lost, and then the incomplete text was copied at a later date when no other manuscript was available.

BIBLIOGRAPHY

PRIMARY SOURCES

MANUSCRIPTS AND FACSIMILE EDITIONS

Budapest, Egyetemi Könyvtár
 Coll. Pray. tom. XVI
Budapest, Magyar Országos Levéltár (MOL) (Hungarian National Archives)
 Diplomáciai Levéltár (DL)
  255
  256
  975
  1142
  1146
  1170
  1221
  1229
  1230
  1298
  1343
  28502
  29673
  30583
  40049
  40166
  40177
  50148
  56727
  57213
  57217
  57222
  86840
  86854
  97856
  105378

Bibliography

I 7, vol. 18, vol. 52, vol. 54
V8, box 1162, no. 844
V8, box 375, no. 63612
Diplomáciai Filmtár (DF) (Photo reproductions of material held in archives elsewhere)
200719
219422
235968
236350
238636
238715
238737
239444
240766
248407
248542
248770
248771
251667
263904
270046
283482
286489
Budapest, Országos Széchenyi Könyvtár (OSzK)
MNy I (*Codex Prayanus*)
Clmae 33
Quart. Lat. 1280
Paris, Bibliothèque Nationale
BN, lat. 8879
Rome, Bibliotheca Vallicellana
B12 ff. 520v–534r
Vatican City, Archivio Segreto Vaticano (ASV)
Archivum Arcis (AA) Armaria
I-XVIII-104
I-XVIII-592
I-XVIII-594
I-XVIII-595
I-XVIII-605
I-XVIII-608
I-XVIII-3104
Instrumenta Miscellanea (Instr. Misc.)
4809
Miscellaneorum Armarium XV, no. 1 (*Liber censuum*)
Registra Vaticana (Reg. Vat.)
9, 11, 12, 13, 14, 15, 16, 17, 18, 19, 20, 22, 25, 29, 32, 39, 41, 43, 44, 45

Érszegi, Géza. ed. *Az Aranybulla* (The Golden Bull of 1222). Facsimile. Budapest: Helikon, 1990.

Bibliography

Lévárdy, Ferenc. *Magyar Anjou Legendárium* (Hungarian Angevin Legendary). Facsimile. Budapest: Helikon, 1973.

Mezey, László and László Geréb. eds. *Képes Krónika* (Illuminated Chronicle). 2 vols. Facsimile. Budapest: Helikon, 1964.

EDITED SOURCES AND SOURCE-COLLECTIONS

Abelard. *Dialogus inter Philosophum, Iudaeum et Christianum*. Edited by Rudolf Thomas. Stuttgart and Bad Cannstatt: Friedrich Frommann, 1970.

Abu-Hámid Al-Garnáti utazása Kelet- és Közép-Európában 1131–1153 (The travels of Abū Hāmid Al-Garnati in Eastern and Central Europe 1131–1153). Edited and translated by Tamás Iványi and György Bakcsi. Budapest: Gondolat Kiadó, 1985. (Hungarian tr. of *Abū Hāmid el Granadino y su relación de viaje por tierras eurasiáticas*. Edited by César E. Dubler. Madrid: Imprenta y Editorial Maestre, 1953 and parts of 'Le Tuhfat al-albāb de Abū Hāmid al-Andalusī al-Garnātī édité d'après les Mss. 2167, 2168, 2170 de la Bibliothèque Nationale et le Ms. d'Alger'. Edited by Gabriel Ferrand. *Journal Asiatique* 207 (July–December 1925): 1–148, 193–303.)

Abū 'l-Fidā', *Takwīm al-buldān*. Edited by Joseph Toussaint Reinaud and William MacGuckin de Slane. Paris, 1840. French tr. Joseph Toussaint Reinaud. *Géographie d'Aboulféda*. 3 vols. Paris, 1848–83.

Adler, Marcus Nathan. *The Itinerary of Benjamin of Tudela*. London: Oxford University Press, 1907.

Alberigo, Joseph, Joseph Dossetti Perikle, P. Joannou, Claudio Leonardi and Paul Prodi. *Conciliorum Oecumenicorum Decreta*. 3rd edn. Bologna: Istituto per le Scienze Religiose, 1973.

Analecta Franciscana, vol. II. Quaracchi: Collegio San Bonaventura, 1887.

Anjoukori Okmánytár (Codex Diplomaticus Hungaricus Andegavensis). Edited by Imre Nagy and Gyula Tasnádi Nagy. 7 vols. Budapest: MTA, 1878–1920.

'Albrici monachi Triumfontium Chronicon'. Edited by Paulus Scheffer-Boichorst. In *MGH SS*, vol. XXIII: 631–950.

'Annales Austriae, Continuatio Sancrucensis II'. Edited by Wilhelmus Wattenbach. In *MGH SS*, vol. IX: 637–46.

'Annales Austriae, Continuatio Praedicatorum Vindobonensium'. Edited by Wilhelmus Wattenbach. In *MGH SS*, vol. IX: 724–32.

'Annales Austriae, Continuatio Vindobonensis'. Edited by Wilhelmus Wattenbach. In *MGH SS*, vol. IX: 698–722.

'Annales Austriae, Historia annorum 1264–1279'. Edited by Wilhelmus Wattenbach. In *MGH SS*, vol. IX: 649–54.

'Annales Colmarienses maiores 1277–1472'. Edited by Philip Jaffé. In *MGH SS*, vol. XVII: 202–32.

'Annales Otakariani'. Edited by Rudolf Köpke. In *MGH SS*, vol. IX: 181–94. Also in *Fontes Rerum Bohemicarum*. Edited by Josef Emler, vol. II: 308–35.

'Annales Sancti Rudberti Salisburgenses'. Edited by Wilhelmus Wattenbach. In *MGH SS*, vol. IX: 758–810.

'Anonymi (P. Magistri) Gesta Hungarorum'. Edited by Emil Jakubovich. In *SRH*, vol. I: 33–117.

Bibliography

'Anonymous Leobiensis'. Edited by Hieronymus Pez. In *Scriptores Rerum Austriacarum Veteres et Genuini*. 3 vols., vol. I: cols. 750–972. Leipzig, 1721–45.
Auvray, Lucien. ed. *Les Registres de Grégoire IX*. 4 vols. Bibliothèque des Ecoles Françaises d'Athènes et de Rome. 2nd ser. Paris: Ernest Thorin, then Albert Fontemoing, 1890–1955.
Bak, János M., György Bónis and James Ross Sweeney. eds. and trs. *The Laws of Hungary* ser. 1. vol. 1. *The Laws of Medieval Hungary 1000–1301*. Bakersfield, Calif.: Charles Schlaks Jr., 1989.
Benisch, A. ed. *Travels of Rabbi Petachia of Ratisbon*. 2nd edn. London: Longman, 1861.
Berger, Élie. ed. *Les Registres d'Innocent IV*. 4 vols. Bibliothèque des Ecoles Françaises d'Athènes et de Rome. 2nd ser. Paris: Ernest Thorin, then E. de Boccard, 1884–1921.
Berthold von Regensburg. Vollständige Ausgabe Seiner Predigten. Edited by Franz Pfeiffer. 2 vols. Vienna: Braumüller, 1862–80.
Bibliografia dell'Archivio Vaticano. Edited by Giulio Battelli. Vatican City: Archivio Vaticano, 1962– .
Blume, Clemens and Guido Maria Dreves. *Analecta Hymnica Medii Aevi*. 55 vols. Leipzig: O. R. Reisland, 1886–1922.
Borsa, Iván. ed. *A Justh család levéltára 1274–1525* (The archives of the Justh family 1274–1525). Budapest: Akadémiai Kiadó, 1991.
Bourel de la Roncière, Charles, Joseph de Loye, Pierre de Cenival and Auguste Coulon. eds. *Les Registres d'Alexandre IV*. 3 vols. Bibliothèque des Ecoles Françaises d'Athènes et de Rome. 2nd ser. Paris: Thorin et fils, then Albert Fontemoing, then E. de Boccard, 1895–1959.
Brevissima chronica magistrorum generalium ordinis Praedicatorum. In *Veterum scriptorum et monumentorum historicorum, dogmaticorum, moralium amplissima collectio*. Edited by Edmond Martène and Ursin Durand. 9 vols. vol. VI: cols. 344–96. Paris, 1724–33.
Budapest történetének okleveles emlékei (Monumenta diplomatica civitatis Budapest), vol. I, *1148–1301*. Edited by Dezső Csánki and Albert Gárdonyi. Budapest: A. Székesfőváros Kiadása, 1936.
Büchler, Alexander [Sándor]. ed. 'Das Judenprivilegium Bélas IV Vom Jahre 1251'. In *Jubilee Volume in Honour of Prof. Bernhard Heller on the Occasion of his Seventieth Birthday*. Edited by Alexander Scheiber, 139–46. Budapest, 1941.
Carpenter, Dwayne E. *Alfonso X and the Jews: An Edition of and Commentary on Siete Partidas 7.24 'De los judíos'*. Berkeley and Los Angeles: University of California Press, 1986.
El-Cazwini's Kosmographie. Part 2: *Die Denkmäler der Länder*. Edited by Ferdinand Wüstenfeld. Göttingen, 1848.
'Chronica Albrici monachi Trium Fontium a monacho novi monasterii Hoiensis interpolata'. Edited by Paulus Scheffer-Boichorst. In *MGH SS*, vol. XXIII: 631–950.
'Chronica Sigeberti Gemblacensis'. Edited by Ludowicus Conradus Bethmann. In *MGH SS*, vol. VI: 300–74.
'Chronici Hungarici compositio saeculi XIV'. Edited by Sándor Domanovszky. In *SRH*, vol. I: 217–505.

Bibliography

'Chronicon Austriacum anonymi'. In *Rerum Austriacarum scriptores*. 3 vols. Edited by Adrian Rauch. Vol. II: 213–300. Vienna, 1793–4. Partially reprinted in *Catalogus*. Edited by Albinus Franciscus Gombos. Vol. I: 504–18.

Chronicon Budense. Edited by József Podhradczky. Buda, 1838.

'Chronicon Francisci Pragensis'. In *Fontes Rerum Bohemicarum*. Edited by Josef Emler. Vol. IV: 347–456.

Chronique dite de Nestor. Tr. Louis Leger. Publications de l'Ecole des langues orientales vivantes, ser. 2, vol. XIII. Paris: Ernst Leroux, 1884.

Codex Cumanicus Cod. Marc. Lat. DXLIX. Edited by Kaare Grønbech. Facsimile edn. Copenhagen: Levin and Munksgaard, 1936.

'Commentariolum de provinciae Hungariae originibus'. In *MOPH*, vol. I: 305–9. Reprint in Nicolas Pfeiffer, *Die Ungarische Dominikanerordensprovinz von ihrer Gründung 1221 bis zur Tatarenwüstung 1241–2*, 143–6. Zurich, 1913.

Corpus Antiphonalium Officii. Edited by Renatus-Joannus Hesbert. Vol. III. *Invitatoria et Antiphonae*. Rome: Herder, 1968. Vol. IV. *Responsoria, versus, hymni et varia*. Rome: Herder, 1970.

Cosmas. 'Chronica Bohemorum libri III usque ad annum 1125'. Edited by Berthold Bretholz. In *MGH SRG*, n.s., 1923. Also in *Fontes Rerum Bohemicarum*. Edited by Josef Emler. Vol. II: 1–198.

'Continuatio Cosmae Pragensis'. In *MGH SS*, vol. IX: 132–209. Also in *Fontes Rerum Bohemicarum*. Edited by Josef Emler. Vol. II: 201–370.

'Cronica Przibiconis dicti Pulkaua'. In *Fontes Rerum Bohemicarum*. Edited by Josef Emler. Vol. V: 3–207.

Dankó, József, ed. *Vetus hymnarium ecclesiasticum Hungariae*. Budapest, 1893.

Digard, Georges, Maurice Faucon, Antoine Thomas and Robert Fawtier. eds. *Les Registres de Boniface VIII*. 4 vols. Bibliothèque des Ecoles Françaises d'Athènes et de Rome. 2nd ser. Paris: Ernest Thorin, then Albert Fontemoing, then E. de Boccard, 1884–1939.

Al-Dimashkī. *Manuel de la Cosmographie du Moyen Age*. Tr. M. A. F. Mehren. Paris, 1874.

Dörrie, Heinrich. *Drei Texte zur Geschichte der Ungarn und Mongolen*. Nachrichten der Akademie der Wissenschaften in Göttingen, Philosophisch-Historische Klasse, 6. Göttingen: Vandenhoeck und Ruprecht, 1956.

Ehrenreich, H. L. ed. *Sepher Ha-Pardes and Liturgical and Ritual Work, Attributed to Rashi*. Deva: bi-Defus ha-Ahim Kattsburg, 1924.

'Emonis Chronicon'. Edited by Ludevicus Weiland. In *MGH SS*, vol. XXIII: 454–523.

Fejér, György. *Codex diplomaticus Hungariae ecclesiasticus ac civilis*. 11 vols. Buda, 1829–44.

Fejérpataky, László. *Kálmán király oklevelei* (Charters of King Coloman). Budapest, 1892.

Fontes Rerum Bohemicarum. Edited by Josef Emler and Jan Gebauer. 8 vols. Prague: Musea Království Českého, Nakladem Nadáni Františka Palackého, 1873–1932.

A Frangepán család oklevéltára. Edited by Thallóczi, Lajos and Samu Barabás. (The archives of the Frangepán family). Vol. I. Monumenta Hungariae Historica Diplomataria 35. Budapest: MTA, 1910.

Friedberg, Aemilius. *Corpus Iuris Canonici*. 2 vols. Leipzig: Tauchnitz, 1879–81. Reprint Graz: Akademische Druck- und Verlagsanstalt, 1959.

Bibliography

Garcia y Garcia, Antonius. *Constitutiones Concilii quarti Lateranensis una cum commentariis glossatorum*. Vatican City: Biblioteca Apostolica Vaticana, 1981.
Gay, Jules and Suzanne Clémencet-Witte. eds. *Les Registres de Nicolas III*. Bibliothèque des Ecoles Françaises d'Athènes et de Rome. 2nd ser. Paris: Albert Fontemoing, then E. de Boccard, 1898–1938.
Geoffroy de Villehardouin. In *Un chevalier à la croisade. L'histoire de la conquête de Constantinople*. Edited by Jean Longnon. Paris: Tallandier, 1981.
'Gerardi de Fracheto Vitae Fratrum Ordinis Praedicatorum necnon cronica ordinis ab anno MCCIII usque ad MCCLIV'. Edited by Benedictus Maria Reichert. In *MOPH*, vol. I.
Golb, Norman, and Omeljan Pritsak. *Khazarian Hebrew Documents of the Tenth Century*. Ithaca and London: Cornell University Press, 1982.
Gombos, Albinus Franciscus. *Catalogus Fontium Historiae Hungaricae*. 4 vols. Budapest: Szent István Akadémia, 1937–43.
Grayzel, Solomon. *The Church and the Jews in the XIIIth Century*. Vol. I: *A Study of Their Relations During the Years 1198–1254, Based on the Papal Letters and the Conciliar Decrees of the Period*. Rev. edn, New York: Hermon Press, 1966. Vol. II: *1254–1314*. Edited by Kenneth R. Stow. New York: Jewish Theological Seminary of America and Detroit: Wayne State University Press, 1989.
Guiraud, Jean. ed. *Les Registres d'Urbain IV*. 4 vols. Bibliothèque des Ecoles Françaises d'Athènes et de Rome. 2nd ser. Paris: Albert Fontemoing, then E. de Boccard, 1899–1958.
Guiraud, Jean and E. Cadier. eds. *Les Registres de Grégoire X et de Jean XXI*. Bibliothèque des Ecoles Françaises d'Athènes et de Rome. 2nd ser. Paris: Thorin et fils, then Albert Fontemoing, then E. de Boccard, 1892–1906.
Gutheil, Jenő. *Az Árpád-kori Veszprém* (Veszprem in the age of the Arpads). 2nd edn. Veszprém: Veszprém Megyei Levéltár, 1979.
Gyöngyösi, Gregorius. *Vitae fratrum eremitarum ordinis sancti Pauli primi eremitae*. Edited by Ferenc L. Hervay. Budapest: Akadémiai Kiadó, 1988.
Hageneder, Othmar, Anton Haidacher *et al.* eds. *Die Register Innocenz III*. Graz, Vienna, Rome and Cologne: Böhlaus, Österreichischen Akademie der Wissenschaften, 1964–97.
Hazai Oklevéltár 1234–1536 (Hungarian charters 1234–1536). Edited by Imre Nagy, Farkas Deák and Gyula Nagy. Budapest, 1879.
Hazai Okmánytár (Codex Diplomaticus Patrius). Edited by Imre Nagy *et al.* 8 vols. Győr and Budapest, 1865–91.
Házi, Jenő. *Sopron szabad királyi város története* (The history of the royal city of Sopron). Part I, vol. I. Sopron: Székely Nyomda, 1921.
'Hermanni Altahensis Annales'. Edited by Philippus Jaffé. In *MGH SS*, vol. XVII: 381–407.
The History of the World Conqueror by 'Ala-ad-Din 'Ata-Malik Juvaini. Tr. John Andrew Boyle. 2nd edn. Manchester: Manchester University Press, 1997.
Hodinka, Antal. ed. and tr. *Az orosz évkönyvek magyar vonatkozásai* (Russian chronicles pertaining to Hungarian history). Budapest: MTA, 1916.
Hube, Romualdus. ed. *Antiquissimae Constitutiones Synodales Provinciae Gneznensis*. St Petersburg, 1856.
Huillard-Bréholles, J. L. A. *Historia Diplomatica Friderici Secundi*. 7 vols. Paris: Henri Plon, 1852–61.

Bibliography

Huszár, Lajos. *Münzkatalog Ungarn, von 1000 bis Heute*. Budapest: Corvina, 1979.
Iacobi de Vitriaco libri duo quorum prior Orientalis sive Hierosolymitanae, alter Occidentalis Historiae nomine inscribitur. Edited by Franciscus Moschus. Douai, 1597. Facsimile Reprint Westmead, Farnborough, 1971.
Isaac ben Moses. *Sefer Or Zaru'a*. Vol. I. Edited by H. Lipa and J. Höschel. Zhitomir, 1862.
Istványi, Géza. 'XIII. századi följegyzés IV. Bélának 1246-ban a tatárokhoz küldött követségéről' (A thirteenth-century note concerning Bela IV's embassy to the Mongols). *Századok* 72 (1938): 270–2.
Jean Sire de Joinville. *Histoire de Saint Louis*. Edited by Natalis de Wailly. Paris: Firmin Didot, 1874.
Johannes of Marignola. *Chronica*. In *Fontes Rerum Bohemicarum*. Edited by Josef Emler. Vol. III: 492–604.
Johannes de Plano Carpini. *Ystoria Mongalorum quos nos Tartaros appellamus*. Edited by Anastasius van den Wyngaert. In *Sinica Franciscana*, vol. I: 27–130. Quaracchi: Collegio San Bonaventura, 1929. *Giovanni di Pian di Carpine: Storia dei Mongoli*. Edited by Paolo Daffinà, Claudio Leonardi, Maria Cristiana Lungarotti, Enrico Menestò and Luciano Petech. Spoleto: Centro Italiano di Studi sull'Alto Medioevo, 1989.
Jordan, Edouard. ed. *Les Registres de Clément IV*. Bibliothèque des Ecoles Françaises d'Athènes et de Rome. 2nd ser. Paris: Thorin et fils, then Albert Fontemoing, then E. de Boccard, 1893–1945.
Jordan of Saxony. 'Libellus de principiis ordinis praedicatorum'. Edited by H. Ch. Scheeben. In *MOPH*, vol. XVI: 25–88.
Karácsonyi, János and Samu Borovszky. eds. *Az időrendbe szedett váradi tüzesvaspróba-lajstrom (Regestrum Varadinense)* (The chronological list of ordeals of Varad). Budapest: A Váradi Káptalan Kiadása, 1903.
Katona, Tamás. ed. *A tatárjárás emlékezete* (The memory of the Mongol invasion). 2nd edn. Budapest: Európa Könyvkiadó, 1987.
Knauz, Ferdinand [Nándor]. *Az esztergomi főegyháznak okmánytára (Codex diplomaticus primatialis ecclesiae Strigoniensis)*. 2 vols. Esztergom, 1863–6.
A nápolyi Margitlegenda. Vita b. Margaritae Hungaricae (Legenda Neapolitana). Esztergom, 1868.
Knauz, Ferdinand [Nándor]. ed. *Monumenta Ecclesiae Strigoniensis*. 3 vols. Esztergom, 1874–1924.
Kniewald, Károly. 'A zágrábi érseki könyvtár MR 126 (XI.szd.) jelzésű Sacramentariumának magyar rétege a MR 67. sz. zágrábi Breviarium (XIII. szd.) megvilágításában' (The Hungarian layer of the MR 126 (eleventh-century) Sacramentary of the episcopal library of Zagreb in the light of the MR 67 Breviary (thirteenth-century) of Zagreb). *Pannonhalmi Szemle* (1938): 36–54.
Kohn, Sámuel. *Héber kútforrások és adatok Magyarország történetéhez* (Hebrew sources and data concerning the history of Hungary). Budapest, 1881. Reprint Budapest: Akadémiai Kiadó, 1990.
Kubinyi, Ferenc. *Árpádkori oklevelek, 1095–1301* (Charters from the Arpad age 1095–1301). Pest, 1867.
Kupfer, Franciszek and Tadeusz Lewicki. eds. *Źródła Hebrajskie do Dziejów Słowian i niektórych innych ludów Środkowej i Wschodniej Europy* (Hebrew sources for the

Bibliography

history of Slavs and some other peoples of Central and Eastern Europe). Wrocław and Warsaw: Polska Akademia Nauk, 1956.
Langlois, Ernest. ed. *Les Registres de Nicolas IV*. 2 vols. Bibliothèque des Ecoles Françaises d'Athènes et de Rome. 2nd ser. Paris: Ernest Thorin, then Albert Fontemoing, 1886–1905.
László, Gyula. *A Szent László-legenda középkori falképei* (The medieval frescoes of the St Ladislaus legend). Tájak-Korok-Múzeumok Könyvtára 4. Budapest: Tájak-Korok-Múzeumok Egyesület, 1993.
'Legenda Sancti Stephanis Regis Maior'. Edited by Emma Bartoniek. In *SRH*, vol. II: 377–92.
'Legenda S. Stephani regis ab Hartvico episcopo conscripta'. Edited by Emma Bartoniek. In *SRH*, vol. II: 401–40.
'Libellus de institutione morum'. Edited by Josephus Balogh. In *SRH*, vol. II: 611–27.
Ligeti, Lajos, tr. *A Mongolok Titkos Története* (The Secret History of the Mongols). Budapest: Akadémiai Kiadó, 1962. Eng. tr. of the same work, Francis Woodman Cleaves. Cambridge, Mass.: Harvard University Press, 1982.
Luard, Henry Richards. ed. *Rerum Britannicarum Medii Aevi Scriptores*. Rolls Series 36. *Annales Monastici*, pt. 2. London, 1865. Reprint Liechtenstein: Kraus Reprint, 1971.
'Magnum Chronicon Belgicum'. In *Ungarische*. Edited by Nicolas Pfeiffer, 178–9.
Magyar diplomáciai emlékek az Anjou korból (Hungarian diplomatical documents relating to the Angevin period). Edited by Gusztáv Wenzel. 3 vols. Budapest, 1874–6.
Magyar Zsidó Oklevéltár (Monumenta Hungariae Judaica). Edited by Sándor Scheiber and Ármin Friss. 18 vols. Budapest: vols. I–IV, Wodianer F. és fia; vols. V–XVIII, Magyar Izraeliták Országos Képviselete, 1903–80.
Mályusz, Elemér and Iván Borsa. eds. *Zsigmondkori oklevéltár* (Charters from the era of King Sigismond). 5 vols. Budapest: Akadémiai Kiadó, 1951–97.
Mansi, Joannes Dominicus. *Sacrorum Conciliorum Nova, et Amplissima Collectio*. 53 vols. Venice and Florence, 1759–1927.
Mansilla, Demetrio. *La documentación pontificia de Honorius III (1216–1227)*. Monumenta Hispaniae Vaticana 2. Rome: Instituto Español de Historia Eclesiastica, 1965.
Marczali, Henrik. Edition of Luxembourg, BN cod. 110, f. 187r. *Magyar Történelmi Tár* (1878): 376.
A magyar történet kútfőinek kézikönyve (Handbook of the sources of Hungarian history). Budapest: Athenaeum, 1901.
Marsina, Richard. ed. *Codex Diplomaticus et Epistolaris Slovaciae*, vol. I. Bratislava: Academiae Scientiarum Slovacae, 1971.
Matthew Paris. *Chronica Majora*. 7 vols. Edited by H. R. Luard. Rolls Series 57. London: 1872–84. Wiesbaden: Kraus Reprint, 1964.
Mollat, Guillaume. ed. *Jean XXII (1316–1334) Lettres communes*. 16 vols. Paris: Albert Fontemoing, then E. de Boccard, 1904–47.
Monumenta Romana Episcopatus Vesprimiensis. Edited by Vilmos Fraknói. 4 vols. Budapest: Római Magyar Történeti Intézet, 1896–1907.
Monumenta Vaticana Historiam Regni Hungariae Illustrantia. Budapest, 1884.
Moravcsik, Gyula. *Az Árpád-kori magyar történet bizánci forrásai (Fontes Byzantini historiae Hungaricae aevo ducum et regum ex stirpe Árpád descendentium)*. 1934. Reprint. Budapest: Akadémiai Kiadó, 1984.

Bibliography

Moule, A. C. 'Textus Trium Novorum Documentorum e Tartari Aquilonari an. 1314–1322'. *Archivum Franciscanum Historicum* 17 (1924): 65–71.
Nagy, Imre *et al.* eds. *Codex diplomaticus domus senioris comitum Zichy de Zich et Vásonkő.* 12 vols. Pest: Magyar Történelmi Társulat, 1871–1931.
Olivier-Martin, Félix. ed. *Les Registres de Martin IV.* Bibliothèque des Ecoles Françaises d'Athènes et de Rome. 2nd ser. Paris: Albert Fontemoing, then E. de Boccard, 1901–35.
Otto of Freising. 'Chronicon'. Edited by Roger Wilmans. In *MGH SS,* vol. xx: 116–301.
Ottokar of Steier. *Österreichische Reimchronik.* 2 vols. Edited by Joseph Seemüller. In *MGH DC,* vol. v: pt. 1.
Pachymérès, Georges. *Relations historiques.* Edited and translated by Albert Failler and Vitalien Laurent. Corpus Fontium Historiae Byzantinae 14, pts. 1 and 2. Paris: Les Belles Lettres, 1984.
'Paltramus seu Vatzo, consul Viennensis: Chronicon Austriacum ad a. 1301'. *Scriptores Rerum Austriacarum Veteres et Genuini.* 3 vols. Edited by Hieronymus Pez. Vol. i: 707–24. Leipzig, 1721–45.
Pauler, Gyula and Sándor Szilágyi. eds. *A Magyar Honfoglalás Kútfői* (Sources of the Hungarian Conquest). Budapest: MTA, 1900. Reprint Budapest: Nap Kiadó, 1995.
Pest megye történetének okleveles emlékei 1002–1599-ig. Edited by László Bártfai Szabó. Budapest: A Szerző Kiadása, 1938.
Peter Ferrand. 'Legenda Sancti Dominici'. Edited by M.-H. Laurent. In *MOPH,* vol. xvi: 209–60.
Petri Venerabilis Adversus Judeorum Inveteratam Duritiem. Edited by Yvonne Friedman. Corpus Christianorum Continuatio Mediaevalis, vol. lviii. Turnholt: Brepols, 1985.
Petrovich, Eduardus and Paulus Ladislaus Timkovics. eds. *Sermones compilati in studio generali Quinqueecclesiensi in regno Ungarie.* Budapest: Akadémiai Kiadó, 1993.
Pierre des Vaux-de-Cernai. *Historia Albigensis.* 3 vols. Edited by Pascal Guébin and Ernest Lyon. Paris: Champion, 1926–39.
'Planctus Destructionis Regni Hungariae per Tartaros'. Edited by Ladislaus Juhász. In *SRH,* vol. ii: 589–98.
Potthast, Augustus. *Regesta Pontificum Romanorum.* 2 vols. Graz: Akademische Druck- und Verlagsanstalt, 1957.
Pray, György. *Dissertationes historico-criticae in annales veteres Hunnorum, Avarum, et Hungarorum.* Vienna, 1774.
Pressutti, Pietro. ed. *Regesta Honorii papae III.* 2 vols. Rome, 1888–1905. Repr. Hildesheim and New York: Georg Olms, 1978.
Prou, Maurice. ed. *Les Registres d'Honorius IV.* Bibliothèque des Ecoles Françaises d'Athènes et de Rome. 2nd ser. Paris: Ernest Thorin, 1886–8.
Rashīd al-Dīn. *The Successors of Genghis Khan.* Tr. John Andrew Boyle. New York and London: Columbia University Press, 1971.
'Relatio Ibrāhīm ībn Ja'kūb de itinere slavico'. Edited and translated by Tadeusz Kowalski. In *Monumenta Poloniae Historica,* n.s., 1. Cracow: Polska Akademia, 1946.
Réthy, László. *Corpus Nummorum Hungariae.* Vol. i: *Az Árpádházi királyok kora* (The age of the Arpads). Budapest: MTA, 1899.
Réthy, László and Günther Probszt. *Corpus Nummorum Hungariae.* Graz: Akademische Druck- und Verlagsanstalt, 1958.

Bibliography

Ricoldo of Montecroce. 'Libellus fratris Ricoldi ad nationes orientales'. Edited by Antoine Dondaine. 'Ricoldiana. Notes sur les œuvres de Ricoldo da Montecroce'. *Archivum Fratrum Predicatorum* 37 (1967): 119–79.
Robert de Cléry. 'De ceux qui se croisèrent'. In *Un chevalier à la croisade. L'histoire de la conquête de Constantinople.* Edited by Jean Longnon. Paris: Tallandier, 1981.
Rogerius. *Carmen Miserabile.* Edited by Ladislaus Juhász. In *SRH*, vol. II: 543–88.
Roger Bacon. *The 'Opus Maius' of Roger Bacon.* Edited by John Henry Bridges. 3 vols. Oxford: Clarendon Press, 1897–1900.
Salfeld, Siegmund. ed and tr. *Das Martyrologium des Nürnberger Memorbuches.* Berlin, 1898.
Scheiber, Alexander [Sándor]. *Jewish Inscriptions in Hungary From the 3rd Century to 1686.* Budapest: Akadémiai Kiadó and Leiden: Brill, 1983.
Schütz, Ödön. tr. 'Kirakos Gandzaketzi Az Örmények története' (A history of the Armenians). In *Kelet-Kutatás. Tanulmányok az orientalisztika köréből.* Budapest: Kőrösi Csoma Társaság, 1977.
Scriptores Rerum Hungaricarum. Edited by Imre Szentpétery. 2 vols. Budapest: MTA, 1937–8.
Seifried Helbling. Edited by Joseph Seemüller. Halle, 1886.
Las Siete Partidas. Tr. Samuel Parsons Scott. Chicago, New York and Washington: Commerce Clearing House, 1931.
'Simonis de Kéza Gesta Hungarorum'. Edited by Alexander Domanovszky. In *SRH*, vol. I: 131–94.
Simon of Kéza: The Deeds of the Hungarians. Edited and translated by László Veszprémy and Frank Schaer. Budapest: Central European University Press, 1999.
Simon de Saint-Quentin: Histoire des Tartares. Edited by Jean Richard. Paris: P. Geuthner, 1965.
Simonsohn, Shlomo. *The Apostolic See and the Jews: Documents: 492–1404.* Studies and Texts 94. Toronto: Pontifical Institute of Mediaeval Studies, 1988.
Spitzer, Shlomo. ed. Hungarian tr. Andrea Strbik. 'Héber nyelvű források Magyarország és a magyarországi zsidók történetéhez' (Hebrew sources concerning the history of Hungary and of Hungarian Jews). Typescript.
Székely oklevéltár. Edited by Károly Szabó and Lajos Szádeczky. 8 vols. Kolozsvár, 1872–98 and Budapest: MTA, 1934.
Szentpétery, Imre and Iván Borsa. *Regesta regum stirpis Arpadianae critico-diplomatica. Az Árpád-házi királyok okleveleinek kritikai jegyzéke* (A critical register of royal charters from the House of Arpad). 3 vols. Budapest: MTA, 1923–87.
Theiner, Augustinus. *Vetera Monumenta Historica Hungariam Sacram Illustrantia.* Vol. I: *1216–1352.* Rome, 1859.
Thomas of Spalato. 'Historia Salonitanorum Pontificum atque Spalatensium'. Edited by F. Rački. In *Monumenta Spectantia Historiam Slavorum Meridionalium.* Vol. XXVI. Zagreb, 1894.
Unger, Emil. *Magyar Éremhatározó* (Guide to Hungarian coins). 2nd edn. Budapest: Magyar Éremgyűjtők Egyesülete, 1974.
'Vincentii Pragensis annales'. Edited by Wilhelmus Wattenbach. In *MGH SS*, vol. XVII: 658–83.
Vives, José. ed. *Concilios visigóticos e hispano-romanos.* Barcelona and Madrid: Instituto Enrique Flórez, 1963.
Wadding, Lucas. *Annales Minorum.* 5 vols. Rome, 1731–3.

Bibliography

Wenzel, Gusztáv, ed. *Árpádkori új okmánytár (Codex diplomaticus Arpadianus continuatus)*. 12 vols. Pest, 1860–74.
Werbőczy István *Hármaskönyve*. Budapest: Franklin Társulat, 1897. Reprint Pécs: Szikra Nyomda, 1989.
William of Rubruck. 'Itinerarium Willelmi de Rubruc'. Edited by Anastasius van den Wyngaert. In *Sinica Franciscana*. Vol. I: 164–332. Quarracchi: Collegio San Bonaventura, 1929.
Yāqūt. *Mu'djam al-buldān*. Edited by F. Wüstenfeld. Leipzig, 1873. French tr. Joseph Toussaint Reinaud. *Géographie d'Aboulféda*. 3 vols. Vol. II: 294–5. Paris, 1848–83.
Zacour, Norman. *Jews and Saracens in the Consilia of Oldradus de Ponte*. Toronto: Pontifical Institute of Mediaeval Studies, 1990.
Zala vármegye története oklevéltár (A history of the county of Zala: charters). 2 vols. Edited by Imre Nagy, Dezső Véghely and Gyula Nagy. Budapest, 1886–90.
Zimmermann, Franz and Carl Werner. eds. *Urkundenbuch zur Geschichte des Deutschen in Siebenbürgen*. 3 vols. Hermannstadt, 1892–1902.
Zimmermann, Lajos. *Árpádházi királyok pénzei: Pótlék a Corpus nummorum Hungariae 1. füzetéhez*. (The coins of kings of the Arpad dynasty: Additions to the first volume of the Corpus nummorum Hungariae). Budapest: MTA, 1907.
Zolnay, László. 'István ifjabb király számadása 1264-ből' (The account of the younger king István from 1264). In *Budapest Régiségei*, no. 21, 79–111. Budapest: Budapesti Történeti Múzeum, 1964.

SECONDARY SOURCES

Abu-Lughod, Janet L. *Before European Hegemony: The World System A.D. 1250–1350*. New York and Oxford: Oxford University Press, 1989.
Abulafia, Anna Sapir. *Christians and Jews in the Twelfth-Century Renaissance*. London and New York: Routledge, 1995.
  Christians and Jews in Dispute: Disputational Literature and the Rise of Anti-Judaism in the West (c. 1000–1150). Variorum Collected Studies Series CS621. Aldershot: Ashgate–Variorum, 1998.
  'Invectives Against Christianity in the Hebrew Chronicles of the First Crusade'. In *Christians and Jews in Dispute*, no. XVIII.
Abulafia, David. 'The Norman Kingdom of Africa and the Norman Expeditions to Majorca and the Muslim Mediterranean'. In *Anglo-Norman Studies VII: Proceedings of the Battle Conference*. Edited by R. Allen Brown, 26–49. Woodbridge: Boydell and Brewer, 1985. Reprinted in Abulafia, *Italy, Sicily and the Mediterranean, 1100–1400*, no. XII. London: Variorum Reprints, 1987.
  Frederick II: A Medieval Emperor. Oxford: Oxford University Press, 1988.
  'Una comunità ebraica della Sicilia occidentale: Erice 1298–1304'. In Abulafia, *Commerce and Conquest in the Mediterranean, 1100–1500*, no. VIII. Aldershot: Variorum, 1993.
  A Mediterranean Emporium: The Catalan Kingdom of Majorca. Cambridge: Cambridge University Press, 1994.
  'Monarchs and Minorities in the Christian Western Mediterranean around 1300: Lucera and its Analogues'. In *Christendom and its Discontents*. Edited by Scott L. Waugh and Peter D. Diehl, 234–63.

Bibliography

'Il Mezzogiorno peninsulare dai bizantini all'espulsione (1541)'. In *Storia d'Italia Annali*. Vol. XI: *Gli ebrei in Italia dall'alto medioevo all'età dei ghetti*. Edited by Corrado Vivanti, pt. 1: 5–44. Torino: Einaudi, 1996.

Actes du XIVe Congrès International des Etudes Byzantines. 3 vols. Edited by Mihai Berza and Eugen Stanescu. Bucharest: Editura Academiei Republicii Socialiste România, 1974–6.

Adams, Jeremy duQuesney. *The Populus of Augustine and Jerome: A Study in the Patristic Sense of Community*. New Haven and London: Yale University Press, 1971.

Agus, Irving A. *Rabbi Meir of Rothenburg: His Life and His Works as Sources for the Religious, Legal, and Social History of the Jews of Germany in the Thirteenth Century*. 2 vols. Philadelphia: Jewish Publication Society, 1947.

Urban Civilization in Pre-Crusade Europe: A Study of Organized Town-Life in North-Western Europe during the Tenth and Eleventh Centuries Based on the Responsa Literature. 2 vols. Leiden: Brill, 1965.

The Heroic Age of Franco-German Jewry: The Jews of Germany and France of the Tenth and Eleventh Centuries, the Pioneers and Builders of Town-Life, Town-Government and Institutions. New York: Yeshiva University Press, 1969.

Ahrweiler, Hélène. 'La frontière et les frontières de Byzance en Orient'. In *Actes du XIVe Congrès International des Etudes Byzantines*. Vol. I: 209–30. Reprinted in Ahrweiler, *Byzance: les pays et les territoires*, no. III. London: Variorum Reprints, 1976.

Akhinazov, Serzhan M. 'Kipcaks and Khwarazm'. In *Rulers from the Steppe*. Edited by Gary Seaman and Daniel Marks, 126–31.

Allsen, Thomas T. *Commodity and Exchange in the Mongol Empire: A Cultural History of Islamic Textiles*. Cambridge: Cambridge University Press, 1997.

Almási, Tibor. 'A beregi egyezmény megkötésének diplomáciai mozzanatai' (Diplomatic events surrounding the agreement of Bereg). *AUSz Acta Historica* 83 (1986): 31–9.

'A Siralmas Ének kézirati hagyományának néhány problémája' (Problems of the manuscript transmission of the Carmen Miserabile). *AUSz Acta Historica* 84 (1987): 51–6.

'Megjegyzések Rogerius magyarországi méltóságviseléséhez' (Remarks concerning the offices filled by Rogerius in Hungary). *AUSz Acta Historica* 86 (1988): 9–14.

'Egy ciszterci bíboros a pápai világuralom szolgálatában: Pecorari Jakab' (A Cistercian Cardinal in the service of papal power: Jacob of Pecorara). *Magyar Egyháztörténeti Vázlatok* (1993, nos 1–2): 129–41.

Altaner, Berthold. *Die Dominikanermissionen des 13. Jahrhunderts: Forschungen zur Geschichte der Kirchlichen Unionen und der Mohammedaner- und Heidenmission des Mittelalters*. Breslauer Studien zur historischen Theologie 3. Habelschwerdt: Frankes Buchhandlung, 1924.

Amitai-Preiss, Reuven. *Mongols and Mamluks: The Mamluk-Īlkhānid War, 1260–1281*. Cambridge: Cambridge University Press, 1995.

Amory, Patrick. 'The Meaning and Purpose of Ethnic Terminology in the Burgundian Laws'. *Early Medieval Europe* 2 (1993): 1–28.

People and Identity in Ostrogothic Italy. Cambridge: Cambridge University Press, 1997.

Anderson, Benedict. *Imagined Communities: Reflections on the Origin and Spread of Nationalism*. Rev. edn. London and New York: Verso, 1993.

Bibliography

Antalóczy, Ildikó M. 'A nyíri izmaeliták központjának, Böszörmény falunak régészeti leletei I' (Archaeological finds at Böszörmény, the center of the Ishmaelites of Nyír). *A Hajdúsági Múzeum Évkönyve* 4 (1980): 131–70.

Auner, Mihály. 'Latinus'. *Századok* 50 (1916): 28–41.

Avneri, Zvi, Marcus Brann, Ismar Elbogen, Aron Freimann, Yakov Guggenheim, Arye Maimon and Hayim Tykocinski. eds. *Germania Judaica*. 4 vols. Breslau: M. and H. Marcus, 1934; Tübingen: Mohr, 1968 and 1987–95.

Babad, Joseph. 'The Jews in Medieval Carinthia: A Contribution to the History of the Jews in the Alpine Countries of Europe'. *Historia Judaica* 7 (1945): 13–28, 193–204.

Baer, Yitzhak. *A History of the Jews in Christian Spain*. 2 vols. 2nd edn. Philadelphia and Jerusalem: Jewish Publication Society, 1992.

Bak, János M. 'Queens as Scapegoats in Medieval Hungary'. In *Queens and Queenship in Medieval Europe*. Edited by Anne J. Duggan, 223–33.

Bakay, Kornél. 'Hungary in the Tenth and Eleventh Centuries'. In *Sacra Corona Hungariae*. Edited by Kornél Bakay, 3–31. Kőszeg: Városi Múzeum, 1994.

Balanyi, György. 'Adatok a ferencrendiek tatárországi missziós működésének történetéhez' (Data concerning the missionary activity of the Franciscans among the Mongols). *Katholikus Szemle* 39 (1925): 70–84.

Balić, Smail. 'Der Islam im mittelalterlichen Ungarn'. *Südost-Forschungen* 23 (1964): 19–35.

Balics, Lajos. *A római katolikus egyház története Magyarországban* (A history of the Roman Catholic Church in Hungary). 2 vols. Budapest: Szent István Társulat, 1888–90.

Bálint, Csanád. 'A kutya a X–XII. századi magyar hitvilágban' (The Dog in X–XIIth Century Hungarian Religious Beliefs). *Móra Ferenc Múzeum Évkönyve 1971/1*. Szeged: Szegedi Nyomda, 1971, 295–315.

'Az európai dirhem-forgalom néhány kérdése' (Some questions concerning the circulation of dirhems in Europe). *Századok* 116 (1982): 3–32.

Balog, Paul and Jacques Yvon. 'Monnaies à légendes arabes de l'orient latin'. *Revue Numismatique* 6th ser., 1 (1958): 133–68.

Balog, Szidónia. *A magyarországi zsidók kamaraszolgasága és igazságszolgáltatása a középkorban* (Medieval Hungarian Jews: their jurisdiction and serfdom of the royal chamber). Művelődéstörténeti értekezések 28. Budapest: Vasutas Szövetség, 1907.

Barfield, Thomas J. *The Perilous Frontier: Nomadic Empires and China*. Cambridge, Mass.: Blackwell, 1989.

Barkaï, Ron. *Christianos y musulmanes en la Espagna medieval*. Madrid: Rialp, 1984.

Baron, Salo Wittmayer. 'Ghetto and Emancipation'. *Menorah Journal* 14 (1928): 515–26.

A Social and Religious History of the Jews. 18 vols. 2nd edn. New York: Columbia University Press, 1967.

'"Plenitude of Apostolic Powers" and Medieval "Jewish Serfdom"'. In *Ancient and Medieval Jewish History*, 284–307. New Brunswick: Rutgers University Press, 1972.

Bartal, Antonius. *Glossarium Mediae et Infimae Latinitatis Regni Hungariae*. Leipzig: Teubner, and Budapest: Franklin Nyomda, 1901.

Barth, Fredrik. ed. *Ethnic Groups and Boundaries: The Social Organization of Cultural Difference*. Bergen and Oslo: Universitets Forlaget, and London: George Allen and Unwin, 1969.

Bibliography

Barthélemy, Dominique. 'Présence de l'aveu dans le déroulement des ordalies (9–13e s.)'. In *L'Aveu: Antiquité et Moyen-Age*, 191–214. Collection de l'Ecole Française de Rome 88. Rome: Ecole Française de Rome, 1986.

Barthes, Roland. 'Histoire et sociologie du vêtement'. *Annales ESC* (1957, no. 3): 430–41.

Bartlett, Robert. 'The Conversion of a Pagan Society in the Middle Ages'. *History* 70 (1985): 185–201.

Trial by Fire and Water: The Medieval Judicial Ordeal. Oxford: Clarendon Press, 1986.

'Colonial Aristocracies of the High Middle Ages'. In *Medieval Frontier Societies*. Edited by Robert Bartlett and Angus MacKay, 23–47.

The Making of Europe: Conquest, Colonization and Cultural Change 950–1350. Princeton: Princeton University Press, 1993. 2nd edn, Harmondsworth: Penguin, 1994.

'Symbolic Meanings of Hair in the Middle Ages'. *Transactions of the Royal Historical Society* 6th ser. 4 (1994): 43–60.

Bartlett, Robert and Angus MacKay. eds. *Medieval Frontier Societies*. Oxford: Clarendon Press, 1989; 2nd edn, 1996.

Bartusis, Mark C. *The Late Byzantine Army: Arms and Society, 1204–1453*. Philadelphia: University of Pennsylvania Press, 1992.

Bates, Michael L. and D. M. Metcalf. 'Crusader Coinage with Arabic Inscriptions'. In *The Impact of the Crusades on Europe*. Edited by Harry W. Hazard and Norman P. Zacour, 421–82. Vol. VI of *A History of the Crusades*. Edited by Kenneth M. Setton. Madison: University of Wisconsin Press, 1989.

Bazzana, André, Pierre Guichard and Philippe Sénac. 'La frontière dans l'Espagne médiévale'. In *Castrum 4: Frontière et peuplement dans le monde méditerranéen au Moyen Age*. Actes du colloque d'Erice-Trapani, 18–25 Septembre 1988, 36–59. Rome: Ecole Française de Rome and Madrid: Casa Velazquez, 1992.

Beaune, Colette. *Naissance de la nation France*. Paris: Gallimard, 1985.

Beckingham, Charles F. and Bernard Hamilton. eds. *Prester John: The Mongols and the Ten Lost Tribes*. Aldershot: Variorum, 1996.

Beckwith, C. I. 'Aspects of the Early History of the Central Asian Guard Corps in Islam'. *AEMAe* 4 (1984): 29–43.

Benkő, Loránd. *A régi magyar személynévadás* (Old Hungarian naming patterns). Budapest: Néptudományi Intézet, 1949.

Hungarian Proper Names. Budapest: Akadémiai Kiadó, 1972.

'Anonymus kunjairól' (Concerning the Cumans of Anonymous). In *Kelet és Nyugat között: Történeti Tanulmányok Kristó Gyula tiszteletére*. Edited by László Koszta, 39–67. Szeged: Szegedi Középkorász Műhely, 1995.

'A helynevek szerepe az Árpád-kori népességtörténeti kutatásokban' (The role of toponyms in research on the demography of the Arpad age). In *Magyarország történeti demográfiája I. A Honfoglalás és az Árpád-kor népessége*. Edited by József Kovacsics, 96–105. Budapest: Központi Statisztikai Hivatal, 1995.

'Anonymus 'kunjainak' személynevei' (The personal names of the Cumans of Anonymous). In Benkő, *Név és történelem: tanulmányok az Árpád-korról*, 40–57. Budapest: Akadémiai Kiadó, 1998.

Benkő, Loránd. ed. *A magyar nyelv történeti-etimológiai szótára* (Historical-Etymological dictionary of the Hungarian Language). 3 vols. Budapest: Akadémiai Kiadó, 1967–76

Bibliography

Bentley, Jerry H. *Old World Encounters: Cross-Cultural Contacts and Exchanges in Pre-Modern Times*. Oxford: Oxford University Press, 1993.

Berend, Nora. 'Medieval Patterns of Social Exclusion and Integration: The Regulation of Non-Christian Clothing in Thirteenth-Century Hungary'. *Revue Mabillon* n.s. 8 (69) (1997): 155–76.

'Medievalists and the Notion of the Frontier'. *Medieval History Journal* 2, no. 1 (1999): 55–72.

'Hungary in the Eleventh and Twelfth Centuries'. In *The New Cambridge Medieval History*. Edited by David Luscombe and Jonathan Riley-Smith. Vol. IV, pt. 2. Cambridge: Cambridge University Press, forthcoming.

'Imitation Coins and Frontier Societies: The Case of Medieval Hungary'. *AEMAe* 10 (1998–9): 5–14.

'How Many Medieval Europes? The "pagans" of Hungary and Regional Diversity in Christendom'. In *The Medieval World*, ed. Janet Nelson and Peter Linehan. London: Routledge, forthcoming.

Bertényi, Iván. 'Magyarország nemzetközi helyzete a tatárjárás után' (The international position of Hungary after the Mongol invasion). In *Unger Mátyás Emlékkönyv*. Edited by Péter Kovács, János Kalmár and László V. Molnár, 15–22. Budapest: MTA Történettudományi Intézet, 1991.

Bigalli, Davide. *I Tartari e l'Apocalisse: ricerche sull'escatologia in Adamo Marsh e Ruggero Bacone*. Florence: La Nuova Italia, 1971.

Billington, Ray Allen. *Westward Expansion: A History of the American Frontier*. New York: Macmillan, 1949.

America's Frontier Heritage. New York: Holt, Reinhart and Winston, 1966.

The American Frontier Thesis: Attack and Defense. Washington: American Historical Association, 1971.

Bishko, Charles Julian. 'The Castilian as Plainsman: The Medieval Ranching Frontier in La Mancha and Extremadura'. In *The New World Looks at its History*. Edited by Archibald R. Lewis and Thomas F. McGann, 47–69. Austin, Tex.: University of Texas Press, 1963. Reprinted in Bishko, *Studies in Medieval Spanish Frontier History*, no. IV. London: Variorum Reprints, 1980.

'The Spanish and Portuguese Reconquest, 1095–1492'. In *A History of the Crusades*. Edited by Kenneth M. Setton. Vol. III: 396–456. Madison, Wis.: University of Wisconsin Press, 1975. Reprinted in Bishko, *Studies in Medieval Spanish*, no. III.

Bitterli, Urs. *Die 'Wilden' und die 'Zivilisierten': Grundzüge einer Geistes- und Kulturgeschichte der europäisch-überseeischen Begegnung*. Munich: Beck, 1976.

Blazovich, László. 'IV. László harca a kunok ellen' (Ladislas IV's war against the Cumans). *Századok* 111 (1977): 941–5.

Blunt, C. E. 'The Coinage of Offa'. In *Anglo-Saxon Coins: Studies Presented to F. M. Stenton*. Edited by R. H. M. Dolley, 50–1. London: Methuen, 1961.

Bogyay, Tamás. 'A bántornyai falképek donátorairól' (The donors of the frescoes at Bántornya). *Ars Hungarica* 14, no. 2 (1986): 147–58.

Boivin, Jeanne-Marie. *L'Irlande au Moyen Age: Giraud de Barri et la Topographia Hibernica (1188)*. Paris: Champion, 1993.

Bolla, Ilona. *A jogilag egységes jobbágyosztály kialakulása Magyarországon* (The development of the legally unified serfdom in Hungary). Értekezések a történeti tudományok köréből, n.s. 100. Budapest: Akadémiai Kiadó, 1983.

Bibliography

Bolsakov, O. G. 'Abu-Hámid al-Garnáti és művei' (Abū Hāmid al-Garnāti and his works). In *Abu-Hámid Al-Garnáti utazása Kelet- és Közép-Európában 1131–1153*, 11–28.
Bonenfant, Paul. 'A propos des limites médiévales'. In *Eventail de l'histoire vivante: hommage à Lucien Febvre.* Vol. II: 73–9. Paris: Librairie Armand Colin, 1953.
Bonfil, Roberto. *Tra due mondi: cultura ebraica e cultura cristiana nel Medioevo.* Naples: Liguori, 1996.
Bónis, György. *A jogtudó értelmiség a Mohács előtti Magyarországon* (Intellectuals trained in law in Hungary before the battle of Mohács). Budapest: Akadémiai Kiadó, 1971.
Bonnefoy, Yves. ed. *Dictionnaire des Mythologies.* 2 vols. Paris: Flammarion, 1993.
Boockmann, Hartmut. *Der Deutsche Orden.* Munich: Beck, 1981.
Borosy, András. 'A XI–XIV. sz. magyar lovasságról' (Concerning the XI–XIVth c. Hungarian cavalry). *Hadtörténelmi közlemények* 9, no. 2 (1962): 119–74.
  'A lovagi haditechnika és a lovagság Magyarországon az Árpád-korban' (Military techniques of knights and chivalry in Hungary in the Arpad age). In *Társadalom- és Művelődéstörténeti tanulmányok. Mályusz Elemér Emlékkönyv.* Edited by Éva H. Balázs, Erik Fügedi and Ferenc Maksay, 47–57. Budapest: Akadémiai Kiadó, 1984.
  'Történetírók a tatárjárásról' (Historians on the Mongol invasion). *Hadtörténelmi Közlemények* 104 (1991): 3–21.
  'A keresztesháborúk és Magyarország' (The Crusades and Hungary). *Hadtörténelmi Közlemények* 109, no. 1 (1996): 3–41; no. 2 (1996): 11–53.
Borsa, Gedeon. 'A kassai kódex hitelességéről' (On the authenticity of the Codex of Kassa). *Magyar Könyvszemle* 88 (1972): 88–90.
Borzsák, István. 'A Nagy Sándor-hagyomány Magyarországon' (Traditions concerning Alexander the Great in Hungary). *Antik Tanulmányok* 30, no. 1 (1983): 1–18.
Boswell, John. *The Royal Treasure: Muslim Communities under the Crown of Aragon in the Fourteenth Century.* New Haven and London: Yale University Press, 1977.
  Christianity, Social Tolerance, and Homosexuality: Gay People in Western Europe from the Beginning of the Christian Era to the Fourteenth Century. Chicago: University of Chicago Press, 1980.
Botka, János. 'A jogállás és a katonai szolgálat kapcsolata a kunok és a jászok török hódítás előtti történetében' (The relationship between legal status and military service in the history of the Cumans and the As before the Ottoman conquest). *Zounok: A Jász- Nagykun- Szolnok megyei Levéltár évkönyve* 11 (1996): 65–75.
Boureau, Alain. 'La guerre des récits: la crémation du Talmud (1240–1242)'. In *L'Evénement sans fin: récit et christianisme au Moyen Age*, 231–51. Paris: Les Belles Lettres, 1993.
Bowlus, Charles R. *Franks, Moravians and Magyars: The Struggle for the Middle Danube, 788–907.* Philadelphia: University of Pennsylvania Press, 1995.
Boyer, Régis. *Le Christ des barbares: Le monde nordique (IXe–XIIIe siècle).* Paris: Cerf, 1987.
Bredero, Adriaan H. *Christendom and Christianity in the Middle Ages: The Relations between Religion, Church, and Society.* Tr. Reinder Bruinsma. 2nd edn. Grand Rapids, Mich.: William B. Eerdmans, 1987.
Brincken, Anna-Dorothee von den. *Fines Terrae: Die Enden der Erde und der vierte Kontinent auf mittelalterlichen Weltkarten.* Hannover: Hahnsche Buchhandlung, 1992.

Bibliography

Bromley, Y. *Ethnic Processes*. Soviet Ethnographic Studies 3. Moscow: Social Sciences Today, 1983.

Browe, Peter. 'Die Hostienschändungen der Juden im Mittelalter'. *Römische Quartalschrift für Christliche Altertumskunde und für Kirchengeschichte* 34 (1926): 167–97.

Die Eucharistischen Wunder des Mittelalters. Breslau: Müller and Seiffert, 1938.

Brown, Elizabeth A. R. 'The Tyranny of a Construct: Feudalism and Historians of Medieval Europe'. *American Historical Review* 79 (1974): 1063–88.

Brown, Peter. *The Rise of Western Christendom*. Oxford: Blackwell, 1997.

Brundage, James A. *Medieval Canon Law and the Crusader*. Madison and London: University of Wisconsin Press, 1969.

Law, Sex and Christian Society in Medieval Europe. Chicago: University of Chicago Press, 1987.

'The Thirteenth-Century Livonian Crusade: Henricus de Lettis and the First Legatine Mission of Bishop William of Modena'. in Brundage, *The Crusades, Holy War and Canon Law*, no. XIV. Aldershot: Variorum Reprints, 1991.

Bulliet, Richard W. 'Conversion to Islam and the Emergence of a Muslim Society in Iran'. In *Conversion to Islam*. Edited by Nehemia Levtzion, 30–51. New York and London: Holmes and Meier, 1979.

Burnett, Charles and Patrick Gautier Dalché. 'Attitudes towards the Mongols in Medieval Literature: The XXII Kings of Gog and Magog from the Court of Frederick II to Jean de Mandeville'. *Viator* 22 (1991): 153–67.

Burns, Robert Ignatius. *The Crusader Kingdom of Valencia: Reconstruction of a Thirteenth-Century Frontier*. 2 vols. Cambridge, Mass.: Harvard University Press, 1967.

Moors and Crusaders in Mediterranean Spain. London: Variorum Reprints, 1978.

'The Parish as a Frontier Institution in Thirteenth-Century Valencia'. *Speculum* 37 (1962): 244–51. Reprint in Burns, *Moors and Crusaders in Mediterranean Spain*, no. VIII.

'Surrender Constitutions: The Islamic Communities of Eslida and Alfandech'. In Burns, *Muslims, Christians and Jews in the Crusader Kingdom of Valencia: Societies in Symbiosis*, 54–78. Cambridge: Cambridge University Press, 1984.

'Christian–Muslim Confrontation: The Thirteenth-Century Dream of Conversion'. In Burns, *Muslims, Christians and Jews in the Crusader Kingdom of Valencia: Societies in Symbiosis*, 80–108.

'King Jaume's Jews: Problem and Methodology'. In Burns, *Muslims, Christians and Jews in the Crusader Kingdom of Valencia: Societies in Symbiosis*, 126–41.

Society and Documentation in Crusader Valencia. Princeton: Princeton University Press, 1985.

'The Significance of the Frontier in the Middle Ages'. In Burns, *Medieval Frontier Societies*. Edited by Robert Bartlett and Angus MacKay, 307–30.

Büchler, Sándor. *A zsidók története Budapesten a legrégibb időktől 1867-ig* (The history of the Jews in Budapest from the beginnings to 1867). Budapest: Izraelita Magyar Irodalmi Társulat, 1901.

Campbell, Mary B. *The Witness and the Other World: Exotic European Travel Writing 400–1600*. Ithaca and London: Cornell University Press, 1988.

Castro, Américo. *España en su historia: cristianos, moros y judíos*. Buenos Aires: Editorial Losada, 1948. Tr. *The Structure of Spanish History*. Princeton: Princeton University Press, 1954.

Bibliography

Chazan, Robert. ed. *Church, State, and Jew in the Middle Ages*. New York: Behrman House, 1980.
  Daggers of Faith: Thirteenth-Century Christian Missionizing and Jewish Response. Berkeley and Los Angeles: University of California Press, 1989.
  Barcelona and Beyond: The Disputation of 1263 and its Aftermath. Berkeley and Los Angeles: University of California Press, 1992.
  European Jewry and the First Crusade. Berkeley, Los Angeles and London: University of California Press, 1996. 1st edn. 1987.
  Medieval Stereotypes and Modern Antisemitism. Berkeley, Los Angeles and London: University of California Press, 1997.
Christiansen, Eric. *The Northern Crusades: The Baltic and the Catholic Frontier 1100–1525*. London: Macmillan, 1980. 2nd edn. Harmondsworth: Penguin, 1997.
Clark, Hugh R. 'Muslims and Hindus in the Culture and Morphology of Quanzhou from the Tenth to the Thirteenth Century'. *Journal of World History* 6, no. 1 (1995): 49–74.
Clauson, Sir Gerard. *An Etymological Dictionary of Pre-Thirteenth-Century Turkish*. Oxford: Clarendon Press, 1972.
Cohen, Jeremy. *The Friars and the Jews: The Evolution of Medieval Anti-Judaism*. Ithaca and London: Cornell University Press, 1982.
  Living Letters of the Law: Ideas of the Jew in Medieval Christianity. Berkeley: University of California Press, 1999.
Cohen, Mark. *Under Crescent and Cross: The Jews in the Middle Ages*. Princeton: Princeton University Press, 1994.
Connell, C. W. 'Western Views of the Origin of the Tartars: An Example of the Influence of Myth in the Second Half of the Thirteenth Century'. *Journal of Medieval and Renaissance Studies* 3 (1973): 115–37.
Constable, Olivia Remie. *Trade and Traders in Muslim Spain: The Commercial Realignment of the Iberian Peninsula 900–1500*. Cambridge: Cambridge University Press, 1994.
Courcelles, Dominique de. *La parole risquée de Raymond Lulle: entre le judaïsme, le christianisme et l'islam*. Paris: J. Vrin, 1993.
Cronon, William, George Miles and Jay Gitlin. eds. *Under an Open Sky: Rethinking America's Western Past*. New York: Norton, 1992.
Curzon of Kedleston, Lord. *Frontiers*. The Romanes Lecture 1907. Oxford: Clarendon Press, 1907.
Czeglédy, Károly. 'Az Árpád-kori mohamedánokról és neveikről' (On the Muslims of the Arpad-age and their names). In *Magyar Őstörténeti Tanulmányok*, 99–104. Budapest Oriental Reprints Series A2. Budapest: Akadémiai Kiadó, 1985. (First published in *Névtudományi előadások a II. Névtudományi Konferencián. Nyelvtudományi Értesítő* 70 (1970): 254–9.)
Csinos, Albin. *Az izmaeliták Magyarországon* (The Ishmaelites in Hungary). Esztergom: Laiszky János Könyvnyomdája, 1913.
Csorba, Csaba. 'A tatárjárás és a kunok Magyarországi betelepedése' (The Mongol invasion and the settlement of the Cumans in Hungary). In *Emlékkönyv a Túrkevei Múzeum fennállásának harmincadik évfordulójára*, 33–68. Túrkeve: Túrkevei Finta Múzeum, 1981.
Dahan, Gilbert. *Les intellectuels chrétiens et les juifs au moyen âge*. Paris: Cerf, 1990.

Bibliography

La polémique chrétienne contre le judaïsme au moyen âge. Paris: Albin Michel, 1991.
Dahan, Gilbert. ed. *Le brûlement du Talmud à Paris 1242–1244*. Paris: Cerf, 1999.
D'Alverny, Marie-Thérèse. 'La connaissance de l'Islam en occident du IXe au milieu du XIIe siècle'. In *L'Occidente e l'Islam nell'Alto Medioevo*. 2 vols. Settimane di Studio del Centro Italiano di Studi sull'Alto Medioevo 12. Vol. II: 577–602. Spoleto, 1965.
'La connaissance de l'Islam au temps de Saint Louis'. In *Septième centenaire de la mort de Saint Louis: Actes des colloques de Royaumont et de Paris*, 235–46. Paris: Les Belles Lettres, 1976.
'Translations and Translators'. In *Renaissance and Renewal in the Twelfth Century*. Edited by Robert L. Benson and Giles Constable, 421–62. Cambridge, Mass.: Harvard University Press, 1982.
Dán, Róbert. 'Mikor űzte ki I. Lajos a zsidókat?' (When did King Louis I expel the Jews?). *Tanulmányok Budapest Múltjából* 24 A Budapesti Történeti Múzeum Évkönyve 1991, 9–15.
Daniel, E. Randolph. *The Franciscan Concept of Mission in the High Middle Ages*. 2nd edn. St Bonaventure, N.Y.: Franciscan Institute, 1992.
Daniel, Norman. *The Arabs and Medieval Europe*. 2nd edn. London: Longman, 1979.
Heroes and Saracens: An Interpretation of the Chansons de Geste. Edinburgh: Edinburgh University Press, 1989.
'The Legal and Political Theory of the Crusade'. In *A History of the Crusades*. Edited by Kenneth M. Setton. Vol. VI: *The Impact of the Crusades on Europe*. Edited by Harry W. Hazard and Norman P. Zacour, 3–38. Madison, Wis.: University of Wisconsin Press, 1989.
'Crusade Propaganda'. In *A History of the Crusades*. Edited by Kenneth Setton. Vol. VI: 39–97.
Islam and the West: The Making of an Image. Rev. edn. Oxford: Oneworld Publications, 1993.
Dávid, Ferenc. *A soproni ó-zsinagóga* (The Old Synagogue of Sopron). Budapest: A Magyar Izraeliták Országos Képviselete, 1978.
Davies, Rees. 'Frontier Arrangements in Fragmented Societies: Ireland and Wales'. In *Medieval Frontier Societies*. Edited by Robert Bartlett and Angus MacKay, 77–100.
Deér, József. *Pogány magyarság, keresztény magyarság* (Pagan Hungarians, Christian Hungarians). Budapest: Királyi Magyar Egyetemi Nyomda, 1938. Reprint Budapest: Holnap Kiadó, 1993.
Demski, Augustin. *Papst Nikolaus III*. Kirchengeschichtliche Studien 6. Münster: H. Schöning, 1903.
D'Eszlary, Charles. 'Les Musulmans Hongrois du Moyen Age (VIIe–XIVe s.)'. *IBLA. Revue de l'Institut des Belles Lettres Arabes* 19 (1956): 375–86.
DeWeese, Devin. *Islamization and Native Religion in the Golden Horde*. Philadelphia: Pennsylvania State University Press, 1994.
Diaconu, Petre. *Les Coumans au Bas Danube aux XIe et XIIe siècles*. Bucharest: Editura Academiei Republicii Socialiste România, 1978.
Dienes, István. *A honfoglaló magyarok* (The conquering Hungarians). Budapest: Corvina Kiadó, 1972.
Diószegi, Vilmos. *A pogány magyarok hitvilága* (The beliefs of pagan Hungarians). Kőrösi Csoma Kiskönyvtár 4. Budapest: Akadémiai Kiadó, 1967.

Bibliography

Diószegi, Vilmos. ed. *Az ősi magyar hitvilág* (Ancient Hungarian beliefs). Budapest: Gondolat Kiadó, 1971.
Dodds, Jerrilynn D. 'Mudejar Tradition and the Synagogues of Medieval Spain: Cultural Identity and Cultural Hegemony'. In *Convivencia: Jews, Muslims, and Christians in Medieval Spain*. Edited by Vivian B. Mann, Thomas F. Glick and Jerrilynn D. Dodds, 113–31. New York: George Braziller, 1992.
Domanovszky, Sándor. *Kézai Simon mester krónikája* (The chronicle of Simon of Kéza). Budapest: MTA, 1906.
'Kézai és a hun-krónika' (Simon of Kéza and the Hun-chronicle). In *Emlékkönyv Károlyi Árpád születése nyolcvanadik fordulójának ünnepére*. Edited by Sándor Domanovszky, 110–32. Budapest, 1933.
Duby, Georges. *Medieval Marriage: Two Models from Twelfth-Century France*. Baltimore: Johns Hopkins University Press, 1978.
Duggan, Anne J. ed. *Kings and Kingship in Medieval Europe*. London: King's College, 1993.
ed. *Queens and Queenship in Medieval Europe*. Woodbridge: Boydell Press, 1997.
Duggan, Lawrence G. ' "For Force is not of God"? Compulsion and Conversion from Yahweh to Charlemagne'. In *Varieties of Religious Conversion in the Middle Ages*. Edited by James Muldoon, 49–62. Gainesville: University of Florida Press, 1997.
Dunlop, D. M. *The History of the Jewish Khazars*. Princeton: Princeton University Press, 1954. New York: Schocken, 1967.
Dvornik, Francis. *The Making of Central and Eastern Europe*. London: Polish Research Centre, 1949.
Eckhardt, Sándor. 'Kun analógiák a magyar ősvalláshoz' (Cuman analogies to traditional Hungarian religion). *Magyar Nyelv* 34 (1938): 242–4.
'Attila a mondában' (Attila in legends). In *Attila és hunjai*. Edited by Gyula Németh, 143–216. Budapest: Magyar Szemle Társaság, 1940. Reprint Budapest: Akadémiai Kiadó, 1986.
Ehrle, Franz. 'Zur Geschichte des Schatzes, der Bibliothek und des Archivs der Päpste im vierzehnten Jahrhundert'. *Archiv für Litteratur- und Kirchen-Geschichte des Mittelalters* 1 (1885): 1–48, 228–364.
'Ein Leben Mohammeds (Adelphus?)'. In *Anecdota Novissima: Texte des vierten bis sechzehnten Jahrhunderts*. Edited by Bernhard Bischoff, 106–22. Stuttgart: Anton Hiersemann, 1984.
Eliade, Mircea. *Shamanism: Archaic Techniques of Ecstasy*. Bollingen Series 76. Princeton: Princeton University Press, 1964.
Elias, Norbert and John L. Scotson. *The Established and the Outsiders*. 2nd edn. London: Sage, 1994.
Elukin, Jonathan. 'From Jew to Christian? Conversion and Immutability in Medieval Europe'. In *Varieties of Religious Conversion*. Edited by James Muldoon, 171–89.
The Encyclopaedia of Islam. 5 vols. Leiden: Brill and London: Luzac, 1913–38. New edn, Leiden: Brill, 1960–. s.v. 'Kipčak', 'Madjar, Madjaristān'.
Encyclopaedia Judaica. 16 vols. Jerusalem: Encyclopaedia Judaica and New York: Macmillan, 1971–2. s.v. 'Moses Or Zaru'a', 'Responsa', 'Synagogue'.
Engel, Pál. *Beilleszkedés Európába a kezdetektől 1440-ig* (Integration into Europe from the beginnings to 1440). Budapest: Háttér Lap- és Könyvkiadó, 1990.
The Realm of St Stephen: A History of Medieval Hungary. London: I. B. Tauris, forthcoming.

Bibliography

Epalza, Mikel de. *Jésus otage: Juifs, Chrétiens et Musulmans en Espagne (VI–XVII siècles)*. Paris: Cerf, 1987.
Epalza, Mikel de and Suzanne Guellouz. *Le Cid: Personnage historique et littéraire*. Paris: Maisonneuve et Larose, 1983.
Erdélyi, László. *Krónikáink atyja Kézai* (The father of our chronicles, Simon of Kéza). Szeged: Prometheus Nyomda, 1933.
Erdélyi, László. ed. *A Pannonhalmi Szent-Benedek-rend története* (The History of the Benedictines at Pannonhalma). 12 vols. Budapest: Stephaneum, 1902–16.
Erdő, Péter. 'A részleges egyházjog forrásszövegei a Magyarországon őrzött középkori kódexekben' (Canon law texts in medieval Hungarian codices) *Magyar Könyvszemle* 108, no. 2 (1992): 301–11.
Éri, István. 'Adatok a kígyóspusztai csat értékeléséhez' (Contribution to the evaluation of the brooch from Kígyóspuszta). *Folia Archaeologica* 8 (1956): 137–52.
Eriksen, Thomas Hylland. *Ethnicity and Nationalism: Anthropological Perspectives*. London and Boulder, Colo.: Pluto Press, 1993.
Érszegi, Géza. 'Eredeti pápai oklevelek Magyarországon (1199–1417)' (Original papal bulls in Hungary (1199–1417)', Ph.D. dissertation. Budapest, 1989.
Érszegi, Géza and László N. Szelestei. 'Fogalmazásmintákat tartalmazó tankönyv töredékei a 14. század első feléből' (Fragments of an early fourteenth-century schoolbook containing model compositions). In *Tanulmányok a középkori magyarországi könyvkultúráról* . Edited by László N. Szelestei, 297–326. Budapest: Országos Széchényi Könyvtár, 1989.
Evans, Robert J. W. 'Frontiers and National Identities in Central Europe'. *The International History Review* 14, no. 3 (1992): 480–502.
Fazekas, István and András Pálóczi Horváth. *A kunok emléke Magyarországon* (The memory of the Cumans in Hungary). Kiskunfélegyháza: Kiskun Múzeum, 1985.
Fazekas, István, László Szabó and István Sztrinkó. eds. *A Jászkunság kutatása 1985*. Kecskemét and Szolnok: Szolnoki Damjanich János Múzeum, 1987.
Febvre, Lucien. 'La Frontière: le mot et la notion'. *Revue de Synthèse Historique* 45 (1928): 31–44. Reprinted in Febvre, *Pour une histoire à part entière*, 11–24. Paris: Ecole Pratique des Hautes Etudes, 1962.
'Limites et frontières'. *Annales ESC* 2 (1947): 201–7.
Fehértói, Katalin. *A XIV. századi magyar megkülönböztető nevek* (Fourteenth-century Hungarian distinguishing names). Budapest: Akadémiai Kiadó, 1969.
Árpád-kori kis személynévtár (Dictionary of personal names of the Arpad age). Budapest: Akadémiai Kiadó, 1983.
Fejérpataky, László. *A királyi kancellária az Árpádok korában* (The royal chancery in the age of the Arpads). Budapest, 1885.
'A Gutkeled-Biblia' (The Gutkeled Bible). *Magyar Könyvszemle* n.s. 1 (1892–3): 5–22.
Fennell, John. *The Crisis of Medieval Russia (1200–1304)*. 5th edn. London and New York: Longman, 1993.
Ferenţ, Ioan. *A kunok és püspökségük* (The Cumans and their bishopric). Tr. Péter Pál Domokos. Budapest: Szent István Társulat, 1981. (Originally published as *Cumanii si episcopia lor*. Baj, 1933.)
Fernández-Armesto, Felipe. *Before Columbus: Exploration and Colonisation from the Mediterranean to the Atlantic 1229–1492*. London: Macmillan, 1987.

Bibliography

Figueira, Robert C. ' "Legatus apostolice sedis": The Pope's "alter ego" According to Thirteenth-Century Canon Law'. *Studi Medievali* 3rd ser., 27, no. 2 (1986): 527–74.
'The Classification of Medieval Papal Legates in the Liber Extra'. *Archivum Historiae Pontificiae* 21 (1983): 211–28.
Fine, John V. A. Jr. *The Late Medieval Balkans: A Critical Survey from the Late Twelfth Century to the Ottoman Conquest.* Ann Arbor: University of Michigan Press, 1994.
Fletcher, Richard A. *The Quest for El Cid.* London: Hutchinson, 1989.
The Conversion of Europe from Paganism to Christianity 371–1386. London: HarperCollins, 1997.
Fodor, István. 'Az osztrogozsszki lelet' (The find from Osztrogozsszk). *Cumania: A Bács-Kiskun megyei múzeumok közleményei* 4 (1976): 255–63.
'Archaeological traces of the Volga Bulgars in Hungary in the Árpád period'. *AOASH* 33 (1979): 315–25.
'Lehettek-e kun sírszobrok Magyarországon?' (Were there Cuman grave statues in Hungary?). In *A Jászkunság kutatása 1985.* Edited by István Fazekas, László Szabó and István Sztrinkó, 3–10. Kecskemét and Szolnok: Szolnoki Damjanich János Múzeum, 1987.
Folz, Robert. *Les saints rois du Moyen Age en Occident VIe–XIIIe siècles.* Brussels: Société des Bollandistes, 1984.
Foucher, Michel. *L'invention des frontières.* Paris: Fondation pour les Etudes de Défense Nationale, 1986.
Fraknói, Vilmos. *A magyar királyi kegyúri jog* (The *jus patronatus* of Hungarian kings). Budapest, 1895.
Magyarország egyházi és politikai összeköttetései a római Szent-Székkel (Hungary's ecclesiastical and political relations to the Holy See). 2 vols. Budapest: Szent István Társulat, 1901–2.
Franklin, Simon and Jonathan Shepard. *The Emergence of Rus 750–1200.* London and New York: Longman, 1996.
Frenz, Thomas. *I documenti pontifici nel Medioevo e nell'età moderna.* Tr. Sergio Pagano. Vatican City: Scuola vaticana di paleografia, diplomatica e archivistica, 1989.
Friedenberg, Daniel M. *Jewish Minters and Medalists.* Philadelphia: Jewish Publication Society of America, 1976.
Medieval Jewish Seals from Europe. Detroit: Wayne State University Press, 1987.
'Jewish Mint Masters of Medieval Hungary'. *The Shekel* 24, no. 4 (1991): 20–5.
Fügedi, Erik. 'Középkori magyar városprivilégiumok' (Medieval Hungarian municipal privileges). In *Tanulmányok Budapest múltjából,* no. 14, 17–107. Budapest várostörténeti monográfiái 22. Budapest: Akadémiai Kiadó, 1961.
Vár és társadalom a 13–14. századi Magyarországon (Castle and society in thirteenth–fourteenth-century Hungary). Értekezések a történeti tudományok köréből 82. Budapest: Akadémiai Kiadó, 1977.
'A befogadó: a középkori magyar királyság' (The medieval kingdom of Hungary: 'a guestland'). *Történelmi Szemle* (1979, no. 2): 355–76.
Kolduló barátok, polgárok, nemesek: tanulmányok a magyar középkorról (Mendicants, burghers, nobles: studies about the Hungarian Middle Ages). Budapest: Magvető Kiadó, 1981.

Bibliography

'Városok kialakulása Magyarországon' (The development of towns in Hungary). In *Kolduló barátok, polgárok, nemesek: tanulmányok a magyar középkorról*, 311–35. Budapest: Magvető Kiadó, 1981.
Castle and Society in Medieval Hungary (1000–1437). Budapest: Akadémiai Kiadó, 1986.
Ispánok, bárók, kiskirályok: a középkori magyar arisztokrácia fejlődése (Ispáns, barons and kinglets: the development of the Hungarian aristocracy). Budapest: Magvető Kiadó, 1986.
'The Aristocracy in Medieval Hungary'. In *Kings, Bishops, Nobles and Burghers in Medieval Hungary*. Edited by János M. Bak, no. IV. London: Variorum Reprints, 1986.
'Das mittelalterliche Königreich Ungarn als Gastland'. In *Kings, Bishops, Nobles and Burghers in Medieval Hungary*, no. VIII.
'La formation des villes et les ordres mendiants en Hongrie'. In *Kings, Bishops, Nobles and Burghers in Medieval Hungary*, no. XII.
'A középkori Magyarország történeti demográfiája' (Historical demography of medieval Hungary). *Történeti Demográfiai Füzetek* 10. Budapest: Központi Statisztikai Hivatal Népességtudományi Kutató Intézet, 1992, no. 1: 7–60.
Fyodorov-Davidov, G. A. *Az Aranyhorda földjén*. Hung. tr. Budapest: Gondolat Kiadó, 1983. Originally published as *Kurgani, idoli, moneti*. Moscow, 1968.
Gaudemet, Jean. 'Le dossier canonique du mariage de Philippe Auguste et d'Ingeburge de Danemark (1193–1213)'. *Revue Historique de Droit Français et Etranger* 62 (1984): 15–29. Reprinted in Gaudemet, *Droit de l'église et vie sociale au Moyen Age*, no. XIV. Northampton: Variorum Reprints, 1989.
Gautier Dalché, Jean. 'Islam et chrétienté en Espagne au XIIe s.: contribution à l'étude de la notion de frontière'. *Hespéris* 46 (1959): 183–217.
Gautier Dalché, Patrick. 'De la liste à la carte: limite et frontière dans la géographie et la cartographie de l'Occident médiéval'. In *Castrum 4: Frontière et peuplement dans le monde méditerranéen au Moyen Age*. Actes du colloque d'Erice-Trapani, 18–25 Septembre 1988, 19–31. Rome: Ecole Française de Rome and Madrid: Casa Velazquez, 1992.
Geary, Patrick. 'Ethnic Identity as a Situational Construct in the Early Middle Ages'. *Medieval Perspectives* 3, no. 2 (1988): 1–17.
Gedai, István. 'A magyar numizmatika keleti vonatkozásai' (Eastern aspects of Hungarian numismatics). *Magyar Numizmatikai Társaság Évkönyve* (1972): 189–93.
Magyar Nemzeti Múzeum, A Magyar aranypénzverés története: vezető (Hungarian National Museum, The history of Hungarian gold minting: a guide). Budapest: Népművelési Propaganda Iroda, 1982.
Geremek, Bronislaw. *Les marginaux parisiens aux XIVe et XVe siècles*. Paris: Flammarion, 1976.
Gerevich, László. ed. *Towns in Medieval Hungary*. Atlantic Studies on Society in Change 65; East European Monographs CCXCVII. Highland Lakes, N.J.: Atlantic Research and Publications and Budapest: Akadémiai Kiadó, 1990.
'The Rise of Hungarian Towns along the Danube'. In *Towns in Medieval Hungary*, 26–50.
Gerézdi, Rabán. 'Veress Endre: Olasz egyetemeken járt magyarországi tanulók anyakönyve és iratai 1221–1864' (Review of Endre Veress: documents concerning Hungarian students at Italian Universities 1221–1864). *Századok* 76 (1942): 338–44.

Gerics, József. 'Adalékok a Kézai-krónika problémájának megoldásához' (On the solution of the problem of Kézai's Chronicle). *Annales Universitatis Scientiarum Budapestinensis de R. Eötvös nominatae. Sectio Historica* 1 (1957): 106–34.

'Az államszuverenitás védelme és a "két jog" alkalmazásának szempontjai XII-XIII. századi krónikáinkban' (Protection of state sovereignty and the use of the 'two laws' in twelfth–thirteenth-century Hungarian chronicles). *Történelmi Szemle* 18 (1975): 353–72.

'Krónikáink és a III. András-kori rendi intézmények friauli-aquileiai kapcsolatairól' (Hungarian chronicles and connections between the institutions of estates and Friaul-Aquileia during the reign of András III). *Filológiai Közlöny* 21 (1975): 309–25.

'Az 'új adomány' jogintézménye a 13. századi magyar okleveles gyakorlatban' (The legal practice of the 'new donation' in thirteenth-century Hungarian charters). *Levéltári Szemle* 36, no. 1 (1986): 21–30.

'Nemesi jog – királyi jog a középkori magyarországi birtoklásban' (Noble rights – royal rights in medieval Hungarian property-holding). In Gerics, *Egyház, állam és gondolkodás Magyarországon a középkorban* (Church, state and thought in Hungary in the Middle Ages), 275–94. Budapest: METEM, 1995.

Gerics, József and Erzsébet Ladányi. 'A magyarországi birtokjog kérdései a középkorban' (Rights concerning landed possessions in medieval Hungary). *Levéltári Szemle* 41, no. 4 (1991): 3–19.

Gieysztor, Aleksander. 'Les Juifs et leurs activités économiques en Europe orientale'. In *Gli Ebrei nell'Alto Medioevo*. 2 vols. Settimane di Studio del Centro Italiano di Studi sull'Alto Medioevo 26. Vol. I: 489–522. Spoleto, 1980.

'The Beginnings of Jewish Settlement in the Polish Lands'. In *The Jews in Poland*. Edited by Chimen Abramsky *et al.*, 15–21. Oxford: Blackwell, 1986.

Gilles, Henri. 'Législation et doctrine canoniques sur les Sarrasins'. In *Islam et chrétiens du Midi (XIIe–XIVe s.)*, 195–213. Cahiers de Fanjeaux 18. Fanjeaux: Edouard Privat, 1983.

Glatz, Ferenc. ed. *Virágkor és pusztulás: A kezdetektől 1606-ig* (Flowering and decline: from the beginnings to 1606). História Könyvtár Atlaszok Magyarország történetéhez 1. Budapest: MTA Történettudományi Intézet, 1995.

Glazer, Nathan and Daniel P. Moynihan. *Beyond the Melting Pot*. Cambridge, Mass.: MIT Press, 1963.

Glick, Thomas F. *Irrigation and Society in Medieval Valencia*. Cambridge, Mass.: Belknap Press, 1970.

Islamic and Christian Spain in the Early Middle Ages. Princeton: Princeton University Press, 1979.

From Muslim Fortress to Christian Castle: Social and Cultural Change in Medieval Spain. Manchester and New York: Manchester University Press, 1995.

Glick, Thomas F. and Oriol Pi-Sunyer. 'Acculturation as an Explanatory Concept in Spanish History'. *Comparative Studies in Society and History* 11 (1969): 136–54.

Göckenjan, Hansgerd. *Hilfsvölker und Grenzwächter im Mittelalterlichen Ungarn*. Quellen und Studien zur Geschichte des Östlichen Europa 5. Wiesbaden: Franz Steiner, 1972.

Goffart, Walter. *Barbarians and Romans A.D. 418–584: The Techniques of Accommodation*. Princeton: Princeton University Press, 1980.

Bibliography

Goitein, S. D. *A Mediterranean Society: The Jewish Communities of the Arab World as Portrayed in the Documents of the Cairo Geniza.* Vol. I: *Economic Foundations.* Berkeley and Los Angeles: University of California Press, 1967. Vol. II: *The Community.* Berkeley and Los Angeles: University of California Press, 1971.
Golab, Kasimir. 'De Philippo Firmano Episcopo eiusque statutis legativis a. 1279'. *Revista Española de Derecho Canonico* 16 (1961): 187–200.
Golb, Norman. *The Jews in Medieval Normandy.* Cambridge: Cambridge University Press, 1998.
Gold, Hugo. *Gedenkbuch der Untergegangenen Judengemeinden des Burgenlandes.* Tel Aviv: Olamenu, 1970.
Golden, Peter B. 'The Polovcii Dikii'. *Harvard Ukrainian Studies* 3–4 (1979–80): 296–309.
— *Khazar Studies: An Historico-Philological Inquiry into the Origins of the Khazars.* 2 vols. Budapest: Akadémiai Kiadó, 1980.
— 'Khazaria and Judaism'. *AEMAe* 3 (1983): 127–56.
— 'Cumanica I: The Quipčaqs in Georgia'. *AEMAe* 4 (1984): 45–87.
— 'Cumanica II: The Ölberli (Ölperli): The Fortunes and Misfortunes of an Inner Asian Nomadic Clan'. *AEMAe* 6 (1986): 5–29.
— 'Nomads and their Sedentary Neighbors in Pre-Činggisid Eurasia'. *AEMAe* 7 (1987–91): 41–81.
— 'The Quipčaqs of Medieval Eurasia: An Example of Stateless Adaptation in the Steppes'. In *Rulers from the Steppe: State Formation on the Eurasian Periphery.* Edited by Gary Seaman and Daniel Marks, 132–57. Ethnographics Monograph Series 2. Los Angeles: University of Southern California and Ethnographics Press, 1991.
— 'The Dogs of the Medieval Qüipčaqs'. In *Varia Eurasiatica: Festschrift für Professor András Róna-Tas,* 45–55. Szeged: Department of Altaic Studies, 1991.
— *An Introduction to the History of the Turkic Peoples: Ethnogenesis and State-Formation in Medieval and Early Modern Eurasia and the Middle East.* Wiesbaden: Otto Harrassowitz, 1992.
— 'The "Codex Cumanicus"'. In *Central Asian Monuments.* Edited by Hasan B. Paksoy, 33–63. Istanbul: Isis Press, 1992.
— 'Cumanica IV: The Tribes of the Cuman-Qipčaqs'. *AEMAe* 9 (1995–7): 99–122.
— 'Wolves, Dogs and Quipčaq Religion'. *AOASH* 50 (1997): 87–97.
— 'Religion among the Qipčaqs of Medieval Eurasia'. *Central Asiatic Journal* 42, no. 2 (1998): 180–237.
González Jiménez, Manuel. 'Frontier and Settlement in the Kingdom of Castile'. In *Medieval Frontier Societies.* Edited by Robert Bartlett and Angus MacKay, 49–74.
Gossiaux, M. 'Ethnicité et pouvoir'. Lecture series at the Ecole des Hautes Etudes en Sciences Sociales, Paris, 1994–5.
Graham, Hugh S. ' "Digenis Akritas" as a Source for Frontier History'. In *Actes du XIVe Congrès International des Etudes Byzantines.* Vol. II: 321–9.
Grierson, Philip. *The Coins of Medieval Europe.* London: Seaby, 1991.
Grønbech, Kaare. *Komanisches Wörterbuch: Türkischer Wortindex zu Codex Cumanicus.* Copenhagen: Munksgaard, 1942.
Grundmann, H. 'Bibliographie des études récentes (après 1900) sur les hérésies médiévales'. In *Hérésies et sociétés dans l'Europe préindustrielle 11e–18e siècles.* Communications et débats du Colloque de Royaumont présentés par Jacques Le Goff. Civilisations et Sociétés 10, 407–67. Paris and La Haye: Mouton, 1968.

Bibliography

Guenée, Bernard. 'Des limites féodales aux frontières politiques'. In *Les Lieux de mémoire*, vol. II: *La Nation*. Edited by Pierre Nora, 2: 10–33. Paris: Gallimard, 1986.

Guichard, Pierre. 'Participation des Méridionaux à la Reconquista dans le royaume de Valence'. In *Islam et chrétiens du Midi (XIIe–XIVe s.)*, 115–31. Cahiers de Fanjeaux 18. Toulouse: Edouard Privat, 1983.

Gumowski, Marian. *Hebräische Münzen im mittelalterlichen Polen*. Graz: Akademische Druck- und Verlagsanstalt, 1975.

Gyárfás, István. *A jász-kunok története* (The history of the As-Cumans). 4 vols. Kecskemét, Szolnok and Budapest, 1870–85. Reprint Budapest: A Jászkunságért Alapítvány, 1982.

A jászkúnok nyelve és nemzetisége (The language and ethnicity of the As-Cumans). Budapest, 1882.

Gyóni, Mátyás. 'Kálizok, kazárok, kabarok, magyarok' (Kaliz, Khazars, Kabars, and Hungarians). *Magyar Nyelv* 34 (1938): 86–92, 159–71.

Györffy, György. *Krónikáink és a magyar őstörténet* (Hungarian chronicles and prehistory). 1948. Reprint Budapest: Balassi Kiadó, 1993.

'A hun-magyar krónika szerzője' (The author of the Hun-Hungarian chronicle). In Györffy, *Krónikáink és a magyar őstörténet*, 152–80.

'A magyar nemzetségtől a vármegyéig, a törzstől az országig' (From the Hungarian clans to the county, from the tribe to the country). *Századok* 92 (1958): 12–87, 565–615.

'Magyarország népessége a honfoglalástól a XIV. század közepéig' (The population of Hungary from the conquest period to the mid-fourteenth century). In *Magyarország történeti demográfiája*. Edited by József Kovacsics, 45–62. Budapest: Közgazdasági és Jogi Könyvkiadó, 1963.

Az Árpád-kori Magyarország történeti földrajza (Historical geography of Arpad-age Hungary). 4 vols. to date. Budapest: Akadémiai Kiadó, 1963–98.

'Thomas à Becket and Hungary'. *Angol Filológiai Tanulmányok* 4 (1969): 45–52.

'Budapest története az Árpád-korban' (A history of Budapest in the Arpad age). In *Budapest története*. 5 vols. Edited by László Gerevich. Vol. I: 217–349. Budapest: Budapest Főváros Tanácsa, 1973–80.

István király és műve (King Stephen and his achievements). Budapest: Akadémiai Kiadó, 1977.

'Gyulafehérvár kezdetei, neve és káptalanjának registruma' (The origins and name of Gyulafehérvár and the registers of its chapter). *Századok* 117 (1983): 1103–34.

Anonymus: rejtély vagy történeti forrás? (The Hungarian Anonymous: enigma or historical source?). Budapest: Akadémiai Kiadó, 1988.

A magyarság keleti elemei (The Eastern elements of the Hungarian people). Budapest: Gondolat Kiadó, 1990.

'Besenyők és magyarok' (Pechenegs and Hungarians). In *A magyarság*, 94–191.

'A XV. századi jász szójegyzék' (A fifteenth-century As wordlist). In *A magyarság*, 316–18.

'A Jászság betelepülése' (Settlement in the Jászság). In *A magyarság*, 312–15.

'A magyarországi kun társadalom a XIII–XIV. században (a kunok feudalizálódása)' (Thirteenth–fourteenth-century Cuman society in Hungary: the feudalization of the Cumans). In *A magyarság*, 274–304.

'A Nagykunság és Karcag a középkorban' (The territories of Greater Cumania and Karcag in the Middle Ages). In *A magyarság*, 305–11.

Bibliography

'A kun és komán népnév eredetének kérdéséhez' (Contribution to the origins of the ethnonyms Kun and Cuman). In *A magyarság*, 200–19.

'A Codex Cumanicus keletkezésének kérdéséhez' (Contribution to the question of the origins of the Codex Cumanicus). In *A magyarság*, 220–41.

'A kipcsaki kun társadalom a Codex Cumanicus alapján' (The Cuman society of Kipchak on the basis of the Codex Cumanicus). In *A magyarság*, 242–73.

'A csatlakozott népek' (Peoples who joined the Hungarians). In *A magyarság*, 43–79.

'A székelyek eredete és településük története' (The origins of the Seklers and the history of their settlement). In *A magyarság*, 11–42.

'Újabb adatok a tatárjárás történetéhez' (New data concerning the history of the Mongol invasion). *Történelmi Szemle* 33, nos. 1–2 (1991): 84–8.

'A honfoglalók száma és az Árpád-kor népessége' (The number of conquering Hungarians and the population during the Arpad age). In *Magyarország történeti demográfiája I. A Honfoglalás és az Árpád-kor népessége* (Historical demography of Hungary I: The population during the Conquest and the Arpad age). Edited by József Kovacsics, 37–41. Budapest: Központi Statisztikai Hivatal, 1995.

'Még egyszer Szűcs Jenő: Az utolsó Árpádok c. művéről' (Reconsidering Jenő Szűcs's book, *The Last Arpadians*). *Századok* 130 (1996): 999–1007.

Pest-Buda kialakulása: Budapest története a honfoglalástól az Árpád-kor végi székvárossá alakulásig (The emergence of Pest-Buda: The history of Budapest from the Conquest to the end of the Arpad age). Budapest: Akadémiai Kiadó, 1997.

Györffy, István. *Magyar nép, magyar föld* (Hungarian nation, Hungarian land). Budapest: Turul, 1942.

Györffy, István and Károly Viski. *A magyarság tárgyi néprajza* (A material ethnography of the Hungarian people). 2 vols. Budapest: Királyi Magyar Egyetemi Nyomda, n.d. (before 1934).

Haas, Peter J. 'The Modern Study of Responsa'. In *Approaches to Judaism in Medieval Times*. 2 vols. Edited by David R. Blumenthal. Vol. II: 35–71. Brown Judaic Studies 57. Chico, Calif.: Scholars Press, 1985.

Hajnik, Imre. *A magyar bírósági szervezet és perjog az Árpád- és vegyesházi királyok alatt* (The Hungarian judicial system and law under the kings of the House of Arpad and following dynasties). Budapest, 1899.

Haldon, J. F. and H. Kennedy. 'The Arab–Byzantine Frontier in the Eighth and Ninth Centuries: Military Organisation and Society in the Borderlands'. *Recueil des Travaux de l'Institut d'Etudes Byzantines* 19 (1980): 79–116.

Halperin, Charles J. 'The Ideology of Silence: Prejudice and Pragmatism on the Medieval Religious Frontier'. *Comparative Studies in Society and History* 26 (1984): 442–66.

Hamilton, Janet and Bernard Hamilton. *Christian Dualist Heresies in the Byzantine World c. 650–c. 1450*. Manchester and New York: Manchester University Press, 1998.

Hanák, Péter. 'Kezdjük újra a régió-vitát?' (Shall we start again the debate over the regions of Europe?). *BUKSZ* (1992, no. 4): 6–10.

Harsányi, András. *A Domonkos-rend Magyarországon a reformáció előtt* (The Dominican Order in Hungary before the Reformation). Debrecen, 1938. Reprint Budapest: Kairosz, 1999.

Harvey, Leonard Patrick. *Islamic Spain 1250–1500*. Chicago and London: University of Chicago Press, 1990.

Bibliography

Haskins, Charles Homer. *Studies in the History of Mediaeval Science.* 2nd edn. Cambridge, Mass., 1927. Reprint New York: Frederick Ungar, 1960.

'The Translators from Greek and Arabic'. In Haskins, *The Renaissance of the Twelfth Century,* 278–302. 6th edn. Cambridge, Mass.: Harvard University Press, 1976.

Hatházi, Gábor. 'A Hantos-széki kunok településtörténete' (The history of the settlement of the Cumans of the seat of Hantos). MA thesis. Budapest: ELTE, 1985.

'14. századi ruhakorongpár Sárosdról és viselettörténeti kapcsolatai' (A fourteenth-century brooch from Sárosd and its connections from the point of view of the history of costume). *Archeologiai Értesítő* 114, no. 1 (1987–8): 106–20.

'A perkátai kun szállástemető (előzetes beszámoló az 1986–8. évi feltárásokról)' (The Cuman mass cemetery of Perkáta: initial report on the excavations of 1986–8). In *A Móra Ferenc Múzeum Évkönyve 1984–85/2,* 651–74. Szeged, 1991.

'Megjegyzések a kun településhálózat megszilárdulásának kérdéséhez' (Remarks concerning the establishment of fixed Cuman settlement). In *Internationales Kulturhistorisches Symposion Mogersdorf 1994,* 27–33. Eisenstadt: Amt der Burgenländischen Landesregierung, 1996.

'A kunok régészeti és történeti emlékei a Kelet-Dunántúlon' (The historical and archaeological remains of the Cumans in the Eastern Dunántúl). Ph.D. dissertation, Budapest: ELTE, 1996.

'Két világ határán: A kun székközpont és magyar mezőváros a középkorban' (On the border of two worlds: Cuman seat and Hungarian agrarian town in the Middle Ages). Typescript.

Havassy, Péter. ed. *Zúduló sasok: új honfoglalók – besenyők, kunok, jászok – a középkori Alföldön és Mezőföldön* (Swooping eagles: new conquerors – Pechenegs, Cumans and As – on the medieval plains). Gyula: Erkel Ferenc Múzeum, 1996.

Helmár, Ágost. *A magyar zsidótörvények az Árpádkorszakban* (Hungarian Jewry laws in the Arpad age). Különlenyomat a pozsonyi királyi katholikus főgymnasium 1878/9. évi értesítőjéből. Pozsony, 1879.

Herde, Peter. 'Christians and Saracens at the Time of the Crusades: Some Comments of Contemporary Medieval Canonists'. *Studia Gratiana* 12 (1969): 359–76.

Herrin, Judith. *The Formation of Christendom.* Princeton: Princeton University Press, 1987.

Heywood, Colin. 'The Frontier in Ottoman History: Old Ideas and New Myths'. In *Frontiers in Question: Eurasian Borderlands 700–1700.* Edited by Daniel Power and Naomi Standen, 228–50.

Hillaby, Joe. 'The London Jewry: William I to John'. *Jewish Historical Studies* 32 (1990–2): 1–44.

Hofstadter, Richard and Seymour Martin Lipset. eds. *Turner and the Sociology of the Frontier.* New York and London: Basic Books, 1968.

Hóman, Bálint. *Magyar pénztörténet 1000–1325* (Hungarian monetary history 1000–1325). Budapest: MTA, 1916. Reprint Budapest: Maecenas Könyvkiadó, 1991.

A magyar királyság pénzügyei és gazdaságpolitikája Károly Róbert korában (The monetary affairs and economic policy in the kingdom of Hungary during the reign of Charles Robert). Budapest: Budavári tudományos társaság, 1921.

Bibliography

A Szt. László-korabeli Gesta Ungarorum és XII–XIII. századi leszármazói (The Gesta Ungarorum from the age of St Ladislas, and its twelfth–thirteenth-century versions). Budapest: MTA, 1925.

A magyar hún-hagyomány és hún-monda (The Hungarian tradition and legend about the Huns). Budapest: Egyetemi Nyomda, 1925.

Hóman, Bálint and Gyula Szekfű. *Magyar történet* (A history of Hungary). 5 vols. 2nd edn. Budapest: Királyi Magyar Egyetemi Nyomda, 1935. Reprint Budapest: Maecenas Könyvkiadó, 1990.

Horn, Maurycy. 'Jewish Jurisdiction's Dependence on Royal Power in Poland and Lithuania up to 1548'. *Acta Poloniae Historica* 76 (1997): 5–17.

Horváth, Ferenc. 'Csengele középkori temploma' (The medieval church of Csengele). *Móra Ferenc Múzeum Évkönyve 1976–77/1*. Szeged: Szegedi Nyomda, 1978, 91–126.

'Régészeti adatok a kunok Dél-alföldi történetéhez' (Archaeological data concerning the history of the Cumans on the Southern Plains of Hungary). In *A Jászkunság kutatása 1985*. Edited by István Fazekas, László Szabó and István Sztrinkó, 66–74.

Horváth, János. *A magyar irodalmi műveltség kezdetei* (The beginnings of Hungarian literary culture). Budapest: Magyar Szemle Társaság, 1931. Reprint Budapest: Akadémiai Kiadó, 1988.

'A hun-történet és szerzője' (The Hun-history and its author). *Irodalomtörténeti Közlemények* (1963): 446–76.

'Anonymous és a kassai kódex' (Anonymous and the Codex of Kassa). In *Középkori kútfőink kritikus kérdései*. Edited by János Horváth and György Székely, 81–110. Budapest: Akadémiai Kiadó, 1974.

Horváth, Lajos. 'Adatok az alánok és a kunok történetéhez' (Data concerning the history of the As and the Cumans). In *A Jászkunság kutatása 1985*. Edited by István Fazekas, László Szabó and István Sztrinkó, 187–214.

Horváth, Tibor and Lajos Huszár. 'Kamaragrófok a középkorban' (Ispáns of the treasury in the Middle Ages). *Numizmatikai Közlöny* 54–5 (1955–6): 21–33.

Housley, Norman J. 'Crusades against Christians: Their Origins and Early Development, c. 1000–1216'. In *Crusade and Settlement*. Edited by Peter W. Edbury, 17–36. Cardiff: University College Press, 1985.

'Frontier Societies and Crusading in the Late Middle Ages'. In *Intercultural Contacts in the Medieval Mediterranean*. Edited by Benjamin Arbel, 104–19. London and Portland, Oreg.: Frank Cass, 1996.

Huszár, Lajos. *A budai pénzverés története a középkorban* (A history of minting at Buda during the Middle Ages). Budapest: Akadémiai Kiadó, 1958.

'Az esztergomi középkori pénzverde' (The medieval mint at Esztergom). *Komárom megyei múzeumok közleményei* 1 (1968): 207–20.

'A középkori magyar pénztörténet okleveles forrásai' (Charters as sources for medieval Hungarian monetary history). *Numizmatikai Közlöny* 70–1 (1971–2): 39–49.

Internationales Kulturhistorisches Symposion Mogersdorf 1994. Eisenstadt: Amt der Burgenländischen Landesregierung, 1996.

Iogna-Prat, Dominique. *Ordonner et exclure: Cluny et la société chrétienne face à l'hérésie, au judaïsme et à l'Islam 1000–1150*. Paris: Aubier, 1998.

Isaac, Benjamin. *The Limits of Empire: The Roman Army in the East*. rev. edn. Oxford: Clarendon Press, 1992.

Bibliography

Isajiw, Wsevolod W. *Definitions of Ethnicity*. Occasional Papers in Ethnic and Immigration Studies. Toronto: Multicultural History Society of Ontario, 1979.
Israeli, Raphael. 'Islamization and Sinicization in Chinese Islam'. In *Conversion to Islam*. Edited by Nehemia Levtzion, 159–76. New York and London: Holmes and Meier, 1979.
Jackson, Peter. 'The Crusade Against the Mongols (1241)'. *Journal of Ecclesiastical History* 42 (1991): 1–18.
'The crisis in the Holy Land in 1260'. *English Historical Review* 95 (1980): 481–513.
Jakubovich, Emil. 'Kún Erzsébet nőtestvére' (Elizabeth the Cuman's sister). *Turul* 37 (1922–3): 14–27.
Jánosi, Monika. 'Az első ún. esztergomi zsinati határozatok keletkezésének problémái' (Questions concerning the genesis of the decisions of the so-called first synod of Esztergom). *AUSz Acta Historica* 83 (1986): 23–9.
'A Szent László-kori zsinatok határozatainak keletkezéstörténete' (The genesis of the decisions of synods in the age of St Ladislas). *AUSz Acta Historica* 96 (1992): 3–10.
Törvényalkotás a korai Árpád-korban (Law-making in the early Arpad-age). Szegedi Középkortörténeti Könyvtár 9. Szeged: Agapé, 1996.
Jeszenszky, Géza. 'Az első magyar rézpénzek' (The first Hungarian copper coins). *Numizmatikai Közlöny* 34–5 (1935–6): 35–47.
Jónás, Ilona. *Árpád-házi Szent Erzsébet* (St Elizabeth of Hungary). Budapest: Akadémiai Kiadó, 1986.
Jordan, William Chester. *The French Monarchy and the Jews: From Philip Augustus to the Last Capetians*. Philadelphia: University of Pennsylvania Press, 1989.
Juhász, Kálmán. *A csanádi püspökség története 1243–1307* (The history of the Bishopric of Csanád 1243–1307). Makó: Makói Nyomda, 1933.
Juraszov, Mihail Konsztantinovics. 'Batu magyarországi hadjáratának jellegéről és a tatárok elvonulásának okairól' (The nature of Batu's Hungarian campaign and the reasons for the withdrawal of the Mongols). *Világtörténet* n.s. (1989, no. 4): 92–103.
Kaczmarczyk, Zdzislaw. 'One Thousand Years of the History of the Polish Western Frontier'. *Acta Poloniae Historica* 5 (1962): 79–109.
Kahler, Frigyes. 'Das Pizetum-Recht'. In *A Debreceni Déri Múzeum Évkönyve 1986*, 179–91. Debrecen: Déri Múzeum, 1987.
Kalmár, János. *Régi magyar fegyverek* (Old Hungarian weapons). Budapest: Natura Szegedi Nyomda, 1971.
Kamen, Henry. *Spain 1469–1714: A Society of Conflict*. 2nd edn. London and New York: Longman, 1991.
Kantorowicz, Ernst. *Frederick the Second 1194–1250*. Eng. tr. E. O. Lorimer. New York: Richard R. Smith, 1931.
Kaizer Friedrich der Zweite: Ergänzungsband. Berlin: Georg Bondi, 1931.
Karácsonyi, János. *A magyar nemzetségek a XIV. század közepéig* (Hungarian clans until the mid-fourteenth century). 3 vols. Budapest: MTA, 1900–1.
'a Hód-tavi csata éve' (The dating of the battle of Lake Hód). *Századok* 35 (1901): 626–36.
'A mérges vipera és az antimoniális: korkép Kún László idejéből' (The poisonous viper and the anti-nun: a view from the age of Ladislas the Cuman). *Századok* 44 (1910): 1–24.

Bibliography

'Kik voltak s mikor jöttek hazánkba a böszörmények vagy izmaeliták?' (Who were the böszörmény or Ishmaelites and when did they arrive in Hungary?). In *Értekezések a történeti tudományok köréből a II. osztály rendeletéből* no. 23, part 7 (1913): 483–98.

'Magyar Sibilla', *Turul* 37, no. 1 (1922–3): 3–13.

Szent-Ferenc rendjének története Magyarországon 1711-ig (The history of the Franciscan Order in Hungary until 1711). 2 vols. Budapest: MTA, 1923–4.

A hamis, hibáskeltű és keltezetlen oklevelek jegyzéke 1400-ig (A register of forged, misdated and undated charters until 1400). Szeged: JATE, 1988.

Karp, Hans-Jürgen. *Grenzen in Ostmitteleuropa während des Mittelalters: Ein Beitrag zur Entstehungsgeschichte der Grenzlinie aus dem Grenzsaum*. Cologne and Vienna: Böhlau Verlag, 1972.

Katz, Jacob. *Exclusiveness and Tolerance: Studies in Jewish–Gentile Relations in Medieval and Modern Times*. Oxford: Oxford University Press, 1961. Reprint Westport, Conn.: Greenwood Press, 1980.

Kedar, Benjamin Z. *Crusade and Mission: European Approaches toward Muslims*. Princeton: Princeton University Press, 1984.

'The Subjected Muslims of the Frankish Levant'. In *Muslims under Latin Rule*. Edited by James M. Powell, 135–74.

'Ungarische Muslime in Jerusalem im Jahre 1217'. *AOASH* 40, nos. 2–3 (1986): 325–7. Reprint in Kedar, *The Franks in the Levant, 11th to 14th Centuries*, no. XV. Aldershot: Variorum, 1993.

'De Iudeis et Sarracenis: On the Categorization of Muslims in Medieval Canon Law'. In Kedar, *The Franks in the Levant, 11th to 14th Centuries*, no. XIII. Aldershot: Variorum, 1993.

Kelly, J. N. D. *The Oxford Dictionary of Popes*. Oxford and New York: Oxford University Press, 1986. Reprint 1990.

Kerny, Terézia. 'Keresztény lovagoknak oszlopa' (A pillar of Christian knights). In *A Szent László-legenda középkori falképei*. Edited by Gyula László, 213–23.

Khazanov, Anatoly. *Nomads and the Outside World*. Cambridge: Cambridge University Press, 1984. 2nd edn, Madison: University of Wisconsin Press, 1994.

Kinder, Hermann and Werner Hilgemann. *The Anchor Atlas of World History*. New York: Doubleday, 1974.

Király, János. *Pozsony város joga a középkorban* (The law of the city of Pozsony in the Middle Ages). Budapest: MTA, 1894.

Kisch, Guido. *The Jews in Medieval Germany: A Study of their Legal and Social Status*. Chicago: University of Chicago Press, 1949.

'The Yellow Badge in History'. *Historia Judaica* 19 (1957): 89–147.

Kiss, Attila. '11th c. Khazar Rings from Hungary with Hebrew Letters and Signs'. *Acta Archaeologica Academiae Scientiarum Hungaricae* 22 (1970): 341–8.

Klaniczay, Gábor. 'Daily Life and the Elites in the Later Middle Ages: The Civilized and the Barbarians'. In *Environment and Society in Hungary*. Edited by Ferenc Glatz, 75–90. Budapest: MTA Történettudományi Intézet, 1990.

'Fashionable Beards and Heretic Rags'. In Klaniczay, *The Uses of Supernatural Power*, 51–78. Cambridge: Polity Press, 1990.

Klaniczay, Gábor and Edit Madas. 'La Hongrie'. In *Hagiographies*. Edited by Guy Philippart. Vol. II: 103–60. Turnhout: Brepols, 1996.

Klaniczay, Tibor and Gábor Klaniczay. *Szent Margit legendái és stigmái* (Legends and the stigmata of St Margaret). Budapest: Argumentum Kiadó, 1994.

Bibliography

Kłoczowski, Jerzy. 'L'Europe centrale et orientale à l'époque de Lyon II'. In *1274: Année charnière: Mutations et continuités*, 503–15. Paris: Les Editions du CNRS, 1977.
Kłoczowski, Jerzy. ed. *Histoire religieuse de la Pologne*. Paris: Le Centurion, 1987.
Kniezsa, István. 'Magyarország népei a XI-ik században' (Peoples of Hungary in the eleventh century). In *Emlékkönyv Szent István király halálának kilencszázadik évfordulóján*. 3 vols. Edited by Jusztinián Serédi. Vol. II: 365–472. Budapest: MTA, 1938.
Knoll, Paul W. 'The Stabilization of the Polish Western Frontier under Casimir the Great 1333–1370'. *The Polish Review* 12, no. 4 (1967): 3–29.
Kohn, Sámuel. '1279. budai zsinat végzései' (Canons of the Synod of Buda, 1279). *Történelmi Tár* (1881): 543–50.
A zsidók története Magyarországon (The history of the Jews in Hungary). Budapest, 1884.
Kollányi, Ferenc. *A magánkegyúri jog hazánkban a középkorban* (Medieval laws concerning proprietary churches in Hungary). Budapest: MTA, 1906.
Komoróczy, Géza. ed. *A zsidó Budapest: Emlékek, szertartások, történelem*. Budapest: MTA Judisztikai Kutatócsoport, 1995. Tr. *Jewish Budapest: Monuments, Rites, History*. Budapest: Central European University Press, 1999.
Kossányi, Béla. 'A XI–XII. századi 'ismaelita' és 'saracenus' elnevezésekről' (Concerning the eleventh- and twelfth-century denominations 'ismaelite' and 'saracenus'). In *Emlékkönyv Károlyi Árpád születése nyolcvanadik fordulójának ünnepére*. Edited by Sándor Domanovszky, 308–16. Budapest: Sárkány Nyomda, 1933.
'A kalizok vallása' (The religion of the Khaliz). In *Emlékkönyv Domanovszky Sándor születése hatvanadik fordulójának ünnepére*, 355–68. Budapest: Királyi Magyar Egyetemi Nyomda, 1937.
Koszta, László. 'Un prélat français de Hongrie: Bertalan, évêque de Pécs (1219–1251)'. *Cahiers d'Etudes Hongroises* 8 (1996): 71–96.
A pécsi székeskáptalan hiteleshelyi tevékenysége (1214–1353) (The *loca credibilia* function of the chapter of Pécs). Pécs: Pécs Története Alapítvány, 1998.
Kovacsics, József. ed. *Magyarország történeti demográfiája I. A Honfoglalás és az Árpád-kor népessége* (The historical demography of Hungary I. The population during the age of conquest and the Arpad period). Budapest: Központi Statisztikai Hivatal, 1995.
'A történeti demográfia válaszai és nyitott kérdései az Árpád-kori népesség számára vonatkozóan' (Questions and answers of historical demography concerning the size of the Arpad-age population). In *Magyarország történeti demográfiája I. A Honfoglalás és az Arpad-kor népessége*, 8–36.
Kőhalmi, Katalin U. *A steppék nomádja lóháton, fegyverben* (The nomads of the steppe on horseback, with their arms). Kőrösi Csoma Kiskönyvtár 12. Budapest: Akadémiai Kiadó, 1972.
Köprülü, Mehmed Fuad. *Les origines de l'Empire Ottoman*. Etudes Orientales 3. Paris: E. de Boccard, 1935.
Islam in Anatolia after the Turkish Invasion (Prolegomena). Tr. Gary Leiser, Salt Lake City: University of Utah Press, 1993.
Kramarovsky, Mark G. 'The Culture of the Golden Horde and the Problem of the "Mongol Legacy"'. In *Rulers from the Steppe*. Edited by Gary Seaman and Daniel Marks, 255–73.

Bibliography

Kriegel, Maurice. 'La prise d'une décision: l'expulsion des Juifs d'Espagne en 1492'. In *Chrétiens, Musulmans et Juifs dans l'Espagne médiévale*. Edited by Ron Barkaï, 253–300. Paris: Cerf, 1994.

Kring, Miklós. 'Kun és jász társadalomelemek a középkorban' (Cuman and As society in the Middle Ages). *Századok* 66 (1932): 35–63, 169–88.

Kristó, Gyula. 'Szempontok korai helyneveink történeti tipológiájához' (Considerations regarding the typology of early Hungarian toponyms). *AUSz Acta Historica* 55 (1976).

— 'Volt-e a magyaroknak ősi hun hagyományuk?' (Did the Hungarians have an ancient Hun tradition?). In *Mítosz és történelem* (Myth and history). Edited by Mihály Hoppál and Márton Istvánovits, 55–64. Budapest: MTA Néprajzi Kutatócsoport, 1978.

— *A feudális széttagolódás Magyarországon* (Feudal disintegration in Hungary). Budapest: Akadémiai Kiadó, 1979.

— *Az Aranybullák évszázada* (The century of the Golden Bulls). 2nd edn. Budapest: Gondolat Kiadó, 1981.

— *Tanulmányok az Árpád-korról* (Essays on the Arpad-age). Budapest: Magvető Kiadó, 1983.

— 'A X. század közepi magyarság "nomadizmusának" kérdéséhez' (On the 'nomadism' of the mid-tenth-century Hungarians). In *Tanulmányok az Árpád-korról*, 51–76.

— *Az Árpád-kor háborúi* (Wars of the Arpad age). Budapest: Zrínyi Kiadó, 1986.

— *A vármegyék kialakulása Magyarországon* (The development of the counties in Hungary). Budapest: Magvető Kiadó, 1988.

— 'Magyar öntudat és idegenellenesség az Árpád-kori Magyarországon' (Hungarian identity and xenophobia in Hungary during the Arpad-age). *Irodalomtörténeti Közlemények* 94 (1990): 425–43.

— 'Öt pondust fizetők és várhospesek' (Those paying five pondus, and hospites settling on castle-lands). *AUSz Acta Historica* 92 (1991): 25–35.

— *A Kárpát-medence és a magyarság régmúltja (1301-ig)* (The history of Hungarians and of the Carpathian Basin until 1301). Szeged: Szegedi Középkorász Műhely, 1993.

— *Die Arpaden-Dynastie: Die Geschichte Ungarns von 895 bis 1301*. Budapest: Corvina, 1993.

— 'Magyarország lélekszáma az Árpád-korban' (The size of Hungary's population in the Arpad age). In *Magyarország történeti demográfiája I. A Honfoglalás és az Árpád-kor népessége*. Edited by József Kovacsics, 42–95.

— *A magyar nemzet megszületése* (The birth of the Hungarian nation). Szeged: Szegedi Középkorász Műhely, 1997.

— 'Vallási türelem az Árpád-kori Magyarországon' (Religious tolerance in Arpad-age Hungary). In *La civiltà ungherese e il cristianesimo: Atti del IV. Congresso Internazionale di Studi Ungheresi Roma–Napoli 9–14 settembre 1996*. 3 vols. Vol. II: 485–96. Budapest and Szeged: Nemzetközi Magyar Filológiai Társaság and Scriptum, 1998.

Kristó, Gyula, Ferenc Makk and László Szegfű. 'Adatok "korai" helyneveink ismeretéhez I' (Data concerning the knowledge of Hungarian early place-names). *AUSz Acta Historica* 44 (1973).

Kristó, Gyula, Ferenc Makk and László Szegfű. 'Szempontok és adatok a korai magyar határvédelem kérdéséhez' (Considerations and data concerning the question of early Hungarian frontier defences). *Hadtörténelmi Közlemények* n.s. 20, no. 4 (1973): 639–58.

Kristó, Gyula. ed. *Korai Magyar Történeti Lexikon (9–14. sz.)* (Dictionary for early medieval Hungarian history: ninth–fourteenth centuries). Budapest: Akadémiai Kiadó, 1994.

Kubinyi, András. 'A királyi várospolitika tükröződése a magyar királyi oklevelek arengáiban' (Evidence of royal urban policy in the arenga of Hungarian royal charters). In *Eszmetörténeti Tanulmányok a Magyar Középkorról*. Edited by György Székely, 275–91. Budapest: Akadémiai Kiadó, 1984.

'Spanyol zsidók a középkori Budán' (Spanish Jews in medieval Buda). In *MZsO*, vol. XII: 19–26.

'A zsidóság története a középkori Magyarországon' (A history of the Jews in medieval Hungary). In *Magyarországi zsinagógák*. Edited by László Gerő, 19–27. Budapest: Műszaki Könyvkiadó, 1989.

'Urbanisation in the East-Central Parts of Medieval Hungary'. In *Towns in Medieval Hungary*. Edited by László Gerevich, 103–49.

'A magyarországi zsidóság története a középkorban' (A history of Hungarian Jews in the Middle Ages). *Soproni Szemle* 49 (1995): 2–27.

'Németek és nem-németek a középkori magyar királyság városaiban' (Germans and non-Germans in the cities of the medieval Hungarian kingdom). In *Internationales Kulturhistorisches Symposion Mogersdorf 1994*, 145–58. Eisenstadt, 1996.

'Nemzetiségi és vallási tolerancia a középkori Magyarországon' (Ethnic and religious tolerance in medieval Hungary). In *Főpapok, egyházi intézmények és vallásosság a középkori Magyarországon* (Prelates, ecclesiastical institutions and religiosity in medieval Hungary), 123–38. Budapest: METEM, 1999. (German tr.: 'Zur Frage der Toleranz im mittelalterlichen Königreich Ungarn'. In *Toleranz im Mittelalter*. Edited by Alexander Patschovsky and Harald Zimmermann, 187–206. Vorträge und Forschungen 45. Sigmaringen: Thorbecke, 1998).

Kulcsár, Zsuzsánna. *Eretnekmozgalmak a XI–XIV. században* (Heretical movements in the eleventh–fourteenth centuries). A Budapesti Egyetemi Könyvtár Kiadványai 22. Budapest: Tankönyvkiadó, 1964.

Kumorovitz, Bernát L. 'A Kálmán kori "cartula sigillata"' (The cartula sigillata from the age of Kálmán). *Turul* 58–60 (1944–6): 29–33.

'A középkori magyar "magánjogi" írásbeliség első korszaka (XI–XII. század)' (The first age of Hungarian 'civil law' literacy: eleventh–twelfth centuries). *Századok* 97 (1963): 1–31. (German version: 'Die erste Epoche der ungarischen privatrechtlichen Schriftlichkeit im Mittelalter'. *Etudes Historiques*, 253–90. Budapest: Akadémiai Kiadó, 1960.)

'Szent László vásár-törvénye és Kálmán király pecsétes cartulája' (The market law of St Ladislas and the sealed 'cartula' of King Kálmán). In *Athleta Patriae: Tanulmányok Szent László történetéhez*. Edited by László Mezey, 85–109. Budapest: Szent István Társulat, 1980.

A magyar pecséthasználat története a középkorban (The history of the use of medieval Hungarian seals). Budapest: Magyar Nemzeti Múzeum, 1993.

Kurcz, Ágnes. *A lovagi kultúra Magyarországon a 13–14. században* (Chivalric culture in Hungary in the thirteenth and fourteenth centuries). Budapest: Akadémiai Kiadó, 1988.

Laarhoven, Jan van. 'Christianitas et réforme grégorienne'. *Studi Gregoriani* 6 (1959–60): 1–98.
Ladner, Gerhart B. 'The Concepts of "Ecclesia" and "Christianitas" and their Relation to the Idea of Papal "Plenitudo Potestatis" from Gregory VII to Boniface VIII'. *Miscellanea Historiae Pontificiae* 18 (1954): 49–77.
Landau, Peter. *Jus patronatus: Studien zur Entwincklung des Patronats im Dekretalenrecht und der Kanonistik des 12. und 13. Jahrhunderts*. Cologne and Vienna: Böhlau Verlag, 1975.
Langmuir, Gavin I. 'From Ambrose of Milan to Emicho of Leiningen: The Transformation of Hostility Against Jews in Northern Christendom'. In *Gli Ebrei nell'Alto Medioevo*. 2 vols. Settimane di Studio del Centro Italiano di Studi sull'Alto Medioevo 26. Vol. 1: 313–68. Spoleto, 1980.
Toward a Definition of Antisemitism. Berkeley, Los Angeles and London: University of California Press, 1990.
'Peter the Venerable: Defense Against Doubts'. In *Toward a Definition of Antisemitism*, 197–208.
'"Tanquam Servi": The Change in Jewish Status in French Law about 1200'. In *Toward a Definition of Antisemitism*, 167–94.
History, Religion, and Antisemitism. Berkeley: University of California Press, 1990.
László, Gyula. 'Adatok a kunok tegezéről' (Data concerning the quiver of the Cumans). *A Néprajzi Múzeum Értesítője* 32 (1940): 52–9.
Lattimore, Owen. 'Origins of the Great Wall of China: A Frontier Concept in Theory and Practice'. *The Geographical Review* 27, no. 4 (1937). Reprinted in Lattimore, *Studies in Frontier History: Collected Papers 1928–1958*, 97–118. London, New York and Toronto: Oxford University Press, 1962.
Lecler, Joseph. *Histoire de la tolérance au siècle de la Réforme*. 1955. Reprint Paris: Albin Michel, 1994.
Lederer, Emma. 'A legrégebbi magyar iparososztály kialakulása' (The genesis of the oldest Hungarian artisan class). *Századok* (1927–8): 510–28.
A középkori pénzüzletek története Magyarországon (1000–1458) (The history of medieval Hungarian financial life 1000–1458). Budapest: Kovács Nyomda, 1932.
'Az egyház szerepe az Árpádkori Magyarországon' (The role of the church in Arpad-age Hungary). *Századok* 83 (1949): 79–105.
'A tatárjárás Magyarországon és nemzetközi összefüggései' (The Mongol invasion of Hungary and its international connections). *Századok* 86 (1952): 327–63.
Lee, A. D. *Information and Frontiers: Roman Foreign Relations in Late Antiquity*. Cambridge: Cambridge University Press, 1993.
Lefebvre, Henri. *La production de l'espace*. Paris: Editions Anthropos, 1974. 3rd edn, 1986.
Le Goff, Jacques. 'Le concile et la prise de conscience de l'espace de la Chrétienté'. In *1274: Année charnière: Mutations et continuités*, 481–9. Paris: Les Editions du CNRS, 1977.
'Le roi dans l'Occident médiéval: caractères originaux'. In *Kings and Kingship in Medieval Europe*. Edited by Anne J. Duggan, 1–40.
Saint Louis. Paris: Gallimard, 1996.
'Centre/Périphérie'. In *Dictionnaire raisonné de l'Occident médiéval*. Edited by Jacques Le Goff and Jean-Claude Schmitt, 149–65. Paris: Fayard, 1999.

Bibliography

Lemarignier, Jean-François. *Recherches sur l'hommage en marche et les frontières féodales*. Travaux et mémoires de l'Université de Lille, n.s. Droit et Lettres 24. Lille: Bibliothèque Universitaire, 1945.
Lerner, Robert E. *The Powers of Prophecy*. Berkeley and Los Angeles: University of California Press, 1983.
Levtzion, Nehemia. ed. *Conversion to Islam*. New York and London: Holmes and Meier, 1979.
Lewicki, Tadeusz. 'Węgry i muzulmanie wegierscy w świetle relacji podróznika arabskiego z XII. w'. *Rocznik Orjentalistyczny* 13 (1937): 106–22.
'Les sources hébraïques consacrées à l'histoire de l'Europe centrale et orientale et particulièrement à celle des pays slaves de la fin du IXe au milieu du XIIIe siècle'. *Cahiers du Monde Russe et Soviétique* 2, no. 2 (1961): 228–41.
'Les commerçants Juifs dans l'Orient Islamique non méditerranéen aux IXe–XIe siècles'. In *Gli Ebrei nell'Alto Medioevo*. 2 vols. Settimane di Studio del Centro Italiano di Studi sull'Alto Medioevo 26. Vol. I: 375–99. Spoleto, 1980.
Lewin, Isaac. 'The Historical Background of the Statute of Kalisz'. In *Studies in Polish Civilization*. Edited by Damian S. Wandycz, 38–53. New York: Institute on East Central Europe, Columbia University and The Polish Institute of Arts and Sciences in America, n.d. (1971?).
Lewis, Archibald. 'The Closing of the Mediaeval Frontier 1250–1350'. *Speculum* 33 (October 1958): 475–83.
Lewis, Bernard. *Cultures in Conflict: Christians, Muslims, and Jews in the Age of Discovery*. Oxford: Oxford University Press, 1995.
Lexikon für Theologie und Kirche. 2nd edn, 10 vols. Edited by Josef Höfer and Karl Rahner. Freiburg: Herder, 1957–65. s.v. 'Honorius'.
Ligeti, Lajos. 'Tőzeg' (Peat). *Magyar Nyelv* 34 (1938): 207–10.
'A magyar nyelv török kapcsolatai és ami körülöttük van' (The relations of the Hungarian language to Turkic, and their context). *Magyar Nyelv* 72 (1976): 11–27.
A Codex Cumanicus mai kérdései (Current questions concerning the Codex Cumanicus). Keleti Értekezések 1. Budapest: Kőrösi Csoma Társaság, 1985.
A magyar nyelv török kapcsolatai a honfoglalás előtt és az Árpád-korban (The relations of the Hungarian language to Turkic prior to the conquest of Hungary and during the Arpad age). Budapest: Akadémiai Kiadó, 1986.
Limerick, Patricia Nelson. *The Legacy of Conquest: The Unbroken Past of the American West*. New York: Norton, 1987.
'The Adventures of the Frontier in the Twentieth Century'. In *The Frontier in American Culture*. Edited by James R. Grossman, 67–102. Berkeley, Los Angeles and London: University of California Press, 1994.
Limerick, Patricia Nelson, Clyde A. Milner II and Charles E. Rankin. eds. *Trails: Toward a New Western History*. Lawrence: University Press of Kansas, 1991.
Linehan, Peter. *The Spanish Church and the Papacy in the Thirteenth Century*. Cambridge: Cambridge University Press, 1971.
'The Spanish Church Revisited: The Episcopal *gravamina* of 1279'. In *Authority and Power: Studies on Medieval Law and Government Presented to Walter Ullmann on his Seventieth Birthday*. Edited by Brian Tierney and Peter Linehan, 127–47. Cambridge: Cambridge University Press, 1980. Reprinted in Linehan, *Spanish Church and Society 1150–1300*, no. IV. London: Variorum Reprints, 1983.

Bibliography

'Segovia: A "Frontier" Diocese in the Thirteenth Century'. *English Historical Review* 96 (1981): 481–508. Reprinted in Linehan, *Spanish Church and Society 1150–1300*, no. V.

'Religion, Nationalism and National Identity in Medieval Spain and Portugal'. In *Religion and National Identity*. Edited by Stuart Mews, 161–99. Studies in Church History 18. Oxford: Blackwell, 1982. Reprinted in Linehan, *Spanish Church and Society 1150–1300*, no. I.

'Frontier and Frontiers in Medieval Spain'. In *The Medieval World*. Edited by Peter Linehan and Janet Nelson. London: Routledge, forthcoming.

Lohrmann, Klaus. *Judenrecht und Judenpolitik im mittelalterlichen Österreich*. Handbuch zur Geschichte der Juden in Österreich 1. Vienna and Cologne: Böhlau Verlag, 1990.

Lomax, John Phillip. 'Frederick II, his Saracens, and the Papacy'. In *Medieval Christian Perceptions of Islam*. Edited by John Victor Tolan, 175–97. New York: Garland, 1996.

Longnon, A. 'Les Toucy en Orient et en Italie au 13e siècle'. *Bulletin de la Société des Sciences Historiques et Naturelles de l'Yonne* 96 (1957): 33–43.

López de Coca-Castañer, José Enrique. 'Institutions on the Castilian–Granadan Frontier, 1369–1482'. In *Medieval Frontier Societies*. Edited by Robert Bartlett and Angus MacKay, 127–50.

Lotter, Friedrich. 'The Crusading Idea and the Conquest of the Region East of the Elbe'. In *Medieval Frontier Societies*. Edited by Robert Bartlett and Angus MacKay, 267–306.

Lourie, Elena. 'A Society Organized for War: Medieval Spain'. *Past and Present* 35 (1966): 54–76.

'A Jewish Mercenary in the Service of the King of Aragon'. *Revue des Etudes Juives* 137 (1978): 367–73. Reprinted in Lourie, *Crusade and Colonisation: Muslims, Christians and Jews in Medieval Aragon*, no. VIII. Aldershot: Variorum, 1990.

'Complicidad criminal: un aspecto insolito de convivencia Judeo-Christiana'. In Lourie, *Crusade and Colonisation: Muslims, Christians, and Jews in Medieval Aragon*, no. XI.

'Mafiosi and Malsines: Violence, Fear and Faction in the Jewish Aljamas of Valencia in the Fourteenth Century'. In Lourie, *Crusade and Colonisation: Muslims, Christians and Jews in medieval Aragon*, no. XII.

Lovag, Zsuzsa. 'A magyar viselet a 11–13. században' (Hungarian costumes in the eleventh–thirteenth centuries). *Ars Hungarica* 2 (1974): 381–408.

Lukács, Zsuzsa. 'A Szent László legenda a középkori magyar falképfestészetben' (The St Ladislas legend on medieval Hungarian frescoes). In *Athleta Patriae: Tanulmányok Szent László történetéhez*. Edited by László Mezey, 161–204. Budapest: Szent István Társulat, 1980.

MacKay, Angus. *Spain in the Middle Ages: From Frontier to Empire 1000–1500*. London: Macmillan, 1977.

'Religion, Culture, and Ideology on the Late Medieval Castilian–Granadan Frontier'. In *Medieval Frontier Societies*. Edited by Robert Bartlett and Angus MacKay, 217–43.

Madas, Edit. 'A "Pécsi Egyetemi Beszédek"' (The university sermons of Pécs). *BUKSZ* 8, no. 4 (1996): 415–19.

Madzsar, Imre. 'A hún krónika szerzője' (The author of the Hun chronicle). *Történeti Szemle* 11 (1922): 75–103.

Bibliography

Maier, Christoph T. 'Crusade and Rhetoric against the Muslim Colony of Lucera'. *Journal of Medieval History* 21 (1995): 343–85.
Preaching the Crusades: Mendicant Friars and the Cross in the Thirteenth Century. Paperback edn. Cambridge: Cambridge University Press, 1998.
Makk, Ferenc. *The Árpáds and the Comneni: Political Relations Between Hungary and Byzantium in the 12th Century*. Budapest: Akadémiai Kiadó, 1989.
'Megjegyzések II. István történetéhez' (Remarks concerning the history of Stephen II). In *Középkori kútfőink kritikus kérdései*. Edited by János Horváth and György Székely, 253–9. Budapest: Akadémiai Kiadó, 1974.
Makkai, László. *A Milkói (kún) püspökség és népei* (The Cuman bishopric of Milkó and its people). Debrecen: Pannonia Könyvnyomda, 1936.
'Les caractères originaux de l'histoire économique et sociale de l'Europe orientale pendant le Moyen Age'. *Acta Historica Academiae Scientiarum Hungaricae* 16 (1970): 261–87.
'Feudalizmus és eredeti jellegzetességek Európában' (Feudalism and original characteristics in Europe). *Történelmi Szemle* (1976, no. 1): 257–77.
Mályusz, Elemér. 'A középkori magyar nemzetiségi politika' (Medieval Hungarian ethnic policies). *Századok* 73 (1939): 257–94, 385–448.
'Le problème de l'assimilation au moyen âge'. *Nouvelle Revue de Hongrie* 64 (1941): 291–301.
'Az izmaelita pénzverőjegyek kérdéséhez' (On the mint-marks of Ishmaelites). *Budapest Régiségei: A Budapesti Történeti Múzeum Évkönyve* 18 (1958): 301–11.
'Die Eigenkirche in Ungarn'. *Wiener Archiv für Geschichte des Slawentums und Osteuropas* 5 (1966): 76–95.
A Thuróczy-krónika és forrásai (The chronicle of Thuróczy and its sources). Tudománytörténeti Tanulmányok 5. Budapest: Akadémiai Kiadó, 1967.
'Árpádházi Boldog Margit' (Blessed Margaret of the House of Arpad). In *Emlékkönyv Károlyi Árpád születése nyolcvanadik fordulójának ünnepére*. Edited by Sándor Domanovszky, 341–84. Budapest, 1933.
Az V. István-kori Gesta (The Gesta from the age of King Stephen V). Értekezések a történeti tudományok köréből, n. s. 58. Budapest: Akadémiai Kiadó, 1971.
Népiségtörténet (Ethnic history). Budapest: MTA Történettudományi Intézete, 1994.
Mandl, Bernát. 'Adalék néhány Magyarországban szereplő középkori zsidó történetéhez' (Additions to the history of some medieval Jews in Hungary). *Magyar Zsidó Szemle* 35 (1918): 58–65.
Mándoky Kongur, István. 'Néhány kún eredetű nagykunsági tájszó' (Some dialect words of Cuman origin in Greater Cumania, Hungary). *Nyelvtudományi Közlemények* 73 (1971): 365–85.
'A kun miatyánk' (The Cuman Pater Noster). *Szolnok Megyei Múzeumi Évkönyv* (1973): 117–25.
'A kun nyelv magyarországi emlékei' (Vestiges of the Cuman language in Hungary). In *Kelet-Kutatás. Tanulmányok az orientalisztika köréből*. Edited by György Kara and József Terjék, 143–51. Budapest: Kőrösi Csoma Társaság, 1976.
A kun nyelv magyarországi emlékei (Vestiges of the Cuman language in Hungary). Karcag: Karcag Város Önkormányzata, 1993.
Manselli, Raoul. 'La res publica christiana e l'Islam'. In *L'Occidente e l'Islam nell'Alto*

Bibliography

Medioevo. 2 vols. Settimane di Studio del Centro Italiano di Studi sull'Alto Medioevo 12. Vol. 1: 115–47. Spoleto, 1965.

Manzano Moreno, Eduardo. 'Christian–Muslim Frontier in Al-Andalus: Idea and Reality'. In *The Arab Influence in Medieval Europe*. Edited by Dionisius A. Agius and Richard Hitchcock, 83–99. Reading: Ithaca Press, 1994.

— 'The Creation of a Medieval Frontier: Islam and Christianity in the Iberian Peninsula, Eighth to Eleventh Centuries'. In *Frontiers in Question: Eurasian Borderlands 700–1700*. Edited by Daniel Power and Naomi Standen, 32–54. London: Macmillan, 1999.

Marcus, Ivan G. *Rituals of Childhood: Jewish Acculturation in Medieval Europe*. New Haven and London: Yale University Press, 1996.

Margalits, Ede. *Magyar közmondások és közmondásszerű szólások* (Hungarian proverbs and sayings). 1896. Reprint. 2nd edn. Budapest: Akadémiai Kiadó, 1993.

Marjai Szabó, László. 'A kunok betelepítése és az állandó szállások kialakulása a Nagykunság területén' (The settlement of the Cumans and the establishment of permanent camps in Greater Cumania). *Az Alföldi Tudományos Intézet Évkönyve* 1 (1944–5): 97–106.

Marosi, Ernő. 'Zur Frage des Quellenwertes mittelalterlicher Darstellungen: "Orientalismus" in der Ungarischen Bilderchronik'. In *Alltag und materielle Kultur im mittelalterlichen Ungarn*. Edited by András Kubinyi and József Laszlovszky, 74–107. Medium Aevum Quotidianum 22. Krems, 1991.

— *Kép és Hasonmás: művészet és valóság a 14–15. századi Magyarországon* (Image and likeness: art and reality in fourteenth- and fifteenth-century Hungary). Budapest: Akadémiai Kiadó, 1995.

— 'Magyarok középkori ábrázolásai és az orientalizmus a középkori művészetben' (Medieval depictions of Hungarians and orientalism in medieval art). In *Magyarok Kelet és Nyugat közt*. Edited by Tamás Hofer, 77–97. Budapest: Balassi, 1996.

Marquart, Josef. 'Über das Volkstum der Komanen'. In *Osttürkische Dialektstudien*. Edited by Willy Bang and Josef Marquart, 25–238. Abhandlungen der königlichen Gesellschaft der Wissenschaften zu Göttingen Philologisch-Historische Klasse, n.s. 13, no. 1. Berlin: Weidmannsche Buchhandlung, 1914; repr. Vandenhoeck und Ruprecht, 1970.

Martin, Jean-Marie. 'Les problèmes de la frontière en Italie méridionale (VIe–XIIe siècles)'. In *Castrum 4: Frontière et peuplement dans le monde méditerranéen au Moyen Age*. Actes du colloque d'Erice-Trapani, 18–25 Septembre 1988, 259–76. Rome: Ecole Française de Rome and Madrid: Casa Velazquez, 1992.

Martini, Aldo. *I sigilli d'Oro dell'Archivio Segreto Vaticano*. Milan: Franco Maria Ricci, 1984.

Matanič, Atanasio G. 'Correnti ereticali in Bosnia (sec. XII–XV)'. In *L'Eglise et le peuple chrétien dans les pays de l'Europe du Centre-Est et du Nord, XIVe–XVe siècles*, 267–73. Collection de l'Ecole Française de Rome 128. Rome: Ecole Française de Rome and Paris: Diffusion de Boccard, 1990.

Matolcsi, János. 'A középkori nomád állattenyésztés kelet-európai jellegzetességei' (Eastern-European characteristics of medieval pastoral nomadism). *Nomád társadalmak és államalakulatok*. Edited by Ferenc Tőkei, 281–306. Kőrösi Csoma Kiskönyvtár 18. Budapest: Akadémiai Kiadó, 1983.

Mayhew, N. J. and Peter Spufford. eds. *Later Medieval Mints: Organisation, Administration and Techniques*. The Eighth Oxford Symposium on Coinage and

Bibliography

Monetary History. British Archaeological Reports, International Series 389. Oxford, BAR, 1988.

Mayr-Harting, Henry. *Two Conversions to Christianity: The Bulgarians and the Anglo-Saxons*. The Stenton Lecture 1993. Reading: University of Reading, 1994.

Mažeika, Rasa. 'Of Cabbages and Knights: Trade and Trade Treaties with the Infidel on the Northern Frontier, 1200–1390'. *Journal of Medieval History* 20 (1994): 63–76.

'Bargaining for Baptism: Lithuanian Negotiations for Conversion, 1250–1358'. In *Varieties of Religious Conversion in the Middle Ages*. Edited by James Muldoon, 131–45. Gainesville: University Press of Florida, 1997.

McCrank, Lawrence J. 'The Cistercians of Poblet as Medieval Frontiersmen: An Historiographic Essay and Case Study'. In *Estudios en Homenaje a don Claudio Sanchez Albornoz en sus 90 años*. 3 vols. Edited by María de Carmen Carlé et al. Vol. II: 313–60. Buenos Aires: Istituto de Historia de España, 1983.

McKitterick, Rosamond. *The Frankish Kingdoms under the Carolingians, 751–987*. London and New York: Longman, 1983.

Mellinkoff, Ruth. 'The Round-topped Tablets of the Law: Sacred Symbol and Emblem of Evil'. *Journal of Jewish Art* 1 (1974): 28–43.

The Mark of Cain. Berkeley, Los Angeles and London: University of California Press, 1981.

Outcasts: Signs of Otherness in Northern European Art of the Late Middle Ages. Berkeley, Los Angeles and Oxford: University of California Press, 1993.

Melloni, Alberto. *Innocenzo IV: La concezione e l'esperienza della cristianità come regimen unius personae*. Genoa: Marietti, 1990.

Méri, István. 'Beszámoló a Tiszalök-Rázompusztai és Túrkeve-Mórici ásatások eredményéről II' (Report concerning the results of the excavations of Tiszalök-Rázompuszta and Túrkeve-Móric). *Archaeologiai Értesítő* 81 (1954): 138–54.

Meslin, Michel. 'Rencontres des religion et acculturation'. In *Rencontres de Religions: Actes du Colloque du Collège des Irlandais tenu sous les auspices de l'Académie Royale Irlandaise*. Edited by Proinsias Mac Cana and Michel Meslin, 15–24. Paris: Les Belles Lettres, 1986.

Metzger, Thérèse and Mendel Metzger. *Jewish Life in the Middle Ages*. Secaucus, N.J.: Chartwell Books, 1982.

Meyerson, Mark D. *The Muslims of Valencia in the Age of Ferdinand and Isabel: Between Coexistence and Crusade*. Berkeley and Los Angeles: University of California Press, 1991.

Meyvaert, Paul. '"Rainaldus est malus scriptor Francigenus" – Voicing National Antipathy in the Middle Ages'. *Speculum* 66 (1991): 743–63.

Mezey, László. 'Szent István XIII. századi verses históriája' (A thirteenth-century rythmical history of St Stephen). In *Magyar Századok: Irodalmi műveltségünk történetéhez*, 41–51. Budapest: Egyetemi Nyomda, 1948.

'A latin írás magyarországi történetéből' (On the history of Latin writing in Hungary). *Magyar Könyvszemle* 82 (1966): 1–9, 205–16, 285–304.

'Anfänge der Privaturkunde in Ungarn und der Glaubwürdige Orte'. *Archiv für Diplomatik* 18 (1972): 290–302.

Miller, David H. and Jerome Steffens. eds. *The Frontier: Comparative Studies*, vol. 1. Norman: University of Oklahoma Press, 1977.

Miquel, André. *La géographie humaine du monde Musulman jusqu'au milieu du 11e siècle*. Paris: EHESS, 1988.

Bibliography

Mollat, Michel. *Genèse médiévale de la France moderne.* Paris: Arthaud, 1977.
Moore, Robert Ian. *The Formation of a Persecuting Society.* Oxford: Blackwell, 1987; paperback edn, 1990.
Móra, Ferenc. 'Ásatások a Szeged-Öttömösi Anjou-kori temetőben' (Excavations in the cemetery of Szeged-Öttömös from the Angevin period). *Archeologiai értesítő* 26 (1906): 18–27.
Moravcsik, Gyula. 'Les relations entre la Hongrie et Byzance à l'époque des Croisades'. *Bibliothèque de la Revue des Etudes Hongroises* 9 (1934): 1–8.
  'Görögnyelvű monostorok Szent István korában' (Greek monasteries in the age of St Stephen). In *Emlékkönyv Szent István király halálának kilencszázadik évfordulóján.* 3 vols. Edited by Jusztinián Serédi. Vol. 1: 389–422. Budapest: MTA, 1938.
  'The Role of the Byzantine Church in Medieval Hungary'. *American Slavic and East European Review* 6 (1947): 134–51.
  'Bizánci császárok és követeik Budán' (Byzantine emperors and their ambassadors at Buda). *Századok* 95 (1961): 832–45.
  'Hungary and Byzantium in the Middle Ages'. In *The Cambridge Medieval History.* Vol. IV, pt. 1: 566–92. Cambridge: Cambridge University Press, 1966.
  Byzantium and the Magyars. Budapest: Akadémiai Kiadó, 1970.
  Byzantinoturcica. 2 vols. Berlin: Akademie Verlag, 1983.
Morgan, David. *The Mongols.* Oxford: Blackwell, 1986. Reprint 1996.
Morris, Colin. *The Papal Monarchy: The Western Church from 1050 to 1250.* Oxford: Clarendon Press, 1989.
Morrison, Karl F. *Understanding Conversion.* Charlottesville and London: University Press of Virginia, 1992.
Mortensen, Lars Boje. 'Saxo Grammaticus' View of the Origin of the Danes and his Historiographical Models'. *Cahiers de l'Institut du Moyen Age Grec et Latin* 55 (1987): 169–83.
Muldoon, James. *Popes, Lawyers and Infidels: The Church and the Non-Christian World 1250–1550.* Philadelphia: University of Pennsylvania Press, 1979.
Muldoon, James. ed. *Varieties of Religious Conversion in the Middle Ages.* Gainesville: University Press of Florida, 1997.
Mundill, Robin R. *England's Jewish Solution: Experiment and Expulsion, 1262–1290.* Cambridge: Cambridge University Press, 1998.
Murphey, Rhoads. 'An Ecological History of Central Asian Nomadism'. In *Ecology and Empire: Nomads in the Cultural Evolution of the Old World.* Edited by Gary Seaman, 41–58. Proceedings of the Soviet–American Academic Symposia. Vol. 1. Los Angeles: University of Southern California and Ethnographics Press, 1989.
Musset, Lucien. 'La pénétration chrétienne dans l'Europe du Nord et son influence sur la civilisation Scandinave'. In *La conversione al cristianesimo nell'Europa dell'alto medioevo.* 2 vols. Settimane di Studio del Centro Italiano di Studi sull'Alto Medioevo 14. Vol. 1: 263–325. Spoleto, 1967.
Nagy, Loránt. 'Adatok a késő Árpád-kori pénzek kormeghatározásához' (Data concerning the dating of late Arpad-age coins). *Numizmatikai Közlöny* 72–3 (1973–4): 43–7.
Nederman, Cary J. and John Christian Laursen. eds. *Difference and Dissent: Theories of Toleration in Medieval and Early Modern Europe.* Lanham: Rowman and Littlefield, 1996.

eds. *Beyond the Persecuting Society: Religious Toleration Before the Enlightenment.* Philadelphia: University of Pennsylvania Press, 1998.
Needleman, Saul and Sondra Needleman. 'Medieval Coins with Hebrew Letters'. *The Shekel* 16, no. 5 (1983): 11–15.
Négyesi, Lajos. 'A muhi csata 1241. április 11' (The battle of Muhi). *Hadtörténelmi Közlemények* 110, no. 2 (1997): 296–310.
Németh, Gyula. ed. *Attila és hunjai* (Attila and his Huns). Budapest: Magyar Szemle Társaság, 1940. Reprint Budapest: Akadémiai Kiadó, 1986.
'Die Volksnamen quman und qūn'. In *Kőrösi Csoma Archivum* 3 (1941–3): 95–109. Reprint Leiden: Brill, 1967.
'Kun László király nyőgérei' (The nökers of King Ladislas the Cuman). *Magyar Nyelv* 49 (1953): 304–18.
'Wanderungen des Mongolischen wortes *nökür* "genosse"'. *AOASH* 3 (1953): 1–23.
Eine Wörterliste der Jassen, der Ungarländischen Alanen. Berlin: Akademie Verlag, 1959.
A honfoglaló magyarság kialakulása (The formation of the conquering Magyars). 2nd rev. edn. Budapest: Akadémiai Kiadó, 1991.
Netanyahu, Benzion. *The Origins of the Inquisition in Fifteenth-Century Spain.* New York: Random House, 1995.
Neubauer, Ad. 'Le Memorbuch de Mayence'. *Revue des Etudes Juives* 4 (1882): 1–30.
New Catholic Encyclopedia. 17 vols. New York and St Louis: McGraw-Hill, 1967–79, s.v. 'Honorius'.
Nirenberg, David. *Communities of Violence: Persecution of Minorities in the Middle Ages.* Princeton: Princeton University Press, 1996.
'The Current State of Mudejar Studies'. *Journal of Medieval History* 24 (1998): 381–9.
Nordman, Daniel. 'Des limites d'état aux frontières nationales'. In *Les Lieux de mémoire*, vol. II: *La Nation*. Edited by Pierre Nora, 2: 35–61. Paris: Gallimard, 1986.
'Frontière, histoire et écologie'. *Annales ESC* (1988, no. 1): 277–83.
Frontières de France: de l'espace au territoire XVIe–XIXe siècles. Paris: Gallimard, 1998.
Norris, H. T. *Islam in the Balkans: Religion and Society between Europe and the Arab World.* London: Hurst, 1993.
Obolensky, Dimitri. *The Bogomils: A Study in Balkan Neo-Manicheism.* Cambridge: Cambridge University Press, 1948.
The Byzantine Commonwealth: Eastern Europe, 500–1453. New York and Washington: Praeger, 1971.
'Byzantine Frontier Zones and Cultural Exchanges'. In *Actes du XIVe Congrès International des Etudes Byzantines.* Vol. I: 303–13.
Oikonomidès, Nicolas. 'L'organisation de la frontière orientale de Byzance aux Xe–XIe siècles et le Taktikon de l'Escorial'. In *Actes du XIVe Congrès International des Etudes Byzantines.* Vol. I: 285–302.
'A propos des relations ecclésiastiques entre Byzance et la Hongrie au XIe siècle: le Métropolite de Turquie'. In *Documents et études sur les institutions de Byzance (VIIe–XVe s.)*, no. xx. London: Variorum, 1976.
Olchváry, Ödön. 'A muhi csata' (The battle of Muhi). *Századok* 36 (1902): 309–25.
Őze, Sándor. ' "A kereszténység védőpajzsa" vagy "üllő és verő közé szorult ország". A nemzettudat átformálódása a 16. század közepén a dél-dunántúli végvári

Bibliography

katonaságnál' (The 'shield of Christendom', or 'the country stuck between anvil and hammer'. The transformation of national identity among the soldiers of the frontier castles in mid-sixteenth-century Southern Dunántúl). In *Magyarok Kelet és Nyugat közt*. Edited by Tamás Hofer, 99–107. Budapest: Balassi, 1996.

Pach, Zsigmond Pál. *Nyugat-európai és magyarországi agrárfejlődés a XV–XVII. században* (Agricultural development in Western Europe and in Hungary in the fifteenth–seventeenth centuries). Budapest: Kossuth, 1963.

Die ungarische Agrarentwicklung im 16–17. Jahrhundert, Abbiegung vom westeuropaischen Entwicklungsgang. Budapest: Akadémiai Kiadó, 1964.

'The Shifting of International Trade Routes in the 15th–17th centuries'. *Acta Historica Academiae Scientiarum Hungaricae* (1968): 287–321.

'A harmincadvám eredete' (The origin of the thirtieth customs tax). Budapest: Akadémiai Kiadó, 1990.

'The Transcarpathian Routes of Levantine Trade in the Middle Ages'. In *Quand la montagne aussi a une histoire: mélanges offerts à Jean-François Bergier*. Edited by Martin Körner and François Walter, 237–46. Bern, Stuttgart, and Vienna: Paul Haupt, 1996.

Pakter, Walter. 'Did the Canonists Prescribe a Jewry-Oath?' *Bulletin of Medieval Canon Law* 6 (1976): 81–7.

Pálfy, Ilona. *A tatárok és a XIII. századi Európa* (The Mongols and thirteenth-century Europe). Hefte des Collegium Hungaricum in Wien 2. Budapest: Királyi Magyar Egyetemi Nyomda, 1928.

Pálóczi Horváth, András. 'A csólyosi kun sírlelet' (The Cuman grave find from Csólyos). *Folia Archaeologica* 20 (1969): 107–34.

'A csólyosi kun sírlelet hadtörténeti vonatkozásai' (The military aspects of the Cuman grave find from Csólyos). *A Móra Ferenc Múzeum Évkönyve 1969/1*. Szeged: Szegedi Nyomda, 1969, 115–21.

'A Felsőszentkirályi kun sírlelet' (Cuman grave find from Felsőszentkirály). *Cumania: A Bács-Kiskun megyei múzeumok évkönyve* 1 (1972): 177–204.

'Situation des recherches archéologiques sur les Comans en Hongrie'. *AOASH* 22, no. 2 (1973): 201–9.

'A kunok megtelepedése Magyarországon' (The settlement of the Cumans in Hungary). *Archaeologiai Értesítő* 101 (1974): 244–59.

'L'immigration et l'établissement des Comans en Hongrie'. *AOASH* 29 (1975): 313–33.

'A Lászlófalván 1969–74-ben végzett ásatások eredményei' (The results of the excavations of 1969–74 in Lászlófalva). *Cumania: A Bács-Kiskun megyei múzeumok évkönyve* 4 (1976): 275–309.

'Le costume coman au Moyen Age'. *Acta Archaeologica Academiae Scientiarum Hungaricae* 32 (1980): 403–27.

'Régészeti adatok a kunok viseletéhez' (Archaeological data concerning the costume of the Cumans). *Archaeologiai Értesítő* 109 (1982): 89–107.

'A kunok feudalizálódása és a régészet' (The feudalization of the Cumans and archaeology). In *Középkori régészetünk újabb eredményei és időszerű feladatai* (New results and current tasks of medieval Hungarian archaeology). Edited by István Fodor and László Selmeczi, 93–104. Budapest: Magyar Nemzeti Múzeum, 1985.

'A Balota pusztai középkori sírlelet' (The medieval grave find from Balota puszta). *Cumania: A Bács-Kiskun megyei múzeumok évkönyve* 11 (1989): 95–145.

Bibliography

Besenyők, kunok, jászok (Pechenegs, Cumans and As). Budapest: Corvina, 1989. Tr. *Pechenegs, Cumans, Iasians: Steppe Peoples in Medieval Hungary.* Budapest: Corvina, 1989.
'Steppe Traditions and Cultural Assimilation of a Nomadic People: The Cumanians in Hungary in the 13th–14th century'. In *Archaeological Approaches to Cultural Identity.* Edited by Stephen Shennan, 291–302. London: Unwin Hyman, 1989. Reprint London: Routledge, 1994.
'Hagyományok, kapcsolatok és hatások a kunok régészeti kultúrájában'. Ph.D. dissertation. Budapest, 1992.
Hagyományok, kapcsolatok és hatások a kunok régészeti kultúrájában (Tradition, connections and influences in the archaeological culture of the Cumans). Karcag: Karcag Város Önkormányzata, 1994.
'Keleti népek bevándorlása és letelepedése a középkori Magyarországon: a kunok példája' (Immigration and settlement of Eastern peoples in medieval Hungary: the example of the Cumans). *Internationales Kulturhistorisches Symposion Mogersdorf 1994,* 17–20. Eisenstadt, 1996.
'Nomád népek a kelet-európai steppén és a középkori Magyarországon' (Nomads on the Eastern European steppe and in Hungary). In *Zúduló sasok.* Edited by Péter Havassy, 7–36.
'A kun betelepedés Kiskunfélegyháza környékén és a város korai története' (Cuman settlement around Kiskunfélegyháza and the early history of the town). In *Múzeumi Kutatások Bács-Kiskun megyében 1995–1996,* 25–33. Edited by Imre Romsics. Kecskemét: Bács-Kiskun Megyei Önkormányzatok Szervezete, 1997.
'Kunok a kelet-európai sztyeppén és Magyarországon' (Cumans on the Eastern European steppe and in Hungary). In *Az Alföld Társadalma* (Society on the Plains). Edited by László Novák, 109–46. Nagykőrös: Arany János Múzeum, 1998.
Pamlényi, Ervin. ed. *A History of Hungary.* London: Collet's, 1975.
Papadopoullos, Theodore. 'The Byzantine Model in Frontier History: A Comparative Approach'. In *Actes du XIVe Congrès International des Etudes Byzantines.* Vol. II: 415–19.
Paravicini Bagliani, Agostino. *Cardinali di Curia e 'familiae' cardinalizie dal 1227 al 1254.* 2 vols. Padua: Antenore, 1972.
Il trono di Pietro: L'universalità del papato da Alessandro III a Bonifacio VIII. Rome: La Nuova Italia, 1996.
Parsons, John Carmi. ed. *Medieval Queenship.* New York: St Martin's, 1993.
Pastoureau, Michel. *Figures et couleurs: Etudes sur la symbolique et la sensibilité médiévales.* Paris: Le Léopard d'Or, 1986.
Couleurs, images, symboles: Etudes d'histoire et d'anthropologie. Paris: Le Léopard d'Or, 1989.
Pastoureau, Michel. ed. *Le vêtement: Histoire, archéologie et symbolique vestimentaires au Moyen Age.* Cahiers du Léopard d'Or 1. Paris: Le Léopard d'Or, 1989.
Patai, Raphael. *The Jews of Hungary: History, Culture, Psychology.* Detroit: Wayne State University Press, 1996.
Patlagean, Evelyne. 'Contribution juridique à l'histoire des Juifs dans la Méditerranée médiévale: les formules grecques de serment'. In Patlagean, *Structure sociale, famille, chrétienté à Byzance IVe–XIe siècle,* no. XIV. London: Variorum Reprints, 1981.

Bibliography

Pauler, Gyula. 'Néhány szó hadi viszonyainkról a XI–XIII. században' (A few words concerning the Hungarian military situation in the eleventh–thirteenth centuries). *Hadtörténelmi Közlemények* 1, no. 4 (1888): 501–26.

A magyar nemzet története az Árpádok korában (The history of the Hungarian nation in the age of the Arpads). 2 vols. 2nd edn, 1899. Reprint Szeged: Állami Könyvterjesztő Vállalat, 1984.

Pelliot, Paul. *Recherches sur les chrétiens d'Asie Centrale et d'Extrême-Orient: Oeuvres post-humes de Paul Pelliot.* Paris: Impr. Nationale, 1973.

Pennington, Kenneth. *The Prince and the Law, 1200–1600: Sovereignty and Rights in the Western Legal Tradition.* Berkeley and Los Angeles: University of California Press, 1993.

Perényi, József. 'A magyar "nemzeti öntudat" fejlődése a 11–13. században' (The development of Hungarian 'national consciousness' in the eleventh–thirteenth centuries). In *Nemzetiség a feudalizmus korában.* Edited by Jenő Szűcs, 83–101. Értekezések a Történeti Tudományok Köréből 64. Budapest: Akadémiai Kiadó, 1972.

Peters, Edward. *The Shadow King: 'Rex inutilis' in Medieval Law and Literature 751–1327.* New Haven and London: Yale University Press, 1970.

Petrovics, István. ' "Új" források a kunok kereszténységre térítéséről?' (New sources concerning the conversion of the Cumans?) *AUSz Acta Historica* 86 (1988): 3–7.

Pfeiffer, Nicolas (Miklós). *Die Ungarische Dominikanerordensprovinz von ihrer Gründung 1221 bis zur Tatarenwüstung 1241–2.* Zurich: Gebr. Leemann, 1913.

A Domonkosrend magyar zárdáinak vázlatos története (A brief history of Hungarian Dominican monasteries). Kassa: Szent Erzsébet Nyomda, 1917.

Pfister, Max. 'Grenzbezeichnungen im Italoromanischen und Galloromanischen'. In *Grenzen und Grenzregionen.* Edited by Wolfgang Haubrichs and Reinhard Schneider, 37–50. Saarbrücken: Saarbrücker Druckerei und Verlag, 1994.

Phillips, J. R. S. *The Medieval Expansion of Europe.* 2nd edn. Oxford: Clarendon Press, 1998.

Pirigyi, István. *A magyarországi görög katolikusok története* (The history of the Greek Catholics in Hungary). Budapest: Görög katolikus hittudományi főiskola, 1990.

A görögkatolikus magyarság története (The history of Greek Catholic Hungarians). Budapest: Ikva, 1991.

Pohl, Artúr. 'Hozzászólás középkori rézpénzeink kérdéseihez I' (Remarks concerning the question of Hungarian medieval copper coins I). *Érem* 29, no. 2 (1973): 56–7.

'Hozzászólás középkori rézpénzeink kérdéseihez II' (Remarks concerning the question of Hungarian medieval copper coins II). *Érem* 31, no. 2 (1974): 5–7.

'A középkori magyar verdejegyrendszer kialakulásának kora' (The period of the genesis of Hungarian mint-marks). *Érem* 30, no. 1 (1974): 6–7.

'A kovarezmiai mohamedánok szerepe a magyar középkori pénzverésben' (The role of Khwarazmian Muslims in medieval Hungarian minting). *A Magyar Numizmatikai Társulat Évkönyve* (1975), 79–85.

'Der Islamische Einfluss auf die Münzprägung Ungarns im 12. Jahrhundert'. *Hamburger Beiträge zur Numismatik* 27–9 (1973–5): 163–8.

Pohl, Walter. 'Telling the Difference: Signs of Ethnic Identity'. In *Strategies of Distinction: The Construction of Ethnic Communities, 300–800.* Edited by Walter Pohl and Helmut Reimitz, 17–69.

Bibliography

Pohl, Walter and Helmut Reimitz. eds. *Strategies of Distinction: The Construction of Ethnic Communities, 300–800*. Leiden: Brill, 1998.
Poliakov, Léon. *Histoire de l'antisémitisme*. 2 vols. Paris: Libr. Gén. Française, 1981.
Pollák, Miksa. *A zsidók Bécsujhelyen: Tanulmány a zsidók történetéhez Alsó-Ausztriában és Magyarországon* (Jews in Wienerneustadt: Essay on the history of the Jews of Lower Austria and Hungary). Budapest: Athenaeum, 1892.
A zsidók története Sopronban a legrégebbi időktől a mai napig (A history of the Jews in Sopron from the earliest times until today). Az izraelita magyar irodalmi társulat kiadványai 6. Budapest, 1896.
Poly, Jean-Pierre and Eric Bournazel. *La Mutation féodale Xe au XIIe siècles*. Nouvelle Clio 16. Paris: Presses Universitaires de France, 1980.
Posch, Fritz. 'Die deutsch-ungarische Grenzentwicklung im 10. und 11. Jahrhundert auf dem Boden der heutigen Steiermark'. *Südost-Forschungen* 22 (1963): 126–39.
Powell, James M. ed. *Muslims under Latin Rule, 1100–1300*. Princeton: Princeton University Press, 1990.
Power, Daniel. 'What did the Frontier of Angevin Normandy Comprise?' In *Anglo-Norman Studies* 17. Edited by Christopher Harper-Bill, 181–201. Woodbridge: Boydell Press, 1995.
Power, Daniel and Naomi Standen. eds. *Frontiers in Question: Eurasian Borderlands 700–1700*. London: Macmillan, 1999.
Pratt, Karen. 'The Image of the Queen in Old French Literature'. In *Queens and Queenship in Medieval Europe*. Edited by Anne J. Duggan, 235–59.
Prawer, Joshua. *The History of the Jews in the Latin Kingdom of Jerusalem*. Oxford: Oxford University Press, 1988. New edn, Clarendon Press, 1996.
Pritsak, Omeljan. 'The Khazar Kingdom's Conversion to Judaism'. *Harvard Ukranian Studies* 2 (1978): 261–81.
'The Polovcians and Rus''. *AEMAe* (1982): 321–80.
Rabikauskas, Paulius. 'La cristianizzazione della Lituania (XIII e XIV secolo)'. In *L'Eglise et le peuple chrétien dans les pays de l'Europe du Centre-Est et du Nord, XIVe–XVe siècles*, 3–11. Collection de l'Ecole Française de Rome 128. Rome: Ecole Française de Rome and Paris: Diffusion de Boccard, 1990.
Radó, Polycarpus. *Libri liturgici manuscripti bibliothecarum Hungariae et limitropharum regionum*. Budapest: Akadémiai Kiadó, 1973.
Rádóczy, Gyula. 'Héber betűjeles Árpád-házi pénzek' (Coins marked with Hebrew letters from the Arpad age). *Numizmatikai Közlöny* 70–1 (1971–2): 33–7.
Rajecky, Benjamin. *Magyarország zenetörténete* (The history of music in Hungary). Vol. 1. Budapest: Akadémiai Kiadó, 1988.
Rákos, István. 'IV. Béla birtokrestaurációs politikája' (King Béla IV's policy of estate reclamation). *AUSz Acta Historica* 47 (1974): 3–29.
Rásonyi, László. 'Les noms toponymiques du Kiskunság'. *Acta Linguistica Academiae Scientiarum Hungaricae* 7 (1958): 73–146.
'Kuman Özel Adlari'. *Türk Kültürü Araştirmalari* 3–6 (1966–9): 71–144.
'Les anthroponymes comans de Hongrie'. *AOASH* 20 (1967): 135–49.
Hidak a Dunán: A régi török népek a Dunánál (Bridges on the Danube: Turkic peoples by the Danube). Budapest: Magvető Kiadó, 1981.
Rassovsky, Dimitri A. 'Pétchénègues, Torks et Béréndés en Russie et en Hongrie'. *Seminarium Kondakovianum* 6 (1933): 1–66.

Bibliography

'Les Comans et Byzance'. In *Actes du IVe Congrès International des Etudes Byzantines. Bulletin de l'Institut Archéologique Bulgare* 9 (1935): 346–54.
'Polovci I' (with French summary). *Seminarium Kondakovianum* 7 (1935): 245–62.
'Polovci II' (with French summary). *Seminarium Kondakovianum* 8 (1936): 161–82.
'Polovci III' (with French summary). *Seminarium Kondakovianum* 9 (1937): 71–85; 10 (1938): 155–77.
Ratzel, Friedrich. *Politische Geographie.* Munich and Leipzig: R. Oldenbourg, 1897. Reprint of 3rd edn, Osnabruck: Zeller, 1974.
Réthy, László. *Magyar pénzverő izmaeliták és Bessarábia* (Hungarian Ishmaelites employed in minting, and Bessarabia). Arad, 1880.
Reynolds, Susan. 'Medieval *Origines Gentium* and the Community of the Realm'. *History* 68 (1983): 375–90.
Fiefs and Vassals: The Medieval Evidence Reinterpreted. Oxford: Oxford University Press, 1994.
Kingdoms and Communities in Western Europe 900–1300. 2nd edn. Oxford: Clarendon Press, 1997.
Rhode, Gotthold. *Die Ostgrenze Polens: Politische Entwicklung, kulturelle Bedeutung und geistige Auswirkung.* Vol. I. Cologne and Graz: Böhlau Verlag, 1955.
Richard, Jean. *La papauté et les missions d'orient au Moyen Age (XIIIe–XVe siècles).* Collection de l'Ecole Française de Rome 33. Rome: Ecole Française de Rome, 1977.
'Chrétiens et Mongols au concile: la papauté et les Mongols de Perse dans la seconde moitié du XIIIe siècle'. In *1274: Année charnière: Mutations et continuités,* 31–44. Paris: Les Editions du CNRS, 1977.
'Les Mongols et l'Occident: deux siècles de contacts'. In *1274: Année charnière,* 85–96 ('Discussion', 97–102).
'Les causes des victoires mongoles d'après les historiens occidentaux du XIIIe siècle'. In Richard, *Croisés, missionnaires et voyageurs: les perspectives orientales du monde latin médiéval,* no. XI. London: Variorum, 1983.
'Le discours missionnaire: l'exposition de la foi chrétienne dans les lettres des papes aux Mongols'. In Richard, *Croisés, missionnaires et voyageurs: les perspectives orientales du monde latin médiéval,* no. XVII.
'L'enseignement des langues orientales en Occident au Moyen Age'. In Richard, *Croisés, missionnaires et voyageurs: les perspectives orientales du monde latin médiéval,* no. XVIII.
'The *Relatio de Davide* as a Source for Mongol History and the Legend of Prester John'. In *Prester John.* Edited by Charles F. Beckingham and Bernard Hamilton, 139–58.
Richardson, Henry Gerald. *The English Jewry under Angevin Kings.* London: Methuen, 1960. Reprint Westport, Conn.: Greenwood Press, 1983.
Riley-Smith, Jonathan. 'The First Crusade and the Persecution of the Jews'. In *Persecution and Toleration.* Edited by W. J. Sheils, 51–72.
The First Crusade and the Idea of Crusading. Philadelphia: University of Pennsylvania Press, 1986. 2nd paperback edn, 1994.
Riley-Smith, Jonathan. ed. *The Oxford Illustrated History of the Crusades.* Oxford and New York: Oxford University Press, 1997.
Robert, Ulysse. *Les signes de l'infamie au Moyen Age: Juifs, Sarrasins, hérétiques, lépreux, gagots et filles publiques.* Paris, 1891.

Bibliography

Róna-Tas, András. *Hungarians and Europe in the Early Middle Ages: An Introduction to Early Hungarian History*. Budapest: Central European University Press, 1999.

Rosty, Zsigmond. *A tatárjárás történelme negyedik Béla király idejében* (A history of the Mongol invasion in the age of Béla IV). Pest, 1856.

Roth, Cecil. *A History of the Marranos*. 4th edn. New York: Schocken Books, 1975.

Roth, Norman. *Jews, Visigoths and Muslims in Medieval Spain: Cooperation and Conflict*. Leiden, New York and Cologne: Brill, 1994.

Rousselle, Aline. ed. *Frontières terrestres, frontières célestes dans l'Antiquité*. Paris: Presses Universitaires de Perpignan, 1995.

Roux, Jean-Paul. 'Fonctions chamaniques et valeurs du feu chez les peuples altaïques'. *Revue de l'Histoire des Religions* 189 (1976): 67–101.

La religion des Turcs et des Mongols. Paris: Payot, 1984.

'Les religions dans les sociétés turco-mongoles'. *Revue de l'Histoire des Religions* 201 (1984): 393–420.

'La religion des peuples de la steppe'. In *Popoli delle Steppe: Unni, Avari, Ungari*. 2 vols. Settimane di Studio del Centro Italiano di Studi sull'Alto Medioevo 35. Vol. II: 513–32. Spoleto, 1988.

Rowell, S. C. 'A Pagan's Word: Lithuanian Diplomatic Procedure 1200–1385'. *Journal of Medieval History* 18 (1992): 145–60.

Lithuania Ascending: A Pagan Empire within East-Central Europe, 1295–1345. Cambridge: Cambridge University Press, 1994.

Rubens, Alfred. *A History of Jewish Costume*. 2nd edn. London: Vallentine, Mitchell, 1973.

Rubin, Miri. *Corpus Christi: The Eucharist in Late Medieval Culture*. Cambridge: Cambridge University Press, 1991.

'Desecration of the Host: The Birth of an Accusation'. *Studies in Church History* 29 (1992): 169–85.

Gentile Tales: The Narrative Assault on Late Medieval Jews. New Haven and London: Yale University Press, 1999.

Ruess, Karl. *Die Rechtliche Stellung der päpstlichen legaten bis Bonifaz VIII*. Görres-Gesellschaft zur Pflege der Wissenschaft im Katholischen Deutschland Sektion für Rechts- und Sozialwissenschaft 13. Paderborn: F. Schöningh, 1912.

Rupp, J. *L'idée de chrétienté dans la pensée pontificale des origines à Innocent III*. Paris: Les Presses Modernes, 1939.

Ryan, James D. 'Conversion vs. Baptism? European Missionaries in Asia in the Thirteenth and Fourteenth Centuries'. In *Varieties of Religious Conversion*. Edited by James Muldoon, 146–67.

Sack, Robert David. *Conceptions of Space in Social Thought: A Geographic Perspective*. London: Macmillan, 1980.

Human Territoriality: Its Theory and History. Cambridge, London and New York: Cambridge University Press, 1986.

Sahlins, Peter. *Boundaries: The Making of France and Spain in the Pyrenees*. Berkeley, Los Angeles and Oxford: Oxford University Press, 1989.

Sánchez-Albornoz, Claudio. *España: un enigma histórico*. 2 vols. Buenos Aires: Editorial Sudamericana, 1956.

El Islam de España y el Occidente. 2nd edn. Colección Austral 1560. Madrid: Espasa-Calpe, 1974.

Saunders, J. J. 'Matthew Paris and the Mongols'. In *Essays in Medieval History*

Bibliography

Presented to Bertie Wilkinson. Edited by T. A. Sandquist and M. R. Powicke, 116–32. Toronto: University of Toronto Press, 1969.

The History of the Mongol Conquests. London: Routledge and Kegan Paul, 1971.

Savage, William W. Jr. and Stephen I. Thompson. eds. *The Frontier: Comparative Studies*. Vol. II. Norman: University of Oklahoma Press, 1979.

Sayers, Jane E. *Innocent III: Leader of Europe, 1198–1216*. London: Longman, 1994.

Scheiber, Sándor. 'Recent Additions to the Medieval History of Hungarian Jewry'. *Historia Judaica* 14 (1952): 145–58.

Héber kódexmaradványok magyarországi kötéstáblákban: A középkori magyar zsidóság könyvkultúrája (Fragments of Hebrew codices in book-bindings in Hungary: the learned culture of medieval Hungarian Jews). Budapest: A Magyar Izraeliták Országos Képviselete, 1969.

'A héber betűjeles Árpád-házi pénzekhez' (Concerning the coins marked with Hebrew letters from the Arpad age). *Numizmatikai Közlöny* 72–3 (1973–4): 91.

Scheiberné, Lívia Bernáth. *A magyarországi zsidóság személy- és családnevei II. József névadó rendeletéig* (Personal and family names of Hungarian Jews until Joseph II's edict on names). A Magyarországi Zsidó Hitközségek Monográfiái 10. Budapest: A Magyar Izraeliták Országos Képviselete, 1981.

Scherer, Johann Egid. *Die Rechtsverhältnisse der Juden in den deutsch-österreichischen Ländern*. Beiträge zur Geschichte des Judenrechtes im Mittelalter 1. Leipzig: Duncker und Humblot, 1901.

Schmieder, Felicitas. *Europa und die Fremden: Die Mongolen im Urteil des Abendlandes vom 13. bis in das 15. Jahrhundert*. Sigmaringen: Thorbecke, 1994.

Schmitt, Jean-Claude. 'Religion populaire et culture folklorique'. *Annales ESC* 31 (1976): 941–53.

La raison des gestes dans l'Occident médiéval. Paris: Gallimard, 1990.

Schneider, Reinhard. 'Lineare Grenzen – Vom Frühen bis zum Späten Mittelalter'. In *Grenzen und Grenzregionen*. Edited by Wolfgang Haubrichs and Reinhard Schneider, 51–68. Saarbrücken: Saarbrücher Druckerei und Verlag, 1994.

Schram, Ferenc. 'A középkori sámánperekről' (Concerning medieval shaman trials). *Ethnographia* 79 (1968): 281–4.

Schreckenberg, Heinz. *Die christlichen Adversus-Judaeos-Texte und ihr literarisches und historisches Umfeld*. 3 vols. Frankfurt am Main: Lang, 1990–4.

Schütz, István. 'Les contacts médiévaux albano-comans reflétés par l'onomastique de Kosovo'. *AOASH* 40 (1986): 293–300.

Schütz, Ödön. 'A mongol hódítás néhány problémájához' (Contribution to certain problems of the Mongol invasion). *Századok* 93 (1959): 209–32.

Seaman, Gary and Daniel Marks. eds. *Rulers from the Steppe: State Formation on the Eurasian Periphery*. Los Angeles: University of Southern California and Ethnographics Press, 1991.

Sella, Pietro. *Le Bolle d'Oro dell'Archivio Vaticano*. Vatican City: Biblioteca Apostolica Vaticana, 1934.

Selmeczi, László. 'The Settlement Structure of the Cumanian Settlers in the Nagykunság'. In *Hungaro-Turcica: Studies in Honour of Julius Németh*. Edited by Gyula Káldy-Nagy, 255–62. Budapest: Eötvös Loránd University, 1976.

'A kunok és jászok emlékanyagának kutatása' (Archaeological research concerning the Cumans and the As). In *Középkori régészetünk újabb eredményei és időszerű*

Bibliography

feladatai. Edited by István Fodor and László Selmeczi, 79–92. Budapest: Magyar Nemzeti Múzeum, 1985.
'Régészeti ásatások a Nagykunságban' (Archaeological excavations in Greater Cumania). In *Tanulmányok a 700 éves Kunhegyesről.* Edited by Ernő Szurmay, 5–16. Kunhegyes: Kunhegyesi Nagyközségi Tanács, 1989.
'A magyarországi "jászkunok" és a tételes vallások (The 'As-Cumans' in Hungary and organized religions). *A Szolnok megyei múzeumok évkönyve* 7 (1990): 207–12.
A négyszállási I. számú jász temető (The As cemetery no. I of Négyszállás). Budapest: Történeti Múzeum, 1992.
'A jászok keresztény hitre térítése a XIII.–XV. században' (The conversion of the As in the thirteenth–fifteenth centuries). In *Egyházak a változó világban* (Churches in a changing world). Edited by István Bárdos and Margit Beke, 159–65. Tatabánya: Komárom-Esztergom Megye Önkormányzata és József Attila Megyei Könyvtár, 1992.
Régészeti-néprajzi tanulmányok a jászokról és a kunokról (Archaeological and ethnographical essays on the As and the Cumans). Folklór és etnográfia 64. Debrecen: KLTE, 1992.
'A négyszállási jász temető (előzetes közlés az 1980. évi feltárásokról)' (The As cemetery of Négyszállás: first publication concerning the archaeological excavations of 1980). In *Régészeti-néprajzi tanulmányok a jászokról és a kunokról,* 135–64.
'Régészeti adatok a jászok szokásaihoz és hiedelemvilágához' (Archaeological data on the customs and beliefs of the As). In *Régészeti-néprajzi tanulmányok a jászokról és a kunokról,* 185–211.
'A kunok nomadizmusának kérdéséhez' (Contribution to the question of Cuman nomadism). In *Régészeti-néprajzi tanulmányok a jászokról és a kunokról,* 87–99.
'A szállástól a faluig: adatok a magyarországi kunok településtörténetéhez' (From camps to villages: data concerning the settlement of the Cumans in Hungary). In *Régészeti-néprajzi tanulmányok a jászokról és a kunokról,* 61–85.
'Nomád települési struktúra a Nagykunságban' (Nomad settlement pattern in Greater Cumania). In *Régészeti-néprajzi tanulmányok a jászokról és a kunokról,* 49–59.
'A kunok és a jászok régészeti kutatásának néhány problémája' (Some problems concerning the archaeological investigation of the Cumans and the As). In *Régészeti-néprajzi tanulmányok a jászokról és a kunokról,* 101–13.
'A magyarországi kunok temetkezése a XIII–XVI. században' (Burial customs of the Cumans of Hungary in the thirteenth–sixteenth centuries). In *Régészeti-néprajzi tanulmányok a jászokról és a kunokról,* 21–47.
'Adatok és szempontok a kunok régészeti kutatásához Szolnok megyében' (Data and methodological considerations about the archaeological investigation of the Cumans in Szolnok county). In *Régészeti-néprajzi tanulmányok a jászokról és a kunokról,* 5–20.
'A jászok etnogenezise' (Ethnogenesis of the As). *Tanulmányok és közlemények.* Edited by Zoltán Újváry, 127–44. Debrecen and Szolnok: Damjanich Múzeum – Kossuth Lajos Tudományegyetem Néprajzi Tanszéke, 1995.
Sénac, Philippe. *L'image de l'autre: Histoire de l'occident médiéval face à l'Islam.* Paris: Flammarion, 1983.

Bibliography

Senga, Toru. 'IV. Béla külpolitikája és IV. Ince pápához intézett "tatár-levele"' (The foreign policy of Béla IV and his 'Mongol letter' addressed to Pope Innocent IV). *Századok* 121 (1987): 584–612.
Shatzmiller, Joseph. 'Jewish Conversion to Christianity in Medieval Europe 1200–1500'. In *Cross Cultural Convergences in the Crusader Period*. Edited by Michael Goodich, Sophia Menache and Sylvia Schein, 297–318. New York: Peter Lang, 1995.
Sheils, W. J. *Persecution and Toleration*. Oxford: Blackwell, 1984.
Shepard, Jonathan. 'Slavs and Bulgars'. In *The New Cambridge Medieval History*. Vol. II. Edited by Rosamond McKitterick, 228–48. Cambridge: Cambridge University Press, 1995.
Shneidman, Jerome Lee. 'Jews as Royal Bailiffs in Thirteenth Century Aragon'. *Historia Judaica* 19 (1957): 55–66.
'Jews in the Royal Administration of Thirteenth Century Aragon'. *Historia Judaica* 21 (1959): 37–52.
Silayev, Alexander. 'Frontier and Settlement: Cumans North of the Lower Danube in the First Half of the Thirteenth Century'. MA thesis. Budapest: Central European University, 1998.
Simmel, Georg. 'Fashion'. *International Quarterly* 10 (1904): 130–55.
Simonsohn, Shlomo. *The Apostolic See and the Jews: History*. Studies and Texts 109. Toronto: Pontifical Institute of Mediaeval Studies, 1991.
Sinor, Denis. 'Quelques passages relatifs aux Comans, tirés des chroniques françaises de l'époque des croisades'. In *Silver Jubilee Volume of the Zinbun-Kagaku-Kenkyusyo, Kyoto University*. Edited by Shigeki Kaizuka, 370–75. Kyoto: Nissha, 1954.
Inner Asia and its Contacts with Medieval Europe. London: Variorum Reprints, 1977.
'Central Eurasia'. In *Inner Asia*, no. I.
'The Mongols and Western Europe'. In *Inner Asia*, no. IX.
'Les relations entre les Mongols et l'Europe jusqu'à la mort d'Arghoun et de Béla IV'. In *Inner Asia*, no. X.
'John of Plano Carpini's Return from the Mongols: New Light from a Luxemburg Manuscript'. In *Inner Asia*, no. XII.
'Le Mongol vu par l'Occident'. In *1274: Année charnière: Mutations et continuités*, 55–72. Paris: Les Editions du CNRS, 1977.
'Taking an Oath over a Dog Cut in Two'. In *Altaic Religious Beliefs and Practices*. Edited by Géza Bethlenfalvy *et al.*, 301–5. Budapest: Research Group for Altaic Studies, Hungarian Academy of Sciences and Department of Inner Asiatic Studies, ELTE, 1992.
ed. *The Cambridge History of Early Inner Asia*. Cambridge: Cambridge University Press, 1990.
S. Kiss, Erzsébet. 'A királyi generális kongregáció kialakulásának történetéhez' (On the history of the origins of the royal general assembly). *AUSz Acta Historica* 39 (1971).
Smalley, Beryl. *The Study of the Bible in the Middle Ages*. 3rd edn. Notre Dame: University of Notre Dame Press, 1978.
Smith, Anthony. *The Ethnic Origins of Nations*. Oxford: Blackwell, 1986.
Smith, Julia M. H. 'Fines Imperii: The Marches'. In *The New Cambridge Medieval History*. Vol. II. Edited by Rosamond McKitterick, 169–89. Cambridge: Cambridge University Press, 1995.

Bibliography

Solymosi, László. 'Hospeskiváltság 1275-ből' (Hospes privileges from 1275). In *Tanulmányok Veszprém megye múltjából*. Edited by László Kredics, 17–100. Veszprém: Veszprém Megyei Levéltár, 1984.

'Egyházi-politikai viszonyok a pápai hegemónia idején (13. század)' (The ecclesiastical and political situation during the hegemony of the papacy in the thirteenth century). In *Magyarország és a Szentszék kapcsolatának ezer éve*. Edited by István Zombori, 47–54.

A földesúri járadékok új rendszere a 13. századi Magyarországon (The new system of manorial revenues in thirteenth-century Hungary). Budapest: Argumentum, 1998.

Southern, Richard W. *Western Society and the Church in the Middle Ages*. The Pelican History of the Church 2. Harmondsworth and New York: Penguin, 1970.

Western Views of Islam in the Middle Ages. 2nd edn. Cambridge, Mass.: Harvard University Press, 1978.

Spahr, Rodolfo. *Le Monete Siciliane dai Bizantini a Carlo I d'Angiò (582–1282)*. Zurich and Graz: Association Internationale des Numismates Professionnels, 1976.

Spinelli, Domenico. *Monete Cufiche battute da Principi Longobardi Normanni e Svevi nel regno delle due Sicilie*. Naples, 1844.

Spufford, Peter. *Money and its Use in Medieval Europe*. Cambridge: Cambridge University Press, 1988.

Spuler, Bertold. *Les Mongols dans l'histoire*. Paris: Payot, 1961.

Stephenson, Paul. 'Manuel I Comnenus, the Hungarian Crown and the "Feudal Subjection" of Hungary, 1162–1167'. *Byzantinoslavica* 57 (1996): 33–59.

Stow, Kenneth R. *Alienated Minority: The Jews of Medieval Latin Europe*. Cambridge, Mass.: Harvard University Press, 1992.

Strayer, Joseph. 'The Political Crusades of the Thirteenth Century'. In *A History of the Crusades*. 6 vols. Edited by Kenneth M. Setton. Vol. II: *The Later Crusades 1189–1311*. Edited by Robert Lee Wolff and Harry W. Hazard, 343–75. Madison, Wis.: University of Wisconsin Press, 1969.

Suarez Fernandez, Luis. *Les Juifs espagnols au Moyen Age*. Paris: Gallimard, 1983.

Sugár, Peter. ed. *A History of Hungary*. London and New York: I. B. Tauris, 1990.

Sullivan, Richard E. *Christian Missionary Activity in the Early Middle Ages*. Aldershot: Variorum Reprints, 1994.

'The Medieval Monk as Frontiersman'. In *The Frontier: Comparative Studies*. Vol. II. Edited by William W. Savage, Jr. and Stephen I. Thompson, 25–49. Norman: University of Oklahoma Press, 1979. Reprinted in Sullivan, *Christian Missionary Activity in the Early Middle Ages*, no. VI.

'Khan Boris and the Conversion of Bulgaria: A Case Study of the Impact of Christianity on a Barbarian Society'. In Sullivan, *Christian Missionary Activity in the Early Middle Ages*, no. IV.

Sümegi, József. 'Az oltáriszentség és a Szent Vér tisztelete a középkori Magyarországon' (The cult of the host and the Holy Blood in medieval Hungary). *Magyar Egyháztörténeti Vázlatok* 3 (1991): 107–19.

Sweeney, James Ross. 'Papal-Hungarian Relations during the Pontificate of Innocent III, 1198–1216'. Ph.D. dissertation. Cornell University, 1971.

'The Problem of Inalienability in Innocent III's Correspondence with Hungary: A Contribution to the Study of the Historical Genesis of Intellecto'. *Mediaeval Studies* 37 (1975): 235–51.

Bibliography

'The Decretal Intellecto and the Hungarian Golden Bull of 1222'. In *Album Elemér Mályusz*, 91–6. Brussels: Les Editions de la Librairie Encyclopédique, 1976.
Synan, Edward A. *The Popes and the Jews in the Middle Ages*. New York: Macmillan, 1965.
'The Popes' Other Sheep'. In *The Religious Roles of the Papacy: Ideals and Realities 1150–1300*. Edited by Christopher Ryan, 389–411. Toronto: Pontifical Institute of Mediaeval Studies, 1989.
Szabó, István. *A falurendszer kialakulása Magyarországon (X–XV. század)* (The development of the village system in Hungary in the tenth–fifteenth centuries). Budapest: Akadémiai Kiadó, 1966.
A középkori magyar falu (The medieval Hungarian village). Budapest: Akadémiai Kiadó, 1969.
Szabó, Károly. *Kun László 1272–1290* (Ladislas the Cuman 1272–1290). Budapest: Franklin Társulat, 1886. Reprint Budapest: Maecenas Könyvkiadó, 1988.
Szabó, László. *A jász etnikai csoport I: A jász etnikum és a jászsági műveltségi egység néprajza* (The As ethnic group I: As ethnicity and the ethnography of the As territorial unit). 2 vols. Szolnok: Szolnoki Múzeum, 1979–82.
Szalay, József. 'Városaink nemzetiségi viszonyai a XIII. században' (Nationality relations in our cities in the thirteenth century). *Századok* 14 (1880): 533–57.
Székely, György. 'La Hongrie et Byzance aux Xe–XIIe siècles'. *Acta Historica Academiae Scientiarum Hungaricae* 13 (1967): 291–310.
'Les contacts entre Hongrois et Musulmans aux IXe–XIIe siècles'. In *The Muslim East: Studies in Honour of Julius Germanus*. Edited by Gyula Káldy-Nagy, 53–74. Budapest: ELTE, 1974.
'Településtörténet és nyelvtörténet. A XII. századi magyar nyelvhatár kérdéséhez' (The history of settlement and linguistic history. On the question of the Hungarian linguistic frontier in the twelfth century). In *Mályusz Elemér Emlékkönyv*. Edited by Éva H. Balázs, Erik Fügedi and Ferenc Maksay, 311–39. Budapest: Akadémiai Kiadó, 1984.
'A honfoglalás kori maradvány népek a Kárpát-medencében (román és német elméletek)' (The population found in the Carpathian Basin at the time of the Hungarian Conquest: Roumanian and German hypotheses). In *Magyarország történeti demográfiája I. A Honfoglalás és az Árpád-kor népessége*. Edited by József Kovacsics, 106–21.
Székely, György. ed. *Magyarország története* (A history of Hungary). Vol. 1, pts. 1 and 2: *Előzmények és magyar történet 1242-ig* (Prehistory and Hungarian history until 1242). Budapest: Akadémiai Kiadó, 1984.
Szekfű, Gyula. 'A magyarság és kisebbségei a középkorban: vázlatok egy hazai kisebbségtörténethez' (Hungarians and minorities in the Middle Ages: a sketch of the history of minorities in Hungary). In Szekfű, *Állam és nemzet: tanulmányok a nemzetiségi kérdésről* (State and nation: essays on the nationality question), 39–53. Budapest: Magyar Szemle Társaság, 1942.
'Még egyszer középkori kisebbségeinkről' (Once again about medieval minorities in Hungary). In Szekfű, *Állam és nemzet*, 54–68.
'A nemzetiségi kérdés rövid története' (A short history of the nationality question). In Szekfű, *Állam és nemzet*, 85–177.
Szentpétery, Imre. 'V. István ifjabb királysága' (The younger kingship of Stephen V). *Századok* 55–6 (1921–2): 77–87.

Bibliography

'IV. László király pecsétváltoztatásai' (The successive seals of King Ladislas IV). *Levéltári Közlemények* 1 (1923): 310–20.

Magyar Oklevéltan (Hungarian Diplomatics). Budapest: Magyar Történelmi Társulat, 1930. Reprint Budapest: Határú Síp Alapítvány, 1995.

Szovák, Kornél. 'Pápai–magyar kapcsolatok a 12. században' (Papal–Hungarian relations in the twelfth century). In *Magyarország és a Szentszék kapcsolatának ezer éve*. Edited by István Zombori, 21–46.

'Lodomér érsek leveleiről' (Concerning the letters of Archbishop Lodomer). In *Egyházak a változó világban*. Edited by István Bárdos and Margit Beke, 141–3. Tatabánya: Komárom-Esztergom Megye Önkormányzata és József Attila Megyei Könyvtár, 1992.

Szűcs, Jenő. 'Társadalomelmélet, politikai teória és történelemszemlélet Kézai Gesta Hungarorumában' (Social and political theories and a view of history in the Gesta Hungarorum of Simon of Kéza). *Századok* 107 (1973): 569–643, 823–78.

Nemzet és történelem (Nation and history). Budapest: Gondolat Kiadó, 1974. Tr. *Nation und Geschichte: Studien*. Budapest: Corvina, 1981.

'Társadalomelmélet, politikai teória és történetszemlélet Kézai Simon Gesta Hungarorumában' (Social and political theories and a view of history in the Gesta Hungarorum of Simon of Kéza). In Szűcs, *Nemzet és történelem*, 415–555. Tr. *Nation und Geschichte: Studien*, 263–328. Also 'Theoretical Elements in Master Simon of Kéza's *Gesta Hungarorum* (1282–1285)'. In *Simon of Kéza: The Deeds of the Hungarians*. Edited and translated by László Veszprémy and Frank Schaer, xxix–civ. Budapest: Central European University Press, 1999.

'"Nemzetiség" és "nemzeti öntudat" a középkorban: szempontok egy egységes fogalmi nyelv kialakításához' ("Nationality" and "national identity" in the Middle Ages: considerations in order to develop a unified conceptual language). In Szűcs, *Nemzet és történelem*, 189–278.

'A kereszténység belső politikuma a XIII. század derekán: IV. Béla király és az egyház' (The internal politics of Christendom in the mid-thirteenth century: King Béla IV and the church). *Történelmi Szemle* 21 (1978): 158–81.

Vázlat Európa három történeti régiójáról (The three historical regions of Europe). Budapest: Magvető Kiadó, 1983. Tr. 'The Three Historical Regions of Europe: An Outline'. *Acta Historica Academiae Scientiarum Hungaricae* 29 (1983): 2–4, 131–84. *Les trois Europes*. Paris: Harmattan, 1985.

'Két történelmi példa az etnikai csoportok életképességéről' (Two historical examples concerning the longevity of ethnic groups). In *Magyarságkutatás. A Magyarságkutató Csoport Évkönyve*. Edited by Csaba Gy. Kiss, 11–27. Budapest: Magyarságkutató Csoport, 1987.

'Szent István Intelmei: az első magyarországi államelméleti mű' (The Admonitions of St Stephen: The first Hungarian constitutional theory). In *Szent István és kora*. Edited by Ferenc Glatz and József Kardos, 32–53. Budapest: MTA Történettudományi Intézet, 1988.

'The Peoples of Medieval Hungary'. In *Ethnicity and Society in Hungary*. Edited by Ferenc Glatz, 11–20. Budapest: Institute of History of the Hungarian Academy of Sciences, 1990.

A magyar nemzeti tudat kialakulása (The genesis of Hungarian ethnic identity). Magyar Őstörténeti Könyvtár 3. Szeged: József Attila Tudományegyetem Magyar Őstörténeti Kutatócsoport, 1992.

Bibliography

Az utolsó Árpádok (The last Arpadians). Budapest: MTA Történettudományi Intézete, 1993.

Taitz, Emily. *The Jews of Medieval France: The Community of Champagne.* London and Westport, Conn.: Greenwood Press, 1994.

Takács, Lajos. *Határjelek, határjárás a feudális kor végén Magyarországon* (Border markers and perambulation of borders at the end of the feudal age in Hungary). Budapest: Akadémiai Kiadó, 1987.

Tardy, Lajos. *A tatárországi rabszolgakereskedelem és a magyarok a XIII–XV. században* (Slave-trade in the Mongol Empire and the Hungarians in the thirteenth–fifteenth centuries). Kőrösi Csoma Kiskönyvtár 17. Budapest: Akadémiai Kiadó, 1980.

Tazbir, Janusz. *A State without Stakes: Polish Religious Toleration in the Sixteenth and Seventeenth Centuries.* Warsaw and New York: Kosciuszko Foundation, 1973.

TeBrake, William H. *Medieval Frontier: Culture and Ecology in Rijnland.* College Station: Texas A. and M. University Press, 1985.

Terbe, Lajos. 'Egy európai szállóige életrajza (Magyarország a kereszténység védőbástyája)' (The history of a European proverb: Hungary, the bulwark of Christendom). *Egyetemes Philológiai Közlöny* 60 (1936): 297–351.

Terestyéni, Ferenc. *Magyar közszói eredetű személynevek az 1211-i tihanyi összeírásban* (Hungarian personal names originating from everyday words in the list of Tihany, 1211). Budapest: Magyar Nyelvtudományi Társaság, 1941.

Thesaurus Linguae Latinae. Stuttgart and Leipzig: Teubner, 1900– , s.v. 'gens'.

Thompson, James Westfall. 'Profitable Fields of Investigation in Medieval History'. *American Historical Review* 18 (1913): 490–504.

Tolan, John Victor. ed. *Medieval Christian Perceptions of Islam.* New York and London: Garland, 1996.

Toubert, Pierre. 'Frontière et frontières: un objet historique'. In *Castrum 4: Frontière et peuplement dans le monde méditerranéen au Moyen Age.* Actes du colloque d'Erice-Trapani, 18–25 Septembre 1988, 9–17. Rome: Ecole Française de Rome and Madrid: Casa Velazquez, 1992.

Török, József. 'A középkori magyarországi liturgia története' (A history of the medieval Hungarian liturgy). In *Kódexek a középkori Magyarországon.* Edited by Csaba Csapodi, 49–66. Budapest: Országos Széchenyi Könyvtár, 1985.

'Szent István tisztelete a középkori magyar liturgiában' (The cult of St Stephen in medieval Hungarian liturgy). In *Szent István és kora.* Edited by Ferenc Glatz and József Kardos. 197–201. Budapest: MTA Történettudományi Intézet, 1988.

Travaini, Lucia. 'A Neglected Cufic Copper Coin of Roger II in Sicily'. *Numismatic Circular* 98, no. 9 (1990): 312–13.

'Entre Byzance et l'Islam: le système monétaire du royaume normand de Sicile en 1140'. *Bulletin de la Société Française de Numismatique* 46, no. 9 (1991): 200–4'.

Tubach, Frederic C. *Index Exemplorum: A Handbook of Medieval Religious Tales.* Folklore Fellows Communications 204. Helsinki: Akademia Scientiarum Fennica, 1969.

Turner, Frederick Jackson. 'The Significance of the Frontier in American History'. In *The Frontier in American History*, chapter 1. 1920. Reprint New York: Holt, Rinehart and Winston, 1962.

Újvári, Péter. ed. *Magyar Zsidó Lexikon* (Hungarian Jewish Encyclopedia). Budapest: Pallas Nyomda, 1929.

Ullmann, Walter. *Principles of Government and Politics in the Middle Ages*. 4th edn. London: Methuen, 1978.
Van Engen, John. 'The Christian Middle Ages as an Historiographical Problem'. *American Historical Review* 91 (1986): 519–52.
Várdy, Steven Béla. *Historical Dictionary of Hungary*. Lanham, Md. and London: Scarecrow Press, 1997.
Vásáry, István. *A régi Belső-Ázsia története* (The history of ancient Inner Asia). Magyar Őstörténeti Könyvtár 7. Szeged: József Attila Tudományegyetem Magyar Őstörténeti Kutatócsoportja, 1993.
Vauchez, André. *La sainteté en Occident aux derniers siècles du Moyen Age*. Rome: Ecole Française de Rome, 1988.
Vékony, Gábor. 'The Role of a March in Ethnic and Political Changes'. *AOASH* 33, no. 3 (1979): 301–14.
Venetianer, Lajos. *A magyar zsidóság története a honfoglalástól a világháború kitöréséig, különös tekintettel gazdasági és művelődési fejlődésére* (A history of Hungarian Jews from the conquest to the world war, with a special emphasis on their economic and cultural development). Budapest, 1922. Reprint Budapest: Könyvértékesítő Vállalat, 1986.
Verlinden, Charles. 'Esclavage et ethnographie sur les bordes de la Mer Noir XIII–XIVe s'. In *Miscellanea Historica in Honorem Leonis van der Essen*, 2 vols. Vol. 1: 287–98. Brussels and Paris: Editions Universitaires, 1947.
L'esclavage dans l'Europe médiévale. 2 vols. Bruges: Rijksuniversiteit te Gent, 1955–77.
Veszprémy, László. 'A Hun-magyar hagyomány alakulása és a tatárjárás' (The development of the Hun-Hungarian tradition and the Mongol invasion). *Hadtörténelmi Közlemények* 104 (1991): 22–33.
'Kézai Simon a "fajtiszta" Magyarországról' (Simon of Kéza about a 'racially pure' Hungary). *Magyar Könyvszemle* 109, no. 4 (1993): 430–3.
Vicaire, Marie Humbert. *Histoire de Saint Dominique*. 2 vols. Paris: Cerf, 1957.
Saint Dominique et ses frères: évangile ou croisade? Paris: Cerf, 1967.
Vives y Escudero, Antonio. *Monedas de las dinastías Arábigo-españolas*. Madrid, 1893.
Vízkelety, András. 'Nomád kori hagyományok vagy udvari-lovagi toposzok?' (Traditions from a nomadic age or courtly topoi?). *Irodalomtörténeti Közlemények* 85 (1981): 243–75.
'Béla hercegnek, IV. Béla király fiának menyegzője' (The wedding of Prince Béla, son of King Béla IV). *Irodalomtörténeti Közlemények* 97 (1993): 571–84.
Vladimirtsov, Boris. *Le régime social des mongols: le féodalisme nomade*. Paris: Adrien Maisonneuve, 1948.
Voegelin, Eric. 'The Mongol Orders of Submission to European Powers, 1245–1955'. *Byzantion* 15 (1940–1): 378–413.
Wacks, Mel. 'Medieval Hungarian Silver Coins with Hebrew Letters'. *The Shekel* 22, no. 5 (1989): 10–11.
Wadl, Wilhelm. *Geschichte der Juden in Kärnten im Mittelalter*. 2nd edn. Klagenfurt: Kärtner Landesarchiv, 1992.
Waldmüller, Lothar. *Die Synoden in Dalmatien, Kroatien und Ungarn Von der Völkwanderung bis zum Ende der Arpaden*. Konziliengeschichte 21. Paderborn and Munich: F. Schöning, 1987.
Wallerstein, Immanuel M. *The Modern World-System: Capitalist Agriculture and the*

Bibliography

Origins of the European World-Economy in the Sixteenth Century. New York, San Francisco and London: Academic Press, 1974.
Watt, John. *The Theory of Papal Monarchy in the Thirteenth Century: The Contribution of the Canonists.* New York: Fordham University Press, 1965.
'The Jews, the Law, and the Church: The Concept of Jewish Serfdom in Thirteenth-Century England'. In *The Church and Sovereignty c. 590–1918: Essays in Honour of Michael Wilks,* 153–72. Studies in Church History Subsidia 9. Oxford: Ecclesiastical History Society, 1991.
Waugh, Scott L. and Peter D. Diehl. eds. *Christendom and its Discontents: Exclusion, Persecution and Rebellion, 1000–1500.* Cambridge, Cambridge University Press, 1996.
Webb, Walter Prescott. *The Great Frontier.* 1951. Lincoln and London: University of Nebraska Press, 1986.
Wehli, Tünde. 'A magyarországi művészet helyzete a tatárjárás körüli években' (The situation of Hungarian art in the years around the Mongol invasion). *Hadtörténelmi Közlemények* 104 (1991): 34–44.
Weinreich, Max. *History of the Yiddish Language.* Tr. Shlomo Noble. Chicago and London: University of Chicago Press, 1980.
Weinryb, Bernard D. *The Jews of Poland: A Social and Economic History of the Jewish Community in Poland from 1100 to 1800.* Philadelphia: Jewish Publication Society of America, 1973.
Wellesz, Gyula. 'Izsák B. Mózes Or Zarua és az esztergomi zsidók' (Isaac B. Moses Or Zarua and the Jews of Esztergom). *Magyar Zsidó Szemle* 20, no. 2 (1903): 148–50.
'Izsák b. Mózes Or Zarua és az üreghi zsidók' (Isaac B. Moses Or Zarua and the Jews of Üreg). *Magyar Zsidó Szemle* 21, no. 4 (1904): 370–3.
Wenskus, Reinhard. *Stammesbildung und Verfassung: Das Werden der Frühmittelalterlichen Gentes.* Cologne and Graz: Böhlau Verlag, 1961.
Wertner, Mór. *IV. Béla király története okirati kútfők nyomán* (A history of King Béla IV based on primary sources). Temesvár, 1893.
Whittaker, C. R. *Frontiers of the Roman Empire: A Social and Economic Study.* Baltimore and London: Johns Hopkins University Press, 1994.
White, Richard. *'It's Your Misfortune and None of My Own': A History of the American West.* Norman and London: University of Oklahoma Press, 1991.
The Middle Ground: Indians, Empires, and Republics in the Great Lakes Region, 1650–1815. Cambridge: Cambridge University Press, 1991.
Wickham, Christopher. 'Frontiere di vilaggio in Toscana nel XII secolo'. In *Castrum 4: Frontière et peuplement dans le monde méditerranéen au Moyen Age.* Actes du colloque d'Erice-Trapani, 18–25 Septembre 1988, 239–51. Rome: Ecole Française de Rome and Madrid: Casa Velazquez, 1992.
Wieczynski, Joseph L. *The Russian Frontier: The Impact of Borderlands upon the Course of Early Russian History.* Charlottesville: University Press of Virginia, 1976.
Wilks, Michael. *The Problem of Sovereignty in the Middle Ages.* Cambridge: Cambridge University Press, 1963.
Will, Edouard and Claude Orrieux. *'Proselytism Juif?' Histoire d'une erreur.* Paris: Les Belles Lettres, 1992.
Williams, Daniel. 'Matthew Paris and the Thirteenth-Century Prospect of Asia'. In *England in the Thirteenth Century.* Edited by W. M. Ormrod, 51–67. Stamford: Paul Watkins, 1991.
Winkler, Ernő. *Adalékok a zsidó eskü középkori történetéhez* (Additions to the medieval history of the Jewry oath). Budapest: Pallas Nyomda, 1917.

Bibliography

'A zsidó esküMagyarországon' (The Jewry oath in Hungary). *Magyar Zsidó Szemle* 44 (1927): 29–47.

Wyrozumski, Jerzy. 'Die Frage der Toleranz im mittelalterlichen Polen'. *Universitas Iagellonica Acta Scientiarum Litterarumque*, vol. MXXV. Studia Germano-Polonica 1. Edited by Krzysztof Baczkowski, Antoni Podraza and Winfried Schulze, 7–19. Cracow: Nakl. Uniwersytetu Jagiellónskiego, 1992.

'Jews in Medieval Poland'. In *The Jews in Old Poland 1000–1795*. Edited by Antony Polonsky *et al.*, 13–22. London and New York: I. B. Tauris, 1993.

Yerushalmi, Yosef H. 'Assimilation and Racial Anti-Semitism: The Iberian and the German Models'. *The Leo Baeck Memorial Lecture no. 26*. New York: Leo Baeck Institute, 1982.

Zajtay, Imre. 'Le Registre de Varad: Un monument judiciaire du début du XIIIe siècle'. *Revue Historique de Droit Français et Etranger* ser. 4, 32 (1954): 527–62.

Zakrzewska-Kleczkowska, Jadwiga. 'Brakteaty z napisami hebrajskimi ze Střelic' (with English summary). In *Sborník II. Numismatického Symposia 1969*. Edited by Jiří Sejbal, 182–97. Brno: Moravské Museum, 1976.

Zichy, István. 'A Képes Krónika miniatűrjei viselettörténeti szempontból' (The miniatures of the Illuminated Chronicle from the point of view of the history of costumes). In *Petrovics Elek Emlékkönyv*. Budapest: Az Országos Magyar Szépművészeti Múzeum barátai és tisztviselői, 1934.

Zichy, Ladomér. *A tatárjárás Magyarországon* (The Mongol invasion of Hungary). Pécs: Veszprémvármegyei Történelmi, Régészeti és Néprajzi Társulat, 1934.

Ziegler, Joseph. 'Reflections on the Jewry Oath in the Middle Ages'. In *Christianity and Judaism*. Edited by Diana Wood, 209–20. Studies in Church History 29. Oxford: Blackwell, 1992.

Zientara, Benedykt. 'Nationality Conflicts in the German-Slavic Borderland in the 13th–14th Centuries and their Social Scope'. *Acta Poloniae Historica* 22 (1970): 207–25.

'Foreigners in Poland in the 10th–15th Centuries: Their Role in the Opinion of the Polish Medieval Community'. *Acta Poloniae Historica* 29 (1974): 5–28.

Zimmermann, Heinrich. *Die päpstliche Legation in der ersten Hälfte des 13. Jahrhunderts*. Görres- Gesellschaft zur Pflege der Wissenschaft im katholischen Deutschland Sektion für Rechts- und Socialwissenschaft. Paderborn: F. Schöningh, 1913.

Zolnay, László. *Buda középkori zsidósága és zsinagógáik* (Jews and their synagogues in medieval Buda). Budapest: Budapesti Történeti Múzeum, 1987.

Zombori, István. ed. *Magyarország és a Szentszék kapcsolatának ezer éve* (A thousand years of the relations between Hungary and the Apostolic See). Budapest: METEM, 1996.

Zsoldos, Attila. 'Terra hereditaria és szabad rendelkezésű birtok (Szempontok a várjobbágyi birtoklás egyes kérdéseinek megítéléséhez)' (Terra hereditaria and landholding with the power of disposition: considerations for solving certain questions of the landholding of the castle-warriors). In *Unger Mátyás Emlékkönyv*. Edited by Péter E. Kovács, *et al.*, 23–37. Budapest: MTA Történettudományi Intézet, 1991.

Az Árpádok és alattvalóik (The Arpads and their subjects). Debrecen: Csokonai Kiadó, 1997.

'Téténytől a Hód-tóig' (From Tétény to Lake Hód). *Történelmi Szemle* 39 (1997): 69–98.

INDEX

Compiled by Laura Napran

Abelard, *see* Peter Abelard
Abū Hāmid, Muslim scholar, 66, 67, 85, 121, 140–1, 212, 241
  on Muslim religious practices, 96, 237–40
  on slavery, 111, 153
Abū 'l-Fidā', 245–6
Abū Zayd (Sa'īd), converted Muslim, 259
Alexander III, pope, 76
Alexander IV, pope, 167, 168, 169–70
Alfonso X (the Wise), king of Castile, 46, 182–3
Al-Kazwīnī, 96
Al-Wansharīshī, 243
András II, king of Hungary, 31, 95 n. 83, 127, 130, 153, 155, 171
  charter to the Saxons, 106
  crusade of 56, 156, 185
  death of, 160
  investigation of Muslims, 159, 160, 213
  protection of Muslims, 157–8
  taxes of, 86, 113, 120
  and Teutonic knights, 33, 213–14
András III, king of Hungary, 121 n. 60, 182
  and Jews, 81, 119, 128
  and non-Christians, 161
Andrew of St Victor, 45
Angevin rulers of Hungary, 4, 120, 171
Anna Comnena, chronicler, 69
Anselmus, converted Jew, 236
Antonio Bonfini, 207
Apulia, 19
Armenians, 40, 104
Árpád dynasty, 4, 21
As, the, 57–8
Attila the Hun, 178, 205–7
Austria
  and Jews 94, 112–13, 200
  war with Hungary, 37

Barcaság, the, 33, 213
Bartholomew, bishop of Pécs, 30

Bartlett, Robert, 7, 11, 253, 271
Batu, Mongol leader, 34, 35, 36
Béla I, king of Hungary, 113 n. 26
Béla III, king of Hungary, 31, 123
Béla IV, king of Hungary, 33, 130, 159, 196, 202, 263
  accession to throne, 120
  admission of Cumans 107, 135, 136, 143, 184, 185
  and civil war, 139, 144, 145, 187, 197
  and conversion of Cumans, 220–1, 261
  frontier ideology of, 38, 163–71, 270
  as godfather of Köten, 98, 218
  as landowner, 132
  and Mongols, 30, 34, 71, 163–71, 176, 188, 254
  petition to Gregory IX, 160
  privileges for Jews, 76–84, 94, 114, 116, 117, 118, 133, 147, 185, 225
  sponsor of missionaries, 214
  and Urban IV, 161
  use of Muslim soldiers, 141
Béla, prince, son of Béla IV, 202
Benedict XII, pope, 90
Benjamin of Tudela, 234
Bereg, oath of, 121, 128, 158–60, 162
Berthold of Aquileia, 165
Bishko, Charles Julian, 8
Bogomils, 58–9
Bohemia, 30, 55
  Jewish trade in, 110
  war with Hungary, 37
Bolesław of Kalisz, 76
Boniak, Cuman chieftain, 246, 247
Boniface VIII, pope, 177
Boris, khan of Bulgaria, 259
Bortz, Cuman chieftain, 214–15, 217
Bosnia, 30
Bruno, bishop of Olomouc, 161, 194, 262
Buda, Synod of, 161, 162, 181, 275–6

Index

Bulgars, 25
  conversion of, 259
  and Cumans, 69, 71
Burns, Robert I., 8, 129
Byzantium, 9, 10 n. 17, 14, 16, 23, 25, 30–1
  and Cumans, 68, 145, 251
  defeat of Pechenegs, 39
  and Muslims, 12, 240, 241

castles, 33, 36, 37, 213
Celestine IV, pope, 165
Charles Robert, king of Hungary, 21, 120
Charles I of Sicily, father of Queen Isabella of Hungary, 175, 194
Chasdai ibn Shaprut, 110
Chernigov, 70
Christianitas, 42–3
Cistercians, 8, 30
Clement IV, pope, 151, 165
Codex Cumanicus, 72
Cohen, Mark, 52
comes camere, see *ispán*
Constance of Aragon, wife of King Imre of Hungary, 31
Constantinople, 19, 31
  Latin Empire of, 166, 251
Croatia, 29–30
crusades, northern, 47
Cumans, 27, 203–4
  burials of, 4, 244–5, 248–52, 253, 255, 257
  clan structure of, 264
  conversion of, 98, 173–4, 184, 186–8, 199, 210, 213–23, 244, 247, 251–4, 259, 271
  costume of, 255–60
  Cuman laws, 89–92, 100, 127–9, 135, 136, 174
  customs of, 97–9
  and Davit' II Ağmašenebeli, king of Georgia, 173
  defeat of Pechenegs, 39
  distrust of, 196–9, 201–2
  in Georgia 11, 69, 72, 144, 148, 173, 183, 264
  hairstyles of, 258–9, 271
  judicial autonomy of, 99–100
  as king's soldiers, 140, 142–8, 178, 197, 201
  as landholders, 134–40
  legal status of, 87–93
  loan-words of, 265–6
  and Mongols, 218;
  names of, 195 n. 29, 252
  origins of, 68
  pictorial representation of, 207–9, 255–6
  raids of, 33, 69
  religious practices of, 244–51
  settlement in Hungary, 27, 35, 39, 40, 54, 56, 71–2
  as slaves in Egypt, 70
  sources for, 72–3
  subjugation of the As, 58
  terminology for, 190–5

Dahan, Gilbert, 52
Daniel, Jewish landholder, 132
Daniel, Norman, 52
Denis, chief treasurer of King András II, 120
distinguishing signs, 114, 161–2
Dominicans, 31, 213–19, 220 n. 151

Elias, Norbert, 272
Eliezer ben Isaac, rabbi, 227–8, 232, 234–5
Erzsébet, queen of Hungary, wife of István V
  conversion of, 261–3
  Cuman origins of, 194, 262
  marriage to István V, 88 n. 56, 218, 261
  as mother of László IV, 171, 177
  as regent, 145, 262–3
Erzsébet, sister of László IV, 175–6, 179

Farkas, Jewish money-lender, 118
Fehérvár, 77
Fernández-Armesto, Felipe, 11
Flanders, 31, 105, 115
Fodor, István, 249
France, 31, 40, 105, 163 n. 59, 175 n. 119
Franciscans, 31, 213, 218, 219, 223
Frederick, duke of Austria
  annexes western Hungary, 30, 164
  charter of privileges to Jews, 76, 78, 80–1, 94, 117
Frederick II, emperor, 46, 164
  crusade of, 156
  and Muslims, 110, 151, 182, 237
Frederick III of Castile, 170
Fredman, Jewish financier, 118, 131
Friedenberg, Daniel, 125
frontiers, historiography of, 4–17
  and Hungary, 27–33
Fügedi, Erik, 104

Galicia, 30, 70
Geary, Patrick, 192
Gerard (Gellért), theologian, 55
Germany, 5, 31, 40, 105
Gertrude of Merania, wife of András II, 31
Gesta Hungarorum of the Hungarian Anonymous, 28–9, 65, 136, 242
Géza II, king of Hungary, 85, 141, 184
Gisela, daughter of Duke Henry II of Bavaria, wife of St István, 19, 20
Golden Bull of 1222, 21, 82 n. 32, 121, 128, 153, 154–5, 157
Gratian, canonist, 212

Index

Gregory IX, pope, 153, 155, 157, 159 n. 41, 199 n. 45, 214 n. 122, 236
  conversion of Cumans, 202, 215, 217
  on crusading, 156
  Decretales of, 160–1
  on Mongol invasion, 164, 165 n. 72
Gregory X, pope, 79 n. 18, 144 n. 177, 172
Györffy, György, 264

Hartvic, author of *Vita* of St István, 20
Henel, *comes camere* of Hungary, 126–7, 128 n. 95, 130, 131–2
heretics, 58–9, 199 n. 45
Holy Land, 17, 50–1, 240
Honorius III, pope, 174, 175 n. 118, 214 n. 122
  on Muslims and Jews, 86, 152–3, 154, 155, 156
hospes privileges, 105–6, 107 n. 121
Hospitallers, 28, 33, 193
Humbert de Romans, 188
Huns, History of, 204 n. 75

Iberia, 1, 2
  frontier of, 6, 9, 12, 13, 17
  Mudejar revolt, 51
  non-Christians in, 48, 49, 52, 85, 109, 129, 148, 151, 156, 196, 199, 243, 259
  raided by Hungarian tribes, 19
  reconquest of, 8 n. 12, 43, 48, 50, 109
  settlers from, 40
Ibn Saʿīd, 242
Ibrāhīm ibn Yaʿqūb, 65, 110, 112
Illuminated Chronicle, 28, 172, 178, 208–9, 256
Imre, king of Hungary, 31
Innocent III, pope, 43, 48, 153–4
Innocent IV, pope, 43, 48, 167 n. 86
  conflict with Frederick II, 182
  conversion of Cumans, 217 n. 129, 220
  on Jews, 45, 149–50
  on Mongols, 165, 193
Ioannes Kinnamos, 141
Isaac ben Moses, rabbi, 95, 228, 234
Isabella, wife of László IV, 175
Ismail ibn Hassan, student of Abū Hāmid, 241
ispán, 20, 25, 27, 82, 120, 121, 124, 125–6, 128, 130
István I (Stephen), saint, king of Hungary, 55, 200 n. 53, 205, 206–7
  Admonitions, 40
  canonization, 19
  Vita, 20, 32, 207
István II, king of Hungary, 173 n. 113
István IV, king of Hungary, 31
István V, king of Hungary, 133, 146, 197
  death of, 172
  as father of László IV, 171
  as 'the younger king', 88, 98, 115, 139, 144, 145, 167, 187, 220
  marriage to Erzsébet, 218, 261, 262, 263
Italy, 31, 40, 105, 115

Jacob ben Isaac, Jewish scholar, 228
Jacob (Giacomo) of Pecorara, cardinal bishop of Palestrina, 158–9, 160, 173
Jaime, king of Aragon, 151
Jean de Joinville, chronicler, 99, 245, 247
Jews, 52
  architecture of, 231 n. 33, 232
  and canon law, 49, 75–6
  cemeteries of, 4, 61 n. 69, 62 n. 72, 229–30
  as collectors of salt revenues, 158 n. 41
  conversion of, 45–6, 210–11, 223, 235–6
  judicial autonomy of, 94–5
  in Khazar Empire, 60–1
  as landholders, 129–33
  legal status of, 74–84, 103 n. 107
  as merchants, 110–15, 230–1
  and minting, 121 n. 59, 124–6, 127 n. 86, 157 n. 34
  as money-lenders, 115–20, 133
  names of, 232–4
  oaths of, 79–80
  persecution of, 48, 199–201
  religious practices of, 45, 226–30
  scholars, 44–5, 229 n. 20
  settlement in Hungary, 40–1, 60–4, 75 n. 2, 184
  streets of, 63, 225 nn. 2 and 3
  terminology for, 190–2
Joachim, viceroy of Croatia and Slavonia, 145
Johannes de Amelio, 90–1
John XXII, pope, 223
John of Plano Carpini, missionary, 47, 169, 246
  History of the Mongols, 53, 98
John of Limoges, abbot of Zirc, 31
John of Wildeshausen, bishop of Bosnia, 159
Jonah, Jew of Pozsony, 200
Joseph, Jew from Buda, 78
Julian, missionary, 163

Káliz, 66, 113, 121
Kalka, battle of, 70
Kálmán (Coloman), king of Hungary
  on Christianity, 55
  laws concerning Muslims, 85, 211–12, 237
  regulations concerning Jews, 75, 110–11, 114, 116, 130
Kalonymos of Worms, rabbi, 234
Kavars, 66

Index

Khazar Empire, 19, 98
  Jews in, 60–1
  Muslims in, 65, 66, 142
Khwarezm
  Cumans in, 69, 216
  Muslims in, 65, 66
Kiev, 70, 112
Klaniczay, Gábor, 203
Komoróczy, Géza, 125
Körmend, 81
Köten, Cuman chieftain, 39, 87, 88 n. 56, 260
  baptism of, 218
  death of, 71, 134, 143, 196

Langmuir, Gavin, 52
László I, saint, king of Hungary, 65 n. 85
  and canonization of King István, 19
  laws concerning Muslims, 85, 237
  legends of, 33, 207
  Life, 28
  prohibitions against Jews, 75
  relics of, 97
László IV (Ladislas), king of Hungary, 102, 118, 131, 188, 194, 263
  assassination of, 177, 178
  Aydua, concubine of, 175
  conflict with Church, 171–8, 180–3, 201, 203, 206
  Cuman laws of, 89–92, 136, 258
  employment of non-Christians, 128, 161
  support of Church, 179–80, 262
  use of Cumans as soldiers, 145–7, 173
  war against Cumans, 27, 139, 179, 197–8, 204, 208
Lateran Council, Fourth, 48, 50, 97, 153, 161
Lattimore, Owen, 16
Lech, battle of, 19
Lecler, Joseph, 51
Le Goff, Jacques, 54
Leopold, duke of Austria, 24
Leopold I, king of Hungary, Habsburg emperor, 91
Levunion, battle of, 69
Lewis, Archibald, 7
Limerick, Patricia, 16
Lithuania, 12, 16, 50, 51, 215, 216
Livonia, 2, 49, 110, 167
Lodomer, archbishop of Esztergom, 173–6, 179, 180–2, 206
Louis IX, saint, king of France, 38, 188
  crusading of, 51, 166
  on Jews, 45, 150–1
Lucas, archbishop of Esztergom, 155
Lyons
  First Council of, 165
  Second Council of, 188

MacKay, Angus, 7, 8
Mamluks, 70, 143
Manuel Comnenos, emperor of Byzantium, 31
Margit (Margaret) of Hungary, saint
  canonization of, 38, 175, 176 n. 123
  miracles of, 222
Maria, wife of Béla IV, 263
Martin IV, pope, 149, 181
Matthias, king of Hungary, 207
McCrank, Lawrence J., 10
Meir, rabbi of Rothenburg, 150
Membrok, Cuman chieftain, 214, 217
Michael Attaleiates, chronicler, 69
Mieszko III, of Poland, 126
Miklós Kán (Nicholas), 263
Mindaugas, prince of Lithuania, 51
minting, 120–6, 127 nn. 86 and 89, 155
missionaries, 19, 30, 49, 84, 210–21
  and Cumans, 72, 98, 184, 188
  of Innocent IV, 48, 165
Mizse, palatine of László IV, 128
monasteries, 31
  Boldva, 197
  Csatár, 118
  order of Saint-Paul, 179
  Pannonhalma, 211, 236
Mongols, 146, 193
  invasion of Hungary, 30, 33–9, 54, 56, 135, 151, 163–71, 186, 218
  conflict with Cumans, 70, 216, 254, 260
  conversion of, 51, 188, 218, 219
  Golden Horde, 70, 218, 219, 254
  and László IV, 176–8
  and Muslims, 134, 141, 242–3
  population loss caused by, 37 n. 113
  and Prester John, 50
  shamans of, 47 n. 18, 246
Moore, R. I., 52
Mstislav Mstislavich, prince of Galicia, 39
Muhi, battle of, 34, 165 n. 72
Muldoon, James, 187
Muslims, 41, 44
  in China, 243
  Christian attitudes toward, 46, 52
  as collectors of salt revenues, 158 n. 41
  conversion of, 47, 53, 85, 86, 154, 184, 210–13, 223, 237–40, 243
  costume of, 4, 259
  as frontier guards, 24
  isolation of, 241–3
  as king's soldiers, 140–2, 143, 238, 240
  as landholders, 133–4
  legal position of, 84–7
  as merchants, 110–15
  as minters, 122–3, 127 n. 89, 239 n. 75
  names of, 240–1

338

and ordeal, 96–7
religious practices of, 46, 238–40, 243
religious scholars of, 85, 96
settlement in Hungary 40, 64–8, 184
in Iberia, 43, 48, 52, 185 n. 173, 237, 243, 259 n. 186
terminology for, 190–2
in treasury, 127

Nekkul, son of Henel, *comes camere* in Austria, 127, 128 n. 95, 130
Németh, Gyula, 146
Nevronius, converted Jew, 236
Nicholas I, pope, 259
Nicholas III, pope, 172, 173, 174, 175 n. 118, 182
Nicholas IV, pope, 150, 174, 177, 259–60
Nordman, Daniel, 14

Odilo of Cluny, 55
Oghuz, 33, 56, 68, 191
Ogodai, Great Khan, 35
Olaf, saint, 207
Otakar II, king of Bohemia, 28, 145, 202, 262
Otto of Freising, 24
Ottokar of Steier, 201–2, 203
Ottoman conquest, 22, 34, 265
Ottonian–Salian Empire, 19

Pechenegs, 19, 69, 173 n. 113, 191
  as frontier guards, 24, 29
  raids of, 28, 32–3, 213
  settlement of, 39, 56–7, 66, 104
Pere III (Peter), king of Valencia and Aragon, 119
Peter Abelard, 44
Peter Damian, 55
Peter the Venerable, 45, 46, 50
Philip of Fermo, papal legate, 172–5, 178, 181, 203
  imposition of Cuman articles, 89, 92, 136, 197, 221, 258
  on Jews and Muslims, 114, 162
Philippe de Toucy, 99
Plano Carpini, *see* John of Plano Carpini
Poland, 17, 25, 30
  and Jews, 94, 110, 115, 227
  and Mongols, 34, 36, 176
Pozsony, 81, 199–200
Premonstratensians, 30
Prester John, 38, 50

Rádóczy, Gyula, 125
Rashi, 228, 230, 234
Rashīd al-Dīn, 247
Rásonyi, László, 252

Robert, archbishop of Esztergom, 155, 157, 158, 159, 160
  conversion of Cumans, 156, 214–15
  conversion of Muslims, 213, 238
Robert de Cléry, 247
Roger Bacon, 70–1
Roger, canon, 30, 71–2, 87–8, 134, 196, 260–1
Rowell, S. C., 12
Rudolph I of Hapsburg, 150
Rus', 36
  chronicle of, 68
  and Cumans, 69, 143, 145, 183, 216, 260
  frontier of, 11, 25
  and Jews, 110, 226, 227

Salian emperors, 30
Samuel, *ispán* of Hungarian treasury, 127
Sancho II, king of Portugal, 160
Saul, Jew from Buda, 77
Saul, Jew from Pest, 77
Scechtinus, Jewish landowner, 131
Scheiber, Sándor, 125, 227, 230, 233
Selmeczi, László, 251
Sicily, 9, 17, 48, 52, 123, 156
Sigismond, king of Hungary, 77–8, 179 n. 145, 225 n. 3
Silesia, duke of, 34
Simon, Aragonese knight, 104–5
Simon of Kéza, chronicler, 102, 147, 179, 198, 203–6, 207, 210
Skylitzes, continuation of, 69
slavery, 95, 110–12, 130, 152 n. 15, 153, 213, 235
Smolensk, 70
Solomon, Jew of Fehérvár, 77
Spain, *see* Iberia
Styria, 30, 143
Sword-Brothers, 49, 110
Szabolcs, Synod of, 113, 211
Szűcs, Jenő, 23, 145, 178, 180, 204

Taksony, prince of Hungary, 65
Teka, Jewish financier, 107, 118, 126, 128 n. 95, 130, 131, 132
Teutonic Knights, 33, 49, 213
Theodoric, Dominican provincial of Hungary, 215
Thompson, James W., 7
Thuróczy, János, chronicler, 207
treasury, 123–4, 154 n. 21
Turner, Frederick Jackson, 6–8, 12, 16

Urban IV, pope, 145, 161, 167–8, 220

Várad, Register of, 96–7, 191
Venice, 30

339

Index

Volga Bulgaria, 65
Volynia, 70

Walloons, 31, 40, 105
Walter, *comes camere* of Hungary, 130–1
Wenceslas, saint, 207
White, Richard, 16
Wid, Hungarian noble, 118
William of Rubruck, missionary, 47, 246, 250

Yāqūt, 67, 85, 96, 141, 238, 239, 241, 242
Yehudah ha-Kohen, rabbi of Mainz, 112, 226
Yuri, son of Könchek, Cuman chieftain, 260

Zeicze, converted Cuman, 222
Zeyhan, Cuman chieftain, 88, 261
Zolnay, László, 115
Zulta, ruler of Hungary, 19

Cambridge Studies in Medieval Life and Thought
Fourth series

Titles in series

1 The Beaumont Twins: The Roots and Branches of Power in the Twelfth Century
   D. B. CROUCH
2 The Thought of Gregory the Great★
   G. R. EVANS
3 The Government of England Under Henry I★
   JUDITH A. GREEN
4 Charity and Community in Medieval Cambridge
   MIRI RUBIN
5 Autonomy and Community: The Royal Manor of Havering, 1200–1500
   MARJORIE KENISTON MCINTOSH
6 The Political Thought of Baldus de Ubaldis
   JOSEPH CANNING
7 Land and Power in Late Medieval Ferrara: The Rule of the Este, 1350–1450
   TREVOR DEAN
8 William of Tyre: Historian of the Latin East★
   PETER W. EDBURY AND JOHN GORDON ROWE
9 The Royal Saints of Anglo-Saxon England: A Study of West Saxon and East Anglian Cults
   SUSAN J. RIDYARD
10 John of Wales: A Study of the Works and Ideas of a Thirteenth-Century Friar
   JENNY SWANSON
11 Richard III: A Study of Service★
   ROSEMARY HORROX
12 A Marginal Economy? East Anglian Breckland in the Later Middle Ages
   MARK BAILEY
13 Clement VI: The Pontificate and Ideas of an Avignon Pope
   DIANA WOOD
14 Hagiography and the Cult of Saints: The Diocese of Orléans, 800–1200
   THOMAS HEAD
15 Kings and Lords in Conquest England
   ROBIN FLEMING
16 Council and Hierarchy: The Political Thought of William Durant the Younger
   CONSTANTIN FASOLT
17 Warfare in the Latin East, 1192–1291★
   CHRISTOPHER MARSHALL
18 Province and Empire: Brittany and the Carolingians
   JULIA M. H. SMITH

19 A Gentry Community: Leicestershire in the Fifteenth Century, *c.* 1422–*c.* 1485
    ERIC ACHESON
20 Baptism and Change in the Early Middle Ages, *c.* 200–1150
    PETER CRAMER
21 Itinerant Kingship and Royal Monasteries in Early Medieval Germany, *c.* 936–1075
    JOHN W. BERNHARDT
22 Caesarius of Arles: The Making of a Christian Community in Late Antique Gaul
    WILLIAM E. KLINGSHIRN
23 Bishop and Chapter in Twelfth-Century England: A Study of the *Mensa Episcopalis*
    EVERETT U. CROSBY
24 Trade and Traders in Muslim Spain: The Commercial Realignment of the Iberian Peninsula, 900–1500*
    OLIVIA REMIE CONSTABLE
25 Lithuania Ascending: A Pagan Empire within East-Central Europe, 1295–1345
    S. C. ROWELL
26 Barcelona and Its Rulers, 1100–1291
    STEPHEN P. BENSCH
27 Conquest, Anarchy and Lordship: Yorkshire, 1066–1154
    PAUL DALTON
28 Preaching the Crusades: Mendicant Friars and the Cross in the Thirteenth Century*
    CHRISTOPH T. MAIER
29 Family Power in Southern Italy: The Duchy of Gaeta and Its Neighbours, 850–1139
    PATRICIA SKINNER
30 The Papacy, Scotland and Northern England, 1342–1378
    A. D. M. BARRELL
31 Peter des Roches: An Alien in English Politics, 1205–1238
    NICHOLAS VINCENT
32 Runaway Religious in Medieval England, *c.* 1240–1540
    F. DONALD LOGAN
33 People and Identity in Ostrogothic Italy, 489–554
    PATRICK AMORY
34 The Aristocracy in Twelfth-Century León and Castile
    SIMON BARTON
35 Economy and Nature in the Fourteenth Century: Money, Market Exchange and the Emergence of Scientific Thought*
    JOEL KAYE
36 Clement V
    SOPHIA MENACHE
37 England's Jewish Solution, 1262–1290: Experiment and Expulsion

ROBIN R. MUNDILL
38 Medieval Merchants: York, Beverley and Hull in the Later Middle Ages
    JENNY KERMODE
39 Family, Commerce and Religion in London and Cologne: A Comparative Social History of Anglo-German Emigrants, c. 1000–c. 1300
    JOSEPH P. HUFFMAN
40 The Monastic Order in Yorkshire, 1069–1215
    JANET BURTON
41 Parisian Scholars in the Early Fourteenth Century: A Social Portrait
    WILLIAM J. COURTENAY
42 Colonisation and Conquest in Medieval Ireland: The English in Louth, 1170–1330
    BRENDAN SMITH
43 The Early Humiliati
    FRANCES ANDREWS
44 The Household Knights of King John
    S. D. CHURCH
45 The English in Rome, 1362–1420: Portrait of an Expatriate Community
    MARGARET HARVEY
46 Restoration and Reform: Recovery from Civil War in England, 1153–1165
    GRAEME J. WHITE
47 State and Society in the Early Middle Ages: The Middle Rhine Valley, 400–1000
    MATTHEW INNES
48 Brittany and the Angevins: Province and Empire, 1157–1203
    JUDITH EVERARD
49 The Making of Gratian's *Decretum*
    ANDERS WINROTH
50 At the Gate of Christendom: Jews, Muslims and 'Pagans' in Medieval Hungary c. 1000–c. 1300
    NORA BEREND
51 Making Agreements in Medieval Catalonia: Power, Order, and the Written Word, 1000–1200
    ADAM J. KOSTO

* *Also published as a paperback*

For EU product safety concerns, contact us at Calle de José Abascal, 56–1º,
28003 Madrid, Spain or eugpsr@cambridge.org.

www.ingramcontent.com/pod-product-compliance
Lightning Source LLC
LaVergne TN
LVHW091528060526
838200LV00036B/529